New Readers Press Dictionary

New Readers Press Dictionary
ISBN 978-1-56420-432-5

Copyright © 2005 New Readers Press
New Readers Press
A Publishing Division of ProLiteracy
1320 Jamesville Avenue, Syracuse, New York 13210
www.newreaderspress.com

Printed in the United States of America
9 8 7 6 5 4 3 2

All proceeds from the sale of New Readers Press materials
support literacy programs in the United States and worldwide.

This dictionary is a joint effort on the part of
Wordsmyth Collaboratory and New Readers Press.

Wordsmyth Collaboratory Staff
President: Robert Q. Parks, Ph.D
Managing Editor: Jan Schwartzberg Douglas
Senior Editor: Lynn Broquist, Ph.D
Associate Editors: Margaret Kelly Moorhoff, Genevieve Kocienda
Design and Layout: Brian Dudla
Production Assistant: Heather Youngman

New Readers Press Staff
Acquisitions Editor: Paula L. Schlusberg, Ph.D
Production Manager: Andrea Woodbury
Technical Specialist: Maryellen Casey
Production Consultant: James Wallace
Cover Design: Kimbrly Koennecke

Contents

About This Dictionary

A dictionary can be an important tool for understanding new words. It can also help you learn more about words you already know. It gives you more than just the meanings of words. It also tells you a lot about how the words are used.

New Readers Press created this dictionary especially for new readers and English language learners. It defines over 5,100 of the most common English words. These words include many that you will need for your studies as well as for everyday life.

The entry for each word tells you a lot about that word. It includes things like the pronunciation, irregular forms, and some common phrases. The definitions use familiar words. Example sentences for most words show how the words are used in talking or writing. The sentences deal with school, work, family life, and many everyday activities. All of the words in the definitions and example sentences are also in the dictionary.

Many words have more than one meaning. This dictionary gives you the most common meanings. Illustrations throughout the dictionary help make meanings clearer. Special features in shaded boxes give more information about some words. These include word families and words that we often confuse.

In the back of this dictionary, there is a special tool, the Word Explorer™. This organizes many common words and shows the relationships among them. The Word Explorer - can help you find a word that you are thinking of but can't remember. It can also help you get ideas for your writing.

We hope that you will enjoy using the *New Readers Press Dictionary*. We hope it will be useful to you in many ways.

Pronunciation Guide

Vowels

Word Guide	Symbol	Pronunciation
pay, l**ate**	ā	pā, lāt
m**e**, m**ea**t	ē	mē, mēt
l**ie**, b**y**	ī	lī, bī
g**o**, m**ow**	ō	gō, mō
c**u**te	ū	kūt
h**a**t	æ	hæt
f**a**ther, p**o**t	a	father, pat
b**e**d, h**ea**d	e	bed, hed
b**oo**t, fr**ui**t	oo	boot, froot
p**u**t, b**oo**k	u	put, buk
b**u**t, **a**lone	ə	bət, əlōn
h**ow**, c**ou**nt	ow	how, kownt
b**oy**, b**oi**l	oy	boy, boyl
b**ou**ght, w**a**ter	aw	bawt, wawter

Consonants

Word Guide	Symbol	Pronunciation
be	b	be
do	d	doo
fit, cou**gh**	f	fit, kawf
give, **g**o	g	giv, gō
him	h	him
gym, **j**oke	j	jim, jōk
key, **c**ap	k	kē, kæp
lie	l	lī
me	m	mē
no	n	nō
si**ng**	ng	sing
pay	p	pā
red	r	red
some, **c**ity	s	səm, sitē
tie	t	tī
vote	v	vōt
was, **wh**y	w	wəz, wī
zebra	z	zēbrə
mea**s**ure	zh	mezhər
chair, wa**tch**	ch	chār, wach
shoe, ma**ch**ine	sh	shoo, məshēn
thin	th	thin
that	th	thæt

The primary stress in a word is shown in **underlined letters.**
A syllable with no stress is shown in plain letters.

make	m<u>āk</u>
machine	mə <u>shēn</u>
merchandise	<u>mər</u> chən dīs

How to Use This Dictionary—Quick Reference Diagram

Guide Words identify the first and last entry words on a page. The words in this dictionary are listed in alphabetical order. You are on the right page when the word you are looking for comes after the first guide word and before the second guide word.

Phrases are shown in **bold, blue type** after the definitions.

Part of speech labels are in *bold, black italic* type. This dictionary uses these part of speech labels:

noun = noun
pl. noun = plural noun
verb = verb
aux. verb = auxiliary verb
adj. = adjective
adv. = adverb
pron. = pronoun
art. = article
prep. = preposition
conj. = conjunction
interj. = interjection
abbrev. = abbreviation

Word Builder boxes show words that are related to the main word in an entry.

Entry words are in **bold, blue type.**

The small number after an entry word shows that there are two or more words with the same spelling but with different meanings.

Illustrations give more information about the meaning of a word.

Definitions are written in plain language. See page 312 for a list of most of the words used in the definitions.

Different meanings, or senses, for a word are numbered, with the most frequent meaning first.

April / arrive

April *noun* (ā prəl) the fourth month of the year.

apron *noun* (ā prən) a piece of clothing that covers the front of the body. An apron helps keep clothes clean.

arch *noun* (arch) a rounded structure over an open space such as a door. *There is an arch over the entrance to the church.*

are *verb* (ar) a form of the verb be that is present tense and used with the pronouns *you, we,* or *they.* It is also used with plural nouns.

area *noun* (ar ē ə) 1. a place or region. *That area of the country has many lakes.* 2. the amount of surface within a certain space. *This room is ten feet wide and twenty feet long, so the area is two hundred square feet.*

area code *noun* (ar ē ə kōd) the first three numbers of a telephone number in the United States and Canada. You dial the area code first, then the telephone number. In the phone number *607-555-1234,* the area code is *607.*

argue *verb* (ar gū) 1. to disagree; quarrel. *The children* **argued over** *which game to play.* 2. to make statements that support your idea or opinion. *His parents argued that a new car would be too expensive.*

argument *noun* (ar gū mənt) an angry discussion by people who disagree. *Mr. and Mrs. Harris had an argument about money.*

arithmetic *noun* (ə rith mə tik) [N] the study of the use of numbers to add, subtract, multiply, and divide. Arithmetic is a basic area of mathematics.

arm¹ *noun* (arm) 1. the part of the body between the shoulder and the wrist. 2. any part that looks like or is used like an arm. *Do not sit on the arm of that chair.*

> **Word Builder: arm +**
> **armchair:** a chair with parts at the sides for resting your arms.
> **armrest:** the part on some chairs for resting your arm.

arm² *verb* (arm) to make ready for war. *The country armed itself against its enemy.*

armed forces *pl. noun* (armd fōr səz) all the military groups of a country. In the United States, the Army, the Navy, the Air Force, and the Marines make up the armed forces.

arms *pl. noun* (armz) things used to attack and hurt other people. Guns and knives are kinds of arms. *Some countries sell arms to other countries.*
bear arms to carry and use weapons. *They have the right to bear arms.*

army *noun* (ar mē) a large group of people brought together by a country to protect the country and fight its enemies. *People may join the army when they are eighteen.*

around *adv.* (ə rownd) 1. in a circle. *The car spun around.* 2. in all directions or to all sides. *He looked around.* 3. (informal) near. *I'll be around if you need me.* 4. in or to the opposite direction. *Michael turned around to look in the mirror.* 5. through an area. *Will you show me around?*
prep. 1. on all sides of. *There are trees around the park.* 2. near. *John had to stay around the house.* 3. in or to places within an area; here and there. *They drove around the country.* 4. in a way that encloses or makes a circle. *This ring is too tight around my finger.* 5. so as to move in a circle. *I walked around the tree.* 6. somewhere near in time or amount; about. *We eat lunch around noon.* | *This watch costs around twenty dollars.*

arrange *verb* (ə rānj) 1. to put in an order. *Joe arranged his books by author.* 2. to make plans for; prepare. *Mrs. Gomez arranged a birthday party for her son.*

arrangement *noun* (ə rānj mənt) 1. the group of things that have been put in order. *I sent a flower arrangement to my friend in the hospital.* 2. a plan. *We have an arrangement to meet for lunch once a week.* | *Who is* **making arrangements** *for the funeral?*

arrest *verb* (ə rest) to stop and hold someone for breaking the law. *The police arrested the criminal.*
noun the act of stopping and holding someone for breaking the law. *The police put the suspect* **under arrest.**

arrival *noun* (ə rī val) coming to or reaching a certain place. *Mr. Sen waited for the arrival of his son at the airport.*

arrive *verb* (ə rīv) to come to or reach a certain place. *The children are hungry when they arrive home after school.*

19

How to Use This Dictionary—Quick Reference Diagram

actress *noun* (ăk tris) a woman or girl who performs in a play, a movie, or a radio or television program.

actual *adj.* (ăk choo əl) real; true; exact. *The actual cost of the plane ticket was higher than I expected.*

actually *adv.* (ăk choo ə lē) as a matter of fact; really. *She actually finished the project on time.*

ad *noun* (ăd) the short form of **advertisement.**

add *verb* (ăd) 1. to put on or with something else to make it larger or better. *I always add sugar to my tea.* | *She added a new doll to her collection.* 2. to use mathematics to find the total of two or more numbers. *You made a mistake when you* **added** *19 to 24.* | *You need to add all the numbers.* 3. to find the sum of a set of numbers. *If you* **add up** *all the numbers, you will get the answer.*

addition *noun* (ə di shən) 1. the process of finding the total of two or more numbers. *The first example of addition that we often learn is 1+1= 2.* 2. anything that is added to something else. *The addition to our house will give us a new bedroom.* | *This baby is an addition to our family.*

address *noun* (ə dres or ăd res) 1. the place where a person lives or works. The address has the street name and number, city, and state. *The president's address is 1600 Pennsylvania Avenue, Washington, D.C., 20500.* 2. a formal speech or talk. *The senator's address was shown on television.*
verb 1. to speak or write to a particular person or group. *He addressed those comments to me, not to you.* 2. to write information that tells where to send something. *I addressed the letter to him in Atlanta.*

adequate *adj.* (ă də kwit) enough; as much as needed. *Is your paycheck adequate?*

adhesive *adj.* (ăd hē siv) able or likely to stick to something. *This tape is so old that it isn't adhesive anymore.*
noun [N] a sticky substance such as glue. *We used some adhesive to fix the broken dish.*

adhesive bandage *noun* (ăd hē siv băn dij) a small piece of cloth or plastic with a sticky material on one side. You use an adhesive bandage to cover a wound and keep it clean.

adhesive bandage

adhesive tape *noun* (ăd hē siv tāp) [N] a long, thin piece of cloth or plastic with a sticky material on one side. You use adhesive tape to attach things to each other. *The doctor used adhesive tape to cover the bandage on my cut.*

adjective *noun* (ă jək tiv) a word that describes a noun. In the sentences "It was a hard test" and "The test was hard," the word *hard* is an adjective.

adjust *verb* (ə jəst) 1. to bring to a better state or position; make fit. *I adjusted my seat belt.* 2. to change in order to fit in; get used to. *Mary will adjust to her new school.*

administration *noun* (əd mi nə strā shən) the people in charge of a group, organization, or business. *The school administration meets with the teachers once a month.*

admiration *noun* (ăd mə rā shən) [N] a feeling of deep respect and approval. *He had* **admiration for** *his teacher.*

admire *verb* (əd mīr) to have a high opinion of; respect. *I admire the hard work you do.*

admission *noun* (əd mi shən) 1. the act of letting someone enter something, or the condition of being allowed to enter. *He was in charge of hospital admissions.* | *She had to fill out many forms before her admission to the hospital.* 2. [N] the price a person must pay to enter. *Admission to the movie is six dollars.*

admit *verb* (əd mit) 1. to let in; allow to enter. *This movie ticket admits one.* | *The restaurant admitted us after a long wait.* 2. to tell the truth. *Did he admit that he broke the window?*

adopt *verb* (ə dəpt) 1. to become a parent of someone by law. *We adopted a baby, so now we have two children.* 2. to accept in an official way, often by voting. *The city adopted a new traffic law.*

Word Builder: adopt +
adopted: having been accepted by law.

adopt or adapt?
Adopt means to accept a new thing as your own. *Adapt* means to make changes because of a new purpose or situation.
Compare:
We adopted a puppy from the animal shelter.
The puppy soon adapted to its new home.

11

Irregular forms of nouns and verbs are in *blue italic* type. For verbs, this dictionary shows both the past tense and past participle, even when the form is the same. For nouns, this dictionary shows the plural form. A list of irregular verbs is on page 270. A list of irregular nouns and adjectives is on page 272.

Example sentences, in italic show how to use the word in a sentence. **Bold** type in an example sentence shows other words that are often used with the entry word.

Pronunciation guides are in parentheses. Some words have more than one pronunciation, usually because people pronounce the word differently in different parts of the country. If pronunciation changes with different parts of speech, the pronunciation is shown with each part of speech. A key to the pronunciation guides is on page 5.

[N] before a definition means that this is a noncount noun. Noncount nouns do not have a plural form.

Cross-references to other entry words are shown in **bold** type in the definition.

Word notes help you decide which word to use when two or more words are often confused because they are similar in some way.

A a

a *art.* (ə or ā) 1. any one of a group or kind. *A house is a place to live.* | *We have a dog.* 2. one of some kind of thing. *I bought a bottle of orange juice and two apples.* 3. any one of a particular group. *Mary is a friend of mine.*

abbreviation *noun* (ə brē vē ā shən) a short form of a word or phrase used in writing. *Mon. is an abbreviation for the word Monday.*

ability *noun* (ə bi lə tē) 1. the power or knowledge to do something. *Most birds have the ability to fly.* | *Your child has many abilities.* 2. [N] skill. *She has a lot of ability as a tennis player.*

able *adj.* (ā bəl) having the power or knowledge to do something. *She is not **able to** walk because she broke her leg.* | *He is **able to** use a computer.*

about *prep.* (ə bowt) concerning. *I read a book about animals.*
adv. more or less; nearly. *I paid about ten dollars for this shirt.* | *I have lived here for about four years.*
about to ready to; very close to doing something. *I was about to leave when the phone rang.*

above *adv.* (ə bəv) at or to a higher place. *There were birds flying up above.*
prep. at, on, or to a higher place than something else. *The plane is flying above the clouds.* | *Put the picture there, and the clock above it.*

abroad *adv.* (ə brawd) in or to another country. *We lived abroad for two years.* | *Joe traveled abroad.*

absence *noun* (æb səns) 1. a time of being away or not present. *My child had three absences from school last month.* 2. [N] a length of time of being away. *Work continued during the boss's absence.*

absent *adj.* (æb sənt) not in the expected place. *Jen was **absent from** work because she was sick.* | *Why were you absent yesterday?*

absorb *verb* (əb zorb) to take in liquid through the surface. *These towels don't absorb water well.*

abuse *verb* (ə būz) 1. to use in a way that is wrong or bad. *If you abuse alcohol, you will hurt your health.* 2. to hurt someone or something by treating it in a bad way. *His father abused him when he was a child.*
noun (ə būs) 1. [N] bad or wrong use. *Drug abuse is a problem for some people.* 2. [N] cruel or harmful treatment. *Child abuse is a crime.*

academic *adj.* (æ kə de mik) having to do with school or what you learn in school. *Teaching is an academic job.* | *My son doesn't like academic work.*

accelerate *verb* (ək se lə rāt) to make something go faster. *The driver accelerated the car.*

> **Word Builder: accelerate +**
> **accelerator:** a device that increases the speed of something, such as the gas pedal in a car.

accept *verb* (ək sept) 1. to say yes when someone wants to give you something. *She accepted the job offer.* | *He was happy to accept her gift.* 2. to allow someone to join a group or organization. *Two colleges accepted my son.*

acceptable *adj.* (ək sep tə bəl) good enough for someone to accept. *My salary raise was quite acceptable.* | *I made some mistakes, but the teacher said my work was acceptable.*

accessory *noun* (ək se sə rē) a thing that you add to something else to make it nicer or better. *Air conditioning is an accessory in many cars.* | *She bought a scarf and other accessories to match her dress.*

accident *noun* (æk sə dənt) 1. something that happens that you did not plan. *We met **by accident**.* 2. a harmful event that happens by chance. *My uncle was hurt in a car accident.*

accident

accidental *adj.* (æk sə den təl) not planned or intended. *Their meeting was accidental.* | *The damage to the car was accidental.*

> **Word Builder: accidental +**
> **accidentally:** by accident.

accommodate *verb* (ə ka mə dāt) to have space for. *This hotel room accommodates four people.*

accomplish *verb* (ə kam plish) to do or finish something, especially a thing that needed a lot of work or effort. *He accomplished his goal of learning to play the piano. | I was lazy yesterday, but I accomplished a lot today.*

account *noun* (ə kownt) the amount of money you have in a bank. *How much money is in your* **bank account?**
on account of because of. *The game was canceled on account of rain.*
take into account to consider; to not ignore. *The judge took the boy's age into account before deciding on a punishment.*

accounting *noun* (ə kown ting) [N] the profession that records the money that a business or a person gets or spends. *Accounting requires knowledge of mathematics.*

accuracy *noun* (æ kyə ri sē) [N] the condition of being right or correct. *Accuracy is important when you balance your checkbook.*

accurate *adj.* (æ kyə rit) free of mistakes; correct. *The newspaper gave an accurate report of the fire.*

Word Builder: accurate +
accurately: in an accurate way.

accuse *verb* (ə kūz) to say that someone has done something wrong or illegal. *The teacher* **accused** *her of cheating on the test.*

accustom *verb* (ə kə stəm) to become used to or familiar with something over time. *She* **accustomed** *herself* **to** *her new life in the city.*

Word Builder: accustom +
accustomed: in the habit of; used to.

ache *verb* (āk) to have a dull pain that lasts a long time. *Tom's legs ached after the long walk.*
noun a dull pain that lasts a long time. *He used an ice pack to relieve the ache in his jaw.*

ache

Word Builder: kinds of aches
backache: a pain in the back.
bellyache: a pain in the belly.
headache: a pain in the head.
stomachache: a pain in the stomach.
toothache: a pain in a tooth.

achieve *verb* (ə chēv) to do or complete something with success. *He wanted to become famous, and he achieved his goal.*

achievement *noun* (ə chēv mənt) something that is completed with success using hard work or skill. *Graduating from college was a great achievement.*

acid *noun* (æ sid) [N] a substance that has a sour taste and can often burn a hole in something that it touches. *The acid in lemons can hurt your stomach.*

acre *noun* (ā kər) a standard unit of area used to measure land. *He bought two acres of land.*

across *prep.* (ə kraws) 1. from one side of something to the other side. *We hung ribbons across the window.* 2. to or on the other side of. *I bought some candy at the store across the street.*
adv. 1. from one side to the other. *He came to a small stream and jumped across.* 2. on or to the other side or end. *She sat across from me at the table.*

act *noun* (ækt) 1. something that is done. *Firefighters perform many acts of courage in their job.* 2. a short performance, or one part of a whole performance, of music, dance, or other entertainment. *The children enjoyed the clown's act.*
verb 1. to do something with purpose or energy. *He acted with courage in battle.* 2. to perform in plays, in movies, or on television. *She acted in the school play.*

action *noun* (æk shən) something that is done for a specific purpose. *The doctor's quick action saved the child's life.*

activate *verb* (æk tə vāt) to cause something to start working. *You will activate the alarm if you open the door.*

active *adj.* (æk tiv) 1. always doing something; busy; full of energy. *My grandfather is very active even though he is old.* 2. used in grammar to describe a form of the verb that emphasizes the person or thing who performs the action. In the sentence "John ate the apple," the verb *ate* is in an active form. In the sentence "The apple was eaten by John," the verb is in a passive form.

activity *noun* (æk ti və tē) a specific thing that is done. *My favorite activity on weekends is soccer.*

actor *noun* (æk tər) a person who performs in a play, a movie, or a radio or television program.

actress *noun* (ǽk tris) a woman or girl who performs in a play, a movie, or a radio or television program.

actual *adj.* (ǽk choo əl) real; true; exact. *The actual cost of the plane ticket was higher than I expected.*

actually *adv.* (ǽk choo ə lē) as a matter of fact; really. *She actually finished the project on time.*

ad *noun* (ǽd) the short form of **advertisement.**

add *verb* (ǽd) 1. to put on or with something else to make it larger or better. *I always add sugar to my tea.* | *She added a new doll to her collection.* 2. to use mathematics to find the total of two or more numbers. *You made a mistake when you **added** 19 **to** 24.* | *You need to add all the numbers.* 3. to find the sum of a set of numbers. *If you **add up** all the numbers, you will get the answer.*

addition *noun* (ə dí shən) 1. [N] the process of finding the total of two or more numbers. *The first example of addition that we often learn is 1+1= 2.* 2. anything that is added to something else. *The addition to our house will give us a new bedroom.* | *This baby is an addition to our family.*

address *noun* (ə drés or ǽd res) 1. the place where a person lives or works. The address has the street name and number, city, and state. *The president's address is 1600 Pennsylvania Avenue, Washington, D.C. 20050.* 2. a formal speech or talk. *The senator's address was shown on television.*
verb 1. to speak or write to a particular person or group. *He addressed those comments to me, not to you.* 2. to write information that tells where to send something. *I addressed the letter to him in Atlanta.*

adequate *adj.* (ǽ də kwit) enough; as much as needed. *Is your paycheck adequate?*

adhesive *adj.* (ǽd hē siv) able or likely to stick to something. *This tape is so old that it isn't adhesive anymore.*
noun [N] a sticky substance such as glue. *We used some adhesive to fix the broken dish.*

adhesive bandage *noun* (ǽd hē siv bǽn dij) a small piece of cloth or plastic with a sticky material on one side. You use an adhesive bandage to cover a wound and keep it clean.

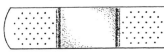

adhesive bandage

adhesive tape *noun* (ǽd hē siv tāp) [N] a long, thin piece of cloth or plastic with a sticky material on one side. You use adhesive tape to attach things to each other. *The doctor used adhesive tape to cover the bandage on my cut.*

adjective *noun* (ǽ jək tiv) a word that describes a noun. In the sentences "It was a hard test" and "The test was hard," the word *hard* is an adjective.

adjust *verb* (ə jást) 1. to bring to a better state or position; make fit. *I adjusted my seat belt.* 2. to change in order to fit in; get used to. *Mary will adjust to her new school.*

administration *noun* (əd mi nə strā shən) people in charge of a group, organization, or business. *The school administration meets with the teachers once a month.*

admiration *noun* (ǽd mə rā shən) [N] a feeling of deep respect and approval. *He had **admiration for** his teacher.*

admire *verb* (əd mīr) to have a high opinion of; respect. *I admire the hard work you do.*

admission *noun* (əd mi shən) 1. the act of letting someone enter something, or the condition of being allowed to enter. *He was in charge of hospital admissions.* | *She had to fill out many forms before her admission to the hospital.* 2. [N] the price a person must pay to enter. *Admission to the movie is six dollars.*

admit *verb* (əd mit) 1. to let in; allow to enter. *This movie ticket admits one.* | *The restaurant admitted us after a long wait.* 2. to tell the truth. *Did he admit that he broke the window?*

adopt *verb* (ə dápt) 1. to become a parent of someone by law. *We adopted a baby, so now we have two children.* 2. to accept in an official way, often by voting. *The city adopted a new traffic law.*

Word Builder: adopt +
adopted: having been accepted by law.

adopt or adapt?
Adopt means to accept a new thing as your own.
Adapt means to make changes because of a new purpose or situation.
Compare:
We adopted a puppy from the animal shelter.
The puppy soon adapted to its new home.

adult *adj.* (ə d̲ə̲l̲t̲) having grown up. *The adult dog weighed seventy pounds.*
noun a person or animal that is done growing. *Children should have an adult with them when they go swimming.*

advance *verb* (əd v̲æ̲n̲s̲) to come or move forward. *The car advanced ten feet.*

advanced *adj.* (əd v̲æ̲n̲s̲t̲) beyond an early or beginning level; in a very developed state. *I'm a good swimmer, so I'm in the advanced class.* | *Their company uses some very advanced technology.*

advantage *noun* (əd v̲æ̲n̲ tij) anything good that you get from something. *The advantages of my new job are better hours and better pay.*
take advantage of 1. to do something to help yourself in a way that is not fair. *I took advantage of my friend by not returning the money I borrowed.* 2. to use something in order to help yourself. *She took advantage of the sale and bought extra cereal.*

adventure *noun* (əd v̲e̲n̲ chər) a trip or activity that is dangerous or exciting. *Ali's journey to America was quite an adventure.*

adverb *noun* (æ̲d̲ vərb) a word that describes a verb, adjective, or other adverb. Many adverbs in English end with the letters *"ly."* In the sentence "That very hungry cat ate extremely quickly," *very, extremely,* and *quickly* are adverbs.

advertise *verb* (æ̲d̲ vər t̲ī̲z̲) 1. to tell about something so people will want to buy it. *Automobile companies advertise their new car models every fall.* 2. to try to find something by putting a notice in a public place. *Acme, Inc.,* **advertised for** *workers in the newspaper.*

advertisement *noun* (æd vər t̲ī̲z̲ mənt) a public notice that tells people about things to buy or things that are happening. *Their advertisement claims that their soap cleans better than before.* | *Did you see the advertisement in the newspaper for the new movie?*

advertisement

advice *noun* (əd v̲ī̲s̲) [N] an idea or opinion that someone gives to help you decide. *My friend gave me good advice on which car to buy.*

advise *verb* (əd v̲ī̲z̲) to give advice to. *His doctor advised him to stop smoking.* | *Did your lawyer* **advise** *you* **about** *the changes in the law?*

> **Word Builder: advise +**
> **adviser, advisor:** a person who advises.

affair *noun* (ə f̲ā̲r̲) 1. an event, matter, or happening. *You should learn more about world affairs.* | *We read about that strange affair in the newspaper.* 2. something that concerns only one person or one particular group; a private matter. *My salary is my affair, not yours.* 3. a love relationship between two people who are not married to each other. *John and Mary* **are having an affair.**

affairs *pl. noun* (ə f̲ā̲r̲z̲) public or business matters. *As mayor, he is always busy with the affairs of the city.*

affect *verb* (ə f̲e̲k̲t̲) to cause a change in. *The bad weather affected my plans to have a picnic.*

afford *verb* (ə f̲ō̲r̲d̲) to have enough money for; be able to pay for. *I can't afford a new car.*

afraid *adj.* (ə f̲r̲ā̲d̲) feeling fear. *She is* **afraid of** *rats.*

after *prep.* (æ̲f̲ tər) later in time than; behind in order or position. *Peter had a snack after school.* | *The first house after the white one is mine.*
conj. following a certain event or time. *A strange thing happened after she left.*

afternoon *noun* (æf tər n̲o̲o̲n̲) the time of day between noon and evening. *School ends in the afternoon.*

afterward *adv.* (æ̲f̲ tər wərd) at a later time. *We saw a movie and went out for pizza afterward.*

again *adv.* (ə g̲e̲n̲) 1. one more time. *Please say that again.* 2. once more; as before. *He was sick for a while, but now he's well again.*

against *prep.* (ə g̲e̲n̲s̲t̲) 1. opposite to something or not in agreement with it. *What you did was against the rules.* | *The manager and the owner seem to be working against each other.* 2. on or touching, so as to be supported by. *Lean the ladder against the house.* 3. in the opposite direction to. *He swam against the tide.*

age *noun* (ā̲j̲) how old a person or thing is. *The boy said his age was twelve.* | *What is the age of this building?*
verb to become older. *Grandfather is aging well.*

aged *adj.* (ā jəd) being old or having lived many years. *She does the housework for her aged grandfather.*

agency *noun* (ā jən sē) a company or group that does business to help other companies or people. An agency can also be part of a government. *The employment agency helped him find work.*

agent *noun* (ā jənt) a person who has the authority to do certain actions for another person. *A travel agent helped me to plan my vacation.*

ago *adv.* (ə gō) in the past. *He lived long ago.* | *My friend called three days ago.*

agree *verb* (ə grē) 1. to have the same opinion or feel the same way. *I **agree with** my friends about most things.* 2. to say yes; consent. *He **agreed to** cut our grass.* 3. to come to an understanding or a decision with another person. *They finally **agreed on** what kind of ice cream to buy.*

agreement *noun* (ə grē mənt) 1. an understanding between people or groups that states what is to be done. *My friends and I **made an agreement** to drive to work together.* 2. [N] the condition of having the same feelings or opinions regarding something. *She and her husband are usually **in agreement** about how to spend money.* | *There is very little agreement between the employees and the management about this matter.* 3. a legal contract. *We signed an agreement to buy that house.*

agriculture *noun* (æ grə kəl chər) [N] the science or activity of farming. Agriculture includes raising crops and animals for food.

Word Builder: agriculture +
agricultural: having to do with agriculture.

ah *interj.* (a) a word used to express surprise, understanding, and other feelings. *Ah! It's so late!* | *Ah, yes, now I understand.*

ahead *adv.* (ə hed) before; in front. *You need to call ahead to get a hotel room.* | *You can go **ahead of** me.*
get ahead to move to a higher position; succeed. *He worked hard to get ahead in his company.*
ahead of time before the time of some event. *You need to buy a ticket ahead of time for the show.*

aid *verb* (ād) to give help to someone. *The doctors aided the sick people.*
noun 1. [N] the help that is given to someone in need. *After her operation, she was glad to have the aid of her neighbors.* 2. a person or thing that helps. *He needs a hearing aid.*

aide *noun* (ād) a person whose job is to help another person. *The teacher's aide helped my son learn to read.*

AIDS *abbrev.* (ādz) a disease that stops the body from being able to protect itself from other diseases. AIDS is spread through body fluids.

aim *verb* (ām) 1. to point something at a thing that you want to hit. *The boy aimed the paper airplane at his friend.* 2. to direct something toward someone. *He aimed his anger at me.* | *She aimed her questions at the children.*
noun intention; purpose; goal. *My aim this month is to finish planting my garden.*

air *noun* (ār) [N] the mixture of gases that is in the space around the earth. People need air to live. *Fish do not breathe air as humans do.*

Word Builder: air +
airbag: a large bag that fills with air to make a cushion when a car crashes. It protects the people in the car.

air conditioning *noun* (ār kən di shə ning) [N] a system that cools air throughout a certain space. Air conditioning is used inside buildings and cars.

aircraft *noun* (ār kræft) [N] any machine that can fly through the air. *Airplanes and helicopters are examples of aircraft.*

air force *noun* (ār fōrs) the branch of a country's military system that uses aircraft.

airline *noun* (ār līn) a business that offers travel by airplane from one place to another. *Which airline will you take when you fly to California?*

airplane *noun* (ār plān) a machine that is heavier than air and that can fly. It has wings and engines.

airplane

airport *noun* (ār pōrt) a large area of land where airplanes come and go. *The airplane took off from the airport.*

aisle *noun* (īl) an open space to walk between rows of seats or shelves. *The aisles are narrow in a small store.* | *The bride walked down the aisle of the church.*

alarm *noun* (ə larm) 1. a bell or other loud noise used to signal danger. *When they heard the fire alarm, they left the building.* 2. the sound of a clock that wakes you up. *I didn't hear my alarm this morning, so I slept late.*

alarm clock *noun* (ə larm klak) a clock that makes a noise to wake you up. *I set my alarm clock for six o'clock in the morning.*

album *noun* (æl bəm) 1. a book with empty pages used for showing photographs, stamps, or other things. *She bought an album for pictures of the new baby.* 2. a recording of music that usually contains several pieces of music. *The singer recorded a new album of songs.*

> **Word Builder: kinds of albums**
> **photo album:** an album that you put photographs in.
> **record album:** a CD or other disk with a collection of songs.

alcohol *noun* (æl kə hawl) [N] a clear liquid made from certain grains and fruits that has an effect on a person's mind and physical ability. Alcohol is in drinks such as beer and wine. It is also used to make some kinds of medicine.

> **Word Builder: alcohol +**
> **alcoholic** (1): containing alcohol.
> **alcoholic** (2): a person who drinks too much alcohol; a person with alcoholism.
> **alcoholism:** a disease caused by the habit of drinking too much alcohol.

alert *adj.* (ə lərt) quick to notice and act. *The alert driver saw the child in the road and quickly stopped the car.*

alike *adv.* (ə līk) in the same way. *My sister and I dressed alike when we were little.*
adj. like one another; similar. *These two shirts are exactly alike.*

alive *adj.* (ə līv) having life; not dead. *Fish need water to stay alive.*

all *adj.* (awl) the whole thing of something or every one of some kind of thing. *I waited all week for her telephone call.* | *All babies cry sometimes.*
pron. 1. each of the people or things being talked about. *The boat carrying ten passengers sank, but all were saved.* 2. the total number or total amount of something. ***All of** the children liked the new teacher.* | *They finished **all of** their work.*

at all to any degree; in any way; used with *not* to make the meaning stronger. *I do not understand this homework at all!*

allegiance *noun* (ə lē jəns) loyalty to a person, country, or belief. *The soldiers gave their allegiance to the king.* | *The children **pledge allegiance** to the flag every morning at school.*

allergic *adj.* (ə lər jik) having an allergy. *Because she is **allergic to** cat hair, she sneezes if she is near a cat.*

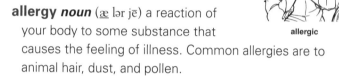

allergic

allergy *noun* (æ lər jē) a reaction of your body to some substance that causes the feeling of illness. Common allergies are to animal hair, dust, and pollen.

allow *verb* (ə low) to say that someone may do something; let; permit. *His mother said no at first, but later she allowed him to go to the late movie.*

allowance *noun* (ə low əns) [N] money that someone receives at regular times or for a particular purpose. *His parents give him his weekly allowance on Saturday.* | *The company's managers get a travel allowance each month.*

all right *adv.* (awl rīt) well enough but not perfect. *He did all right on the test, but he could have done better.*
adj. not harmed or damaged; safe. *The car accident was bad, but the driver was all right.*
interj. yes; OK. *All right, if you really want me to go with you, I'll go.*

almost *adv.* (awl mōst) not quite all; nearly. *I am almost finished with this book.* | *My daughter is almost five years old.*

alone *adj.* (ə lōn) 1. being in a place with no other people. *He was alone on the island.* 2. without anyone or anything else. *You alone will have to make this decision.*
adv. without anything or anyone else. *She works alone.*
leave alone to keep away from a person or thing. *She didn't want to talk, so we left her alone.* | *Leave my things alone.*

along *prep.* (ə lawng) over the line that something makes; in a line that goes next to something. *We ran along the path.* | *We drove along the ocean.*
adv. in the company of other people. *Do you want to **come along with** us to the park?*

aloud *adv.* (ə lowd) in a voice that people can hear. *The teacher read aloud to the children.*

alphabet *noun* (æl fə bet) all the letters of a language that you use when you write it. We say or write an alphabet in a special order. *The English alphabet begins with A and ends with Z.*

alphabetical *adj.* (æl fə be tə kəl) arranged in the order of the alphabet. *The students' names were in alphabetical order.*

Word Builder: alphabetical +
alphabetically: in alphabetical order.

already *adv.* (awl re dē) 1. before now or before some other time. *I already have a form and don't need another one.* | *When I arrived at the station, the train had already left.* 2. so soon. *Have the guests arrived already?*

also *adv.* (awl sō) too; in addition. *I bought a jacket, and I also bought a hat.*

alternative *noun* (awl tər nə tiv) one of two or more choices. *Our two alternatives are walking or taking a taxi.* *adj.* different in a way that gives you a choice. *Paying by credit card and paying in cash are alternative ways to pay for something.*

although *conj.* (awl thō) used when two parts of a sentence are true but seem to disagree with each other. *Although he is smart, school is difficult for him.* | *We bought the car although it was expensive.*

altogether *adv.* (awl tə ge thər) if you count or include everything. *Altogether, the price is ten dollars.*

aluminum *noun* (ə loo mi nəm) [N] a strong, light metal with a silver color. It is used to make things such as cooking pots and foil.

always *adv.* (awl wāz) 1. at all times; without stopping; forever. *She has two jobs, so she is always busy.* | *The stars are always in the sky.* 2. every time. *He always arrives at work early.* 3. at any time. *If you have a question, you can always ask me.*

a.m. *abbrev.* (ā em) the time between twelve o'clock in the night and twelve o'clock in the day; morning.

am *verb* (æm) a form of the verb *be* that is present tense and used with the pronoun *I*.

amaze *verb* (ə māz) to surprise very much. *The large size of the fish amazed everyone.*

Word Builder: amaze +
amazed: showing great wonder or surprise.
amazement: great wonder or surprise.
amazing: causing great wonder or surprise.

ambition *noun* (æm bi shən) a strong desire to reach a goal; the goal that someone wants to reach. *He has a strong ambition to become a lawyer.* | *Her ambition was to become famous.*

ambitious *adj.* (æm bi shəs) having or showing a strong desire to reach a goal or have success in general. *Carlos is an ambitious young man who plans to become a doctor.*

ambulance *noun* (æm byə ləns) a vehicle that carries people who are sick or hurt to a hospital. *When he fell off the roof, his wife called for an ambulance.*

ambulance

amendment *noun* (ə mend mənt) an official change made to a bill, law, or other document. *The first ten amendments to the U.S. Constitution are called the Bill of Rights.*

amenity *noun* (ə me ni tē) something that makes a place or an occasion more convenient, pleasant, or comfortable. *The hotel offered many amenities, including a restaurant and a swimming pool.*

America *noun* (ə me ri kə) 1. another name for the **United States** that people in the United States use. 2. North America, South America, or both. *They have done a lot of traveling in **the Americas.***

American *adj.* (ə me ri kən) of or having to do with the United States or its people or language. *The American people elect their president every four years.* *noun* a person who was born in or is a citizen of the United States.

American Revolution *noun* (ə me ri kən re və loo shən) the war in which the American people won their independence from England. *The American Revolution took place from 1775 to 1783.*

ammonia *noun* (ə mōn yə) [N] a liquid with a strong smell made from a chemical gas and water. Ammonia is used in some cleaning products and in fertilizers.

among *prep.* (ə məng) 1. together with or in the middle of. *She is comfortable among her friends. | There were some shells among the stones. | We walked among the trees.* 2. with a share for each. *The bread was shared among ten people.*

among or between?
Among is used when talking about three or more people or things.
Between is used when talking about two people or things.
Compare:
Bill and Ben divided the pizza between themselves.
Tony, Tom, and Tim divided the pizza among themselves.

amount *noun* (ə mownt) a measure; quantity. *He put a small amount of butter on his bread. | What amount of money is in the account?*

amphibian *noun* (æm fi bē ən) a small animal that is born in water and then lives on land for part of its life. Frogs and toads are kinds of amphibians.

amuse *verb* (ə mūz) to cause to smile or laugh. *His funny stories amuse us.*

amusement *noun* (ə mūz mənt) something that amuses or entertains; fun. *My favorite amusement is riding a bike.*

amusing *adj.* (ə mū zing) entertaining; funny. *Maria told an amusing story.*

an *art.* (æn) another word for **a.** It is used before words that start with vowel sounds. *There is **an apple** for you and **an orange** for me. | It is **an honor** to meet you.*

analyses *pl. noun* (ə næ lə sēz) plural of **analysis.**

analysis *noun* (ə næ lə sis) *analyses* a careful study of the parts of something in order to understand more about the whole. *The teacher's analysis of the book helped us understand its importance.*

analyze *verb* (æ nə līz) to separate into parts for close study; examine and explain. *If we analyze the problem, perhaps we can solve it.*

ancestor *noun* (æn se stər) a person in your family who lived a long time before you were born. *Her ancestors came to America from Africa.*

anchor *noun* (æng kər) 1. a heavy object that is attached to and dropped from a boat or ship to keep it from moving. *The captain dropped the boat's anchor into the water.* 2. the main person who reports the news on a television or radio program.

anchor

ancient *adj.* (ān shənt) very old; from a long time ago. *Rome is an ancient city with many ancient buildings.*

and *conj.* (ænd) 1. with; also; along with; as well as. *We ate cake and ice cream. | John wore a suit, and Mary wore a dress.* 2. added to; plus. *Six and six equals twelve.*

anemia *noun* (ə nē mē ə) [N] a physical problem caused by having too few red blood cells or having red blood cells that are not working in the right way. People with anemia may feel tired and weak.

anger *noun* (æng gər) [N] a strong feeling caused when someone or something has done something wrong to you or when you think that something is bad or not fair. *His mean words filled me with anger.*
verb to make angry. *Her lies angered me.*

angle *noun* (æng gəl) the figure made by two lines coming from a single point. *Every triangle has three angles.*

angry *adj.* (æng grē) feeling or showing anger. *Liz was **angry at** George for coming late.*

animal *noun* (æ nə məl) 1. one of a large group of living things that is not a plant. Animals can move around by themselves to find food. 2. a living creature that is not a plant or a human. *We saw many animals at the zoo. | They have cows, chickens, and other animals on their farm.*

ankle *noun* (æng kəl) the joint between the leg and the foot.

announce *verb* (ə nowns) 1. to tell or make known. *They announced the birth of their first baby.* 2. to report on the action of an event, often on radio or television. *He announces all the football games on this channel.*

Word Builder: announce +
announcer: a person who announces.

announcement *noun* (ə nowns mənt) a public or formal statement. *The newspaper prints wedding announcements once a week.*

annoy *verb* (ə <u>noy</u>) to cause someone to be angry or upset. *Their loud music annoyed the neighbors.*

annual *adj.* (<u>æn</u> ū əl) 1. happening once every year. *The state fair is an annual event.* 2. of or having to do with a year; yearly. *Her annual salary is thirty thousand dollars.*

another *adj.* (ə <u>nə</u> thər) 1. being one more just like the others; a different one. *May I have another piece of bread?* 2. of a different kind; not the same. *She lives in another country.*
pron. 1. a different one; a new one. *Since that dish is broken, I'll buy another.* 2. one that is just like the others. *I've already had two cookies, but I'd like another.*
another one one more of the same kind. *She returned the broken toaster to the store and got another one.*

answer *noun* (<u>æn</u> sər) 1. what you say or write after someone asks you a question; a reply. *I want an answer to my question.* 2. the solution to a problem. *You will find the right answer if you think about it.* | *The teacher said my answers on the test were all correct.*

answering machine *noun* (<u>æn</u> sər ing mə <u>shēn</u>) a machine that records a telephone message. *I left a message on your answering machine when you were out.*

ant *noun* (<u>ænt</u>) a small insect, often red or black. Ants live in large groups in the ground.

ant

anthem *noun* (<u>æn</u> thəm) a song of praise, often for one's country. *Everyone stood as the band played the national anthem.*

Word Builder: kind of anthem
national anthem: the official anthem of a nation. "The Star-Spangled Banner" is the national anthem of the United States.

antibiotic *noun* (æn ti bī <u>a</u> tik) a medicine that can destroy or prevent the growth of disease and infection. *I took an antibiotic for my sore throat.*

antiseptic *noun* (æn tə <u>sep</u> tik) a substance or drug used to stop disease or infection. *The doctor put an antiseptic on the wound.*

anxiety *noun* (æng <u>zī</u> ə tē) [N] a feeling of being worried, nervous, or afraid that something bad will happen. *I have anxiety about flying in a plane.*

anxious *adj.* (<u>ænk</u> shəs) feeling worried, nervous, or afraid about something. *She was anxious as she waited to see the doctor.*

any *adj.* (<u>e</u> nē) 1. one or some of a certain thing, no matter which, how much, or how many. *You may sit at any table.* | *Do you have any money?* 2. each and every. *Any child can learn.* 3. even a very small amount of; used after *not. I do not want any trouble.*
pron. an amount of something; a number of; used in questions or with *not. Did you spend* **any of** *your money?* | *There aren't* **any of** *those rolls left.*
adv. at all; to a degree. *Is he any better today?*

anybody *pron.* (<u>e</u> nē ba dē) [N] any person; anyone. *Anybody can enjoy this movie.*

anyhow *adv.* (<u>e</u> nē how) in any case; anyway. *I do not have a map, but I will go anyhow.*

anymore *adv.* (<u>e</u> nē <u>mōr</u>) 1. any longer. *After she moves to the city, we will not see her anymore.* 2. at the present time; these days; used with *not. People do not ride in carriages much anymore.*

anyone *pron.* (<u>e</u> nē wən) any person; anybody. *Does anyone know where my book is?*

anything *pron.* (<u>e</u> nē thing) any thing or subject whatever. *Is there anything you have not told me?*
noun [N] a single thing; a thing of any kind. *Do you know anything about physics?*
adv. in any way; at all. *He is not anything like his father.*

anyway *adv.* (<u>e</u> nē wā) in any case; anyhow; no matter what happens. *She was sick but went to school anyway.*

anywhere *adv.* (<u>e</u> nē wār) to or in any place or direction; at any place. *She liked adventure and was not afraid to go anywhere.* | *I can't find my glasses anywhere.*

apart *adv.* (ə <u>part</u>) 1. away from each other in time or space. *We keep our cat and dog apart.* | *Jim and his sister are three years apart in age.* 2. into pieces. *The lamp fell apart when I dropped it.*

apartment *noun* (ə <u>part</u> mənt) one or more rooms that people live in and that are part of a building. *Jack's apartment has a bedroom, a bathroom, a kitchen, and a living room.*

Word Builder: apartment +
apartment complex: a group of apartment houses.
apartment house: a large building that has many apartments in it.

apologize *verb* (ə pa̱ lə jīz) to say that you are sorry. *I apologized for being late to the meeting.*

apology *noun* (ə pa̱ lə jē) a statement that you are sorry for something that you did. *I hope she'll **accept** my **apology** for forgetting our appointment. | I'm calling because I **owe** you an **apology**.*

apostrophe *noun* (ə pa̱ strə fē) 1. a punctuation mark (')used to show where one or more letters or numbers have been left out. *Wouldn't for would not and '87 for1987 use apostrophes this way.* 2. a punctuation mark (') used to show possession. *Susan's clothes and citizens' rights use apostrophes this way.*

apparent *adj.* (ə pær ənt) easy to see; clear. *It is apparent that you didn't cook dinner yet.*

Word Builder: apparent +
apparently: in a way that seems to be true.

appeal *noun* (ə pēl) [N] the ability to get interest and attention. *That toy has great appeal for young children.* **verb** 1. to seem interesting or attractive to someone. *Chocolate appeals to many people.* 2. to request that a higher court change the decision of a lower court. *The lawyer appealed the case to the Supreme Court.*

appear *verb* (ə pēr) 1. to begin to be seen. *A dark shape appeared in the distance.* 2. to seem. *Jared appears to be smart.* 3. to come before the public. *My favorite singer will appear on television tonight.*

appearance *noun* (ə pēr əns) 1. the act of arriving and becoming able to be seen. *We were surprised by the appearance of a stranger at our house.* 2. the way something seems or looks. *That dog has a friendly appearance. | Your appearance is important in a job interview.*

appetizer *noun* (æ pə tī zər) a small amount of food or drink served before a meal.

apple *noun* (æ pəl) a firm, round fruit with red, green, or yellow skin. Apples grow on trees.

apple

Word Builder: apple +
apple pie: a pastry filled with cooked apples. Apple pie is used as a symbol of American values.
applesauce: a soft food made of cooked apples.

appliance *noun* (ə plī əns) a piece of equipment that people use to help them do work at home. Ovens and refrigerators are some kinds of appliances.

applicant *noun* (æ pli kənt) a person who applies for a job or some other thing. *The applicant is waiting for his interview. | That university accepts only half of the applicants.*

application *noun* (æ pli kā shən) a request in writing. *Mrs. Johnson **filled out** a job **application**.*

apply *verb* (ə plī) 1. to lay on. *He applied paint to the walls and ceiling.* 2. to make a formal request, often for employment or permission to enter an institution. *Mr. Kane **applied for** a job at the supermarket. | My daughter **applied to** the bank for a job.*

appoint *verb* (ə poynt) to name someone to a particular office or duty. *The mayor appointed a new police chief.*

appointment *noun* (ə poynt mənt) an arrangement to meet or to do something at a particular time. *You need to **make an appointment** with the doctor.*

appreciate *verb* (ə prē shē āt) to feel or show thanks for something. *Dorothy appreciated her neighbor's help.*

appreciation *noun* (ə prē shē ā shən) [N] a feeling of thanks. *Mr. Jones expressed his appreciation to his employees for their hard work.*

approach *verb* (ə prōch) to come or go near to. *Be careful when you approach a strange dog.*

appropriate *adj.* (ə prō prē ət) right for a certain time and place; proper. *Jeans and a T-shirt are not appropriate clothes for a formal wedding.*

approval *noun* (ə proo vəl) the act of approving. *You need the approval of your doctor before you can leave the hospital.*

approve *verb* (ə proov) 1. to say that you accept something; to say yes to something. *The bank approved Sam's loan application.* 2. to have a good opinion of someone or something. *Mrs. Garcia doesn't approve of people who smoke.*

approximate *adj.* (ə prak sə mit) close in amount or time, but not exact. *The mechanic told us the approximate cost to repair the car. | What is the approximate time that you will arrive?*

Word Builder: approximate +
approximately: almost exactly; about.

April *noun* (ā prəl) the fourth month of the year.

apron *noun* (ā prən) a piece of clothing that covers the front of the body. An apron helps keep clothes clean.

arch *noun* (arch) a rounded structure over an open space such as a door. *There is an arch over the entrance to the church.*

are *verb* (ar) a form of the verb *be* that is present tense and used with the pronouns *you, we,* or *they.* It is also used with plural nouns.

area *noun* (ār ē ə) 1. a place or region. *That area of the country has many lakes.* 2. the amount of surface within a certain space. *This room is ten feet wide and twenty feet long, so the area is two hundred square feet.*

area code *noun* (ār ē ə kōd) the first three numbers of a telephone number in the United States and Canada. You dial the area code first and then the telephone number. In the phone number *607-555-1234,* the area code is *607.*

argue *verb* (ar gū) 1. to disagree; quarrel. *The children* **argued over** *which game to play.* 2. to make statements that support your idea or opinion. *His parents argued that a new car would be too expensive.*

argument *noun* (ar gū mənt) an angry discussion by people who disagree. *Mr. and Mrs. Harris had an argument about money.*

arithmetic *noun* (ə rith mə tik) [N] the study of the use of numbers to add, subtract, multiply, and divide. Arithmetic is a basic area of mathematics.

arm[1] *noun* (arm) 1. the part of the body between the shoulder and the wrist. 2. any part that looks like or is used like an arm. *Do not sit on the arm of that chair.*

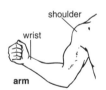

shoulder
wrist
arm

> **Word Builder: arm +**
> **armchair:** a chair with parts at the sides for resting your arms.
> **armrest:** the part on some chairs for resting your arm.

arm[2] *verb* (arm) to make ready for war. *The country armed itself against its enemy.*

armed forces *pl. noun* (armd fōr səz) all the military groups of a country. In the United States, the Army, the Navy, the Air Force, and the Marines make up the armed forces.

arms *pl. noun* (armz) things used to attack and hurt other people. Guns and knives are kinds of arms. *Some countries sell arms to other countries.*
bear arms to carry and use weapons. *They have the right to bear arms.*

army *noun* (ar mē) a large group of people brought together by a country to protect the country and fight its enemies. *People may join the army when they are eighteen.*

around *adv.* (ə rownd) 1. in a circle. *The car spun around.* 2. in all directions or to all sides. *He looked around.* 3. (informal) near. *I'll be around if you need me.* 4. in or to the opposite direction. *Michael turned around to look in the mirror.* 5. through an area. *Will you show me around?*
prep. 1. on all sides of. *There are trees around the park.* 2. near. *John had to stay around the house.* 3. in or to places within an area; here and there. *They drove around the country.* 4. in a way that encloses or makes a circle. *This ring is too tight around my finger.* 5. so as to move in a circle. *I walked around the tree.* 6. somewhere near in time or amount; about. *We eat lunch around noon.* | *This watch costs around twenty dollars.*

arrange *verb* (ə rānj) 1. to put in an order. *Joe arranged his books by author.* 2. to make plans for; prepare. *Mrs. Gomez arranged a birthday party for her son.*

arrangement *noun* (ə rānj mənt) 1. the group of things that have been put in order. *I sent a flower arrangement to my friend in the hospital.* 2. a plan. *We have an arrangement to meet for lunch once a week.* | *Who is* **making arrangements** *for the funeral?*

arrest *verb* (ə rest) to stop and hold someone for breaking the law. *The police arrested the criminal.*
noun the act of stopping and holding someone for breaking the law. *The police put the suspect* **under arrest.**

arrival *noun* (ə rī vəl) coming to or reaching a certain place. *Mr. Sen waited for the arrival of his son at the airport.*

arrive *verb* (ə rīv) to come to or reach a certain place. *The children are hungry when they arrive home after school.*

arrow *noun* (ăr ō) 1. a thin stick with a point on one end. An arrow is a kind of weapon. *The hunter shot a deer with an arrow.* 2. a sign with a shape like this weapon. An arrow is used to point out a place or show which way to go. *Follow the arrow to the exit.*

art *noun* (art) [N] things that are made by humans and that people think have beauty or deep meaning. Music, films, written works, and paintings are examples of art. *We looked at the art on display.*

article *noun* (ar tə kəl) 1. one thing out of a group of similar things. *She put several **articles of clothing** into her suitcase.* 2. a piece of writing in a newspaper, magazine, or book. *Did you read the article about the president's speech?* 3. the word *a* or *an* or *the*. Articles are used before nouns to express whether the noun is a specific example of something or whether the noun is a general example of something.

artificial *adj.* (ar tə fĭ shəl) made by people; not natural. *Those flowers are artificial, not real.*

artificial respiration *noun* (ar tə fĭ shəl re spə rā shən) [N] a way to help a person who has stopped breathing by pushing air into and out of the lungs.

artist *noun* (ar tist) a person who works at or who has skill at painting, music, or any other form of art.

as *adv.* (ăz) equally; to an equal degree. *He is smart, but his sister is just as smart.*
　　conj. 1. in the same way or manner that; to the same degree. *He doesn't love you as I do!* 2. at the same moment; when. *One machine stopped as the other machine started.* 3. because. *As I was tired, I went to bed.* 4. at a point during some action or during the same time period as another action. *As I was walking to work, I saw a car accident.* | *As she was sleeping, her parents were packing for their trip.*
　　prep. in the position or function of. *He has a job as a mechanic.*
　　as...as to the same degree or in the same amount that something else is. *She is as tall as her mother now.* | *I don't have as many friends as you have.*
　　as if how it would be if. *He looked as if he had not slept for days.*
　　as of beginning on; from. *As of tomorrow, my son will be old enough to drive a car.*

ash *noun* (ăsh) the soft gray powder that remains after something burns. *The cigarette ash fell to the floor.*

ashamed *adj.* (ə shāmd) feeling bad about yourself, usually because you did something wrong; feeling shame. *She was ashamed of herself for cheating on the test.*

aside *adv.* (ə sīd) 1. on or toward the side. *As we came toward each other on the sidewalk, she stepped aside.* 2. away or to a separate place. *She pushed her vegetables aside and ate her meat.* | *He stood aside while his parents talked to his teacher.*

ask *verb* (ăsk) 1. to put a question to someone. *He asked me what time it was.* | *The teacher asked the student her name.* 2. to make a request of someone. *His mother asked him to close the window.* 3. to put a question to someone for information about something. *She **asked about** his trip to Chicago.* 4. to request something. *I **asked for** the salt, but she gave me the sugar.*

asleep *adj.* (ə slēp) in a state of sleep. *Please be quiet while the baby is asleep.* | *I was so tired, but I couldn't fall asleep.*

asphalt *noun* (ăs fawlt) [N] a black, sticky substance that is mixed with small rocks and becomes hard. People use asphalt to make roads.

aspirin *noun* (ă spər in) [N] a drug that people use to take away pain and bring down fever. *The doctor told him to take two tablets of aspirin for his headache.*

aspirin

assault *noun* (ə sawlt) 1. the crime of attacking someone. *Hitting someone is an assault.* 2. an attack made by armed forces. *The army began its assault on the enemy base.*
　　verb to make an assault on; attack. *The strange man assaulted her as she was walking home.*

assembly *noun* (ə sem blē) 1. [N] the process of joining things together to make a whole thing. *Assembly of the bicycle took all afternoon.* 2. a part of state government that makes laws. *Ms. Berg was elected to the state assembly.* 3. [N] the coming together of people for a particular purpose. *Freedom of assembly is an important right of the American people.*

assembly line *noun* (ə sem blē līn) a way of putting together a product in a factory. The product moves along a line of people, and each person adds a part until the product is finished.

assign *verb* (ə sīn) 1. to choose someone to do a particular thing. *His boss assigned him to work the night shift.* 2. to give a particular thing for someone to do. *The teacher assigned homework.*

Word Builder: assign +
assignment: a piece of work that has been assigned.

assist *verb* (ə sist) to give help to someone. *The nurse assisted the doctor with the operation.*

Word Builder: assist +
assistance: the act of assisting.
assistant: a person who assists.

associate *verb* (ə sō shē āt) 1. to join with other people as friends or partners. *At age ten, some girls don't want to associate with boys.* 2. to connect one thing with another thing in your mind. *I associate fall with going back to school.*
noun (ə sō shē it) a person who is active with someone else in operating a business; a partner. *He discussed the decision with his associate.*

associate's degree *noun* (ə sō shē its di grē) a degree that you get after finishing a program of studies at a community college. *Mark earned an associate's degree in accounting.*

association *noun* (ə sō shē ā shən) a group of people who join together for a common purpose or interest. *I am a member of the parent association at my daughter's school.*

assume *verb* (ə soom) to think that something is true without knowing the facts or asking about them. *Everyone assumed they were rich because they had a big house, many cars, and a swimming pool.*

assure *verb* (ə shur) to cause someone to feel certain or say something to make someone feel certain. *The mother's gentle voice assures the baby that he is safe. | His lawyer assured him that there was no problem.*

astonish *verb* (ə sta nish) to surprise someone very much. *The news astonished us.*

Word Builder: astonish +
astonishing: causing great surprise.
astonishment: great surprise.

astronaut *noun* (æ strə nawt) a person whose job is to travel and work in space.

astronaut

at *prep.* (æt) 1. in or near a place. *We had dinner at a restaurant.* 2. used to say the particular time that an action happens. *I will meet you for lunch at one o'clock.* 3. in the direction of; toward. *We looked at the moon. | The baby smiled at her mother. | He aimed the gun at the target.*

ate *verb* (āt) past tense of **eat.**

athlete *noun* (æth lēt) a person who takes part in sports or other physical activities.

athletic *adj.* (æth le tik) having to do with sports and other physical activities. *That athletic equipment is in poor condition. | She has a lot of athletic ability.*

atlas *noun* (æt ləs) a book of maps. *We looked at the atlas to plan our trip.*

ATM *abbrev.* (ā tē em) an abbreviation for *automated teller machine.* An ATM is a machine for getting money without going into a bank.

atmosphere *noun* (æt məs fēr) 1. [N] gases that are in the space around the earth. 2. [N] the feeling of a particular place. *That restaurant has a warm and pleasant atmosphere.*

atom *noun* (æ təm) the smallest possible unit of a chemical element. *Water is a substance that contains two kinds of atoms.*

atomic *adj.* (ə ta mik) having to do with atoms or energy from atoms. *Many countries use atomic energy to produce electricity.*

attach *verb* (ə tæch) to join, fasten, or connect. *He attached the telephone wire to the wall.*

Word Builder: attach +
attachment: something that can be attached to another thing.

attack *verb* (ə tæk) to begin to cause violent or serious harm to. *The cat attacked the mouse. | The army attacked the enemy. | The disease attacked his lungs.*
noun an action with the purpose of hurting or destroying. *The army's attack was a terrible surprise.*

attempt *verb* (ə tempt) to try. *He attempted to help the woman stand up after she fell.*
noun an effort to do or accomplish something. *Her attempt to read every book in the library will not succeed.*

attend *verb* (ə tend) to be present at a place for some particular purpose. *Did you attend the wedding?* | *The law says that children must attend school.*

attendance *noun* (ə ten dəns) [N] the act of being present at an event. *He was pleased by his father's attendance at his graduation.* | *Teachers record the attendance of students.*

attention *noun* (ə ten shən) [N] the act of directing your mind to something, especially by listening or watching. *The movie held our attention for three hours.* | *The teacher could not get the children's attention.*
pay attention to direct your mind to something. *The television was on, but she wasn't paying attention to it.*

attic *noun* (æ tik) the space in a house that is under the roof and over the ceiling of the top floor. People often store things in the attic.

attitude *noun* (æ ti tood) a way of feeling or thinking about something or someone. *When her attitude toward school improved, her grades got better.*

attorney *noun* (ə tər nē) a person whose job is to give legal advice and to speak for people in court; lawyer.

attract *verb* (ə trækt) to cause to come near. *The restaurant's bright colors attract many customers.* | *Light attracts insects.*

attractive *adj.* (ə træk tiv) having qualities that attract people, such as a pleasant appearance or character. *He is attractive enough to be a movie star.*

audience *noun* (aw dē əns) a group of people gathered to see or hear something. *The audience laughed at all his jokes.*

audio *adj.* (aw dē ō) having to do with sound or using sound. *We bought a new audio system.*

August *noun* (aw gəst) the eighth month of the year.

aunt *noun* (ænt or ant) the sister of one's mother or father, or the wife of one's uncle.

author *noun* (aw thər) a person who writes books, stories, plays, or other works.

authorities *pl. noun* (ə thôr i tēz) (used with *the*) police or other people in government. *You must report crimes to the authorities.*

authority *noun* (ə thôr i tē) 1. [N] the right or power to make decisions and rules that affect other people. *The teacher has the authority to discipline students.* | *Congress has the authority to declare war.* 2. a person who has the most power or control in a particular situation. *The manager is the authority in this restaurant.*

auto *noun* (aw tō) a short form of **automobile.**

auto body *noun* (aw tō ba dē) the main part of a car; the part of a car that you sit inside. *The auto body was damaged in the accident.*

automated *adj.* (aw tə mā təd) able to operate without the help or work of a human. *My doctor's office has an automated telephone system.*

automatic *adj.* (aw tə mæ tik) working or operating by itself. *This house has an automatic heating system.*

> **Word Builder: automatic +**
> **automatically:** in an automatic way.

automobile *noun* (aw tə mə bēl) another word for **car.** *She prefers to travel by automobile.*

automobile

autumn *noun* (aw təm) the season of the year between summer and winter; fall.

auxiliary *adj.* (awg zil yə rē) serving to help or support. *We can use auxiliary power if the electricity shuts off.*

auxiliary verb *noun* (awg zil yə rē vərb) a part of the verb phrase in a sentence that shows tense or is used to make questions. In the phrases "She is sleeping" and "Do you like it?", *is* and *do* are auxiliary verbs.

available *adj.* (ə vā lə bəl) able to be used; possible to get. *The baseball field is now available for the season.* | *That video isn't available in this store.*

> **Word Builder: available +**
> **availability:** the condition of being available.

avenue *noun* (æ və noo) a wide street. *There was a lot of traffic on the avenue.*

average *noun* (æ və rij) 1. a usual amount or kind; something that is ordinary. *The temperature this winter was the average for our area.* 2. the number that results when you add two or more numbers together and then divide them by the number of numbers. *The average of four, six, and two is four: four plus six plus two divided by three is four.*
adj. usual or typical; ordinary. *The average person in this country does not exercise enough.*

avoid *verb* (ə <u>voy</u>d) to keep away from. *He always tries to avoid hard work.*

awake *verb* (ə <u>wāk</u>) *awoke, awoken* 1. to wake someone from sleep. *Please awaken me in the morning before you go.* 2. to come out of sleep. *I awoke when I heard the dog bark.*
adj. not sleeping. *She is awake, so you don't have to whisper.*

award *verb* (ə <u>wōr</u>d) to give as a prize or honor. *The college awards scholarships to students with high grades.*
noun a prize given for a special achievement; honor. *The mayor presented her with an award for her volunteer work.*

aware *adj.* (ə <u>wār</u>) knowing or conscious. *I **am aware of** the hole in my shirt.*

Word Builder: aware +
awareness: the state of being aware.

away *adv.* (ə <u>wā</u>) 1. in another direction or to another place. *He walked away.* 2. from a person's keeping or possession. *She gave away my secret.* | *Latoya wants to give away all her toys.*
adj. 1. in another place; not present. *She is away from home this week.* 2. in the distance. *He was ten miles away.*

awful *adj.* (<u>aw</u> fəl) very bad; terrible; of poor quality. *She had an awful pain in her stomach.* | *The food is awful at that restaurant.*

awkward *adj.* (<u>awk</u> wərd) without physical skill or grace. *My brother is an awkward dancer.*

awoke *verb* (ə <u>wōk</u>) past tense of **awake.**

awoken *verb* (ə <u>wō</u> kən) past participle of **awake.**

ax *noun* (<u>æk</u>s) a tool with a blade attached to the end of a long handle. An ax is used for chopping wood.
ax

axle *noun* (<u>æk</u> səl) a bar on which a wheel or wheels turn. *The right rear axle on his car was broken in the accident.*

B b

baby *noun* (ba̅ be̅) a very young girl or boy. *The baby cried because she was hungry.*

baby-sit *verb* (ba̅ be̅ sit) to take care of children while their parents are away. *He **baby-sits for** his cousins when his aunt and uncle go out.*

> **Word Builder: baby-sit +**
> **baby-sitter:** a person who baby-sits.

bachelor *noun* (bæch lər) a man who has not married. *He was a bachelor for most of his life.*

bachelor's degree *noun* (bæch lərz də gre̅) a degree that you get after finishing a program of studies at a college or university. *Mark earned a bachelor's degree in mathematics from the state university.*

back[1] *noun* (bæk) 1. the part of the body that is on the side opposite the chest and between the neck and hips. 2. the side opposite the front. *The kitchen is in the back of the house.* | *Put your name on the back of this paper.* 3. a part of an object that supports the part of the body opposite the chest. *I leaned against the back of the chair.*
verb to cause something to move with its back part first. *He backed the car out of the garage.*
adj. located behind the front part. *The children rode in the back seat of the car.*
in back behind. *There was a big truck in back of our car.*

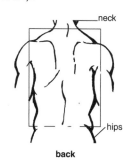

back

back[2] *adv.* (bæk) 1. in the direction of things that are behind something or someone. *The police officer told the people to move back.* | *Could you move your car back? I can't get out.* 2. to a place where you were before; to an earlier time. *He went back to his car to get his glasses.* | *I thought back to when I was very young.* 3. in return or in reply. *Joe hit Bob, and Bob hit back.* | *She left a message, but I forgot to call her back.*
back and forth 1. from side to side or backward and forward. *I rocked the baby back and forth in its cradle.* | *The children like to swing back and forth in that tree.* 2. making trips again and again between two positions or places. *The police officer walked back and forth in front of the building.*

background *noun* (bæk grownd) 1. the part of a picture or scene that is toward the back or seems to be far away. *The artist painted a castle with mountains in the background.* 2. all of a person's experience, education, and family history. *His background in law prepared him for his career as a judge.*

backward (backwards) *adv.* (bæk wərd) 1. toward things that are behind something. *I pulled the swing backward and then let it go.* 2. with the back part first. *If you walk backward, be careful not to trip.* 3. with the last part first; in a way that is the opposite of the usual way. *Can you count backward from one hundred to one?*

bacon *noun* (ba̅ kən) [N] salted and smoked meat from the back and side of a pig. Bacon is usually cut into long, thin pieces for cooking.

bacteria *pl. noun* (bæk ter e̅ ə) very small living things that you cannot see. Some kinds of bacteria cause diseases.

bad *adj.* (bæd) 1. not good in behavior or quality. *Please don't be bad while the guests are here.* | *That picture was taken with a bad camera.* 2. not pleasant or nice. *It is hard to like a person who has a bad attitude.* 3. not healthy; harmful. *Sugar is bad for your teeth.* 4. rotten; spoiled. *Don't eat the bad meat.*

badge *noun* (bæj) a pin or small piece of cloth that people wear to show that they belong to a group, have a particular job, or have done something special. *My brother's army uniform has many badges on it.*

badly *adv.* (bæd le̅) 1. not well; in a bad way. *He sings badly.* 2. very much. *I want a new car badly.*

> **bad or badly?**
> *Bad* is an adjective that means not good.
> *Badly* is an adverb that means in a bad way.
> Compare:
> *He had a bad accident.*
> *I feel bad about your accident.*
> *He rode the bike badly and fell.*

bag *noun* (bæg) 1. a soft container used to hold things. Bags are made of materials such as cloth, paper, plastic, or leather. *The bag of flour split open.* 2. a suitcase or other container carried by hand. *You left your bag on the bus.*

baggage *noun* (b<u>æ</u> gij) [N] suitcases, bags, or trunks used to carry things during travel. *Where do we pick up our baggage in this airport?*

baggage

bail *noun* (b<u>ā</u>l) money left with a court of law to make sure that a person will appear in court. *The judge set bail at three hundred dollars. | Her boyfriend is out on bail.*

bake *verb* (b<u>ā</u>k) to cook in an oven using dry heat. *I baked a birthday cake.*

> **Word Builder: bake +**
> **baker:** a person who bakes.
> **bakery:** a place where baked goods are made or sold.

balance *noun* (b<u>æ</u> lins) 1. [N] the state of being steady in body or mind. *The dancer kept her balance while standing on her toes.* 2. an amount of money that remains in an account that can be used or must still be paid. *She was glad to see a large balance in her bank account. | He was not happy to see a large balance in his credit card account.*
verb 1. to hold steady. *The seal balanced a ball on its nose.* 2. to subtract the amount of money that you have taken out of your bank account from the amount of money you have put into it. *I balance my checkbook every month.*

bald *adj.* (b<u>aw</u>ld) having little or no hair on the head. *When he took off his hat, I noticed he was bald.*

bale *noun* (b<u>ā</u>l) a large, tight group of objects tied together with something like string or wire. *Bales of hay were stacked in the barn.*

> **Word Builder: bale +**
> **baler:** a machine that makes bales.

ball *noun* (b<u>aw</u>l) a round or nearly round object. *They made a ball of snow.*

balloon *noun* (bə l<u>oon</u>) a bag made of rubber that is filled with air and used as a toy. *He blew up a balloon and gave it to his daughter.*

banana *noun* (bə n<u>æ</u> nə) a long, curved, soft fruit with a thick yellow skin. *Bananas grow in bunches on tropical trees.*

band[1] *noun* (b<u>æ</u>nd) 1. a group of people who play music together. *My brother plays guitar in the band.* 2. a group of people or animals acting together. *The police discovered a band of criminals.*

band[2] *noun* (b<u>æ</u>nd) a thin piece of material that holds several objects together. *She put a rubber band around the pencils.*

bandage *noun* (b<u>æ</u>n dij) a piece of cloth used to protect or cover a wound or other injury. *I put a bandage on the cut.*
verb to cover with a bandage. *The doctor bandaged my leg.*

Band-Aid *noun* (b<u>æ</u>n dād) (trademark) a name for a kind of small bandage.

bang *noun* (b<u>æ</u>ng) 1. a sudden, loud sound. *She slammed the door with a bang.* 2. a sudden, hard hit or blow. *He fell and got a bang on his head.*
verb to hit loudly or violently. *Tom banged the drum. | She slipped and banged her head on the counter.*

bangs *pl. noun* (b<u>æ</u>ngz) hair cut straight across the forehead. *Marta's bangs cover her eyebrows.*

bank[1] *noun* (b<u>æ</u>ngk) the ground at the edge of a river or stream. *We pulled the canoe up on the bank.*

bank[2] *noun* (b<u>æ</u>ngk) a business for holding, borrowing, or exchanging money. *He got a loan from the bank.*

> **Word Builder: bank +**
> **bankbook:** a small book that gives details about a person's bank account.
> **banker:** a manager who works in a bank.

bank account *noun* (b<u>æ</u>ngk ə kownt) the money that you keep in a bank. *He took some money out of his bank account.*

bar *noun* (b<u>ar</u>) 1. a piece of solid material, usually in the shape of a block. *There were two bars of soap in the bathtub.* 2. a place where drinks with alcohol are served. *You must be 21 to drink alcohol in a bar in the United States.*

barbecue *noun* (b<u>ar</u> bə kū) 1. an outdoor party at which meat and vegetables are cooked over an open fire. *Every summer we have a barbecue for the whole neighborhood.* 2. the piece of equipment that is used to cook a meal outside. *This barbecue uses gas as fuel.*
verb to cook meat or vegetables over an open fire outside.

barber *noun* (b<u>ar</u> bər) a person whose job is to cut or style hair and beards.

> **Word Builder: barber +**
> **barbershop:** the workplace of a barber.

bar code *noun* (bar kōd) a set of dark bars on a light background printed on the labels of goods and mail. A bar code is scanned by a computer that reads information such as price.

bare *adj.* (bār) wearing no clothing or covering; naked. *It's too cold to go outside with bare legs.*
verb to show something or tell something that had not been seen or heard before. *The little girl didn't want to bare her stomach, even for the doctor. | The newspaper bared the truth about the politician.*

barely *adv.* (bār lē) almost not at all. *Please speak louder. I can barely hear you.*

bargain *noun* (bar gən) something that you buy at a good price, especially if it is worth more than what you paid. *I got this jacket on sale. It was a real bargain!*
verb to discuss the price of something before you buy it. *Mrs. Clark bargained with the salesman for a lower price on the car she wanted.*

bark[1] *noun* (bark) the sound a dog makes. *That little dog has a loud bark.*
verb to make the sound of a dog or to speak in a loud voice, like a dog. *Our neighbor's dog barked all night. | The officer barked orders to the soldiers.*

bark[2] *noun* (bark) the outside cover of a tree. *The oak tree has rough bark.*

barn *noun* (barn) a large building on a farm where you keep equipment or animals and their food. *The farmer led the cows into the barn.*

barrel *noun* (bær əl) a large round container with a flat top and bottom that is used to keep liquids. Barrels are often made of wood. *They store wine in barrels.*

barrier *noun* (bær ē ər) something that stops things or people from coming in or going out, such as a fence or wall. *There is a barrier around the area where the accident happened. | A bandage creates a barrier against germs.*

base *noun* (bās) 1. the part that supports something or that something stands on. *The lamp has a square base.* 2. the bottom part of something. *They chopped at the base of the tree.* 3. a place that is the center of activity for a group. *Soldiers live and work on the army base.* 4. the bag at one of the four corners of a baseball or softball field. *The batter ran to first base.*
verb 1. to use as the main place. *They **based** their company **in** New York. | The computer company **is based in** California.* 2. to use something to make something else. *The author **based** the story **on** her childhood. | This movie **is based on** a famous book.*

baseball *noun* (bās bawl) 1. [N] a game played by two teams of nine people each. You get points when you hit the ball with a bat and then run around four bases. *People usually play baseball in the summer.* 2. the small, hard ball used in the game of baseball. *He hit the baseball hard, and I caught it.*

baseball

basement *noun* (bās mənt) the space in a building that is under the ground. People often use it for storing things, and the heating system is usually located there.

bases *pl. noun* (bā sēz) plural of **basis.**

basic *adj.* (bā sik) 1. forming the base of something; being the central or most important element. *The basic structure of the house is very simple, but they have added many things.* 2. necessary as a base. Things that are basic need to be learned first or done first. *I studied basic science in my first year of high school. | Words like go, house, and cold are basic English words.* 3. simple; having only necessary things. *I just need a basic camera.*

basics *pl. noun* (bā siks) things you need to know in order to do something. *Children learn the basics of reading and writing in school.*

basin *noun* (bā sin) a large bowl. A basin usually holds water to wash with. *Ronald filled the basin and washed the dishes in it.*

basis *noun* (ba̅ sis) *bases* a part of something on which other parts are built and depend. *Trust is the basis of friendship.* | *The Constitution is the basis of government in the United States*

basket *noun* (bæ skit) a container made of thin pieces of wood, metal, or other materials that are woven together. *Donna put her groceries in the shopping basket.*

basketball *noun* (bæ skit bawl) 1. [N] a game played by two teams of five people each. You get points when you throw a ball through a metal ring and net. *Basketball is very popular in the United States.* 2. the large ball used in this game.

bat[1] *noun* (bæt) a heavy stick that you use to hit the ball in baseball, softball, and other sports. *The baseball player swung at the ball with his bat.*

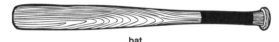

bat

bat[2] *noun* (bæt) a small animal that flies at night. Bats have wings, but they are mammals, not birds.

batch *noun* (bæch) an amount of something made at the same time or considered as a group. *I made a batch of cookies.*

bath *noun* (bæth) the act of sitting in water and cleaning yourself. *Ralph **takes a bath** every evening.*

Word Builder: bath +
bathmat: a mat on the floor near a bathtub to absorb water.
bathroom: a room where people wash and use the toilet.
bathtub: a large tub in which a person can wash.

bathe *verb* (ba̅th) 1. to give a bath to; wash. *Anna bathed her baby.* 2. to have a bath. *Some people bathe every day.* 3. to swim. *We bathed in the pool.*

batter[1] *verb* (bæ tər) to hit hard again and again in a way that causes harm or damage. *The two fighters battered each other.* | *The storm battered the island.*

Word Builder: batter +
battered: injured by having been beaten.
battery: the crime of causing injury to a person.

batter[2] *noun* (bæ tər) [N] a thick mixture of flour, eggs, liquid, and other things. Batter is used to make things such as cake. *Tim mixed the batter and poured it into a pan.*

battery *noun* (bæ tə re̅) a device that makes electricity by using chemical reactions. Batteries give power to many things, including cars, toys, and watches. *The car wouldn't start because its battery was dead.*

battle *noun* (bæ təl) a fight between two opposing sides. *Many soldiers died in the battle.*
verb to fight or struggle against. *The firefighters battled the fire.*

bay[1] *noun* (ba̅) a body of water with land around it but that is open to the sea on one side. *The ship sailed into the bay.*

bay[2] *noun* (ba̅) a section of a building that is apart from the rest of the building and that is used for a specific purpose. *The truck backed into the loading bay.* | *The garage has two bays.*

be *verb* (be̅) *was/were, been* 1. to live or exist. *There was a railroad here a long time ago.* 2. used to tell the particular place or position of a person or thing. *They are at home.* | *My building is on the corner.* 3. used to connect the subject of a sentence to a noun or adjective that describes it. *She is a doctor.* | *He is sick.* 4. used with a present participle to show a continuing action. *It is raining.* 5. used with the present participle to say that some action is planned in the future. *I am leaving for Chicago tomorrow.* 6. used before the past participle of another verb to connect the subject of the sentence to actions done to it. *All of the furniture was moved yesterday.*

beach *noun* (be̅ch) the land at the edge of a lake, ocean, or other body of water. A beach is often formed of sand or small stones. *We took a vacation at the beach.*

beak *noun* (be̅k) the hard part of a bird's mouth. *The crow has a pointed beak.*

beam *noun* (be̅m) 1. a long, strong piece of wood or metal that supports parts of a building. *Skyscrapers are built with steel beams.* 2. light sent out from something. *The sun's beams warmed us.* | *This flashlight has a bright beam.*
verb to send out over a long distance. *The radio station beams its signal to a large area.*

bean *noun* (be̅n) the seed of certain plants that is eaten as a vegetable.

bear¹ *verb* (bār) *bore, born (borne)* 1. to hold up or support. *The foundation bears the weight of the building.* 2. to live with something although it is difficult or not pleasant. *She bore the pain bravely.* | *I can't bear to see you cry.* 3. to give birth to. *She bore eight children.*

bear² *noun* (bār) a large mammal with thick hair and a short tail. Bears eat plants and other animals. *The big white bear swam in the icy water.*

beard *noun* (bērd) the hair that grows on the face, especially on the chin.

bearing *noun* (bār ing) a machine part that holds another moving part and allows it to move with less friction. Bearings are often used to help wheels turn.

beat *verb* (bēt) *beat, beaten* 1. to hit again and again. *He beat the drum.* | *Don't beat your child.* 2. to win against. *Leila beat her sister at tennis.* 3. to mix hard. *Beat the eggs.*
noun a regular sound in music from instruments such as a drum. *We danced to the beat of the music.*

Word Builder: beat +
beater: a device used to beat eggs, cream, or other liquid food.
beating: punishment in the form of physical violence.

beaten *verb* (bē tən) past participle of **beat.**

beautiful *adj.* (bū tə fəl) very nice to see, hear, or feel. *These flowers are beautiful.* | *We read a beautiful poem.*

beauty *noun* (bū tē) 1. [N] the quality of being pleasant to see, hear, or feel. *I love the beauty of nature.* 2. a person or thing that is pleasant to see. *Veronica is a beauty.*

became *verb* (bi kām) past tense of **become.**

because *conj.* (bi kəz or bi kawz) for the reason that. *He went to college because he wanted a better job.*

because of *prep.* (bi kəz əv or bi kawz əv) used to introduce the reason for something. *The banks are closed today because of the holiday.* | *They hired her because of her experience.*

become *verb* (bi kəm) *became, become* to grow or come to be. *David became ill.* | *My son became a teacher.*

bed *noun* (bed) a soft place or piece of furniture used for resting or sleeping. *American hotels usually have two beds in each room.*

Word Builder: bed +
bedroom: a room where people sleep and keep their clothing.
bedspread: a cloth cover for a bed.
bedtime: the time when someone goes to sleep.

bee *noun* (bē) a black and yellow insect that sometimes stings. Some kinds of bees make honey from flowers.

bee

beef *noun* (bēf) [N] meat from a cow.

been *verb* (bin) past participle of **be.**

beep *noun* (bēp) a short, high sound that acts as a signal. *The microwave oven made a beep when the food was ready.*

beer *noun* (bēr) 1. [N] a drink made from grain. Beer contains alcohol. 2. [N] a drink without alcohol made from the roots of certain plants.

beet *noun* (bēt) a dark red root that people eat as a vegetable.

before *adv.* (bə fōr) at an earlier time; in the past. *Sam thought he had read this book before.*
prep. 1. earlier than; previous to. *Cinderella forgot to leave before midnight.* 2. in front of; ahead of. *She stood before the door and knocked.*
conj. earlier than the time when something else happens. *I always brush my teeth before I go to bed.*

began *verb* (bi gæn) past tense of **begin.**

begin *verb* (bi gin) *began, begun* 1. to do the first step in a process; start. *You may begin as soon as the teacher gives you the test paper.* | *The movie will begin soon.* 2. to take the first step of something; start doing something. *She began her speech by telling with a joke.*

beginning *noun* (bi gi ning) 1. the first part of something. *The beginning of this movie is exciting.* 2. the earliest time at which something happens or exists. *She was hard to talk to from the beginning.*

begun *verb* (bi gən) past participle of **begin.**

behave *verb* (bi hāv) 1. to act in a certain way. *If you behave badly, we will have to go home.* | *The dog is behaving in a strange way.* 2. to act in a proper manner. *Those children know how to behave in a restaurant.*

behavior *noun* (bə h̄av yər) 1. [N] typical actions of a person, animal, thing, or group. *Crying a lot is normal behavior for babies.* | *We are studying animal behavior in our class.* 2. [N] the way a person or thing acts or does something. *Her mother gave her a reward for her good behavior.* | *His behavior at the party embarrassed his wife.*

behind *prep.* (bə hīnd) 1. in or at the back of; on the other side of. *Who is standing behind this door?* 2. at a stage or position less advanced than. *John is one year behind his brother in school.* 3. at a time later than. *The second train arrived five minutes behind the first.* 4. giving support to. *The people are behind the mayor's plan to build a new library.*
adv. slower than expected or required; not keeping to the usual or necessary schedule. *I am behind in my work.* | *She is behind in her rent.*

being *noun* (bē ing) any living creature. *Humans are intelligent beings.*

belief *noun* (bə lēf) 1. [N] a strong opinion. *My teacher has a belief that all children can learn.* 2. [N] trust in a person, thing, or idea; confidence. *My mother's belief in me helped me to succeed.* 3. an idea thought of as true; something people believe. *Many people **hold the belief** that there is life after death.*

believe *verb* (bə lēv) 1. to accept as honest or true. *Can you believe his crazy story?* 2. to think something and feel some confidence about it; suppose. *I believe they will arrive before noon.* 3. to have a strong belief in something that people cannot prove is true or not. *Many people **believe in** God.*

bell *noun* (bel) a hollow metal cup that makes a ringing sound when you hit it. *When the bell rings, class is over.*

bell

belly *noun* (be lē) the part of the body below the chest and above the legs that contains the stomach and intestines.

belong *verb* (bə lawng) 1. to be owned by. *The shirt **belongs to** me.* 2. to be a member of. *Mary **belongs to** a sports club.* 3. to have as a proper place or situation. *This knife belongs in the kitchen.* | *The children belong in school.*

Word Builder: belong +
belongings: things that belong to a person.

below *adv.* (bə lō) in or to a lower place; beneath. *They were on the deck of the ship but then went below when it began to rain.*
prep. 1. under; beneath. *His apartment is on the floor below my apartment.* 2. lower than, in rank or value. *His grade on the test was below mine.*

belt *noun* (belt) 1. a piece of cloth, leather, or other material that you wear around the waist. *You need to wear a belt with those pants.* 2. a continuous band of rubber or other material used to drive a machine or carry materials. *That car needs a new fan belt.* | *Our factory uses several conveyor belts.*

Word Builder: belt +
belt loop: a strip of cloth that holds a belt to a skirt, a pair of pants, or other piece of clothing.

bench *noun* (bench) 1. a long seat, often made of wood and without a back. *Let's sit on this bench and look at the lake.* 2. a table for working on, often with space for tools. *The bench in the garage has tools on it.*

bend *verb* (bend) **bent, bent** 1. to cause something that was straight to have the shape of a curve or angle. *He bent the nail by mistake.* | *I hurt my arm, and now I can't bend it.* 2. to change to a shape of a curve or angle. *The branch bent as the child climbed on it.* | *The arm bends at the elbow.* 3. to lean your upper body from the waist. *He **bent over** to pick up the napkin from the floor.* 4. to change direction in a curving way. *The road bends sharply just in front of my house.*

beneath *prep.* (bə nēth) 1. under; lower than; below. *His name is beneath my name on the list.* 2. covered by; under. *Amy walked in the rain beneath the umbrella.*

benefit *noun* (be nə fit) anything that does someone good or gives an advantage. *I'm sure you will get a lot of benefit from your education.*
verb to gain something good. *My son benefited from the counselor's advice.*

benefits *pl.* **noun** (be nə fits) 1. money from a government program. *She receives benefits because of a disability.* 2. something that you get, in addition to money, from your job. *Some benefits are health insurance and paid vacation leave. My company provides excellent medical benefits to its employees.*

bent *adj.* (bent) not straight; curved. *This nail is bent.*
verb past tense and past participle of **bend.**

berry *noun* (be̱ rē) any of several soft, small fruits. Berries grow on bushes or trees. *Strawberries are my favorite kind of berry.*

beside *prep.* (bə si̱d) next to; at the side of. *The dog is walking beside its owner.*

besides *prep.* (bə si̱dz) in addition to. *Besides her regular job, she also has a part-time job.*

best *adj.* (best) superlative of **good**; better than all others. *That's the best pie I've ever eaten! | Martin is my best friend.*
adv. 1. superlative of **well**; better than any other. *Out of all those students, he writes best.* 2. superlative of **well**; better than in any other way. *She works best in the morning.*

bet *verb* (bet) *bet, bet* 1. to agree to pay if your guess about some future event is wrong. *I bet you a dollar that it will snow tomorrow.* 2. to be sure about an event or action. *I bet he was late again yesterday.*
noun the amount of money you promise to pay if your guess about a future event is wrong. *Jack **placed a bet on** one of the horses in the race.*

better *adj.* (be̱ tər) 1. comparative of **good**; of a higher quality than something else. *This TV is good, but that one is better. | This is one of the better restaurants in town.* 2. healthy again; no longer sick or injured. *Is she better after the operation?*
adv. 1. comparative of **well**; in a way that is higher in quality than some other. *She dances better than I do.* 2. comparative of **well**; better than in some other way. *These plants grow well in the shade, but they will grow better in the sun.*
had better used to state or warn that something bad might happen if you do not do something; should. *I'd better take an umbrella with me in case it rains. | You had better do what the teacher says.*

between *prep.* (bə twe̱n) 1. in the area that separates. *Bob stood in line between Joe and Kate.* 2. from one thing to another thing when comparing. *There are not many differences between my bike and yours.* 3. during a set time period. *Come for lunch between noon and one.*

beverage *noun* (bev rəj) any liquid for drinking that people enjoy. Juice and wine are beverages. *Would you like a beverage with your meal?*

beyond *prep.* (bē ya̱nd) past the farthest side of; farther on or later than. *The post office is two blocks beyond the school. | He never stays at work beyond closing time at the store.*

bicycle *noun* (bi̱ si kəl) a light vehicle with two wheels, one behind the other. You make the wheels turn by pushing on pedals. *Peggy rides a bicycle to work instead of driving a car.*

big *adj.* (big) 1. large in size, number, or weight. *Elephants are big animals. | He has a big collection of stamps.* 2. important. *Choosing a college is a big decision.*

bike *noun* (bi̱k) a short form of **bicycle**.

bilingual *adj.* (bī li̱ng gwəl) 1. able to speak two languages well. *There are many bilingual people in the United States.* 2. written or spoken in two languages. *We use a bilingual dictionary when we do our Spanish homework.*

bill¹ *noun* (bil) 1. a statement that a business sends to a customer to show how much the customer must pay for goods or services that the business provided. *Did you pay the telephone bill yet?* 2. a piece of paper money. *Mrs. Perez paid with a ten-dollar bill.* 3. a law that people in government are considering but have not voted on yet. *Do you think the Senate will **pass** the new education **bill?***
verb to send a statement of how much money a customer owes. *The electric company bills us every month. | You don't have to pay now. We will bill you.*

bill

bill² *noun* (bil) the hard part of a bird's mouth.

billboard *noun* (bil bōrd) a large board that shows advertisements outdoors. Billboards are often seen next to major roads.

billion *noun* (bil yən) the word for the number 1,000,000,000.

Bill of Rights *noun* (bil əv ri̱ts) the first ten amendments to the U.S. Constitution. The Bill of Rights lists the basic rights of U.S. citizens and residents.

bin *noun* (bin) a container or space for putting things or storing things such as wood, potatoes, or coal. *He filled the bin with more logs.* | *Please put those newspapers in the bin. We can recycle them.*

bind *verb* (bīnd) **bound, bound** to tie together with a rope or something like a rope. *This machine binds stacks of newspapers.*
in a bind in a bad or difficult situation. *I'm in a bind since I don't have a ride to work.*

biology *noun* (bī a lə jē) [N] the study of how living things grow, function, and develop. *We studied how cells divide in biology class.*

biotech *noun* (bī o tek) [N] a short form of **biotechnology.**

biotechnology *noun* (bī ō tek na lə gē) [N] the science that uses very small living things to make things such as medicine. *Scientists use biotechnology to invent new antibiotics.*

bird *noun* (bərd) an animal with two wings, two feet, and feathers. Most birds can fly.

birth *noun* (bərth) the process or fact of a child being born. *Birth can be difficult for both mother and baby.* | *In the United States, most births take place in a hospital.*
give birth to bring a child into the world. *She gave birth to twins last Monday.*

Word Builder: birth +
birth date: the day when you were born; date of birth.
birthday: the anniversary of the day when you were born.
birthplace: the place where you were born.

bit[1] *noun* (bit) a small amount or a little piece of something. *I'd like just a bit of ice cream.* | *Dan tore the paper into bits.*

bit[2] *verb* (bit) past tense of **bite.**

bite *verb* (bīt) **bit, bitten** to cut with the teeth. *That dog bit me.* | *Tom bit into the apple.*
noun 1. a wound caused by teeth or other mouth parts. *This mosquito bite itches.* 2. the amount that you take into your mouth at one time. *He took a bite of cake.*

bitten *verb* (bi tən) past participle of **bite.**

bitter *adj.* (bi tər) 1. having a strong taste that is neither sweet nor sour. *That old coffee tastes bitter.* 2. full of anger, hate, or sorrow. *They are bitter enemies.*

black *adj.* (blæk) 1. having the color of the night sky. 2. taken without cream or milk. *Jan drinks her coffee black.*

Word Builder: black +
blackboard: another name for chalkboard.

blade *noun* (blād) 1. the part of a knife, scissors, or other tool that cuts. *This old knife has a dull blade.* 2. a thin, flat part that pushes something as it moves. *This electric fan has four blades that spin around.*

Word Builder: blade +
blade guard: a cover for a blade that is part of many tools.

blame *verb* (blām) to say that someone or something is the cause of something bad. *Mrs. Martin blamed her for breaking the glass.* | *The team blamed its loss on bad luck.*
noun responsibility. *I took the blame for the mistake.*

blank *adj.* (blængk) without marks or writing. *The teacher gave us each a blank sheet of paper.*
noun a space where something is left out or missing. *Fill in the blanks on this form.*

blanket *noun* (blæng kət) a large piece of material that you put on a bed to make it warm. It is often made of wool. *Some people put an extra blanket on their bed in winter.*

blast *noun* (blæst) 1. a loud and sudden sound. *The blast of the siren woke me.* 2. an explosion. *A bomb caused the blast.*
verb to open up with an explosion. *They blasted a tunnel for the mine.*

bleach *verb* (blēch) to make white or light in color by using a chemical or the light of the sun. *He bleaches his socks and underwear.* | *The sun bleached her hair.*
noun [N] a substance that you use to make something white or light in color. *Some people add bleach to their laundry.*

bleachers *pl. noun* (blē chərz) long, flat seats placed in rows with each row higher than the one before. *We sat in bleachers at the football stadium.*

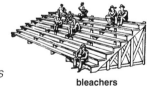
bleachers

bled *verb* (bled) past tense and past participle of **bleed.**

bleed *verb* (blēd) **bled, bled** to lose blood. *Matt's knee bled from a cut.*

blend *verb* (blend) to mix completely so that there no longer seem to be separate parts. *We blend flour, eggs, sugar, and milk to make cake batter.*
noun 1. a mixture. *The cook added a blend of spices to the soup.* 2. two or more consonants that are next to each other in a word and that you pronounce together. *The word* **street** *starts with the blend* str.

Word Builder: blend +
blender: a small appliance that blends foods.

blew *verb* (bloo) past tense of **blow**[2].

blind *adj.* (blīnd) not able to see. *A dog led the blind man across the street.*
noun a window cover often made of cloth or thin pieces of metal or plastic. *Open the blinds and look out the window.*

blizzard *noun* (bli zərd) a strong storm with a lot of snow and wind that lasts for a long time. *We could not leave the house until the blizzard was over.*

block *noun* (blak) 1. a solid piece of hard material with flat sides. *The wall is made of concrete blocks.* 2. an area in a city or town with four streets around it. The distance of one of the sides is also called a block. *Let's take a walk around the block.* | *He lives one block from the store.*
verb to close off by putting something in the way. *A tree fell and blocked the road.*

blood *noun* (bləd) [N] the red liquid that flows through the body. Blood carries oxygen and other substances that the body needs.

blossom *noun* (bla səm) the flower of a plant that makes the seed or fruit. *The apple trees are covered with white blossoms.*
verb to produce flowers. *The apple trees blossom before they grow fruit.*

blossom

blouse *noun* (blows) a loose shirt for women.

blow[1] *noun* (blō) a quick, hard hit by the hand or by a hard object. *The boxer fell down after a blow to his chin.*

blow[2] *verb* (blō) *blew, blown* 1. to be in fast motion, as the air. *The wind blew all night.* 2. to be carried along by the wind. *My cap blew into the water.* 3. to force air out of the mouth. *She blew on the baby's fingers to warm them.* 4. to move or force along by means of an air current. *The wind blew the leaves into the street.* 5. to empty by forcing air through. *She blew her nose into a handkerchief.*
blow out to stop the burning of something with the movement of air. *She blew out the candles.*
blow up 1. to destroy or be destroyed through an explosion. *In many action movies, cars often blow up.* 2. to fill with air or gas. *Let's blow up the balloons.*

blown *verb* (blōn) past participle of **blow**[2].

blue *adj.* (bloo) having the color of the sky on a clear bright day.

board *noun* (bōrd) 1. a flat, cut piece of wood. *We are going to make shelves out of these boards.* 2. a group of people who manage or direct something. *The board of education will choose a new school principal.*
verb to get into or on something that is used for transportation. *It's time to board the airplane.*

boat *noun* (bōt) a vehicle, smaller than a ship, that moves on water. *We got into the boat and sailed down the river.*

bodily *adj.* (ba də lē) having to do with the human body. *Parents want to keep their children from bodily harm.*

body *noun* (ba dē) 1. all the physical parts that make up a person or animal. *The elephant has a very large body.* 2. a large or main part of anything. *The body of the car is blue.* 3. a particular mass of land, water, or other matter. *Oceans and lakes are bodies of water.*

boil *verb* (boyl) 1. to change from a liquid to a gas by heating. 2. to heat a liquid until it starts to turn into a gas. *You should boil the water before you pour it over the tea leaves.* 3. to cook in very hot water. *I like to boil eggs for breakfast.*
boil over to boil until the liquid flows out of a container. *Turn off the gas before the soup boils over!*

Word Builder: boil +
boiler: a large appliance that supplies heat by boiling water to make steam.

bold *adj.* (bōld) 1. having courage; having little or no fear. *The bold man jumped into the river to save the drowning child.* 2. set in heavy type that stands out. *The word* **bold** *is in bold print.*

boll *noun* (bōl) the part of the cotton plant that holds the seeds.

bolt *noun* (b͞olt) 1. a metal bar that slides into an opening in a door. It keeps the door closed. *If you live in a big city, it's a good idea to have a bolt on your door.* 2. a metal screw with a flat end. A bolt screws into a matching nut. 3. a large roll of cloth. *She cut two yards of cloth from the bolt.*

bomb *noun* (bam) a metal shell filled with explosives. *The bomb destroyed the building.*

bond *noun* (band) 1. something that joins, ties, or fastens together. *This glue makes a powerful bond.* 2. a feeling or shared interest that joins people together. *She **has** a special **bond with** her daughter.* | *I still have strong bonds of friendship with people from my high school.* 3. a piece of paper that a government or business gives when it borrows money. A bond promises to pay back the sum of money along with interest. *They invested their money in **stocks and bonds.***

bone *noun* (b͞on) a hard part inside of a person or animal. *He fell and broke a bone in his arm.*

book *noun* (buk) 1. sheets of paper that are put together between two covers. The sheets can be empty or have writing or pictures on them. *I like books about animals.* 2. (usually plural) a financial or business record. *He **keeps the books** for the company.* **verb** to arrange for something ahead of time so that it is saved for you. *I booked a table at your favorite restaurant.* | *Did you book the airplane flights?*

> **Word Builder: book +**
> **bookcase:** a piece of furniture for storing books.
> **bookmark:** a strip of paper or other material used to mark the place in a book.
> **bookshelf:** a shelf on which you store books.
> **bookstore:** a store that sells books.

bookkeeping *noun* (buk k͞e ping) [N] the practice of keeping records of the money taken in and paid out by a business. *Bookkeeping requires good math skills.*

boot *noun* (b͞oot) a covering for the foot and lower part of the leg, usually made of leather or rubber. **verb** to start a computer by loading the operating system or giving it the first instructions to start. *You must **boot up** the computer every time you turn it on.*

boot

border *noun* (bor dər) 1. the outer part; edge. *There is a fence along the border of our yard.* 2. the line between two countries or other areas that have a government. *You must show your passport at the border.*

bore[1] *verb* (b͞or) past tense of **bear**[1].

bore[2] *verb* (b͞or) to make someone tired or lose interest by being dull. *News programs bore most children, but my son thinks they're interesting.*

bored *adj.* (b͞ord) feeling tired because of having to do something that is not interesting. *I felt bored during the long drive.*

boring *adj.* (b͞or ing) dull; having no interesting features. *The movie was so boring that we fell asleep.*

born *adj.* (born) brought into life by birth. *A child born in California is a U.S. citizen.*

borne *verb* (b͞orn) past participle of **bear**[1].

borrow *verb* (bar ō) to take something and promise to return it. *May I borrow your book for a few days?* | *He **borrowed** fifty dollars **from** me but never paid it back.*

boss *noun* (baws) a person who gives work to other people and tells them what to do; manager. *The boss explained the new office procedures.*

both *adj.* (b͞oth) one and the other of two things or people. *Both students got high grades.* **pron.** the one in addition to the other. *Bill couldn't decide between the two shirts, so he got both.* **conj.** used with *and* to show that two things are being included. *Both girls and boys can play basketball.*

bother *verb* (ba thər) 1. to annoy or give trouble to. *The loud noise is bothering us.* 2. to disturb or interrupt. *Don't bother me while I'm studying.* 3. to make the necessary effort. *Tanya never bothers to smile.*

bottle *noun* (ba təl) a container with a narrow neck used to hold or pour liquids. A bottle is usually made of glass or plastic. *I bought a bottle of milk and a bottle of soda at the store.*

bottom *noun* (ba təm) 1. the lowest or deepest part of something. *There is more space to write at the bottom of the page.* | *There are a lot of coins in the bottom of my bag.* 2. the side of something that is under the main part. *The bottoms of your shoes are dirty.* | *That's the bottom of the box. You have to turn it over.*

bought *verb* (<u>bawt</u>) past tense and past participle of **buy.**

bounce *verb* (<u>bowns</u>) 1. to spring back or up after hitting against a surface. *The ball bounced down the stairs.* 2. (informal) to be returned to you by a bank because there is not enough money in your checking account. *The check that I wrote at the supermarket bounced.*

bound[1] *adj.* (<u>bownd</u>) 1. held by ties; feeling as if tied. *Because of the snowstorm, we were bound to the house.* 2. certain; sure. *She is **bound to** be angry after what you did.*
verb past tense and past participle of **bind.**

bound[2] *adj.* (<u>bownd</u>) on the way to; headed. *This train is **bound for** Chicago.*

boundary *noun* (<u>bown</u> drē) something that marks the edge or limit. *The fence is the boundary of our neighbor's property.*

bow[1] *verb* (<u>bow</u>) to bend the head or upper body forward toward the feet in order to greet or show respect to someone. *The actors bowed to the audience at the end of the play.*

bow[2] *noun* (<u>bō</u>) 1. a weapon used for shooting arrows. A bow is made of a thin, curved piece of wood or other material with a tight string between the two ends. *He went hunting with a bow and arrow.* 2. a knot that is easy to make loose; a knot used for decoration. *My little boy is learning to tie his shoes with a bow now.* | *Let's use a red bow on this present.*

bow

bowl[1] *noun* (<u>bōl</u>) a deep, round dish used for holding food or liquid. *She served the soup in bowls.*

bowl[2] *verb* (<u>bōl</u>) to play the game of bowling. *He bowls very well.*

bowling *noun* (<u>bō</u> ling) [N] a game in which you roll a heavy ball along a long, smooth wood surface toward heavy pins that stand at the far end. You get points by knocking over as many pins as you can.

box[1] *noun* (<u>baks</u>) a container made of stiff material that usually has four sides, a bottom, and a lid. *I put my old books in a box.*

Word Builder: box +
box cutter: a tool with a short, sharp blade used for opening boxes.

box[2] *verb* (<u>baks</u>) to fight with the hands as a sport. *Kyle boxes at the community center.*

Word Builder: box +
boxer: a person who boxes; a fighter.
boxing: the sport of fighting with the hands.

boy *noun* (<u>boy</u>) a male child. *There are four boys and five girls on the team.*
interj. used to express surprise. *Boy, that is hard to believe!*

boycott *verb* (<u>boy</u> kat) to refuse to buy, use, or go to in order to make a protest or bring about a change. *Customers are boycotting the supermarket while the employees are on strike.*

boyfriend *noun* (<u>boy</u> frend) a favorite male friend with whom you have a romantic relationship. *Juliet was sad when her boyfriend had to leave town.*

bra *noun* (<u>bra</u>) underwear for women that supports the breasts.

brace *noun* (<u>brās</u>) 1. something that steadies or gives support to. *Julie wears a back brace when she lifts heavy things.* 2. (usually plural) metal wires and bands attached to the teeth to make them straight and bring them into proper position. *I wore braces on my teeth for two years.*

bracelet *noun* (<u>brā</u> slit) a piece of jewelry worn around the wrist or arm. *She was wearing a bracelet made of gold and diamonds.*

brag *verb* (<u>bræg</u>) to speak in a way that is too proud about something you do or have. *We're tired of listening to him **brag about** his new car.*

brain *noun* (<u>brān</u>) the organ in the body that controls thought, movement, and feeling.

brake *noun* (<u>brāk</u>) a device used to slow or stop the motion of a vehicle or machine. *You should have the brakes on your car inspected every year.* | ***Put on the brakes!*** *There's a dog!*
verb to operate the part on a vehicle that makes it stop. *She braked when she saw the child in the road.*

brake pedal *noun* (<u>brāk</u> pe dǝl) a device in a vehicle that you push with your foot in order to slow or stop the vehicle.

bran *noun* (<u>bræn</u>) [N] the outer layer of wheat and other cereal grains.

branch *noun* (brænch) 1. a woody part of a tree or bush that grows out from the trunk. 2. a part or division of the main part of something. *We chose a bank that has a branch near our house.* | *Geometry is a branch of mathematics.* | *The U.S. government has three branches.*

brand *noun* (brænd) a kind of product made by one particular company. *Which brand of peanut butter do you prefer?*

brand-new *adj.* (brænd noo) having never been used before; completely new. *We drove our brand-new car home from the car dealer.*

brass *noun* (bræs) [N] a bright, yellow metal that is used to make hardware and other things. *The horns in an orchestra are made out of brass.*

brave *adj.* (brāv) ready to face pain or danger; showing courage. *The brave pilot flew alone through the storm.*

> **Word Builder: brave +**
> **bravely:** in a brave way.
> **bravery:** courage.

bread *noun* (bred) [N] a food made with grains such as wheat or corn. Water, oil, and other ingredients are added to the grains, and the mixture is baked.

break *noun* (brāk) a period of time when something stops. *We **took a break** from our work to eat lunch.* *verb* **broke, broken** 1. to make something come apart into pieces. *She broke the candy into two pieces for the children.* | *He broke his arm when he fell.* 2. to damage something so that you cannot use it. *If you hit the TV, you'll break it.* 3. to stop operating because of damage. *My watch broke.*
break down to stop working. *My car broke down on the highway.*
break in(to) to enter by force without permission. *Someone broke into the car and stole the radio.* | *How did the thief break in?*
break up 1. to end a relationship. *Gary and Mary broke up.* 2. to stop. *The police broke up the fight.*

breakdown *noun* (brāk down) 1. a failure to operate. *The breakdown of the bus made the children late for school.* 2. a serious failure of a person's mind or body. *After her breakdown, she was in the hospital for three weeks.*

breakfast *noun* (brek fəst) the first meal of the day, which people usually eat in the morning.

breast *noun* (brest) 1. the front part of the body between the neck and the stomach; chest. 2. one of the two glands on the human chest, usually bigger on women than on men. Babies get milk from female breasts.

breath *noun* (breth) 1. [N] the air that goes into and out of the body through the nose or mouth. *The police tested his breath for alcohol.* 2. a single act of taking in and letting out air. *The doctor told me to **take a deep breath.***

breathe *verb* (breth) to take air into and out of the lungs. *Humans cannot breathe underwater.*

breeze *noun* (brēz) a light or gentle wind. *A breeze feels nice on a hot summer day.*

brick *noun* (brik) a very hard block of clay. People use bricks to make walls.

bride *noun* (brīd) a woman on her wedding day. *In America, a bride usually wears a white dress.*

bridge *noun* (brij) a structure that goes over something such as a river or road so that people can travel from one side to the other.

brief *adj.* (brēf) taking only a little time; short. *We had only a brief conversation because he was in a hurry.*

briefcase *noun* (brēf kās) a flat container that is often made of leather and has a handle. It is used for carrying things like documents or books between home and work or while traveling.

briefcase

bright *adj.* (brīt) 1. giving a lot of light. *The stars look bright in the clear night sky.* 2. strong or clear in color or shine. *The house is bright yellow.* 3. intelligent; smart. *All of the children in her class are bright.*

brights *pl. noun* (brīts) lights on the front of your car when you use your high beams. *The driver coming toward me was using his brights, so I couldn't see well.*

brilliant *adj.* (bril yənt) 1. very shiny. *The diamond in her ring was brilliant.* 2. very intelligent. *My science teacher is brilliant.*

bring *verb* (bring) *brought, brought* 1. to take or carry something from one place to another. *Please bring a pencil and a calculator when you come to class.* 2. to take someone to a place. *John brought his girlfriend to the party.*

bring up 1. to take care of a child until the child is an adult. *Her parents died, so her grandparents brought her up.* 2. to put a subject or idea into conversation. *Don't bring up money again. I don't want to talk about it.*

> **bring or take?**
> *Bring* usually means to carry something with you when you come.
> *Take* usually means to carry something with you when you go.
> Compare:
> *Bring your notebook when you come to class.*
> *Take your test papers when you go home.*

broad *adj.* (brawd) wide. *This bird has a broad chest but a short body.* | *She has a broad knowledge of history.*

broadcast *verb* (brawd kæst) *broadcast, broadcast* to send over television or radio. *The radio station broadcasts the news at seven o'clock.*
noun a show or any other thing that people send over television or radio. *Millions of people watched that special broadcast on television.*

broccoli *noun* (bra kə lē) [N] a common green vegetable with flowers that look like small trees.

brochure *noun* (brō shoor) a small set of attached pages with writing and often pictures that people use to advertise or explain something. *This brochure from the hotel has pictures of the rooms and information about prices.*

broil *verb* (broyl) to cook by very high, direct heat. *I broiled the meat and then put sauce on it.*

broke *verb* (brōk) past tense of **break.**
adj. (informal) having no money to spend or to live on. *He spent all his money and is now broke.*

broken *adj.* (brō kən) in pieces or not working anymore. *Can you fix this broken toy?* | *That bird has a broken wing.*
verb past participle of **break.**

brook *noun* (bruk) a small stream. *The children caught fish in the brook.*

broom *noun* (broom) a long handle with a brush on one end. People use it for moving loose dirt on a flat surface such as a floor.

brother *noun* (brə thər) a male person who has the same mother or father as another person.

brought *verb* (brawt) past tense and past participle of **bring.**

brown *adj.* (brown) having the color of coffee beans or chocolate.
verb to make or become brown in cooking. *I browned the meat in the frying pan.*

bruise *verb* (brooz) to hurt a part of your body without breaking the skin. *He fell and bruised his knee.*
noun an injury that does not break the skin. It often gives pain and leaves a blue mark.

brunch *noun* (brənch) a meal that is breakfast and lunch together. People eat brunch in the late morning.

brush *noun* (brəsh) a tool for cleaning, painting, and other things. It has a handle and a tight group of stiff fibers on one end. *I bought him a brush and comb for his hair.*
verb to use a brush on something. *I brush my teeth every night.*
brush up on to study something again because you forgot some of your knowledge. *She's taking a class to brush up on her English.*

bubble *noun* (bə bəl) a small amount of gas surrounded by another substance. *Bubbles form in water when it boils.*

buck *noun* (bək) an informal word for dollar. *Can I borrow five bucks from you?*

bucket *noun* (bə kət) an open container with round sides, a flat bottom, and a curved handle at the top. *We carried the water in a bucket.*

bucket

buckle *noun* (bə kəl) a device that fastens two ends. *The belt buckle is made of silver.*
verb to join or fasten with this device. *You should buckle your seatbelt every time you ride in a car.*

buddy *noun* (bə dē) (informal) friend. *He likes to go fishing with his buddies.*

budget *noun* (bə jit) 1. a plan for how a person or a group will receive and spend money during a certain period. *The school makes a new budget every year.* 2. the amount of money that someone can spend during a certain time or for certain purposes. *Our food budget is usually higher during the winter months.*
verb to plan the use of something. *He budgets his time well.*

bug *noun* (bəg) 1. (informal) an insect or any similar small animal. *People call spiders and ants bugs.* 2. (informal) an illness. *She did not come to school all week because she had a bug.* 3. a mistake or fault that keeps something from working right. *Sometimes it is hard to fix bugs in a computer program.*
verb (informal) to bother or annoy. *Please don't bug me while I'm trying to read.*

build *verb* (bild) *built, built* to make something by joining together different parts. *Are you going to build a new house?*

Word Builder: build +
builder: a person who builds; a person who works in construction.

building *noun* (bil ding) a structure that people have made, such as a house, a store, or a school. A building has a door, a roof, rooms, and outside walls. *They live in a large building with many apartments.*

built *verb* (bilt) past tense and past participle of **build.**

bulb *noun* (bəlb) the round glass part of an electric light. *Please change the bulb. The old bulb burned out.*

bull *noun* (bul) an adult male of cattle and some other animals.

bulldozer *noun* (bul dō zər) a heavy vehicle with a large blade on the front that pushes things such as soil or rocks. *The bulldozer cleared the ground to make it ready for building.*

bullet *noun* (bu lit) a small metal object shot from a gun. *The soldiers fired bullets at the enemy.*

bulletin *noun* (bu lə tin) a public announcement about something of current interest. *Did you hear the bulletin on the radio about the big snowstorm?*

bulletin board *noun* (bu lə tin bȯrd) a public board where you put notices and other things that you want people to read. *There is a bulletin board with announcements of jobs and events at the community center.*

bump *noun* (bəmp) a small swelling or raised area. *She got a bump on her head after she fell.* | *Watch out for the bump in the road!*
verb 1. to hit against something by accident. *Our car bumped the car that was parked in front of it.* 2. to cause to hit something against another object. *He bumped his head on the cabinet door.*
bump into 1. (informal) to meet by chance. *I bumped into my neighbor at the grocery store.* 2. to hit against something with some force; to cause something to hit against. *His car bumped into a truck and caused some damage.*

Word Builder: bump +
bumpy: covered with bumps.

bumper *noun* (bəm pər) the heavy bar on the front and back of a vehicle. A bumper protects the vehicle from damage.

bun *noun* (bən) a small form of bread made for one person. Some kinds of buns are plain, and some are sweet. *Did you bring the hamburger buns?* | *I had a bun for breakfast.*

bunch *noun* (bənch) 1. a group of things of the same kind that are attached to each other. *Please buy two bunches of bananas.* 2. (informal) any group or collection. *She went to the movie with a bunch of friends.*

bundle *noun* (bən dəl) a number of things that you tie or wrap together so you can carry them. *We brought in bundles of logs for the fire.*

bureau *noun* (byu rō) 1. an office or department of a business or government that is responsible for specific kinds of work. *John works for a credit bureau.* | *The Federal Bureau of Investigation is part of the U.S. government.* 2. a piece of furniture with drawers. People often keep clothes in a bureau.

burger *noun* (<u>bər</u> gər) a short form of **hamburger.**

burglar *noun* (<u>bər</u> glər) a person who enters a building without permission in order to steal something. *We woke up and thought we heard a burglar downstairs.*

> **Word Builder: burglar +**
> **burglary:** the crime of breaking into a building to steal things.

burn *verb* (<u>bər</u>n) **burned (burnt), burned (burnt)** 1. to be on fire. *The forest burned for three days.* 2. to cause to be on fire. *He burned his trash in the backyard.* 3. to hurt or damage by too much heat. *She burned her hand on the stove.*
burn down to destroy or be destroyed by burning. *A fire burned the house down.* | *Their house burned down.*
burn out 1. to stop burning or giving off heat. *The candle burned out.* | *The lightbulb burned out.* 2. to become so tired that you want to stop doing something. *She burnt out after years of working overtime.*
noun an injury caused by heat or fire. *He got a burn from touching a hot pan.*

burnt *verb* (<u>bər</u>nt) a past tense and past participle of **burn.**

burst *verb* (<u>bər</u>st) **burst, burst** 1. to break, open up, or explode suddenly. *The balloon burst.* 2. to cause to suddenly break or open up. *He blows up paper bags and bursts them.*

bury *verb* (<u>be</u> rē) to cover in the ground with dirt. *When our grandmother died, we buried her next to our grandfather.* | *The dog buried its bone.*

bus[1] *noun* (<u>bə</u>s) a long motor vehicle with many rows of seats that carries many people. *Anthony takes the bus to work every day.*

bus

> **Word Builder: bus +**
> **bus station:** a building where many buses stop so that people can get on or off.
> **bus stop:** the place where a bus stops so people can get on or off.

bus[2] *verb* (<u>bə</u>s) to clear dishes, cups, and other things from a table in a restaurant. *Kenny busses tables in a restaurant downtown.*

bush *noun* (<u>bush</u>) a low plant like a small tree. *There is a row of bushes in front of that house.*

business *noun* (<u>biz</u> nis) 1. [N] the work that a person does to earn money; profession. *What business are you in?* | *He bought a new suit for business.* 2. the activity of buying and selling goods and services in order to make money. *He wants to **go into business** with a partner.* 3. an organization that sells goods or services in order to make money. *She owns two businesses. One is a gift shop, and the other is a restaurant.* 4. [N] the amount of buying and selling within a period of time. *Business was bad last year.* 5. [N] a duty, concern, or interest. *Don't ask me about that. It's none of your business.* 6. [N] activities of organizations that buy and sell goods or services, or activities of customers in relation to these organizations. *Our company **does** a lot of **business with** foreign companies.* | *I enjoy **doing business** at my bank.*

> **Word Builder: business +**
> **businessman:** a man who works in business.
> **businessperson:** a person who works in business.
> **businesswoman:** a woman who works in business.

busy *adj.* (<u>bi</u> zē) 1. doing something or working on something. *The mechanic is busy putting the engine back together.* | *I am too busy to go to the movies today.* 2. full of work or activity. *Saturday is a busy day at the supermarket.* 3. being used; not available. *Marta tried to call me, but the phone was busy.*

but *conj.* (<u>bə</u>t) 1. used to show a contrast with what was just said. *Mary likes onions, but Joe doesn't.* 2. except that. *They wanted to play baseball, but it rained.* 3. except. *We did **nothing but** talk all night.*
prep. except. *No one went but me.*

butcher *noun* (<u>bu</u> chər) a person whose job is to cut and sell meat.

butter *noun* (<u>bə</u> tər) [N] a solid yellow fat made from milk. *I like a lot of butter on toast.*

> **Word Builder: butter +**
> **buttermilk:** a sour drink made from milk.
> **butterscotch:** a candy made from butter and brown sugar.

butterfly *noun* (<u>bə</u> tər flī) a flying insect with four large wings that often have bright colors.

buttocks *pl. noun* (<u>bə</u> təks) the rounded parts of the human body at the base of the spine that are used to sit on.

button *noun* (bə tən) 1. a small, round, flat thing that fastens clothing by fitting through a hole. *My new jacket has brass buttons.* 2. a small object that you press to make something start or stop. *Push this button to start your computer.* **verb** to fasten with buttons. *Please button your shirt.*

button

Word Builder: button +
buttonhole: a hole in clothing through which a button is fastened.

buy *verb* (bī) *bought, bought* to get in return for paying money. *He buys groceries at the supermarket.* | *My son bought a new car.*

buzz *noun* (bəz) a low noise caused by something moving fast. *I heard the bees buzz before I saw them.*

by *prep.* (bī) 1. next to; near. *That house is by a lake.* 2. through the means of. *We traveled by train in Japan.* 3. made through the work of. *I've read three books by that author.* 4. at or before a certain time. *You need to be at work by eight o'clock.* 5. through the action of. *He was hit by a car.* 6. in agreement with. *You have to play by the rules.* 7. according to a unit of measure. *This store sells apples by the pound.* **adv.** past in space or time. *A train sped by.* | *Many years have gone by.*

bye-bye *interj.* (bī bī) (informal) another word for **good-bye.** *The little girl waved and said, "Bye-bye."*

C c

cab *noun* (kăb) 1. a short form of **taxicab.** 2. the enclosed part of a truck with a seat for the person who drives. *There is room for the driver and one passenger in the cab.*

cabbage *noun* (kăbij) a vegetable with large green or purple leaves that form a round head.

cabin *noun* (kăbin) 1. a small house, built in a simple or rough way. *They live in a cabin made of logs.* 2. a room in a ship or airplane. *There are more than three hundred seats in the cabin of that jet.*

cabinet *noun* (kăbə nit) 1. a piece of furniture with shelves and doors. People have cabinets in kitchens, bathrooms, and other places. 2. (often capitalized) a group of officials who give advice to the head of a government. *The Cabinet met with the president to discuss plans.*

> **Word Builder: cabinet +**
> **cabinetmaker:** a person who makes furniture out of wood.

cable *noun* (kā bəl) 1. a thick, strong rope made of steel. *Some bridges hang from heavy cables.* 2. wrapped wires that carry electricity. *The monitor and keyboard are connected to the computer by cables.* 3. a form of television in which the sound and picture signals are sent by a special wire rather than through the air. *You can only get that channel **on cable.***

cafeteria *noun* (kăf ə tēr ē ə) a restaurant where people choose their own food and then carry it to a table. *We usually eat lunch in the employee cafeteria.*

caffeine *noun* (kă fēn) [N] a substance in coffee, tea, chocolate, and some other foods. Caffeine can make your heart beat fast and keep you awake. *Sandra drinks tea without caffeine so she can sleep better.*

cage *noun* (kāj) a space closed in by wires or bars and used to hold animals. *Our pet birds live in a pretty cage.*

cake *noun* (kāk) 1. a sweet food made of batter and cooked in an oven. *I've baked a cake for my cousin's wedding.* 2. a flat, round portion of food that is baked or fried. *We had fish cakes for lunch.* 3. a hard mass of some substance. *Buy three cakes of soap.*
verb to become a hard mass. *Clean your boots before the mud cakes on them.* | *Your boots are caked with mud.*

cake

calcium *noun* (kăl sē əm) [N] a soft, silver-white substance. Calcium is found in things such as rocks, shells, and milk. The body uses calcium to build strong bones and teeth.

calculate *verb* (kăl kyə lāt) to add, subtract, multiply, or divide in order to find an answer to a number question. *He calculated the cost of a dozen oranges at fifty cents each.*

calculator *noun* (kăl kyə lā tər) a small machine used to add, subtract, multiply, or divide numbers.

calendar *noun* (kăl ən dər) 1. a page or set of pages that shows the days, weeks, and months of a year. *We hang a new calendar on the wall every January.* 2. a list of events arranged in the order in which they happen. *The library posts a calendar of special events on the Web.*

calf[1] *noun* (kăf) *calves* a young cow or bull. A young whale or elephant is also called a calf.

calf[2] *noun* (kăf) *calves* the round part at the back of the leg below the knee.

call *verb* (kawl) 1. to say in a loud voice or shout out. *She called his name.* | *He **called for** help.* 2. to tell someone to come. *Our host **called** us **to dinner.*** 3. to telephone. *Please call me next week.* | *I can't talk now. Can I call you back later?* 4. to name. *She called her child Isaiah.*
noun 1. the sound made by a bird or animal. *The crow's call sounds like "caw caw."* 2. an instance of speaking to someone by telephone. *We got her call early this morning.* 3. a short visit. *He **paid** her **a call.***
call off to decide not to do; cancel. *We called off the picnic because of the storm.*

> **Word Builder: call +**
> **caller:** a person who calls.

calm *adj.* (kam) 1. not moving; still. *The wind is calm today.* 2. not excited. *A good nurse stays calm at the sight of blood.*
    calm down to become calm or calmer. *I told the angry child to calm down.*

calorie *noun* (kæ lə rē) a unit for measuring the amount of energy that a food makes in the body. The more calories something has, the more energy it gives. *Lettuce is low in calories, and doughnuts are high in calories.*

calves *pl. noun* (kævz) plural of **calf**.

camcorder *noun* (kæm kōr dər) a small machine that records moving pictures and sound. *Paul made a video of the wedding with his new camcorder.*

came *verb* (kām) past tense of **come**.

camera *noun* (kæm rə) a device for making photographs. *James took a picture of me with his digital camera.*

camp *noun* (kæmp) 1. an outdoor area where tents or shelters are set up to live in for a time. *We set up camp on a flat, clear place in the forest.* 2. a place with activities for children when they are not in school. Children stay overnight at some camps. *My son **goes to camp** for a few weeks every summer.*
    verb to set up a temporary shelter, such as a tent. *Let's camp here by the river.*

Word Builder: camp +
camper: a person who camps.
campfire: an outdoor fire.
campground: a large area where people can camp.
camping: the activity of staying in a camp or living for a short time in a tent for recreation.
campsite: a specific place that is good for camping.

---

campaign *noun* (kæm pān) a set of planned actions carried out in order to make something happen. *Radio and television are part of this advertising campaign.* | *The candidate gave many speeches during his campaign for office.*
    verb to follow a plan of action in order to achieve something in politics. *The candidate is **campaigning for** mayor.*

can[1] *verb* (kæn) 1. to be able to; have the ability to. *She can play the piano.* 2. to have the power or right to. *Only the boss can hire and fire employees.* 3. to have permission to do something. *Can I go outside now?* | *You can't smoke inside the restaurant.* 4. to have the possibility of happening or of being a certain way. *It can snow even in late spring in this area.* | *That man can't be her father. He's much too young.*

can[2] *noun* (kæn) 1. a round metal container for food or other products. *I opened a can of soup.* 2. a large container for waste. *Tom put the garbage can out by the curb.*

Word Builder: can +
can opener: a small machine that you use to open cans.

---

cancel *verb* (kæn səl) 1. to decide not to do; call off. *She canceled her doctor's appointment because she couldn't get a ride there.* 2. to mark, cross out, or change to keep from being used again. *The bank cancels checks.* | *The post office cancels stamps.*

cancer *noun* (kæn sər) a disease in which certain cells grow much faster than they should. Cancer can affect many different body parts, such as the lungs, breasts, and brain.

candidate *noun* (kæn də dāt) 1. a person who wants to be elected to a certain position. *The **candidates for** mayor will speak on TV tonight.* 2. a person who has applied for a job. *The human resources department is interviewing several candidates this week.*

candle *noun* (kæn dəl) a stick of wax with a string through the middle. The string burns and gives off light. *Mrs. Murphy lit the candles on the birthday cake, and her daughter blew the candles out.*

flame
string
candle

candy *noun* (kæn dē) [N] a sweet food made of sugar, or some other sweet substance, and flavors such as chocolate. *Eating too much candy is bad for your teeth.*

cane *noun* (kān) a stick made of metal or wood that helps someone walk. *She had to walk with a cane after she broke her hip.*

cannot *verb* (kæ nat or kæ nat) another spelling of *can not*.

canoe *noun* (kə noo) a small, narrow boat with curved sides and pointed ends. You move a canoe through water using a long stick with one wide flat end. *We went across the lake in a canoe.*

cap *noun* (kæp) 1. a soft hat with a part that sticks out in the front. *A cap is part of a baseball player's uniform.* 2. a round top for a bottle or other container. *Please put the cap back on the bottle.* 3. an upper limit. *The company has a salary cap.*

capable *adj.* (kā pə bəl) having the skill or power to do what is needed. *I know a capable mechanic who can fix your car.* | *He is **capable of** fixing anything.*

capacity *noun* (kə pæ si tē) 1. the amount that can be held in a particular space. *The gas tank has a capacity of 12 gallons.* | *The room has a capacity of one hundred people.* 2. a power or ability. *He has the capacity to be a great musician.*

capital *noun* (kæ pi təl) 1. the city where the government of a country or state is located. *The capital of the United States is Washington, D.C.* | *The capital of Texas is Austin.* 2. [N] the money or other wealth owned by a business. *The company invested a lot of capital in new equipment.*
adj. 1. being the larger form of a letter of the alphabet. *T is a capital letter, but t is not.* *Write the first letter of your name as a capital letter.* 2. able to be punished by death. *Murder is a capital crime.*

capitalize *verb* (kæ pi tə līz) to write or print in capital letters. *Capitalize the first letter of a person's name.*

capitol *noun* (kæ pi təl) 1. the building where the people who make the laws of a state meet. *Members of the state assembly met in the capitol for a vote.*
2. (capitalized) the building in which the U.S. Congress meets. *The Capitol is on a hill in Washington, D.C.* | *The Senate and the House of Representatives meet in the Capitol.*

capital or capitol?
A *capital* is a city where the government of a state or country is.
The *Capitol* is the name of the building where the U.S. Congress meets.
Compare:
The capital of California is Sacramento.
The capital of the United States is Washington, D.C.
The Capitol is in Washington, D.C.

captain *noun* (kæp tin) 1. a leader. *The president of that company is known as a captain of industry.* | *Nancy is the captain of her soccer team.* 2. the chief officer of a ship or airplane. *The captain sailed the ship across the ocean.*

caption *noun* (kæp shən) words that describe a picture in a magazine, book, or newspaper. *The caption identified the people in the photograph.*

car *noun* (kar) 1. a vehicle with four wheels and a motor. It is used to carry people on roads. *She got in the car and drove away.*
2. a part of a vehicle that runs along a specific path, such as a railroad. *This train has ten cars for passengers and one car for baggage.*

car

Word Builder: car +
carpool: a group of people who drive to work together.
carport: an area outside of a house with a roof under which you park a car.
car wash: a business that washes cars.

carbohydrate *noun* (kar bō hī drāt) one kind of substance that makes up food. There are large amounts of carbohydrates in fruit, bread, and other plant foods. Carbohydrates provide energy for the body.

carcinogen *noun* (kar si nə jin) a substance that causes cancer. *Some chemicals in cigarette smoke are carcinogens.*

card *noun* (kard) 1. a small piece of plastic or thick paper with information about a person. *I found her company's name on her **business card.*** | *His student **identification card** has his photograph on it.* 2. one of a set of small pieces of thick paper used for playing games. These cards have designs, and often numbers, printed on them. *We each get seven cards to start the game.* 3. a small, thick piece of paper used for sending a message to another person. *My friend sent me a card for my birthday.*

cardboard *noun* (kard bōrd) [N] a stiff material made of layers of paper. Most boxes are made of cardboard.

care *verb* (kār) 1. to watch over or protect. *Aunt Jane* **cared for** *me while I was sick.* 2. to like. *Sam doesn't* **care for** *onions.* 3. to have an opinion or concern about something. *What movie do you want to watch tonight? I don't care.* | *He didn't care what other people said about him.*
noun 1. [N] serious attention. *Do this important job with care.* 2. worry or concern. *She acts as if she doesn't have a care in the world.* 3. [N] the act of watching over something or keeping it safe. *Care of a pet includes giving it food, water, and a place to sleep.*
take care of to give attention to someone and do things to keep that person safe. *The clinic takes care of sick people.* | *My mother takes care of the baby while I'm at work.*

> **Word Builder: care +**
> **careful:** acting with care.
> **careless:** acting without care.

career *noun* (kə rēr) the work a person chooses to do through life. *She wants to have a career as a scientist.*

cargo *noun* (kar gō) the goods carried by a ship, airplane, or other vehicle. *The truck is carrying a cargo of fruit.*

carpenter *noun* (kar pən tər) a person who builds or repairs houses and other things made of wood.

carpet *noun* (kar pit) a covering for floors made of heavy cloth or a similar material. *There is a wool carpet in the dining room.*

carriage *noun* (kær ij) a vehicle with no engine for carrying people. You push or pull a carriage to make it move. *She put her baby in the baby carriage.* | *Before cars were invented, many people traveled in carriages pulled by horses.*

carrot *noun* (kær ət) a long orange root that people eat as a vegetable.

carrots

carry *verb* (kær ē) 1. to take from one place to another. *She carried my suitcase up the stairs.* | *The pipe carries water to your house.* 2. to hold or be able to hold. *This van carries seven passengers.* 3. to hold before birth. *Mrs. Perez is carrying twins.* 4. to have in order to sell. *The store carries many different products.*
carry out to do what has been planned; to start and complete something. *It will take a year to carry out the plans for the new building.*

cart *noun* (kart) 1. a small, light vehicle moved by hand and used to carry things. *Most grocery stores have carts for their customers to use.* 2. an open vehicle with two wheels used to carry a heavy load. An animal or a vehicle usually pulls a cart. *The farmer loaded the cart with hay.*

carton *noun* (kar tən) a box made of heavy paper or cardboard. *Milk, cereal, and eggs come in cartons.*

cartoon *noun* (kar toon) 1. a picture or set of pictures that makes people laugh or think. Cartoons often have words that show what a character is thinking or saying. *Our newspaper has one political cartoon every day.* 2. a motion picture made from a set of pictures. *The kids watch cartoons on TV every Saturday.*

case[1] *noun* (kās) 1. an instance or example of something. *There are four cases of the flu in our department.* 2. what is true or actual. *It is not the case that Jill fell first.* 3. a matter that the police or a court must consider. *The police are investigating a murder case.* | *The judge will decide this divorce case.*
in case if it happens that; if. *Take this umbrella in case it rains.* | **In case of** emergency, pull the alarm.

case[2] *noun* (kās) a container for holding, carrying, or keeping things safe. *Put your glasses in the case so they don't break.*

cash *noun* (kæsh) money in the form of bills and coins. *Will this be cash or charge? I'll pay* **with cash.**
verb to exchange for money in the form of bills and coins. *I cashed my check at the bank.*

cashier *noun* (kæ shēr) a person whose job is to take the money when a customer pays for something.

cash register *noun* (kæsh re ji stər) a machine with a drawer that holds money and records information about it as it comes in or out. Most stores and restaurants use a cash register.

cassette *noun* (kə set) a small plastic box that holds film or tape on which people record sound or pictures. A cassette can go into a camera, recording device, or playing device. *We want to watch a video, but the cassette is broken.*

castle *noun* (kæ səl) a large, strong building built in the past and used as a defense against attacks. *The prince built his castle on a high hill.*

casual *adj.* (kæ zhoo əl) 1. done without much attention or planning. *The boss made only casual checks of my work.* 2. not formal. *We can wear casual clothes in this restaurant.*

cat *noun* (kæt) 1. a small, common mammal with four legs and a long tail. *People often keep cats as pets.* 2. a large wild animal. *Tigers and lions are kinds of cats.*

catalogue (catalog) *noun* (kæ tə lawg) an organized list of things for sale. Catalogues usually give a short description of each item on the list. *The store didn't have the shoes in my size, so I ordered them from the catalogue.*

catch *verb* (kæch) *caught, caught* 1. to take hold of something that is moving. *My sister caught the ball.* | *The dog caught the rabbit.* 2. to discover and surprise. *The teacher caught him cheating on the test.* 3. to step inside a bus, train, or airplane in time to ride. *We caught the last bus.* 4. to become sick with an illness that goes from one person to another. *I **caught** the flu **from** my son.*
catch up 1. to reach something that is ahead of you. *Slow down. Let me **catch up with** you!* 2. to finish something that you needed to finish earlier. *It's important to **catch up on** homework if you have been absent from school.*

category *noun* (kæ tə gŏr ē) a particular type of thing within a larger group; class. *The books in the library are arranged by category.* | *Dogs are one category of animals.*

cater *verb* (kā tər) to supply food or service for a special event. *Our company catered two wedding parties.*

cattle *pl. noun* (kæ təl) large mammals that people keep for their milk, meat, and skin. *Cows are a kind of cattle.*

caught *verb* (kawt) past tense and past participle of **catch.**

cause *noun* (kawz) 1. something that makes a thing happen. *A cigarette was the cause of the fire.* 2. a purpose that people think is important and will give their efforts to. *They are working for the cause of world peace.*
verb to make something happen. *The sleepy driver caused the car accident.* | *The rain caused them to cancel the game.*

caution *noun* (kaw shən) [N] care and attention to safety. *You need to **use caution** when you ride your bike on busy streets.*
verb to give a warning to someone. *I **cautioned** her **about** the slippery roads.*

cave *noun* (kāv) a natural hole in the earth. *A cave is big enough for a person or animal to enter.*

cavity *noun* (kæ və tē) a hollow place or hole. *The dentist found three cavities in my teeth.*

cc *abbrev.* (sē sē) used on a letter or message to show that you are sending a copy of this message to another person.

CD *abbrev.* (sē dē) an abbreviation for **compact disc.**

CD-ROM *abbrev.* (sē dē ram) an abbreviation for **compact disc read-only memory.**

ceiling *noun* (sē ling) the part of a room that is over your head. *We painted the ceiling white and the walls blue.*

celebrate *verb* (se lə brāt) to honor something or make it special by giving gifts or doing things that people enjoy. *Our family celebrates holidays with a special dinner.* | *We celebrated her birthday with a big party.*

celebration *noun* (se lə brā shən) a party or anything else that people do to honor a special event. *The city's Independence Day celebration included a parade and fireworks.*

cell *noun* (sel) 1. a single unit of animal life or plant life. *The human body is made of many kinds of cells.* 2. a small room in a prison or jail. *The prisoner had to stay in his cell most of the day.*

cellar *noun* (se lər) a room that is built under the ground. People use it for storing things.

cell phone *noun* (sel fōn) a telephone that operates without wires. *She called me on her cell phone from her car.*

cell phone

cement *noun* (sə ment) [N] a gray powdered material that becomes hard when you add water. Cement is used to make concrete.

cemetery *noun* (se mə te rē) a place where the bodies of dead people are put in the ground.

cent *noun* (sent) a unit of money in many countries. One hundred cents equals one U.S. dollar.

center *noun* (<u>sen</u> tər) 1. the middle of something. *The center of the earth is very hot.* 2. a place of activity that many people come to from different places. *We went to the shopping center on Saturday.* | *They need more nurses at the medical center.* 3. a place, person, or thing that is the main object of attention or interest. *New York City is a center of business in the United States.* | *She likes to be the* **center of attention** *at a party.*

central *adj.* (<u>sen</u> trəl) being in the center. *The library is in the central part of town.*

century *noun* (<u>sen</u> chə rē) a period of time equal to one hundred years. *The United States became a country a little more than two centuries ago.*

cereal *noun* (<u>sēr</u> ē əl) 1. any plant whose grains are used for food. *Some cereals are wheat, corn, and oats.* 2. [N] food made from grain that people eat for breakfast. *The kids eat cereal with milk most days.*

ceremony *noun* (<u>se</u> rə mō nē) a set of actions that someone performs to mark a special occasion. *They invited only a few guests to the wedding ceremony.*

certain *adj.* (<u>sər</u> tən) 1. sure; having no doubt. *I'm certain she is still alive.* 2. particular; definite. *She buys only a certain brand of juice.* | *The club admits a certain number of people every year.*

> **Word Builder: certain +**
> **certainly:** yes, indeed; of course.

certainty *noun* (<u>sər</u> tən tē) a fact that cannot be argued with. *It is a certainty that she will win the prize.*

chain *noun* (<u>chān</u>) 1. circles of metal or another material that are joined together in a line. *He put his dog on a chain outside.* 2. a group of businesses of the same kind that have the same owner. *My cousin owns a chain of hotels.*

chair *noun* (<u>chār</u>) a piece of furniture for one person to sit on. A chair has four legs, a back, and sometimes arms.

back
arm
seat
back
chair

chalk *noun* (<u>chawk</u>) [N] a type of soft, white stone. Chalk is made into long, thin shapes used for writing or drawing. *The teacher wrote on the blackboard with chalk.*

> **Word Builder: chalk +**
> **chalkboard:** a board in a classroom; blackboard. You write on a chalkboard with chalk.

challenge *noun* (<u>chæ</u> linj) 1. an invitation to join a fight or competition. *He accepted the challenge to enter the race.* 2. an interesting or difficult problem. *English spelling is a challenge for anyone.*
    verb to invite someone to enter a competition or to do something that requires courage or skill. *He* **challenged** *her* **to** *climb the cliff.* | *She* **challenged** *him* **to** *a tennis match.*

chamber *noun* (<u>chām</u> bər) a large room or meeting hall used by people in government to make and discuss laws. *There are two chambers in the U.S. Capitol: one for the House of Representatives and one for the Senate.*

chance *noun* (<u>chæns</u>) 1. how likely it is that something will happen; possibility. *There is still some chance that he will live.* | *What are your chances of winning the lottery?* 2. opportunity; possibility. *Please call me when you get a chance.* | *I would like the chance to travel someday.* 3. a risk; a possibility of success or failure. *He* **took a chance** *and opened a new business.* 4. the quality of happening without any human control or planning. *I won the game* **by chance,** *not by skill.*

change *verb* (<u>chānj</u>) 1. to make different. *They changed the color of their kitchen.* | *I always* **change** *my* **clothes** *after work.* 2. to become different. *You have changed since the last time I saw you.*
    noun 1. the act of making something different or the fact of being different than before. *The school made two changes in the menu this month.* | *You can see many changes in the children this year.* 2. money in smaller bills or coins in exchange for a larger bill or coin. *I got change for a twenty: a ten-dollar bill, a five-dollar bill, four one-dollar bills, and four quarters.* 3. coins. *Some change fell out through a hole in his pocket.* 4. the money that you receive in return when you pay more money than the price of something. *Mark paid for the newspaper with a five-dollar bill, and the cashier gave him his change.*

channel *noun* (<u>chæ</u> nəl) 1. a long, narrow body of water that joins two larger bodies of water. 2. a radio or television station. *I changed the channel because I wanted to watch another program.*

chapter *noun* (<u>chæp</u> tər) one of the main parts of a book. *The last chapter of this novel is the most exciting.*

character *noun* (k̲æ̲r̲ ək tər) 1. [N] all the things that make a person, place, or thing different from others. *This neighborhood has a friendly character.* 2. [N] moral qualities of a person. *Honesty is part of his character.* 3. a person in a story, play, or movie. *That actor always plays evil characters.* | *The main character in the movie is a woman.*

> **Word Builder: character +**
> **characteristic:** a particular quality of a person or thing.
> **characterize:** to describe a person's character.

charge *verb* (c̲h̲a̲r̲j) 1. to state in an official way that someone may be responsible for a crime. *The police* **charged** *her* **with** *shoplifting.* 2. to supply with power or energy. *He charged the battery.* 3. to ask for a certain amount of money as the price of something. *That restaurant charges a dollar for a cup of coffee.* 4. to pay for something with a credit card. *He charged his purchases instead of paying cash.* 5. to rush forward in order to attack. *The soldiers charged the enemy.*
noun a price you have to pay for something. *The charge for that telephone call was very high.*
in charge having the power and responsibility for doing or deciding something. *Who is* **in charge of** *this department?* | *The supervisor is* **in charge of** *quality control.*

chart *noun* (c̲h̲a̲r̲t) a sheet that gives information in the form of a table or graph. *The sales manager pointed to the numbers on his chart.*

charter *noun* (c̲h̲a̲r̲ tər) an official document that a government gives to a business or other group. The charter states that the group has a right to exist and explains its purpose.
verb to rent something for a short time for a group of people. *The school chartered a bus for a trip to the museum.*

chase *verb* (c̲h̲ā̲s̲) to follow with the purpose of catching; run after. *The police chased the person down the street.*

chat *verb* (c̲h̲æ̲t̲) to talk in an informal, easy way. *I chat with my friends at lunch.*

cheap *adj.* (c̲h̲ē̲p̲) 1. having a low price. *Vegetables are cheap at the farmer's market.* 2. of poor quality. *Cheap clothing wears out fast.*

cheat *verb* (c̲h̲ē̲t̲) to act in a way that is not honest in order to get something from someone. *The man cheated the woman by taking her money for work he did not do.*

check *noun* (c̲h̲e̲k̲) 1. a written order to a bank to pay money from an account. *I pay my bills by check.* 2. a bill for food and drink at a bar or restaurant. *The waiter gave us the check after we finished our meal.*
verb 1. to look at something in order to make sure that it is right or correct. *Please check the door to make sure it is locked.* 2. to give something to someone to keep for you while you travel or for a short time. *We checked our bags at the ticket counter before we got on the plane.* | *The restaurant has a place to check our coats.*
check in to say in an official way that you have arrived. You check in at a hotel before you stay there and at an airport before you fly.
check off to make a mark next to things on a list that are already correct, completed, or not needed anymore. *I checked off each person's name on the list after I called them.*
check out 1. to pay for something in a store where there are different lines for people to pay. *It takes a long time to check out at the grocery store.* 2. to say in an official way that you are leaving your hotel room and to pay the bill. *We have to check out before noon.*
check up on to try to get information about what someone is doing. *My son doesn't like it when we check up on him.*

checkbook *noun* (c̲h̲e̲k̲ buk) a small book of forms that can be used to pay for something with money from a bank account. *I wrote a check from my checkbook to pay the bill.*

checkbook

check-cashing card *noun* (c̲h̲e̲k̲ k̲æ̲s̲h̲ ing k̲a̲r̲d̲) a card given by a store. It allows a person to write a check to buy something from that store. *I can pay for my groceries with a check if I bring my check-cashing card.*

checkup *noun* (c̲h̲e̲k̲ əp) an examination of a person or thing to discover if there are any problems. *My daughter has to go to the doctor for a checkup.*

cheek *noun* (c̲h̲ē̲k̲) either side of the face between the nose and the ear.

cheer *noun* (ch<u>er</u>) 1. [N] happy or good feelings. *We are filled with cheer during the holiday season.* 2. a shout to show that you are happy about or approve of something. *The crowd let out a cheer when the team made a goal.*
verb to shout in order to show that you like something. *They cheered the team.*

cheerful *adj.* (ch<u>er</u> fəl) full of happy or good feelings. *My sister is always cheerful when she returns from school.*

cheese *noun* (ch<u>ez</u>) [N] a solid food made from milk.

chef *noun* (sh<u>ef</u>) a person whose job is to cook in a restaurant.

chemical *noun* (k<u>e</u> mə kəl) a substance used in or made by a chemical process. *The drain cleaner contains strong chemicals.*
adj. having to do with the science of chemistry. *Salt is a chemical compound.*

chemistry *noun* (k<u>e</u> mi str<u>e</u>) [N] the structure and function of elements and their compounds, or the study of this.

cherry *noun* (ch<u>e</u> r<u>e</u>) a small, round fruit with red skin and flesh. *Cherries grow on trees.*

chest *noun* (ch<u>est</u>) 1. the upper front part of the body between the neck and waist. 2. a large, strong box with a lid, used for holding things. *She stores blankets in a wooden chest.*

chew *verb* (ch<u>oo</u>) to break apart and make soft with the teeth. *Chew food before you swallow it.*

chewing gum *noun* (ch<u>oo</u> ing gəm) [N] a soft, sweet substance that you chew for a long time but do not swallow.

chicken *noun* (ch<u>i</u> kən) a common bird that people raise on farms for its meat and eggs.

chief *noun* (ch<u>ef</u>) the most powerful or important person in a group; leader. *The chief of police was in charge of the investigation.*
adj. most important; main. *Potatoes are the chief crop of Idaho.*

child *noun* (ch<u>ild</u>) **children** a young human. *The child held her mother's hand.*

Word Builder: child +
childbirth: the birth of a child.
childhood: the time of life when you are a child.
childish: acting like a child.
childless: having no children.
childlike: like or appropriate to a child.

children *pl. noun* (ch<u>il</u> drən) plural of **child.**

chill *noun* (ch<u>il</u>) 1. a feeling of cold and shaking in the body caused by a low temperature. *She got a chill when she walked out the door without her coat on.* 2. a sudden, cold feeling caused by fear. *That scary part of the movie* **gave** *me* **a chill.**
verb to cause to become cold or colder. *She chilled the bottles of water.*

Word Builder: chill +
chilly: causing or feeling a chill; cool.

chimney *noun* (ch<u>im</u> n<u>e</u>) a tall, hollow structure that carries smoke up through a building and to the outside. *The chimney on my house is made of brick.*
chimney

chin *noun* (ch<u>in</u>) the part of the face below the mouth and above the neck.

china *noun* (ch<u>i</u> nə) 1. [N] a hard, delicate material that cups and plates are made from. *Mary has plates made of fine china.* 2. [N] plates, dishes, and cups. *Please clear the china from the table.*

chip *noun* (ch<u>ip</u>) 1. a small piece broken or cut from a hard material. *A chip flew off the stone when I hit it with a hammer.* 2. a space that remains when a small piece has broken off. *I dropped the plate, and now it has a chip in it.* 3. a small, thin piece of food. *I bought a bag of potato chips.* 4. a small, electronic part of a computer. *This computer has a powerful new chip.*
verb to cause a small piece to break off from the surface of something. *I chipped my tooth.*

Word Builder: kinds of chips
chocolate chip: a very small piece of chocolate.
potato chip: a very thin slice of potato fried in oil.

chisel *noun* (ch<u>i</u> zəl) a tool with a sharp metal edge attached to a handle. A chisel is used for cutting stone, wood, or metal.

chocolate *noun* (<u>cha</u> klət) 1. [N] a food substance used to make candy and other sweet foods. Chocolate is made from the ground beans of a tropical plant. *I put a lot of chocolate in these cookies.* 2. a piece of candy made with this food and sugar. *He gave her a box of chocolates.*

choice *noun* (<u>choys</u>) 1. a decision that you make about something you want. *It was hard to make the right choice.* 2. the thing or person chosen. *Jack was our choice for club president.*

choke *verb* (<u>chōk</u>) to stop breathing because something is in the throat. *A piece of food got stuck in my throat, and I choked.*
noun a piece of equipment that controls the amount of air that mixes with the gasoline in an engine.

choose *verb* (<u>chooz</u>) *chose, chosen* 1. to pick one or more things or people from a group. *Paul chose three books from the library.* 2. to decide between different possibilities. *We chose to go to a movie instead of a concert.*

chop *verb* (<u>chap</u>) to cut with a sharp tool such as an ax or knife. *He chopped wood.* | *She chopped onions to put them into the soup.*
noun a thick piece of meat with a bone in it. *Would you like lamb chops for dinner?*
chop off to cut something with one strong, quick motion so that one part separates from the main part. *Be careful with that machine! You could chop off your finger.*

chore *noun* (<u>chōr</u>) 1. a regular job around the house or at work. *His chores are doing the laundry and taking out the garbage.* 2. something that is difficult or not pleasant to do. *Gardening is a pleasure for some people but a chore for others.*

chorus *noun* (<u>kōr</u> is) 1. a group of people who sing together. *Sue joined the chorus at her church.* 2. a part of a song that is repeated. *The chorus of the song is easy to remember.*

chose *verb* (<u>chōz</u>) past tense of **choose.**

chosen *verb* (<u>chō</u> zən) past participle of **choose.**

chuck *noun* (<u>chək</u>) a part of a drill. The chuck holds the long metal piece that cuts the hole.

church *noun* (<u>chərch</u>) a building used for Christian religious services. *The bell rang in the church tower.*

cigarette *noun* (<u>si</u> gə <u>ret</u>) a short, narrow tube of thin paper that contains cut tobacco for smoking. *Cigarettes cause health problems.*

circle *noun* (<u>sər</u> kəl) 1. a line that curves so that one end meets the other. The line is made up of points that are all the same distance from the center. *The ring has the shape of a circle.* 2. anything that has a round, closed shape. *The children sat in a circle and listened to a story.*

circuit *noun* (<u>sər</u> kət) the complete path followed by an electric current. *When you turn off the switch, the circuit opens and the light goes off.*

circuit breaker *noun* (<u>sər</u> kət <u>brā</u> kər) a safety device that stops the flow of electricity in a circuit when there is too much electricity going through it. *Circuit breakers protect against fire.*

circular *adj.* (<u>sər</u> kyə lər) having the shape of a circle; round. *She moved her arm in a circular motion.*
noun a piece of printed matter with advertisements that is given to many people. *There is a circular from the supermarket in today's newspaper.*

circular saw *noun* (<u>sər</u> kyə lər <u>saw</u>) a saw with a round blade that turns at a high speed.

circular saw

circulation *noun* (<u>sər</u> kyə <u>lā</u> shən) 1. [N] the movement of blood through the body. *My hands get cold because I have poor circulation.* 2. [N] the movement of something, such as money or news, from person to person or place to place. *The new stamps are now **in circulation.** | That nasty joke has been **in circulation** for too long.*

circus *noun* (<u>sər</u> kəs) a show that travels from town to town to entertain people. People and trained animals perform inside a ring. *My son loved the clowns and tigers at the circus.*

citizen *noun* (<u>si</u> tə zən) a person who is a member of a country because of being born there or being accepted as a member by law. *In the United States, only citizens can vote.*

citizenship *noun* (<u>si</u> tə zən ship) [N] rights of being a citizen. *Luis got his citizenship after living in America for ten years.*

city *noun* (<u>si</u> tē) a large and important town where many people live and work. *Chicago is one of the largest cities in the United States.*

civic *adj.* (sĭ vĭk) having to do with being a citizen. *It is your civic responsibility to obey the law.*

civil *adj.* (sĭ vəl) 1. having to do with the activities of citizens, but not of religious or military groups. *Charles and Susan were married in a civil ceremony, not in church.* 2. using good manners; polite. *She behaves in a civil way toward everyone.*

civil rights *pl. noun* (sĭ vəl rīts) certain rights, such as the right to vote and own property. In the United States the Constitution promises these rights to citizens. *Martin Luther King, Jr., was a leader in the fight for civil rights for all Americans.*

civil war *noun* (sĭ vəl wōr) a war between different groups within one country. *The Civil War in the United States began in 1861 and ended in 1865.*

claim *verb* (klām) to state as true. *He claimed that his father was seven feet tall.*
noun a demand for something as one's right. *After he died, his oldest son made a claim to all his property.*

clam *noun* (klăm) an animal with a soft body and a hard shell that often lives in water. People eat some kinds of clams.

clamp *noun* (klămp) a thing used to hold two objects or pieces together. *The carpenter used a clamp to hold two boards together while the glue dried.*

clan *noun* (klăn) a group of people from the same family. *The Smith clan got together at the beach last summer.*

clap *verb* (klăp) to hit your hands together again and again to show that you like something. *Everyone clapped when the show was over.*

class *noun* (klăs) 1. a group of people, things, or animals that are similar in certain ways; kind. *Cars race against cars of the same class.* 2. a group of people who have a similar economic or social position in society. *Many people in the American middle class own their own homes.* 3. a group of students who study something together with a teacher. *Our art class meets Tuesday evenings.*

Word Builder: class +
classmate: a person who is in the same class as you.
classroom: a room in a school where a class meets.

classify *verb* (klă sə fī) to put in groups according to things that are similar. *People classify trees by the kind of leaves they have.*

Word Builder: classify +
classified advertisements: newspaper advertisements that are in groups according to what a person or business wants to sell or is looking for.

clause *noun* (klawz) a group of words in a sentence that has a subject and a verb. A clause can be part or all of a sentence. In the sentence "I was tired, so I went to bed," there are two clauses connected by *so.*

claw *noun* (klaw) 1. a thin, sharp, curved nail on the foot of an animal. *The cat scratched me with its claws.* 2. a part that looks or acts like a claw. *Use the claw of the hammer to pull out the nails.*

claw

clay *noun* (klā) [N] a kind of wet earth that becomes hard when you heat it. You use clay to make bricks, pots, and other things.

clean *adj.* (klēn) not dirty. *I took a clean dish from the shelf.*
verb to remove dirt or stains from; make clean. *Clean your shoes outside.*
clean out to empty many things from something. *She cleaned out her closet.*
clean up to wash or clean. *Please clean up your room.*

cleanse *verb* (klenz) to make clean or pure. *The nurse cleansed the skin before putting the bandage over the wound.*

Word Builder: cleanse +
cleanser: a liquid or powder used for cleaning.

clear *adj.* (klēr) 1. easy to see through; without color or dirt. *He covered the bowl with clear plastic wrap.* | *We swam in the clear water.* 2. easy to understand. *Her directions were very clear.* 3. used to describe the sky when there are no clouds or when there is little pollution or dust. *It was a clear, cold day.*
verb to make free of anything in the way. *They **cleared** the path **of** branches.* | *They **cleared** the branches **from** the path.*
clear up to become bright or clear. *The weather is clearing up.*

Word Builder: clear +
clearly: in a way that is clear or easy to understand.

clerk *noun* (klərk) 1. a person whose job is to sell goods to customers in a store. 2. a person whose job is to record, organize, and keep information so that it is easy to find. *She works as a clerk in a lawyer's office.*

clever *adj.* (kle vər) having a quick mind; smart. *Anna is a clever girl who does well in school.*

click *noun* (klik) a slight, sharp sound. *I heard the click of her shoes on the floor.*
verb to cause to make a slight, sharp sound. *To open the program, move the mouse to the icon and click it twice.*

cliff *noun* (klif) a high, steep surface of rock. *It is dangerous to stand near the edge of a cliff.*

climate *noun* (klī mit) the usual weather conditions in a place. *Alaska has a cold climate.*

climb *verb* (klīm) 1. to travel up or go toward the top. *He climbed until he reached the top of the mountain. | The airplane climbed fast into the air.* 2. to move up something using your feet and sometimes your hands and other parts of your body. *We climbed the stairs to the roof. | My daughter loves to climb trees.*

cling *verb* (kling) *clung, clung* to stick to something or hold close. *A piece of food is clinging to your chin. | The baby is clinging to her mother.*

clinic *noun* (kli nik) a place that gives medical treatment to people who do not need to stay in a hospital. *Angela went to the clinic to get medicine for her sore throat.*

clip[1] *verb* (klip) to cut with a tool with sharp edges such as scissors. *He clipped an article from a magazine. | She clipped her nails.*

Word Builder: clip +
clippers: a tool for clipping.

clip[2] *noun* (klip) a device that holds or fastens. It is usually made of light metal or plastic. *She found a clip to hold the pages of her report together. | I need a clip for my hair.*
verb to hold together or attach by means of a clip. *You should clip those papers together. | He **clipped** his name tag **to** his shirt.*

Word Builder: kinds of clips
hair clip: a clip for holding hair in place.
paper clip: a clip for holding pieces of paper together

clock *noun* (klak) a thing for measuring and showing the time. *There is a small clock next to her bed.* **verb** to record the time you arrive at or leave work. *Edward **clocked in** at eight o'clock and **clocked out** at four o'clock.*

face
hands
clock

clockwise *adj., adv.* (klak wīz) moving in the same direction as a clock's hands. *He gave the knob on the radio a clockwise turn. | Tighten the screw by turning it clockwise.*

clog *verb* (klag) to block passage through something. *Hair and dirt are clogging the pipe. | We can't use the sink now because the drain is clogged.*

close *verb* (klōz) 1. to shut. *Close the door.* 2. to end; finish. *She closed her speech with a funny story.* 3. to become shut. *The elevator doors closed.*
adj. (klōs) 1. near in space or time. *The school is **close to** downtown. | It is **close to** the end of the movie.* 2. near in relation. *I invited my close friends to the party.*
adv. in a close way; near. *She held her baby close.*

Word Builder: close +
closely: in a close way.
closing: the end or last part of something.

closet *noun* (kla zit) a small room or space for storing things such as clothes or supplies. *She hung her dresses in the closet. | The mop and broom are in the janitor's closet.*

cloth *noun* (klawth) 1. [N] material made by weaving. *She wears a coat made of cloth, not fur.* 2. a piece of woven material used for a particular purpose. *She used a cloth to clean the table.*

Word Builder: kinds of cloths
dust cloth: a small piece of cloth that you wipe things with to remove dust.
tablecloth: a large cloth that covers a table.
washcloth: a small cloth that you wash with.

clothes *pl. noun* (klōz or klōthz) things that you wear to cover the body; clothing. *The children always wear clean clothes to school.*

Word Builder: clothes +
clothesline: a rope that you hang wet clothes on to dry.
clothespin: a clip for holding clothes to a clothesline.

clothing *noun* (klō thing) [N] things that you wear to cover the body; clothes. *She prefers dark clothing.*

cloud *noun* (klowd) a white or gray mass of small drops of water high in the sky above the earth. *The dark clouds told us a storm was coming.*

Word Builder: cloud +
cloudy: having many clouds.

clown *noun* (klown) an actor who wears odd clothes, does amusing tricks, and paints his or her face in order to make people laugh. *We saw many clowns at the circus.*

club *noun* (kləb) 1. a heavy stick that is used as a weapon. *The police officer carried a club.* 2. a group of people who meet for a special purpose. *My friend belongs to a book club.* 3. a black shape with three round parts that can be found on a playing card; a card marked with this shape. *The three of clubs is considered bad luck in some card games.* 4. a place for evening entertainment where there is usually music, food, and drinks with alcohol. *That club has a good band tonight.*

clue *noun* (kloo) something that helps to solve a problem or mystery. *The detective found many clues at the scene of the crime.*

clung *verb* (kləng) past tense and past participle of **cling.**

cluster *noun* (klə stər) a small group of similar things that are close together or are attached to each other. *Steve took a cluster of grapes from the bowl.* | *English has many consonant clusters, such as* str, spl, *and* scr.

clutch *verb* (kləch) to hold tight. *The baby clutched her toy bear.*
noun a part for working the gears of the engine in a car or truck. In a car with a standard transmission, the pedal for the clutch is on the left.

coach *noun* (kōch) 1. a person who trains and teaches people in sports. *The football team has a new coach.* 2. a section of seats on an airplane or train. Tickets for this section are the least expensive. *Brian traveled in coach to save money.* 3. a public bus. *We took a coach from Chicago to New York City.*
verb to train, teach, or prepare. *She coaches soccer.* | *He coaches the team.*

coal *noun* (kōl) [N] a hard black or dark brown substance that is found in the earth. People burn coal for heat and energy. *People who mine coal have a dangerous job.*

coast *noun* (kōst) the land next to the ocean. *New York City is on the east coast of the United States.*
verb to move without effort or energy. *The children coasted down the hill on a sled.*

coat *noun* (kōt) 1. a piece of clothing that people wear over their clothes. It covers the body, arms, and some of a person's legs and is usually used to keep warm. 2. the fur or body hair of an animal. *Our cat has a shiny, gray coat.* 3. a covering or layer of a liquid, which usually becomes dry. *These walls need another coat of paint.*
verb to cover with a layer. *The bread was coated with melted cheese.*

collar
lapel
sleeve
coat

cocoa *noun* (kō kō) 1. [N] a powder made by removing oil from chocolate. *I need two cups of cocoa for my cake.* 2. [N] a warm drink made with cocoa, sugar, and milk or water. *The children love to drink cocoa after playing in the snow.*

code *noun* (kōd) 1. a set of rules or laws. *The **dress code** at school states that students may not wear shorts or jeans.* 2. a system of symbols or signals used in place of letters and numbers. Code is used to send a message when you want to hide its meaning. *The army officer sent secret messages in code.*

coffee *noun* (kaw fē) [N] a dark brown drink made from the beans of a tropical plant.

Word Builder: coffee +
coffee break: a rest from work when you eat a snack and drink coffee or other things.
coffee cake: a sweet cake often served with coffee.
coffeepot: a pot for making and serving coffee.
coffee table: a low table placed in front of a sofa.

coil *noun* (koyl) something that is wound into many connected rings. *There is a coil of rope in that cabinet.* | *Bring me that coil of copper wire.*

coin *noun* (koyn) a piece of metal money that is small, flat, and round. *Pennies, nickels, dimes, and quarters are all coins.*

cold *adj.* (kōld) 1. without heat or warmth. *This room is very cold.* | *January is a cold month.* 2. feeling a lack of warmth. *I was cold, so I put an extra blanket on the bed.*
noun 1. low temperature in the environment. *The cold was awful when I walked to work.* 2. a common sickness that often causes coughing and a runny nose. *My son **caught a cold** from his friend at school.*

collar *noun* (ka lər) the part of a piece of clothing that goes around the neck. *The boys had to wear both a shirt with a collar and a tie.*

collate *verb* (kō lāt) to separate into groups of pages, which are all in correct order. *We have twenty copies of each of the twelve pages. Now we need to collate them.*

collect *verb* (kə lekt) to gather together. *The teacher collected her students' work.*
adj., adv. requiring payment for a telephone call from the person who receives the call. *I made a collect phone call to my sister in Hawaii.* | *I called her collect.*

collection *noun* (kə lek shən) a group of things of the same type that someone has brought together. *Phil has a large collection of stamps.*

college *noun* (ka lij) a school that you go to after high school. Most college programs require four years of study. *If you want to be a doctor, you must go to college.*

collision *noun* (kə li zhən) an act of things coming together with force. *There was a collision between a car and a truck on the highway.*

colon *noun* (kō lən) a punctuation mark (:). It is often used to introduce a series, quotation, or explanation.

colony *noun* (ka lə nē) a place that is under the control of a distant country. People from that country often move to and live in the colony. *America was a colony of England before it became independent.*

color *noun* (kə lər) a quality of light as our eyes see it. Red, blue, and yellow are some colors. *My computer monitor can show thousands of colors.*

Word Builder: color +
colorful: having many colors or having bright colors.

color-blind *adj.* (kə lər blīnd) not able to see a difference between certain colors. *Red and green look the same to people who are color-blind.* | *Many animals are color-blind.*

column *noun* (ka ləm) 1. a tall, thin part of a building. A column helps support a building. *The Capitol in Washington, D.C., has many columns.* 2. a section of print or writing that runs down a page, not across. *This dictionary page has two columns.* | *I added a column of numbers.*

column

comb *noun* (kōm) a thin piece of plastic or other material that has teeth along one side. It is used to smooth or arrange hair.
verb to remove the knots from hair or make it smooth with a comb. *I comb my daughter's hair every day.*

combination *noun* (kam bə nā shən) things that are brought together or combined. *The soup had a combination of chicken and vegetables.*

combine *verb* (kəm bīn) to bring or join together into a whole. *He combined flour and water to make dough.*
noun (kam bīn) a machine used to gather crops. A combine cuts and cleans the grain. *The farmer used a combine to harvest wheat.*

combustible *adj.* (kəm bə stə bəl) able to catch fire and burn. *Gasoline is combustible.*

come *verb* (kəm) *came, come* 1. to move or travel toward you. *Come here, please.* 2. to arrive or enter. *Here she comes now!* | *I came into the room through the window.* 3. to appear in a certain place or position in relation to other things or people. *The letter C comes after the letter B.* | *In tonight's performance, my daughter comes after your son.*
come across to discover or find by chance. *I came across a new recipe in that magazine.*
come from to be born in or to have as your home. *Her father comes from Mexico.*
come out to become known to many people. *The story of the crime came out in the newspaper.*
come over to come from one place to another to visit or talk with someone, used only when people are in the same town, area, or space. *Some friends came over to my house last night.*
come through to continue to live or exist. *Mr. Jackson came through his illness.* | *The building came through the flood.*
come up to enter a conversation. *The subject of politics always comes up when my brother visits.*

comedy *noun* (ka mə dē) a play, film, story, or television show that is funny. *Which do you like better, comedies or mysteries?*

comfort *verb* (kəm fərt) to make someone feel less pain or worry. *Barbara comforted her sick baby.*
noun a pleasant condition that comes from not having worry, pain, or a difficult life. *The rich family lived in comfort.*

comfortable *adj.* (kəmf tər bəl) giving or feeling comfort. *She wears comfortable shoes so her feet don't hurt.* | *He feels comfortable in his new house.*

comma *noun* (ka mə) a punctuation mark (,). It is used to separate words, phrases, or other parts of a sentence. It is also used in writing large numbers.

command *verb* (kə mænd) to lead and control. *The general commands his troops.*
noun an instruction that you must obey; order. *The dog learned to follow a few commands.*

commander-in-chief *noun* (kə mæn dər in chēf) the person in charge of all the armed forces of a country. In the United States the commander-in-chief is the president.

commerce *noun* (ka mərs) [N] the buying and selling of goods or services; business. *The United States has increased its commerce with Mexico.* | *Cities are centers of commerce.*

commercial *adj.* (kə mər shəl) having to do with trade or business. *The commercial part of town has many stores.*
noun an advertisement on television or radio. *The car sounds wonderful in the commercial.*

commit *verb* (kə mit) 1. to promise to give a thing such as money or time or your own effort and to not change your decision to give it. *We have **committed** this money **to** our children's education.* | *She has decided to **commit herself to** her new job.* 2. to do; perform. *He **committed a crime.***

committee *noun* (kə mi tē) a group of people who meet to discuss and make decisions about a particular matter. *The bank's loan committee meets twice a week.*

common *adj.* (ka mən) 1. shared in equal parts by all members of a group. *My friends and I have a common interest in football.* 2. usual; easy to find. *Pigeons are common in our part of the country.* | *Snow is common in winter.*
in common owned or used together; shared. *My brother and I have several friends in common.*

Word Builder: common +
commonly: usually, often.

common sense *noun* (ka mən sens) [N] the ordinary good judgment that is part of a person's intelligence or that is learned through experience. *It is common sense to wear a jacket when it is cold outside.*

communicate *verb* (kə mū nə kāt) to exchange ideas or information. *I communicate with my best friend by telephone.*

communication *noun* (kə mū nə kā shən) [N] the sharing or exchange of messages, information, or ideas. *Reading and writing are important forms of communication.* | *E-mail is a new **means of communication.***

communism *noun* (kam yə ni zəm) [N] a system of government in which all factories, farms, and other valuable things are owned and controlled by the government.

communist *noun* (kam yə nist) a person who supports **communism.**

community *noun* (kə mū ni tē) 1. a particular area where a group of people live. *A new store opened in my community.* 2. a group of people who live close together or who have the same interests. *Education is important to the immigrant community.*

community college *noun* (kə mū ni tē ka lij) a small college that serves a community. Most courses of study at a community college take one or two years. *Kimberly graduated from a community college with a degree in nursing.*

commute *verb* (kə mūt) to ride or drive a certain distance to and from work or school. *Michelle commutes from her home to her office in the city.* | *She commutes by bus.*

compact *adj.* (kam pækt) small; able to fit in a small space. *They bought a compact washing machine for their small apartment.* | *Cynthia drives a compact car, not a van.*
verb (kəm pækt) to press things together to make them fit into a smaller space. *That machine compacts cans so they can be recycled.*

compact disc *noun* (kam pækt disk) a flat, round plastic piece on which music or information is stored. You can play a compact disc on a computer or special machine. *Anthony bought his favorite band's latest compact disc.*

compact disc

company *noun* (k<u>əm</u> pə nē) 1. a business firm or organization. *Our company hired many new workers this year.* 2. [N] a guest or guests. *We had company for dinner last night.* 3. [N] another person who stays with you. *I need company because I don't like to be alone.*

comparative *adj.* (kəm <u>pær</u> ə tiv) of or involving comparison. *Here is a book about comparative methods of farming.*
noun the form of an adjective or adverb that expresses the idea of comparison. The words *better, faster,* and *more beautiful* are comparatives.

compare *verb* (kəm <u>pār</u>) 1. to consider two or more things and decide how they are different or similar to each other. *I compared the two kinds of soup and decided this one is better.* 2. to say that one thing is like another thing. *He **compared** her eyes **to** the stars in the sky.*

> **compare to or compare with?**
> *Compare to* is used to show that something is like another thing.
> *Compare with* is used when you look at two things to find out whether they are the same or different.
> Compare:
> *She compared her boyfriend to a movie star.*
> *She compared her old car with her new car.*

comparison *noun* (kəm <u>pær</u> i sən) the act of comparing or the result of being compared. *My grandfather likes to **make comparisons between** his native country and the United States.*

compensation *noun* (kam pən <u>sā</u> shən) [N] something that you get in return for doing something; something that you get in exchange for damage or loss. *They received fair compensation for the work they did.* | *Debra received compensation for her injuries from the accident.*

compete *verb* (kəm <u>pēt</u>) to try to win or get something that others are also trying to get. *The two friends **competed for** the highest grade in the class.* | *Those two companies have always **competed against** each other.*

competition *noun* (kam pə <u>ti</u> shən)
1. [N] the process or act of trying to win. *Many businesses fail because of too much competition.*
2. a situation where people compete, such as a contest or game. *My sister won the swimming competition.*

competition

competitive *adj.* (kəm <u>pe</u> ti tiv) having a strong desire to win or do better than other people. *She is a competitive person, so she always tries to do her best.*

competitor *noun* (kəm <u>pe</u> ti tər) a person, group, or thing that competes. *That new company is our strongest competitor.* | *My brother and I were competitors in the race.*

complain *verb* (kəm <u>plān</u>) to say that something is wrong or that you are not happy with something. *She **complained about** the cold weather.* | *He complained that the soup was too salty.*

complaint *noun* (kəm <u>plānt</u>) 1. an act of complaining. *He **made** several **complaints** to the company about errors on his bill.* 2. a formal charge or accusation. *I filed a complaint with the police after I was robbed.*

complete *adj.* (kəm <u>plēt</u>) having all of the parts that are necessary; whole. *We can't play cards because I don't have a complete deck.*
verb to finish. *He completed the test in one hour.*

> **Word Builder: complete +**
> **completely:** all.

complex *adj.* (kəm <u>pleks</u> or <u>kam</u> pleks) not simple. *A computer is a complex machine.* | *English spelling is complex.*
noun (<u>kam</u> pleks) a structure that has several parts that are connected, or a group of structures that are built according to a similar plan. *They built a large housing complex on that land.*

complicated *adj.* (<u>kam</u> pli kā tid) not simple; having many parts that are connected in various ways. *The process for making cars is complicated.* | *He gave complicated instructions for using the new software.*

compliment *noun* (<u>kam</u> plə mənt) an expression of praise or approval. *He **gave** her a **compliment on** the report she wrote.*
verb to give praise or express approval. *The teacher **complimented** us **on** our work.*

compose *verb* (kəm <u>pōz</u>) 1. to form or be the parts of. *These twenty people compose the class.* | *The class **is composed of** people from many different countries.* 2. to write a new piece of music. *She has composed several songs.*

composition *noun* (kam pə zi shən) 1. [N] the way the parts of something are put together. *The scientists studied the composition of rocks from the moon.* 2. a piece of writing or music that has required thought and imagination to make. *The teacher asked us to write a composition about the Bill of Rights.* | *His musical compositions are beautiful.*

compound *noun* (kam pownd) something made up of two or more parts or elements. *Water is a compound.* **adj.** having to do with a word that has two or more parts or a sentence made up of two or more main clauses. *Bathroom is a compound word. "I went to the store, and I bought some bread " is a compound sentence.*
verb (kəm pownd) to figure and pay interest on the interest that you have earned combined with the principal. *The bank* **compounds interest** *four times a year.*

comprehend *verb* (kam prə hend) to understand. *Do you comprehend the instructions?*

compromise *noun* (kam prə mīz) a certain type of agreement in which two sides disagree about something in the beginning but come to agree after each side gives up something. *They both wanted to use the car every day, but they finally* **reached a compromise.**
verb to make a compromise. *She wanted to go to a movie and I wanted to stay home, so we compromised by renting a video.*

compulsory *adj.* (kəm pəl sə rē) required or necessary. *This test is compulsory for graduation.*

compute *verb* (kəm pūt) to find an answer to a number problem by using basic mathematics. *Let's compute the score to see who won the game.*

computer *noun* (kəm pū tər) an electronic machine that is used to store, sort, and work with information at a high speed.

computer

con *noun* (kan) a reason against something. *We argued the* **pros and cons** *of her suggestion.*

concentrate *verb* (kan sən trāt) 1. to make purer or stronger by taking away parts that are not necessary. To concentrate some substances, you remove the water they contain. *If you boil this sauce for a long time,*

it will concentrate and get thick. 2. to give your attention or thought to one thing only. *Please don't talk to me now so I can* **concentrate on** *my work.*
noun something in a pure form, with most of the water removed. *We don't have any fresh juice, but we have some concentrate.*

concentration *noun* (kan sən trā shən) [N] close attention. *This problem is difficult and requires concentration.*

concept *noun* (kan sept) a general idea or thought. *The concept of marriage is different in different countries.* | *My youngest child has difficulty learning new concepts.*

concern *verb* (kən sərn) 1. to have to do with something; be connected with something. *This matter is between your father and me. It does not concern you.* 2. to make someone worried. *Her bad attitude about school concerns me.*
noun worry or anxiety. *I understand your concern for your family.*

concerned *adj.* (kən sərnd) worried. *I'm very* **concerned about** *my mother's health these days.*

concerning *prep.* (kən sər ning) having to do with; about. *The teacher spoke to us concerning our son's absence.*

concert *noun* (kan sərt) a performance of music in front of an audience. *We are going to a concert in the city this weekend.*

conclude *verb* (kən klood) 1. to bring to an end; finish or complete. *We concluded the meeting and went out for lunch.* 2. to think about something and form an opinion. *The principal concluded that the child had done nothing wrong.*

conclusion *noun* (kən kloo zhən) 1. an ending or result. *The conclusion of the book was a surprise.* 2. an opinion that you form after thinking about many things. *What is your conclusion about how the accident happened?*

concrete *adj.* (kan krēt) able to be seen and touched; real. *Pencils are concrete objects, but ideas are not.*
noun (kan krēt) [N] a hard, strong building material. *Bridges and sidewalks are often made from concrete.*

condiment *noun* (kan də mənt) a kind of food that you eat with another food to add flavor. *Some popular condiments are ketchup and mustard.*

condition *noun* (kən di shən) 1. [N] a state of health or fitness for use. *My grandmother has been in bad condition since she fell. | These shoes are old, but they are in good condition.* 2. things that affect comfort or safety. *Conditions in the factory have improved under the new management.* 3. something that must happen or exist before something else can happen. *Being a citizen is a condition for being able to vote.*

conduct *noun* (kan dəkt) [N] the way a person acts; behavior. *People expect good conduct from leaders in government.*
verb (kən dəkt) 1. to lead or guide. *She conducted a tour of the museum. | He conducted the orchestra.* 2. to carry electricity through or along something. *Copper conducts well. | Plastic does not conduct electricity.*

> **Word Builder: conduct +**
> **conductor (1):** a thing that conducts electric current.
> **conductor (2):** a person who leads an orchestra.
> **conductor (3):** a person who collects tickets on a train.

cone *noun* (kōn) 1. a solid figure that is round at one end and pointed at the other end. 2. anything shaped like a cone. *The orange cones in the road warn drivers to be careful.*

> **Word Builder: kinds of cones**
> **ice cream cone:** a thin cookie in the shape of a cone. You put ice cream in the open end of the cone.
> **warning cone:** a large, bright-colored cone placed in a road to warn drivers of danger.

conference *noun* (kan frəns) a meeting of people who have the same job or similar interests. The purpose of the meeting is to share information and opinions. *The teachers have a conference every month.*

confess *verb* (kən fes) to admit as true. *She confessed that she took the wallet. | He **confessed to** stealing the money.*

confession *noun* (kən fe shən) the act of admitting that you have done something wrong or that you have certain feelings. *She went to the police station and **made a confession.** | His confession about his love was a surprise to her.*

confidence *noun* (kan fi dəns) [N] a sense of trust or faith in a person or thing. *The passengers **have confidence** in the pilot. | He was a great singer before he **lost** his **confidence.***

confident *adj.* (kan fi dənt) having trust or faith; sure that something will happen. *We are confident that our team will win.*

confidential *adj.* (kan fi den shəl) told in private; only for certain people, not for the public. *The information in this letter is confidential.*

confine *verb* (kən fīn) to keep within limits. *The storm confined me to the house. | Please confine your questions to this one topic.*

confine

> **Word Builder: confine +**
> **confined:** close, tight.

conflict *verb* (kən flikt) to be in strong opposition to. *My opinion of the new mayor conflicted with my wife's.*
noun (kan flikt) 1. a strong difference of opinion. *There is a **conflict between** the workers and the management at that company.* 2. a fight, battle, or war. *The conflict between the two countries caused the deaths of many people.*

confuse *verb* (kən fūz) to make something difficult to understand or follow. *Her complicated directions confused me, and I got lost. | The broken road sign confused the drivers.*

confusion *noun* (kən fū zhən) 1. [N] the state of being confused. *The missing road sign caused a lot of confusion for drivers.* 2. [N] a lack of order or sense. *When we heard the alarm, there was confusion about what to do.*

congratulate *verb* (kən græ chə lāt) to praise and express pleasure when a good thing happens to someone. *His friends **congratulated him on** getting his driver's license.*

congratulations *interj.* (kən græ chə lā shənz) used to express your pleasure when something good happens to someone. *Congratulations! You passed the test! | **Congratulations on** your new baby!*
pl. noun an expression of pleasure when a good thing happens to someone. *I offered her **congratulations on** her marriage.*

congress *noun* (<u>kang</u> grəs) the branch of a national government that makes laws. *The two parts of the U.S. Congress are the Senate and the House of Representatives.*

Word Builder: congress +
congressman: a man who is a member of the U.S. House of Representatives.
congresswoman: a woman who is a member of the U.S. House of Representatives.

conjunction *noun* (kən <u>jəngk</u> shən) a word that connects words, phrases, clauses, or sentences. *And, but, because,* and *before* are examples of conjunctions.

connect *verb* (kə <u>nekt</u>) to join together. *The plumber connected the two pipes.*

connection *noun* (kə <u>nek</u> shən) 1. a relationship or association. *There is often a connection between drugs and crime.* 2. the state of being connected. *Can I call you back? This is a bad connection, and I can't hear you well.*

conscience *noun* (<u>kan</u> shəns) [N] the sense that helps a person decide what is right and wrong. *My conscience will not allow me to lie.*

conscious *adj.* (<u>kan</u> shəs) able to feel, think, hear, and see. *Dave fell and hit his head, but he was still conscious.*

Word Builder: conscious +
consciousness: the state of being conscious.

consent *verb* (kən <u>sent</u>) to give permission or approval. *They **consented to** her going on a trip with her friends.* **noun** the permission for or approval of a plan or action. *Pat had his parents' consent to drive their car.*

Word Builder: consent +
consent form: a form that you fill out and sign to give your permission for someone to do something.

consequence *noun* (<u>kan</u> sə kwens) that which follows; result. *Her stomach pain was a consequence of eating too much.*

conservation *noun* (kan sər <u>vā</u> shən) [N] the protection of natural resources such as soil, water, or forests from harm. *Water conservation is important for people's health.*

conservative *adj.* (kən <u>sər</u> və tiv) wanting things to stay as they are; not wanting change. *The conservative teachers opposed getting rid of the school's dress code.* **noun** a person who is against rapid change in politics, government, or society.

conserve *verb* (kən <u>sərv</u>) to keep safe from loss, destruction, or waste. *We are conserving water by taking short showers instead of baths.*

consider *verb* (kən <u>si</u> dər) to think about something in a serious way. *She is considering getting a new job.*

consideration *noun* (kən si dər <u>ā</u> shən) 1. [N] attention or thought given with care. *The teacher gives some consideration to the problems of each student.* 2. [N] respect or concern for the needs of others. *Please show each other some consideration.*

consist *verb* (kən <u>sist</u>) to be made up or formed of something. *The United States consists of fifty states.*

consistent *adj.* (kən <u>si</u> stənt) having a regular style or pattern; not changing. *He has a consistent way of throwing the ball.*

consonant *noun* (<u>kan</u> sə nənt) a sound in a language made by stopping or restricting the flow of air through the mouth with the tongue, teeth, or lips. The sounds represented by the letters *k, b, s,* and *m* are examples of consonants in English.

constant *adj.* (<u>kan</u> stənt) going on without a pause. *The dog's constant barking annoyed the neighbors.*

Word Builder: constant +
constantly: all the time; without stopping.

constitution *noun* (kan st ə <u>too</u> shən) 1. the system of basic laws that govern a nation, state, or other organization. *Members of the new government wrote a new constitution for the nation.* 2. (sometimes capitalized) the written record of the basic laws of a country. *The Constitution of the United States states the rights of citizens.*

construct *verb* (kən <u>strəkt</u>) to build; put together. *They constructed the garage in three days.*

construction *noun* (kən <u>strək</u> shən) 1. [N] the act or process of building. *Construction of the new mall will begin next year.* 2. [N] the job or business of building things such as houses, roads, or other structures. *If you work in construction, you use many tools.*

construction

consult *verb* (kən s<u>a</u>lt) to speak with someone or look up something to gain advice or information. *Bob consulted the doctor about his pain.* | *I consulted the dictionary to check the spelling of a word.*

consumer *noun* (kən s<u>oo</u> mər) a person who buys goods or services. *Consumers spend a lot of money during the holidays.*

contact *noun* (<u>kan</u> tækt) 1. the touching of two things or people. *He got a shock when his hand **came into contact with** the wire.* 2. communication. *She is **out of contact with** her family.* | *He is **in contact with** his old friends.*
verb to speak or write to someone; communicate. *I contacted my friend about our weekend plans.*

contain *verb* (kən t<u>ā</u>n) to hold or have within. *Many foods contain sugar.*

container *noun* (kən t<u>ā</u> nər) something, such as a box, bottle, or can, that contains or can contain something else. *I placed the container of ice cream in the freezer.*

contaminate *verb* (kən t<u>æ</u> mə n<u>ā</u>t) to ruin, infect, or make dirty by touching or adding something harmful. *Lead can contaminate drinking water.*

Word Builder: contaminate +
contaminated: ruined, dirty, or infected.

contemporary *adj.* (kən t<u>em</u> pə r<u>ār</u> e) of or belonging to the present time; current; modern. *Many older people do not like contemporary music.*

content *adj.* (kən t<u>ent</u>) wanting no more than what you already have; satisfied. *She is content with her life.*

contents *pl. noun* (<u>kan</u> tents) things that are inside something. *The contents of the box fell out when I dropped it.*

contest *noun* (<u>kan</u> test) a sport or game that people try to win to get a prize; competition. *My nephew won first prize in the math contest.*
verb (kən t<u>est</u>) to argue against; challenge. *He is contesting the terms of the contract.*

context *noun* (<u>kan</u> tekst) the setting of a word or phrase that affects its meaning. *The meaning of the word fly changes depending on its context.*

continent *noun* (<u>kan</u> ti nənt) one of the earth's seven largest areas of land. *The continent of South America has many countries, including Brazil.*

continent

continue *verb* (kən t<u>in</u> ū) 1. to keep happening or being; to last for a long time. *The snow continued to fall.* | *The party continued until late into the night.* 2. to begin again after a pause. *The runner fell, but he got back up and continued the race.*

Word Builder: continue +
continual: happening without stopping.

continuous *adj.* (kən t<u>in</u> ū əs) going on without stopping; not ending. *There is a continuous flow of water from the pipe.*

contract *noun* (<u>kan</u> trækt) 1. an agreement between people that is supported by the law. A lease is an example of a contract. *He **broke** his **contract** when he left the company.* 2. the document that shows a legal agreement. *Sign your name at the bottom of the contract.*
verb (kən tr<u>ækt</u>) to become smaller. *Metal contracts when it becomes cold.*

contraction *noun* (kən tr<u>æk</u> shən) 1. the strong, painful action of muscles in which they become tight, such as before and during the birth of a baby. *Sheila had contractions for ten hours before her baby was born.* 2. a short form of two words, where the missing letters are replaced by an apostrophe. *I'm is the contraction of I am.*

contrast *verb* (kən tr<u>æst</u>) to compare in order to show differences. *The book contrasted the lives of women a hundred years ago with the lives of women today.*
noun (<u>kan</u> træst) 1. the state of being different; difference. *The contrast between the two boys was noticeable.* 2. the degree of difference between light and dark colors. *There is a lot of contrast in this photograph.*

contribute *verb* (kən tri b<u>ū</u>t) to give something for a purpose. *She contributed time and money to the animal shelter.*

contribution *noun* (kan trə b<u>ū</u> shən) something that is given for a purpose. *They made a contribution to the local museum.*

control *verb* (kən trōl) 1. to use power to manage or command. *The government controlled the newspapers and radio stations.* 2. to hold back or restrain. *It is hard to control insects in our garden.* | *They built a dam to control the river.*

noun 1. the ability to handle or manage; power or authority. *She **lost control of** her car and crashed.* | *The supervisor **has control over** the shipping department.* 2. something used to guide or operate a vehicle or other type of machine. *The pilot used the controls to land the airplane safely.* | *This button is the volume control for the TV.*

convenient *adj.* (kən vēn yənt) easy to use; good for someone's needs, purposes, or comfort. *Meet with me when it is convenient for you.* | *A washing machine is a convenient appliance.*

convention *noun* (kən ven shən) 1. a formal meeting where people discuss particular issues. *There is a convention for doctors this weekend.* 2. a way of doing something that is accepted by most people. *It is a convention to say "You're welcome" when someone thanks you.*

conversation *noun* (kan vər sā shən) talk between people. *There is little time for conversation at work.*

convert *verb* (kən vərt) to change into a different form or state. *This sofa **converts to** a bed.* | *He **converted to** his wife's religion.*

convey *verb* (kən vā) 1. to carry from one place or person to another. *Large trucks are used to convey goods across the country.* 2. to communicate; express. *The picture conveys a feeling of joy.* | *I think this sentence doesn't convey your meaning well.*

conveyor belt *noun* (kən vā yər belt) a machine with a continuous moving part that carries things from one place to another. *The conveyor belt moved the product from one workstation to the next.*

convict *verb* (kən vikt) to find someone guilty of a crime. *After a long trial, the jury convicted her of assault.* **noun** (kan vikt) a person who has been found guilty of a crime. *It's hard to get a job if you have been a convict in the past.*

convince *verb* (kən vins) to cause someone to believe or accept. *His doctor convinced him to stop smoking.* | *Advertisements convince many people to buy products.*

cook *verb* (kuk) to prepare food for eating by using heat. *She cooked macaroni and cheese for dinner.*
noun a person who cooks. *The cook tried a new recipe this evening.*

cook

Word Builder: cook +
cookbook: a book with recipes and directions for cooking.
cookout: a meal that is cooked and eaten outdoors; barbecue.
cookstove: a stove.
cookware: pots, pans, and other things for cooking food.

cookie *noun* (ku kē) a small, sweet, flat cake. *Her favorite snack is milk and cookies.*

cooking *noun* (ku king) [N] the act or process of preparing food or meals. *I enjoy cooking for my family and friends.*

cool *adj.* (kool) 1. a little cold; not warm. *It was a cool spring day.* 2. calm and under control. *He stays cool in an emergency.* 3. (informal) great; good. *This game is really cool.*
verb to make less warm. *The fan cooled the room.*
cool off 1. to become cool. *We cooled off by swimming in the lake.* 2. to become calmer or less upset. *It took him a long time to cool off after the fight.*

Word Builder: cool +
coolant: a liquid that cools the engine of a car or other machine.
cooler: a container that keeps food cold.

cooperate *verb* (ko a pər āt) 1. to work with other people for a common purpose. *Margaret and I **cooperated on** a new project at work.* 2. to do what someone else asks without complaint. *The crowd of people **cooperated with** the police.*

cooperation *noun* (kō a pər ā shən) [N] the act of working together. *The two leaders hope for **cooperation between** their two countries.*

cooperative *adj.* (kō a pər ə tiv) willing to work together. *If you'd be more cooperative, we could finish this job sooner.*
noun an apartment house in which the people who live there own their apartment.

cop *noun* (kap) an informal word for **police officer.**

copier *noun* (ka pē ər) a short form of **photocopier.**

copper *noun* (<u>ka</u> pər) [N] a red-brown metal. It is often used to make wires that carry electricity and pipes that carry water.

copy *noun* (<u>ka</u> pē) 1. something that looks exactly like another thing. *That picture is a copy of the original painting.* 2. one of a number of books, magazines, or pictures that were printed at the same time. *I have a copy of that book.*
verb to make a copy of. *I copied the information from the report into my notebook.*

copy machine *noun* (<u>ka</u> pē mə shēn) another name for **photocopier.**

cord *noun* (<u>kōr</u>d) 1. a thick string. *Pull the cord to open the curtain.* 2. a covered wire that carries electricity to a piece of equipment such as a television or lamp. *I plugged the cord for the computer into the outlet.*

core *noun* (<u>kōr</u>) the center of something. *The core of the earth is extremely hot.* | *The seeds are in the core of an apple.*

corn *noun* (<u>kōr</u>n) [N] a tall plant with rows of yellow or white seeds that are eaten as a vegetable.

corner *noun* (<u>kōr</u> nər) 1. the place where two lines, walls, paths, roads, or streets meet. *The bank is on the corner of Madison Street and Washington Avenue.* | *I put my desk in the corner of the room.*

corporation *noun* (kōr pər <u>ā</u> shən) an organization formed by a group of people to operate a business.

correct *verb* (kə <u>rekt</u>) to fix the mistakes in; change to make right. *She corrected the report before she gave it to her supervisor.*
adj. with no mistakes. *The student gave the correct answer.*

Word Builder: correct +
correctly: in the correct way.

correction *noun* (kə <u>rek</u> shən) something right put in place of something wrong. *The teacher made corrections to my essay.*

corrode *verb* (kə <u>rōd</u>) to cause damage by a slow chemical process. *Rust had corroded the car.*

corrosion *noun* (kə <u>rō</u> zhən) [N] damage caused by a slow chemical process. *Salt on the roads caused the corrosion of the car.*

corrosive *adj.* (kə <u>rō</u> səv) causing or likely to cause damage over time. *The chemical had a corrosive effect on the machine.*

cost *noun* (<u>kawst</u>) *cost, cost* the amount of money charged or paid for something. *The cost of cereal is higher than it used to be.*

cottage *noun* (<u>ka</u> tij) a small house. *We rented a cottage by the lake last summer.*

cotton *noun* (<u>ka</u> tən) 1. [N] a soft white fiber from a plant that grows in warm parts of the world. It is used to make thread and cloth. 2. thread or cloth made from this plant. *My shirt is made of cotton.*

couch *noun* (<u>kowch</u>) a comfortable seat with a back and arms for two or more people; sofa.

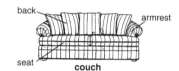

back   armrest

seat   **couch**

cough *verb* (<u>kawf</u>) to push out air and other substances from the lungs, making a noise in the throat. People cough because of illness or when they breathe in something such as smoke or dust.
noun [N] an illness that causes a person to cough. *She is taking medicine for her cough.*

Word Builder: cough +
cough drop: a candy with medicine to help stop a cough.
cough syrup: a liquid medicine to help stop a cough.

could *verb* (<u>kud</u>) 1. used to express that there was ability to do something in the past, or that an action or state was possible in the past. *She could swim even when she was very little.* | *He could be very kind sometimes.* | *I couldn't sleep last night.* 2. used as a past form of *can* after verbs in the past tense that report speech or thoughts. *I can drive a truck, and I told him that I could drive one!* | *He knew that he could finish on time.* 3. used in present or future time to talk about a possibility that is not certain; often used in polite requests or offers. *Maybe I could do it tomorrow.* | *Could you help me with this?* | *I could bring it to you now, if you'd like.* 4. used to say that someone may be able to do something, or that something is possible, only if something else happens or if something else were true. *If I order the parts today, I could fix your car next week.* | *If I made more money, I could buy a car.*

council *noun* (<u>kown</u> səl) a group of people chosen to make decisions or give advice. *The city council recommended that taxes be lowered.*

counselor *noun* (<u>kown</u> sə lər) a person who gives advice. *The school counselor helped my daughter choose her courses.*

count *verb* (<u>kown</u>t) to give each thing in a group a number to learn how many there are. *Hasani counted the coins in his pocket.*
　count on to depend on or trust a person. *Can I count on you to take care of your little sister tonight?*

Word Builder: count +
countless: being too many to count.

counter *noun* (<u>kown</u> tər) 1. a long, high table. People sit on stools or stand at a counter to eat, prepare food, or do business. 2. a person or thing that counts. *The counter we used for our game was easy to read.*

Word Builder: counter +
countertop: the top of a counter.

counterclockwise *adj., adv.* (kown tər <u>klak</u> wīz) moving in the direction opposite to the hands of a clock. *He gave the knob on the radio a counterclockwise turn.* | *Loosen the screw by turning it counterclockwise.*

country *noun* (<u>kən</u> trē) 1. a large area of land where people live under the same government or have the same culture; nation. *China is a country in Asia.* 2. [N] the land outside of towns and cities. *The Millers live in the country on a farm.*

county *noun* (<u>kown</u> tē) a section of a U.S. state with its own government. *New Jersey has 21 counties.*

couple *noun* (<u>kə</u> pəl) 1. a group of two. *I ate **a couple of** cookies.* 2. two people who are together by marriage or who are in a romantic relationship. *I met a nice couple at the party.*

coupon *noun* (<u>koo</u> pan) a small, printed piece of paper. A coupon gives a person a lower price on something. *I have a coupon for 50 cents off the price of a loaf of bread.*

courage *noun* (<u>kər</u> ij) [N] the ability to face fear or danger. *It takes courage to stand up for what you believe in.*

course *noun* (<u>kors</u>) 1. the direction or way along which something moves. *The course of the river twists and turns.* 2. passage through time. *Brian has done many good things in the course of his life.* 3. a set of classes in a subject. *I took a science course last fall.* 4. a part of a meal. *Dessert is the last course in an American meal.*
　of course used to show that you agree with or are sure of something. *Of course I want to come with you!*

court *noun* (<u>kort</u>) 1. a place where legal matters are heard. *The judge kept order in the court.* 2. an open space where people play games or sports. *We went to the tennis court to play tennis.*

Word Builder: court +
courthouse: the building where a judge hears legal cases.
courtroom: the room in a courthouse where a judge hears legal cases.

courtesy *noun* (<u>kər</u> tə sē) good, polite manners. *She had the courtesy to open the door for her grandmother.*

cousin *noun* (<u>kə</u> zən) the son or daughter of an aunt or uncle.

cover *verb* (<u>kə</u> vər) 1. to put or spread something over or on something else. *Cover your bicycle so it doesn't get wet in the rain.* 2. to protect from possible loss; insure. *Our insurance covers both cars.* 3. to give attention to something; include. *Our textbook covers many topics.* 4. to take the place of someone who is absent. *You take a break, and I'll cover for you.*
　noun something that you put on something else to protect it. *Put the cover back on the can of paint.* | *The cover of a book keeps the pages from being torn.*

covering *noun* (<u>kə</u> vər ing) something that covers or hides. *A tablecloth is a covering for a table.*

cow *noun* (<u>kow</u>) the adult female of **cattle** and some other animals. People keep cows for their milk, meat, and skin.

COW

Word Builder: cow +
cowboy: a boy or man who cares for cattle.
cowgirl: a girl or woman who cares for cattle.
cowhand: a person who cares for cattle.

coward *noun* (<u>kow</u> ərd) a person who does not have the courage to face danger, pain, or something difficult. *I'm a coward about speaking in front of an audience.*

co-worker *noun* (kō wər kər) a person who works with another person. *My co-workers are very helpful.*

CPU *abbrev.* (sē pē ū) an abbreviation for *central processing unit.* The CPU is the main part of a computer.

crack *verb* (kræk) 1. to break apart with a sharp sound. *The tree branch cracked in the storm.* 2. to break, but not into separate pieces. *The plate cracked, but it can still be used.*
noun a break in something. *There is a crack in the glass.*

cracker *noun* (kræ kər) a thin, hard food made from dough and cooked in an oven.

cradle *noun* (krā dəl) a small bed for a baby that can move from side to side.

craft *noun* (kræft) 1. an activity that requires skill with the hands. *It takes many years to learn the craft of a good carpenter.* 2. [N] a boat, ship, airplane, or space vehicle, or a group of these. *We sailed the small craft across the lake.*

crafts *pl. noun* (kræfts) activities that use the hands to make things that decorate or are useful in a home. *The children love doing crafts at school.*

cramp[1] *noun* (kræmp) a sharp pain in a muscle that suddenly becomes tight. *A leg cramp kept her from finishing the race.*

cramp[2] *verb* (kræmp) to limit by keeping in a small space. *The short bed cramped his long legs.*

> **Word Builder: cramp +**
> **cramped:** having little space in which to move.

crash *verb* (kræsh) to destroy with great force and loud noise. *He crashed his new car into the wall.*
noun 1. a loud noise of things breaking. *There was a huge crash when the shelf fell down.* 2. a violent accident. *No one was hurt in the car crash.*

crate *noun* (krāt) a box for shipping made of wood or other material. *We packed the computer in a crate.*

crawl *verb* (krawl) to move along the ground on the hands and knees. *The baby crawled to his mother.*

crayon *noun* (krā an) a colored stick or pencil made of wax. A crayon is used for drawing and coloring. *My child enjoys using crayons to draw pictures.*

crazy *adj.* (krā zē) 1. (informal) having a mental illness, or acting as if you have one. *Don't believe what she says. She's crazy.* 2. (informal) very enthusiastic; excited. *Jane is **crazy about** dancing.* 3. showing poor judgment; not sensible. *He was crazy to drive home during the blizzard.*

cream *noun* (krēm) 1. [N] the part of whole milk that contains fat. Butter is made from cream. 2. [N] a thick liquid used on the skin to clean it or make it softer.

create *verb* (krē āt) to bring into being. *The chef created a new dish.*

creation *noun* (krē ā shən) 1. [N] the act of creating or of causing something to exist. *The creation of this famous statue took three years.* 2. something that is made. *The art students displayed their creations at the fair.*

creative *adj.* (krē ā tiv) able to make or do something new or with imagination. *Lucas is a creative artist.* | *That creative inventor designed a new kind of wheelchair.*

creature *noun* (krē chər) a living person or animal. *Owls, bats, and birds are creatures that can fly.*

credit *noun* (kre dit) 1. [N] the right or ability to buy things now but not pay until later. *Her credit is good at the clothing store.* | *She bought a bicycle **on credit**.* 2. [N] approval or praise given to a person or group for something that has been done. *I **give** him **credit** for trying so hard.* | *She got all the credit for my great idea.* 3. a unit of study in school. *I earned three credits in English last semester.*
verb to add to a person's account. *When you make a deposit, the bank will credit your account.*

credit card *noun* (kre dit kard) a card from a bank or store that lets a person buy things and pay for them later. *I used my credit card to buy a sweater.*

credit union *noun* (kre dit ūn yən) a financial association made up of members. A credit union is similar to a bank, but its members can borrow money at lower interest rates.

creek *noun* (krēk) a stream that is smaller than a river. *We went fishing in the creek.*

crew *noun* (kroo) a group of people who work together. *The road crew finished putting a new surface on the highway.*

crib *noun* (krib) a bed with high sides all around for a baby or young child to sleep in.

crib

crime *noun* (krīm) 1. something that people do that is against the law. *Stealing is a crime.* 2. [N] illegal activity in general. *Police try to* **fight crime.** | *There is more crime in a city than in this small town.*

criminal *noun* (kri mi nəl) a person who commits a crime.

crippled *adj.* (kri pəld) a word used to describe a person or animal that is not able to use its arms or legs. *The crippled man got out of his wheelchair with difficulty.*

crises *pl. noun* (krī sēz) plural of **crisis.**

crisis *noun* (krī sis) **crises** a situation that is difficult or hard to deal with. *The murder of the president caused a crisis in the country.*

criteria *pl. noun* (krī tēr ē ə) plural of **criterion.**

criterion *noun* (krī tēr ē ən) **criteria** a standard or test by which to judge or decide. *Power is only one criterion of a car's quality.*

critical *adj.* (kri ti kəl) 1. likely to find fault. *She is critical of the cafeteria food.* 2. serious or dangerous. *He is in critical condition at the hospital.*

criticism *noun* (kri ti si zəm) [N] the act of judging what is good or bad in something. *The coach's criticism helped us learn to be better players.*

criticize *verb* (kri ti sīz) to find problems or mistakes in. *I feel bad when he criticizes what I say.*

crock *noun* (krak) a container made of clay. *I put the crock on the shelf.*

crop *noun* (krap) plants grown on a farm. *Corn is an important crop.*

cross *noun* (kraws) an upright line with another line across it. *A cross is used as a symbol in churches.* **verb** 1. to move across something from one side to the other. *Look both ways before you cross the street.* 2. to meet together and then move past. *Main Street crosses*

Elm Street at the corner.

cross out to remove something by drawing a line through it. *If the information on the form is not correct, cross it out.*

Word Builder: cross +
cross-eyed: having both eyes pointing in toward the nose.
crossroad: a road that crosses another road.
crosswalk: a part of the road that is marked off for people to cross on foot.

crossword puzzle *noun* (kraws wərd pə zəl) a word game in which a person must guess words and enter them in a pattern of squares, one letter in each square. *The crossword puzzle was very difficult to solve.*

crow *noun* (krō) a common black bird with a loud call.

crowd *noun* (krowd) a large number of people gathered together. *There was a crowd at the baseball game.* **verb** to press, push, or pack tightly together. *He crowded cardboard boxes into the tiny closet.*

Word Builder: crowd +
crowded: being full of people or things.

crown *noun* (krown) 1. a metal object worn on the head by kings and queens. Crowns are often made of gold or silver. 2. an artificial cover for a tooth.

crown

cruel *adj.* (krool) willing to cause pain or suffering; not caring if you hurt someone or something. *The country's cruel leader did nothing to help the people.*

crumb *noun* (krəm) a tiny piece that breaks or falls from bread or other food. *We cleaned cake crumbs off the table after the birthday party.*

crush *verb* (krəsh) to make smaller or flatter by pounding or pressing. *You must crush a box before you recycle it.*

crust *noun* (krəst) the hard, brown layer on the outside of cooked foods. *The pie crust was delicious.*

cry *verb* (krī) to have tears fall from your eyes as the result of pain, sadness, or another strong feeling. *The baby cried when he lost his toy.* **noun** a loud shout or yell. *I let out a cry when we won.*

crystal *noun* (kri stəl) 1. a clear rock that has a regular shape. Diamonds and grains of salt are crystals. 2. [N] glass of very high quality. *That beautiful vase is made of crystal.*

cub *noun* (kəb) the young of some mammals that eat meat, such as bears and lions. *The mother tiger protected her cub.*

cube *noun* (kūb) 1. a solid figure with six square faces all the same size, or any similar solid figure. *He placed the statue on a metal cube.* 2. something that has this shape. *I put ice cubes in my drink.*

cucumber *noun* (kū kəm bər) a long vegetable with hard green skin and white flesh.

cuddle *verb* (kə dəl) to hold in a gentle and loving way. *Mrs. Garcia cuddled her baby.*

Word Builder: cuddle +
cuddly: soft and pleasant to cuddle.

cuff *noun* (kəf) the piece of material that is folded over at the bottom of a sleeve or pant leg. A cuff is often sewn in place.

culture *noun* (kəl chər) the language, ideas, inventions, and art of a particular group of people. *American culture has been influenced by the cultures of people from other countries.*

Word Builder: culture +
cultural: having to do with culture.

cup *noun* (kəp) a small, open container used for drinking. *I drank tea from a cup.*

cupboard *noun* (kə bərd) a piece of furniture with shelves to store food, dishes, or other things.

curb *noun* (kərb) the border or edge of a street. It is usually made of concrete and raised higher than the road. *The driver parked the car next to the curb.*

cure *noun* (kūr) something that makes a sick person healthy or well. *Scientists are searching for a cure for cancer.*
verb to cause to become free of a disease. *Antibiotics cure many people who have infections.*

curiosity *noun* (kūr ē a si tē) [N] the desire to learn or know. *He read his grandmother's journal with great curiosity.*

curious *adj.* (kūr ē əs) eager to learn or know. *She was curious about how stars were formed.*

curl *verb* (kərl) to make into a curved shape. *Terry curled her hair.*
noun an individual ring of hair. *I just love your baby's curls.*

Word Builder: curl +
curly: having many curls.

currency *noun* (kər ən sē) the money that is used in a country. *The dollar is the basic unit of U.S. currency.*

current *adj.* (kər ənt) of or happening in the present time. *My current number is in the phone book.*
noun 1. a mass of liquid or air that flows in one direction. *It is hard to swim **against the current.** | The kite rose on a current of air.* 2. the flow of electricity. *Copper wire conducts current.*

curse *verb* (kərs) 1. to make a statement that wishes harm on someone. *He cursed his enemy.* 2. to swear at. *She cursed at the dog for digging up her flowers.*

curtain *noun* (kər tən) a piece of cloth that hangs in a window or other opening to shut out light or to cover something. *I bought new curtains for the livingroom windows.*

curve *noun* (kərv) 1. a line that bends smoothly in one direction without any straight parts. *She drew a curve with the marker.* 2. an area where a road or path bends. *Drive slowly around the curve.*
verb 1. to cause to have a round, bent shape. *The carpenter curved the edge of the shelf with his tools.* 2. to take the shape of a curve; bend. *The road curves to the left at the top of the hill.*

Word Builder: curve +
curved: having a rounded shape.

custodian *noun* (kə stō dē ən) a person whose job is to take care of a building by cleaning or repairing it.

custom *noun* (kə stəm) a way of acting that is usual or accepted for a person or a social group. *Shaking hands when you meet someone is a common custom in the United States.*

customer *noun* (kə stə mər) a person who buys products or services. *The store held a special sale for its regular customers.*

cut *noun* (kət) the act or result of opening or breaking something with a sharp tool; wound; tear. *I got a cut on my hand while chopping vegetables.*

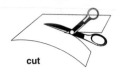

cut

verb cut, cut to divide or break open with a sharp tool such as a knife, saw, or scissors. *The barber cut my hair. | I cut my hand with that knife. | She cut wood for the fire.*

cut down to remove with a saw or ax. *He cut down the large tree in the front yard.*

cut out to remove part of something with a sharp tool. *He cut out the coupon from the paper.*

cute *adj.* (kūt) attractive or pleasing. *Your baby looks cute in that outfit.*

cutoff switch *noun* (kət awf swich) a device that turns off a machine by stopping the flow of electricity. *If there is a problem, use the cutoff switch to stop the machine immediately.*

cycle *noun* (sī kəl) a group of events that repeat at regular times. *Summer follows spring in the cycle of seasons.*

cylinder *noun* (si lən dər) a solid figure that is shaped like a can.

D d

dad *noun* (dăd) an informal word for **father**.

daily *adj.* (dā lē) happening or done every day. *She is taking her daily walk in the park.*
adv. each day. *I read the newspaper daily.*

dairy *noun* (dār ē) a business that makes and sells milk and milk products such as butter and cheese. *I buy fresh milk from the dairy.*
adj. made from milk or having to do with milk products. Milk, butter, cheese, and yogurt are dairy products. *He works in the dairy department at the grocery store.*

dam *noun* (dăm) a wall built across a river or stream to stop the flow of water. *The dam was built to help control floods.*

damage *noun* (dăm məj) [N] any harm or injury that makes something less useful or valuable. *The storm caused damage to many houses.*
verb to harm or injure. *The movers damaged some furniture.* | *Insects damaged the crops.*

Word Builder: damage +
damaged: having damage.

damp *adj.* (dămp) wet, but not very wet. *The towel was still damp.*

dance *verb* (dăns) to move the feet and body to music. *Everyone danced when the band started playing.*
noun a party or gathering where people come to dance. *The school dance is on Saturday night.*

dance

Word Builder: dance +
dancer: a person who dances.
dancing: the act of moving the body with rhythm.

danger *noun* (dān jər) something that may harm or injure a person. *Firemen face many dangers in their work.*

dangerous *adj.* (dān jə rəs) likely to cause harm; not safe. *The path along the edge of the cliff is dangerous.*

dare *verb* (dār) to try to get someone to do something as a test of courage. *I dared her to eat a bug.* | *He dared me to jump into the river.*

dark *adj.* (dark) 1. having little or no light. *It was a dark night.* 2. not light in color. *Brown is a dark color.*

Word Builder: dark +
darkness: the state of being dark.

dash *verb* (dăsh) to move fast; rush. *He dashed across the street before the light changed.*
noun a punctuation mark (—). It is used in writing to show a break in speech or thought.

dashboard *noun* (dăsh bōrd) the part of a car or other vehicle that contains the instrument that shows how fast the car is going, the controls for heat, a place to put things, and other instruments.

data *pl. noun* (dā tə) facts, figures, or other pieces of information that can be used in different ways. *Computers are used to store large amounts of data.* | *Data about the U.S. population is collected every ten years.*

database *noun* (dā tə bās) information in a computer that is arranged so that it can be changed or searched. *The librarian searched the database to find books on my topic.*

date *noun* 1. a particular day or point in time. *What is today's date?* 2. an appointment to meet for a social event. *We made a date to have dinner.*
out of date not modern or in fashion. *My father's clothes are out of date.*

daughter *noun* (daw tər) a person's female child. *I have one daughter and one son.*

dawn *noun* (dawn) the first light of day that appears in the morning. *He woke up at dawn.*

day *noun* (dā) 1. the period between the time that the sun rises and sets. *He spent the whole day at the beach.* 2. a standard unit used to measure time. One day equals 24 hours.

Word Builder: day +
daylight: light from the sun that you see during the day.
daytime: the time when the sun lights the earth.
daywork: work that is paid one day at a time.

day care *noun* (dā kār) [N] care during the day for children too young for school. *I picked up my children from day care.*

dead *adj.* (ded) no longer alive. *His grandmother is living, but his grandfather is dead.*

> **Word Builder: dead +**
> **deadly:** causing death.

deaf *adj.* (def) not able to hear. *Many deaf people learn to talk with their hands.*

deal *verb* (dēl) *dealt, dealt* 1. to handle or give your attention to. *We must **deal with** this problem carefully. | I don't have time to **deal with** these bills right now.* 2. to act or behave toward other people. *She is honest in the way she **deals with** people.* 3. to do business; trade. *My uncle **deals in** truck tires.* 4. to give out cards to people who are playing in a card game. *It's your turn to deal the cards.*
noun 1. an agreement or bargain. *We **made a deal** to share the money equally.* 2. a quantity or degree. *A million dollars is **a great deal of** money.*

> **Word Builder: deal +**
> **dealer (1):** a person whose business is buying and selling.
> **dealer (2):** a person who deals the cards in a card game.

dealt *verb* (delt) past tense and past participle of **deal.**

dear *adj.* (dēr) 1. much loved. *My dear friend Janet is coming to visit.* 2. (capitalized) used as a greeting that begins a letter. *Dear Ms. Flynn, thank you for the gift.*

death *noun* (deth) the end of life in any living thing. *Her death came after a long illness.*

debit *noun* (de bət) an amount of money taken out of or owed on an account. *My bank account shows a debit of ten dollars for the check I wrote.*
verb to subtract or charge with an amount. *The bank debited my savings account a hundred dollars.*

> **Word Builder: debit +**
> **debit card:** a card from your bank that lets you withdraw money from an ATM.

debt *noun* (det) something owed to another person. *I paid all my debts except the five dollars I owe my sister.*

decade *noun* (de kād) a unit of time equal to ten years. *A person who is 90 years old has been alive for nine decades.*

decay *verb* (də kā) to break down or become destroyed by a slow, natural process. *Leaves decay on the forest floor.*
noun [N] the process of breaking down or becoming destroyed. *Daily brushing helps prevent tooth decay.*

deceit *noun* (də sēt) [N] the act of lying. *She used deceit to get what she wanted.*

deceive *verb* (də sēv) to cause someone to believe something that is not true; lie to. *He deceived us about his age.*

December *noun* (də sem bər) the twelfth month of the year.

deceptive *adj.* (də sep təv) Causing someone to believe something that is not true. *Deceptive advertising is against the law.*

decide *verb* (də sīd) 1. to choose between different possibilities or to find an answer in your mind to a problem or question. *My mother decided to go back to school. | He decided that he would look for another job.* 2. to announce the answer to a problem or question that involves other people; settle. *The judges decided the winner of the competition.* 3. to make a choice between different things. *He **decided on** a used car instead of a new one.*

decision *noun* (də si zhən) the act or result of deciding. *I have **made the decision** not to go to school this summer. | What was your decision about moving?*

deck *noun* (dek) 1. a floor on a ship or on the outside of a house that people can walk or sit on. *The restaurant has a deck for dining outdoors.* 2. a pack of playing cards. *I opened a new deck of cards for the game.*

deck

declaration *noun* (de klə rā shən) an official or formal announcement or statement, or the document that contains it. *The American colonies made a declaration of war against England.*

Declaration of Independence *noun* (de klə rā shən əv in də pen dəns) the public document by which America declared its freedom from England in 1776. *The original Declaration of Independence is on display in Washington, D.C.*

declare *verb* (də klãr) 1. to announce in a formal way. *Congress declared war.* 2. to say in a strong or firm way. *She declared that she would never speak to him again.*

decorate *verb* (de kə rāt) 1. to make more attractive by adding things. *We decorated the room with balloons for the party.* 2. to put furniture and other things in a room to make a pleasant appearance. *My sister decorated her new home with modern furniture and bright colors.*

decoration *noun* (de kə rā shən) something used to decorate or to make something else more beautiful. *I will use flowers and lights as decorations at my party.*

decrease *verb* (də krēs) to become less or smaller. *The price of gas has decreased.* | *Her interest in television has decreased since she started reading.*
noun (dē krēs) the act of becoming less or smaller. *We are hoping for a **decrease in** gas prices.*

deduct *verb* (də dəkt) to subtract one amount from another. *You can deduct certain expenses from your taxes.*

Word Builder: deduct +
deductible: able to be deducted on a tax return.
deduction: something that is deducted on a tax return.

deep *adj.* (dēp) having a lot of space below or behind a certain point; reaching far down or back. *The lake is very deep in the middle.* | *His cut was deep and needed stitches.*

deer *noun* (dēr) *deer* a large mammal with long, thin legs. Deer eat only plants. People hunt or keep deer for their meat.

deer

defeat *verb* (də fēt) to beat in a game or battle. *He defeated me in tennis.*

defective *adj.* (də fek təv) not perfect; having a fault or wrong part. *We returned the defective television to the store.*

defend *verb* (də fend) to protect from harm; guard. *He defended his brother from the angry dog.* | *The army is ready to defend the city.*

defense *noun* (də fens) 1. [N] the act of protecting or guarding, or a thing that protects or guards. *The government spends a lot of money on national defense.* |

They built a fort **as a defense against** attacks. 2. [N] an explanation or excuse for something. *His defense was that he had picked up her wallet by mistake.*

define *verb* (də fīn) to explain the meaning of a word or phrase. *This dictionary defines hundreds of words.*

definite *adj.* (de fə nət) 1. clear or exact. *I have no definite plans for Friday night.* | *I have a definite reason for wanting it this way.* 2. having clear and certain limits. *There is a definite number of balls that must go into each box.* 3. known for certain; sure. *Do you have definite proof that she took your money?*

Word Builder: definite +
definitely: known for sure; certainly.

definition *noun* (de fə ni shən) a statement of the meaning of a word or phrase. *This dictionary gives two definitions for the word* choke.

degree *noun* (də grē) 1. [N] a measure or amount. *Skiing takes a high degree of skill.* 2. a unit for measuring temperature. *The temperature today is 82 degrees.* 3. a title given by a university or college to a student who has completed a program of study. *He has a degree in business.*

delay *verb* (də lā) 1. to put off until a later time. *We delayed our vacation until we had saved more money.* 2. to cause to be late. *Rain delayed the game.*
noun the condition or an instance of being stopped or delayed. *Her delay in getting home was caused by a traffic jam.*

delete *verb* (də lēt) to remove from a written work. *A computer can delete a mistake with a click of the mouse.*

deli *noun* (de lē) the short form of **delicatessen.**

deliberate *adj.* (də li bə rət) said or done because of desire or plan; on purpose. *I know he hurt you, but his action was not deliberate.* | *That was a deliberate insult to the teacher!*

delicate *adj.* (de lə kət) easy to break or hurt. *I handled the delicate vase as gently as I could.* | *The old woman is in delicate health.*

delicatessen *noun* (de lə kə te sən) a shop that sells cheese, cooked meats, and other foods that are ready to eat. *We often get lunch at the delicatessen.*

delicious *adj.* (də li shəs) having a pleasing taste or smell. *This apple pie is delicious.*

delight *noun* (də l<u>ī</u>t) [N] a great pleasure. *It was a delight to see you again after so many years.*
verb to give great pleasure to. *He delighted us with his jokes.*

Word Builder: delight +
delighted: happy.
delightful: causing delight.

deliver *verb* (də l<u>i</u> vər) 1. to send or bring to a particular person or place. *Jim delivers newspapers to the people in this neighborhood.* 2. to give birth to or help give birth to. *She delivered a baby boy yesterday.* | *The doctor delivers babies at the hospital.*

delivery *noun* (də l<u>i</u> və rē or də l<u>iv</u> rē) 1. an act of bringing or sending something to a particular person or place. *The furniture store offers free delivery to its customers.* 2. the act of giving birth. *She had an easy delivery with her second child.*

demand *verb* (də m<u>æ</u>nd) to ask for with force; order. *She demanded her money back.*
noun something that must be done. *With a job and three kids, there are many demands on my time.*

democracy *noun* (də m<u>a</u> krə sē) a government in which the people have power in a direct way or through representatives whom they elect.

democratic *adj.* (de mə kr<u>æ</u> tək) 1. believing that all people should be treated as equals. *We try to be democratic at club meetings by letting everyone take part in discussions.* 2. having to do with a democracy. *Our democratic government gives the vote to adult citizens.* 3. (capitalized) of the Democratic Party, one of the major political parties in the United States. *John F. Kennedy was a Democratic president.*

Democratic Party *noun* (de mə kræ tək par tē) one of the major political parties in the United States. *The donkey is the symbol of the Democratic Party.*

demonstrate *verb* (<u>de</u> mən strāt) 1. to show how to do something. *The physical education teacher demonstrated some new exercises.* 2. to take part in a public activity to show you are for or against something. *People demonstrated for women's rights.*

dentist *noun* (<u>den</u> təst) a doctor who takes care of the teeth and mouth.

dentist

deny *verb* (də n<u>ī</u>) 1. to say that something is not true. *She denied that she lost the necklace.* 2. to say no to. *My boss denied my request for a raise.*

deodorant *noun* (dē <u>ō</u> də rənt) [N] a substance that you put on the skin under your arms so that you do not have a bad odor. *He showers and puts on deodorant every day.*

depart *verb* (də p<u>art</u>) to leave; go away. *The train will depart in five minutes.*

department *noun* (də p<u>art</u> mənt) a separate part of a government, school, business, or other large organization. *He works in the shipping department.* | *You get a driver's license from the motor vehicle department.*

department store *noun* (də p<u>art</u> mənt st<u>ōr</u>) a large store with separate departments. Each department sells a certain type of goods. *We went to a department store to buy shoes for me and a toy for my son.*

depend *verb* (də p<u>end</u>) 1. to need the help or presence of. *Children **depend on** their parents for food and shelter.* 2. to be decided by. *The price of this paper **depends on** how much you buy.*
it depends used to say that you cannot decide until you have more information. *Do you want to go to the movies? It depends. I might have to baby-sit.*

Word Builder: depend +
dependable: able to be depended on.

dependent *noun* (də p<u>en</u> dənt) a person who needs the help of another person in order to live. *I have two dependents, my son and my daughter.*

deport *verb* (də p<u>ōrt</u>) to make a person leave a country. *The government deported some people who were living in the United States illegally.*

deposit *verb* (də p<u>a</u> zət) to put into a bank account. *I deposit my paycheck every week.*
noun 1. the money that you put into your bank account. *I **made a deposit** of fifty dollars to my savings account.* 2. the money that you give to someone to guarantee that you will pay or do something. *I had to pay a security deposit equal to one month's rent for my new apartment.*

depress *verb* (də pres) 1. to cause to be sad. *His failure depressed him.* 2. to push in or down. *If you depress that button, the machine will start.*

Word Builder: depress +
depressed: feeling unhappy.

depression *noun* (də pre shən) 1. [N] a sad feeling that can last a long time and cannot always be explained. *She is taking medicine for depression.* 2. an economic state in which business is very bad and many people have no work and are poor. *My grandparents lived through the depression of the 1930s.*

depth *noun* (depth) [N] the distance from top to bottom or from front to back. *The lake has a depth of 400 feet. | She measured the length, width, and depth of the box.*

describe *verb* (də skrīb) to tell or write about. *He described the places he saw on his vacation.*

description *noun* (də skrip shən) the act of telling about something in detail; the results of that act. *She gave a good description of the person who stole her purse.*

desert[1] *noun* (de zərt) a very dry area with few plants growing in it. *Most of North Africa is desert.*

desert[2] *verb* (də zərt) to leave someone or something behind when you should stay. *He deserted his wife and children.*

deserve *verb* (də zərv) to have earned something or have a right to something. *He deserves our respect.*

design *verb* (də zīn) to draw plans for the form or structure of something. *She designs and makes her own clothes. | He designed an addition to his house.*
noun 1. a plan that shows how to build something. *The city council approved the design for the new library.* 2. a drawing made by an artist for a specific purpose. *She drew some new designs for winter coats.* 3. a drawing that uses a pattern. *Our curtains have a design of flowers on them.*

designate *verb* (de zəg nāt) 1. to stand for or mean. *Red designates danger.* 2. to choose for a particular job or purpose. *The manager **designated** him **as** the supervisor. | The boss designated her to take care of the mail.*

Word Builder: designate +
designated driver: a person who is chosen by some people to drink no alcohol so that he or she can safely drive the others.

desire *verb* (də zīr) to want or wish for. *Both countries desire peace after years of war.*
noun a feeling of wanting something; wish. *She has a lot of pain, but she has a strong desire to live.*

Word Builder: desire +
desirable: pleasing or attractive.

desk *noun* (desk) a piece of furniture with a flat surface used for writing, using a computer, or reading. Desks usually have drawers where you keep paper, pens, and other supplies.

desk

desperate *adj.* (de spə rət or de sprət) 1. having almost no way to escape from or solve. *The people in the burning building were in a desperate situation.* 2. having a great need. *She was **desperate for** water.*

Word Builder: desperate +
desperately: in a desperate way.

despite *prep.* (də spīt) without being changed or stopped by. *He kept driving despite the blizzard.*

dessert *noun* (də zərt) a sweet food served at the end of a meal. *What would you like **for dessert**: cake or ice cream?*

destroy *verb* (də stroy) to damage something so that it cannot be fixed. *Their barn was destroyed by a fire.*

destruction *noun* (də strək shən) [N] the state of being destroyed. *The flood left destruction in its path.*

detail *noun* (dē tāl) a small item; a particular thing. *The mechanic explained every detail of the engine.*
in detail including every small thing. *Tammy described her new dress in detail.*

detain *verb* (də tān) to stop or keep from moving. *The police detained the suspect. | Heavy traffic detained me.*

detect *verb* (də tekt) to discover or notice. *He detected anger in her voice. | She detected the smell of smoke.*

Word Builder: detect +
detector: a machine that detects something.

detective *noun* (də tek təv) a person whose job is to find information that will solve crimes. A detective is often a police officer.

detergent *noun* (də tər jənt) a liquid or powder used for washing things. *I have two kinds of detergent: one for dishes and one for clothes.*

determination *noun* (də tər mə nā shən) 1. [N] the quality of continuing to work at something even when it is difficult. *We admired his determination to finish the project on time.* 2. a decision. *The judge's determination was that the defendant had to return the money.*

determine *verb* (də tər mən) to decide or set. *We determined the date for our wedding.*

develop *verb* (də ve ləp) 1. to grow or cause to grow. *His muscles developed when he started lifting weights.* | *He wanted to develop his muscles.* 2. to treat with chemicals in order to make a photograph. *He develops his own film.*

development *noun* (də ve ləp mənt) 1. an important event. *The president spoke about the latest developments in the war.* 2. [N] the act of working on something until it is done. *The development of the new mall took several years.*

device *noun* (də vīs) an invention or machine used for a specific purpose. *The computer is a device that has changed the way people work.* | *This device can peel apples.*

devil *noun* (de vəl) an evil spirit or being thought to cause evil in the world. *Some people believe that devils cause people to do bad things.*

DHS *abbrev.* (dē āch es) an abbreviation for *Department of Homeland Security.* The DHS is the part of the U.S. government that deals with immigration and naturalization. It also tries to protect the country from terrorism.

diabetes *noun* (dī ə bē tēz) [N] a serious disease in which there is too much sugar in a person's blood.

diagnose *verb* (dī əg nōs) to find out what is making someone sick. *The doctor diagnosed him with anemia.*

diagram *noun* (dī ə græm) a drawing or plan that shows the parts of something or how the parts work together. *He drew a diagram of the car.*

dial *noun* (dī əl) a flat, round device that controls a machine or measures something. *When you want to turn off the machine, turn this dial to the left.* | *That dial shows how many miles we have driven the car.* *verb* to enter a telephone number into a telephone by turning a dial or pushing the buttons. *Molly picked up the phone and dialed my number.*

dialog box *noun* (dī ə lag baks) a window that appears in a computer program to ask for information from the person using the computer. When you want to print a document, for example, a dialog box appears and asks you how many copies you want.

dialogue (dialog) *noun* (dī ə lag) a talk between two or more people or between characters in a play, film, or book. *This movie has a lot of action but not much dialogue.*

dial tone *noun* (dī əl tōn) the steady sound in a telephone that shows the line is open. When you hear the dial tone, you can enter the number of the person you want to call.

diameter *noun* (dī æ mə tər) a straight line from one side of a circle to the other side that passes through the center. *The wheels on the truck have a large diameter.*

diamond *noun* (dī mənd) 1. a clear mineral that is the hardest natural substance. Diamonds are used in jewelry and also as tools to cut hard materials. 2. a shape with four straight, equal sides and four points. The base of a diamond is one of its points. *Part of a baseball field is a diamond.* 3. a playing card that has the shape of a diamond or diamonds on it.

diaper *noun* (dī pər) underwear for a baby made of soft cloth or paper. You fold a diaper between the baby's legs and fasten it at the waist. *Her baby is still in diapers.*

dice[1] *pl. noun* (dīs) a pair of die[3]. Dice are often used in games. *Maggie rolled the dice.*

dice

dice[2] *verb* (dīs) to cut into small pieces. *He diced the potatoes and fried them.*

dictionary *noun* (dik shə nār ē) a book that lists the words of a language, with information about their meaning, spelling, and pronunciation.

did *verb* (did) past tense of **do.**

die[1] *verb* (dī) 1. to stop living; become dead. *His father died last year.* | *The plant died because he never watered it.* 2. to lose force or stop running. *The car's engine died.*

die[2] *noun* (dī) a tool for forming, cutting, or stamping material such as metal or plastic.

die³ *noun* (dī) *dice* a small block with six square sides. Each side has between one and six marks on it. Dice are used in many games.

die press *noun* (dī pres) a large machine for cutting or stamping metal.

diet *noun* (dī ət) 1. the usual food and drink of a person or animal. *The diet of a baby is usually his mother's milk. | The cow's diet is grass.* 2. a special way of eating to improve your health or to lose weight. *He is on a low-salt diet because of high blood pressure.* *verb* to eat less food or choose certain foods in order to improve health or lose weight. *He dieted for three months and lost ten pounds.*

Word Builder: diet +
dietary: having to do with diet.

differ *verb* (di fər) 1. to be not the same as. *The twins look alike, but they differ in many ways.* 2. to have a different opinion; disagree. *You and I differ on this issue.*

difference *noun* (di frəns) the condition of being not the same. *Are there any important differences between these two televisions?*
make a difference to be important or have an effect. *It makes no difference to me whether you stay or go. | That teacher made a real difference in my life.*

different *adj.* (di frənt) 1. not the same. *Three different buses stop at this corner. | The shirt he's wearing today is **different from** the one he wore yesterday.* 2. various. *She has many different pairs of shoes.*

difficult *adj.* (di fə kəlt) hard to do or understand. *The president has to make many difficult decisions. | That book was difficult for me.*

Word Builder: difficult +
difficulty: something that is difficult.

dig *verb* (dig) *dug, dug* to make a hole by removing dirt, sand, or other material. *She dug in the garden to prepare for planting.*

digest *verb* (dī jest) to break down food into substances that the body can use. *Your body digests food more slowly at night.*

digestion *noun* (də jes chən or dī jes chən) [N] the process by which the body changes food into substances it can use. *People say that some kinds of tea are good for digestion.*

digital *adj.* (di jə təl) 1. showing information by a row of numbers. *I wear a digital watch because it's easy to read.* 2. using information in the form of an electronic signal. *Digital cameras don't need film.*

dignity *noun* (dig nə tē) [N] a belief in your own value or worth. *She behaved **with dignity** in spite of her troubles.*

dim *adj.* (dim) having little or no light. *It's hard to read in that dim corner.*

dime *noun* (dīm) a coin of the United States and some other countries equal to ten cents.

dine *verb* (dīn) to eat a meal, usually in a formal way. *We dined at a nice restaurant last night.*

Word Builder: dine +
diner (1): a person who dines at a restaurant.
diner (2): an informal restaurant.

dinner *noun* (di nər) the main meal of the day. *In our family, we usually eat dinner around six o'clock.*

dinosaur *noun* (dī nə sawr) a kind of animal that lived millions of years ago. Some dinosaurs were the largest animals that ever lived on land.

dinosaur

diode *noun* (dī ōd) a device that allows electricity to flow in only one direction. *Some diodes give off a bright light.*

dip *verb* (dip) to put into a liquid for a short time. *He dipped his toes into the water. | She dipped the doughnut in the coffee.*
noun [N] a thick liquid food served in a bowl. You eat it by dipping other pieces of food into it with your fingers. *She served chips and onion dip at her party.*

diploma *noun* (də plō mə) an official piece of paper stating that a student has earned a degree or finished a course of study. High schools, colleges, and universities give out diplomas.

direct *verb* (də rekt) 1. to give instructions or information to. *Can you direct me to the nearest phone?* 2. to manage or control. *The chief of police directs the police force.* 3. to send or aim toward a person or place. *I directed my question to the mayor.* | *I directed the beam of light to the roof.*
adj. going in a straight line or on a straight course. *I'll show you the most direct route to my house.*

Word Builder: direct +
director: a person who directs or who gives directions.

---

direct deposit *noun* (də rek də pa zət) a way of getting paid so that the money goes straight into your bank account. You receive a notice of deposit instead of a paycheck.

direction *noun* (də rek shən) the way in which someone or something faces or travels. *Houses on this street face in one direction.* | *Which direction did they go?*

directions *pl. noun* (də rek shənz) information on which way to go or how to do something. *We stopped at a gas station and asked for directions to the stadium.* | *The directions for the new camera were confusing.*

directory *noun* (də rek tə rē) a list with information about people or businesses. *I found his phone number in the telephone directory.*

dirt *noun* (dərt) 1. [N] loose earth or soil. *The dog is digging in the dirt.* 2. [N] a material such as mud or dust. *His clothes were covered with dirt.*

dirty *adj.* (dər tē) 1. not clean. *The windows were so dirty that you could hardly see out of them.* 2. not pleasant to do. *Give someone else the dirty work.*

disability *noun* (dis ə bi lə tē) a physical or mental condition that makes you not able to do something. *She can't climb stairs because of her disability.* | *He has a job in spite of his disability.*

disabled *adj.* (dis ā bəld) not able to do certain things because of a physical or mental condition. *Parking spaces close to the store are for disabled people.*

disadvantage *noun* (dis əd væn təj) 1. a condition that makes it more difficult to succeed. *Not knowing English is a disadvantage if you live in the United States.* 2. a reason for something being not very good. *One disadvantage of this car is that it uses a lot of gas.*

disagree *verb* (dis ə grē) to have a different opinion or not agree. *I **disagree with** you about the election.*

disappear *verb* (dis ə pēr) to be no longer seen. *The plane disappeared in the clouds.*

disappoint *verb* (dis ə poynt) to cause someone to feel sad because of not doing or receiving something. *Tony's poor grades disappointed his parents.*

Word Builder: disappoint +
disappointed: feeling sad because of not doing or receiving something.
disappointment: the sad feeling caused by not doing or receiving something.

---

disapprove *verb* (dis ə proov) to not approve of someone or something. *She **disapproved of** some of her son's friends.*

disaster *noun* (də zæ stər) a sudden event that causes a lot of damage. *The earthquake was a disaster for the town.*

disc *noun* (disk) 1. a thin, round object used for storing information. *I saved the document on a compact disc.* 2. any thin, flat, round object. *The children like to catch and throw a large plastic disc.*

disc

discard *verb* (də skard) to throw out or away. *We discarded some old newspapers.*

discharge *verb* (dəs charj) 1. to remove from a job; to fire. *The manager discharged a worker who was always late.* 2. to shoot or fire off. *The police officer discharged her weapon.*

discipline *noun* (di sə plən) [N] the training of the body or mind to behave in a certain way. *She believes in strict discipline for her children.*
verb to punish in order to correct behavior. *He disciplined his dog for jumping on people.*

discount *noun* (dis kownt) an amount taken away from the full price. *Tina got a discount on the dress because it was dirty.*
verb (dis kownt) to reduce the price on goods or services for sale. *The store owner discounted the bread because it was a day old.*

discount

discover *verb* (də sk̲ə̲ vər) 1. to find or see before anyone else. *He discovered oil on his property.* 2. to learn or find out about through study or by watching. *We discovered that it was easy to use e-mail.*

Word Builder: discover +
discovery: something that is discovered.

discriminate *verb* (də sk̲ri̲ mə nāt) 1. to treat someone worse than others because he or she belongs to a particular group of people. *It is illegal to **discriminate against** people based on their race or sex.* 2. to see a clear difference. *He could not **discriminate between** the two brands of soda.*

discrimination *noun* (də skri mə n̲ā̲ shən) [N] the act of treating some people worse than others. *Discrimination in the workplace is against the law.*

discuss *verb* (də sk̲əs̲) to talk together about something. *We discussed plans for our vacation.*

discussion *noun* (də sk̲ə̲ shən) the act of talking or writing about something. *Gary and I had an interesting **discussion about** computers.*

disease *noun* (də z̲ēz̲) a condition that causes harm to a person's health. *Many diseases are caused by germs.*

disgust *verb* (dəs g̲əst̲) to cause a strong feeling against something; to cause someone to feel sick. *The sight of the dead animal in the road disgusted her.*
noun [N] a strong feeling against something. *He was filled with disgust when he heard the terrible news.*

dish *noun* (d̲ish̲) 1. a container for serving or holding food, such as a plate, cup, or bowl. *We cleared the table and washed the dishes.* 2. a certain kind of prepared food. *Tacos are a dish from Mexico.*

Word Builder: dish +
dishcloth: a cloth for washing dishes.
dish rack: a rack for drying dishes.
dishrag: a cloth for washing dishes.
dish towel: a towel for drying dishes.
dishwasher: an appliance for washing dishes.

dishonest *adj.* (dis a̲ nəst) not honest. *They had to fire the dishonest employee.*

dismiss *verb* (dəs m̲is̲) 1. to send away or allow to go away. *The teacher dismissed her class.* 2. to remove

from a job; fire. *The company dismissed twenty workers.*

dispense *verb* (də sp̲ens̲) to give out one piece at a time. *This machine dispenses candy.*

Word Builder: dispense +
dispenser: a person or thing that dispenses.

display *verb* (də spl̲ā̲) to cause to be seen; show. *The store displayed cards on a rack.*
noun 1. anything put out in order to be seen. *We looked over the display of fine jewelry.* 2. the screen of a computer on which information is shown. *This computer has a large color display.*

dispose *verb* (də sp̲ō̲z) to give or throw away. *We need to **dispose of** these old clothes.*

dispute *verb* (də sp̲ūt̲) to question whether something is true or correct. *He disputed her claim to the property.*
noun an argument; a thing that people do not agree on. *Mr. Ash and I settled our dispute about the fence.*

dissolve *verb* (də z̲alv̲) to mix completely with a liquid. *He dissolved sugar in his tea.* | *Sugar dissolves in water.*

distance *noun* (d̲i̲ stəns) the measure of space between things or places. *The distance from our house to the gas station is one mile.*

distance learning *noun* (d̲i̲ stəns lər nēng) [N] a form of education where the students are not in the same place as the teacher. Distance learning often happens by means of computers. *This college offers courses by distance learning.*

distant *adj.* (d̲i̲ stənt) far away in time or space. *Dinosaurs lived in the distant past.* | *My brother moved to a distant country.*

distinct *adj.* (də st̲ingkt̲) 1. different or separate. *There are many distinct kinds of dogs.* 2. clear to see, hear, or understand. *There was a distinct change in her mood.*

distinguish *verb* (də st̲ing̲ gwəsh) to tell apart by seeing differences. *It was hard to distinguish the twin brothers.*

distract *verb* (də st̲rækt̲) to draw away a person's attention. *Street noise **distracted** him **from** his work.*

distribute *verb* (də st̲ri̲ būt) to divide into parts and give out to each person or group. *The supervisor distributed safety goggles to the workers.*

distribution *noun* (di strə bū shən) [N] the act of giving something out to each person or group. *We took over distribution of the newspaper in our neighborhood.*

district *noun* (di strəkt) an area of a country, city, or other place used for a particular purpose. *We went shopping in the business district of the city.*

disturb *verb* (də stərb) 1. to interrupt by making noise or doing something that draws away attention. *The party next door disturbed our sleep.* | *I'm sorry to disturb you, but I have one more question.* 2. to upset or trouble. *Violence in movies disturbs me.*

dive *verb* (dīv) *dove (dived), dived* to move down from a high place at high speed, with the head or front part first. *I dived into the pool.* | *The eagle dove from the sky.*

divide *verb* (də vīd) 1. to separate into parts. **Divide** this cake **into** eight pieces. | *The argument divided the council.* 2. to separate a number into equal sets of another number. *Can you **divide** six **by** two?* | *Six **divided by** two is three.* 3. to become separated into two or more parts. *The river **divides into** two small streams.*

dividend *noun* (di və dend) a share of profits paid to people who own all or part of a company. *ABC Corporation paid a dividend of 12 cents a share to people who own its stock.*

division *noun* (də vi zhən) 1. a unit or group in government, business, the military, schools, sports, and other institutions. *The company has one division for sales and one for research.* | *The Chicago Cubs are in the Central Division of the National Baseball League.* 2. [N] the process in mathematics that you use to find how many sets of one number are in another. *We used division to find out how many nickels are in seven dollars.*

divorce *noun* (də vōrs) the ending of a marriage as recognized by law. *Her parents **got a divorce** three years ago.*

Word Builder: divorce +
divorced: no longer married because of divorce.

dizzy *adj.* (di zē) having a feeling of spinning around and being about to fall. *The ride at the amusement park made him dizzy.*

DMV *abbrev.* (dē em vē) an abbreviation for *Department of Motor Vehicles*. The DMV is the name most often used for the government office of each state that gives licenses to drive vehicles and registrations to owners of vehicles.

do *verb* (doo) *did, done* 1. to complete; perform. *I did everything you asked me to do.* 2. to cause or bring about. *The accident did a lot of damage to the car.* 3. to work at. *Carol is doing her homework.* 4. to perform. *He is doing well at his new job.* 5. used to introduce a question with most verbs in the present tense. *Do you want to go to the movies?*
do over to do again. *If you don't do this right the first time, you will have to do it over.*
have to do with to be about or be connected with something. *That book has to do with changes in technology.* | *Her job has something to do with the Internet.*

DOB *abbrev.* (dē ō bē) an abbreviation for *date of birth*.

dock[1] *noun* (dak) 1. a raised, flat surface that is built out into the water. *The boats are tied up at the dock.* 2. a raised, flat surface used to load trucks or trains. *The truck backed up to the dock where the cartons were stacked.*

dock[2] *verb* (dak) to take away part of someone's pay. *She was docked for being late.* | *The supervisor docked five dollars from her pay.*

doctor *noun* (dak tər) 1. a person whose job is to treat and give medicine to sick people or animals. 2. a person who has a doctorate, the highest degree at a university.

doctorate *noun* (dak tə rət) the highest degree that you get after finishing an advanced program of studies at a university. You can call a person *doctor* after he or she has earned a doctorate. *Dr. Jones has a doctorate in physics.*

document *noun* (dak yə mənt) 1. a written or printed paper that gives information or proof of something. Licenses and passports are kinds of documents. 2. a file made with a word processor. Documents can contain text, pictures, charts, and sounds.

dog *noun* (dawg) a kind of mammal with four legs and a tail. People keep dogs as pets. Dogs help people guard buildings and animals.

dog

doll *noun* (dal) a toy made to look like a baby, child, or other person. *My daughter likes to play with dolls.*

dollar *noun* (da lər) the main unit of money in the United States and many other countries. One U.S. dollar is equal to 100 cents.

dolly *noun* (da lē) a piece of equipment for moving heavy objects. A dolly has small wheels, a flat surface for holding things, and handles for pushing.

domestic *adj.* (də me stək) 1. having to do with the home or family. *On the weekends, I do domestic chores.* | *Acts of domestic violence are crimes.* 2. from the country where you live. *He buys domestic cars, not foreign cars.*

dominant *adj.* (da mə nənt) most powerful. *The United States became one of the dominant nations during the 1900s.*

done *verb* (dən) past participle of **do.**

donkey *noun* (dang kē) a mammal in the same family as the horse. People use donkeys for riding and for pulling or carrying heavy loads.

donut *noun* (dō nət) another spelling of **doughnut.**

door *noun* (dōr) 1. an opening through which you enter or leave a room or building. *She walked up to the front door and rang the bell.* 2. a way of reaching the inside of a vehicle or other closed object. *Did you close the refrigerator door?* | *This car has four doors.*

door

Word Builder: door +
doorbell: a bell near the front door of a house. You ring it if you want to enter.
doorknob: a round part on a door. You hold and turn the doorknob to open the door.
doorman: a person whose job is to greet and open the door for people at an apartment house.
doorway: the part of a building that contains the door. You enter through the doorway.

dosage *noun* (dō səj) [N] the amount of a medicine that a person should take and how often in one day he or she should take it. *The dosage of the drug is one teaspoon three times a day.* | *The information about dosage is on the label.*

dose *noun* (dōs) an amount of medicine that a person should take at one time or at certain times in a day. *He took a dose of his medicine before going to bed.*

dot *noun* (dat) 1. a small, round mark or spot. *This shirt is blue with white dots.* 2. a small mark made by a pencil or pen, or printed; a period. *The teacher told her to put a dot over her i.* 3. the pronunciation of the punctuation mark (.) that is used in addresses on the World Wide Web. *You can write to the president at president@whitehouse.gov, or "president at whitehouse dot gov."*

double *adj.* (də bəl) 1. two times the amount or number. *I got double pay for working on Sunday.* | *He made a double batch of cookies.* 2. made for two people. *I have a double bed.*
double-check *verb* to check something twice to make sure it is correct. *The store manager double-checked the receipts at the end of the day.*
double-click *verb* to press the button of a computer mouse twice. *Double-click on the icon to open the file.*

doubt *verb* (dowt) to not be certain or confident about something; to think that something might not be true. *He doubts that he passed the test.* | *I'll try, but I doubt that I can finish this work before five o'clock.*
noun a feeling of not being certain or sure. *He **has doubts about** his ability to succeed.*

dough *noun* (dō) [N] a thick mixture of flour and a liquid such as water or milk. You make bread, cookies, and other things to eat out of dough. *Anne formed the dough into a loaf and baked it.*

doughnut *noun* (dō nət) a small, sweet cake shaped like a ring that is cooked in deep fat. *His favorite snack is coffee and doughnuts.*

dove *verb* (dōv) a past tense of **dive.**

down *adv.* (down) 1. from a higher to a lower position. *The rain came down.* 2. to a lower or worse level. *Turn down the radio.* | *His grades have gone down.*
prep. 1. to a lower position or level. *They walked down the stairs.* 2. along; through. *We ran down the street.*
adj. (informal) sad; not happy. *He has been feeling down since the accident.*

Word Builder: down +
downward: toward a lower level; down.

down payment *noun* (down pā mənt) money to pay for part of the price of something that is very expensive. *We made a down payment of five hundred dollars for the car and got a loan for the rest of the purchase price.*

downstairs *adv.* (down stārz) at, to, or on a lower floor. *The washing machine is downstairs. | I went downstairs to the basement.*
   adj. of a lower floor. *We vacuumed the downstairs rooms.*
   noun the lower floor of a building. *The downstairs doesn't have any heat yet.*

downtown *adv.* (down town) in or to the business area of a town or city. *We went downtown to go shopping. | She took a bus downtown.*
   noun the business area of a town or city. *His apartment is close to downtown.*

dozen *noun* (də zən) a group of twelve. *Eggs are sold by the dozen.*

Dr. *abbrev.* 1. an abbreviation for **Doctor.** 2. an abbreviation for **Drive,** used when writing an address.

draft *noun* (dræft) 1. a piece of writing or a picture that needs more work to be finished. *He wrote the first draft of the report.* 2. the choosing of people for military duty or for certain sports teams. *He went to war because of the draft. | The best football players are chosen early in the draft.* 3. a current of air in a closed space. *The draft in this room is making me cold.*

drag *verb* (dræg) to pull along with effort. *We dragged the logs down the path.*

drain *verb* (drān) to remove a liquid from something through a pipe. *You should drain the bathtub after your bath.*
   noun a device, such as a pipe, through which a liquid flows. *The drain in the kitchen sink is clogged.*

drank *verb* (dræengk) past tense of **drink.**

drapes *pl. noun* (drāps) long, heavy curtains. *She closed the drapes to keep out the sun.*

draw *verb* (draw) *drew, drawn* 1. to make a picture with a pen, pencil, or other writing tool. *She drew some flowers. | He likes to draw.* 2. to pull out or remove. *Who will draw the winning ticket from the bowl?*

drawback *noun* (draw bæk) a thing that keeps something from being good or from having success. *One drawback of this job is the long hours. | Her only drawback is that she doesn't like to use computers.*

drawer *noun* (drōr) a part of a desk, chest, or other piece of furniture that you can keep things in. It is like an open container that slides in and out. *She keeps pens and pencils in one drawer and paper in another.*

drawing *noun* (draw ing) 1. a picture or design made with a pen, pencil, or other writing tool. *That's a beautiful drawing of your house.* 2. [N] the act of making pictures with a pen, pencil, or other writing tool. *His hobby is drawing.*

drawn *verb* (drawn) past participle of **draw.**

dream *noun* (drēm) 1. an event in which changing pictures or images come into your mind as you sleep. *Last night I **had a dream** that I was flying.* 2. a strong hope or wish. *Her dream is to become a doctor.*
   verb dreamed (dreamt), dreamed (dreamt) to see pictures or images in your mind while you sleep. *I dreamed about a magic place last night.*

dress *noun* (dres) a piece of clothing for girls or women. A dress covers the body from the shoulders to the legs. *She decided to wear a dress instead of pants.*
   verb 1. to put clothing on. *She dressed her baby in warm clothes.* 2. to put clothes on oneself. *She dressed nicely for dinner.*
   dress up to wear formal or fancy clothes. *Are you going to dress up for the party?*
   get dressed to put clothes on. *She woke up, got dressed, and had breakfast.*

> **Word Builder: dress +**
> **dress code:** rules that tell you what you may or may not wear in a place.
> **dressed:** wearing clothes.
> **dressmaker:** a person who makes dresses and other women's clothes.
> **dress shop:** a shop that sells dresses and other women's clothing.

dresser *noun* (dre sər) a piece of furniture with drawers or shelves for holding clothing. *He keeps some of his clothing in a dresser and some in a closet.*

dressing *noun* (dre sing) [N] a thick liquid often made with oil, vinegar, and other things. Dressing is a condiment often used on salads. *What kind of dressing would you like with your salad?*

dressy *adj.* (dre sē) formal in style of clothing. *You need to wear something dressy to the wedding.*

drew *verb* (droo) past tense of **draw.**

dried *verb* (drīd) past tense and past participle of **dry.**

drift *verb* (drift) to be carried along by wind or water. *The snow drifted across the road. | The boat drifted in the sea.*

drill *noun* (dril) a tool used to make holes in wood, metal, and other materials.
verb to make a hole using this tool. *She drilled a hole in the wall for a picture hook.*

power drill

drill press *noun* (dril pres) a machine for making holes in metal. *He operates a drill press in the factory.*

drink *verb* (dringk) *drank, drunk* 1. to take in a liquid that contains alcohol through your mouth. *It is dangerous to drink and drive.* 2. to take liquid into your body through your mouth. *I drink orange juice every morning.*
noun a liquid that you take in through your mouth, or a certain amount of liquid. *Apple juice is her favorite drink. | **Take a drink of** water.*

drip *verb* (drip) 1. to come down in drops. *Water is dripping from the ceiling.* 2. to let drops flow down. *The faucet in the bathtub drips.*

drive *verb* (drīv) *drove, driven* 1. to operate a vehicle. *She drove to work today, but she usually takes the bus.* 2. to take or carry in a vehicle. *I will drive her to the hospital.* 3. to make something move by using force. *I drove the nail deep into the wood.* 4. to operate a car, truck, or other vehicle. *He was so sick that he wasn't able to drive.* 5. to travel in a car, truck, or other vehicle. *He doesn't like to take the bus or train, so we always drive into the city.*
noun 1. a trip in a car or other vehicle. *It's only a short drive to my office.* 2. a road for cars and other vehicles to travel on. *Drive is often part of the name of a road. Her address is 123 Maple Drive.* 3. a device in a computer for copying or storing information. *The new computer has a CD and DVD drive.*

Word Builder: drive +
driveway: a road that leads from a street to a building.

driven *verb* (dri vən) past participle of **drive.**

driver *noun* (drī vər) a person who drives, or a person whose job is to drive. *He is a truck driver.*

Word Builder: driver +
driver's license: a license that allows you to drive a car or other vehicle.
driver's seat: the seat in the front of a car or other vehicle where the driver sits.
driver's side: the side of a car or other vehicle where the driver enters and sits.

drop *noun* (drap) 1. a very small amount of liquid with a round shape. *Drops of rain fell on the windshield.* 2. a decrease in amount. *Store owners expect a drop in business after the holidays.*
verb 1. to fall to a lower level. *The coins dropped out of his pocket.* 2. to fall in amount. *The temperature drops after the sun goes down.* 3. to let something fall. *I dropped my keys when I got out of the car.*
drop in to visit someone. *The next time you're in our neighborhood, please drop in.*
drop off to let someone get out of a vehicle. *I'll drop you off at your apartment on my way home.*
drop out to stop taking part in; to leave before finishing. *She dropped out of the chorus because she was too busy. | He dropped out of school and went to work full time.*

drop or fall?
Drop means to cause something to move to a lower position.
Fall describes the action in which something moves to a lower position.
Compare:
Don't drop the baby! Don't let him fall!
The baby fell from the step.

drove *verb* (drōv) past tense of **drive.**

drown *verb* (drown) to die under water because of lack of air. *The child fell into the river and drowned.*

drug *noun* (drəg) 1. a substance used to cure a disease or help people who have physical problems; medicine. *The doctor gave him a drug for his cough. | She takes a drug for pain.* 2. a substance that causes a change in the body and mind. *He went to jail for selling illegal drugs.*

drugstore (drug store) *noun* (drəg stōr) a store that sells medicine and other things for your body as well as things such as candy, magazines, and newspapers.

drug test *noun* (drəg test) a test of the body to discover if a person is using drugs that are illegal. *The company makes all employees take a drug test.*

drum *noun* (drəm) 1. an instrument for playing music that has a hollow round shape and a tight covering over an open end. You play a drum by hitting its surface with your hands or sticks. 2. a round container with a flat top and bottom. *The oil is stored in drums.*

drunk *adj.* (drəngk) having had too much alcohol to drink. *It is against the law to drive when you are drunk.*
verb past participle of **drink.**

> **Word Builder: drunk +**
> **drunkard:** a person who drinks too much alcohol; alcoholic.

dry *adj.* (drī) 1. not wet; without any water. *If you don't hang up the towels, they will not get dry. | There has been no rain, so the river is dry.* 2. having little or no water or other liquid. *This year we had a dry summer. | This cake is too dry.*
verb to make something dry. *Be sure to dry your hair before you go outside.*

> **Word Builder: dry +**
> **dryer:** an appliance for drying clothes or hair.

dry-cleaning *noun* (drī clē ning) [N] a method of cleaning clothes that uses chemicals instead of water.

dryer *noun* (drī ər) a machine for drying something, such as wet hair or clothes. *I use a hair dryer after I wash my hair. | Put the wet laundry into the dryer.*

dryer

duck[1] *noun* (dək) a bird with a short neck and large feet that lives in or near water. People hunt or keep ducks for their meat.

duck[2] *verb* (dək) to lower your head or body to avoid something that might hit you. *I ducked when she threw the pillow at me. I You will have to duck when the boat goes under the bridge.*

due *adj.* (doo) 1. owed to someone as a debt or because it is deserved. *There are still a few hundred dollars due on the loan. | This money is due to me because I worked hard for it.* 2. required or expected to arrive. *The payment is due next week. | Her baby is due in January.* 3. caused by. *The game was canceled* **due to** *the rain.*

dues *pl. noun* (dooz) the money that members of a group or club must pay to remain part of the group. *I pay part of my union dues every week.*

dug *verb* (dəg) past tense and past participle of **dig.**

dull *adj.* (dəl) 1. not interesting; boring. *The class was dull, so she fell asleep.* 2. not sharp. *You cannot slice a tomato with a dull knife.* 3. lasting a long time but not felt in a sharp way. *The nurse asked whether the pain in his side was dull or sharp. | I feel a dull pain in my leg after I exercise.* 4. not bright, shiny, or having much color. *They painted their house a dull gray.*

dumb *adj.* (dəm) 1. not smart; stupid. *It was a dumb idea to cut your own hair. | Her brother says she's dumb, but I think she's smart.* 2. not able to speak. *She has been deaf and dumb since childhood.*

dump *verb* (dəmp) to let something fall out of a container. *The truck dumped the garbage at the landfill. | Don't dump the paint into the sink!*
noun a place owned by a town or city where people can bring garbage. *We took our trash to the town dump.*

during *prep.* (door ing) 1. all through a certain period of time. *My daughter goes to camp during the summer.* 2. at some point within a certain period of time. *She arrived during the night.*

dust *noun* (dəst) [N] tiny, dry pieces of dirt or other material that are in the air and collect on surfaces. *There was a lot of dust behind the TV set.*
verb to clean tiny pieces of dirt from a surface. *I dusted all the shelves.*

> **Word Builder: dust +**
> **dust bag:** a bag that you attach to a vacuum cleaner to hold dust.
> **dust cloth:** a cloth for wiping dust.
> **dustpan:** a pan that you sweep dust into.
> **dusty:** covered in dust.

duster *noun* (də stər) a person or thing that removes dust.

duty *noun* (doo tē) 1. something that a person should do because it is right or fair. *It is the duty of parents to take care of their children.* 2. things a person must do in a particular job or position. *One of the duties of a police officer is to direct traffic.* 3. a tax on things that people bring into a country if they bought them in another country.
on duty in the process of doing one's job. *When he is not on duty, the guard goes outside to smoke.*

DVD *abbrev.* (dē vē dē) an abbreviation for *digital versatile disk.* A DVD is a flat, round plastic object that can store information from a computer, a movie, or other material.

E e

each *adj.* (ēch) every one of two or more things. *The child had a cookie in each hand.* | *The president shook hands with each employee.*
pron. every one of a group. *Many children came to the party, and each brought a gift.*
adv. for, to, or from each one. *They gave the children a dollar each.*

each other *pron.* (ēch ə thər) used to express that each of two people or things does the same action to the other. *They bought each other a present.*

eager *adj.* (ē gər) wanting very much. *We were **eager for** the game to start.* | *They are eager to see her.*

eagle *noun* (ē gəl) a large, strong bird that hunts small animals and fish.

ear *noun* (ēr) either of the two organs of the body used for hearing.

earlobe — ear

Word Builder: ear +
earache: an ache in the ear.
earmuffs: a warm covering for the ears.
earplugs: small pieces that you put into your ears to block noise.
earring: a piece of jewelry worn in the ear.

early *adv.* (ər lē) 1. near the beginning of something. *I like to get up early in the morning.* 2. before the usual or expected time. *I arrived early for my appointment.*
adj. 1. near the beginning of a time period. *We see these flowers in the early spring.* 2. before the usual or expected time. *We had an early dinner on Sunday.* | *I was ten minutes early for my interview.*

earn *verb* (ərn) 1. to receive money for work that you have done. *She earns more money in her new job than in her old job.* 2. to receive something because of hard work or good behavior. *He earned that award through a lot of effort.* 3. to receive money as profit. *Does your bank account earn much interest?*

earth *noun* (ərth) 1. the third planet from the sun. *People live on the earth.* 2. [N] the outer layer of our planet; ground. *When the wind stopped, the kite fell to the earth.* 3. [N] soil or dirt. *We can't plant crops when the earth is frozen.*

earthquake *noun* (ərth kwāk) a strong shaking in a part of the earth's surface. *An earthquake is a dangerous event.*

ease *noun* (ēz) [N] the absence of problems, effort, or pain. *It was difficult work, but she did it with ease.*

east *noun* (ēst) 1. [N] the direction in front of you when you face the rising sun. 2. (often capitalized) the eastern part of a country or area. *New York City is in the East.*
adj. from, of, or in the east. *There's an east wind blowing.*
adv. from, in, or toward the east. *I've been driving east.*

eastern *adj.* (ē stərn) having to do with or located in the east. *We traveled in the eastern part of the country.*

easy *adj.* (ē zē) 1. not difficult. *She wants an easy job.* | *She helped her younger brother find an easy book.* 2. without trouble or worry; comfortable; relaxed. *He leads an easy life.*

Word Builder: easy +
easily: with no difficulty; in an easy way.

eat *verb* (ēt) *ate, eaten* to take food into the body through the mouth. *Do you eat meat?*

eaten *verb* (ē tən) past participle of **eat.**

EBT *abbrev.* (ē bē tē) [N] an abbreviation for *electronic benefits transfer*. EBT is a government program that gives money to people who need food and other things.

economic *adj.* (e kə na mik) having to do with money and the production of goods and services. *Economic conditions are getting better now, so people are spending more money.*

economics *noun* (e kə na miks) [N] the study of how money, goods, and services are produced and used within a country.

economy *noun* (i ka nə mē) all the money and production of goods and services of a certain place, such as a state or country. *The new factory will help the state's economy.*

edge *noun* (ej) 1. a line where two sides or surfaces meet. *He rested his arms on the edge of the counter.* | *That knife has a sharp edge.* 2. the border or outside line. *We saw a deer at the edge of the forest.*

edit *verb* (e̱ dit) to prepare written materials by correcting mistakes and making other changes. *My husband edited my résumé before I sent it.*

editor *noun* (e̱ di tər) a person whose job is to read and correct pieces of writing. *The editor made few changes in the author's new book.*

editorial *noun* (e di to̱r e̱ əl) an article in a newspaper, or a statement on television, that gives a personal opinion. *The newspaper printed an editorial against the war.*

educate *verb* (e̱ jə ka̱t) to give knowledge or understanding of something through teaching or training. *The responsibility of a school is to educate children.*

education *noun* (e j ə ka̱ shən) 1. [N] the act or process of giving or receiving instruction. *Teaching reading is an important part of education in schools.* 2. [N] the knowledge a person gets through learning. *A high school education is necessary for most jobs.*

effect *noun* (i fe̱kt) 1. something that happens because of something else. *A good teacher can **have** a great **effect on** students. | That medicine **had** no **effect** on me.* 2. the condition of being in active operation. *The new rules **go into effect** tomorrow. | The city passed a new law about dogs, but it's not **in effect** yet.*

effective *adj.* (i fe̱k tiv) 1. able to produce a result that you want. *That's a very effective medicine.* 2. in operation. *This rule is effective immediately.*

efficiency *noun* (i fi̱ shən se̱) [N] the ability to do something well without much waste. *We checked the efficiency of the different washing machines before we chose one to buy.*

efficient *adj.* (i fi̱ shənt) operating well without much waste. *This is an efficient clothes dryer.*

effort *noun* (e̱ fərt) 1. [N] the use of physical or mental energy. *It took a lot of effort to move all that furniture.* 2. [N] a use of energy in trying to do something; attempt. *Let's make one more effort to finish this work before we go home.*

egg *noun* (eg) 1. an object that contains a baby animal in a shell. The insides of an egg are often cooked and eaten. 2. a cell in a female animal or in some kinds of plants that can develop into a new individual after it is fertilized.

nest

eggs

eight *noun* (a̱t) the word for the number 8.

eighteen *noun* (a̱ te̱n) the name for the number 18.

eighth *adj.* (a̱th) next after seventh.
   noun one of eight equal parts of a whole.

eighty *noun* (a̱ te̱) the word for the number 80.

either *adj.* (e̱ thər or i̱ thər) 1. one or the other of two things or people. *You can have either the pie or the cake, not both.* 2. each of two things or people. *There is a lamp on either side of the bed.*
   pron. one or the other. *No, thanks. I don't want either. | Either is OK with me.*
   conj. a word used to tell of two possibilities or choices. *He is **either** outside **or** in the basement. | You can **either** go with us **or** stay here.*
   adv. used in negative sentences to mean *also*. *He doesn't have a car, and I don't either.*

eject *verb* (i je̱kt) to move something out with force. *He ejected the noisy kids from the library. | The CD player is broken and won't eject the CD.*

elbow *noun* (e̱l bo̱) 1. the joint between the upper and lower arm. 2. anything shaped or bent like this joint. *She used an elbow to connect the two pipes.*

elderly *adj.* (e̱l dər le̱) a polite word for **old.** *This is a home for elderly people.*

elect *verb* (i lekt) 1. to choose by means of voting. *They elected her as president.* 2. to choose or decide. *They elected to educate their children at home instead of in school.*

election *noun* (i lek shən) the process of choosing a person to serve in government by voting. *In the United States, the election of the president takes place every four years.* | *Elections for city council are next week.*

electric *adj.* (i lek trik) using or having to do with electricity. *He plays an electric guitar.* | *These wires carry electric current.*

electrical *adj.* (i lek tri kəl) having to do with electricity. *You should not do electrical work yourself because it's dangerous.*

electric eye *noun* (i lek trik ī) a device that gives off an electric signal as a reaction to light or motion. *Electric eyes are used in alarms because they can sense motion.*

electrician *noun* (i lek tri shən) a person whose job is to put in or fix electric equipment.

electricity *noun* (i lek tri si tē) [N] a kind of energy that is used for light and heat and for making things operate. *Lightning is a natural form of electricity.* | *This small heater uses a lot of electricity.*

electronic *adj.* (i lek tra nik) using or having to do with a system that uses electricity. *Computers and televisions are electronic machines.*

element *noun* (e lə mənt) 1. a basic part of any whole. *One element of this recipe is missing.* 2. a pure, simple chemical substance that has only one kind of atom. *There are more than one hundred different elements. Gold and oxygen are examples of elements.*

elementary *adj.* (e lə men tər ē) 1. having to do with the most basic or simplest parts of something. *Learning the alphabet is an elementary part of reading and writing.* 2. having to do with early education. *Reading and arithmetic are part of elementary education.*

elementary school *noun* (e lə men tər ē skool) a school for the first four to eight years of a child's education.

elephant *noun* (e l ə fənt) a very large mammal with thick, gray skin and a very long nose. Elephants live in Africa and Asia.

elephant

elevator *noun* (e lə vā tər) 1. a device that carries people or things from one floor to another in a building. An elevator is like a small room or platform that moves up and down. 2. a grain storage structure equipped to lift and pour out grain; grain elevator.

eleven *noun* (ə le vən) the word for the number 11.

eligibility *noun* (e li jə bi li tē) [N] the state or condition of having the things necessary to do or be chosen for something. *Eligibility for voting depends on whether you are a citizen.*

eligible *adj.* (e li jə bəl) having the required things that allow you to do something or be chosen for something. *Only children under twelve years old are eligible to enter the contest.* | *You are not eligible to vote if you are not a citizen.*

eliminate *verb* (ə li mə nāt) to remove or destroy. *He is trying to eliminate weeds from his garden.*

else *adj.* (els) 1. different; other. *They gave the job to someone else.* 2. in addition; more. *Do we have time to do anything else?*
adv. 1. in addition; in another way. *Where else would you like to go?* | *How else can I explain this?* 2. if not. *Hurry up **or else** you will be late.*

elsewhere *adv.* (els wār) in or to another place; somewhere else. *I'll go elsewhere to play my music.*

e-mail *noun* (ē māl) a message that you write and send from one computer to another; electronic mail. *Did you get the e-mail that I sent this morning?*
verb to send a message or image by computer. *They e-mailed pictures of their new baby to their friends.*

embarrass *verb* (em bær əs) to make someone feel shame. *When something embarrasses me, my face gets red.* | *My behavior embarrassed my sister.*

Word Builder: embarrass +
embarrassed: feeling uncomfortable or ashamed.
embarrassing: causing someone to become uncomfortable or ashamed.
embarrassment: a feeling of being made uncomfortable or ashamed.

emergency *noun* (i mər jən sē) a sudden dangerous situation that requires immediate action or help. *Fires and floods are kinds of emergencies. | This is an emergency! Call the doctor!*

emit *verb* (i mit) to send out or give off. *Lightbulbs emit light.*

emotion *noun* (i mō shən) a strong feeling such as love, hatred, or fear. *When my grandparents came to this country, they felt many different emotions.*

Word Builder: emotion +
emotional: showing emotion.

emphases *pl. noun* (em fə sēz) plural of **emphasis.**

emphasis *noun* (em fə sis) *emphases* 1. [N] the special importance that is attached to something. *Teachers of young children **put** a lot of **emphasis on** reading.* 2. [C] the attention or strength given to a particular sound, word, phrase, or idea. *In the word* father, *the emphasis is on the sound* fa.

emphasize *verb* (em fə sīz) to give particular attention to something. *The president emphasized the importance of education.*

empire *noun* (em pīr) a group of nations under one ruler. *The queen sent soldiers to expand her empire.*

employ *verb* (im ploy) 1. to use. *Doctors employ many different instruments during an operation.* 2. to provide a job for someone or get services from someone in exchange for payment. *Our company employs over two hundred people.*

Word Builder: employ +
employed: having a job.
employee: a person who is employed; a worker.
employer: a company or person who hires people to do work.

employment *noun* (im ploy mənt) [N] the condition of having a job for which you receive payment. *His employment at that store lasted six years.*

empty *adj.* (emp tē) holding or containing nothing. *I thought I had put my shoes in the box, but it is empty.*
verb to remove what is inside of something; make empty. *Please empty the garbage can.*

empty

enclose *verb* (in klōz) 1. to put something around a thing to separate it from other things or people. *They enclosed their backyard with a fence.* 2. to include something inside another thing. *She enclosed a letter in the package.*

encourage *verb* (in kər ij) to give hope or courage to someone; give confidence or support. *Her praise encouraged me to continue playing the piano. | His parents encouraged him to play sports.*

encyclopedia *noun* (in sī klə pē dē ə) a book or set of books that has information on a wide variety of subjects. *I read an article about atoms in the encyclopedia.*

end *noun* (end) 1. the point at which anything that has length starts or stops. *Please tie a knot at the end of the string. | There is a stop sign at the end of the road.* 2. a point in time at which something stops or finishes. *We look forward to going home at the end of the day.* 3. the last part. *I cried at the end of the movie.*
verb 1. to cause to stop; finish. *A bad injury ended his dream of becoming a football player.* 2. to stop. *The class will end at three o'clock. | Their marriage ended in divorce.*
end up to come to be in a place or situation that you did not plan to be in. *We ended up not going to the movies because it was too late.*

Word Builder: end +
ending: the last part of something.
endless: without end.

endorse *verb* (in dōrs) 1. to give support to; approve of. *He endorsed her for governor.* 2. to sign your name on the back of a check. *Endorse the check, and the teller will cash it.*

enemy *noun* (e nə mē) a person who hates or wants to harm another. *The king made many enemies among his people.*

energetic *adj.* (e nər je tik) full of energy; active. *He is over 80 years old, but he is still very energetic.*

energy *noun* (e nər jē) [N] the ability to have force or power or to do work. There are many kinds of energy such as physical, electrical, nuclear, or chemical. *His construction job requires that he have a lot of energy. | The power plant operated on nuclear energy.*

engage *verb* (in gāj) 1. to make a set of things start to work by fitting them together. *Use the lever to engage the gears.* 2. to get or use the service of someone; hire. *The company engaged ten new workers.* 3. to involve yourself in something; to take part in. *You should engage in more activities on the weekends.*

engaged *adj.* (in gājd) having a plan to marry someone. *Mary is **engaged to** John.*

engagement *noun* (in gāj mənt) 1. a promise to marry; a period of time before the marriage. *Jane and Jim announced their engagement last week.* | *Their engagement lasted two years.* 2. a meeting with someone at a certain time. *I have an engagement at two o'clock.*

engine *noun* (en jin) a machine that uses energy from a source such as gasoline or electricity to do work. *Some new cars have electric engines.*

engineer *noun* (en ji nēr) 1. a person whose job is to plan and design structures, systems, or machines. 2. a person who runs an engine, especially the engine of a train.

engineering *noun* (en ji nēr ing) [N] the study and practice of using mathematics and science to do practical things such as designing and building structures, tools, and machines.

English *noun* (ing glish) [N] the main language of the United States and many other countries. English comes from England, a country in Europe.

enjoy *verb* (in joy) 1. to find pleasure in something. *I enjoy skating.* 2. to experience pleasure or happiness in some activity. *She **enjoyed herself** at the party.*

enjoyable *adj.* (in joy ə bəl) giving pleasure. *That was an enjoyable trip to the city.*

enjoyment *noun* (in joy mənt) [N] the pleasure or satisfaction that you get from doing something. *I get enjoyment from going to see movies with my friends.*

enough *adj.* (i nəf) as much or as many as needed or required. *I have enough money to pay my bills.* | *There are enough people here for a softball team.*
adv. in a way or to a degree that is needed or required. *The job doesn't pay enough.* | *She is old enough to vote.*

enroll *verb* (in rōl) 1. to put someone's name on an official list. *Parents must enroll their young children in school.* 2. to put your name on an official list. *I enrolled in an evening class at the college.*

enter *verb* (en tər) 1. to come or go into. *I entered the house by the front door.* 2. to take part in or join. *We entered the race.* | *He entered the university.* 3. to record on a list or to type into a computer. *Enter the number of the check that you wrote into the register.* | *Enter your password into the computer to start it.*

enterprise *noun* (en tər prīz) a business organization. *Their software enterprise made huge profits last year.*

entertain *verb* (en tər tān) 1. to amuse; keep someone interested. *She entertained me with stories about her travels.* 2. to have someone as a guest. *We entertained four guests at dinner last night.*

entertainment *noun* (en tər tān mənt) [N] something that amuses or interests. *We can see many kinds of entertainment at the circus.*

enthusiasm *noun* (in thoo zē æ zəm) [N] a strong, happy interest in something. *He has more enthusiasm for playing the piano than for anything else.* | *He listened to my ideas with a lot of enthusiasm.*

entire *adj.* (in tīr) 1. having all the parts; whole. *She watched the entire program.* 2. whole; every one of a group. *The entire department is unhappy about the new work rules.* | *We need the entire set of tools to do the job right.*

entitle *verb* (in tī təl) to give a right or legal claim to. *Citizenship entitles you to vote.* | *A driver's license entitles you to drive a car.*

entrance *noun* (en trins) 1. the act of entering. *Everyone applauded the president's entrance.* 2. a place through which you enter. *The main entrance to the building faces the street.*

entrée *noun* (an trā) the main course of a meal. *Would you like fish or meat for your entrée?*

entry *noun* (en trē) 1. [N] an act or instance of entering. *A visa is needed for entry into most countries.* 2. an area for entering. *The entry into the building was blocked by a crowd of people.* 3. something that is added to a written list or record. *He made an entry in his notebook.*

Word Builder: entry +
entry-level: a low or first level of employment.

envelope *noun* (en və lōp) a folded paper covering for a letter or other papers you mail. You write the address and put a stamp on an envelope before you mail it.

envelope

environment *noun* (in vī ərn mənt) 1. the objects and conditions that exist in a place and influence how people feel and develop. *A safe environment is important for the proper development of a child.* | *Problems with the boss create a bad work environment.* 2. everything that surrounds living things and affects growth and health; the natural world. *Taking care of the environment is crucial for the survival of all living things.*

> **Word Builder: environment +**
> **environmental:** having to do with the environment.
> **environmentally:** in a way that affects the environment.

equal *adj.* (ē kwəl) 1. having the same value, measure, or amount as something else. *The two sisters are of equal height.* 2. the same for everyone. *We all have an equal chance of winning the game.*
verb to be the same as. *Two plus two equals four.*

equality *noun* (i kwa li tē) [N] the condition, fact, or quality of being equal. *The female students wanted equality with the male students.*

equal rights *pl. noun* (ē kwəl rīts) the same rights for all people. *The Constitution guarantees equal rights.*

equator *noun* (i kwā tər) the imaginary circle around the middle of the earth. *Temperatures around the equator tend to remain the same all year.*

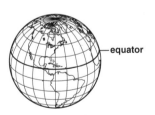
equator

equip *verb* (i kwip) to provide with what is needed to do an activity or job. *She equipped herself for work with a new briefcase.*

> **Word Builder: equip +**
> **equipped:** having the equipment that you need to do something.

equipment *noun* (i kwip mənt) [N] anything made for a particular use. Jobs and sports often require special equipment. *We bought a lot of new equipment for our hiking trip, including a tent.*

equivalency *noun* (i kwi və lən sē) [N] the condition of being equal in value. *She is studying for her high school equivalency.*

equivalent *adj.* (i kwi və lənt) the same as or equal to another in force, value, measure, or meaning. *Three feet is equivalent to one yard.*
noun something that is the same or equal. *One dollar is the equivalent of 100 pennies.*

era *noun* (e rə) a period of time in history. An era often begins or ends with an important event. *Franklin D. Roosevelt was president during the World War II era.*

erase *verb* (ə rās) to remove by rubbing away. *He erased the wrong answer and wrote the correct answer.*

> **Word Builder: erase +**
> **eraser:** a thing used to erase.

error *noun* (e rər) a mistake in thought or action; something that is wrong. *I corrected the errors on my math test.*

escape *verb* (i skāp) to get free from something; to get away. *The prisoner **escaped from** jail.* | *The dog escaped out the front door.*

escort *noun* (e skört) a group of people who travel with someone to protect or to show respect to that person. *The president always travels with an escort.*
verb (ə skört) to go with someone to a place; to take someone to a place. *My friend escorted me to the movie.* | *The nurse escorted me into the doctor's office.*

ESL *abbrev.* (ē es el) an abbreviation for *English as a Second Language*. ESL is the study of English for people whose first language is not English.

ESOL *abbrev.* (ē es ō el) an abbreviation for *English for Speakers of Other Languages*. ESOL is the study of English for people whose first language is not English.

especially *adv.* (i spe shə lē) 1. better or more than usual; to a great degree. *The food is especially good at this restaurant.* | *I'm especially tired tonight.* 2. in particular. *The trip will be expensive, especially if we go by plane.* 3. for one reason or purpose in particular. *I bought this bracelet especially for you.*

essay *noun* (e sā) a short piece of writing on a particular subject that contains the ideas and opinions of the author. *Have you completed your English essay?*

establish *verb* (i stæ blish) to start or make something that did not exist before. *He established a new business last year.*

establishment *noun* (i stæ blish mənt) 1. [N] the act of establishing. *We celebrated the establishment of a new school in our town.* 2. a business, or a place of business. *We always get our hair cut at that establishment.*

estate *noun* (i stāt) 1. a piece of land with a large house on it. *Her family owned a huge estate in the country.* 2. all the property of a person or family; the property left by someone when he or she dies. *After my grandfather died, his estate went to my mother and my uncle.*

estimate *verb* (e sti māt) to make a guess about the amount, size, or worth of something. *We estimated the taxes we would have to pay.*
noun (es tə mit) a guess about the amount, size, or value of something. *The mechanic gave me an estimate for the car repair.*

etc. *abbrev.* (et se tə rə) an abbreviation for **et cetera**.

et cetera *adv.* (et se tə rə) and others of the same kind. *There were all kinds of fruit in the basket—apples, oranges, peaches, bananas, et cetera.*

ethnic *adj.* (eth nik) of or relating to a group of people with its own language, history, or culture. *Our community celebrates many ethnic holidays.*

ethnicity *noun* (eth ni si tē) the condition of being a member of a group sharing the same language, history, or culture. *It is against the law to discriminate against someone because of his or her ethnicity.*

evacuate *verb* (i væk ū āt) to leave or to empty of people for safety reasons. *The firefighters evacuated the burning building.* | *The police evacuated the people from the valley before the flood.*

evaluate *verb* (i væl ū āt) 1. to judge or set the value of. *The magazine evaluated ten new cars.* 2. to judge or measure something by studying it with care. *Teachers use tests to evaluate how much their students have learned.*

evaluation *noun* (i væl ū ā shən) 1. a report that tells the value or quality of something. *Martin's boss gave him a good evaluation.* 2. a careful study of something in order to judge it or measure it. *I scheduled an evaluation of my daughter's hearing.*

even *adj.* (ē vin) 1. smooth, level, or flat. *The children play ball on a field where the ground is nice and even.* 2. at the same level or height. *The snow is even with the tops of my boots.* 3. equal in quantity or measure. *I gave my children an even number of cookies.* 4. in the same amount all over. *The painter put an even coat of paint on the walls.* 5. able to be divided by two. *Six is an even number, but five is not.*
adv. 1. used to emphasize something as surprising or not expected. *That's so easy that even I can do it!* 2. used to emphasize the degree of difference between the things that you are comparing. *Kit runs fast, but her sister runs even faster.* 3. used before *though* and *if* to give these words more force. **Even though** *we tried hard, we lost the game.* | *I would not leave this company* **even if** *the other company paid me more.*
verb to cause to be equal. *The other team soon* **evened up** *the score.*

even

evening *noun* (ēv ning) the period between late afternoon and night; the early part of the night. *I walk my dog every morning and evening.*

event *noun* (i vent) something that happens, especially an important thing that happens. *The newspaper reports on current world events.*

ever *adv.* (e vər) 1. at some time; at any time. *Have you ever flown in an airplane?* 2. at all times; always. **Ever since** *the accident, we are more careful.*

every *adj.* (ev rī) each member or part of a group. *Every person got a prize.* | *Every seat in the theater was taken.*
every other every second one. *I go swimming every other day.*

each or every?
Use *each* when you want to emphasize one person or thing in a group at a time.
Use *every* when you want to emphasize the group as a whole, but as made up of individual people or things.
Compare:
Each child got to choose one treat.
Every child in the class is important.
She put each loaf of bread on the shelf.
Every item in the store has an SKU.

everybody *pron.* (ev rē ba dē) each and all persons; every person. *Everybody gets a turn with the game.*

everyday *adj.* (ev rē dā) ordinary or common; happening daily. *You should not wear your everyday clothes for special occasions. | His everyday activities always included a long walk.*

everyone *pron.* (ev rē wən) each and every person; everybody. *Everyone in my family has red hair.*

everything *pron.* (ev rē thing) every part; all. *I ate everything on my plate.*

everywhere *adv.* (ev rē wār) in every place; in all places. *I looked everywhere for my keys.*

evict *verb* (i vikt) to force someone to leave a rented property. *The landlord evicted the man from his apartment because he could not pay the rent.*

eviction *noun* (i vik shən) the process of being forced to leave a property. *My friend faces eviction from his apartment if he cannot pay the rent.*

evidence *noun* (e və dins) [N] something that gives proof of or a reason to believe something. *The police searched for evidence at the scene of the crime.*

evil *adj.* (ē vəl) having very bad character or behavior. *The evil leader killed thousands of his people.*

exact *adj.* (ig zækt) 1. having no mistakes; correct. *Check the dictionary to find the exact spelling of a word.* 2. not allowing anything to be different from something else. *This is an exact copy of the painting.*

exam *noun* (əg zæm) the short form of **examination.** *We will have a math exam tomorrow. | You must pass a health exam before you can play football.*

examination *noun* (ig zæ mi nā shən) 1. the act of examining or testing. *The mechanic's examination of my car showed that it needed new tires.* 2. a test of skill used to see how much a person knows or can do. *Before you can become a lawyer, you must pass an examination.*

examine *verb* (ig zæ min) to look at in a close, thorough way. *The doctor examined my eyes and ears.*

example *noun* (əg zæm pəl) 1. something that shows what a group of things is like. *An apple is an example of a fruit.* 2. a model that you should either copy or avoid. *Jack's father tried to be a good example for him.*
for example used to say that you will now give an example or examples. *Farmers grow many kinds of crops, for example, wheat, corn, and oats.*

excavate *verb* (ek skə vāt) to dig up and remove material from. *The bulldozer excavated an area for the foundation of the new house.*

excavate

excavation *noun* (ek skə vā shən) [N] the act or process of digging out or removing material. *Excavation for the new basement is complete.*

exceed *verb* (ik sēd) to go beyond or do more than. *Don't exceed the speed limit.*

excellent *adj.* (ek sə lint) very good or much better than others. *Her excellent test grades show how hard she studies.*

except *prep.* (ik sept) apart from; not including. *The store is open every day except Sunday.*

exception *noun* (ik sep shən) something that is different from the general rule. *The form* went *is an* **exception to** *the rule that past tense forms end in* ed. *| All of my friends are married,* **with the exception of** *Sarah.*

exchange *verb* (iks chānj) to give something in return for something else; trade. *I exchanged this blouse for one in a different color.*
noun 1. the act of giving or getting one thing in return for another; trade. *The exchange of rings is a part of some wedding ceremonies.* 2. a place where things are bought, sold, or traded. *My mother buys and sells on the stock exchange.*

excite *verb* (ik sīt) to increase the feelings of; to increase energy. *The first snow of the year always excites children.*

excitement *noun* (ik sīt mənt) [N] the state of being excited. *She was filled with excitement when she heard the good news.*

exclaim *verb* (iks klām) to say in a loud voice and with strong feeling. *"I won!" exclaimed the woman.*

exclamation mark *noun* (ek sklə mā shən mark) a punctuation mark (!). It is used after a word or words that express strong feeling. It is also called an exclamation point.

excuse *verb* (iks kūz) to forgive. *Please* **excuse** *me* **for** *stepping on your foot.* | *She* **excused** *him* **for** *forgetting her birthday.*
noun (iks kūs) a reason that you give in order to explain something. *My excuse for being late is that I missed the bus.*

executive *noun* (ig ze kyə tiv) a person who manages or directs a business or government. *The company's top executives met to discuss how to increase sales.*

executive branch *noun* (ig ze kyə tiv brænch) one of the three branches of the government in the United States. The job of the executive branch is to carry out the laws of the country. The president and various departments make up the executive branch. *The Department of Defense, Department of State, and Department of Health and Human Services are some parts of the executive branch.*

exercise *noun* (ek sər sīz) 1. [N] an activity that improves the health of the body or mind. *Swimming is good physical exercise.* | *Doing crossword puzzles is good mental exercise.* 2. a particular way to use your muscles to make them strong. *He learned some new exercises for his arms and shoulders.*
verb 1. to put into practice; make use of. *He failed to exercise his right to vote.* 2. to do physical activity. *I exercise in the gym every morning.*

exhaust *verb* (ig zawst) 1. to use all of; use up. *The campers exhausted their supply of food and had to catch fish.* 2. to make tired; wear out. *The long day at the factory exhausted her.*
noun [N] the smoke or gas given off by an engine. *The exhaust from the old car filled the garage with smoke.*

exhibit *verb* (ig zi bit) to show or present for view. *Michael exhibits his paintings at the art gallery.* | *Maura rarely exhibits her feelings to strangers.*
noun a display or show. *There is a new exhibit of photographs at the museum.*

exist *verb* (ig zist) to be real; to live. *She does not believe that ghosts exist.* | *Insects existed before humans.*

existence *noun* (ig zi stins) [N] the condition of being alive or real. *Dinosaurs are no longer* **in existence.** | *She believes in the existence of life on other planets.*

exit *noun* (ek sit) a way out. *She left the theater through the rear exit.*
verb to go out; leave. *He exited through the back door.*

expand *verb* (ik spænd) 1. to make larger or wider. *The supermarket expanded its parking lot.* 2. to become larger or wider. *The stomach expands when a person eats.*

expect *verb* (ik spekt) 1. to think that something will happen or arrive. *We expect that the project will be done in June.* | *They expected a letter from their son.* 2. to believe that someone will do something or act in a certain way because it is right or necessary. *She expects her children to obey her.* | *People expect a doctor to have a lot of knowledge.*

expectation *noun* (ek spek tā shən) a belief or hope concerning what is possible in the future. *Their* **expectation of** *higher pay made the workers happy.* | *That teacher* **has** *high* **expectations** *for her students.*

expense *noun* (ik spens) the money needed to buy or do something; cost. *His parents work hard to afford the expense of new school clothes.*

expensive *adj.* (ik spen siv) costing a lot of money; having a high price. *She wanted the most expensive sandals in the store.* | *New cars are expensive.*

experience *noun* (ik spēr ē ins) 1. something that a person has done or lived through. *The war was a terrible experience for everyone.* 2. [N] understanding or skills gained from practice or activity. *We need a worker with two years of computer experience.* | *Captain Black* **has** *a lot of* **experience** *with that kind of boat.*
verb to feel or know. *He experienced defeat for the first time.* | *She experienced pain after the accident.*

Word Builder: experience +
experienced: having experience.

experiment *noun* (ik <u>spe</u> rə mənt) a test used to discover something not known, such as the cause of something. *Scientists performed experiments on several new kinds of plastic.*
verb to perform an experiment; to explore by trying different things. *The cook experimented until he found the right spices for his dish.*

experiment

expert *noun* (<u>ek</u> spərt) someone who knows a great deal about a particular thing. *He is an expert on the history of the American West.*

expiration *noun* (ek spər <u>ā</u> shən) [N] the last time something can or should be used. *I must get a new driver's license before the expiration of my old one.*

Word Builder: expiration +
expiration date: the last day on which something can or should be used. An expiration date is often printed on food or medicine packages.

expire *verb* (ik <u>spīr</u>) to no longer be able to be used. *My driver's license expires in May.*

explain *verb* (ik <u>splān</u>) 1. to give information so that another person can understand something. *The teacher explained the directions to the students.* 2. to give reasons for. *Please explain why you were not at work this morning.*

explanation *noun* (ek splə <u>nā</u> shən) the act or process of making something clear. *Her explanation of the process helped me understand it.*

explode *verb* (ik <u>splōd</u>) to suddenly break into very small pieces with great noise and energy. *Our car tire exploded after we drove over some nails.*

exploration *noun* (ek splər <u>ā</u> shən) 1. the act of exploring new or unknown places. *The early exploration of the great river was filled with danger.* 2. the act of examining or looking at something in detail. *The book is an exploration of the animals of Africa.*

explore *verb* (ik <u>splōr</u>) 1. to travel in order to discover or search for something. *We explored the forest in hope of finding rare kinds of animals.* 2. to try to understand something by looking at it in detail. *Let's explore this idea.*

Word Builder: explore +
explorer: a person who explores.

explosion *noun* (ik <u>splo</u> zhən) the act or noise of breaking open with great force; burst. *They heard the explosion of fireworks in the distance.*

explosive *adj.* (ik <u>splo</u> siv) able to cause an explosion. *Gasoline and fire make an explosive combination.*
noun a substance that is able to cause an explosion. *Dynamite is an explosive.*

explosives

expose *verb* (ək <u>spōz</u>) to show something that you usually cannot see. *We pulled up the carpet and exposed the wood floor.*

exposure *noun* (ik <u>spō</u> zhər) [N] the condition of being open to weather or to a substance. *The exposure of your skin to the sun can cause it to burn.* | *Wear gloves to protect yourself against exposure to this chemical.*

express *verb* (ik <u>spres</u>) to make thoughts or feelings known by saying or writing. *The president's speech expressed his ideas on education.*
adj. without stopping; fast. *We sent the important letter by express mail.*

expression *noun* (ik <u>spre</u> shən) 1. the act of telling or showing thoughts or feelings. *His gift was an expression of his love.* 2. a common saying. *My brother often uses the expression more or less.* 3. an action of the face or body that is able to make feelings known. *She has tears in her eyes and a sad expression on her face.*

extend *verb* (ik <u>stend</u>) 1. to make longer in size or time. *We extended the ladder so that it would reach the top of the tree.* | *The government extended his work permit.* 2. to reach or stretch over an area. *These mountains **extend for** many miles.*

Word Builder: extend +
extended: long or longer than usual.

extension *noun* (ik <u>sten</u> shən) 1. something that makes another thing larger or longer; addition. *They are building an extension to the old school building.* 2. an extra amount of time. *The teacher gave her an extension on her homework.* 3. an extra telephone line connected to the main line. *Dial the number for the office and ask for Mr. Swan's extension.*

exterior *adj.* (ik <u>stēr</u> ē ər) on the outside of something. *The exterior walls of our house are green.*
noun the outside or outer part. *The exterior of the car has a lot of rust.*

external *adj.* (ik st<u>ər</u> nəl) of the outside or outer part. *He cleaned only the external surfaces of the oven.*

extra *adj.* (<u>ek</u> strə) more than is expected or usual. *I asked for extra time to finish the test.*
adv. to a higher degree; more than is usual. *The fabric of those jeans is extra thick.*

extreme *adj.* (ik str<u>ē</u>m) 1. far beyond what is usual or reasonable. *I do not agree with your extreme ideas.* 2. very great; to the highest degree. *She is in extreme pain.*
noun the farthest point or greatest degree. *His moods go from one extreme to the other.*

Word Builder: extreme +
extremely: in or to the greatest degree.

eye *noun* (<u>ī</u>) either of two organs in the body used to see. *My eyes are tired after working at the computer all day.*

eye

Word Builder: eye +
eyecup: a small cup for washing the eye.
eyestrain: a condition where the eyes are tired and sore because they have been used too much.
eyewash station: a special sink or other place in a workplace for washing the eyes.
eyewear: eyeglasses or goggles.

Word Builder: parts of the eye
eyeball: the entire eye, including the part that is inside your head.
eyebrow: a row of hair on the face above the eye.
eyelash: the small hairs that grow on the eyelid or below the eye.
eyelid: the small piece of skin that you move to close your eye.

eyeglasses *pl. noun* (<u>ī</u> glæ siz) round pieces of special glass or plastic held in a frame and worn on the face. Eyeglasses help people see better. *She got a new **pair of eyeglasses.***

F f

fabric *noun* (fǽ brək) [N] a cloth that is woven; material. *The shirt is made of a very soft fabric.*

face *noun* (fās) 1. the part of the head containing the eyes, nose, and mouth. 2. a look or expression that shows feelings. *Why do you have such a sad face?* **verb** to turn or be in a position so that the front is to a particular direction. *Our house faces the road.*

facility *noun* (fə sí lə tē) a building made or used for a particular activity. *The new sports facility will have evening basketball.*

fact *noun* (fækt) something said or known to be true. *It is a fact that water covers most of the earth's surface.* **in fact** in reality; really; indeed. *He's not short. In fact, he's quite tall.*

factor *noun* (fǽk tər) one of the causes of something; something that makes a difference in a result. *Lower housing costs were a factor in our decision to move.*

factory *noun* (fǽk tə rē) a building or set of buildings where products are made by machines. *That factory makes shoes.*

smokestack

factory

fade *verb* (fād) 1. to lose color. *Her black shirt faded after she washed it.* 2. to disappear little by little. *The sound of the train **faded away** into the distance.*

> **Word Builder: fade +**
> **faded:** having little or no color.

fail *verb* (fāl) 1. to not succeed in trying to do something. *Rick **failed in** his effort to start a new business.* 2. to stop working. *The engine failed, so we walked home.* 3. to not do something that is necessary or important. *She failed to pay her taxes on time.* 4. to receive a grade below passing in a test or course of study. *Sue failed her driving test.*

failure *noun* (fāl yər) a person or thing that fails or does not succeed. *The scientist's experiment was a failure.*

faint *adj.* (fānt) 1. weak or slight. *There is a faint smell of fish in the kitchen.* | *We heard a faint whisper.* 2. very tired, dizzy, or about to pass out. *She **felt faint** after standing in the sun for hours.* **verb** to pass out. *Paul faints at the sight of blood.*

fair¹ *adj.* (fār) 1. giving equal treatment. *Mrs. Jones tries to be fair to each of her children.* | *They divided the money in a way that was fair.* 2. according to the rules. *If you don't play the game in a fair way, I won't play it with you.*

fair² *noun* (fār) an event with games, shows, foods, crafts, and other activities. At some fairs, farm animals and farm products are shown and judged. *My pig won a prize at the state fair.*

fairly *adv.* (fār lē) 1. in a just or honest way. *The judge decided the case fairly.* 2. to a degree that is not high but not low. *She is doing fairly well in school.*

faith *noun* (fāth) 1. [N] trust or confidence. *I have faith that I will do well on the test.* 2. religious belief or practice. *Going to church on Sunday was part of his faith.*

faithful *adj.* (fāth fəl) 1. giving loyalty to a person, cause, or idea. *My dog is a faithful friend.* | *She is faithful to the things she believes in.* 2. staying close to fact. *She gave a faithful account of the accident.*

fall *verb* (fawl) **fell, fallen** 1. to move from a higher position to a lower position. *At the end of the play, the curtain fell.* | *He fell from the top of the tree.* 2. to become less; go down in amount or degree. *The price of gasoline fell last month.* | *The students' voices fell to a whisper when the teacher walked in.* 3. to start to be in a particular condition or position; become. *Sue and David were just friends, but last summer they fell in love.* | *He fell behind in his work because he was sick.*
noun the season of the year between summer and winter; autumn.
fall apart to break into pieces. *The cheap toy fell apart after two days.*
fall down to fall to the ground. *Kim slipped on the ice and fell down.*

fallen *verb* (faw lən) past participle of **fall.**

false *adj.* (fawls) 1. not true or not correct. *"The world is flat" is a false statement.* 2. not real; artificial. *She's wearing false eyelashes.*

fame *noun* (fām) [N] the condition of being known by many people. *He **gained fame** as an actor after his last big movie.*

familiar *adj.* (fə míl yər) 1. known by many people. *The audience sang along with the familiar song.* 2. having some knowledge of. *She is **familiar with** that part of town.*

family *noun* (fæm lē) 1. all of the people related to you by blood or marriage. *I have a large family with many cousins, aunts, and uncles.* 2. a group of living things that are related because they are similar in some way. *Lions and tigers are members of the cat family.*

famous *adj.* (fā məs) recognized or liked by the public. *That man is a famous actor.*

fan[1] *noun* (fæn) a machine that makes air move by means of blades that spin. *It's so hot that I can only sleep with the fan on.*

fan[2] *noun* (fæn) a person who is very interested in a sport or art, or in a person who does that activity. *The football fan painted his face in the team colors.*

fancy *adj.* (fæn sē) grander or more special than average. *She wore a fancy dress to the wedding.* | *We bought some fancy cheese for our party.*

fantastic *adj.* (fæn tæ stək) excellent; wonderful. *This food is fantastic!* | *She is a fantastic dancer.*

far *adv.* (far) 1. at or to a long distance in space or time. *We traveled far.* | *Far in the past, people lived in caves.* 2. very much. *My cold is far worse today.*
adj. distant in space or time. *I don't want to walk there because it's too far.*
so far until this point; until the present. *The new worker is doing very well so far.*

fare *noun* (far) the price paid to ride on a bus, train, taxi, or airplane. *The bus fare is only fifty cents for children.*

farm *noun* (farm) an area of land or water used to raise certain kinds of crops or animals. *Those salmon come from a fish farm.*
verb to raise crops or animals. *Many families farm for a living.*

farmer *noun* (far mər) a person who owns or runs a farm. *The farmer planted some new crops in the spring.*

farther *adv.* (far thər) comparative of **far**; at or to a greater distance; further. *Jim rode farther than Charlie did.*
adj. comparative of **far**; more distant. *His office is* **farther from** *the center of town than mine is.*

farthest *adj.* (far thəst) superlative of **far**; most distant. *Hawaii is the* **farthest** *state* **from** *Washington, D.C.*
adv. superlative of **far**; to or at the greatest distance. *I threw the ball farthest.*

fashion *noun* (fæ shən) 1. [N] the style of clothes or way of acting that is popular. *What's the fashion in skirts this summer?* 2. the manner or way of something. *He behaved* **in** *an odd* **fashion** *last night.*

fashionable *adj.* (fæ shə nə bəl) following current styles; popular. *Your new jacket is quite fashionable.*

fast[1] *adj.* (fæst) 1. moving or operating with speed. *He's a fast runner.* | *She drives a fast car.* 2. ahead of the correct time. *That clock is five minutes fast.*
adv. with speed; quickly. *He came home fast when his mother called him for dinner.*

fast[2] *verb* (fæst) to eat no food. *She had to fast for twelve hours before the operation.*

fasten *verb* (fæ sən) 1. to join two sides of something together so that it is closed. *The policeman fastened the badge to his uniform.* 2. to close tight or cause to stay closed with a lock, buttons, or other device. *She fastened her suitcase.* | *Fasten your seatbelts, please.*

> **Word Builder: fasten +**
> **fastener:** a thing used to fasten, such as a zipper, clip, or button.

fast food *noun* (fæst food) [N] food from a restaurant that is made and eaten right away. Fast food is usually not expensive. *It is not healthy to eat too much fast food.*

fast food

fat *adj.* (fæt) 1. having too much weight. *That cat is so fat that he can't jump.* 2. thick or wide. *How many pages does that fat book have?*
noun [N] a white or yellow substance that contains oil and is found in animals and plants. *Ducks have a lot of fat to keep them warm.* | *Whole milk has fat in it.*

fate *noun* (fāt) 1. [N] events that happen in someone's life. *His fate was to get married and have five children.* 2. [N] the power that some people believe decides what will happen in life. *Fate was on her side when she won the contest.*

father *noun* (fa thər) a male parent.

fatigue *noun* (fə tēg) [N] the condition of being tired in body or mind. *The hospital nurses are suffering from fatigue.*

faucet *noun* (faw sət) a device for turning on and off the flow of liquid from a pipe or container. *Mike turned off the faucet when he was done washing.*

fault *noun* (fawlt) responsibility for a mistake or error. *Whose fault is it that the work didn't get done?*

favor *verb* (fā vər) to give special treatment to; prefer. *It's not fair when a parent favors one child over another.* **noun** something kind you do for someone else. *Would you please* **do** *me a* **favor** *and get some milk at the store?*
in favor of in support of. *Most senators voted in favor of the new law.*

favorable *adj.* (fā və rə bəl) giving an advantage. *The favorable winds made it a good day to fly a kite.*

favorite *adj.* (fā və rət or fāv rət) liked over all others. *Oranges are my favorite fruit.*

fax *noun* (fæks) 1. a machine for sending and receiving pages over telephone lines to or from another machine of this kind. *We will send this application by fax so it arrives on time.* 2. a paper copy of a document that is sent by this machine. *Did we receive the fax from the lawyer's office?*

fear *noun* (fer) [N] a strong feeling you get when you expect danger or pain. *Her fear of fire is based on a bad experience.*
verb to be frightened of. *I fear high places.*

Word Builder: fear +
fearful: having or showing fear.
fearless: having or showing no fear.

---

feast *noun* (fēst) a large meal with many different types of foods. *Every Sunday my grandmother cooks a feast for the whole family.*

feather *noun* (fe thər) one of the soft and light parts of a bird that grows from the skin and covers the body. *That bird has beautiful red and orange feathers.* **feather**

feature *noun* (fē chər) 1. a part of the face such as the eyes, nose, or chin. *A baby has tiny features.* 2. a part or quality of something. *The best feature of that house is the large kitchen.*

February *noun* (fe broo ār ē) the second month of the year.

fed *verb* (fed) past tense and past participle of **feed.**

federal *adj.* (fe də rəl) having to do with a system of government that unites several states under a central government. *The leader of the federal government is the president.*

fee *noun* (fē) an amount of money asked or paid for a service. *Doctors and lawyers often charge high fees.*

feed *verb* (fēd) **fed, fed** 1. to provide food for or give food to. *Did you feed the dog this morning?* 2. to put something into; supply. *Lisa fed the fire with sticks.* | *Many small streams feed the lake.*
noun [N] food for birds and animals, such as seeds or grain. *A truck delivered feed for the horses.*

feel *verb* (fēl) **felt, felt** 1. to experience something by the sense of touch. *Can you feel this bump on my head?* 2. to experience a sense of your physical or mental condition. *I feel fine.* 3. to have a belief or opinion. *I'm not sure how I* **feel about** *your idea.*
feel like to have a desire for or interest in. *I feel like going to a movie.*

feeling *noun* (fē ling) 1. [N] the ability to sense things by touch. *After the accident he lost all feeling in his right hand.* 2. an emotion. *Love, anger, joy, and fear are human feelings.*

feet *pl. noun* (fēt) plural of **foot.**

fell *verb* (fel) past tense of **fall.**

fellow *noun* (fe lō) a man or boy. *He's a good fellow.* **adj.** belonging to the same group, having the same job, or sharing the same interests. *The president began his speech with "My fellow countrymen." | Scott and his fellow students raised money for the school trip.*

felony *noun* (fe lə nē) a serious crime such as murder or robbery.

felt[1] *verb* (felt) past tense and past participle of **feel.**

felt[2] *noun* (felt) [N] a cloth made of wool that has been pressed instead of woven together. *The children cut shapes out of felt.*

female *noun* (fē māl) any person or animal of the sex that produces eggs or gives birth. *There are more females than males in my family. | Two of the puppies were females.*
adj. being a member of the sex that produces eggs and gives birth. *We saw a female bird sitting on her nest.*

fence *noun* (fens) a structure used to mark off an area or to keep animals or people in or out. *We built a fence around our house.*

fender *noun* (fen dər) a metal guard over the wheel of a truck, car, or bicycle. *My car fender was bent in the accident.*

fern *noun* (fərn) a family of plants with large green leaves shaped like feathers. Ferns do not make flowers or seeds.

fern

fertile *adj.* (fər təl) 1. producing or able to produce farm crops or other plant life. *The soil in river valleys is fertile.* 2. producing or able to produce young, seeds, fruit, or eggs. *The most fertile cows give birth every year.*

fertilize *verb* (fər tə līz) 1. to make able to support plants and crops. *Farmers fertilize their fields.* 2. to make able to produce young, seeds, fruit, or eggs. *Bees fertilize the flowers.*

fertilizer *noun* (fər tə lī zər) [N] a natural or chemical substance that you add to soil to make it better for growing plants. *Some gardeners use bone meal as a fertilizer.*

festival *noun* (fe stə vəl) a group of shows, events, or special activities usually planned around a type of food, a season, or a kind of art or music. *We tried maple syrup at the maple festival.*

fetch *verb* (fech) to bring back or cause to come; get. *Go and fetch your tools.*

fever *noun* (fē vər) [N] a body temperature higher than normal that is usually caused by illness. *I stayed home from work because I **had** a high **fever**.*

few *adj.* (fū) only a small number of. *Few people become millionaires.* | *There are few seats left.*
noun a very small number. *Few of my friends are married.*
a few a small number of things or people. *I have a few questions to ask you.*
quite a few some; more than you might expect. *Quite a few students were sick last week.*

fiber *noun* (fī bər) a small, thin structure like a thread that can be found in plants, animals, or minerals. *My sweater is made from cotton and wool fibers.* | *Fibers make up the muscles of your body.*

FICA *abbrev.* (fī kə) an abbreviation for *Federal Insurance Contributions Act*. FICA is the law that gets money for Social Security and Medicare from companies and the people who work for those companies.

fiction *noun* (fik shən) [N] writing that tells a story from an author's imagination. *She enjoys reading about facts, but I enjoy reading fiction.*

field *noun* (fēld) 1. a wide area of open land. *That field is planted with wheat.* 2. an open area where sports events take place. *My school has football and baseball fields.*

fierce *adj.* (fērs) wild and dangerous. *A fierce tiger escaped from the zoo.*

fifteen *noun* (fif tēn) the word for the number 15.

fifth *adj.* (fifth) next after fourth.
noun one of five equal parts of a whole.

fifty *noun* (fif tē) the word for the number 50.

fight *noun* (fīt) a battle or argument. *The fight between the two armies began at dawn.* | *My husband and I **had a fight over** money.*
verb fought, fought 1. to use weapons, physical action, mental strength, or words for the purpose of winning an argument, gaining power, or defending yourself. *Many people fought and died in the war.* | *Some boys are fighting outside the school building.* | *The workers and management **fought over** higher pay.* 2. to battle or struggle against someone or something. *He is fighting the champion tonight.* | *She fought cancer for many years.*

figure *noun* (fig yər) 1. a number or other symbol in writing that is not a letter of the alphabet. Some examples of figures are *3* and *&*. 2. the shape of a human body. *His figure hasn't changed in twenty years.*
verb to find an answer to by using numbers. *I figured the cost of the party by adding up how much I spent on food and drinks.*
figure out to begin to understand something or solve a problem by using your mind. *I finally figured out how this new phone works.*

file[1] *noun* (fīl) 1. a place for keeping documents or other objects safe and in order. A file can be something that holds papers or a space on a computer. *She put the report in a file with the other reports.* | *He saved the message as a text file on the hard drive.* 2. the documents or other objects that are kept in this way. *Schools keep files on all their students.*
verb 1. to put or keep safe and in order in a particular place. *The secretary filed the reports in alphabetical order.* 2. to present or send a formal document. *Have you filed your tax return yet?*

Word Builder: file +
file cabinet: a piece of furniture for holding many paper files.

file[2] *noun* (fīl) a hard, thin tool used to shape or smooth wood, metal, plastic, or other hard material. *I used a file to smooth my nails.*

fill *verb* (fil) 1. to cause to become full; put as much as possible into. *He filled the bag with leaves.* 2. to prepare or make up. *The pharmacy **filled** my **prescription** for cough medicine.*
fill in 1. to give or write down information. *I filled in the blanks on the application form.* 2. to take the place of. *Can you fill in for me at work?*
fill out to complete by giving information. *Tenzin had to fill out a form to get his library card.*

film *noun* (film) 1. [N] a thin layer or coating. *There was a film of dust on the desk.* 2. [N] a thin piece of material that is covered with a substance that changes in the light to make photographs and movies. *Is there film in the camera?* 3. a movie. *What film did you see last night?*

filter *noun* (fil tər) a device used to remove dirt or other solids from liquids or gases that pass through it. *A car has an oil filter.*
verb to remove dirt or other solids from a liquid or gas by passing it through a device. *This device filters the water as it comes out of the tap.*

final *adj.* (fī nəl) 1. happening at or being the end of something; last. *The mystery was not solved until the final chapter of the book.* 2. not to be changed. *The decision of the court was final.*

Word Builder: final +
finally: at last.

finance *noun* (fī næns) [N] the business of managing money. *People who work for a bank must know about finance.*
verb (fə næns) to provide money for. *Taxes financed the new highway.*

finance charge *noun* (fī næns charj) an amount charged by a person or business that lends money. *The finance charge is 5 percent of the purchase price.*

financial *adj.* (fə næn shəl) having to do with money. *The company is having financial problems.*

financial aid *noun* (fə næn shəl ād) [N] money provided for students to help pay bills. *He applied to the university for financial aid.*

find *verb* (fīnd) *found, found* 1. to come upon after losing or searching for. *Alex found his father's lost watch.* 2. to discover. *The explorers found a pass through the mountains.*
find out to discover; learn. *Did you find out what time the movie starts?*

fine[1] *adj.* (fīn) 1. very good; excellent. *That was a fine meal.* 2. very thin or delicate. *The baby has such fine hair.* 3. in good health or condition. *I feel fine now.*

fine[2] *noun* (fīn) an amount of money charged as a punishment for a crime or offense. *When you get a traffic ticket, you will have to pay a fine.*

finger *noun* (fing gər) one of the five long parts at the end of the hand.

Word Builder: finger +
fingernail: the hard piece that grows at the end of each finger.
fingertip: the end of each finger.

finish *verb* (fi nəsh) to reach or cause the end of; complete. *Hurry and finish your homework so you can play.*

fire *verb* (fīr) 1. to shoot. *Don't fire that gun!* 2. to let go or dismiss from a job. *The boss fired him for always being late to work.*
noun 1. [N] the heat, light, and flames made when something burns. *Fire destroyed their home.* 2. an instance of burning, as in a stove or furnace, or as something that harms or destroys other things. *We lit a fire in the fireplace. | There was a big fire at that old warehouse.*
catch fire to start to burn. *The paper caught fire when the burning match touched it.*
on fire burning. *Help! The house is on fire!*

firefighter *noun* (fīr fī tər) someone who works to put out fires, either for pay or as a volunteer.

firehouse *noun* (fīr hows) a building to keep trucks and other equipment for fighting fires.

fireman *noun* (fīr mən) *firemen* a male firefighter.

fireplace *noun* (fīr plās) a brick or stone space in a building that you build a fire in. A fireplace has a way to let smoke go to the outside of the building. *A fireplace is a nice way to warm a room.*

fireproof *adj.* (fīr proof) difficult to set on fire, or difficult to damage or destroy with fire. *Firefighters wear fireproof suits to protect them from the flames.*

fireworks *pl. noun* (fīr wərks) things that burn or explode to make noise and colored lights. *There was a display of fireworks on the Fourth of July.*

firm[1] *adj.* (fərm) 1. not soft. *I would rather sleep on a firm mattress.* 2. not likely to be changed; steady. *She has very firm opinions on government.*

firm[2] *noun* (fərm) a business or small company. *The firm that I work for is ten years old.*

first *adj.* (fərst) before all others in time or place. *She was the first person at work today.*
noun the beginning. *It's hard to use a computer* **at first.**
at first on the first occasion or in the beginning. *At first, I really liked my job, but now I'm not happy with it.*

first aid *noun* (fərst ād) [N] the medical help given to hurt or sick persons before they can get to a doctor. *The nurse gave the patient first aid.*

fish *noun* (fish) [N] an animal that lives in water and does not breathe air. Fish have bones inside their bodies and scales on their skin. People catch fish for their meat. Tuna, shark, and salmon are kinds of fish.
verb to catch or try to catch a fish. *People **fish for** salmon in this river.*

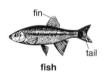
fish

fishing *noun* (fi shing) [N] the activity of catching or trying to catch fish. *My sister enjoys fishing in the creek.*

fishing pole *noun* (fi shing pōl) a long, thin pole with a line and a hook attached to one end that is used to catch fish. *Most fishing poles come in parts that disconnect to make them easier to carry.*

fist *noun* (fist) a hand with the fingers bent under tight.

fit *adj.* (fit) strong and healthy. *Cora is very fit because she exercises daily.*
verb fit, fit to be the right shape and size for. *Does the shirt fit him?*
noun the way in which something fits. *These shoes are a perfect fit.*
fit in to feel a sense of belonging. *You fit in well at your new job.*

Word Builder: fit +
fitted: having a close fit.

five *noun* (fiv) the word for the number 5.

fix *verb* (fiks) 1. to repair. *Do you think you can fix my bike?* 2. to make or prepare. *Eric fixed a delicious dessert.*

flag *noun* (flæg) a piece of cloth with special colors and designs used as a symbol of a country or organization. *The flag of the United States is red, white, and blue.*

flame *noun* (flām) the hot, bright gas that you see when something burns. *Flames leaped from the roof of the burning house.*

flammable *adj.* (flæ mə bəl) able to catch on fire. *Dry leaves are very flammable.*

flannel *noun* (flæ nəl) [N] a soft material made of wool or cotton used for warm clothing and bedcovers. *Shirts made of flannel are very comfortable.*

flash *noun* (<u>flæsh</u>) 1. a sudden, bright light that shines and then disappears. *The flash of lightning was followed by a clap of thunder.* 2. a light on a camera that you use to take pictures when it's dark. *This camera comes with an automatic flash.*

> **Word Builder: flash +**
> **flashcard:** a card you use to help you learn something, such as spelling or math facts. You write the thing you want to learn on the card and try to remember it.
> **flashlight:** a lamp with a strong beam that you hold in your hand.

flat *adj.* (<u>flæt</u>) 1. having a surface that does not have higher and lower places; smooth; even. *It is important that a tennis court be flat.* 2. having little or no air. *The flat tire on his car made him late for work.*

flavor *noun* (<u>flā</u> vər) the particular way something tastes. *Salt brings out the flavor of some foods.*
verb to give a different or special taste to. *The chef flavored the soup with pepper and onion.*

> **Word Builder: flavor +**
> **flavoring:** a substance, such as a spice, that gives a different or special flavor to a food or drink.

flea market *noun* (<u>flē</u> mar kət) a market where used goods are sold for low prices. Flea markets are usually outdoors. *I often find great bargains at the flea market in my town.*

fled *verb* (<u>fled</u>) past tense and past participle of **flee.**

flee *verb* (<u>flē</u>) *fled, fled* to run away or escape. *Burglars usually flee when a dog barks.*

flesh *noun* (<u>flesh</u>) 1. [N] the soft parts of the human or animal body that lie between the skin and the bones. Flesh includes muscle and fat. *An injury to your flesh can be very painful.* 2. [N] the soft part under the skin of a fruit or vegetable. *The flesh of a peach is sweet and juicy.*

flew *verb* (<u>floo</u>) past tense of **fly**[1].

flexible *adj.* (<u>flek</u> sə bəl) 1. able to bend without breaking. *Give the baby some flexible toys.* 2. able to change in order to fit new situations. *They had a flexible plan for the day's activities.*

flight *noun* (<u>flīt</u>) 1. an act of moving through air or space by flying. *Many scientists have studied the flight of birds.* 2. a trip on a plane from one place to another. *His flight to New York leaves in two hours.* 3. a series of stairs between two floors of a building. *We carried the furniture up three flights.*

flight attendant *noun* (<u>flīt</u> ə ten dənt) a person whose job is to help passengers on an airplane during a flight.

flip *verb* (<u>flip</u>) to throw in such a way as to cause to turn over or spin. *He flipped the pancakes so the other side would cook.*

float *verb* (<u>flōt</u>) to rest on the surface of a liquid without sinking. *The girl floated on her back in the water.*

flock *noun* (<u>flak</u>) a group of animals or birds of one kind that stay or are kept together. *The farmer watched over his flock of sheep.* | *A flock of ducks landed on the shore.*

flood *noun* (<u>fləd</u>) a sudden, strong flow of water onto land that should not be underwater. *Our house was destroyed in the flood.*
verb 1. to cover or fill with a flow of water. *The rains flooded the fields.* 2. to fill with too much of something. *Local radio stations were flooded with telephone calls.*

floor *noun* (<u>flōr</u>) 1. the lowest surface of any building or structure. *The floor of our old car is rusted.* 2. a level of a building. *Her office is on the tenth floor.*

floppy *adj.* (<u>fla</u> pē) hanging in a loose way; easy to bend. *Kyle's pet rabbit has floppy ears.*

> **Word Builder: floppy +**
> **floppy disk:** a plastic disk for a computer that stores data.

floss *noun* (<u>flaws</u>) [N] a soft thread used for cleaning between the teeth. *Use floss before you brush your teeth.*

flour *noun* (<u>flowr</u>) [N] the ground meal of wheat or other grain. Flour is used to make bread, cake, and other foods.

flow *verb* (<u>flō</u>) to move in a smooth, steady stream. *The river flows to the sea.* | *Sand flowed through her fingers.*
noun [N] the steady movement of liquids. *They stopped the flow of water by building a dam.*

flower *noun* (<u>flow</u> ər) the colored part of a plant that makes fruit or seeds. Flowers often have a pleasant smell. *He has many beautiful flowers growing in his garden.* **verb** to produce flowers. *Cherry trees flower every spring.*

flower

flown *verb* (<u>flōn</u>) past participle of **fly**[1].

flu *noun* (<u>floo</u>) [N] the short form of **influenza.**

fluctuation *noun* (flək choo <u>ā</u> shən) a change or movement up and down or back and forth. *Fluctuations in temperature are common in spring.*

fluff *noun* (<u>fləf</u>) [N] a soft, light material, such as pieces of wool, cotton, or hair from an animal. *She brushed a piece of fluff from her blouse.*
verb to make something lighter or softer by shaking. *She fluffed her pillow before getting into bed.*

Word Builder: fluff +
fluffy: containing fluff; soft and light.

fluid *noun* (<u>floo</u> əd) a liquid. *It is important to drink plenty of fluids.*

flunk *verb* (<u>fləngk</u>) (informal) to fail as a student, on a test or in a course. *If you flunk the class, you will have to repeat it.*

flush *verb* (<u>fləsh</u>) to wash, clean, or empty with a rush of water. *I flushed my eyes after I got dust in them.* | *I flushed the toilet.*

flute *noun* (<u>floot</u>) an instrument for playing music. It is a long tube made of metal or wood that you play by blowing into a hole at one end.

flute

fly[1] *verb* (<u>flī</u>) *flew, flown* 1. to move through the air by means of wings. *The birds flew over the house.* 2. to travel in an aircraft. *They will fly to Los Angeles next week.* 3. to cause to move through the air. *She flies jets.* | *He is flying a kite.*

fly[2] *noun* (<u>flī</u>) a small common insect with two wings. Sometimes flies carry disease. *There are many flies in the house today.*

focus *noun* (<u>fō</u> kəs) [N] the area of greatest attention or activity. *The focus of the report was changes in the economy.*

verb 1. to turn or move to make a clear image. *Lee focused the camera lens.* 2. to direct to a central point. *You should* **focus your attention on** *your driving.* 3. to direct your attention to something. *She couldn't* **focus on** *her work with all the noise.*

fog *noun* (<u>fag</u> or <u>fawg</u>) [N] a thick mass, like a cloud, made of tiny drops of water that float in the air near the ground. *It is difficult to drive in fog.*

Word Builder: fog +
foggy: full of or covered by fog.

foil *noun* (<u>foyl</u>) [N] a very thin sheet of a metal that you can bend or fold. *Cover the food with foil before you put it away.*

fold *verb* (<u>fōld</u>) to bend something so that one part lies on top of another part. *She folded the letter before putting it in the envelope.*

folk *adj.* (<u>fōk</u>) having to do with the art forms in the tradition of a group of people. *They enjoyed an evening of folk music.*

folks *pl. noun* (<u>fōks</u>) 1. (informal) parents or family members. *I'm having dinner with my folks tonight.* | *All of her folks live in Texas.* 2. (informal) people. *My neighbors are really nice folks.*

follow *verb* (<u>fa</u> lō) 1. to come or go after or behind. *He followed me down the street.* 2. to take place after. *A party will follow the wedding.* 3. to understand. *Did you follow the story he told?*

Word Builder: follow +
follower: a person who follows.

follow-up *adj.* (<u>fa</u> lō əp) serving to check something again at a later time. *The doctor ordered a follow-up visit.*

fond *adj.* (<u>fand</u>) having or showing feelings of love. *He has fond memories of his grandparents.*

food *noun* (<u>food</u>) [N] anything that living creatures eat. *Scientists are studying ways to grow more food.* | *Honey is food for bees.*

food stamps *pl. noun* (<u>food</u> stæmps) a government program that pays for food. People who do not have enough money to buy food can apply for food stamps.

fool *noun* (<u>fool</u>) a person who has poor sense or judgment. *Max is a fool to think he could get up late and get to school on time.*
verb to trick into believing something that is not true. *He fooled his friend with a card trick.*
fool around to behave in a silly way. *He was fooling around when he should have been working.*

foolish *adj.* (<u>foo</u> ləsh) having poor sense; silly. *It was foolish to go out in the snow without a coat.*

foot *noun* (<u>fut</u>) *feet* 1. the part at the end of the leg that has toes. 2. a standard unit used to measure length. One foot equals 12 inches.

football *noun* (<u>fut</u> bawl) 1. [N] in the United States and Canada, a game played by two teams. You get points by carrying, kicking, or throwing a ball to one end of a long field. *Football is a popular sport in the United States.* 2. the leather ball used in this game. *Sue wants a new football for her birthday.* 3. the name for soccer in countries other than the United States and Canada.

for *prep.* (<u>for</u>) 1. used to show the purpose or aim of an action. *They are working for peace.* | *He was heading for the door.* 2. used to show who is to receive something or how it is to be used. *The gift is for Julie.* | *I put some money aside for a new bike.*
conj. since; because. *I don't know if the house is big or small, for I've never seen it.*

> **for or since?**
> *For* tells how long an action or state has continued over time.
> *Since* tells when an action or state began.
> Compare:
> *I have lived here for five years.*
> *I have lived here since 1999.*

forbade *verb* (for <u>bæd</u>) past tense of **forbid.**

forbid *verb* (fər <u>bid</u>) *forbade, forbidden* to give orders that prevent some action; to not allow. *Her parents forbid her to smoke.*

forbidden *verb* (fər <u>bi</u> dən) past participle of **forbid.**

force *noun* (<u>fors</u>) 1. [N] power, energy, or physical strength. *The force of the wind knocked down the trees.* 2. a group of people with a common goal or activity. *She is a member of the police force.*

verb to make or cause to do something by using strength or power. *Ivan forced her to tell the truth.*

forecast *verb* (<u>for</u> kæst) *forecast, forecast* to say that something is likely to happen. *The weather report forecasts rain for this afternoon.*
noun a guess or estimate about something that will happen in the future. *I'm waiting to hear the weather forecast.*

forehead *noun* (<u>for</u> hed) the part of the human face above the eyes and below the hair.

foreign *adj.* (<u>faw</u> rən) in, from, or having to do with a country that is not one's own. *For people who live in Mexico, English is a foreign language.*

> **Word Builder: foreign +**
> **foreigner:** a person who was born in or is from a foreign country.

forest *noun* (<u>for</u> əst) a large area of land covered with many trees and other plants. *Many animals live in the forest.*

forever *adv.* (fə <u>re</u> vər) continuing for all time. *Dinosaurs are gone forever.*

forgave *verb* (fər <u>gav</u>) past tense of **forgive.**

forget *verb* (fər <u>get</u>) *forgot, forgotten* to not remember. *Don't forget to lock the door when you go out.*

forgive *verb* (fər <u>giv</u>) *forgave, forgiven* to excuse or not be angry with someone. *Forgive me for not remembering your birthday.*

forgiven *verb* (fər <u>gi</u> vən) past participle of **forgive.**

forgot *verb* (fər <u>gat</u>) past tense and past participle of **forget.**

forgotten *verb* (fər <u>ga</u> tən) past participle of **forget.**

fork *noun* (<u>fork</u>) 1. a tool with a handle and two or more points used for eating or lifting food. *Eat meat with a fork and soup with a spoon.* 2. the point where something divides into two or more branches, or one of the branches. *Turn right at the fork in the road.* | *We followed the left fork of the river.*

forklift *noun* (<u>fork</u> lift) a machine or small truck used to lift and move heavy objects. *Many factories move pallets with a forklift.*

form *noun* (fŏrm) 1. the shape or structure of something. *He arranged the chairs in the form of a circle.* | *She presented the results of the survey in the form of a graph.* 2. a document with empty spaces for writing in information. *She **filled out a form** to apply for a passport.* 3. a type or kind of something. *She has a rare form of cancer.*
verb to make, build, or give a shape to. *He formed the clay into a pot.*

formal *adj.* (fŏr məl) 1. following accepted rules or standards of behavior; legal; official. *He made a formal request for parental leave to his supervisor.* | *A lease is a formal document.* 2. following special rules or tradition. *Their parents want them to have a formal wedding.* 3. proper and serious, not relaxed and easy. *You need to use more formal language in a job interview.*

former *adj.* (fŏr mər) 1. happening in or having to do with the past; previous. *He was a great baseball player in his former career.* 2. being the first of two. *Of the two choices, she preferred the former.*

Word Builder: former +
formerly: in the past.

formula *noun* (fŏrm yə lə) 1. a group of words or symbols used to express a standard way of doing something, or a way to find an answer to a problem. *The teacher taught the formula to find out the area of a triangle.* | *We are looking for a formula for success.* 2. exact instructions for how to make something. *Our company is using a new formula in its cleaning products.* 3. a liquid food for babies; artificial milk. *My doctor recommended a different formula for my baby.*

fort *noun* (fŏrt) a strong building used for defense or for soldiers to live in. *The army built a fort on the hill above the river.*

forth *adv.* (fŏrth) forward in time or location; used most often in the phrase *back and forth. She swam back and forth across the pool.*

fortunate *adj.* (fŏr chə nət) having good fortune; lucky. *You are fortunate to receive such a good education.*

Word Builder: fortunate +
fortunately: happening because of good luck.

fortune *noun* (fŏr chən) 1. a large amount of money or wealth. *She made her fortune buying and selling land.* 2. [N] a person's luck; the results of experiences during a person's life. *Some say it was her fortune to become a great leader.*

forty *noun* (fŏr tē) the word for the number 40.

forward *adv.* (fŏr wərd) 1. toward a place or time that is further on or in the future; ahead. *The line for tickets finally moved forward.* 2. toward the front. *The chairs face forward in a movie theater.* | *The doctor turned her face forward to look in her eyes.*

forwards *adv.* (fŏr wərdz) 1. toward a place that is farther ahead. *The band marched forwards across the football field.* 2. toward the front. *She was looking at her friend when the teacher asked her to face forwards.*

fought *verb* (fawt) past tense and past participle of **fight.**

foul *adj.* (fowl) 1. not pleasant to taste, smell, or look at. *Those old socks give off a foul odor.* 2. falling outside of the lines that mark an area for fair play in a sport. *He hit a foul ball.*

found *verb* (fownd) past tense and past participle of **find.**

foundation *noun* (fown dā shən) 1. the base of something such as an action, substance, structure, or opinion. *He has enough money to give his business a good foundation.* | *Your ideas about her are completely without foundation.* 2. the stone or concrete structure that holds up a building from beneath. *A house built on a strong foundation will last many years.*

fountain *noun* (fown tən) a spray of water made by a machine, or the structure from which the water flows. *There is a drinking fountain in the hall.*

four *noun* (fŏr) the word for the number 4.

fourteen *noun* (fŏr tēn) the word for the number 14.

fourth *adj.* (fŏrth) next after third.
noun one of four equal parts of a whole.

fox *noun* (faks) a wild mammal that has a pointed nose, pointed ears, and a long, thick tail.

fox

fracture *noun* (fræk chər) a break or crack. *The fracture in his leg took six weeks to heal.*
verb to break or cause a break in. *She fractured her arm.*

frame *noun* (frām) 1. a simple structure that supports a larger object. *The builders have finished the frame for the new house. They will put up the walls next week.* 2. a border that fits around something. *I need a* **picture frame** *for this photograph.* | *The new frames for the windows are aluminum.*

fray *verb* (frā) to become thin from washing or use. *This kind of fabric frays soon after you wash it.*

free *adj.* (frē) 1. not held back or under the control of another person; not in prison. *The prisoner forgot what it was like to be free.* 2. having a type of government that is controlled by all the people and that gives rights to all the people. *We are lucky to live in a free nation.* 3. without cost. *That store gives a free balloon to every child.* 4. empty; not in use. *Is this seat free?*
adv. without being held back or under control. *The dog likes to run free.*
verb to set loose; make free. *Jeremy freed the animal from the cage.*
for free for no money; at no cost. *When you buy ten cups of coffee, you get the next cup for free.*

Word Builder: free +
freely: in a free way.

freedom *noun* (frē dəm) 1. [N] the condition of being free to act or move as one wishes. *Under the new government, people have freedom to travel inside and outside the country.* | *The employees have freedom to wear whatever clothes they want.* 2. a specific right. *Freedom of speech is a right enjoyed by all Americans.*

freeway *noun* (frē wā) a long, wide public road with no stop signs or traffic lights. Vehicles travel very fast on freeways.

freeze *verb* (frēz) *froze, frozen* 1. to make into ice or become solid from cold temperatures. *Rivers and lakes often freeze in the winter.* 2. to feel very cold in your body. *I'm freezing. I want to go inside.* 3. to make food extra cold and solid in order to keep it fresh. *Freeze the meat if you do not plan to cook it right away.*

Word Builder: freeze +
freezer: a very cold refrigerator that freezes foods.
freezing: very cold.

freight *noun* (frāt) [N] goods shipped by boat, plane, train, or truck. *The truck is carrying hundreds of pounds of freight.*

French fries *pl. noun* (french frīz) potatoes cut into long pieces and cooked in hot fat.

frequent *adj.* (frē kwənt) happening often or repeated often. *We make frequent trips to the store for milk.*

Word Builder: frequent +
frequently: often.

fresh *adj.* (fresh) just made, received, cleaned, or experienced. *They enjoyed a fresh cup of tea.* | *Please put on a fresh shirt.*

friction *noun* (frik shən) 1. [N] the rubbing of one object or surface against another. *If you rub two sticks together, the friction will create heat and sparks.* 2. [N] disagreement between people or groups of people; conflict. *It upsets me that there is so much friction in our family.*

Friday *noun* (frī dā) the sixth day of the week. Friday comes between Thursday and Saturday.

friend *noun* (frend) a person whom you know well and like and who likes you. *Sheila and I have been friends since we were children.*

friendly *adj.* (frend lē) pleasant toward others. *I try to be friendly toward people that I don't like.* | *Our town is a friendly place.*

friendship *noun* (frend ship) the state or condition of being a friend. *Their friendship has lasted for many years.*

frighten *verb* (frī tən) to cause fear in someone; to make someone afraid. *The fierce dog frightened the children.*

Word Builder: frighten +
frightened: feeling fear; scared.
frightening: causing fear; scary.

frog *noun* (frag or frawg) a small, jumping animal with smooth, wet skin, long back legs, and no tail. Frogs live in or near water. frog

from *prep.* (frəm) 1. used to show a starting point in place or time. *We ran from his house to mine.* | *We are meeting her one hour from now.* 2. used to tell the source of something. *Joe is from Kentucky.* | *Wood comes from trees.* 3. used to show distance. *It is 200 miles from here to New York City.* 4. used to show cause. *They were tired out from sledding.*

front *noun* (frənt) 1. the most forward part or side of something. *The entrance is at the front of the building.* 2. the position or place at the head or beginning. *He went to the front of the line.* 3. the forward edge of a mass of cold or warm air. *It started to rain as the cold front came closer.*

frost *noun* (frawst) [N] a thin, light, white covering of water or ice. *This morning, the grass is covered with frost.*
verb to put a sweet covering on. *She frosted the cake.*

frosting *noun* (fraw sting) [N] a sweet covering for cake. Frosting is usually made of sugar, butter, and flavoring. *We had chocolate cake with vanilla frosting.*

frown *verb* (frown) to turn the corners of the mouth down to show that you are not happy. *Why are you frowning?*
noun the look on your face when you are unhappy or upset. *I could tell by his frown that he didn't like the food.*

froze *verb* (frōz) past tense of **freeze.**

frozen *verb* (frō zən) past participle of **freeze.**
adj. changed into a solid or made hard by freezing. *Ice is frozen water.*

fruit *noun* (froot) the part of a plant that has seeds and flesh, such as an apple or berry.

frustrate *verb* (frə strāt) to prevent from happening or being done. *Bad weather frustrated our plans for a picnic.*

Word Builder: frustrate +
frustrated: feeling frustration.
frustrating: causing frustration.

---

frustration *noun* (frəs strā shən) [N] a feeling that something is stopping you from getting something or doing something. *There is a lot of frustration among the workers in that office.*

fry *verb* (frī) to cook in hot butter, oil, or other fat. *Would you like to fry these vegetables or steam them?*

frying pan *noun* (frī ing pæn) a shallow pan with a long handle used to cook food. *Do you have a cover for the frying pan?*

frying pan

fuel *noun* (fūl) anything such as wood or gasoline that is burned as a source of energy. *A car cannot operate without fuel.*

full *adj.* (ful) holding as much as possible. *The trunk is full, so put your suitcase in the back seat.*

Word Builder: full +
fully: in full; so as to be complete.

---

full-time *adj.* (ful tīm) involving or working the standard number of hours per week. In America, it is forty hours. *James has a full-time job.*

fume *noun* (fūm) gas, smoke, or a smell that is not pleasant or healthy. *Breathing the paint fumes made him dizzy.*

fun *noun* (fən) [N] something that amuses, entertains, or pleases. *Flying the kite was a lot of fun.*
make fun of to laugh at or make jokes about. *The kids made fun of me when I was young because I wore glasses.*

function *noun* (fəngk shən) the purpose for which an object or a person is used. *The function of a police officer is to keep the peace. | The function of scissors is to cut things.*
verb to run or operate. *The city cannot function in a normal way without electricity. | The heart functions by pumping blood.*

funeral *noun* (fū nə rəl) a ceremony for a person who has died. *Many friends and relatives attended Mr. Newman's funeral.*

fungi *pl. noun* (fəng gī) plural of **fungus.**

fungus *noun* (fəng gəs) *fungi* a kind of living thing that is similar to a plant but that cannot make its own food. Some kinds of fungi are mushrooms and mold[2].

funny *adj.* (fə nē) 1. causing laughter or amusement. *John likes to tell funny stories.* 2. strange or odd; unusual. *There was a funny smell in the attic.*

fur *noun* (fər) 1. [N] the soft, thick hair that covers the bodies of certain animals such as a bear or rabbit. *In winter, the bear's fur becomes very thick.* 2. the skin of an animal that has such hair, used in the making of clothing or other objects. *The jacket is made of rabbit fur.*

furious *adj.* (fūr ē əs) full of anger. *She was furious that he took all of her money.*

furnace *noun* (fər nəs) a large appliance for making heat by burning gas, oil, coal, or wood.

furnish *verb* (fər nəsh) to supply with furniture. *They still have not furnished their apartment.*

Word Builder: furnish +
furnished: having or including furniture.

furniture *noun* (fər nə chər) [N] objects such as chairs, tables, and beds used to fill a living area. *My grandmother bought beautiful new furniture for my bedroom.*

further *adv.* (fər thər) comparative of **far;** at or to a greater distance. *We drove further today than we did yesterday.*
adj. 1. comparative of **far;** more distant. *Los Angeles is* **further from** *New York than Chicago is.* 2. more. *Are there any further questions?*

farther or further?
Farther and *further* have the same meaning. You can use either *farther* or *further* as an adverb to describe a distance in space or time. But it is more common to use *further* in other adverb senses and as an adjective.
Compare:
Drive farther until you reach the traffic light.
I want nothing further from him.
Do you have any further questions?

furthest *adj.* (fər thəst) superlative of **far;** most distant. *My house is the furthest one from the corner.*
adv. superlative of **far;** to or at the greatest distance or extent. *My father went furthest in education of anyone in his family.*

fuse *noun* (fūz) a short wire in an electric system. A fuse prevents too much electricity from flowing through the system. *This car has about fifteen fuses, including one for the headlights and one for the power windows.*

future *noun* (fū chər) [N] a time that is still to come. *He hopes to become a teacher in the future.*

G g

gain *verb* (gān) 1. to get. *He worked hard to gain respect.* 2. to get more of something that you already have. *I gained some weight.*

gallon *noun* (gǽ lən) a standard unit used to measure liquid. *Gasoline is sold by the gallon.*

gamble *verb* (gǽm bəl) to risk money or other things on the way a game, race, or other event will end. *She gambled on the horse race and lost 50 dollars.*

game *noun* (gām) a form of play or sport having certain rules and equipment for play. *We enjoyed a game of chess.* | *My whole family went to the football game.*

gang *noun* (gǽng) a group of people who do things together. These things may be just for fun or may involve crime. *A gang of high school kids were playing basketball in the park.* | *Gangs are responsible for a lot of crime in the city.*

gap *noun* (gǽp) a space or opening between two things. *I have a gap between my two front teeth.* | *She will fix the gap in the fence tomorrow.*

garage *noun* (gə rǽzh) 1. a building or part of a building used for keeping cars, trucks, or other vehicles. *We parked our car in the downtown garage while we went shopping.* 2. a business for repairing cars, trucks, or other vehicles. *Our old car is at the garage for repairs again.*

garbage *noun* (gǽr bəj) [N] food or other things that are thrown away. *There was a lot of garbage in the street after the festival.*

garbage

Word Builder: garbage +
garbage can: a large can in which you put garbage.

garden *noun* (gǽr dən) an area of land used for growing flowers or vegetables. *I grow tomatoes and beans in my garden.*
verb to plant or take care of a garden. *My family gardens in the summer.*

Word Builder: garden +
gardener: a person who gardens for fun or for work.
gardening: the activity of planting and taking care of a garden.

garment *noun* (gǽr mənt) any piece of clothing. *It is wise to separate garments by color before washing.*

gas *noun* (gǽs) 1. [N] a form of matter that is neither liquid nor solid. Oxygen is an example of a gas. *Poisonous gas was leaking from the factory.* 2. [N] a short form of gasoline. *We should get gas before we get on the highway.*

gasoline (gasolene) *noun* (gǽ sə lēn) [N] a liquid that burns and is used as fuel for engines. *Most automobiles run on gasoline.*

gas station *noun* (gǽs stā shən) a place where people buy gas, oil, and some other supplies for a car. *There is a gas station on the next street.*

gate *noun* (gāt) a place where people or things enter or leave. *You have to check in at the gate before you get onto the airplane.* | *We climbed over the fence because there was no gate.*

gather *verb* (gǽ thər) to bring together into one place; collect. *We gathered the apples from under the tree.* | *We gathered the children together and took them home.*

gauze *noun* (gawz) [N] a thin cotton cloth often used to cover a wound. *Keep gauze on the wound until it heals.*

gauze pad *noun* (gawz pǽd) a piece of thin cotton, woven material that is made into a covering for a wound. *Tape the gauze pad over your cut, and it will heal faster.*

gave *verb* (gāv) past tense of **give.**

gear *noun* (gēr) 1. a part of a machine that causes another part to move because of teeth that connect the two moving parts. *I shift the gears in my car as I increase speed.* 2. [N] any equipment, clothes, or tools used for some particular purpose. *The hikers packed their camping gear. The workers put on their safety gear before climbing up the ladder.*

Word Builder: gear +
gearshift: a part in a car for changing from one gear to another.

GED *abbrev.* (jē ē dē) an abbreviation for *General Educational Development.* You can take the GED test and get a diploma if you did not finish high school.

geese *pl. noun* (gēs) plural of **goose.**

gender *noun* (jen dər) the sex of a person or animal. *It is against the law to discriminate against someone because of gender.*

general *adj.* (je̱ nər əl or je̱n rəl) 1. having to do with a group as a whole; including or concerning the whole group. *The general public is invited to the meeting.* | *The general opinion of the teachers was positive.* 2. not detailed; not specific. *He gave us a general idea of what the new building would look like.*
noun an officer of high rank in the military. *The general was known for making good decisions in battle.*
in general 1. not considering details that do not agree with the rule; usually; generally. *In general, her work is perfect. This mistake was unusual.* | *I like students, in general.* 2. looking at the group as a whole; not concerning any particular member of a group. *I was talking about cats in general. I wasn't talking about this particular cat.*

generally *adv.* (je̱ nə rə le̱ or je̱n rə le̱) 1. in most ways; not considering any details that do not agree. *The doctor said my grandmother was generally healthy but should get more rest.* 2. usually. *We generally get home around six o'clock.*

generation *noun* (je̱ nə ra̱ shən) the entire group of people who were born around the same time. *People of my grandmother's generation did not have television.*

generous *adj.* (je̱ nə rəs) willing to give or share. *She is a generous person who gives a lot of time to help other people.* | *He is **generous with** his money.*

genius *noun* (je̱n yəs) 1. [N] an intelligence much greater than what most people have. *This young child's ability in mathematics shows her genius.* 2. a person who has this level of intelligence. *All of the professors are smart, but this new professor is a genius.*

gentle *adj.* (je̱n təl) 1. not intending to cause pain or trouble to other people or animals; kind. *The veterinarian was gentle with the sick cat.* 2. soft, not hard or violent. *A gentle breeze blew through the leaves.* | *The nurse spoke in a gentle voice.*

Word Builder: gentle +
gently: in a gentle way.

gentleman *noun* (je̱n təl mən) *gentlemen* 1. a polite man. *A gentleman apologizes when he has hurt someone.* 2. a polite word for **man.** *I believe this gentleman was next in line.*

geography *noun* (je̱ a̱ grə fe̱) 1. [N] the study of the earth's surface, climate, landforms, and bodies of water. 2. [N] physical features of a region or place on the earth. *The geography of Asia includes many mountains.*

geometry *noun* (je̱ a̱ mə tre̱) [N] the study in mathematics of objects and shapes such as lines, angles, circles, and triangles.

geometry

germ *noun* (jərm) a very, very small living thing that causes illness. *It is important to wash your hands to get rid of germs.*

get *verb* (ge̱t) *got, gotten* 1. to gain; obtain. *I got some apples at the supermarket.* 2. to become sick with. *I think I'm getting a cold.* 3. to cause to do a particular thing or to be in a particular state. *It is difficult to get my son to eat vegetables.* | *It was hard to get the piano into the house.* | *I can't get this window open.* 4. to understand. *Do you get the meaning?* 5. to have the opportunity to do something that you enjoy. *The kids are excited because they get to stay overnight with their cousins.* 6. to arrive. *I get to work at eight o'clock every day.* 7. to become; to enter a different state. *She is getting angry.* | *What time did you get back last night?* | *He fell, and he couldn't get up.* 8. to begin the doing of something; start. *Let's get going early in the morning.*
get across to become understood or make something understood. *He makes mistakes in English, but he gets his ideas across.*
get along to have a smooth relationship with someone without any problems. *Your two little girls get along so well. They never seem to argue.* | *He doesn't **get along with** his roommate.*
get off to leave a public vehicle after riding. *Could you tell me where to get off the bus?*
get on to enter a public vehicle in order to ride. *I got on the bus and found a seat.*
get out to leave. *We got out of school early today.* | *He is getting out of prison next month.*
get over to become healthy again after an illness or feel better after a bad experience. *I'm getting over the flu.* | *He's finally getting over his wife's death.*
get up to rise from bed. *I have to get up early tomorrow.*

GFCI *abbrev.* (jē ef sē ī) an abbreviation for *ground fault circuit interrupter*. A GFCI is a device that shuts down an electric circuit when it senses a sudden loss of power. It protects people from severe electric shocks.

gift *noun* (gift) something a person gives without wanting anything in return; a present. *I gave her a gift after she helped me move to my new apartment.*

girl *noun* (gərl) a female child. *There are seven girls and eight boys in my class.*

girlfriend (girl friend) *noun* (gərl frend) 1. a favorite female friend with whom you have a romantic relationship. *He gave flowers to his girlfriend.* 2. a friend who is a female. *She invited all her girlfriends to her party.*

give *verb* (giv) *gave, given* 1. to present someone with something without expecting its return. *She gave me a new hat and gloves.* | *My supervisor gave me my pay envelope.* 2. to put into someone's hands. *Could you give me that telephone book over there?* 3. to provide someone with something. *We gave medical aid to the injured passengers.*
give away 1. to give someone something without asking for payment. *He gave away all his furniture.* 2. to give some information that is secret or would be a surprise to someone. *Don't give away the movie ending.*
give in to agree to something you don't want to agree to, especially after a long argument. *I finally gave in to my son and let him drive my new car.*
give up 1. to stop. *He gave up playing football after breaking his hand.* 2. to stop trying to do something. *She gave up playing the violin because it was too difficult.*

given *verb* (gi vən) past participle of **give.**
prep. considering; taking into account. *Given the cold weather, I'll wear my winter coat.* | *Given her experience, I'm not surprised that she does the job well.*

given name *noun* (gi vən nām) a person's first name, given at birth. *Her given name is Mary.*

glad *adj.* (glæd) happy that a good thing has happened or will happen. *I am so glad my exams are over!* | *We are very glad that you can come.*

gland *noun* (glænd) an organ in the body that produces liquid substances from materials in the blood. *The glands in my neck are swollen.*

glass *noun* (glæs) 1. [N] a hard, clear material. Glass is used to make things such as windows, bottles, and mirrors. *The glass in the front window is cracked.* 2. a container used for drinking, usually made of glass. *I bought new glasses for the dinner party.*

glasses *pl. noun* (glæ səz) a short form of **eyeglasses.**

 glasses

> **Word Builder: kinds of glasses**
> **safety glasses:** special glasses that protect the eyes; goggles.
> **sunglasses:** glasses that protect your eyes from the sun.

gloat *verb* (glōt) to feel or show pleasure when you have succeeded more than others or when someone else has failed at something. *Secretly, Maria gloated when her rich brother lost his money.*

globe *noun* (glōb) 1. the world; planet Earth. *She traveled around the globe.* 2. a round ball with a map of the earth on it, or anything shaped like a ball. *The students looked at the globe to find Spain.*

glory *noun* (glōr ē) 1. [N] great honor, praise, or fame. *The team earned glory after winning the world championship.* 2. [N] great beauty. *I still remember the glory of the view from the top of the mountain.*

glove *noun* (gləv) a covering for the hand that has separate parts for each finger and the thumb.

glow *noun* (glō) [N] a steady light, especially the light given off by something very hot. *The fire's glow lit the path.*
verb to shine with bright light from being very hot. *The coals were so hot that they glowed.*

glue *noun* (gloo) [N] a thick, sticky liquid used to join things together. *The children used glue to stick the pieces of paper together.*
verb to fasten or hold with glue or as if with glue. *I glued the broken pieces back together.* | *His eyes were **glued to** the television.*

go *verb* (gō) *went, gone* 1. to move; travel. *I go to school by bus.* | *We went to the beach on Saturday.* 2. to move away from a place; leave. *We will miss her when she goes.* 3. to reach from one point to another. *The driveway goes from the house to the road.* 4. to pass. *Time goes fast when you are busy.* 5. to make a certain sound. *The engine went "bang!"* 6. to become. *The milk has gone sour.* 7. to belong with something else or belong in a certain place or position. *This price tag goes with that shirt, not this one.* | *The stamp goes on the right side of the envelope.*

go out to stop burning. *It's cold because the fire went out.*

be going to used as an auxiliary verb to express that someone has a plan to do something or that some action or state seems likely based on certain evidence. *I'm going to call the doctor tomorrow.* | *Come inside now. It's going to rain.*

goal *noun* (gōl) 1. a result or end that a person wants and works for; aim or purpose. *Her goal is to become a doctor.* 2. the area in certain sports into which a player must move a ball or other object in order to score. *The soccer player kicked the ball into the goal.*

goat *noun* (gōt) a mammal with rough hair and horns. People keep goats for their milk and meat.

goat

god *noun* (gad) a being that is worshipped and believed to have special powers over nature or life. *The people of ancient Greece believed in many different gods.*

goggles *pl. noun* (ga gəlz) a special clear cover that you wear over your eyes to protect them. *You should wear goggles when you work with dangerous chemicals.*

gold *noun* (gōld) [N] a soft, heavy, yellow metal that is valuable and used to make jewelry.
adj. having the color of the metal gold, or bright yellow.

Word Builder: gold +
golden: being like gold in color or some other way.

gone *verb* (gawn or gan) past participle of **go.**
adj. used completely; not here anymore. *The candy is gone.*

good *adj.* (gud) 1. having qualities that are desired. *That was a good movie.* | *She makes good soup.* 2. morally right. *A good person helps other people.* 3. pleasant.

We had a good time at the park. 4. well; healthy; comfortable. *I feel good today.*
noun something that causes an improvement; advantage. *The new laws were for the good of all the people.*
for good forever; permanently. *He has moved to New York for good.*

good or well?
Good is an adjective.
Well is the adverb form of *good.*
Compare:
He is a good baseball player.
He hits the ball well.

good-bye *interj.* (gud bī) a word used when you are leaving or when ending a telephone call. *Good-bye! I'll see you when I get back.* | *Good-bye! I'll talk to you later.*

goods *pl. noun* (gudz) things to buy and sell. *Factories produce goods, and stores sell them.* | *That shop is known for its baked goods.*

goose *noun* (goos) *geese* a bird with a long neck and large feet that lives in or near water. People hunt or keep geese for their meat.

got *verb* (gat) 1. past tense and past participle of **get.** 2. informal pronunciation of the phrase **have got.**

gotten *verb* (ga tən) past participle of **get.**

govern *verb* (gə vərn) to rule or lead. *The king governed the country.*

Word Builder: govern +
governor: a person who governs. In the United States, a governor is the elected leader of a state.

government *noun* (gə vərn mənt) the group of people that has power to make laws and important decisions for a community, state, or nation. *The city government decided to build a public swimming pool.*

grab *verb* (græb) to take hold of suddenly or with force. *The man grabbed his hat and ran out.*

grace *noun* (grās) 1. [N] beauty in form, style, motion, or behavior. *She moved with the grace of a dancer.* 2. [N] a prayer said before, or sometimes after, eating. *We bowed our heads and said grace.*

Word Builder: grace +
graceful: moving with grace.

grade *noun* (grād) 1. a level, degree, or rank in a scale, including mark or evaluation in school. *These eggs are the top grade.* 2. a rank of students in a school based on the age of children, or all the students in a school who are in that rank. *Chris is in second grade. | The whole sixth grade went to the museum yesterday.*

gradual *adj.* (græ joo əl) happening by degrees that are small and even. *There was a gradual change in the weather. | The tree showed gradual growth.*

> **Word Builder: gradual +**
> **gradually:** by degrees, one small step at a time.

graduate *noun* (græ joo ət) a person who has finished the required studies at a high school or college. *You must be a high school graduate to apply for this job.*
adj. having to do with a level of study beyond a bachelor's degree. *My son is a graduate student now, working on his master's degree.*
verb (græ joo āt) to successfully finish required studies at a school or college. *She will **graduate from** high school this spring.*

graduation *noun* (græ joo ā shən) 1. [N] the act or process of successfully completing required studies at a high school or college. *Everyone must pass this class for graduation.* 2. the ceremony at which students receive a diploma or degree after successfully finishing school. *My family will come to my college graduation.*

grain *noun* (grān) 1. [N] the small hard seeds of plants such as wheat or rice. Grain is used for food and often ground into flour. *Chickens eat grain.* 2. any kind of plant that produces seeds that are used for food. *Rice, wheat, and corn are grains.* 3. any tiny, hard piece of something. *You spilled some grains of sugar on the floor.* 4. [N] the pattern that runs through wood, cloth, or other material. *By looking at the grain, he can tell which kind of wood the table is made of.*

grain

gram *noun* (græm) the international standard unit used to measure weight.

grammar *noun* (græ mər) [N] the study of the way the words of a language are put together and used for communication.

grand *adj.* (grænd) of the highest rank; very important. *The grand prize was a new car.*

grandchild *noun* (grænd chīld) the child of one's son or daughter.

granddaughter *noun* (græn daw tər) the female child of one's son or daughter.

grandfather *noun* (grænd fa thər) the father of a person's mother or father.

grandmother *noun* (grænd mə thər) the mother of a person's father or mother.

grandparent *noun* (grænd paer ənt) the father or mother of one's parent; a grandmother or grandfather.

grandson *noun* (grænd sən) the male child of one's son or daughter.

grape *noun* (grāp) a small fruit with purple or green skin. Grapes are used to make wine, juice, or other food products.

grapefruit *noun* (grāp froot) a large, round, sour fruit with yellow or pink skin. Grapefruits grow on trees.

graph *noun* (græf) a drawing that shows information and the relationships between pieces of that information. *This graph shows the change in world population in the past fifty years.*

grasp *verb* (græsp) 1. to take hold of with a hand. *He grasped the suitcase by its handle.* 2. to understand or get the meaning of. *He grasped the rules of the game quickly.*
noun mental or physical power over something; control. *The new leader has a powerful grasp on the people. | She has a good grasp of mathematics.*

grass *noun* (græs) [N] a short green plant with narrow pointed leaves that usually covers fields and yards. *My son hates to cut the grass.*

grave *noun* (grāv) a hole dug in the ground where a dead body is buried. *She visits her husband's grave every Sunday.*

gravel *noun* (græ vəl) [N] a loose mixture of small stones and sometimes sand. *The parking lot is covered with gravel.*

gravity *noun* (græ və tē) 1. [N] the force by which all objects in the universe are attracted to each other. *Objects fall to the ground because of the pull of gravity.* 2. [N] a very serious nature or manner. *She needed an operation because of the gravity of her injuries. | He spoke with gravity.*

gravy *noun* (grā vē) [N] a hot liquid made from flour and the juice of cooked meat. Gravy is a sauce used on meat.

gray (grey) *adj.* (grā) having the color that results from mixing black and white substances.

grease *noun* (grēs) 1. [N] a thick, oily material used on a machine to allow the parts to rub together smoothly while the machine is working. *The gears on this bicycle need some grease.* 2. [N] melted or soft animal fat. *Bacon leaves a lot of grease in the pan after it has been cooked.*

great *adj.* (grāt) 1. very large in size or number. *A great crowd came to see the parade.* 2. of very high quality, ability, or importance. *Shakespeare was a great writer who lived hundreds of years ago.* 3. (informal) very good. *This is great ice cream.*

greed *noun* (grēd) [N] a great desire for more wealth and possessions than one needs or deserves. *His greed for power caused many people to hate him.*

Word Builder: greed +
greedily: in a way that shows greed.
greedy: having or showing greed.

green *adj.* (grēn) having the color of grass or a young leaf.

greenhouse *noun* (grēn hows) a building used to grow plants all year long. A greenhouse usually has a glass roof and walls. *She grows tomatoes in the winter in the greenhouse.*

greet *verb* (grēt) to use words or simple actions that show pleasure or respect when you meet someone or start a letter. *She always says "Hi" when she greets people, never "Hello." | She **greeted** her guests **with** a smile and a bow.*

greeting *noun* (grē ting) words or actions used to show pleasure or respect when you meet someone or start a letter. *She waved a friendly greeting as she got off the bus. | The usual greeting in a letter begins with the word Dear.*

grew *verb* (groo) past tense of **grow**. *My son grew one inch in one month!*

grill *noun* (gril) a frame of metal bars used to hold foods for cooking over flames. *We cooked the chicken on the grill.*
verb to cook on a grill. *We grilled hamburgers for dinner.*

grin *verb* (grin) to smile broadly so that the teeth are showing. *She grinned when she heard the good news.*
noun a wide smile that shows the teeth. *Emil's grin told us he liked the gift.*

grind *verb* (grīnd) **ground, ground** 1. to crush into very small pieces or a powder. *He ground the coffee very fine.* 2. to make something sharper or smoother by rubbing it against a hard surface. *He ground the edge of the knife on a stone.*

Word Builder: grind +
grinder: a machine that grinds.

grip *noun* (grip) a tight hold on something. *I felt the grip of his hand on my wrist.*
verb to grasp or hold firmly. *The little boy gripped his mother's hand.*

groceries *pl. noun* (grō sə rēz) food and other supplies for the home that people buy at a store. *I went shopping for groceries.*

groceries

grocery *noun* (grō sə rē) a store where food and other supplies for the home are sold. *My parents run a small grocery.*
adj. having to do with food products and supplies for the home as they are grouped together for sale. *I bought some bread and milk at the grocery store.*

groom *noun* (groom) a man on his wedding day. *The groom kissed the bride.*
verb to make clean and neat in appearance. *He went upstairs to groom himself before dinner. | She groomed the horse after her ride.*

Word Builder: groom +
grooming: care of the skin and hair.

gross *adj.* (grōs) 1. before anything is taken out; total. *Your gross pay for the week will be eight hundred dollars.* 2. large and able to be seen by anyone. *The mayor made a gross mistake by firing the popular police chief.*
noun twelve dozen; 144. *The store ordered five gross of lightbulbs.*

ground[1] *noun* (grownd) 1. [N] the earth's solid surface or the soil covering it; land. *The leaves fell to the ground.* | *He dug a hole in the ground.* 2. the reason or reasons for saying or doing something. **On** *what* **grounds** *are you making this complaint?* | *What are their* **grounds for** *divorce?* 3. a body, such as the earth, that electricity flows through and that completes an electric circuit.
verb to connect to a body that electricity flows through and that completes an electric circuit. *It is important to ground electrical appliances that you use near water.*

ground or land?
Use *land* when talking or writing about a part of the earth that is not water.
Use *ground* when talking or writing about the surface of the earth, not the air.
Compare:
Our family bought some land to start a farm.
The leaves fell to the ground.

ground[2] *verb* (grownd) past tense and past participle of **grind.**
adj. having been made into very small pieces. *We made hamburgers from the ground beef.*

grounds *pl. noun* (growndz) 1. tiny pieces of solid matter, such as coffee, that settle at the bottom of a liquid. 2. an area of land around a large building or institution such as a school or prison. *We took a walk around the grounds of the hospital.*

groundskeeper *noun* (growndz kē pər) a person responsible for taking care of an area of land such as a park, sports field, or land around a school.

group *noun* (groop) a collection of people, things, or ideas that are in one place or have important things in common. *A large group of people were standing in front of the building.* | *Put the green chairs in one group and the white chairs in another.*
verb to put with other items that are similar; classify. *The librarian grouped the books by topic.*

grow *verb* (grō) *grew, grown* 1. to become larger; increase. *She grew an inch over the summer.* 2. to become. *The weather grew warmer.*
grow up to become an adult. *I want to be a doctor when I grow up.*

grown *verb* (grōn) past participle of **grow.**

grownup *noun* (grōn əp) an adult person. *Sometimes children like to act like grownups.*

growth *noun* (grōth) 1. the process of growing. *Teenagers experience rapid growth.* | *That town had a large growth in population during the 1990s.* 2. an area of tissue that is not normal. *The doctor removed a growth from my arm.*

guarantee *noun* (gær ən tē) a promise that something you have bought will work well. If it does not, the store must either repair it or give you a new one. *There is a two-year guarantee on my new computer.*
verb to promise; to make someone feel sure about something *The salesman guaranteed my satisfaction with the new car.*

guard *verb* (gard) to protect or pay close attention to something in order to keep it safe. *The dog guarded the sheep.* | *The soldier guarded the entrance.*
noun a person whose job is to watch out for danger or protect property. *There were guards around the president's house.*

guardrail *noun* (gard rāl) a metal bar that keeps people from falling over a high place. *The car drove into the guardrail.*

guess *verb* (ges) to give an answer or opinion without enough information to be certain. *Can you guess how many pennies are in this jar?* | *When I didn't know an answer on the test, I just guessed.*

guest *noun* (gest) 1. a person who visits another person's home. *Please offer our guest some more potatoes.* 2. a customer at a hotel or restaurant. *This hotel usually has older guests.*

guidance *noun* (gī dəns) [N] advice. *The school counselor gave her guidance about what classes to take in high school.*

guide *verb* (gīd) to direct or lead someone to a place or around an unfamiliar area. *The librarian guided us to the books about snakes.* | *A young man guided us around the museum.*
noun a person who shows the way or leads others. *The guide led us up the mountain.*

guideline *noun* (gīd līn) a rule that helps someone to do something in the best way. *The book gave guidelines about how to fish.*

guilty *adj.* (gil tē) responsible for breaking a law or doing something wrong. *The judge sent the guilty man to prison.*

guitar *noun* (gə tar) an instrument for playing music. It has a hollow body and a long neck to which strings are attached. You play a guitar by picking on the strings.

guitar

gum[1] *noun* (gəm) [N] a short form of **chewing gum.**

gum[2] *noun* (gəm) the flesh inside the mouth around the base of the teeth. *My dentist examined my gums.*

gun *noun* (gən) 1. a weapon with a tube made of metal from which bullets are fired. *Children should never be around guns.* 2. a tool that has the shape of a gun. *We used a spray gun to paint the house.* | *We used a nail gun to build the table.*

Word Builder: kinds of guns
glue gun: a gun that heats and shoots glue.
nail gun: a gun that shoots nails.
staple gun: a gun that shoots staples.

gutter *noun* (gə tər) 1. a low area that continues along the edge of a road, or a pipe under the lower edge of a roof that carries water away. *The gutters were flooded after the heavy rain.* | *Our gutters are clogged with leaves.* 2. a long open passage on each side of a bowling lane that stops the ball from crossing into another lane.

guy *noun* (gī) 1. (informal) a boy or man. *What's that guy doing?* 2. (informal) used in the plural form to mean people, including males and females. *Why don't you guys come with us?*

gym *noun* (jim) a short form of **gymnasium.**

gymnasium *noun* (jim nā zē əm) a building or large room that has equipment for physical education, sports, and games. *We have two gymnasiums in our school.*

gymnastics *noun* (jim næ stəks) [N] a sport based on physical exercises that require great strength and balance. The exercises are often done on a mat and with special equipment such as bars and ropes.

gymnastics

H h

habit *noun* (hæ bət) 1. a regular action. *He is **in the habit of** washing the dishes right after dinner.* 2. a fixed, repeated action, often done without meaning or wanting to. *She has an annoying habit of tapping her toes.*

hacksaw *noun* (hæk saw) a saw used to cut metal. *She used a hacksaw to cut through the bolt.*

had *verb* (hæd) past tense and past participle of **have.**

hail *noun* (hāl) [N] round pieces of frozen rain that fall from the sky. *The hail was loud as it hit the roofs of cars and buildings.*
verb to fall or pour down as frozen rain. *It is getting colder and may hail tomorrow if it doesn't rain.*

hair *noun* (hār) 1. a single, thin structure like a thread that grows on the body of humans and some animals. *The baby has a few hairs on his head now.* 2. [N] a mass of hairs growing on the head or skin. *His hair is brown. | He shaves the hair off his face.*

> **Word Builder: hair +**
> **hairbrush:** a brush for the hair.
> **haircut:** a way of cutting the hair on your head.
> **hairdresser:** a person whose job is to cut and style hair.
> **hairnet:** a net to cover the hair and keep it in place.

half *noun* (hæf) *halves* one of two equal parts of a whole. *Two is half of four. | I gave half of my sandwich to my sister.*

halfway *adv.* (hæf wā) to or at the middle point between two places. *I was halfway to work when the bus broke down.*

hall *noun* (hawl) 1. a long space in a building that people walk through to go from one room to another. *Mr. Brown's office is at the end of the hall.* 2. a large room or public building for meetings or social events. *John and Mary rented a hall for their wedding. | The city council meets at City Hall.*

Halloween *noun* (hæ lə wēn) a holiday celebrated on October 31. On Halloween, children wear special clothes and go from house to house asking for candy or other treats.

halt *verb* (hawlt) to stop or pause. *Work halted while everyone ate lunch.*

halves *noun* (hævz) plural of **half.**

ham *noun* (hæm) [N] salted, smoked meat from the back leg of a pig.

hamburger *noun* (hæm bər gər) ground meat; a round, flat mass of ground meat that is cooked and served on bread. *Mr. Martin bought two pounds of hamburger at the market. | We ordered hamburgers for lunch.*

hammer *noun* (hæ mər) a tool with a heavy metal head on a handle. A hammer is used to hit things such as nails.
verb to hit or strike with a hammer; pound. *He hammered nails into the wood.*

hamper *noun* (hæm pər) a large container for holding dirty clothes before they are washed. *Lina emptied the hamper into the washing machine.*

hand *noun* (hænd) 1. the part at the end of the arm that has fingers. *She's holding a kitten in her hands.* 2. a person who does physical work for pay. *The farmer hired several hands for the harvest.* 3. a small device that moves around the front of a clock and points to the numbers. *The children are learning about the minute hand and hour hand now.*
verb to give or pass to with the hand. *Please hand me an apple.*
by hand with the use of your hands, or by human effort without the help of any machines. *They make all their clothes by hand.*
hand over to give up control of. *We handed over the car to the new owners.*
hand out to give to each person. *The teacher handed out books to her class.*

handbag *noun* (hænd bæg) a bag used to carry small personal things; purse. *She keeps her wallet in her handbag.*

handle
clasp
handbag

handbook *noun* (hænd buk) a book that gives information on a specific subject. *Tom found the answer to his question about the new computer in the handbook.*

handful *noun* (hænd fəl) the amount that can be held in a single hand. *She took a handful of candy.*

handicap *noun* (hæn dē kæp) anything that makes things harder or keeps a person from doing better. *Despite the handicap of being blind, she graduated from college.* | *His greatest handicap is not believing in himself.* **verb** to put at a disadvantage. *His fear of speaking up handicapped him in class.*

handicapped *adj.* (hæn dē kæpt) having a physical or mental condition that makes it harder to do certain things. *That parking space is reserved for handicapped people.*

handkerchief *noun* (hæng kər chəf) a small piece of thin cloth that you use to clean your nose. *She blew her nose into her handkerchief.*

handle *noun* (hæn dəl) the part of an object that you hold in order to lift or move the object. *Lift the pot off the stove by its handle.*

handlebars *pl. noun* (hæn dəl bɑrz) a curved bar with handles on a bicycle or other vehicle with two wheels. *The brakes on this bicycle are attached to the handlebars.*

handmade *adj.* (hænd mād) made by hand or with hand tools, not by machine. *That's a beautiful handmade sweater.*

handout *noun* (hænd owt) a piece of paper with advertising or other writing on it that is given out for free. *The teachers passed out the handouts to the class.*

handrail *noun* (hænd rāl) a long, narrow structure that a person holds for support. *When you go down the stairs, make sure you use the handrail.*

handsaw *noun* (hænd saw) a saw with a handle at one end.

handshake *noun* (hænd shāk) the holding and shaking of hands between two people when they meet or say good-bye. *I greeted my guest with a handshake.*

handshake

handsome *adj.* (hæn səm) 1. having an attractive, healthy appearance. *He is a handsome man.* 2. large in amount. *She was given a handsome reward.*

hand truck *noun* (hænd trək) a small vehicle with two wheels and handles for moving heavy things. *Put the boxes on the hand truck and bring them inside.*

handwriting *noun* (hænd rī ting) [N] words written by hand with a pen or pencil, or the way in which the letters of words are written. *Is this your handwriting on this envelope?* | *The students are practicing their handwriting.*

handy *adj.* (hæn dē) 1. easy to reach and use; near. *Do you have a pencil handy?* 2. useful. *The hammer is a handy tool.* 3. having skill at something. *He's handy with cars and trucks.*

hang *verb* (hæng) **hung, hung** 1. to attach to a point without support from below. *She hung a pair of curtains.* | *Let's hang the painting above the couch.* 2. to lean over or out of something. *He hung out of the window.* **noun** the idea or skill of how to do something. *My daughter got the hang of riding a bike.* **hang around** to stay in a place for no purpose. *He likes to hang around at the mall with friends.* **hang up** 1. to end a telephone call by pressing a button or putting the telephone down in the part that holds it. *You will hear a noise from the phone if you forget to hang it up.* 2. to put on a hook or other device to keep things off the floor. *Hang up your coat, please.*

Word Builder: hang +
hanger: a device for hanging clothes on a rack.

happen *verb* (hæ pən) 1. to take place; occur. *Two important events happened recently. My sister got married, and I changed jobs.* | *What happened? You're all wet.* 2. to occur or take place by chance. *They happened to arrive at the same time.*

happy *adj.* (hæ pē) feeling glad, pleased, or comfortable. *Nina is a happy baby.* | *She was happy with her new job.*

Word Builder: happy +
happiness: the condition of being happy.

happy hour *noun* (hæ pē owr) a period of one or two hours in the late afternoon when some bars offer lower prices on drinks. *Let's go to happy hour after work on Friday.*

harass *verb* (hə ræs) to trouble or make threats against someone again and again. *The police harass young people who hang out in the park.*

harassment *noun* (hə rǽs mənt) [N] the crime of behavior that threatens another person again and again. *The police charged Paul with harassment because he would not stop calling his former girlfriend.*

Word Builder: one kind of harassment
sexual harassment: a situation where an employer asks an employee to do something sexual in exchange for an advantage at work.

harbor *noun* (har bər) a safe area of water where people can leave their boats. *We saw several boats in the harbor.*

hard *adj.* (hard) 1. not soft; solid. *I fell on the hard ground.* 2. not easy; difficult. *Physics is a hard subject for some people.* 3. giving a strong effort. *We are happy to have a hard worker on our team.* 4. asking for a lot of effort. *Ms. Johnson is a hard boss.*
adv. 1. with much effort. *He worked hard on the farm.* | *I thought long and hard about what you told me.* 2. with great force or strength. *It rained hard last night.* | *He hit me hard.*

Word Builder: hard +
harden: to make hard or harder.
hardworking: giving a strong effort.

hard disk *noun* (hard disk) a part inside of a computer for storing information. *Linda saved all the documents on the hard disk.*

hard hat *noun* (hard hæt) a strong hat made of hard plastic. It protects the heads of people who work in dangerous places such as mines or construction areas. *You may not enter the building site without a hard hat.*

hard hat

hardly *adv.* (hard lē) almost not at all. *Her voice is so quiet I can hardly hear it.*

hardware *noun* (hard wār) 1. [N] tools and equipment used for making and fixing things. Hardware is usually made of metal. Bolts, screws, and hinges are pieces of hardware. 2. [N] computer parts and equipment. Computer hardware includes all the parts of a computer that make it work, except for the programs.

harm *noun* (harm) [N] a hurt or injury. *No harm came to the lost child.*
verb to hurt or injure. *Too much sun can harm the skin.*

harmful *adj.* (harm fəl) causing harm; dangerous. *Smoking is harmful to your health.*

harsh *adj.* (harsh) 1. rough and not pleasing. *She has a harsh voice.* 2. severe or strict. *The president believes in harsh punishment for criminals.*

harvest *noun* (har vəst) [N] the gathering of ripe crops, or the amount gathered. *The farmer hired people to help with the harvest.* | *There was a good harvest of grapes this year.*
verb to gather in a crop. *Many farmers use large machines to harvest wheat from the fields.*

Word Builder: harvest +
harvester: a machine that harvests crops.

has *verb* (hæz) present tense of **have,** used with *he, she,* or *it,* or with singular nouns. *He has two sisters.* | *The horse has a long tail.*

haste *noun* (hāst) [N] speed that is too great. *I wrote the report **in haste,** so I made a lot of mistakes.*

hat *noun* (hæt) a covering for the head worn for warmth, protection, or decoration.

hatch *noun* (hæch) an opening in the floor, roof, or side of a building or vehicle. Hatches are often found on ships.

hate *verb* (hāt) to have a very strong bad feeling toward something; to not like in any way. *The people hated their cruel leader.* | *I **hate it when** you yell at me.* | *She hates to get up early.*

hatred *noun* (hā trəd) [N] a feeling of hate. *She feels **hatred for** people who are cruel to animals.*

haul *verb* (hawl) 1. to pull or carry with force. *We hauled the garbage can out to the street.* 2. to carry from one place to another in a truck. *Mr. Clark hauls freight for a living.*

have *verb* (hăv) *had, had* 1. to own; possess. *She has five dollars.* 2. to experience; feel. *We always have a good time at the movies.* 3. to include or contain. *Our team has ten members.* 4. to think about or hold in mind. *I have a great idea.* 5. to give birth to. *Mother is having a baby in the hospital.* 6. to eat or drink. *He's having dinner now.* | *Let's have a cup of coffee.* 7. used with a past participle to express a completed action. *They have gone.* | *He has finished the sandwich.* | *We had just arrived home when the phone rang.*

have got (present tense only) to own; possess. *I've got a pen that you can use.*

have got to (present tense only) have to; must. *I've got to leave here by six o'clock.*

have to 1. to have the necessity to do something; be required to; must. *I have to be at the office by nine o'clock.* 2. used to make a strong statement about something based only on logic, not knowledge. *This has to be her house. It's the only one that is red.*

hawk *noun* (hawk) a bird with a short beak and sharp claws. Hawks catch and eat small animals.

hawk

hay *noun* (hā) [N] grass or another plant like grass that has been cut, dried, and stored for animal food. *The cows in the barn eat hay all winter.*

hazard *noun* (hăz ərd) a danger or risk. *There were many hazards on the steep mountain trail.*

> **Word Builder: hazard +**
> **hazardous:** dangerous; being a hazard.

he *pron.* (hē) the male human being or animal that is being discussed or was recently referred to. *Where is your brother? He is at school.*

head *noun* (hed) 1. the top part of a human or animal body that contains the brain and has eyes, ears, a nose, and a mouth. 2. the person who is the leader of a group. *She is the head of the agency.* 3. the top or most important part of a thing. *The teacher sat at the head of the table.* 4. the side of a coin that shows a person's face. *President Lincoln is on the head of a penny.*
adj. of the highest rank. *He is the head chef at the restaurant.*
verb 1. to move in a certain direction. *His car is heading south now.* | *He came home and headed for the kitchen.* 2. to cause to go in a certain direction or

on a certain path. *She headed the car south down the highway.*

headlight *noun* (hed līt) a bright light on the front of a vehicle. *Turn your headlights on when you drive at night.*

heal *verb* (hēl) to become healthy or whole again. *Her broken leg healed in about a month.*

health *noun* (helth) [N] the condition of one's body or mind. *She was in bad health from years of smoking.*

healthy *adj.* (hel thē) 1. being free from sickness. *Will you be healthy enough to play basketball tomorrow?* 2. having to do with a good mind and body. *A good diet is important to a healthy life.*

hear *verb* (hēr) *heard, heard* 1. to receive sound with the ears. *Did you hear that noise?* 2. to find out; learn. *I heard that he was quitting his job.* 3. to experience an event using your ears. *I heard a great song on the radio this morning.* | *Did you hear the president's speech?*

> **hear or listen?**
> *Hear* means to use the ears in a natural way, without thinking about it.
> *Listen* means to use the ears on purpose.
> Sometimes *hear* and *listen* are very close in meaning, but *hear* is more concerned with the action of your mind and ears, while *listen* is more concerned with having something as part of your experience of life.
> Compare:
> *I hear birds singing outside.*
> *I listen to music while I work.*
> *I heard the weather report this morning.*
> *I listen to the weather report every morning.*

heard *verb* (hərd) past tense and past participle of **hear.**

heart *noun* (hart) the organ in the body that controls the flow of blood.
by heart by memory. *She knows the song by heart.*

heart attack *noun* (hart ə tăk) an event in which the blood supply to the heart suddenly stops. This causes damage to the heart muscle and sometimes death. *He **had a heart attack,** and he's in the hospital.*

heat *noun* (hēt) [N] the state of being very warm; warmth. *This furnace gives off a lot of heat.* | *Rent on this apartment includes heat and hot water.*
verb to cause to become warm or hot. *We heated the soup on the stove.* | *We heat our house with wood during the winter.*

heat up to make or become warm or hot. *I heated up the cold coffee.* | *The room heated up.*

> **Word Builder: heat +**
> **heater:** the appliance that heats a room or a building.
> **heating:** the appliances and other parts that give heat in a building.

heaven *noun* (he̲ vən) [N] a place that some people believe exists. It is where a god or gods live or the place where people go after they die.

heavy *adj.* (he̲ ve̅) 1. having much weight. *I couldn't lift the heavy box by myself.* 2. of great size or amount. *There was a flood after the heavy rain.*

hedge *noun* (he̲j) a solid row of bushes, used as a kind of fence. *The gardener trimmed the hedge around the front yard.*

heel *noun* (he̲l) 1. the rounded, back part of the foot. 2. the part of a shoe under the back part of a human foot. *Some people wear shoes with high heels.*

height *noun* (hi̲t) 1. the distance from the bottom to the top. *The height of that building is one hundred feet.* 2. how tall a person is. *My son's height is now four feet.* 3. the highest point. *She's at the height of her success.* | *At the height of the sale, there were hundreds of people at the store.*

held *verb* (he̲ld) past tense and past participle of **hold.**

helicopter *noun* (he̲ lə kap tər) a type of aircraft that is held in the air and moved along by spinning blades attached to its top side. *The helicopter landed on the roof of the building.*

hell *noun* (he̲l) [N] a place that some people believe exists. It is where evil spirits live and where bad people are punished after they die.

hello *interj.* (he̲ lo̅ or hə lo̅) used as a greeting or to begin a telephone call. *Hello! It's good to see you!* | *Hello. This is Paul. May I speak with Nina?*

helmet *noun* (he̲l mət) a hard covering worn to protect the head. *You should wear a helmet when you ride a bicycle.*

football helmet

help *verb* (he̲lp) 1. to do part of the work for someone. *I helped my friends move to a new apartment.* 2. to save someone from harm or danger. *We all tried to help him when he fell.* 3. to avoid or keep from doing something. *I could not help noticing that his hair was dirty.* | *Don't walk those streets at night if you can help it.* 4. to take for yourself. *Help yourself to some pie.*
noun [N] the act of giving help. *The house is on fire! Call for help!*
interj. used to express serious trouble. *Help! I'm drowning!*

help out to assist. *He helps out in his daughter's class once a week.*

> **Word Builder: help +**
> **helper:** a person or thing that helps.
> **helpful:** able and willing to give help.
> **helpless:** needing help.
> **help wanted:** a notice asking for people to apply for a job.

hen *noun* (he̲n) an adult female chicken. People keep hens for their eggs and meat.

her *pron.* (hər) the female person or animal already talked about; the form of **she** that is used as the object of a verb or that is used after a preposition. *Please tell her what I said.* | *I went with her to the store.*
adj. of or belonging to her; a possessive form of **she.** *Is this her desk?*

here *adv.* (he̲r) at or to this place. *Please come here.* | *When will you get here?*

hero *noun* (he̲r o̅) 1. a person who has courage and who is a model for others. *People said the firefighter was a hero after he saved someone from the burning building.* 2. the main male character of a book or movie. *The hero wins against his enemy at the end of the movie.*

hers *pron.* (hərz) the one or ones that belong to her; a possessive form of **she.** *My job is hard, but hers is harder.* | *This is her mother's hat, not hers.*

herself *pron.* (hər self) 1. a word used to show that an action is done to or in connection with the same female person who performs the action. *My sister hurt herself when she fell.* | *She bought herself a necklace.* | *She took a picture of herself.* 2. she and no one else. *She herself did all the work.*

hesitate *verb* (he̲ zə ta̅t) to stop or pause because of not feeling sure. *I hesitated before diving into the pool.*

hey *interj.* (ha̅) used to get attention. *Hey! I'm over here.*

hi *interj.* (hi̲) (informal) "Hello!" *Hi! How are you?*

hid *verb* (hi̲d) past tense of **hide.**

hidden *adj.* (hi dən) not in view; secret. *That box has a hidden lock.*
verb past participle of **hide.**

hide *verb* (hīd) *hid, hidden* 1. to put or keep from view. *Did you hide the present under the bed?* 2. to make or keep yourself out of view. *The child hid from his father.*

high *adj.* (hī) 1. reaching up a great distance. *We climbed to the top of the high mountain.* 2. at a given distance from the ground. *That branch is ten feet high.* 3. above what is usual. *The train traveled at a high speed.* 4. expensive. *The price was too high.*

high school *noun* (hī skool) a school that begins with grade nine or ten and ends with grade twelve. *You get a diploma when you graduate from high school.*

highway *noun* (hī wā) a large, important public road. *We took the highway from New York to Philadelphia.*

hike *verb* (hīk) to take a long walk in the country for fun or exercise. *We hiked seven miles through the forest.*

hill *noun* (hil) a raised area of land smaller than a mountain. *We rode our bikes up and down the hill.*

him *pron.* (him) the male person or animal already talked about; the form of **he** that is used as the object of a verb or that is used after a preposition. *Can you see him?* | *Please walk with him to the car.*

himself *pron.* (him self) 1.a word used to show that an action is done to or in connection with the same male person who performs the action. *He burned himself while cooking.* | *My husband bought himself some new power tools.* | *He looked at himself in the mirror.* 2. he and no one else. *He finished all the work himself.*

hinge *noun* (hinj) a device attached to one side of a door, or to a lid or window. A hinge allows the door to open and close. *That door is held to its frame by three metal hinges.*

hip *noun* (hip) the joint that connects the leg to the body.

hire *verb* (hīr) to give a job to. *The company hired many people to work in the new factory.*

his *pron.* (hiz) the one or ones that belong to him; a possessive form of **he.** *This is my office. His is down the hall.* | *Those shirts are his.*
adj. of or belonging to him; a possessive form of **he.** *This is his wallet.*

history *noun* (hi stə rē or hi strē) [N] the study of events that happened in the past.

hit *verb* (hit) *hit, hit* 1. to strike. *He hit me with the back of his hand.* | *She hit the drum with a stick.* | *They threw a stone, and it hit the window.* 2. to reach or get to. *The car hit its top speed.*
noun someone or something that is very popular. *The movie was a big hit with young people.*

hitchhike *verb* (hich hīk) to get or try to get a free ride in a vehicle. *We hitchhiked home after our car broke down.*

hobby *noun* (ha bē) an interest or activity that you do for fun. *Her favorite hobby is making dolls.*

hockey *noun* (ha kē) 1. [N] a game played on ice by two teams. Each person wears skates and carries a long stick. 2. [N] a game played on a grass field by two teams. Players get points by pushing a ball into a net with their stick.

hockey

hoe *noun* (hō) a tool with a thin, flat blade at the end of a long handle. It is used for breaking up the soil. *I used a hoe to prepare my garden before I planted seeds.*

hold *verb* (hōld) *held, held* 1. to support and contain, usually within your hand or hands. *I picked up the kitten and held it gently.* | *The little girl held her spoon in her mouth.* 2. to keep for a certain time. *Our neighbors will hold our mail until we return.* | *He **held** the **office** of president for four years.* 3. to contain within a particular area. *The theater holds two hundred people.* 4. to have. *Let's hold a meeting.*
hold on 1. to wait. *Hold on a minute. I'll be ready to go soon.* 2. to hold an object for the support or safety of your body or because you do not want to lose it. *The child **held on** tight **to** the guardrail.* | *Hold on to your balloon, or it will fly away!*
on hold waiting to complete a telephone call. *The person who answered the phone **put** me **on hold.***

hole *noun* (hōl) an open or hollow place in something. *We dug a small hole for the seeds.* | *She has a hole in her jeans.*

holiday *noun* (ha lə dā) 1. a day to remember or celebrate something. Many businesses close and people do not go to school or work on a holiday. *Thanksgiving and New Year's Day are holidays.* 2. a day or period of freedom from work or school; time off. *They enjoyed their summer holiday.*

hollow *adj.* (ha lō) 1. having an empty space on the inside. *Basketballs are hollow.* 2. curving in or down. *We hid in a hollow place in the ground.* | *The hungry child has hollow cheeks.*

holy *adj.* (hō lē) 1. relating to a god or religion. *Many people believe that church is a holy place.* 2. showing very strong religious beliefs. *The priest lives a holy life.*

home *noun* (hōm) 1. the place where a person or animal lives. *I went home and went to bed.* | *The forest is home to many animals.* 2. a place where people who cannot take care of themselves live and are cared for. *Our town's group home is for children with no parents.*
adv. to or toward the place where you live. *I take the bus home after work.*

Word Builder: home +
homeless: having no home.
homemade: made at home, not in a factory.
homeroom: the classroom where you meet in the morning so the teacher can take attendance.
homesick: feeling sad because you are away from your home and family.
homework: the work for school that you do at home.

homeland *noun* (hōm lænd) the country where your home is. *Her homeland is the United States, but she lives in Canada.*

honest *adj.* (a nəst) 1. sincere; felt to be true. *He gave me an honest answer to my question.* 2. having the character of a person who does not lie, steal, or cheat. *I believe what she said because she's an honest person.* | *I gave him the key to my house because I think he's honest.* | *The honest students didn't cheat on the test.*

Word Builder: honest +
honesty: the condition of being honest.

honey *noun* (hə nē) 1. [N] a thick, sweet liquid made by bees. 2. sweet one; dear. *I love you, Honey.*

honk *noun* (hangk) a loud sound made by some animals or by a vehicle as a warning. *We heard the honk of a goose in the sky above us.*
verb to cause to make a loud sound. *I honked the horn at a boy who had run into the street.*

honor *noun* (a nər) 1. [N] high public value or respect. *The mayor holds a place of honor in our community.* 2. [N] good and honest behavior. *A person of honor will not cheat her friends.*
verb to show respect or admiration for. *He is a good son who honors his parents.* | *We honored our mother on her birthday with a special dinner.*

hood *noun* (hud) 1. a covering for the head and neck that may be attached to a coat or other piece of clothing. 2. the metal lid that covers a car's engine. *The mechanic lifted the hood to check the oil.*

hook *noun* (huk) 1. a curved piece that is used for holding, hanging, or pulling things. A hook is made of metal, plastic, or another hard material. *We put a hook into the wall to hold the picture.* 2. a curved metal piece with a sharp point that you use for catching fish. *Matt removed the hook from the fish's mouth.*

hook

hop *verb* (hap) to make a short, quick jump, sometimes on one foot. *The rabbit hopped across the yard.* | *The little girl hopped on her left foot and then on her right foot.*

hope *noun* (hōp) 1. [N] a feeling or chance that something that you want to happen will happen. *They have hope for a better life for their children.* | *Is there any hope that she will recover?* 2. a wish for something that one thinks could come true; desire. *It is my hope to become a vice president at the bank.*
verb to wish for something that you believe may happen. *I hope that I get that job.* | *I hope it doesn't rain this afternoon.*

Word Builder: hope +
hopeful: showing or feeling hope.
hopeless: showing or feeling no hope.

hope or wish?
Hope means to want something that is possible.
Wish means to want something that is probably not possible.
Compare:
I hope I pass the test.
I wish I were ten years younger.

horizon *noun* (hə rī zən) the line where the earth and the sky appear to meet. *The sun seems to sink below the horizon.*

horizontal *adj.* (har ə zan təl or hōr ə zan təl) in a line with the surface of the earth. *Most people sleep in a horizontal position.*

horn *noun* (hōrn) 1. a hard, hollow growth on the head of certain mammals. Goats and sheep are some animals that have horns. 2. an instrument for playing music, usually made of metal. Horns have the shape of a tube that is wide at one end and narrow at the other. 3. a device used to make a loud warning sound. *Dad **blew the horn** on his car to warn the dog.*

horrible *adj.* (hōr ə bəl or har ə bəl) 1. causing a feeling of fear or horror. *She had a horrible dream.* 2. very ugly or bad. *The dog made a horrible mess in the kitchen.*

horror *noun* (hōr ər or har ər) [N] a strong feeling of fear or shock. *I jumped in horror when I heard the loud scream.*

horse *noun* (hōrs) a large mammal with long legs and a long tail. People often use horses for riding.

horse

Word Builder: horse +
horseback: the back of a horse; the part of a horse that you ride on.
horsepower: a unit of energy used to measure the power of engines.

hose *noun* (hōz) 1. a tube of rubber or plastic through which a liquid can pass. *You can use a hose to water the garden.* 2. [N] (used with a plural verb) socks or other covering for the feet and legs. *I need a new **pair of hose** to wear with that dress.*

hospital *noun* (ha spə təl) a place where sick or hurt people go to find care or help. *Mr. Walker had to go to the hospital for an operation.*

host *noun* (hōst) a person who takes care of guests in a home or greets customers in a restaurant. *Our host served pizza and drinks at his party.*

hot *adj.* (hat) 1. holding or giving off great heat. *The hot soup was delicious. | It's hot out today.* 2. causing a burning feeling in the mouth. *Some people can't eat hot peppers.* 3. (informal) liked by many people at the current time. *That style of jeans was hot last year.*

hot dog *noun* (hat dawg) meat that is ground up, mixed with spices, and shaped into a tube for eating. A hot dog is often served on a roll.

hotel *noun* (hō tel) a place with many rooms and beds where people pay money to sleep and eat meals. *Steve stayed in a hotel when he was on vacation.*

hot water bottle *noun* (hat waw tər ba təl) a soft container made of rubber that you fill with hot water. It is used to put heat on a sore or cold part of your body.

hour *noun* (owr) 1. a standard unit used to measure time. There are 24 hours in one day. 2. a time of the day when you do certain things. *I like to take a walk during my lunch hour.*

house *noun* (hows) a building in which people live. *This neighborhood has houses, stores, and a school.*
verb (howz) to provide living space for people or animals. *The university houses some students in apartments. | The cows are housed in a barn.*

Word Builder: house +
housewares: things used in the kitchen of a house, such as utensils.
housewife: a woman who does not work outside of the home.
housework: the work of keeping a house clean and safe.

household *noun* (hows hōld) the group of people, such as a family, that lives together in one place. *Paul's household includes his wife, children, and brother.*

housekeeper *noun* (hows kē pər) a person whose job is to take care of a house, hotel, or other place where people stay.

housekeeping *noun* (hows kē ping) [N] the job of taking care of a house, hotel, or other place where people stay. Some parts of housekeeping are cleaning the rooms and making the beds.

House of Representatives *noun* (hows əv re prə zen tə təvz) one of the two parts of the U. S. Congress. The other part is the Senate.

housing *noun* (how zing) [N] houses or living places as a group. *The city is building housing for senior citizens.*

how *adv.* (how) 1. by what manner or means. *How is cheese made?* 2. in what way, state, or condition. *How are you feeling?* 3. to what amount or degree. *How big is he?* 4. for what purpose or reason. *How are you going to use this?*
conj. the way in which. *Do you know how I can get to the highway? | I don't know how to fix it.*

however *adv.* (how e ver) no matter what or how. *However you do, I will be proud.*
conj. in spite of that; yet. *It is raining; however, it is not cold.*

HR *abbrev.* (āch ar) an abbreviation for **human resources.**

hubcap *noun* (həb kæp) a round metal cover over the center of the wheel of a car.

hug *verb* (həg) to put your arms around another person to show that you like him or her. *I hugged my little sister before I said good-bye.*
noun a hold using both arms. *I **gave** my husband **a hug.***

huge *adj.* (hūj) very large in size or amount. *He is a huge man. | She ate a huge number of potato chips.*

human *adj.* (hū mən) having to do with or belonging to people. *Speaking is a human activity. | Fingers and toes are part of the human body.*
noun a person. *Humans are a kind of animal.*

human resources *adj.* (hū mən rē sōr səz) having to do with the people who work for a business. *If you have a question about your benefits, talk to someone in the human resources department.*
pl. noun the people who work for a business. *That company wants to lower the amount it spends on human resources.*

humid *adj.* (hū məd) having a high amount of water in the air. *Hot, humid weather is uncomfortable.*

humor *noun* (hū mər) [N] a quality that makes people laugh or feel amused. *The story was filled with humor. | She has a good **sense of humor.***

hundred *noun* (hən drəd) the name for the number 100.

hung *verb* (həng) past tense and past participle of **hang.**

hunger *noun* (həng gər) [N] the need or want for food. *Hunger is a problem around the world. | Some people **feel** less **hunger** in the morning than at night.*

hungry *adj.* (həng grē) feeling a need or want for food. *It is hard for a hungry child to study well. | I'm **hungry for** dinner.*

hunt *verb* (hənt) 1. to find and kill animals for food or sport. *Uncle Dan likes to hunt. | He hunts deer in the fall.* 2. to try to find. *He **hunted for** his lost keys.*

hunt

hurry *verb* (hə rē) to move or act with speed. *If we don't hurry, we'll miss the bus.*
hurry up to go faster. *Hurry up, or you'll be late.*
in a hurry needing to move quickly to do something. *I can't talk now. I'm in a hurry.*

hurt *verb* (hərt) *hurt, hurt* to cause pain or harm to. *Joe hurt his arm. | Jean hurt my feelings.*
noun physical or mental pain. *The hurt went away when I took aspirin.*

husband *noun* (həz bənd) the man to whom a woman is married.

hut *noun* (hət) a small house or shelter. A hut is sometimes made of dry grass or mud. *The people in that village live in round huts.*

hyphen *noun* (hī fən) a punctuation mark (-). It is used to join the parts of some compound words, for example, "brand-new." It is also used to divide a word at the end of a line of writing if there is not enough space for the whole word.

I i

I *pron.* (ī) the one who is speaking or writing. *I left yesterday.* | *I am the farmer's son.*

ice *noun* (īs) [N] frozen, solid water. *The lake is covered with ice in winter.*
verb to make very cold. *He iced the bottles of soda for the party.*

Word Builder: ice +
iced: served cold or with ice.

ice cream *noun* (īs krēm) [N] a sweet, frozen food made by mixing cream, sugar, and other things. Ice cream is made in many different flavors.

ice cream
cone

ice pack *noun* (īs pæk) a bag filled with ice or something like ice. You put an ice pack on a hurt place to make it feel better. *Mary put an ice pack on her knee after she bruised it.*

icicle *noun* (ī sə kəl) a long, thin piece of ice that hangs from something. *There were icicles hanging from the roof.*

icon (ikon) *noun* (ī kan) a small picture on the screen of a computer. When you click on an icon with the mouse, the computer does a certain action. *Click twice on this icon to start the word processing program.* | *Click on that icon to open the document.*

icy *adj.* (ī sē) covered with ice. *Drive slowly on icy roads!*

ID *abbrev.* (ī dē) an abbreviation for **identification.**

idea *noun* (ī dē ə) any thought or picture formed in the mind. *Do you have any ideas about what to eat tonight?*

ideal *adj.* (ī dēl) seen as perfect or best. *Teaching is the ideal job for Mark.*

identical *adj.* (ī den tə kəl or ə den tə kəl) the same in every way. *My shoes are **identical to** my friend's.* | *The brothers are identical twins.*

identification *noun* (ī den tə fə kā shən) [N] something that proves who a person is. A passport is a form of identification. *The guard checks the identification of every person who enters the building.*

identify *verb* (ī den tə fī) to find out or show who someone is or what something is. *She identified him as the criminal.* | *He is good at identifying trees.*

identity *noun* (ī den tə tē) all the things by which a person or thing is known to be himself, herself, or itself. *The police tried to find out the identity of the criminal.*

if *conj.* (if) 1. on the condition that; in the event that. *If it rains tomorrow, they will cancel the game.* | *Would you buy a new car if you had enough money?* 2. accepting that it is true that. *If you are hungry, why don't you eat something?* 3. whether. *I don't know if he wants to go to the zoo.*

ignition *noun* (ig ni shən) the part that turns the engine on in a car or other vehicle. *To start your car, put the key into the ignition and turn it.*

ignorance *noun* (ig nə rəns) [N] the lack of education or information. ***Ignorance of** the law can get you into trouble.*

ignorant *adj.* (ig nə rənt) without knowledge or education. *Many people are still **ignorant of** the new law.* | *I'm ignorant about history because I didn't study it in school.*

ignore *verb* (ig nōr) to refuse to recognize or notice. *She ignored me at the dance.*

ill *adj.* (il) not healthy; sick. *He became ill with fever.*

illegal *adj.* (i lē gəl) against the law or rules. *It is illegal to steal.*

illiterate *adj.* (i li tə rət) not able to read or write. *He used to be illiterate, but he learned how to read and write.*

illness *noun* (il nəs) sickness or disease. *She missed a day of work because of illness.* | *Tuberculosis is a serious illness.*

illustrate *verb* (i lə strāt) to provide pictures to go along with written material. *He illustrated the children's book with pictures of dinosaurs.*

Word Builder: illustrate +
illustrated: having pictures.

illustration *noun* (i lə strā shən) a picture or drawing used to explain or decorate written material. *This dictionary has an illustration on every page.*

image *noun* (i məj) a picture of a person or thing. *The dollar bill has an image of George Washington.*

imaginary *adj.* (i m̆æ jə nār ē) existing only in the mind. *Some children have an imaginary friend.*

imagination *noun* (i m̆æ jə nā shən) the power of the mind to make a thought or picture of something that is not real. *She uses her imagination to write stories.*

imagine *verb* (i m̆æ jən) to form a picture of something in the mind. *Can you imagine having a million dollars?*

immediate *adj.* (i m̆ē dē ət) happening right away. *He wrote an immediate answer to the letter.*

Word Builder: immediate +
immediately: very soon; without delay.

immigrant *noun* (i̲ mə grənt) a person who moves from the country where he or she was born to another country. *My parents are immigrants from Poland.*

immigrate *verb* (i̲ mə grāt) to come to live in a country where you were not born. *My parents immigrated to the United States from Mexico.*

immigration *noun* (i mə grā shən) [N] the act of coming to live in a new country. *About 120 years ago, the U.S. government first approved the immigration of people from Korea.*

impact *noun* (im̲ pækt or əm pækt) 1. the coming together of objects with great force. *The impact of the bus against the tree cracked the windshield.* 2. a strong and powerful effect. *The senator's speech on gun control had a great impact on voters.*

importance *noun* (im pōr təns) [N] the quality or condition of being important. *The doctor talked about the importance of a healthy diet.*

important *adj.* (im pōr tənt) 1. having great meaning or value. *Health care is an important issue for many people.* 2. having great power or influence. *The mayor of our city is an important person.*

impossible *adj.* (im pa̲ sə bəl) not able to happen or to be done. *It's impossible to open that window.* | *It is impossible for her to run as fast as her son.*

impress *verb* (im pres) to have a strong effect on the mind or feelings. *Joe's excellent work impressed his boss.*

Word Builder: impress +
impressive: causing a strong effect on the mind or feelings.

improve *verb* (im proov) 1. to make better. *Salt and pepper improved the sauce.* 2. to become better. *Richard improved slowly after the accident.* | *Her grades in school have improved this year.*

improvement *noun* (im proov mənt) 1. [N] the act of making something better than it was. *The teacher noticed an improvement in his handwriting.* 2. a change that makes something better than it was. *The Clarks made several improvements to their house.*

in *prep.* (in) 1. surrounded or contained by; living or located at. *They were caught in the rain.* | *The sandwich is in the refrigerator.* | *He lives in the city.* 2. during or before the end of a period of time. *He finished the work in ten minutes.* 3. to or toward the inside of. *He got in his car.* 4. using; with. *She spoke in a loud voice.* **adv.** to, toward, or into a place. *May I come in?*

inch *noun* (inch) a standard unit used to measure length. Twelve inches equals one foot.

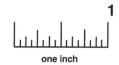
one inch

incinerate *verb* (in si̲ nə rāt) to burn completely. *The hospital incinerates its waste.*

Word Builder: incinerate +
incinerator: a machine that incinerates things. Incinerators are used as a way to get rid of trash.

incineration *noun* (in si̲ nə rā shən) [N] the complete burning of something. *Incineration of the garbage happens in a special furnace.*

inclination *noun* (in klə nā shən) a natural tendency toward. *She has an inclination to sleep a lot.*

incline *verb* (in klīn) to be likely to; to usually think or feel in a certain way. *I'm inclined to agree with you.* **noun** (in klīn) a line that goes up or down at an angle from a flat surface. *The old bus couldn't make it up the hill's steep incline.*

include *verb* (in klood) 1. to have or contain as a part of the whole. *The new clock includes batteries.* | *The list includes his name.* 2. to put into a group or class. *She often included her little sister when she played with her friends.* | *I included the two new members on our member list.*

income *noun* (in kəm) the money you get from work you do or property you own. *That lawyer has a high income.* | *Rent from the apartments provides income to the owner of the building.*

income tax *noun* (<u>in</u> kəm tæks) a tax on the income of a person or business. *Your employer will deduct income tax from your pay each week.*

incompetent *adj.* (in <u>kam</u> pə tənt) without the skills or knowledge needed to do something well. *The company tries to get rid of incompetent employees.*

incomplete *adj.* (in kəm <u>plēt</u>) not complete; not finished. *Work on the new house is incomplete.*

increase *verb* (in <u>krēs</u>) 1. to make larger or more in number. *The company increased the salaries of the managers.* 2. to become larger or more in number. *Her salary increased last year.* | *The population of our town is increasing.*
noun (<u>in</u> krēs) an addition in size or amount. *There has been an increase in the number of people in this city in recent years.*

indeed *adv.* (in <u>dēd</u>) without any question or doubt. *I do indeed like the new restaurant.*

indent *verb* (in <u>dent</u> or <u>in</u> dent) to begin to write or type farther to the right on the first line of a piece of writing. *Indent the first line of a new paragraph.*

independence *noun* (in də <u>pen</u> dəns) [N] freedom from outside control. *People in America fought for **independence from** England.*

Independence Day *noun* (in də <u>pen</u> dəns dā) a U.S. national holiday celebrated on July 4 to remember the signing of the Declaration of Independence from England in 1776; Fourth of July.

independent *adj.* (in də <u>pen</u> dənt) 1. not ruled by another person or government. *Mexico is an independent nation.* 2. not needing the support or advice of another person. *She earns enough money to be an independent person.*

index *noun* (<u>in</u> deks) a list of subjects, names, or other information in a book, with page numbers given for each thing on the list. *Look at the index in the back of the book.*

Indian *noun* (<u>in</u> dē ən) 1. a member of any of the peoples who have lived in North or South America since before people from Europe arrived. 2. a person who was born in or is a citizen of India.

indicate *verb* (<u>in</u> də kāt) to show or point out. *Can you indicate your street on the map?*

individual *adj.* (in də <u>vi</u> joo əl) single, separate, or different from others. *You need to water each individual plant.*
noun a single human being; person. *Each individual in this country has certain rights.*

indoor *adj.* (<u>in</u> dōr) located or happening inside a house or building. *There is an indoor swimming pool at the community center.*

indoors *adv.* (in <u>dōrz</u>) in or into a building. *They went indoors when it started to rain.*

induce *verb* (in <u>doos</u>) to cause. *If you swallow that kind of poison, you should induce vomiting immediately.*

industrial *adj.* (in də <u>strē</u> əl) having to do with industry. *She works at a factory in the industrial park.*

industry *noun* (<u>in</u> də strē) a number of companies that make a particular product. *The automobile industry employs thousands of people.*

infant *noun* (<u>in</u> fənt) a child in the first months of life. *Infants need a lot of care.*

infant

infect *verb* (in <u>fekt</u>) to spread disease to. *Cover your mouth when you cough so you won't infect others.*

infection *noun* (in <u>fek</u> shən) a disease caused by germs. *He got an infection from a dirty wound.*

infectious *adj.* (in <u>fek</u> shəs) able to be spread to others. *The flu is an infectious disease.*

infinitive *noun* (in <u>fi</u> nə təv) the simple form of a verb that has no subject and does not show time of an action. It is usually formed by the word *to* followed by the base form of a verb. In the sentence "I want to leave now," "to leave" is an infinitive.

influence *noun* (<u>in</u> floo əns) a thing or person who can affect another thing or person. *My mother was a big influence in my life.* | *The war had an influence on the country's future.*
verb to affect. *Your ideas have influenced my thinking.*

influenza *noun* (in floo <u>en</u> zə) [N] an infectious disease in humans and some animals. Influenza causes fever, coughing, and muscle pain. It is often called "the flu."

inform *verb* (in <u>form</u>) to give knowledge to; tell. *They informed me that today is your birthday.*

123

informal *adj.* (in fōr məl) not formal in appearance or language. *The company allows employees to wear informal clothing to the office on Fridays. | Don't use informal language when you write a business letter.*

information *noun* (in fŏr mā shən) [N] knowledge or facts about any thing or event. *The newspaper is full of information. | My friend gave me information about the new movie.*

ingredient *noun* (in grē dē ənt) one of the parts of a mixture. *Flour, sugar, eggs, and cocoa are some ingredients of chocolate cake.*

inhale *verb* (in hāl) to breathe in. *Richard became sick after he inhaled chemicals at work.*

inherit *verb* (in he rət) to receive from a person who has died. *James inherited land and money from his grandfather.*

initial *adj.* (i ni shəl) first. *I was nervous before my initial visit to the doctor.*
noun the first letter in a person's name. *President Franklin Delano Roosevelt's initials were "FDR." | Put your signature on this line, and put your initials here.*

injure *verb* (in jər) to harm or damage. *He injured his leg in a car accident.*

injury *noun* (in jə rē) any damage to a part of the body that causes pain or a problem in how the part functions. *Hospitals treat many kinds of injuries, such as broken bones, cuts, and burns.*

ink *noun* (ingk) [N] a colored liquid in pens. *The teacher says we need to write with black or blue ink.*

in-law *noun* (in law) a relative by marriage; usually used with the words *mother, father, sister,* and *brother. My mother-in-law lives with us.*

inner *adj.* (i nər) located inside. *The inner walls of the house are painted yellow.*

innocent *adj.* (i nə sənt) not guilty of a crime. *George told the judge that he was innocent.*

input *noun* (in put) 1. [N] the information that is put into a computer. *This computer has a program that processes financial input.* 2. [N] an opinion, advice, or help. *I would like your input on the new work plan.*
verb to put or cause to be put into a computer; enter. *The secretary input the sales data yesterday.*

inquire *verb* (in kwīr) to try to find out by asking. *My boss inquired about my absence from work.*

inquiry *noun* (in kwə rē) a process of looking for true or correct information. *The government **conducted an inquiry into** defense spending.*

INS *abbrev.* (ī en es) an abbreviation for *Immigration and Naturalization Service*, which is now United States Citizenship and Immigration Services (USCIS).

insect *noun* (in sekt) a small animal with a hard covering over its body. Most kinds of insects have a body that is divided into three parts. Most insects also have three pairs of legs and one or two pairs of wings.

insect

insecticide *noun* (in sek tə sīd) a poison used to kill insects. *The farmer sprayed insecticide over his fields.*

insert *verb* (in sərt) to put in. *She inserted the plug in the socket.*

inside *prep.* (in sīd) in the inner part of; within. *Please don't wear your shoes inside the house. | What's inside that box?*
adv. into or to the inner part. *She went inside when it started to rain.*
noun (in sīd) the inner part or side. *The inside of this jacket is made of silk.*
inside of within the area or time of. *The cat is inside of the box. | He will be here inside of an hour.*
inside out having the inner surface facing out. *I put my socks on inside out this morning.*

inspect *verb* (in spekt) to look at with care in order to find any problems. *He inspected the machines to make sure they were safe.*

Word Builder: inspect +
inspector: a person who inspects or who does inspections.

inspection *noun* (in spek shən) the act of looking at with care in order to find any problems. *The restaurant passed the health department inspection.*

inspire *verb* (in spīr) to give someone the desire or courage to do something. *My parents' achievements inspired me to write a book about them.*

install *verb* (in stawl) to put into position and make ready for use. *She installed a new refrigerator in the kitchen.*

Word Builder: install +
installer: a person who installs things, such as appliances or carpet.

instance *noun* (in stəns) an example or occasion. *His gift was an instance of generous behavior.* | *In this instance, I will excuse you.*
   for instance as an example; for example. *I've lived in many cities, for instance, New York, Los Angeles, and Chicago.*

instant *noun* (in stənt) a very short amount of time; moment. *He disappeared* **in an instant.**
   adj. needing very little preparation in order to be ready to eat or drink. *I made instant coffee for myself and instant pudding for the children.*

instead *adv.* (in sted) in place of; rather. *I don't care for the mountains, so let's go to the beach instead.*
   instead of in place of. *She chose tea instead of coffee.*

instinct *noun* (in stingkt) a natural behavior that is not learned. *Instinct makes birds fly south in winter.*

institution *noun* (in stə too shən) a public organization set up for a specific purpose. *Hospitals, churches, prisons, and schools are examples of institutions.*

instruct *verb* (in strəkt) to teach. *My boss instructed me in how to use a computer.*

> **Word Builder: instruct +**
> **instructor:** a person who instructs.

instruction *noun* (in strək shən) [N] the act of teaching or giving knowledge. *Does the school offer* **instruction in** *swimming?*

instructions *pl. noun* (in strək shənz) a statement of how to do something. *Follow the instructions in the manual before using your new oven.*

instrument *noun* (in strə mənt) 1. a tool or mechanical device used for special work. *The dentist has a special instrument for cleaning teeth.* 2. a device for recording or measuring. *An airplane pilot uses many instruments when flying a plane.* 3. a thing used for making music. Pianos and horns are instruments. *Many children learn to play a musical instrument in school.*

insulate *verb* (in sə lāt) to cover with a material that reduces or stops the movement of heat, electricity, or sound. *We insulated our house to save money on our heating bill.* | *If a wire is not well insulated, it can cause an electrical fire.*

insulation *noun* (in sə lā shən) [N] the material used to prevent loss of heat. *We installed insulation in the attic.*

wall
insulation

insult *verb* (in səlt) to speak to someone in a way that hurts them. *She insulted her friend by saying he was stupid.*
   noun (in səlt) a rude statement or action that hurts someone's feelings. *He shouted* **insults at** *his brother.* | *Leaving the party early was* **an insult to** *the host.*

insurance *noun* (in shoor əns) [N] a promise of a company to pay money to you if certain accidents happen. You pay the company a regular amount of money for this protection. *After the fire, we got enough money from our insurance to buy a new house.*

insure *verb* (in shoor) to promise to pay money in case of loss or harm. *Some companies will not insure young drivers.* | *My house* **is insured against** *fire and theft.*

intelligence *noun* (in te lə jəns) [N] the ability to learn, think, and understand. *The scientist is a person of high intelligence.*

intelligent *adj.* (in te lə jənt) having a great ability to learn, think, and understand. *My son is intelligent and does well in school.*

intend *verb* (in tend) 1. to have a plan in your mind to do something; plan. *I intend to leave early in the morning.* | *I'm sorry. I didn't really intend to say that.* 2. to have in your mind for a specific purpose. *He intended the books for his sister.*

intention *noun* (in ten shən) a plan. *He went to college with the intention of getting a degree.*

interest *noun* (in trəst) 1. [N] the desire to learn or know about something. *The teacher* **took an interest in** *his student's work.* 2. [N] the money that is paid for the use of another person's money. *The bank will* **pay interest on** *the money in our account.*
   verb to cause to want to learn or know about something. *Computers interest me.*

interesting *adj.* (in trə sting) causing attention or interest. *He read an interesting article in the newspaper.*

interest rate *noun* (in trəst rāt) the rate at which interest is paid by a bank. An interest rate is given as a percent. *The interest rate on her savings account is three percent.*

interface *noun* (in tər fās) 1. programs that allow communication between a person and a computer or between computers. *A new interface allowed all the computers in the company to communicate with each other.* 2. the way a computer program appears on the screen to the person who uses the program. *Computer programs for children often have a colorful interface.*

interfere *verb* (in tər fēr) to block or prevent. *Noise from the party next door **interfered with** her sleep.*

interior *adj.* (in tēr ē ər) being inside or within. *The interior walls of the house had water damage.*
noun the inside area of a house, building, or car. *Mr. Adams's new car has a leather interior.*

interjection *noun* (in tər jek shən) a word or expression that shows strong feeling. *"Oh, no!" is an interjection.*

internal *adj.* (in tər nəl) located on the inside. *The heart is an internal organ.*

international *adj.* (in tər næ shə nəl) of or having to do with two or more countries. *The United Nations is an international organization.*

Internet *noun* (in tər net) [N] the world's largest computer network, which is made up of millions of computers that are linked together. Some parts of the Internet are the World Wide Web and e-mail. *My home computer is connected to the Internet.*

interpret *verb* (in tər prət) to understand in a particular way. *I interpreted her smile to mean that she agreed. | We had to interpret a poem in English class.*

interrogate *verb* (in te rə gāt) to question for a long time for an official purpose. *The police interrogated the suspect for several hours.*

interrupt *verb* (in tə rəpt) to begin to speak before someone else has finished speaking. *Please don't interrupt me while I'm speaking.*

intersect *verb* (in tər sekt) to meet or cross at a point. *There is a stop sign where these roads intersect.*

intersection *noun* (in tər sek shən) the place where two or more lines, roads, or other straight things meet. *Be careful when you cross a busy intersection.*

intersection

interstate *adj.* (in tər stāt) having to do with or connecting two or more states. *The federal government regulates interstate trade.*
noun a large road that runs through two or more states. *We took the interstate from Los Angeles to Chicago.*

interview *noun* (in tər vū) 1. a meeting between a person who has applied for a job and the person who is offering the job. The person who wants the job must answer questions about his or her experience and qualifications. *She applied for six jobs and got three interviews.* 2. a conversation in which someone asks questions of a person in order to learn more about that person. *This magazine often publishes interviews of movie stars. | Tenzin spent a long time preparing for his naturalization interview.*
verb to have an interview with or of. *The supervisor interviewed several people for the open position.*

into *prep.* (in too) 1. to the inside of. *Go into the room.* 2. against. *The clowns bumped into each other.* 3. to the condition or form of. *The rain turned into snow during the night.* 4. to a particular situation or action. *He went into business for himself.*

introduce *verb* (in trə doos) to present one person to another person for the first time. *Hello, Jim. May I introduce you to my wife, Nancy?*

introduction *noun* (in trə dək shən) 1. a part at the beginning of a book that explains what is in the book. *He read the introduction to see if the book interested him.* 2. [N] a book or course of study for people who know nothing about the subject. *Mr. Jackson took a class called Introduction to Computers.*

invent *verb* (in vent) to make something that has never been made before. *Do you know who invented television?*

Word Builder: invent +
inventor: a person who has invented something.

invention *noun* (in ven shən) something made for the first time; the result of inventing. *Thomas Edison is known for many inventions.*

inventory *noun* (in vən tōr ē) a complete list of things in a place, like a store. *The store manager hires extra people to* **take inventory** *once a year.*

Word Builder: inventory +
inventory sheet: the piece of paper where you record information when you take inventory.

invest *verb* (in vest) to put into use for the purpose of making more money. *He invested his money in a new company and hoped it would make him more money.*

investigate *verb* (in ve stə gāt) to look at closely so as to get information and learn the facts. *The police are investigating the crime.*

investigation *noun* (in ve stə gā shən) a thorough search to get true information. *The police* **conducted an investigation** *into illegal drug use.*

investment *noun* (in vest mənt) money that is put into use for the purpose of making more money. *I made an investment in some rental property.*

invisible *adj.* (in vi zə bəl) not able to be seen. *Air is invisible.*

invitation *noun* (in və tā shən) a formal request to someone asking hiim or her to go somewhere or do something. *I received an invitation to their wedding in the mail.*

invite *verb* (in vīt) to ask in a polite way to go somewhere or do something. *Mike invited me to have dinner with him.*

invoice *noun* (in voys) a statement that shows how much you owe for things or services given to you. *Mr. Garcia received an invoice for the shipment of books that he received.*

involve *verb* (in valv) to have as a necessary part; include. *Police work involves danger. | Please don't involve me in your problems.*

Word Builder: involve +
involvement: the state of being involved.

inward *adv.* (in wərd) in or toward the inside or center. *The door opens inward.*

iron *noun* (ī ərn) 1. [N] a heavy gray metal. Iron is mixed with other metals to make steel. 2. a small device with a handle and a flat surface that you make very hot. You use an iron to make cloth smooth.
verb to make smooth with an iron. *I ironed some shirts.*

iron

Word Builder: iron +
ironing: clothes that need to be ironed.
ironing board: a special table that you iron clothes on.

irregular *adj.* (i reg yə lər) 1. not even in some way. *The dirt road has an irregular surface.* 2. not following the general rules of grammar or spelling. *English has many irregular verbs.*

irrigate *verb* (i rə gāt) to bring in water for land or crops. *The farmer irrigated the dry land so he could grow corn.*

irrigation *noun* (i rə gā shən) [N] the act of supplying water to land or crops. *Much of the water from the river is used for irrigation.*

irritant *noun* (i rə tənt) something that makes part of your body sore. *Smoke is an irritant that makes the eyes red.*

irritate *verb* (i rə tāt) 1. to anger or annoy. *It irritates me when you tap your fingers on the table.* 2. to make sore or red. *The detergent irritated his skin.*

is *verb* (iz) a form of the verb **be** that is used with *he, she, it,* and with singular nouns. *She is happy, and so is he. | It is raining today. | The book is on the shelf.*

island *noun* (ī lənd) an area of land surrounded by water on all sides. *Hawaii is a group of islands.*

isolate *verb* (ī sə lāt) to set apart in order to make alone. *The doctors isolated the sick child. | His house is isolated in the woods.*

Word Builder: isolate +
isolated: separate and alone; far from others.
isolation: the act of keeping someone or something separate and alone.

issue *noun* (i shoo) 1. something that is produced and sent out. *Did you get the June issue of this magazine?* 2. a subject being talked about or questioned. *They discussed the issue of joining a union.*

it *pron.* (it) 1. the thing or animal that has been or will soon be mentioned. *She bought a newspaper and read it.* | *Flying is faster than driving, but I don't like it.* | *The dog barked, but it didn't bite.* | *It's too salty—this soup!* 2. a word used in sentences when the person or thing that is the logical subject is mentioned after the verb. In the sentence "It is nice to see you," "to see you" is the logical subject. *It was important to finish the work on time.* | *It was a terrible thing that he did.* 3. a word used with the verb *be* to give stronger emphasis to the information that follows. *It was his sister who called, not his wife.* 4. the general situation; often used as a subject in statements about time, weather, or distance. *It's six o'clock.* | *It's raining.* | *It's ten miles from here to the next town.*

itch *verb* (ich) to have a feeling on the skin that makes you want to rub it with your fingernails. *The insect bite on my arm itches.*

item *noun* (I təm) a separate thing in a group or list. *I have a list of six items to buy at the store.*

itemize *verb* (I tə mīz) to say or write each separate thing in a group or list. *They itemized their deductions on their tax return.*

its *adj.* (its) belonging to or having to do with the one already mentioned. *I have a dog. Its coat is black, but its tail is white.*

itself *pron.* (it self) its own self; used to show that an action is done to the same thing that does that action. *The cat cleaned itself.*

J j

jack *noun* (jăk) 1. a machine for lifting a heavy object. 2. the face card with the lowest value in a set of cards. The jack is pictured as a young man in uniform. 3. a part that allows you to connect to a source of electricity. *The telephone plugs into a jack in the wall.*

jacket *noun* (jă kət) a short coat or the top part of a suit.

jackhammer *noun* (jăk hă mər) a large tool with a motor used to dig in rock or other hard material.

jail *noun* (jāl) a building in which a government keeps people who have broken a law. *The judge sentenced him to three months in jail.*

jam¹ *verb* (jăm) to force into a small space. *She jammed her big foot into the little shoe.*
noun a large gathering or mass that slows or stops movement. *We were stuck in a traffic jam. | The copier won't work because of a paper jam.*

> **Word Builder: jam +**
> **jammed:** blocking the movement or flow of something through a tight space.

jam² *noun* (jăm) [N] a sweet spread made by cooking crushed fruit and sugar.

janitor *noun* (jă nə tər) a person whose job is to clean and take care of a building.

January *noun* (jăn ü ār ē) the first month of the year.

jar *noun* (jär) a round container with a wide mouth. A jar is often made of glass and has a lid. *That jar has peanut butter in it.*

jaw *noun* (jaw) 1. either or both of the two bones that frame the mouth and hold the teeth. *My jaw was tired after my dentist appointment.* 2. either of two parts of a tool that close or hold something like the bones of the mouth. *Clara held the bolt in the jaws of the pliers.*

jealous *adj.* (je ləs) 1. afraid of losing someone's love or attention to another person. *She became jealous when her parents spent so much time with the new baby.* 2. feeling angry or sad when you want what another person has. *He was **jealous of** his friend's new car. | She is **jealous of** her sister's fame and success.*

jeans *pl. noun* (jēnz) pants made from a heavy, often blue, cotton cloth. *Sue is not allowed to wear jeans to the office.*

jelly *noun* (je lē) [N] a soft food that is usually spread on bread. Jelly is made from fruit juice and sugar. *James made a sandwich with peanut butter and jelly.*

jersey *noun* (jər zē) 1. a shirt made of soft cloth that you pull on over the head. *This football team wears blue and gold jerseys.* 2. [N] a soft woven material often made of cotton or wool.

jet *noun* (jet) an airplane with engines that give off a flow of heated gases to cause forward movement. *They flew from New York to Chicago by jet.*

jewel *noun* (joo əl) a special stone that has been cut and made smooth. Jewels are used to make jewelry. *Diamonds and rubies are jewels.*

jewelry *noun* (joo əl rē) [N] things made of special stones and metal worn on the body for decoration. Rings, necklaces, and bracelets are some kinds of jewelry.

jewelry

jigsaw *noun* (jig saw) a kind of **saw¹** that has a narrow, thin metal blade for cutting sharp corners or curved designs. Jigsaws usually have an electric engine.

job *noun* (jäb) 1. a regular position for which a person is paid to do particular duties. *Does your job require you to wear a uniform?* 2. a particular piece of work. *Cleaning the windows was a big job.*

jog *verb* (jäg) to run at a slow rate for exercise. *She jogs every day after work.*

join *verb* (joyn) 1. to put, bring, or fasten together. *The children joined hands.* 2. to become a member of. *Will you join the softball team?*

joint *noun* (joynt) a place where two or more parts come together or are connected. *A person's hand and arm come together at the wrist joint. | We glued the joint where the leg meets the top of the table.*

joke *noun* (jōk) a short story with a funny ending that is told to make people laugh. *My uncle loves to **tell jokes.***
verb to say things that you think will make people laugh. *David and John are very funny when they are joking with each other. | Don't be angry. I was just joking.*

journal *noun* (jər nəl) a written record of a person's experiences, thoughts, or daily events. *Anna **keeps a journal.** | She writes in her journal every day.*

joy *noun* (joy) [N] a strong feeling of being happy. *Mrs. Perez was **filled with joy** when her daughter graduated from high school.*

judge *noun* (jəj) a person whose job is to hear and decide matters in a court of law.
verb to form an opinion about something. *Don't judge a book by its cover. | Can you judge the distance between here and there?*

judgment (judgement) *noun* (jəj mənt) 1. [N] the ability to make decisions about what to do. *I can't decide for you. You need to use your own judgment. | His decision to drive after drinking showed poor judgment.* 2. a decision made by a judge or court. *We heard about the judgment of the court on TV.*

judicial *adj.* (joo di shəl) having to do with judges, courts, or their activities. *The Supreme Court is part of the **judicial branch** of the federal government.*

jug *noun* (jəg) a container for liquids. A jug usually has a handle and a narrow part for pouring. *Milk comes in plastic jugs.*

jug

juice *noun* (joos) the natural liquid from plants or meats. The liquid from fruits is used for drinking.

> **Word Builder: juice +**
> **juicy:** full of juice.

July *noun* (ju lī) the seventh month of the year.

jump *verb* (jəmp) to push yourself into the air with a strong movement of your legs. *She jumped over the fence.*

June *noun* (joon) the sixth month of the year.

junior *adj.* (joon yər) used as a name, or after a name when a person's name is the same as his father's name. *Junior* is written *Jr. John Smith's son is named John Smith, Jr., but everyone just calls him Junior.*
noun a student in the third year of study at a high school or college in the United States.

junior high school *noun* (joon yər hī skool) a school before high school in the United States. Junior high school usually includes grades seven, eight, and nine. *Our son was in elementary school last year, but now he's in junior high school.*

junk *noun* (jəngk) [N] things that have little worth. *I'd like to throw away some of that old junk.*

jury *noun* (joor ē) in a court of law, a group of people that decides if a person is guilty or not guilty. *The jury took five days to make its decision.*

just *adj.* (jəst) balanced, reasonable, and fair. *This judge is a just person. | That is a just law. | Do you think that was a just punishment for the crime?*
adv. 1. a very short time ago. *He just left.* 2. only. *He ate just a few bites of cake.* 3. by a very small amount. *Kim just missed the bus.* 4. exactly. *That's just the point I meant to make.* 5. nothing more than. *He won't understand that because he's just a child.*
just about almost; nearly. *Tim is just about ten years old. | I'm just about finished with lunch.*

justice *noun* (jə stəs) 1. [N] the principle or quality of fairness. *The United States promises justice for all.* 2. [N] the way the law is carried out through the courts. *Some people think justice should be severe.* 3. a judge of a high court. *There are nine justices of the Supreme Court.*

K k

karate *noun* (kə ra̱ tē) [N] a way to protect and guard yourself without weapons, using your hands and feet. *I'm taking a class in karate at the youth center.*

karate

keep *verb* (ke̱p) **kept, kept** 1. to hold or continue to hold. *The bank will keep your money for you.* 2. to put or store. *You should keep milk in the refrigerator.* 3. to cause to remain in a certain state or position. *Please keep the baby quiet.* | *Keep the dog outside for a few minutes.* 4. to continue. *Keep going along this road until you get to Main Street.*
keep on to continue to do something. *Josie kept on dancing, even after the music stopped.*
keep out to stay away or cause to stay away from a place. *Please **keep out of** my room while I'm studying.* | *The sign on the gate said "Keep Out."*

kept *verb* (ke̱pt) past tense and past participle of **keep.**

ketchup (catsup) *noun* (ke̱ chəp) [N] a thick red mixture made with tomatoes and spices. Ketchup is a condiment.

key *noun* (ke̱) 1. a metal object cut in a special way so it can open or close locks. *I gave my neighbor a key to my house.* 2. something that allows or helps someone to achieve something. *Hard work is the key to success.* 3. a part of a machine or instrument that does something when you press it. *This computer keyboard has keys for numbers, letters, and functions.* | *The piano is an instrument with many keys.*
adj. most important; main. *We discussed only the key points of the article.*

keyboard *noun* (ke̱ bōrd) a row or rows of keys on a machine or instrument. *Most computers come with a keyboard.* | *Pianos and organs are instruments with a keyboard.*

keypad *noun* (ke̱ pæd) a small, flat part with keys or buttons that send a signal to an electronic machine. Computers, telephones, calculators, and remote controls have keypads. *Many computer keyboards have a small keypad for numbers.*

kick *verb* (ki̱k) to strike with the foot. *She kicked the ball.*

kid[1] *noun* (ki̱d) (informal) a child or young person. *Kids aren't allowed to see that movie.*

kid[2] *verb* (ki̱d) (informal) to say something that may not be true in order to make someone laugh or to laugh at someone. *She was just kidding when she said that.* | *Please don't kid me about my new haircut!*

kidnap *verb* (ki̱d næp) to take and hold a person by force in order to get money or some other valuable thing. *Two men kidnapped the son of the company president.*

Word Builder: kidnap +
kidnapper: a person who kidnaps another person.
kidnapping: the crime of taking and holding a person by force.

kidney *noun* (ki̱d nē) either of the two organs in the body that remove water and waste from the blood.

kill *verb* (ki̱l) to cause to die. *The hunter killed a deer.*

kind[1] *adj.* (kī̱nd) gentle, good, and caring. *It was kind of you to help your grandmother do her shopping.*

kind[2] *noun* (kī̱nd) a type; sort. *What kind of dog is that?*
kind of rather; in some ways. *He's actually kind of nice.*

kindergarten *noun* (ki̱n dər gar tən) a class for young children that introduces some school activities. Children in kindergarten are usually five years old. *Lily learned the alphabet in kindergarten.*

king *noun* (ki̱ng) a male ruler of a country who is not elected and whose mother or father was usually a ruler before him.

Word Builder: king +
kingdom: the land ruled by a king or queen.

kiss *verb* (ki̱s) to touch or press with the lips as a sign of love or respect. *I kissed my son good night.*

kit *noun* (ki̱t) 1. a group of things together in one place for a particular use. *She keeps bandages and antiseptic in the firstaid kit.* 2. a group of parts and materials used to make something. *I built that model car from a kit.*

kitchen *noun* (ki̱ chən) a room where people cook and store food.

kite *noun* (kīt) a toy that you fly in the air at the end of a long string. It is made of a light frame covered with paper or plastic.

kitten *noun* (ki tən) a young cat. *She has had her pet cat since it was a kitten.*

knee *noun* (nē) the joint between the upper and lower part of the leg.

kneel *verb* (nēl) *knelt, knelt* to rest on the knee or knees. *She knelt down and prayed.*

knelt *verb* (nelt) past tense and past participle of **kneel.**

knew *verb* (noo) past tense of **know.**

knife *noun* (nīf) *knives* a tool with a handle and a thin, sharp blade, used for cutting. *He cut the meat with a knife.*

blade   **knife**   handle

knit *verb* (nit) to make by joining together pieces of heavy thread by machine or by hand with long needles. *She knit a sweater.*

knives *noun* (nīvz) plural of **knife.**

knob *noun* (nab) a rounded piece on a door, drawer, or machine. *Lee turned a knob on the radio to change the station.*

knock *verb* (nak) to hit a door in order to make noise. *Please knock before you enter the room.*
knock down to make a person or object fall to the ground. *Another player knocked him down on the field. | The dog knocked down the lamp.*
knock over to make an object fall to its side. *The wind knocked over the empty bottle.*

knot *noun* (nat) a tying together of material such as rope or string that is used to fasten. *She tied her shoelaces in a tight knot.*

know *verb* (nō) *knew, known* 1. to have information in your mind that you have learned. *He knows your name.* 2. to have previous experience with someone or something; be familiar with. *He knows car engines. | She knows his parents.* 3. to have the skill to be able to. *Do you **know how** to ski?*

knowledge *noun* (na ləj) 1. [N] information, understanding, or skill. *Working in a restaurant gave Jim a good knowledge of cooking.* 2. [N] the state of having information about something. *Alice left home without her parents' knowledge.*

known *verb* (nōn) past participle of **know.**

L l

lab *noun* (lăb) a short form of **laboratory.**

label *noun* (lā bəl) a small piece of paper or cloth that is attached to an object. A label gives information about what the object contains, how to use it, or who owns it. *The label in my sweater says to wash it in cold water. | I typed the address on a label and taped it to the package.*
verb to mark with a label, or attach a name to something. *The school asked the parents to label their children's clothes.*

labor *noun* (lā bər) 1. [N] hard work or effort. *Finishing the building required many hours of labor.* 2. [N] the physical effort and pain of giving birth to a baby. *She was in labor for eight hours.*
verb to do hard work with little rest. *My grandfather labored six days a week in a hot, noisy factory.*

laboratory *noun* (lă brə tōr ē) a place used for scientific experiments or for teaching about science or other subjects. *Scientists test food for safety in a laboratory.*

Labor Day *noun* (lā bər dā) a holiday to honor working people. In the United States and Canada, Labor Day is on the first Monday in September.

lace *noun* (lās) 1. [N] a cloth made of fine threads that has holes in it as part of the design. *Grandmother's tablecloth is made of lace.* 2. a string used to hold two edges together. *She has white laces in her shoes.*
verb to tie together with a string passed through holes in two edges. *Lace your shoes so that they stay on your feet.*

lack *noun* (lăk) [N] the condition of being without something that is needed. *She canceled her vacation because of a lack of money.*
verb to be without something that is needed. *He was so weak that he lacked the strength to stand up.*

ladder *noun* (lă dər) 1. a structure with steps that you use to climb up to high places. You can move a ladder from one place to another. 2. a way of moving up to a

higher level in steps. *She climbed the company ladder to become president.*

Word Builder: kinds of ladders
extension ladder: a ladder that you make taller by extending a smaller attached ladder.
hook ladder: a ladder with hooks at the top that you attach to a roof or window.
platform ladder: a ladder with a platform at or near the top for holding things.
stepladder: a small ladder with flat steps that can stand without support.
straight ladder: a simple ladder with straight sides.

ladies' room *noun* (lā dēz room) a room in a public place with toilets and sinks used by women and girls.

lady *noun* (lā dē) a polite word for woman or girl. *Ladies and gentlemen, may I have your attention, please?*

laid *verb* (lād) past tense and past participle of **lay**[1].

lain *verb* (lān) past participle of **lie**[2].

lake *noun* (lāk) a large body of fresh or salt water that has land all around it. *Let's go swimming in the lake.*

lamb *noun* (lăm) 1. a young sheep. *There are many lambs in the field.* 2. [N] the meat of a young sheep. *We are having lamb for dinner.*

lamp *noun* (lămp) a device that uses electricity, oil, or gas to produce light. A lamp usually stands on a desk, table, or floor.

lamp

lance *noun* (lăns) a weapon with a long pole and pointed metal head.
verb to cut open with a small sharp tool. *The doctor lanced the infection on my foot.*

land *noun* (lănd) 1. [N] the solid part of the earth's surface. *Fish live in the sea, and tigers live on land.* 2. [N] some part of the surface of the earth. *They bought some land and built a house.* 3. a country or nation. *The princess lived in a land far away.*
verb to arrive on the ground or other surface. *The plane couldn't land because of the fog.*

Word Builder: land +
landing: the space at the top of the stairs.
landlady: a woman who gets money by renting property.
landlord: a person who gets money by renting property.

landfill *noun* (lănd fĭl) a place where trucks bring waste from cities and towns.

landscape *noun* (lănd skāp) the land and sky that you can see from one point. *When you look out her window, you can see a beautiful landscape.*
verb to change a piece of land by doing such things as planting trees, bushes, or other plants and changing the shape of the surface. *They will landscape the yard by making it flat and planting trees.*

Word Builder: landscape +
landscaper: a person whose job is to landscape property.

lane *noun* (lān) 1. a marked path for vehicles or people going in one direction. *The new highway has four lanes. | These lanes of the swimming pool are for older adults.* 2. a narrow country road or city street. Lane is used mostly in road names. *They live at 123 East Lane.*

language *noun* (lăng gwəj) 1. [N] the system of spoken or written words that people use to communicate thoughts, ideas, or feelings. *It surprises adults that children can learn language so quickly.* 2. words or signs that a particular group of people uses to communicate with each other. *He can speak two languages, English and Spanish.*

lap *noun* (lăp) the front of the body from the waist to the knees when you are sitting. *She held the baby on her lap.*

large *adj.* (lärj) big in size or amount. *We will need to buy a large pizza for this many people. | There was a large number of people at the meeting.*

lasagna *noun* (lə zä nyə) [N] a pasta dish made with wide, flat noodles, tomatoes and other vegetables, cheese, and meat.

laser *noun* (lā zər) a device that makes a very strong, narrow beam of light. *The doctor used a laser to perform the operation.*

last¹ *adj.* (lăst) 1. coming after or behind all others. *Our house is the last house on the street. | He was the last student to finish the test.* 2. coming just before the present time; most recent. *Last night was so cold, but today is much warmer. | The last time I went to the doctor was two years ago.* 3. being the only one remaining. *I saved the last piece of cake for you.*

last² *verb* (lăst) 1. to continue through time; to not end. *The movie lasted for two hours.* 2. to stay in satisfactory condition or remain able to be used. *These shoes were cheap, but they lasted for a long time.*

last name *noun* (lăst nām) a family name. *Johnson and Smith are very common last names in the United States.*

latch *noun* (lăch) a device that fastens or locks a door, window, or gate.

latch

late *adj.* (lāt) 1. happening after the usual or expected time. *I was late to work because I missed the bus.* 2. happening near the end of a period of time. *We got back home in the late evening. | It's late. Let's go to bed.*
adv. after the usual or expected time. *The bus arrived late.*

lately *adv.* (lāt lē) in the past but near to the present time; recently. *She called a few months ago, but she has not called lately.*

later *adj.* (lā tər) comparative of **late.** *The later flight to Chicago is at ten o'clock.*
adv. 1. comparative of **late.** *The bus came even later today than yesterday!* 2. at some following time or future time. *We went shopping, and later we went to the post office. | Let's finish this now. We can eat later.*

latest *adj.* (lā təst) 1. superlative of **late.** *Some students are often late, but he is always the latest student.* 2. most recent. *Did you hear the latest news about the accident?*
adv. superlative of **late.** *I can sleep latest on Saturdays.*

latex *noun* (lā teks) [N] a thick liquid used to make rubber, paint, and glue. *Paint made with latex is easy to clean. | The nurse's thin gloves are made of latex.*

laugh *verb* (lăf) to smile and make sounds with your mouth. People usually laugh when something is funny to them, but laughing can express other feelings also. *Some children laughed when the new student fell down. | We **laughed at** all his jokes.*

laughter *noun* (lăf tər) [N] the act or sound of laughing. *I could hear laughter in the next room.*

Laundromat *noun* (lawn drə măt) (trademark) a place where people pay to use washing machines and clothes dryers. *She does her laundry at the laundromat.*

laundry *noun* (lawn drē) 1. [N] the clothing, sheets, and other things that you plan to wash. *I put all my laundry in a big bag and took it downstairs.* 2. a room or business where you wash your laundry or pay someone to wash it.
do the laundry to wash your clothes or other things that are dirty. *I always do the laundry on Sunday.*

law *noun* (law) 1. [N] the set of rules that people in a society must follow. *The law is very complicated. Lawyers must study it for many years.* 2. any one rule that a government makes and that people must follow. *Every state has laws about driving and drinking.*
against the law not allowed by the law. *Driving without a driver's license is against the law.*
break the law to do something that is not allowed by the law. *If he breaks the law, he will go to prison.*

> **Word Builder: law +**
> **lawful:** according to the law; allowed by law.
> **lawfully:** in a lawful way; legally.
> **unlawful:** against the law; not allowed by law.

lawn *noun* (lawn) an area of land where people plant grass and cut it to keep it short. *The lawn was green.*

lawyer *noun* (loy ər) a person whose job is to give legal advice and to speak for people in court.

lay[1] *verb* (lā) *laid, laid* 1. to put something down so that it is flat against a surface. *Please lay the tablecloth on the table. | It was cold, so we laid another blanket on the bed.* 2. to produce an egg. *The hen laid an egg.*
lay off to stop a person's employment, usually because there is not enough work. *The car company laid off one hundred workers last month.*
lay out to spread or arrange something on a surface. *The children laid out the forks and spoons on the table. | I laid out the pattern on the material.*

> **lay or lie?**
> *Lay* means to put or place on a flat surface.
> *Lie* means to be or stay in a flat position.
> These words are easy to confuse, because their meanings are similar and the past tense of *lie* is *lay.*
> Compare:
> *Lay the mail on the table.*
> *He laid the mail on the table.*
> *Lie down if you are tired.*
> *Yesterday, I lay down for a short rest.*

lay[2] *verb* (lā) past tense of **lie**[2].

layaway *noun* (lā ə wā) [N] a plan to buy something from a store by paying a part of the price every week. You get the thing after you have paid the whole price. *If you don't have the money for the coat now, you can buy it* **on layaway.**

layer *noun* (lā ər) a covering of something that lies over a surface, or a substance that forms the first surface on which other coverings of the same material lie. *All the furniture had a thin layer of dust on it. | The workers put down the first layer of cement. | We made a cake with three layers.*

layover *noun* (lā ō vər) a short stay between parts of a trip. *We had a layover in Los Angeles because we had to change planes.*

lazy *adj.* (lā zē) not wanting to work or use effort. *I felt lazy yesterday and slept all afternoon.*

lead[1] *verb* (lēd) *led, led* 1. [N] to direct someone; guide. *He led us through the hotel to our room.* 2. to command or direct the activities of a group of people. *The president led the nation during a difficult time. | He led the orchestra for many years.* 3. to have the most active or controlling part in some activity. *Who will lead the meeting today?* 4. to be first among others. *Look! Your horse is leading in the race!*

lead[2] *noun* (led) a very heavy, soft, gray metal. Lead is poisonous.

leader *noun* (lē dər) a person who directs or guides others or who has the most power in a group. *The men followed their leader into the woods. | He was a strong and powerful leader of the army.*

leaf *noun* (lēf) *leaves* a flat part of a plant or tree that grows from the stem or branch. A leaf is usually green. *Many leaves fell from the tree during the wind storm.*

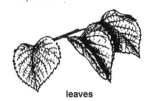

leaves

league *noun* (lēg) a group of people who have joined together for a special purpose. *Some countries formed a league to work for peace in the world. | His parents play in a bowling league on Thursday nights.*

leak *noun* (lēk) an opening or crack in a thing that lets something go through it. *There was a leak in the water pipe.*
verb to allow something to pass through an opening or crack in a way that was not intended. *We keep a bucket on the floor because the ceiling leaks.*

> **Word Builder: leak +**
> **leaky:** having a leak.

lean[1] *verb* (lēn) 1. to bend in a certain direction. *He leaned backwards.* 2. to rest your body by putting some of your weight on something. *He **leaned against** the wall as he talked on the phone.* | *Don't **lean on** that table! It will fall over.*

lean[2] *adj.* (lēn) having little fat. *My mother buys very lean meat.*

leap *verb* (lēp) *leaped (leapt), leaped (leapt)* to jump into the air either straight up or across a distance. *The frog leaped from the rock into the water.*

learn *verb* (larn) to get knowledge about something through study or experience. *If you study harder, you will learn more.* | *He learned the job by watching the other people.*

> **Word Builder: learn +**
> **learner:** a person who learns.
> **learning:** knowledge gained through study.

learner's permit *noun* (lar narz par mit) a paper that you get from the state that gives you permission to learn to drive. You must have a learner's permit before you get a driver's license. *My son just got his learner's permit, so I'm teaching him how to drive.*

lease *noun* (lēs) an agreement to pay to use another person's property for a certain period of time. *The lease for our apartment is for one year.*

leash *noun* (lēsh) a chain or kind of leather rope attached to the collar of an animal. *It is against the law here to walk your dog without a leash.*

—leash

least *adj.* (lēst) a superlative of **little;** smallest in size, amount, or degree. *She had **the least** difficulty of all the students because she studied hard.*
adv. a superlative of **little;** in or to the smallest amount or degree. *Of all the people at work, I like him least.* | *That book was the least interesting of the three.*

at least 1. not less than. *They will invite at least fifty guests, maybe more.* 2. used to name one good thing that still exists in a bad situation. *We didn't have any heat in the house, but at least we had hot water.*

leather *noun* (le thar) [N] a material made from the skin of an animal. People make shoes, bags, and many other things from leather.
adj. made of leather. *She bought a pair of leather boots.*

leave[1] *verb* (lēv) *left, left* 1. to go away from a place. *Their plane left Los Angeles at noon.* 2. to not take something with you when you go away. *They were not home, so I left the package by their door.* | *Oh no! I left my keys in the car!* 3. to let something stay in the same condition that it was before. *Please leave the door open when you go out.* 4. to go away. *What time are you leaving tomorrow?*
leave off to stop an activity before finishing. *We left off reading at page nine.*
leave out to not put something in; to not include. *She made a cake, but she left out the sugar by mistake.*

leave[2] *noun* (lēv) a permitted period of vacation or absence. *The soldier received two weeks' leave to be with his family.*

> **Word Builder: kinds of leave**
> **family medical leave:** time away from work to take care of someone in your family who is sick.
> **parental leave:** time away from work to take care of a new baby in your family.
> **personal leave:** time away from work to take care of personal business.
> **sick leave:** time away from work because you are sick.

leaves *pl. noun* (lēvz) plural of **leaf.**

led *verb* (led) past tense and past participle of **lead**[1].

LED *abbrev.* (el ē dē) an abbreviation for *light emitting diode.* An LED is an electric device that gives off a bright light. *When you turn the computer on, an LED lights up.*

left[1] *adj.* (left) being on the side of the body where the heart is. The opposite of left is right. *The pocket goes **on the left side.***
noun the side of the body where the heart is. *He looked to the left and right before crossing the street.*

left[2] *verb* (left) past tense and past participle of **leave**[1].

left-handed *adj.* (left hæn dəd) having more ability with the left hand than with the right. *This pair of scissors is made for left-handed people.*

leftover *adj.* (left ō vər) still remaining after everything else has been used. *I made a doll's dress with the leftover material from the curtains.*

leftovers *noun* (left ō vərz) food that remains after you have finished eating a meal. *We can eat the leftovers for lunch tomorrow.*

leg *noun* (leg) 1. the part of the body between the hip and the ankle. 2. something similar to a leg in appearance and use. *One of the table's legs is broken.*

legal *adj.* (lē gəl) 1. having to do with law. *A contract is a legal agreement.* | *I don't understand this legal language.* 2. allowed by law. *She is a legal resident of this country.*

legislation *noun* (le jə slā shən) [N] law or laws made by a government. *Congress* **passed** *new* **legislation** *to protect the air and water.*

legislative *adj.* (le jə slā təv) having to do with the branch of government that has the power to make laws. *The Senate is part of the legislative branch of the U.S. government.*

legislature *noun* (le jə slā chər) a part of a government that has the power to make or change laws. *The state legislature voted to change the tax laws.*

legume *noun* (le gūm) plants whose seeds are eaten as a vegetable. Beans and peas are legumes.

leisure *noun* (lē zhər) [N] freedom from work; free time. *She does not have much leisure since she started her new job.*

lemon *noun* (le mən) a small, sour fruit with yellow skin. Lemons grow on trees.

lemon

lend *verb* (lend) *lent, lent* to let someone use something that is yours. When you lend a thing to someone, you expect that person to return it to you. *It was raining hard, so I lent her my umbrella.*

length *noun* (lengkth) 1. the distance from one end of something to the other. *The length of this curtain is five feet.* 2. the amount of time from the beginning to the end of something. *The length of the movie was three hours.*

lens *noun* (lenz) a piece of clear material such as glass that bends light as light passes through it. *I went to the eye doctor to get new lenses for my glasses.*

lent *verb* (lent) past tense and past participle of **lend.**

less *adv.* (les) 1. a comparative form of **little;** to a smaller degree or amount. *We go out for dinner much less now than we used to.* | *He reads less than she does.* 2. to a smaller degree. *The coffee today is less strong than usual.*
  adj. comparative form of **little;** smaller in degree or amount. *I have less money than she has.*
  noun a smaller amount. *I have less than you have.*

lesson *noun* (le sən) a period of instruction with a teacher, or a specific group of things to be learned or studied together. *I have a piano lesson every Monday afternoon.* | *The second lesson in the book was more difficult than the first.*

let *verb* (let) *let, let* to allow. *He lets the dog sleep on the bed.*
  let go to stop holding; set free. *Don't* **let go of** *your brother's hand!* | *I caught a fish, but I let it go.*
  let's contraction of *let us* used to suggest an action for people to do together. *Let's order pizza for dinner.* | *Let's go!*

letter *noun* (le tər) 1. a mark in writing that represents a sound in a language. *A and Z are the first and last letters of the English alphabet.* 2. a message in writing that usually goes by mail to another person. *I'm writing a letter to my sister.*

lettuce *noun* (le təs) [N] a variety of green plant with large leaves that are eaten as a vegetable. Lettuce is often eaten in salad.

level *adj.* (le̱ vəl) 1. having a flat, even surface. *The ground here is level and easy to walk on.* 2. being of the same height or position as another thing. *The paintings should be **level with** each other.*
noun 1. position in height, stage, or rank. *People have different levels of ability in sports.* | *The level of the water in the river was high after the rain.* 2. a tool that shows if a surface is parallel to the ground.

lever *noun* (le̱ vər) 1. a basic tool used to lift something or open something by lifting it out. 2. a handle used to control or set the position of a part in a machine.

liability *noun* (lī ə bi̱ lə te̱) 1. [N] the condition of being responsible for payment under the law. *Some insurance will protect you against liability in case of a car accident.* 2. a thing that someone is responsible for paying, such as a debt. *His liabilities include a car loan and a student loan.*

liberal *adj.* (li̱ bər əl) generous. *The cook used a liberal amount of pepper in this soup.* | *He was liberal in his praise of his grandchildren.*
noun a person who wants a government that supports social change, equal rights, and personal freedom.

liberal arts *pl. noun* (li̱ bər əl a̱rts) subjects that make up a certain college degree program. A liberal arts program gives general knowledge of various subjects, not training for a specific job.

liberty *noun* (li̱ bər te̱) 1. [N] freedom from control by another person or another government. *Independence Day celebrates the liberty of the United States.* 2. the right or power to act and choose freely. *They have the liberty to vote for anyone they want.*

librarian *noun* (lī bra̱r e̱ ən) a person who has special training to work in a library.

library *noun* (lī̱ bra̱r e̱) a place in a town or school where you can borrow books, recorded music, and other materials.

library

lice *pl. noun* (lī̱s) plural of **louse.**

license *noun* (lī̱ səns) the legal permission to do some-thing, or the paper or card that shows legal permission. *My brother got his driver's license today.* | *A restaurant needs a license to sell wine or beer.*

license plate *noun* (lī̱ səns pla̱t) a small metal sign on a motor vehicle that usually has both numbers and letters. The license plate shows that it is legal to drive the vehicle on public roads.

lick *verb* (li̱k) to pass the tongue over or along the surface of something. *He licked the stamp before putting it on the envelope.*

lid *noun* (li̱d) a cover for a container that can be opened or removed. *Where is the lid for the juice bottle?*

lie[1] *noun* (lī̱) a false statement that is said on purpose. *He told his boss a lie about why he was late.*
verb to make a false statement on purpose. *He lied when he said he was busy.* | *She **lied about** her income.*

lie[2] *verb* (lī̱) *lay, lain* 1. to be in or move into a flat or resting position. *I spent all morning lying in bed.* | *The dog lay on the floor, sleeping.* 2. to rest or remain. *The cat walked over the books that lay on the table.* | *Those clothes have lain on your floor for three weeks!*
lie down to put yourself into a flat, resting position. *Lie down if you are tired.*

life *noun* (lī̱f) *lives* 1. [N] the thing that is in humans, animals, and plants that allows them to grow and to produce more creatures like themselves. Things like rocks do not have life. 2. [N] something that is alive; all living things as a group. *The scientists are looking for evidence of life on other planets.* 3. the time between birth and death. *My grandmother has had a long life.*

lift *verb* (li̱ft) 1. to pick up; raise. *We lifted the canoe from the water.* 2. to bring higher in position or condition; raise. *The cheerful song lifted their spirits.*
noun 1. a machine used for raising or carrying. *They went up the mountain on the ski lift.* 2. a ride given to a person who is traveling on foot. *I saw that she was tired, so I gave her a lift in my car.*

light[1] *noun* (lī̱t) 1. [N] the form of energy that makes it possible for the eye to see. The sun produces light. *There is less light during the day in winter.* 2. something that gives off light. *Turn off the light when you go to bed.*
adj. pale in color. *He has very light hair.*
verb *lit, lit* to cause to catch on fire. *After I light the candles, we can sing "Happy Birthday."*

Word Builder: light +
lighter: a small device that makes a flame. You use it to light a cigarette.
lighting: lamps and other things that give light.

light[2] *adj.* (līt) 1. not heavy or full. *My backpack was light enough to carry all day.* 2. not serious or important. *She did some light reading before going to bed.* 3. not filling, heavy, or strong. *It is a good idea to have only a light meal in the evening.*

Word Builder: light +
lightly: with little weight or force.

---

lightbulb *noun* (līt bəlb) a glass object that fits into a lamp or similar device and produces light. *We need to **change the lightbulb** in the ceiling light.*

lightning *noun* (līt ning) [N] the natural electricity produced in clouds and appearing as a bright flash of light in the sky. *Lightning usually occurs during summer thunderstorms.*

light switch *noun* (līt swich) the part of a light that you move to turn it on or off, or a device on a wall that you can use in the same way. *Most rooms have at least one light switch on the wall.*

like[1] *prep.* (līk) 1. the same as or similar to. *He is just like his father.* 2. in the character of someone or something; in the same manner. *She talks like her mother.*

---

like or as?
Like is a preposition that means *similar to.*
As is a preposition and a conjunction. When a preposition, it means *in the position or function of.* When a conjunction, it means *in the same way that* and is used to introduce a subject and verb.
Compare:
He wants a car like the one in the advertisement.
She works as an automobile mechanic.
He bought a new car, as he said he would.

---

like[2] *verb* (līk) 1. to find pleasure in; enjoy. *I like books, and I like to read.* | *They like watching movies.* 2. to have good and caring feelings about someone. *I really like my teacher a lot.*

likely *adv.* (lī klē) probably; possibly. *It will most likely rain tomorrow.*

limb *noun* (lim) 1. one of the large branches of a tree. *The worker cut the dead limb from the tree.* 2. an arm or leg in humans, or a leg or wing of an animal. *The pilot of the plane lost two of his limbs in the crash.*

limit *noun* (li mət) the point at which something ends; an edge or border. *The limit of our yard is that line of trees.*
verb to not allow the movement or progress of something beyond a certain point; restrict. *Tight clothes limit the movement of your body.* | *We limited our game to two hours.*

Word Builder: limit +
limited: having limits; not wide or broad.
unlimited: having no limits.

---

line[1] *noun* (līn) 1. a long, thin mark. *Sign your name on the line at the bottom of the form.* 2. a string, rope, or wire. *The telephone company put up new lines in front of my apartment.* 3. a row of people or things. *The line for tickets went all the way around the block.* 4. a group of words that serves as a unit of a larger work. *This is the most beautiful line in the poem.*
verb to mark with a line or lines. *I used a ruler to line my paper.*
line up to form a line, one person after the other. *Everyone lined up in front of the theater to buy tickets.*

line[2] *verb* (līn) to put a layer of material such as paper or cloth inside of something. *The tailor lined the jacket with silk.*

Word Builder: line +
lined: having a lining.
lining: the inner layer of a coat or other piece of clothing.

---

linen *noun* (li nən) 1. [N] a kind of cloth. *Linen is a comfortable fabric to wear in hot weather.* 2. cloth articles made for covering a bed or for use around the house. *Sheets, napkins, and towels are examples of linens.*

liner *noun* (lī nər) something that covers the inside of an object to protect it. *I always put in a plastic bag as a liner for the garbage can.*

link *noun* (lingk) 1. one of the separate closed pieces of a chain. *My chain bracelet fell off my arm because a link broke.* 2. anything that joins or connects. *There is a **link between** their family and ours because of marriage.* | *I feel a powerful link to my friends.*

lion *noun* (lī ən) a large, strong mammal in the cat family that lives in Africa and Asia. Male lions have long hair around the head and neck.

lion

lip *noun* (lip) 1. the part of the body on the upper or lower edge of the mouth. 2. the edge of a container such as a cup; rim. *Milk dripped from the lip of the cup.*

lipstick *noun* (lip stik) [N] a substance used for coloring the lips. *Lipstick comes in many colors.*

liquid *noun* (li kwəd) 1. [N] a form of matter that can flow and is neither a solid nor a gas. Water is the most common kind of liquid on earth. *This container holds a lot of liquid.* 2. an amount or kind of liquid. *Drink plenty of liquids such as water or orange juice while you're sick.*

liquor *noun* (li kər) [N] a liquid that people drink that contains a lot of alcohol. *They bought some bottles of liquor for the party.* | *They don't sell liquor in that restaurant.*

list *noun* (list) names, numbers, or things placed one after another in a written form. *I made a list of everything I need to buy at the store.*

listen *verb* (li sən) to pay attention to what can be heard. *Listen carefully to the teacher's directions.*

> **Word Builder: listen +**
> **listener:** a person who listens.

list price *noun* (list prīs) the price of an article as it appears in a list of products made by the same company. The list price is usually the price that the company recommends.

lit *verb* (lit) past tense and past participle of **light**[1].

liter *noun* (lē tər) the international standard unit used to measure liquids.

literacy *noun* (li tə rə sē) [N] the state of being able to read or write. *The literacy rate is high in the United States and Canada.*

literate *adj.* (li tə rət) able to read and write. *She can read Spanish, but she is not literate in English yet.*

literature *noun* (li tə rə chər) [N] stories, poems, plays, and other written works that people consider to have value in a culture. *She studied the literature of many countries before she became a teacher.*

litter *noun* (li tər) 1. [N] pieces of wastepaper and other objects scattered around a place. *We cleaned up the litter along the side of the road.* 2. a group

litter

of young animals born to one mother at one time. *My cat had a litter of six kittens.*
verb to make messy by scattering wastepaper or other objects. *He littered the floor with bits of paper.*

little *adj.* (li təl) 1. small in size. *The kittens are still little, but they are growing fast.* 2. young. *He is still too little to go to school.* 3. not much. *We have very little money.*
adv. 1. a small amount. *He sleeps very little at night.* 2. not very often. *We see each other very little now.*
a little 1. a small amount of something. *I have a little time now, so we can talk.* 2. to a small degree or for a small amount of time. *I'm a little tired right now.* | *I studied a little before dinner.* 3. sometimes, but not very often. *She baby-sits a little.*
little by little by small degrees or amounts. *Little by little, he learned everyone's name in the school.* | *Pour the water in little by little.*

live[1] *verb* (liv) 1. to be alive; be in an active state. *We live in a very interesting time in history.* 2. to support oneself in life. *I can **live on** very little money.* 3. to stay for a long time; exist in a place. *We live in the city, but he lives in a cabin in the mountains.*

live[2] *adj.* (līv) 1. being alive; having life. *We saw live baby chickens at the farm.* 2. carrying electric current. *The electricians were careful to step around the live wires.* 3. being watched or heard by people at the same moment that the action is taking place. *The TV program was a live broadcast.* | *They have live music at that restaurant.*

> **Word Builder: live +**
> **lively:** full of life and energy.

liver *noun* (li vər) 1. an organ in the body near the stomach whose most important function is to clean the blood. 2. [N] the liver of certain animals used as food. *My cat loves liver.*

lives *pl. noun* (līvz) plural of **life.**

living *adj.* (li ving) having life. *All living things need water.*
noun the way in which a person earns money; occupation. *She makes her living as an artist.*

living room *noun* (li ving room) a room in a home in which people can relax or gather together. A living room usually has a couch and comfortable chairs.

load *noun* (lōd) an amount of something carried. *The train carried a load of logs.*
verb 1. to put things on or in something in order to carry them. *They loaded the truck with boxes of food.* 2. to put something into a piece of equipment. *Did you load the camera with film?* | *The policeman loaded his gun.* 3. to enter a vehicle for transportation. *The passengers are now **loading onto** the airplane.*

Word Builder: load +
loaded: full.
loader: a machine that carries heavy things to another place.

loaf *noun* (lōf) **loaves** bread or other food made in one whole piece. *I bought a loaf of bread.* | *Salmon loaf is a very tasty dish.*

loan *noun* (lōn) money or something else that is borrowed or lent. *He got a loan from the bank to help pay the bills.* | *He thanked me for the loan of my chairs.*
verb 1. to give something with the understanding that it will be returned. *Will you loan me a suitcase for my trip?* 2. to lend money that must be paid back with interest. *The bank loaned money to her family.*

loaves *pl. noun* (lōvz) plural of **loaf.**

lobby *noun* (la bē) 1. a large open room inside the entrance of a hotel, theater, or other large building. *We'll wait for you in the lobby after we buy our tickets.* 2. a group that tries to influence people who make laws to vote in a way that supports what the group wants. *The senior citizens' lobby is very powerful in Washington.*
verb to try to influence people who make laws to vote in a way that supports what the group wants. *They went to Washington and **lobbied for** new laws to protect the environment.*

local *adj.* (lō kəl) 1. having to do with a particular place such as a neighborhood or town. *They called the local police for help.* 2. making many stops. *The local train takes longer because it stops at every station.*

locate *verb* (lō kāt) 1. to find the position or place of. *Have you located the school?* 2. to put or set in a certain place. *He located his business in the city.*

location *noun* (lō kā shən) 1. a place or position. *I marked the location of my house on the map.* 2. a specific place where something is located. *This is a poor location for a restaurant.*

lock *noun* (lak) a device used to prevent people from taking something or to keep something closed. *Put a lock on your bicycle when you leave it.* | *You need a new lock for this door.*
verb to use a lock to keep other people from opening something or taking something. *We locked all of the doors.* | *This window is locked.*

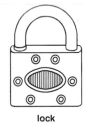
lock

lock out to make someone not able to enter a place. *She locked herself out of her car by accident.* | *The management locked the workers out of the factory during the strike.*
lock up to lock a place or thing so that others cannot get into it or take it. *Lock up your bicycle when you park it.* | *Lock up the house when you leave.*

locker *noun* (la kər) a small container that can be locked. It is used to keep clothes and personal things. *There are rows of metal lockers along the walls at school.*

lodge *noun* (laj) a cabin or shelter meant to be used by people doing outdoor activities. *The men stayed in a lodge during their hunting trip.*
verb 1. to live in a place for a short time. *They lodged with friends while the house was being repaired.* 2. to be or become caught or stuck in a certain position. *The kite lodged in the tree.*

lodging *noun* (la jing) a place to live in for a short time. *Their company will pay for their food and lodging during their trip.*

log *noun* (lag) 1. a large, thick piece of a tree that has been cut down and is ready for sawing, burning, or building. *Frank sawed logs to burn in the fireplace.* 2. a record of important events or activities that often includes the times that these things occured. *The plane's log showed that we had traveled 300 miles.* | *The company keeps a log of all phone calls and visitors who come into the office.*
log off to command a computer to end an activity. *Log off the computer before you turn it off.*
log on to enter a computer system. *A password is needed to log on to my computer.*

logbook *noun* (lag buk) a book that holds a record of important events or activities that often includes the times that these things occured. *Please write down how many copies you made on the copy machine in the logbook.*

logic *noun* (la̱ jək) [N] reasoning and careful thought. *Don't try to guess the answer. Use your logic.*

logical *adj.* (la̱ jə kəl) something that makes sense; reasonable. *It seems logical to keep your job until you find a new one. | It's not logical to get angry about something that hasn't happened.*

lonely *adj.* (lo̱n lē) without company; alone. *If you feel lonely, call a friend.*

long *adj.* (lawng) 1. covering a great distance or time. *There was a long line at the post office. | The runners were very tired after the long race.* 2. of a particular length in time or size. *The movie was two hours long.* **noun** a great period of time. *I've got the motor running, so I can't stay here* **for long.**

as long as since; on the condition of. *As long as you are paying, I will go to dinner.*

Word Builder: long +
long-distance: having to do with telephone service to a place that is far away.
long-range: having to do with a time in the future or a place in the distance.
long-sleeved: having long sleeves.
long-term: lasting for a long time.

look *verb* (lu̱k) 1. to use the eyes to see. **Look at** *the beautiful sunset!* 2. to seem or appear. *The big dog looked dangerous. | It looks as if it's going to rain. | You look tired this morning.* 3. to try to find; search. *She* **looked for** *her lost keys.*
noun the act of looking. *Please* **take a look at** *this report.*

look after to take care of. *My best friend looked after my dog while I was away.*

look forward to to be excited about something that will happen in the future; wait for eagerly. *I'm looking forward to my vacation.*

look like (informal) used to make a statement that may or may not be true based on what you can see or what you know at the present time; look as if. *It looks like we're going to win this game. | You look like you need a rest.*

look on to watch an activity as someone else performs it. *The boss looked on as we worked.*

look out to pay attention to avoid danger. *Look out when you cross that street.*

look over to examine. *I looked over the papers carefully before I signed them.*

look up to search for and find some desired

information in a book. *I looked up the names of all the U.S. presidents in a history book.*

loop *noun* (loop) the rounded shape made when a piece of string or rope curves back and crosses itself. *The end of the rope was tied into a loop.*

loop

loose *adj.* (loos) 1. not held back in any way; free. *The prisoner tried to get his hands loose.* 2. not joined or attached in a tight manner. *There is a loose button on your shirt. | You need to tighten this loose screw.*

Word Builder: loose +
loosen: to make loose or looser.

lord *noun* (lawrd) a person who rules. *The most powerful lord ruled the largest region of the country.*

lose *verb* (looz) *lost, lost* 1. to no longer have something because you do not know where it is. *I lost my watch.* 2. to fail to keep possession of something. *I just lost a quarter in this candy machine. | He lost all of his money by gambling.* 3. to fail to win. *They lost the contest.* 4. to experience the reducing or disappearing of something. *She lost a lot of weight when she was sick. | My grandfather lost his hearing. | I lost my confidence when I failed the first test.*

Word Builder: lose +
loser: a person who loses; a person who has lost.

loss *noun* (laws) 1. a failure to win; defeat. *The team was unhappy about its loss.* 2. a failure to keep or continue. *The loss of his friendship made me very sad.* 3. a decrease in size or amount. *The loss of ten pounds made him look very thin.* 4. the act of losing. *The loss of my glasses is a problem for me.*

lost *adj.* (lawst) 1. not able to be found; no longer in possession. *They finally found their lost puppy.* 2. not won. *The basketball team was unhappy about the lost games this season.* 3. not knowing where you are, or not knowing how to find your way. *We left the path and* **got lost** *in the woods.*
verb past tense and past participle of **lose.**

lost and found *noun* (lawst ən fownd) [N] a place where lost things are kept until the owner claims them. *Check the lost and found at school for your missing book.*

lot *noun* (la̱t) 1. a large amount or number. *We bought* **a lot of** *food for the party.* 2. a piece of land. *My brother hopes to build a house on the new lot that he just bought.*

lotion *noun* (lō shən) [N] a liquid that people use on their skin to protect it. *I use lotion on my hands.*

lottery *noun* a game in which people buy tickets with numbers on them for a chance to win a large amount of money. *Paul's chances of winning the lottery are small, but he buys tickets anyway.*

loud *adj.* (lowd) having a large amount of sound. *The dish made a loud crash when it fell to the floor.*

> **Word Builder: loud +**
> **loudly:** in a loud way.

loudspeaker *noun* (lowd spē kər) a piece of electronic equipment that makes sound louder and broadcasts it in one area, such as a room or hall. *The school makes announcements on the loudspeaker.*

louse *noun* (lows) *lice* a very small insect without wings. Lice live on the bodies of people and other animals from which they suck blood. People's hair is a common place for lice.

louse

love *noun* (ləv) 1. [N] a strong feeling of liking and caring about another person or thing. *She has a deep love for her children.* 2. a strong interest in or liking for something. *He has a great love for music.*
verb to have a strong feeling of caring about and liking a person or thing. *My parents love each other and have a happy marriage. | My daughter loves her dog.*
in love the condition in adults of having a very strong liking for someone and a strong desire to be with that person. *I haven't known her for very long, but I think I'm **in love with** her. | My parents met when they were young, and they soon **fell in love**.*

> **Word Builder: love +**
> **lover:** a person you are in love with.
> **loving:** showing love.

lovely *adj.* (ləv lē) beautiful in appearance. *Mom looked lovely in her new dress.*

low *adj.* (lō) 1. close to the ground or bottom; not high. *The wall is low enough for us to step over it.* 2. below the normal level. *The water in the lake was too low for sailing.* 3. not loud. *I heard the low sound of a train in the distance.*

lower *verb* (lō ər) 1. to cause to move to a position below; let down. *Lower the boat into the water.* 2. to make less loud. *Please lower your voice in the library.*

loyal *adj.* (loy əl) showing faithfulness to someone or something. *She was a loyal friend.*

loyalty *noun* (loy əl tē) the condition of being faithful or loyal. *The soldiers showed great loyalty to their country during the war.*

luck *noun* (lək) 1. [N] something that happens by chance. *It was luck that brought them together.* 2. [N] good fortune; success. *Have you had luck in your search for the lost kitten?*

lucky *adj.* (lə kē) resulting from or having good fortune. *My father is a lucky man to have a job that he loves.*

lug *noun* (ləg) a large nut that has an opening at only one end. *Car tires have several lugs holding them in place.*
verb to carry or drag. *He lugged the heavy box up the stairs.*

> **Word Builder: lug +**
> **lug nut:** another word for lug.
> **lug wrench:** a wrench that you use on a lug nut.

luggage *noun* (lə gəj) [N] suitcases and bags for carrying one's things on trips. *Check your luggage at the gate before you enter the plane.*

lumber *noun* (ləm bər) [N] wood cut into boards or beams
for use in building. *The carpenter brought a lot of lumber to build the barn.*

lunch *noun* (lənch) a light meal eaten in the middle of the day.

> **Word Builder: lunch +**
> **lunch box:** a box with a handle in which you carry your lunch.
> **lunch break:** a break during which you eat lunch.
> **lunchroom:** a room in a workplace or school where people eat lunch.
> **lunchtime:** the time during which you eat lunch.

lung *noun* (ləng) either of the two organs in the body that control breathing.

lunge *verb* (lənj) to make a sudden movement toward something. *He lunged forward to stop the child from falling.*

M m

macaroni *noun* (mæ kə rō nē) [N] a form of pasta in the shape of hollow tubes.

machine *noun* (mə shēn) a piece of equipment with a system of parts that work together to do or make something. *I clean my clothes in a washing machine.*

machinery *noun* (mə shē nə rē) [N] machines in general. *Workers are repairing the street with noisy machinery.*

mad *adj.* (mæd) angry. *I was **mad at** him for forgetting to pick me up.*

made *verb* (mād) past tense and past participle of **make.**

magazine *noun* (mæ gə zēn) a large, thin book with stories, pictures, articles, and advertisements. Magazines are printed and sold at regular times. *His favorite sports magazine appears once a week.*

magic *noun* (mæ jik) 1. [N] the mysterious control of physical forces or events through special actions or words. *In the story, the bad queen used magic to hurt the kind princess.* 2. [N] tricks that entertain by suggesting mysterious control. *He did magic, including making a rabbit jump out of a hat, at the children's party.*

magician *noun* (mə ji shən) a person who has skill in magic and entertains people with tricks.

magnet *noun* (mæg nit) an object that has the power to pull things made of iron toward itself. *She attaches things to the refrigerator with magnets.*

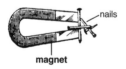
nails
magnet

magnetic *adj.* (mæg ne tik) 1. having to do with magnets and the way they work. *Certain metals are magnetic.* 2. having the power to attract people. *The new governor is a magnetic speaker.*

maid *noun* (mād) a woman whose job is to take care of and clean a house or hotel rooms. *The Smiths have a maid who comes in twice a week.*

maiden name *noun* (mā dən nām) the last name of a woman before she marries and begins to use her husband's last name. *Mrs. Stein's maiden name is Green.*

mail *noun* (māl) [N] letters, packages, and other things sent and received through an official system. *Our town's post office handles thousands of pieces of mail every day.*
verb to send something through the official system. *I mailed a card to my cousin.*

Word Builder: mail +
mailbox: a box for holding mail to be delivered or collected.
mail carrier: a person who carries letters and other mail from house to house.
mailman: a man who carries letters and other mail from house to house.
mailroom: the room in a workplace where people receive, sort, and send mail.

main *adj.* (mān) most important. *The main entrance to the building is on State Street.*

maintain *verb* (mān tān) to keep in good condition. *It can be expensive to maintain a car.*

maintenance *noun* (mān tə nəns) [N] the act of keeping something in good condition. *The janitor is in charge of building maintenance.*

major *noun* (mā jər) 1. the military rank above captain. *Dina is a major in the army.* 2. a student's main field of study at a college or university. *Don's major is physics.*
adj. very important. *The economy is a major issue in the campaign for president.*

majority *noun* (mə jawr i tē) [N] a number or amount that is more than half. *The majority of people in our neighborhood live in apartments.*

make *verb* (māk) *made, made* 1. to perform an action. *Stop making so much noise!* 2. to put in order or prepare. *She makes the beds every morning.* | *He makes dinner every night.* 3. to cause something to exist by putting parts together; build. *They made a table out of wood.* 4. to cause to have a feeling or condition. *The news about the accident made him sad.* 5. to force someone to do something, or cause a thing to do something. *I made my son clean his room.* | *The wind made her hat fly away.* 6. to earn. *The head of the company makes a lot of money.*
noun the brand of something. *What make of car is that?*
make do to manage, even if you have too little. *It is hard to **make do on** one paycheck.*
make it to succeed in arriving somewhere or attending something. *I'm sorry. I can't make it to your party on Sunday.*

make up 1. to form or be the parts of. *My family is* **made up of** *my parents, my brother, and me.* 2. to do something to make things right again. *He brought flowers to* **make up for** *hurting his girlfriend's feelings.* 3. to invent something using your mind. *She made up an excuse to stay home from school.* 4. to become friends again after a fight. *Carol and Ron made up.*

makeup *noun* (mā kəp) [N] cream, powder, or other things you put on your face to change the way it looks or to make it look better. *Jane wears makeup every day.*

male *adj.* (māl) having to do with a person or animal of the sex that does not produce eggs or give birth. *A beard is usually a male feature.*
noun a person or animal of the sex that does not produce eggs or give birth. *The police believe that the thief is a male.*

mall *noun* (mawl) a large indoor or open area that contains shops, restaurants, or other buildings. *I went shopping and had lunch at the mall.*

mallet *noun* (mæ lit) a hammer with a short handle and a round head made of wood, rubber, or some other material.

mammal *noun* (mæ məl) an animal that feeds its babies with milk from the mother. Dogs, whales, and humans are mammals.

man *noun* (mæn) **men** an adult male human being. *I met that man at work.*

manage *verb* (mæ nij) 1. to direct or control. *She manages a grocery store.* 2. to succeed in doing something, even if you have problems. *Anna* **managed to** *finish school while working full time.*

management *noun* (mæ nij mənt) [N] people who own or run a business. *Labor and management negotiated a new contract.* | *This store is under new management.*

manager *noun* (mæ ni jər) the person whose job is to lead a business or a department, or project of a business.

mandatory *adj.* (mæn də tōr ē) required; necessary. *There is a mandatory waiting period before you get your license.*

mankind *noun* (mæn kīnd) [N] all human beings. *Pollution is an issue that is important to mankind.*

manner *noun* (mæ nər) a way of doing something. *She has an awkward manner of speaking.*

manners *pl. noun* (mæ nərz) polite behavior. *Your son has very good manners.*

manual *adj.* (mæn ū əl) using the hands or worked by hand. *He was hired to do manual labor.* | *This car has a manual transmission.*
noun a book of instructions. *Maggie read the manual to learn how to use the new computer.*

manufacture *verb* (mæn yə fæk chər) to make by machine in large quantities. *This factory manufactures car parts.*

Word Builder: manufacture +
manufacturing: the business of making things by machine in large quantities.

many *adj.* (me nē) a large number of. *There are many rooms in the hotel.*
noun a large number of persons or things. *Many of the children got sick.* | *Many of the chairs were broken.*

many or much?
Many is used with words for things that we can count.
Much is used with words for things that we cannot count.
Compare:
Do you have many things to do today?
Do you have much work to do today?
I didn't eat many cookies.
I didn't drink much milk.

map *noun* (mæp) a picture of an area of the earth or sky drawn or printed on a flat surface. *This map shows the streets, parks, and important buildings in Chicago.*

map

maple *noun* (mā pəl) a tree with hard wood and flat leaves that change color and fall off in autumn. Maple trees produce a sweet liquid that people make into syrup.

marathon *noun* (mær ə than) 1. a race in which people run 26.2 miles. *Thousands of people run in the Boston Marathon.* 2. any activity that requires great effort over a long period of time. *Their climb up the mountain was a real marathon.*

March *noun* (march) the third month of the year.

march *verb* (march) to walk with steady, regular steps together with others. *Several bands marched in the parade.*

margarine *noun* (mar jə rin) [N] a food used in place of butter. Margarine is made of vegetable oil, milk, coloring, and other ingredients.

marines *pl. noun* (mə rēnz) a military group that fights both on land and at sea. In the United States, the marines are part of the navy. *Jim joined the marines after high school.*

marital *adj.* (mær i təl) having to do with marriage. *Lenny and Lena enjoy good marital relations.*

Word Builder: marital +
marital status: whether you are married, single, divorced, or separated.

mark *noun* (mark) 1. a spot, line, or other shape that can be seen on a surface. *The wet glass left a mark on the table.* 2. a grade on a school test, report, or other work. *Megan gets good marks in school.*
verb 1. to put a spot, line, or other shape on. *Barbara marked the front door with her dirty hands.* 2. to give a grade to. *The teacher marked the tests and returned them.*
mark down to lower the price of. *The store marked down the winter clothes in February.*
mark up to raise the price of. *That store marked up toys before the holidays.*

Word Builder: mark +
marker: a pen with a thick tip.

market *noun* (mar kit) a place where people buy and sell things. *Fruits and vegetables are sold at the farmers' market.*

marriage *noun* (mær ij) the state of two people being united by law. *Their marriage lasted for fifty years.*

marry *verb* (mær ē) 1. to become someone's husband or wife according to the law. *John married Tina on Saturday.* 2. to join two people as partners for life in an official ceremony. *The priest married them in a church.* | *They were married by a judge.*

Word Builder: marry +
married: having a partner in marriage.

mask *noun* (mæsk) a covering that hides all or part of the face. *The children wore frightening masks for Halloween.*

mask

mass *noun* (mæs) 1. a thing or group of things with no form or structure. *He took a mass of clay and made it into a pot.* 2. the amount of matter in a body or object. *The mass of this brick is greater than the mass of that book.*
adj. having to do with large numbers of people. *TV is a form of mass communication.*

master *noun* (mæ stər) a person with power or control. *The captain is the master of the ship.*
verb to develop skill in or knowledge of something. *He mastered tennis.*

master's degree *noun* (mæ stərz də grē) a degree that you get after finishing an advanced program of study at a college or university. *He has a master's degree in science.*

mat *noun* (mæt) a piece of material that is used to cover a small area of a floor or other surface. *Wipe your shoes on the mat before you enter.*

match[1] *noun* (mæch) a thin piece of wood or thick paper with a material on the end that burns when you strike it against something. *She used a match to light the cigarette.* | *He keeps a box of matches near the stove.*

match[2] *noun* (mæch) a game or competition. *We won the soccer match because we practiced hard.*
verb 1. to bring together because of being equal or the same. *The object of the game is to match pairs of cards.* 2. to be alike in some way, such as size or color. *Your socks don't match.*

mate *noun* (māt) a marriage partner or close friend. *My parents say that they are mates for life.*
verb to come together to produce babies. *Their two dogs mated and had ten puppies.*

material *noun* (mə tē rē əl) 1. anything used for building or making new things. Wood, metal, paint, and paper are examples of materials. *They delivered the building materials to the construction site.* | *I have to buy materials for my art class.* 2. [N] cloth. *Karin bought some material for a new dress.*

maternity *adj.* (mə tər ni tē) having to do with the time when a woman is carrying a child before she gives birth. *She wore maternity clothes while she was pregnant.*

math *noun* (mæth) the short form of **mathematics.**

mathematics *noun* (mæ thə mæ tiks) [N] the study of numbers, amounts, and shapes, and the relationships among them.

matter *noun* (mæ tər) 1. [N] all substances of the universe that can be seen, touched, or measured. Matter includes solids, liquids, and gases. 2. [N] a problem or trouble. *What is **the matter with** you?* **verb** to have importance. *It does not matter to me whether you stay or leave.*

mattress *noun* (mæ tris) layers of soft material held together by an outer layer of strong fabric. A mattress is used to sleep on. *Joe had to buy new sheets and blankets to fit his new mattress.*

mature *adj.* (mə choor) 1. grown in full. *A mature oak tree is very tall.* 2. developed in mental or physical qualities. *Her oldest son has a mature attitude for a teenager.*

maximum *noun* (mæk sə məm) the largest possible amount or number. *A maximum of two hundred people are allowed in this room.*

may *verb* (mā) 1. to be allowed to. *You may speak to the doctor now.* | *May I sit here?* 2. used to express that some action or state is possible but not certain. *He may come tonight, or he may come in the morning.*

May *noun* (mā) the fifth month of the year.

maybe *adv.* (mā bē) it may be so; perhaps. *Maybe the sun will come out today.*

mayonnaise *noun* (mā yə nāz) [N] a thick, light-colored mixture made of eggs, oil, and other things. Mayonnaise is a condiment.

mayor *noun* (mā ər) the head of government in a village, town, or city.

me *pron.* (mē) the person who is speaking or writing; the form of **I** that is used as the object of a verb or that is used after a preposition. *The dog bit me.* | *He gave it to me.*

meal[1] *noun* (mēl) 1. an occasion when people prepare and eat food at a specific time. *Many Americans eat three meals a day.* 2. a group of foods eaten at one time. *Joe ate a meal of beans and rice.*

meal[2] *noun* (mēl) [N] corn, wheat, or other grain that has been ground. *This machine grinds corn into meal.*

mean[1] *verb* (mēn) *meant, meant* 1. to intend to express. *What do you mean?* | *I mean what I say.* 2. to give a particular idea or message. *The word* tomorrow *means the day after today.* | *These dark clouds mean that a storm is coming.*

mean[2] *adj.* (mēn) not nice; nasty or cruel. *The mean dog bit the child.*

meaning *noun* (mē ning) the message that is intended by words, signs, pictures, or other forms of expression. *The meaning of* mandatory *is required or necessary.*

means *pl. noun* (mēnz) a way to do or complete something. *Cars are a means of transportation.*

meant *verb* (ment) past tense and past participle of **mean**[1].

meanwhile *adv.* (mēn wīl) during the same period of time. *I drove all night to get home; meanwhile, my family was waiting for me.*

measles *noun* (mē zəlz) [N] a disease that causes a fever and red spots on the skin. Measles usually affects children.

measure *verb* (me zhər) 1. to find out the exact size of something. *He measured the room before he bought a new rug.* 2. used to say how long, wide, or large something is. *This board measures three feet in length.* | *This room **measures** 12 feet **by** 10 feet.*

measure

measurement *noun* (me zhər mənt) the exact size of something that you find out by measuring. *The measurements of the rug are three feet by six feet.* | *We need to **take the measurements of** the room.*

measures *pl. noun* (me zhərz) things that are done to get a particular result. *The police are **taking** new **measures** to fight crime.*

meat *noun* (mēt) [N] the flesh of animals when used as food. *What kind of meat do you want, beef or pork?*

Word Builder: meat +
meatpacking: having to do with preparing the meat of animals for use as food.

mechanic *noun* (mə kæ nik) a person whose job is to make and repair tools, machines, and motors.

mechanical *adj.* (mə kæ ni kəl) made of or having to do with machines or motors. *Cars have many mechanical parts.*

medal *noun* (me dəl) a flat, small piece of metal used as an honor or reward. A medal usually has a design or words on it. *She won a gold medal in the race.*

media *pl. noun* (mē dē ə) the means of bringing information to large numbers of people through newspapers, magazines, radio, computers, and television. *The media gave a lot of attention to the election.*

medic *noun* (me dik) a person who gives medical help, especially in the military. *John was a medic in the army.*

medical *adj.* (me di kəl) having to do with the study or practice of medicine. *After years of medical school, she became a doctor.*

Medicaid *noun* (me di kād) a program of the U.S. government that pays for health care for people who cannot pay for it themselves.

Medicare *noun* (me di kār) a program of the U.S. government that pays for health care for older people or people who no longer work.

medication *noun* (me di kā shən) a medicine. *She takes medication for high blood pressure.*

medicine *noun* (me di sən) 1. a drug or other substance used to treat an illness or injury. *I gave my baby some medicine for his cough.* 2. the science of learning about and treating diseases and injuries. *There are many different jobs in the field of medicine.*

meditate *verb* (me di tāt) to clear the mind for a period of time as a way to relax. *She meditates before yoga class.*

medium *adj.* (mē dē əm) middle or average in size or amount. *I ordered a medium soda, not a large.*

meet *verb* (mēt) *met, met* 1. to see and begin to know someone; be introduced to. *My parents met my boyfriend yesterday.* 2. to come together and share company by plan or by chance. *We decided to meet at the restaurant at seven o'clock.* | *I was surprised to meet my teacher at the store yesterday.*

meeting *noun* (mē ting) a gathering of people for a particular purpose. *Our company has weekly staff meetings.*

melt *verb* (melt) to change from a solid to a liquid through heat. *The wax melted as the candle burned.*

—melt

member *noun* (mem bər) one of the people or things in a group. *Are you **a member of** this club?*

Word Builder: member +
membership: the state of being a member of something.

memo *noun* (me mō) a short form of **memorandum**.

memorandum *noun* (me mə ræn dəm) a written message between people who work in the same business. *The boss explained the new rules in a memorandum to everyone in the department.*

memorize *verb* (me mə rīz) to learn something well enough that it stays in your memory. *He memorized the words to the song.*

memory *noun* (me mə rē) 1. [N] the ability to remember information or experiences. *She has a good memory for numbers.* 2. an experience, person, or thing that one remembers. *I have happy memories of my visit with you.* 3. the part of a computer that stores information. *New computers have a lot of memory.*

men *pl. noun* (men) plural of **man.**

mend *verb* (mend) to repair or fix. *He mended his torn jeans.*

men's room *noun* (menz room) a room in a public place with toilets and sinks used by men and boys.

mental *adj.* (men təl) having to do with the mind and thinking. *She has a mental illness and can't live alone.* | *The old man still had all his mental powers.*

Word Builder: mental +
mentally: by using the mind; in a way that has to do with the mind.

mention *verb* (men shən) to speak about something in a few words. *Sam mentioned that he was going away for the weekend.*

menu *noun* (men ū) a list of foods served at a restaurant. *The server gave a menu to each customer.*

merchandise *noun* (mər chən dīs) [N] things that people buy or sell. *The spring merchandise has just arrived at the store.*

merchant *noun* (mər chənt) a person who owns a shop or other business that is involved with buying and selling.

mercy *noun* (mər sē) [N] kind treatment by a person who has some power over another person. *The judge showed mercy to the man who stole the car.*

merit *noun* (me rit) value or high quality. *That idea has merit.* | *In this company, your salary is based on merit.*

merry *adj.* (me rē) cheerful and happy. *Everyone was merry at the wedding party.*

mess *noun* (mes) a state of being dirty or not neat. *My room was a mess.*
    mess around (informal) to play with no purpose. *Stop messing around with my tools!* | *Those boys always mess around together after school.*
    mess up 1. (informal) to make something messy. *The children messed up the living room.* 2. (informal) to ruin or cause a problem with something. *Being sick messed up his plans for the weekend.* | *He really messed up his car in that accident.*

message *noun* (me sij) spoken or written information sent from one person or group to another. *There are three messages on the answering machine.*

messenger *noun* (me sən jər) a person who carries and delivers messages and packages.

messy *adj.* (me sē) not neat; in a mess. *Please clean your messy room!*

met *verb* (met) past tense and past participle of **meet.**

metal *noun* (me təl) a kind of chemical element, such as copper, iron, and aluminum, that can move heat or electricity. *Many tools, car parts, and pieces of jewelry are made of metal.*

Word Builder: metal +
metalworker: a person who builds things from metal.

meter[1] *noun* (mē tər) the international standard unit used to measure length.

meter[2] *noun* (mē tər) a device that measures or records distance, speed, time, quantity, or degree. *Many homes have gas and electricity meters.*

method *noun* (me thəd) a regular or proven way of doing something. *He has his own method of working.*

metric *adj.* (me trik) having to do with the international system of measure. *Most countries other than the United States use the metric system.*

mice *pl. noun* (mīs) plural of **mouse.**

microwave *noun* (mī krō wāv) an appliance that heats food or liquids very quickly.

microwave

middle *noun* (mi dəl) the place, point, or position that is in the center of or halfway from each end of a thing. *The boat is in the middle of the lake.* | *Don't stand in the middle of the road.*

middle age *noun* (mi dəl āj) [N] the period of human life that comes between youth and old age. *Where do you plan to live when you reach middle age?*

middle school *noun* (mi dəl skool) a school that includes middle grades, usually grades six through eight. *Children go to middle school after elementary school and before high school.*

midnight *noun* (mid nīt) twelve o'clock at night. *I told my son he had to be home by midnight.*

might[1] *verb* (mīt) 1. used to show that something is possible in the present or future but is not certain. *We might go away next weekend, but we're not sure yet.* | *She might not be home now.* 2. used as a past form of **may** after verbs in the past tense that report speech or thoughts. *I may actually leave early today, although I told her I might stay.* 3. used to express that something is a possibility only if something else happens or if something else were true. *If you ask me politely, I might tell you.* | *If you were older, you might understand better.*

might[2] *noun* (mīt) [N] force or physical strength. *The child used all her might to open the jar.*

Word Builder: might +
mighty: having might or power.

migrant *adj.* (mī grənt) moving from place to place. *Migrant workers work here in June for the strawberry harvest.*
    noun a person who travels from place to place to find work. *Migrants harvest grapes, apples, lettuce, and other farm crops.*

mild *adj.* (mīld) not harsh; gentle. *We had a mild winter, with only a little snow.*

mile *noun* (mīl) a standard unit used to measure long distances.

mileage *noun* (mī ləj) 1. the distance in miles from one place to another, or the distance traveled in one trip. *What is the mileage from here to Chicago? | Our mileage today was much less than yesterday because of the snow.* 2. the number of miles that a vehicle can travel per unit of fuel. *Our new car gets better mileage than our old one.*

military *adj.* (mi lə te rē) having to do with soldiers or armies. *Dan wore a military uniform.*
noun [N] the armed forces. *Did you serve in the military?*

milk *noun* (milk) [N] a white liquid made by female mammals as food for their babies. Many people drink the milk of cows.

milk carton

Word Builder: milk +
milkshake: a drink made from milk, ice cream, and flavoring.

mill *noun* (mil) 1. a machine that crushes whole or solid substances. *Please grind these coffee beans in the coffee mill.* 2. a building or factory where raw materials are changed into products such as cloth, flour, or lumber. *The steel mill in the town employed many workers.*

million *noun* (mil yən) the word for the number 1,000,000.

millionaire *noun* (mil yə nar) a person whose money and property are worth at least one million dollars. *She became a millionaire when she sold the company she started.*

mind *noun* (mīnd) the part of a person that thinks, understands, remembers, imagines, and feels. *Lee has a curious mind and loves to learn.*
verb to think something is bad or not pleasant; often used in questions and with *not* to say that something is acceptable to you. *I do not mind cooking, but I hate cleaning. | **Would** you **mind if** I open the window?*
change one's mind to make a different decision from the one made before. *I ordered coffee, but I changed my mind.*
make up one's mind to decide after thinking for some time. *I can't make up my mind. I like both of them.*
never mind used to tell someone to forget about something or to not worry about something. ***Never mind about** the money you owe me. | Never mind. I can come back later.*

out of one's mind not able to think with a clear mind; crazy. *If she marries that man, she is out of her mind!*

mine¹ *pron.* (mīn) the one or ones that belong to me; a possessive form of **I**. *This is your seat. Mine is over there. | That book is mine.*

mine² *noun* (mīn) a hole or area of holes made in the earth from which coal, gold, silver, or other things are taken. *West Virginia is known for its coal mines.*
verb to dig out; take out from under the earth. *People mine copper in Montana.*

Word Builder: mine +
miner: a person who works in a mine.
mining: the activity of digging in the earth for minerals.

mineral *noun* (mi nə rəl) a substance in the earth that does not come from an animal or a plant. Some minerals, like iron and calcium, are important for human health.

minimum *noun* (mi nə məm) the smallest possible amount or number. *There is an age minimum for this movie.*

minister *noun* (mi ni stər) 1. a person who has the authority to perform or help at the religious services of some religions. *Tony and Maria were married by a minister in church.* 2. a person who is the head of a government department in some countries. *She is the minister of defense in Canada.*

minor *adj.* (mī nər) less important or serious than others of the same kind. *My problem is a minor one compared to yours.*
noun a person under the age of an adult as recognized by law. *Minors cannot vote.*

minority *noun* (mi nar i tē) 1. a number or amount that is less than half. *A minority of students protested the new rules.* 2. a group of people who are different from the larger population in some way. *Many countries have laws that protect minorities.*

mint *noun* (mint) 1. a plant with a strong, pleasant smell whose leaves are used as a flavoring. *I put mint in my iced tea for flavor.* 2. a candy that is flavored with these leaves. *She offered mints after dinner.*

minus *prep.* (mī nəs) made less by subtracting. *Ten minus three is seven.*

minute *noun* (mi nət) 1. a standard unit used to measure time. One minute equals 60 seconds. 2. a very short period of time. *Would you please come inside for a minute?*

Miranda rights *pl. noun* (mə ræn də rīts) specific rights that a person has about what he or she can do or say after being arrested by the police. *The police told the suspect her Miranda rights when they arrested her.*

mirror *noun* (mir ər) a smooth surface that shows an image of whatever is in front of it. *Many bathrooms have a mirror above the sink.*

misbehave *verb* (mis bə hāv) to act or behave in a bad way. *The children misbehaved in the restaurant.*

miscellaneous *adj.* (mi sə lā nē əs) made up of many different kinds. *There is a pile of miscellaneous junk in the garage.*

misdemeanor *noun* (mis də mē nər) a crime that is less serious than a felony. The punishment for a misdemeanor is less than one year in prison.

miss[1] *verb* (mis) 1. to fail to hit, catch, reach, cross, or touch. *He missed the ball.* | *I missed the plane.* 2. to fail to see, hear, or understand. *He missed what I said.* 3. to feel sad or lonely without someone or something. *She missed her friend.*

Word Builder: miss +
missing: not able to be found; lost.

Miss[2] *noun* (mis) the title used before the name of a girl or woman who is not married. *The name of our teacher is Miss Jones.*

mission *noun* (mi shən) a special job given to a person or group of people. *The soldiers are on a mission to destroy the enemy base.*

mist *noun* (mist) [N] a mass or cloud of tiny water drops in the air. *There was mist on the mountain.*

mistake *noun* (mi stāk) a thought or action that is not correct. *I made a mistake when I called her Eileen instead of Elaine.* | *The teacher noticed a few mistakes on the test.*
verb mistook, mistaken to confuse someone or something with another. *I mistook him for his brother.*

mistaken *verb* (mi stā kən) past participle of **mistake.**

mistook *verb* (mi stuk) past tense of **mistake.**

misuse *noun* (mis ūs) [N] a wrong use. *Misuse of a saw can be dangerous.*
verb (mis ūz) to treat in a wrong or bad way. *He misused the bicycle, and now it doesn't work.*

miter saw *noun* (mī tər saw) a kind of **saw**[1] used to make special cuts in wood.

mitten *noun* (mi tən) a covering for the hand, with one part for the thumb and another part for all the fingers.

mix *verb* (miks) to put different things together so that the parts become one. *If you mix yellow and blue paint, you will get green.*
noun something that is made of parts or substances that you put together with a liquid. *We need to add milk to the cake mix.*
mix up to confuse. *Don't mix up the cables when you are charging a car battery.*

Word Builder: mix +
mixer (1): a soft drink that you mix with alcohol.
mixer (2): a machine that you use to mix batter or dough.
mixer (3): a party at which people who don't know each other meet.

mixing bowl *noun* (miks ing bōl) a bowl in which things can be combined in food preparation. Mixing bowls come in many different sizes.

mixing bowl

mixture *noun* (miks chər) something that is made by two or more things that are mixed together. *Dough is a mixture of flour, water, and other ingredients.*

mobile home *noun* (mō bəl hōm) a house that can be moved but stays in one place for a long time. *Many mobile homes are in a special area with utilities and other amenities.*

model *noun* (ma dəl) 1. a small copy of something. *We make a model of a new machine before we build it full size.* 2. a particular type or style of a product. *The salesman showed us a newer model of car.* 3. a person whose job is to show new clothing by wearing it for customers or for photographs. *Magazines show photographs of models wearing beautiful clothes.*

modern *adj.* (ma dərn) having to do with the present or current times. *Modern computers are smaller and faster than old computers.*

moist *adj.* (moyst) wet; damp. *I used a moist towel to clean the counter.*

moisture *noun* (moys chər) [N] a small amount of liquid in the air or on a surface. *The light rain left moisture on the ground.*

mold¹ *noun* (mōld) a hollow form used to give a particular shape to a soft or liquid substance that is poured into it. *The workers poured cement into a mold for the curb.*
verb to work into a certain shape or form. *She molded the clay into a human head.*

mold² *noun* (mōld) [N] a fungus that grows on the surface of plant or animal materials such as food or leather. *Don't eat this bread. It has mold on it.*

mole *noun* (mōl) a small, dark spot on the skin. *She has a mole on her cheek.*

mom *noun* (mam) (informal) another word for **mother.**

moment *noun* (mō mənt) a very short amount of time. *May I talk with you for a moment?*

Monday *noun* (mən dā) the second day of the week. Monday comes between Sunday and Tuesday.

money *noun* (mə nē) [N] coins or paper bills of a country that are used to buy things or pay for services. *How much money do we have in the bank?*

money order *noun* (mə nē ōr dər) a paper that you use like a check to pay a specific amount of money. You buy a money order and pay for it with cash. *Money orders are a safe way to pay bills.*

monitor *noun* (ma ni tər) 1. a device used to collect information about the operation or condition of someone or something. *James was attached to a heart monitor while he was in the hospital.* 2. a screen for a computer that shows information. *Working in front of a computer monitor all day is tiring.*
verb to observe something in order to get information. *The supervisor monitors our daily progress.*

monitor

monkey *noun* (məng kē) a small, intelligent mammal in the same family as humans. Monkeys often live in places with a warm climate.

monster *noun* (man stər) a large, frightening creature that is not real. *He likes to read books about monsters.*

month *noun* (mənth) one of the twelve parts of a year. *What month were you born in?*

monthly *adj.* (mənth lē) happening once a month. *Our monthly meetings take place on the second Tuesday of each month.*

monument *noun* (man yə mənt) something built in memory of a person, event, or special act. *There are many famous monuments in Washington, D.C.*

mood *noun* (mood) a person's general feeling of emotion at a certain time. *Too much work has put him in a bad mood.*

moon *noun* (moon) an object that circles around a planet. *Earth has one moon.*

mop *noun* (map) a tool with cloth at the end of a stick that is used to clean floors and other things. *I usually sweep the floor before I use the mop.*
verb to clean with this tool. *He mops the kitchen floor at least once a week.*

moral *adj.* (mōr əl) 1. having to do with what is right and what is wrong in how a person acts. *Many people go to a religious leader for help with moral decisions.* 2. following rules of right or fair behavior. *People expect moral behavior from teachers.*

morals *pl. noun* (mōr əlz) ideas or habits of behavior that have to do with what is right and what is wrong. *A person with good morals will not cheat or steal.*

more *adj.* (mōr) comparative form of **many** or **much;** in a greater number, amount, or degree. *They have many books, but even more magazines.* | *They have more money than we do.*
noun a greater amount or degree. *He makes a good salary, but he would like to make more.*
adv. 1. comparative form of **much;** to a greater degree. *He eats more than I do.* | *I like him very much, but I like his wife more.* 2. in or to a greater amount or degree. *She is more beautiful now than when she was younger.* 3. a greater number of times or for a longer period of time. *I need to visit my sister more.* | *Do you want to swim more or go home?*

morning *noun* (mōr ning) the early part of the day, beginning when the sun rises and ending at noon. *The children leave for school at eight in the morning.*

mortgage *noun* (m**ōr** gij) a written agreement by which an institution, such as a bank, agrees to lend money so you can buy a property. The institution holds a claim to this property until you pay back all the money. *Most people sign a mortgage when they buy a home.*

moss *noun* (maws) [N] a small, green plant without flowers. Moss grows on rocks, trees, and wet ground.

most *adj.* (m**ōst**) superlative of **many** or **much;** in the greatest number, amount, or degree. *Most people like ice cream. | This is the most fun I've ever had.* *noun* the greatest number or amount. *His brother and sister have some of the money, but he has most of it.* *adv.* 1. superlative of **much;** in the greatest amount or to the greatest degree. *We all talked a lot, but you talked most. | I like this one most.* 2. to the greatest degree. *That was the most difficult question on the test.*

Word Builder: most +
mostly: for the most part; almost all.

motel *noun* (m**ō** t**el**) a hotel that has places to park near the rooms for those who travel by car. *It will be necessary for us to spend the night in a motel on our trip.*

moth *noun* (mawth) a flying insect with four large wings. Most moth wings have dull colors.

mother *noun* (m**ə** thər) a female parent.

motion *noun* (m**ō** shən) the act of moving or changing places. *The motion of the car made me sick.*

motion picture *noun* (m**ō** shən p**ik** chər) a story that is told by means of recorded pictures and sound; film or movie. *He likes to watch old motion pictures on TV.*

motivate *verb* (m**ō** tə v**āt**) to make someone want to do something. *A good teacher motivates her students to learn. | Fear of cancer motivated him to quit smoking.*

motor *noun* (m**ō** tər) a machine that causes motion or power. *The mechanic repaired the motor in the car.*

Word Builder: motor +
motorboat: a small boat with a motor.
motorist: a person who drives a car or other motor vehicle.
motor vehicle: a vehicle with a motor, such as a car or truck.

motorcycle *noun* (m**ō** tər s**ī** kəl) a vehicle with two wheels, a heavy frame, and an engine. *You should wear a helmet when you ride a motorcycle.*

mound *noun* (mownd) a raised amount of something; pile. *The children made a big mound out of sand.*

mountain *noun* (mown tən) a landmass with great height and steep sides. It is much higher than a hill. *She likes to hike and climb in the mountains.*

mourn *verb* (mawrn) to feel great sadness over the loss of something. *Mr. Diaz mourned the death of his father.*

mouse *noun* (mows) *mice* 1. a very small animal with gray or brown hair, sharp teeth, and a long, thin tail. 2. a small device used with computers to choose and move things on the computer screen.

computer mouse

Word Builder: mouse +
mouse pad: a soft pad under a computer mouse.

mouth *noun* (mowth) the part of the body through which an animal eats, breathes, and makes sounds. The mouth is on the face below the nose.

move *verb* (moov) 1. to change position or place. *Let's move to better seats up front.* 2. to be in motion. *The dog moved quickly when I called him.* 3. to change the place of one's home or business. *They are moving to California next month.* 4. to change the position or place of. *I moved my bed to the other side of the room.* 5. to cause to have strong or powerful feelings. *We were moved to tears by his story.*
noun an action or motion. *The dog **made a move** toward the cat.*
move in to bring your possessions into a new place where you will live or work. *Have you moved into your new house yet?*
move out to leave a home or business, taking all your things with you. *We will **move out of** our apartment this weekend.*
move over to change position to make room for another person. *I will move over so you can sit on the couch, too.*

movement *noun* (moov mənt) a motion or way of moving. *The dancers performed some beautiful movements.*

movie *noun* (moo vē) 1. a motion picture; film. *I enjoy watching movies.* 2. (plural) the showing of a motion picture. *Let's go to the movies.*

mow *verb* (mō) to cut down with a blade or machine. *He mowed grass to earn some money.*

mower *noun* (mō ər) a machine with blades for cutting grass or other plants.

mph *abbrev.* (em pē āch) an abbreviation for *miles per hour.*

Mr. *abbrev.* (mi stər) a title of respect often used before a man's last name.

Mrs. *abbrev.* (mi səz) a title of respect often used before a woman's last name if she is married.

Ms. *abbrev.* (miz) a title of respect often used before a woman's last name. It does not give information about whether a woman is married.

MSDS *abbrev.* (em es dē es) an abbreviation for *Material Safety Data Sheet.* An MSDS tells the proper, safe way to handle a particular substance.

much *adj.* (məch) great in degree or amount. *There isn't much time before you have to leave.*
noun a great amount or number. *They don't have much, but they are happy.*
adv. to a great degree. *My other friends don't like him very much.*

mud *noun* (məd) [N] wet earth that has turned soft. *The dog was covered in mud.*

Word Builder: mud +
muddy: full of or covered with mud.

muffin *noun* (mə fən) a type of bread that tastes similar to cake and has a small, round shape. *Would you like a corn muffin or a peach muffin?*

mug *noun* (məg) a large, heavy cup with a handle, often used for hot drinks. *I drink coffee from a mug.*
verb to attack and try to rob someone on the street or in some other public place. *A criminal mugged Ms. Jones last night.*

mug

mule *noun* (mūl) an animal with a horse as its mother and a donkey as its father. People use mules for riding or carrying heavy loads.

multiplication *noun* (məl tə pli kā shən) [N] an operation with two numbers in which one number indicates how many times the other number is added. *Four times three in multiplication is the same as adding four groups of three.*

multiply *verb* (məl ti plī) to figure the answer of a problem by doing multiplication. *You get twelve when you multiply four by three.*

mumps *noun* (məmps) [N] a disease that most often affects children. It causes the glands around the neck and in other areas to swell.

murder *noun* (mər dər) the crime of killing a person. *He **committed a murder** before he was arrested.*
verb to kill a person in a way that is deliberate or cruel. *He murdered two people and will be in prison for the rest of his life.*

muscleS *noun* (mə səl) the soft pieces of flesh in animals and humans that make the bones move. *Joe has weak muscles because he never exercises.*

muscular *adj.* (məsk yə lər) having muscles that are large or strong. *People who play tennis often have muscular arms.*

museum *noun* (mū zē əm) a building where objects that are important to history, art, or science are kept and shown to the public. *They enjoyed seeing the paintings and statues in the art museum.*

mushroom *noun* (məsh room) a kind of fungus with a stem and a cap. Some mushrooms can be eaten as a vegetable, and others are poisonous.

music *noun* (mū zik) [N] pleasant sounds made by voices or instruments. *People clapped their hands when they heard the music.*

Word Builder: music +
musical (1): having to do with music.
musical (2): a play with songs and other music.

musician *noun* (mū zi shən) a person who has skill at playing, singing, or writing music.

must *verb* (m<u>ə</u>st) 1. used to express necessity to do something; to be required to; have to. *Humans must breathe in order to live.* | *Children must attend school.* 2. used to make a strong statement about something based only on logic, not knowledge. *That woman must be her sister. She looks just like her.* | *He is not answering the phone, so he must be out.* 3. used with *not* to express that some action is not allowed. *Employees must not use this machine without proper training.*

---

must or have to?

Have to and *must* usually have the same meaning.
Have to is used in everyday conversation.
Must is used in writing or in a formal setting.
Have to and *must* have different meanings when used with *not.*
Compare:
You have to leave tomorrow.
You must leave tomorrow.
You do not have to leave tomorrow. (You can leave tomorrow if you want, or you can stay, or you can leave some other time.)
You must not leave tomorrow. (You do not have permission to leave tomorrow.)

---

mustache *noun* (m<u>ə</u> stæsh) the hair that grows above the upper lip. *He has a long mustache.*

mustache

mustard *noun* (m<u>ə</u> stərd) [N] a thick brown or yellow mixture with a strong taste. Mustard is a condiment.

my *adj.* (m<u>ī</u>) of or belonging to me; the possessive form of **I.** *This is my seat, not yours.*

myself *pron.* (mī <u>self</u>) 1. used to show that an action is done to or in connection with the speaker, who is the same person who performs the action. *Because of my injury, I couldn't dress myself.* | *I wrote myself a note.* | *I looked at myself in the mirror.* 2. I and no one else. *I myself will take care of this, not my secretary.*

mysterious *adj.* (mi <u>stē</u> rē əs) not known and not able to be explained. *A mysterious light appeared in the sky.*

mystery *noun* (<u>mi</u> stə rē) 1. a matter that is secret or that cannot be known or explained. *What happened to the dinosaurs is a mystery.* 2. a movie, play, book, or other piece of writing that is usually about a crime. *I like to read mysteries and adventure stories.*

N n

nacho *noun* (na chō) a piece of tortilla that is spread with cheese and sometimes other food and then cooked.

nail *noun* (nāl) 1. a thin, pointed piece of metal with a flat top. You hammer nails into pieces of wood or other material in order to fasten them together. *We hammered nails into the new roof.* 2. a hard, thin growth on the end of a finger or toe. *I cut my nails so it would be easier to play the piano.*

nail

Word Builder: kinds of nails
fingernail: the nail at the end of each finger.
toenail: the nail at the end of each toe.

naked *adj.* (nā kid) wearing no clothing; bare. *The naked baby splashed in the bathtub.*

name *noun* (nām) a word or group of words by which something or someone is known. *What is the name of the street where you live? | My name is Jesse.*
verb to give a name to. *I named my kitten Fluffy.*

nap *noun* (næp) a short period of sleep, often during the day. *You will feel better after a short nap.*

napkin *noun* (næp kin) a piece of cloth or paper that you use to keep your mouth, hands, and clothes clean while you eat. *My mother always used cloth napkins for dinner.*

narrow *adj.* (nær ō) 1. not wide. *The bus could not pass through that narrow street.* 2. limited or not changing in ideas or opinions. *People with narrow minds often don't trust new ideas.*
verb to make less wide. *The police narrowed the area of their search for the lost child.*

nasty *adj.* (næ stē) 1. very bad to look at, smell, or taste. *Rotten eggs have a nasty smell.* 2. mean or rude; not kind. *You should apologize for saying such a nasty thing to your sister.* 3. causing harm, trouble, or danger. *He had a nasty fall on those broken steps.*

nation *noun* (nā shən) a country made up of people living under their own government. *The United States became a nation in 1776.*

national *adj.* (næ shə nəl) 1. belonging to one particular nation. *Baseball is the national sport of the United States.* 2. having to do with the whole country, not just one part of it. *The economy is a national issue.*

nationality *noun* (næ shə næ lə tē) the condition of belonging to a particular nation by having been born there or by becoming a citizen. *My grandfather's nationality was Mexican.*

native *adj.* (nā tiv) 1. being the place of birth of a person, or having to do with a person's place or situation of birth. *He missed his native country. | She is a native speaker of English.* 2. belonging to a person or persons because of their place of birth. *Spanish is his native language.*
noun a person born or raised in a particular place. *Mr. Howe is a native of Canada.*

Native American *noun* (nā tiv ə me ri kən) a member of any of the peoples who have lived in North or South America since before people from Europe arrived.

natural *adj.* (næ chər əl) 1. of or produced by nature. *The forest is the natural home of many animals. | She uses only natural ingredients in her cooking.* 2. not pretended or forced. *Your smile looks more natural in this photograph.*

naturalize *verb* (næ chər ə līz) to become or to make someone a citizen; give the rights of a citizen to someone. *The judge naturalized several people who had moved to the United States from other countries.*

Word Builder: naturalize +
naturalization: the process of becoming a citizen of a country.

naturally *adv.* (næ chər ə lē) 1. by nature. *She is a naturally curious child.* 2. of course; without a doubt. *Naturally, I will pass the test.*

nature *noun* (nā chər) 1. [N] the basic character and qualities of a person or thing. *It's not in her nature to be mean. | It is the nature of a lion to hunt.* 2. [N] the physical world and living things in their natural state; all things that are not made by people. *A camping trip is a good way to experience nature.*

naughty *adj.* (naw tē) 1. not behaving or obeying. *The naughty girl hit her sister.* 2. bad or not proper. *Martha told a naughty joke that offended me.*

navy *noun* (nā vē) 1. the part of a nation's military organization that fights wars on or over the sea. *My grandfather served in the navy during World War II.* 2. a dark blue color. *Navy is a good choice for a business suit.*

Nazi *noun* (nat sē) a member of the political party that held power in Germany from 1933 to 1945.

near *adv.* (nēr) 1. to, at, or within a short distance from a person or thing. *I recognized his face as he came near.* 2. close in time. *People are happy because spring is near.*
adj. closer; not far. *Their house is on the near side of the lake.* | *Will I see you in the near future?*
prep. at or close to. *He bought a house near the ocean.*

nearby *adj.* (nēr bī) located close at hand; not far away. *His mother works at a nearby supermarket.*
adv. in a place that is close by. *Stay nearby in case we need your help.*

nearly *adv.* (nēr lē) almost; just about but not quite. *We are nearly there.*

neat *adj.* (nēt) clean and in proper order, or liking to keep things that way. *Tom's desk is neat because he is a neat person.*

Word Builder: neat +
neatly: in a neat way.

necessarily *adv.* (ne sə ser i lē) certain to be. *Rich people are not necessarily happy.*

necessary *adj.* (ne sə ser ē) being something that you must have or must do; needed; required. *Food and water are necessary for life.* | *A TV is not really a necessary thing.* | *It is necessary for you to sign all the forms.*

necessity *noun* (nə se si tē) a person or thing that is needed. *Sleep is a necessity for good health.*

neck *noun* (nek) 1. the part of the body that connects the head to the rest of the body. 2. the narrow top section of something. *The neck of the bottle was very narrow.*

necklace *noun* (ne kləs) a piece of jewelry worn around the neck. *She always wears a pearl necklace.*

necktie *noun* (nek tī) a strip of cloth worn around the neck, usually by men. *When Mr. Lopes gets dressed up, he wears a silk necktie.*

necktie

need *noun* (nēd) 1. something that you want or must have. *I have a need to be with my family.* 2. the lack of something that is necessary. *The crops are **in need of** rain.* | *There is a need for skilled workers at the factory.*
verb to require. *Humans need water to live.*

needle *noun* (nē dəl) 1. a thin tool with a sharp point at one end. Some needles have a hole at the other end, and you put thread through the hole. Needles are used for sewing or knitting. *I sewed the buttons on the shirt with a needle.* 2. a very thin metal tube with a sharp point. Doctors and nurses use this kind of needle to put medicine in or take out blood from the body. *The nurse drew my blood with a needle.*

negative *adj.* (ne gə tiv) 1. saying or meaning *no*. *He gave a negative answer to the question.* 2. bad or harmful. *A bad teacher can have a **negative effect on** students.*

neglect *verb* (nə glekt) 1. to give too little attention to; not take care of. *Claude was so busy that he neglected his health.* | *It's wrong to neglect your children.* 2. to forget or fail to do. *I neglected to call my mother yesterday.*
noun [N] the act or result of not taking care of something. *The house was falling apart after years of neglect.*

negotiable *adj.* (nə gō shə bəl) able to be discussed and agreed on. *Before she hired me, the supervisor said that wages and benefits were negotiable.*

negotiate *verb* (nə gō shē āt) to try to come to an agreement with another person or group. *We negotiated with the dealer before we agreed on a purchase price for the car.*

negotiation *noun* (nə gō shē ā shən) a discussion intended to help people agree on something. *Negotiations between the two countries led to a peace treaty.*

neighbor *noun* (nā bər) a person who lives close to someone else. *New neighbors just moved into the house across the street.*

Word Builder: neighbor +
neighboring: next to.

neighborhood *noun* (nā bər hud) an area in a city, town, or other place that is different from other areas in some way. *There are many young children in my neighborhood.*

neither *conj.* (n$\bar{e}$ thər or n$\bar{i}$ thər) not one or the other of two; not either. **Neither** the cat **nor** the dog came into the house.

nephew *noun* (nef ū) the son of a brother or sister.

nerve *noun* (nərv) 1. one of the long, thin parts of the body that carries messages to and from the brain and other parts of the body. Nerves give you the sense of touch and let you feel heat and pain. 2. [N] the courage to do something difficult. *He didn't have the nerve to ask his boss for a raise.* 3. [N] behavior that shows courage but no respect. *She has **a lot of nerve** to lie to the boss.* 4. (plural) fear or anxiety. *The bad news brought on his attack of nerves.*

nervous *adj.* (nər vəs) 1. showing or feeling worry or fear. *Jamie is a nervous person.* | *That big dog is making me nervous.* 2. having to do with nerves. *He suffers from a nervous illness.*

nest *noun* (nest) 1. a structure of sticks and other material that birds make to hold their eggs. *There's a bird building its nest in that tree.* 2. any place or structure that animals use to hold their eggs. *Some turtles make nests in the sand on beaches.*

net[1] *noun* (net) a material that is made of threads or strings that are woven in a way that leaves open spaces between them. *When you play tennis, you must hit a ball over a net.* | *He caught a fish and lifted it out of the water with a fishing net.*

net

net[2] *adj.* (net) available after you take away taxes and deductions. *Her gross pay is 300 dollars a week, but her net pay is only 220 dollars.*

Word Builder: net +
net pay: the amount of pay you take home; the amount you earn after deductions.
net weight: the weight of a product minus the weight of the package it is in.

network *noun* (net wərk) 1. a system of people or things that are connected. *He has a network of friends whom he has known since he was young.* 2. a group of radio or television stations, or a company that controls such a group. *Some television networks in the United States are ABC, CBS, and NBC.* | *This network owns several television stations.* 3. a system of computers that are connected to other computers. *The Internet is the largest computer network in the world.*

neutral *adj.* (noo trəl) 1. not taking any side in an argument. *Mary remained neutral when her children had a fight.* 2. matching most other colors well. *Gray is a neutral color.*
noun the position of gears where no power is being sent to the wheels from the engine. *She put the car in neutral before she turned off the engine.*

never *adv.* (ne vər) not at any time; not at all. *It never snows in Puerto Rico.*

new *adj.* (noo) 1. recently arrived, made, born, or discovered. *Have you seen the new movie yet?* | *Kathy and Ken have a new baby.* | *This computer uses new technology.* 2. not old or used before. *She bought a new car with a DVD player.*

newcomer *noun* (noo kə mər) a person who arrived not long ago. *Mr. Miller is a newcomer to the neighborhood.*

news *noun* (nooz) 1. [N] new information about important events. The news is presented on television or radio or in a newspaper or magazine. *I watch the news on TV every evening.* 2. [N] new information about people and the things that they do. *Have you heard the news? Lucy just gave birth to twins!*

newspaper *noun* (nooz pā pər) a set of large sheets of paper with reports about recent events, advertisements, and other information. Most newspapers are printed and sold every day or once a week. *When I get a newspaper, I read the sports section first.*

next *adj.* (nekst) coming just after; following. *I get off the bus at the next stop.*
adv. nearest in position. *The chief of police sat **next to** the mayor.*
next door in the house or apartment closest to someone. *We live **next door to** a nice family.*

nice *adj.* (n$\bar{i}$s) 1. having good behavior; polite. *Theresa has some nice friends.* 2. enjoyable; pleasant. *The weather is nice today.* | *I had a nice talk with my brother.*

Word Builder: nice +
nicely: in a nice way.

nickel *noun* (ni kəl) a coin of the United States and some other countries equal to five cents.

niece *noun* (n$\bar{e}$s) a daughter of a brother or sister.

night *noun* (nīt) the period between the time when the sun sets in the evening and when it rises in the morning. *You can see the stars at night.*

Word Builder: night +
nightgown: a dress that you sleep in.
nightmare: a scary dream.
nightstand: a small table next to a bed.
nighttime: night.

nine *noun* (nīn) the word for the number 9.

nineteen *noun* (nīn tēn) the word for the number 19.

ninety *noun* (nīn tē) the word for the number 90.

ninth *adj.* (nīnth) next after eighth.
noun one of nine equal parts of a whole.

nit *noun* (nit) the egg of a louse.

no *adv.* (nō) it is not so; used to say that you refuse or that you do not agree with or accept something. *Would you like a drink? No, thank you. | No, I don't agree with you.*
adj. not any. *There is no milk left. | There are no meetings at work today.*

noble *adj.* (nō bəl) 1. belonging to a class of people with a high rank or title. *When she married a prince, she became part of a noble family.* 2. showing a strong, excellent mind or character. *You risked your life to save that child! That was a noble act.*

nobody *pron.* (nō ba dē) no one; no person. *I asked a question, but nobody answered.*

nod *verb* (nad) to move the head up and down in order to greet or agree with someone. *Nancy nodded when her son asked if he could have a cookie.*

noise *noun* (noyz) 1. a sound. *There was no noise coming from the room. | She heard noises in the basement.* 2. [N] a loud, harsh, or unpleasant sound. *The noise at the construction site was very loud.*

Word Builder: noise +
noisy: making a lot of noise.

nominate *verb* (na mə nāt) to choose for an office; to name for an honor. *He was nominated for vice president. | We nominated her project for the science prize.*

noncount *adj.* (nan kownt) not able to be counted. In grammar, *noncount* describes a noun that cannot take a plural form because the meaning is a thing that cannot be counted. Noncount nouns are often substances like water, mud, or steel. *This dictionary uses* [N] *to show that a noun is noncount.*

none *pron.* (nən) 1. no person or thing; not one. *None of the cookies are left.* 2. not any. *Bad food is better than none.*

nonpolluting *adj.* (nan pə loo ting) causing no **pollution.** *It is good to use nonpolluting cleaners in your home.*

nonprescription *adj.* (nan prə skrip shən) for sale without a **prescription.** *Aspirin is a nonprescription drug.*

nonresident *noun* (nan re zə dənt) a person who is not a legal **resident** of a particular place. *Nonresidents of a state have to pay more at a state university than residents of that state.*

nonsense *noun* (nan sens) [N] words that have no meaning or make no sense. *I wanted to have a serious discussion, but she was just talking nonsense.*

nontoxic *adj.* (nan tak sik) not causing harm or damage to the body; not **toxic.** *This spray contains only nontoxic chemicals.*

nontraditional *adj.* (nan trə di shən əl) not usual or **traditional.** *I have a nontraditional family: my daughter, my sister, my partner, and me.*

noodle *noun* (noo dəl) a flat, hard, narrow piece of food that is made from flour, eggs, and water. You cook noodles in hot water to make them soft.

noon *noun* (noon) twelve o'clock in the middle of the day. *It is usually hottest at noon.*

no one *pron.* (nō wən) no person; nobody. *The house was dark, and no one was home.*

nor *conj.* (nōr) used to introduce a negative phrase or clause, especially after a phrase using *neither*. *He is* **neither** *honest* **nor** *clever.*

normal *adj.* (nōr məl) close to what is usual, average, or standard. *My height is normal for my age.*

Word Builder: normal +
normally: usually; most of the time; in a normal way.

north *noun* (nōrth) [N] the direction to the left of a person facing the rising sun.

northern *adj.* (nōr thərn) in, to, from, or having to do with the north. *Montana is in the northern United States. | A cold northern wind was blowing.*

nose *noun* (nōz) the organ of the body that controls breathing and smelling. The nose is in the middle of the face.

nose

not *adv.* (nat) in no way; at no time. *You must not open that door. | It did not snow last month.*

note *noun* (nōt) 1. a short written record or message. *I wrote him a note to remind him to buy milk. | The student **took** careful **notes** in class.* 2. a single sound in music. *The guitar player missed a note at the beginning of the song.*
verb 1. to pay close attention to and make a record of. *The manager noted the time of each employee's arrival.* 2. to mention or observe. *She noted that she liked the wallpaper.*

nothing *noun* (nə thing) 1. [N] not anything. *There is nothing to eat in the refrigerator.* 2. [N] a value of zero. *This necklace is worth nothing.*
adv. not at all. *The show was nothing like what we had expected.*
for nothing for no purpose. *He's not home? Then we came all this way for nothing!*

notice *noun* (nō təs) 1. a written warning, news, or sign of something. *There is a notice on cigarette packs about the dangers of smoking.* 2. a formal statement that you intend to end a job or arrangement. *He **gave** his boss two weeks' **notice.***
verb to see or observe. *I noticed that you wore a new shirt today.*

noun *noun* (nown) a word that names a person, place, or thing. In the sentence "Mary likes TV and reading," *Mary*, *TV*, and *reading* are nouns.

novel *noun* (na vəl) a long piece of writing that tells a story from the author's imagination. *This novel is about people who lived over a hundred years ago.*

November *noun* (nō vem bər) the eleventh month of the year.

now *adv.* (now) 1. at this time; in these times. *If we leave now, we won't be late for school. | More women work outside the home now.* 2. without delay. *Come here now.*
from now on from the present moment into the future. *I will be on time from now on.*
now and then sometimes but not always. *We go to that restaurant now and then.*
now that because of the fact; since. *We can make the music louder now that she's gone.*

nowhere *adv.* (nō wār) 1. not anywhere; in no place. *You can find these animals nowhere else in the world.* 2. at or to no place. *We drove for hours, but we got nowhere.*
noun 1. the state of not existing or seeming to not exist. *They came out of nowhere.* 2. a place that is far away or not well known. *Some people say that our town is in the middle of nowhere.*

nozzle *noun* (na zəl) a narrow tube on the end of a pipe or hose. A nozzle controls the flow of a liquid or gas.

nuclear *adj.* (noo klē ər) coming from or using the central part of atoms. *The United States has nuclear weapons. | People use nuclear power to make electricity.*

nuisance *noun* (noo səns) a person or thing that annoys. *The barking dog was a nuisance to the neighbors.*

numb *adj.* (nəm) not able to feel; having no feeling. *The dentist gave me medicine that made my gums numb.*

Word Builder: numb +
numbness: the state of being numb.

number *noun* (nəm bər) 1. a unit with a fixed value that is used to count or to tell the position of something. You can write a number as a word or a symbol, such as *nine* or *9*. Bank tellers work with numbers all day. 2. [N] the total amount or quantity. *The theater can hold a large number of people.*

numerous *adj.* (noo mər əs) many. *I have numerous uncles, aunts, and cousins.*

nurse *noun* (nərs) a person whose job is to care for sick and injured people.
verb 1. to give medical care to. *She nursed her son back to health.* 2. to feed from a breast. *Mothers nurse their babies.*

nursery *noun* (nər sər ē) 1. a room where babies or young children sleep or play. 2. a place where plants or trees are grown for sale. *We went to the nursery to buy a tree.*

nut *noun* (nət) 1. a large seed that you can eat that grows in a hard shell. 2. a small piece of metal with a hole in the middle. *This nut is the wrong size for this bolt.*

nut

nutrition *noun* (noo tri shən) [N] the process of eating healthy food for living and growing. *A veterinarian knows a lot about animal nutrition.*

oak *noun* (ōk) a tree with strong, hard wood and flat leaves that change color and fall off in autumn. Oak trees produce small, round nuts.

oat *noun* (ōt) the seed of a plant that is used as food for people and animals.

oath *noun* (ōth) a serious promise. *He **took an oath** to tell the truth in court.*

oatmeal *noun* (ōt mēl) [N] a dried food made from oats. People cook oatmeal with water.

obey *verb* (ō bā) to do what someone tells you to do. *The soldier obeyed the officer's orders.*

object *noun* (ab jekt) 1. anything that has shape or form and can be seen or touched. *The only object in the room was a chair.* 2. the purpose of a particular activity. *The object of the game is to get rid of all your cards.* 3. a noun or noun phrase that is affected by the action of a verb in a sentence. In the sentence "The dog bit the man," *the man* is the object.
verb (əb jekt) to show negative feelings about something. *The store owner objected when we walked in without shoes.* | *I **object to** your rude language.*

obligation *noun* (a bli gā shən) something that someone should or should not do because of a law or moral principle. *You have an obligation to pay back the loan.*

observe *verb* (əb zərv) to watch with care. *The nurse observed a patient.*

obtain *verb* (əb tān) to get; gain. *He obtained his college degree in just three years.*

obvious *adj.* (ab vē əs) easy for anyone to see or understand; clear. *It was obvious that he liked her a lot.*

occasion *noun* (ə kā zhən) 1. an instance or time of something happening. *He has been late **on** many **occasions.** | We only go out to dinner **on** special **occasions.*** 2. a special event. *Holidays at their house are always fancy occasions.*
on occasion sometimes. *On occasion, she likes to eat ice cream.*

occasionally *adv.* (ə kā zhə nə lē) sometimes, but not very often. *We go to that restaurant occasionally.*

occupation *noun* (ak yə pā shən) the work a person does to earn a living; profession. *Teaching is the occupation of most members of her family.*

> **Word Builder: occupation +**
> **occupational:** having to do with an occupation or a workplace.

occupy *verb* (ak yə pī) to fill or use space or time. *A bed occupies a lot of space in a room.* | *How do you occupy your free time?*

> **Word Builder: occupy +**
> **occupied:** filled.

occur *verb* (ə kər) 1. to take place; happen. *Where were you when the crime occurred?* 2. to appear in your thoughts. *It never **occurred to** me to invite her to the party until you suggested it.*

ocean *noun* (ō shən) a part of the large body of salt water that covers most of the earth's surface. *We went to the shore and swam in the ocean.*

o'clock *adv.* (ə klak) of or according to the clock. *Our train leaves at five o'clock.*

five o'clock

October *noun* (ak tō bər) the tenth month of the year.

odd *adj.* (ad) 1. different from what is usual; strange. *Joe wore odd pants with green stripes and purple dots.* 2. not able to be divided by two; not even. *Three is an odd number.*

odor *noun* (ō dər) a smell, often a bad one. *A strange odor filled the kitchen.*

of *prep.* (əv) 1. belonging to. *That house is the home of my friend.* 2. made from. *I wear clothes of a light material when the weather is hot.* 3. used to state a cause. *He died of heart failure.* 4. containing. *She ate a bowl of soup.* 5. about. *I thought of you yesterday.*

off *adv.* (awf) 1. away from a point or position. *The cat ran off.* 2. so as not to be supported or connected. *She got on her bike but soon fell off.* | *Turn off the lights before you go to bed.* 3. away from a job or duty. *She **took** a year **off** when she had a baby.* | *I **have** Friday **off** this week.*
prep. so as to be separated or away from. *Please take your feet off the table!*
adj. not running or in operation. *The engine is off.*

offend *verb* (ə fend) to cause to be angry or upset. *Cruelty to animals offends most people.* | *I was offended when he called me a liar.*

offense *noun* (ə fens) 1. the act of breaking a law or rule or doing something wrong; crime; sin. *After the drunk driver's third offense, the judge sent him to jail.* 2. [N] a feeling of being angry or upset. *I* **take offense** *at your remarks.*

offensive *adj.* (ə fen siv) causing anger or hurt feelings. *His rude comments were offensive to everyone.*

offer *verb* (aw fər) to present something to be accepted or refused. *I offered a toy to the baby.*
    noun something that you present to be accepted or refused. *We* **made an offer** *of a thousand dollars for the car.*

office *noun* (aw fis) 1. a place where people do business work. *Mr. Fleck has a desk with a computer in his office.* 2. an important position in government or business. *Karen* **held the office of** *mayor for ten years.* | *She was* **in office** *for a long time.*

officer *noun* (aw fi sər) 1. a person who has authority in a government or business. 2. a person who has the power to command and lead others in the armed forces. Soldiers must obey the commands of their officers.

officer

official *noun* (ə fi shəl) a person who holds an office in a business or government. *The city officials met to discuss the new highway.*
    adj. approved by an authority; formal and public. *There was an official celebration of the town's 200th birthday.*

often *adv.* (aw fən) at frequent times. *Children are often sick in the first year of school.*

oh *interj.* (ō) a word used to express surprise, pain, or other feelings. *Oh! I can't believe you did that!*

oil *noun* (oyl) 1. [N] a slippery liquid that comes from minerals, animals, plants, or chemicals. *Vegetable oil is used for cooking, while pine oil is used to make cleaners.* 2. [N] a liquid found beneath the earth's surface that is used for fuel and to run machines. *The furnace uses oil for fuel.*

ointment *noun* (oynt mənt) a soft substance used for healing that contains some kind of oil. You rub ointment into the skin. *I put ointment on the burn on my arm.*

OK (or okay) *adj.* (ō kā or ō kā) all right; good. *That restaurant is OK, but this one is excellent.* | *She felt sick yesterday, but she is OK now.*
    adv. all right; well enough. *He did OK on the test.*
    interj. all right; yes. *OK, I'll do it for you.*

old *adj.* (ōld) 1. having lived or existed for many years; not young or new. *That old man is my grandfather.* | *That building is 200 years old.* 2. of a past time; former. *My mother showed me her old neighborhood.*

old-fashioned *adj.* (ōld fæ shənd) looking or being like past styles, manners, or ways of behaving. *She wore a long, old-fashioned dress.*

olive *noun* (a liv) a small fruit with green or black skin. Olives grow on trees and are used to make oil for cooking.

on *prep.* (an) 1. above and supported by. *There is a book on the shelf.* 2. in contact with; touching. *He put his hand on her shoulder.* | *She put paint on the brush.* 3. into or in the direction of. *He got on the train.* | *Her house is on the right.* 4. at the time of; at the moment of. *We moved into our new apartment on Wednesday.* | *He smiled on hearing the joke.* 5. in a state or process of. *The house was on fire.* 6. by means of. *We spoke on the phone.*
    adv. 1. into a state of operation or activity. *Turn the lights on.* 2. forward through time or space. *The movie went on for four hours.* | *Every year they move on to another place to work.*
    adj. running or in operation. *The lights are on.*

once *adv.* (wəns) 1. at one time in the past. *She was once a teacher, but that was a long time ago.* 2. only one time. *Tim gets his hair cut once a month.*
    conj. if something ever happens, or anytime that something happens; when. *Once you feed that cat, she will come back every day.* | *Once someone explains something to me, I never forget.*
    at once now; without any delay. *We must leave at once.*

one *adj.* (wən) being a single thing or person. *Each of you may have one candy.*
    noun the word for the number 1.
    pron. 1. a person or object that is not named but is part of a group. *One of the girls on the team hurt her knee.* 2. any person; a person who is not named. *One can't be right all the time.*

oneself (one's self) *pron.* (wən self) a word used to show that an action is done to or in connection with the same person who performs that action. *One must learn how to support oneself.* | *One should give oneself more chances to succeed.* | *One should take care of oneself to stay healthy.*
by oneself alone or without help. *One can accomplish more by oneself than by working with others.*

one-way *adj.* (wən wā) 1. moving or allowing to move in a single direction. *That is a one-way street.* 2. going to another place and not returning. *She bought a one-way ticket to New York.*

onion *noun* (ən yən) a round vegetable with a sharp taste and smell. Onions grow in the ground.

onion

on-line *adj.* (an līn) connected to a computer or computer network. *The library now has an on-line catalogue.*
adv. while under the direct control of another computer, or while connected to a computer network. *She can work on-line from her computer at home.*

only *adv.* (ōn lē) at least; just. *If he would only listen to me, he would be much better off.*
adj. alone or single; being without others. *She was the only person who got to work early today.*
conj. except that; but. *I would have gone, only I couldn't find a baby-sitter.*

onto *prep.* (an too) to a position on or on top of. *They walked onto the stage.* | *I put the vase onto the shelf.*

open *adj.* (ō pən) 1. not shut or closed. *A cool breeze came through the open window.* 2. prepared to do business. *That supermarket is open twenty-four hours a day.*
verb to change from being shut or closed. *I opened the door to let the dog in.*

Word Builder: open +
opener: a device that opens cans or other things.

opening *noun* (ō pə ning) 1. a hole or empty space. *She looked through an opening in the fence.* 2. a job or position that has not yet been filled. *There is an opening for a nurse at the hospital.*

operate *verb* (a pər āt) 1. to work or run. *This new lamp operates on batteries.* 2. to cut open a human body in order to repair it. *The doctor **operated on** the patient's heart.* 3. to control the working of something. *She*

operates a drill press at work. | *He's learning how to operate his new computer.*

operation *noun* (a pər ā shən) 1. [N] the act or process of working or running. *This factory has been **in operation** for many years.* 2. a process in which a doctor repairs or removes a part of the body. *She **had an operation on** her lung.*

operator *noun* (a pər ā tər) 1. a person whose job is to control a machine. *He is a bulldozer operator.* 2. a person who works for a telephone company or other companies and connects telephone calls or gives information to people who call the company. *I dialed zero to speak with the operator.*

opinion *noun* (ə pin yən) what you think about something or somebody. ***In my opinion,** everyone should vote in the election.*

opponent *noun* (ə pō nənt) a person who fights, plays, or takes a position against another person.

opportunity *noun* (a pər too nə tē) a chance for a better situation. *The new job is a wonderful opportunity.*

oppose *verb* (ə pōz) to think, act, or be against. *The school employees opposed the idea of a longer school day.*

opposite *adj.* (a pə zit or a pə sit) 1. on the side that is across from another; facing. *His house is on the opposite side of the street from mine.* | *The two children stood on opposite sides of the room.* 2. as different as possible. *He and his father always seem to have opposite opinions.*
noun a person or thing that is completely different from another. *Cold is **the opposite of** hot.*
prep. across from; facing. *They are building their house opposite mine.*

opposition *noun* (a pə zi shən) [N] the state of being against something. *I expressed my **opposition to** the city's plan for a new highway.*

or *conj.* (ōr) used to indicate a choice between two or more things. *What flavor of ice cream do you want, vanilla, chocolate, or strawberry?* | *You can go or you can stay.*

oral *adj.* (ōr əl) 1. spoken, rather than written; carried out by speaking. *The teacher asked me to give an oral report.* 2. having to do with the mouth. *The doctor gave her some oral medicine that tastes terrible.*

orange noun (ōr ənj) a round, sweet fruit with orange skin. Oranges grow on trees.
adj. having the color that comes from mixing red and yellow substances.

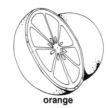

orange

orchestra noun (ōr kə strə) a group of musicians who play different kinds of instruments and perform together. *The orchestra gave a concert at the theater.*

order verb (ōr dər) 1. to tell someone to do something in a strong way; give a command to someone. *The police ordered everyone to leave the area.* 2. to ask for something to be delivered or made. *She ordered a dress from the catalogue.* | *Excuse me, but I ordered chicken, not beef.*
noun 1. a direction or command. *Soldiers have to follow orders.* 2. a request for goods to be made or delivered, or the goods themselves. *She placed an order for the new carpet.* | *Her order was a hamburger and French fries.* 3. the way something is organized or arranged in space or time. *The names are listed in alphabetical order.* 4. [N] the condition of something. *The car is old, but it is in good **working order.***
in order to for the purpose of; so that. *In order to finish the job today, we must begin early.*
out of order not working; broken. *The phone was out of order.*

ordinary adj. (ōr də nār ē) 1. usual or normal. *His ordinary way of doing things is to be slow and careful.* 2. without special qualities; common. *Today was an ordinary day. Nothing exciting happened.*

organ noun (ōr gən) 1. a part of plants or animals that performs a special task. The heart, stomach, and skin are examples of organs. 2. a large instrument for making music. It has one or more keyboards and may also have pedals. You play an organ by pressing the keys or pedals, which forces air through pipes.

organization noun (ōr gə nə zā shən) a group of people who act together for some purpose. *The parent-teacher organization raises money for the school.*

organize verb (ōr gə nīz) 1. to set in order; arrange in a particular way. *I organized my books by subject.* 2. to build a union of workers. *The workers in the hotel have organized.*

origin noun (ōr ə jin) the point or place from which something comes; source. *What is the origin of his ideas?*

original adj. (ə ri jə nəl) 1. first; earliest. *The original owner of our car had it for ten years.* | *Of all the movies in the Star Wars series, I like the original one best.* 2. new or fresh. *She has an original idea for a book.*

Word Builder: original +
originally: at first.

OSHA abbrev. (ō shə) an abbreviation for *Occupational Safety and Health Administration.* OSHA is a department of the U.S. government that deals with health and safety in workplaces.

other adj. (ə thər) 1. different from the one or ones mentioned. *I don't want this wrench. I want the other wrench.* 2. the one remaining out of two or more. *I hurt this arm, so I have to lift things with my other arm.* 3. happening not long ago. *I forgot my wallet the other day, but I have it now.* | *It was nice to see you the other day.*
noun the one of two or more that remains. *The first son went to college, and the other began a job.*
pron. 1. the remaining one. *You take this cookie, and I'll take the other.* 2. everyone except for yourself. *The others stayed at the party after I left.*

otherwise adv. (ə thər wīz) 1. in a different or other way. *Everyone says it's a good movie, but I think otherwise.* 2. under other conditions; except for that. *I'm feeling sick. Otherwise, I would go with you.* 3. in other ways. *He made one mistake. Otherwise, his test was perfect.*

ought verb (awt) 1. used to express that some action is a good or important thing for someone to do. *You **ought to** take your medication every day.* 2. used to express what is expected or likely, based on logic. *He said "twelve o'clock," so he **ought to** be here soon.* 3. used to express someone's opinion of the correct behavior or state of something, even if it is not what is real. *She thinks rich people **ought to** help poor people.* | *Why is this towel here? It **ought to** be in the bathroom.*

ounce noun (owns) 1. a standard unit used to measure weight. There are sixteen ounces in one pound. 2. a standard unit used to measure liquid. There are 32 ounces in one quart.

our adj. (owr) of or belonging to us; a possessive form of **we.** *Why are those people sitting in our seats?*

ours pron. (owrz) the one or ones that belong to us; a possessive form of **we.** *Their car is bigger than ours.*

ourselves *pron.* (owr <u>selvz</u>) 1. a word used to show that an action is done to or in connection with the speaker and others, and that these people are the same people who perform the action. *We saw ourselves in the video.* | *We bought ourselves some snacks.* | *We can take care of ourselves.* 2. we and no one else. *We did the work ourselves.*

out *adv.* (<u>owt</u>) 1. away from the center or inside of something. *Go out through this door.* | *Pour all the water out of the bottle.* 2. so as to be not working; off. *Turn the lights out.*
prep. through. *My advice to you goes in one ear and out the other.* | *He walked out the door.*
adj. 1. not present. *Dr. Jones is out right now.* 2. not working. *The light is out.*
out of 1. used to tell what something is made from. *These shoes are made out of leather.* 2. not having any more of something. *We're out of milk, so I'm going to the store.*

outbreak *noun* (<u>owt</u> brāk) a sudden beginning of a disease among people. *There was an outbreak of flu last month.*

outdoor *adj.* (owt <u>dōr</u>) happening or used outside of any building. *Harry likes outdoor sports.* | *They are building an outdoor pool.*

outdoors *adv.* (owt <u>dōrz</u>) not inside any structure; outside. *Most children like to play outdoors.*

outer *adj.* (<u>ow</u> tər) of or having to do with the part most distant from the center. *Many families choose to live in the outer areas of the city.* | *This candy has an outer layer of chocolate.*

outfit *noun* (<u>owt</u> fit) a set of clothes. *He bought two new outfits for the baby.*

outing *noun* (<u>ow</u> ting) a trip away from home or school for pleasure. *The baby loves outings with his father.* | *The children went on an outing to the museum.*

outlet *noun* (<u>owt</u> let) 1. an opening that allows something to go out. *You need to have an outlet for the smoke.* 2. the point in a room where you attach a wire to a source of electricity. *Plug the cord into the outlet.*

outline *noun* (<u>owt</u> līn) 1. a line showing the outside edge of a figure or object. *She drew an outline of the house.* 2. a short plan of the main ideas of a book, speech, or report. *She wrote an outline of the report before she wrote the first draft.*

outlook *noun* (<u>owt</u> luk) [N] what may come in the future. *The outlook for tomorrow's weather is good.*

outrage *noun* (<u>owt</u> rāj) 1. an act that causes a strong feeling of anger because it is bad, wrong, or violent. *The murder of the child was an outrage.* 2. [N] the anger caused by a terrible thing. *We felt outrage when we heard about the crime.*
verb to cause anger and shock in. *The cruel actions of the soldiers outraged the citizens.*

outrageous *adj.* (owt <u>rā</u> jəs) 1. wrong or harmful to an extreme degree. *Kicking the dog was an outrageous thing to do.* 2. beyond normal or acceptable limits. *Five hundred dollars is an outrageous price for a pair of shoes.*

outside *noun* (owt <u>sīd</u> or <u>owt</u> sīd) the outer side or surface. *We washed the outside of the car, but the inside is still dirty.*
adv. in or to a place beyond the limits of an enclosed space. *He opened the door and went outside.*
prep. on, in, or to the space beyond the limits of an enclosed space. *The cat watched the bird outside the house.* | *The tennis ball landed outside the line.*

outstanding *adj.* (owt <u>stæn</u> ding) 1. better than most others; excellent. *She is an outstanding student.* 2. not paid yet. *I have to pay my outstanding bills.*

oven *noun* (ə vən) a piece of equipment that you cook food in. An oven has a large metal box with a door. *My new apartment has a gas oven, not an electric one.* | *You can bake or roast food in an oven.*

stove top
oven

over *prep.* (<u>ō</u> vər) 1. above; higher than. *She held the umbrella over her head.* 2. across to the other side of something. *I jumped over the fence.* 3. on top of something in a way that covers it. *I pulled the blanket over my head.* 4. in the time of; during. *We've had a lot of snow over the last few days.* | *What did you do over the weekend?* 5. by the means of. *We talked over the phone.*
adv. 1. to your location or to someone else's location, or to this or that place. *Some friends came over for dinner last night.* | *I can come over tomorrow night if you prefer.* 2. to the side. *Please move over.* 3. again from the beginning. *You'll have to do this work over if you do it wrong the first time.* 4. down and to the side; down. *The tree bent over in the wind.* | *The big dog knocked the child over.*

adj. 1. more than. *My son is over six feet tall.*
2. finished; done. *The movie is over at midnight.*
all over in every part of something; everywhere. *People all over the world love children.*

---

over or above?
Above means at a higher place.
Over means above while moving across something.
Compare:
There is a plane above us.
The plane flew over our house.

---

overall *adv.* (ō vər <u>awl</u>) in general. *Overall, our team had a good season.*
adj. (<u>ō</u> vər awl) including all; general. *Their overall goal was to save enough money for a new car.*

overalls *pl. noun* (<u>ō</u> vər awlz) work pants made of heavy cloth, with a part that covers the chest and goes over the shoulders. Overalls have many pockets. *The carpenter wears overalls or jeans to work every day.*

overcast *adj.* (<u>ō</u> vər kæst) gray and full of clouds. *The sky has been overcast all week.*

overcame *verb* (ō vər <u>kām</u>) past tense of **overcome.**

overcome *verb* (ō vər <u>kəm</u>) *overcame, overcome*
1. to win against; defeat. *She overcame all the other players.* | *He overcame many problems.* 2. to cause to be weak or no longer conscious. *The chemical fumes overcame him.* | *He was overcome by fumes.*

overdose *noun* (<u>ō</u> vər dōs) a larger amount of a drug than your doctor says you should take. *An overdose of aspirin will make you sick.*
verb to become very sick or die from taking too much of a drug. *She overdosed on cough medicine and had to go to the hospital.*

overdue *adj.* (ō vər <u>doo</u>) not paid or returned on time. *I forgot to pay this bill, and now it is overdue.* | *These library books are overdue.*

overflow *verb* (ō vər <u>flō</u>) 1. to flow over the top edge of a container. *He forgot to turn off the faucet, and the sink overflowed.* | *Water overflowed from the sink.* 2. to be or become full or too full. *The stadium overflowed with people.*

Word Builder: overflow +
overflowing: too full; with the contents flowing over the top edge.

---

overnight *adv.* (ō vər <u>nīt</u>) from the evening of one day until the morning of the next day. *We stayed at our friends' house overnight because of the snowstorm.*
adj. (<u>ō</u> vər nīt) lasting or staying one night. *We took the overnight train.*

oversleep *verb* (ō vər <u>slēp</u>) *overslept, overslept* to sleep longer than you should. *I overslept and was late for work.*

overslept *verb* (ō vər <u>slept</u>) past tense and past participle of **oversleep.**

over-the-counter *adj.* (ō vər thə <u>kown</u> tər) used to describe drugs that you can buy in a store without seeing a doctor first. *Aspirin is an over-the-counter drug.*

overtime *noun* (<u>ō</u> vər tīm) hours that you work beyond regular working hours. *We get paid more for overtime.*
adv. more than the regular amount of time. *I worked ten hours overtime last week.*

overweight *adj.* (ō vər <u>wāt</u>) having too much weight; too heavy. *The veterinarian said that my dog is ten pounds overweight.*

owe *verb* (<u>ō</u>) to have to pay; be in debt to someone. *I owe 500 dollars to my landlord.*

owl *noun* (<u>owl</u>) a bird with large eyes that hunts for food at night.  owl

own *adj.* (<u>ōn</u>) belonging to oneself or itself alone. *My son bought his car with his own money.*
verb to have or possess something, especially by law. *We used to rent a house, but now we own a house.*
on one's own alone or without anyone's help. *She's living on her own now.* | *You'll have to get the money on your own.*

Word Builder: own +
owner: a person who owns something.

---

oxygen *noun* (<u>ak</u> sə jən) [N] a gas that is part of air. It has no color or smell. Most living things need oxygen to live.

ozone *noun* (<u>ō</u> zōn) [N] a gas that is a form of oxygen. Ozone is made when oxygen reacts with an electrical charge.

P p

pace *noun* (pās) 1. one step in the movement of walking. *She moved forward two paces.* 2. the rate of movement; how fast something moves. *The pace of the game was slow.* | *We walked at a fast pace.*
verb to walk across an area and back many times. *He paced the floor of the hospital waiting for news from the doctor.*

pack *noun* (pæk) 1. a container for carrying things on the back. *She carries her books and papers in a pack.* 2. a group of things arranged together in a container; package. *He bought a pack of cigarettes and a pack of cards.*
verb to put in a container for carrying or storing. *The farmer packed the fruit into crates.* | *He packed his suitcase.*

package *noun* (pæ kij) a thing or group of things that are wrapped together. *I bought a package of doughnuts.*

pad *noun* (pæd) 1. a block of soft material used for protection or comfort. *Football players wear shoulder pads.* | *I need a pad for this hard seat.* 2. a thick piece of soft, clean material used to cover and protect a wound or to take in liquid. *The nurse used a gauze pad to clean the cut.* 3. a group of paper sheets glued together at one edge. *I keep a pad of paper next to the telephone.* 4. a block of material used for cleaning surfaces or dishes. *Please use that soft pad to wash the glasses.*

page *noun* (pāj) one side of a sheet of printed or written paper. *This book has 200 pages.*

paid *verb* (pād) past tense and past participle of **pay.**

pail *noun* (pāl) a container with steep sides and a handle; bucket. *We need a pail to carry the water.*

pain *noun* (pān) 1. [N] a bad or terrible feeling in your body that is usually caused by injury or illness. *I have a lot of pain in my back in the mornings.* 2. a specific instance of hurt. *She couldn't stand up because of the pain in her stomach.* 3. [N] hurt feelings; sorrow. *Her mother's death caused her great pain.*

> **Word Builder: pain +**
> **painful:** causing physical or mental pain.
> **painless:** causing no pain.

paint *noun* (pānt) a liquid that is used on surfaces to give color or protect the surface. *I used blue paint in my room.*
verb 1. to cover with paint. *We painted the outside of the house white.* 2. to make a picture or design using paint. *An artist painted a picture of my mother.*

> **Word Builder: paint +**
> **paintbrush:** a brush used for painting.
> **painter:** a person who paints.

painting *noun* (pān ting) 1. a picture that someone has painted. *That museum has many famous paintings.* 2. the act of using paint for art or for covering surfaces of buildings. *My brother does house painting in the summer.* | *We are studying painting in art class.*

pair *noun* (pār) 1. two things that are the same and are used together. *I bought a new pair of shoes yesterday.* 2. a single object consisting of two parts joined together. *I need a pair of scissors.*

pajamas *pl. noun* (pə ja məz) a loose shirt and pants worn for sleeping.

palace *noun* (pæ lis) the official home of a king or queen or other person of high rank, or a fancy home where a king or queen might live.

pale *adj.* (pāl) light in color. *Her face was so pale that I thought she was sick.*

pallet *noun* (pæ lit) a flat surface on which goods are stored. A pallet can be moved from place to place.

> **Word Builder: pallet +**
> **palletize:** to stack things on pallets.
> **pallet jack:** a machine for lifting pallets.

palm *noun* (pam) the inner surface of the hand. *She says she can tell the future by looking at your palm.*

pan *noun* (pæn) an open, metal container for cooking or baking. *You need a large frying pan to cook all those eggs.*

pan

pancake *noun* (pæn kāk) a flat, round cake made from flour, eggs, and milk.

panic *noun* (pæ nik) [N] a sudden, strong fear or anger that causes people to act without thinking. *Because of their panic, many people were killed in the fire.*
verb to feel or be overcome by a sudden, strong fear. *She panics whenever she has to give a speech.*

pants *pl. noun* (p<u>æ</u>nts) a piece of clothing that covers the body from the waist down, with separate parts for each leg.

pantyhose *noun* (p<u>æ</u>n tē hōz) [N] (used with a plural verb) thin stockings for women that cover the feet and the lower body up to the waist. *These pantyhose are too dark to wear with that dress.*

paper *noun* (p<u>ā</u> pər) 1. [N] a thin material often used to write on, to wrap objects, and to make things such as containers. *I need a **piece of paper** to write a letter.* | *He wrapped the presents in red paper.* 2. a single piece or sheet of this material. *Write your name at the top of your paper.* 3. any written or printed document. *They lost their birth records and other important papers in the fire.*

paperback *noun* (p<u>ā</u> pər bæk) a book having a soft paper cover.

parade *noun* (pə r<u>ād</u>) groups of people moving down a public street together to celebrate something. *We love to hear the music and watch the marching bands in the parade.*

paragraph *noun* (p<u>ær</u> ə græf) a group of sentences in writing that develop an idea together. Each new paragraph begins on a new line. *Our teacher told us to write three paragraphs about an interesting person.*

parallel *adj.* (p<u>ær</u> ə lel) going in the same direction and being the same distance apart at every point. Parallel lines never meet or cross each other. *The row of trees is parallel to the road.*

parent *noun* (p<u>ær</u> ənt) a mother or a father.
verb to act as a parent to. *He has questions about how to parent his children.*

parental *adj.* (pə r<u>en</u> təl) having to do with being a parent. *She lost her parental rights when she allowed the couple to adopt her baby.*

parentheses *noun* (pə r<u>en</u> thə sēs) plural of **parenthesis.**

parenthesis *noun* (pə r<u>en</u> thə sis) *parentheses* either of a pair of marks used in writing ( ). They are used to enclose information that is not part of the main sentence. They are also used as symbols in mathematics.

park *noun* (park) an area of public land that anyone can use for rest and enjoyment. *The town park has a playground, a swimming pool, and a picnic area.*
verb to put a car or other vehicle in a particular place for a short time. *The driver parked the bus in front of the school.*

park

parking lot *noun* (p<u>ar</u> king lat) a special area where people can park their cars. *She had an accident in the supermarket parking lot.*

parking meter *noun* (p<u>ar</u> king mē tər) a device that stands next to a parking space on a street. You put money in it to pay for parking.

part *noun* (p<u>art</u>) 1. a separate piece or section of a whole. *Doctors have to study all the parts of the human body.* | *We can't find all the parts for that toy.* 2. an important element of something. *Part of the reason that he quit his job was the low pay.* 3. a piece or section of a machine that can be removed. *The garage is ordering some special parts for my car.*
adv. in some amount. *He is part happy and part sad about leaving.*
take part in to involve yourself in; be active in. *Many children like to take part in sports.*

participate *verb* (par t<u>i</u> sə p<u>ā</u>t) to take part; to become involved. *The teachers hope that all the parents will participate in this important school event.*

participle *noun* (p<u>ar</u> ti si pəl) a form of a verb that can function as an adjective, noun, or other part of speech. In the sentence "Fixing the broken machine was tiring," the words *fixing*, *broken*, and *tiring* are participles.

particle *noun* (p<u>ar</u> ti kəl) a tiny amount or small piece. *There's a particle of dirt on your glasses.*

particular *adj.* (pər t<u>ik</u> yə lər) being the only one that you have in mind out of many possibilities; specific; special. *He drinks only one particular kind of coffee, not just any coffee.* | *The store didn't have the particular battery that I needed.*
in particular special or specific. *He laughed at nothing in particular.* | *Can I get you anything in particular?*

particularly *adv.* (pər t<u>ik</u> yə lər lē) 1. in or to an unusual or special degree. *I was particularly careful when I filled out the application.* 2. especially; specifically. *Everyone in my family loves animals, particularly horses.*

partly *adv.* (part lē) in some degree or amount; in part. *The accident was partly my fault.*

partner *noun* (part nər) 1. someone who owns and runs a business with another person. *My brother and I are partners in business.* 2. a person who shares in an activity with another person. *Each child works with a partner in science class.* 3. a husband, wife, or other person in a similar relationship. *Bob and his partner live together.*

part-time *adj.* (part tīm) less than **full-time.** *She has a part-time job.*
adv. less than full-time. *He works part-time.*

party *noun* (par tē) 1. an event in which a group of people comes together to celebrate or have fun. *My daughter invited ten children to her birthday party.* 2. a group of people who share the same political opinions and beliefs. *Are you a member of a political party?*

pass *noun* (pæs) a free ticket, or a ticket that you buy, that lets you enter anytime you want. *We bought a summer pass for the swimming pool.*
verb 1. to go past; move beyond. *It's dangerous to pass another car on a hill.* | *You will pass the police station before you come to the traffic light.* 2. to complete with success. *She passed the mathematics test.* 3. to hand, throw, or move to someone else. *Please pass the salt.* | *I passed the ball to another player.* 4. to live through; spend. *How do you pass your time since you stopped working?* 5. to approve or make into law. *The legislature passed a new law against drunk driving.*
pass away used as a polite expression for **die.** *Her father had cancer and passed away last year.*
pass out 1. to faint. *I almost passed out from the heat.* 2. to give something to each of many people. *The teacher passed out the test papers.*

passage *noun* (pæ sij) 1. the act of moving from one place or state to another. *The passage across the ocean was very difficult.* | *She is not afraid of the passage from life to death.* 2. a way to go through something.

There is an underground passage between these buildings. 3. an official approval. *They hoped for quick passage of the new law.*

passbook *noun* (pæs buk) a book that keeps a record of money that is added to or taken out of a bank account.

passenger *noun* (pæ sin jər) a person who is not driving but travels in an automobile, bus, train, or other vehicle.

passive *adj.* (pæ siv) 1. not being active or being part of an activity. *Watching television is a passive activity.* 2. used in grammar to describe a form of the verb that emphasizes the person or thing who is affected by the action of the verb. *"Excellent bikes are produced by a company in New England"* is a sentence that uses a passive verb form. *"A company in New England produces excellent bikes"* uses an active verb form.

passport *noun* (pæs pōrt) an official document that shows that a person is a citizen of a country.

password *noun* (pæs wərd) a secret word or phrase that allows you to enter a place or to get information. *To get your account information, you have to enter your password.*

past *adj.* (pæst) 1. having to do with an earlier time; former. *In past times, many people died young.* | *The past president was less active than the current president.* 2. having ended just now; having happened recently. *The phone has rung ten times during the past hour.* | *We finally finished the project this past Tuesday.* 3. having to do with the form of a verb that shows that the action happened in the past. *Looked, went,* and *bought* are past forms of verbs.
noun all of the time before now. *We cannot change what happened in the past.*
prep. 1. after. *It's five minutes past five o'clock.* 2. beyond; farther away than. *The post office is two buildings past the bank.*

pasta *noun* (pa stə) [N] a food made from flour, eggs, and water and dried in various shapes. You cook pasta in boiling water before you eat it.

pasta

paste *noun* (pāst) 1. [N] a mixture used to stick paper or other light materials together. *You can make paste at home with flour and water.* 2. any soft, thick, liquid substance. *Do you use tomato paste in your sauce?*
verb 1. to use paste to stick something to something else. 2. to add something into a computer text that you have taken from another text in your computer.
I pasted a paragraph from my old document into this document.

pat *verb* (pæt) to touch softly with something flat, such as your hand. *He patted the dough to make it flat.* | *She patted the dog's head.*

patch *noun* (pæch) 1. a small piece of material used to cover a hole or to protect an injury. *My pants have patches over my knees.* | *He had to wear a patch after he hurt his eye.* 2. an area that is part of a larger area but is different from it in color or some other way. *There is a patch of skin on my arm that itches.*
verb to repair or make stronger with one or more patches. *My mother patched my torn sweater.*

path *noun* (pæth) a narrow road or way. *We walked on a path through the woods.* | *The town is making a bicycle path around the park.*

pathogen *noun* (pæth ə jən) a tiny living thing that causes disease. Viruses, bacteria, and other germs are pathogens.

patience *noun* (pā shəns) [N] the ability to stay calm when you are faced with pain or trouble. *Good parents have a lot of patience.*

patient *noun* (pā shənt) a person or animal that is getting treatment from a doctor. *My father was a patient in the hospital.*
adj. able to stay calm when faced with pain, trouble, or a long wait. *The teacher was patient with the rude child.*

patriot *noun* (pā trē ət) a person who loves, supports, and defends his or her country. *George Washington was a patriot.*

pattern *noun* (pæ tərn) 1. an arrangement of shapes, lines, letters, numbers, or colors that can be repeated or used again and again. *The new dishes have a pattern with leaves and flowers.* 2. a guide; model. *Lay the pattern carefully over the fabric.*

pause *noun* (pawz) a short stop. *There was a pause before the second act of the play.*
verb to stop for a short time. *I paused for a moment to catch my breath.*

pave *verb* (pāv) to cover with concrete or some other material to make a hard, flat surface. *Workers pave roads during the spring and summer.*

pavement *noun* (pāv mənt) [N] the hard surface on a road or other flat area. *Walk on the pavement, not on the grass.*

pavilion *noun* (pə vil yən) a building with open sides. *We had a picnic at the pavilion in the park.*

paw *noun* (paw) the foot of a mammal with four legs and curved nails or claws, such as a dog or cat. *My dog hurt its front paw.* paw

pay *noun* (pā) [N] the money or something else of value that is given for work. *The workers get their pay every two weeks.*
adj. needing payment of money to work. *I used the pay phone at the store.*
verb paid, paid 1. to give money in exchange for receiving something. *He paid his bill at the restaurant.* | *He* **paid** *ten dollars* **for** *the meal.* 2. to be worth doing or be good for you. *It pays to work hard.* | *Crime does not pay.*

pay back to pay the money that you owe to someone. *I paid back the ten dollars I borrowed from her.*

pay off 1. to finish making payments on something. *He paid off his college loan.* 2. to bring good results or reward. *His hard work paid off when he was given a raise in pay.*

> **Word Builder: pay +**
> **paycheck:** payment of your wages in the form of a check.
> **payday:** the day when you get paid at work.
> **pay stub:** the part of your paycheck that you keep. It shows your wages and deductions.

payment *noun* (pā mənt) an instance of giving money to pay for something. *He **makes a payment on** his car loan every month.*

payroll *noun* (pā rōl) a list of people who are paid at a workplace and the amount of money for each person. *That large company has hundreds of people on its payroll.*

P.E. *abbrev.* (pē ē) an abbreviation for **physical education.**

pea *noun* (pē) a small, round, green seed that grows on a climbing plant and is eaten as a vegetable.

peace *noun* (pēs) 1. [N] a time when there is no war or fighting. *That country has been* **at peace** *for many years.* 2. [N] a quiet or calm situation. *Let your father watch TV* **in peace.** | *I need some peace so I can finish this work.*

peaceful *adj.* (pēs fəl) 1. quiet; calm. *The sleeping baby looked peaceful.* 2. without war or fighting. *The two countries enjoyed a peaceful relationship.*

peach *noun* (pēch) a soft, sweet fruit with pink or orange skin. *Peaches have a large seed and grow on trees.*

peak *noun* (pēk) the highest part of a mountain, or the highest part of anything. *We could see peaks with white snow in the distance.* | *She is at the peak of her career.*

peanut *noun* (pē nət) a seed like a nut that grows under the ground. *Peanuts can be prepared and eaten in many ways.*

pear *noun* (pār) a firm, sweet fruit with red, green, or brown skin. Pears grow on trees.

pear

pearl *noun* (pərl) a smooth, hard, round object that is worn as jewelry. *A pearl is formed inside the shell of some sea animals.*

peasant *noun* (pe zənt) a poor person who lives and works on a small piece of land or on someone else's farm. *My grandparents were peasants in Mexico before they came to the United States.*

pecan *noun* (pi kan or pē kæn) a nut that has a thin, smooth shell.

peculiar *adj.* (pə kūl yər) strange or odd. *He wore a peculiar purple hat.*

pedal *noun* (pe dəl) a part pushed by the foot to run or control a machine. *Some cars have three pedals: one for the brake, one for the gas, one for the clutch.* | *You operate the sewing machine with this pedal.* **verb** to operate or use a pedal or pedals. *She pedaled her bike up the hill.*

pedestrian *noun* (pə de strē ən) a person who is walking. *Pedestrians should walk on the sidewalk.*

pediatrician *noun* (pē dē ə tri shən) a doctor who takes care of children.

peek *verb* (pēk) to look for a short time or in secret. *I peeked through the window to see who was there.* **noun** a quick or secret look. *He* **took a peek** *at the newspaper before he gave it to me.*

peel *verb* (pēl) to pull, tear, or cut the outer covering from something. *He peeled an orange and ate it.* **noun** the outer layer or skin of some fruits and vegetables. *Bananas have a thick, yellow peel.*

pen *noun* (pen) a long, thin tool used for writing or drawing in ink.

pencil *noun* (pen səl) a long, thin tool used for writing or drawing. *Pencils are made of a narrow stick of wood with a black or colored center.*

penicillin *noun* (pe nə si lən) [N] a kind of medicine for treating illnesses or infections. *The dentist gave her penicillin for the infection in her tooth.*

penny *noun* (pe nē) a coin of the United States and some other countries equal to one cent.

pension *noun* (pen shən) the money that a company or government pays at regular times to a person who is no longer working. *Mrs. Davis gets a monthly pension now that she is retired.*

people *pl. noun* (pē pəl) plural of **person.**

pepper *noun* (pe pər) 1. a spice that comes from dried berries or seeds of certain plants. 2. a hollow fruit of a plant that varies in size, shape, and color. *Peppers can have either a hot or sweet taste. They are eaten as a vegetable or used to add flavor to other foods.*

per *prep.* (pər) for each. *His new job pays ten dollars per hour.*

percent *noun* (pər sent) one part of each hundred, or an amount expressed as part of one hundred. *Ten percent of one hundred is ten.* | *The price of houses rose by four percent.*

> **Word Builder: percent +**
> **percentage:** an amount expressed as a fraction of one hundred.

perfect *adj.* (pər fect) free from mistakes or faults; excellent. *Nobody's perfect! | The weather is perfect today.*
verb (pər fect) to make something as good as possible. *Susan has perfected her word-processing skills.*

Word Builder: perfect +
perfectly: in a perfect way.

perform *verb* (pər form) 1. to present for the entertainment of an audience. *He performed a song that he wrote himself.* 2. to do what has been decided or planned. *Doctors perform operations. | The mayor performs many duties.*

performance *noun* (pər for məns) 1. a particular entertainment shown to an audience. *The theater was filled for the final performance of the play.* 2. one's way of working or operating. *Mark's supervisor rated his job performance. | Regular maintenance will improve your car's performance.*

perfume *noun* (pər fūm) a liquid that you put on your skin to make it smell pleasant. Perfume is made from flowers or other substances. *She wears perfume when she goes out in the evening.*

perhaps *adv.* (pər hæps) it is possible that; maybe. *Perhaps I will see you tomorrow.*

peril *noun* (per il) something that puts you in danger. *When the child fell into the icy water, his life was in peril.*

period *noun* (pēr ē əd) 1. a section of time with a set beginning and end. *We will be on vacation for a period of three weeks.* 2. a punctuation mark (.). It is used at the end of a sentence or after an abbreviation.

perish *verb* (per ish) to die by violence or in some other sudden way. *Many people perished in the earthquake.*

Word Builder: perish +
perishable: likely to spoil or rot.

permanent *adj.* (pər mə nənt) lasting or intended to last forever or for a long time; not temporary. *Ronald finally got a permanent job. | Please write your permanent address on the application.*
noun a style for the hair that lasts for several months. You put special chemicals on the hair to make it curl. *Angela got a permanent last week.*

permission *noun* (pər mi shən) the approval to do something, given by a person with authority. *I gave my daughter permission to go to the movies with her boyfriend.*

permit *verb* (pər mit) to allow; let. *Will you permit me to go to the dance?*
noun (pər mit) a written statement that officially allows someone to do something; license. *He got a building permit for the new porch. | The officer asked to see his fishing permit.*

persecute *verb* (pər sə kūt) to treat someone in a cruel way because of race, religion, political ideas, or some other difference. *Some governments persecute citizens who oppose their policies.*

persist *verb* (pər sist) to continue or keep doing something in a firm, steady way. *Freezing weather persisted for several weeks. | Ruth persisted in her job search.*

person *noun* (pər sən) *people, persons* a human being. *Every person who lives in this country has certain rights.*
in person being present rather than on the phone or radio or in photographs or movies. *I met the actor in person after I saw him in the movie.*

persons or people?
The usual plural form of *person* is *people*. But you can use *persons* in formal language.
Compare:
She invited almost twenty people to a barbecue.
The capacity of the theater is 795 persons.

personal *adj.* (pər sə nəl) 1. belonging to only one person and usually not for other people to share, be concerned with, or see; private. *He removed all his personal things from his desk when he quit his job. | I can't tell you about that! It's personal.* 2. of or about the care of the body. *Keeping clean is an important personal habit.* 3. concerning a person as an individual human being and not as part of a group or organization. *My boss did me a personal favor by letting me borrow his car. | You can't make personal phone calls at work.*

Word Builder: personal +
personally: in a way that relates to one's own self.

personality *noun* (pər sə næ lə tē) all of the qualities of a person that make that person different from others. *One twin has a cheerful personality, while the other is more serious.*

personnel *noun* (pər sə <u>nel</u>) 1. [N] all of the people who work for a business or other organization. *The manager thanked the company's personnel for their hard work.* 2. [N] the department in a company that deals with people who work in that company and often hires new workers. *You should talk to personnel about benefits and company policies.*

persuade *verb* (pər <u>swād</u>) 1. to cause someone to do something through reasoning or arguing. *His wife persuaded him to look for a better job.* 2. to cause someone to believe something. *She persuaded her mother that buying a new car was a good idea.*

pet *noun* (pet) an animal people keep in their home for company and pleasure. *Juan has a kitten for a pet.*
verb to pat or touch with a slow, loving motion. *My sister wanted to pet all the cats at the animal shelter.*

petition *noun* (pə <u>ti</u> shən) a formal, written request by many people that is made to a person in authority. *Many parents signed the petition asking the school board to lower taxes.*

petroleum *noun* (pə <u>trō</u> lē əm) [N] a thick oil found beneath the earth's surface that is made into gasoline, heating oil, and other products.

pharmacy *noun* (<u>far</u> mə sē) a place where medicine is prepared and sold. *I take my prescriptions to the pharmacy in the supermarket.*

phase *noun* (<u>fāz</u>) a particular stage of development or of a process. *Teenagers go through many phases as they become adults.*

phone *noun* (<u>fōn</u>) a short form of **telephone.**
verb to call on the telephone. *The doctor will phone him tomorrow.*

phone

phone number *noun* (<u>fōn</u> nəm bər) a short form of **telephone number.**

photo *noun* (<u>fō</u> tō) a short form of **photograph.**

photocopier *noun* (<u>fō</u> tō ka pē ər) a machine that makes copies by photographing them. *There is a photocopier in the library.*

photocopy *noun* (<u>fō</u> tō ka pē) a copy of a document or other printed material made by a photocopier. *Many people keep a photocopy of important papers.*
verb to make a copy of something with a photocopier.

photograph *noun* (<u>fō</u> tə græf) a picture made by using a camera that records an image. *I have photographs of my children in my wallet.*
verb to take a photograph of. *My sister photographs the family when we get together during the holidays.*

photographer *noun* (fə <u>ta</u> grə fər) a person whose job is to take photographs.

photo ID *noun* (<u>fō</u> tō ī <u>dē</u>) a card with a person's name and photograph. A photo ID is used to prove that a person is who he says he is. *Many workplaces require a photo ID for employees.*

phrase *noun* (<u>frāz</u>) 1. a group of words forming part of a sentence but not having both a subject and a verb. *In the kitchen* and *taking a shower* are phrases. 2. a short and familiar expression. *"Have a nice day"* is a common phrase in the U.S.

physical *adj.* (<u>fi</u> zi kəl) 1. of the body. *She did hard physical training to prepare for the race.* 2. things that can be seen and touched. *He is not interested in physical possessions. He only cares about his education.*
noun an examination of the body given by a doctor. *It is important that children get a yearly physical to stay healthy.*

physical education *noun* (<u>fi</u> zi kəl e jə <u>kā</u> shən) [N] the instruction in sports, exercise, and care of the human body as taught in a school.

physician *noun* (fə <u>zi</u> shən) a doctor of medicine.

physics *pl. noun* (<u>fi</u> ziks) the study of matter and energy. Physics includes the study of light, heat, sound, and electricity.

piano *noun* (pē <u>æ</u> nō) a musical instrument with a keyboard and many wire strings. A piano is played by pressing keys that cause small hammers to strike the strings.

pick¹ *verb* (<u>pik</u>) 1. to choose from a group. *Management picked one person from each department to be on the committee.* 2. to gather by pulling off or out. *She picked cat hair off her sweater.*
pick out to choose. *Pick out the puppy you want to take home.*
pick up 1. to lift up by hand. *The nurse picked up the baby when he began to cry.* 2. to make neat by putting objects in order. *I picked up my room, which was a mess.*

pick[2] *noun* (pik) a sharp, pointed tool used for digging or breaking up rocks or other hard substances. *He used an ice pick to cut a hole in the ice.*

pickle *noun* (pi kəl) a cucumber or another vegetable or fruit that is preserved with salt and a liquid.

pickup truck *noun* (pi kəp trək) a small truck with a large open area for carrying things. *The construction worker put her tools into the back of her pickup truck.*

picnic *noun* (pik nik) an informal meal that is eaten outdoors, usually in a park or other place in nature. *We **had a picnic** on the beach by the lake.*

Word Builder: picnic +
picnic basket: a basket in which you carry food to a picnic.
picnic blanket: a blanket that you spread on the ground and on which you have a picnic.
picnic table: a table that is outside and at which people have picnics.

picture *noun* (pik chər) a painting, drawing, or photograph. *The hall was lined with pictures of the presidents of the United States.*
verb to make an image of someone or something in one's mind; imagine. *It's hard to picture your parents as children.*

pie *noun* (pī) a cooked dish that has a crust made of dough and a thicker layer of fruit, meat, or something else on top of it. Sometimes it has another layer of crust on top of that.

piece *noun* (pēs) 1. a section or part separated from the whole. *I ate a piece of pizza for lunch.* 2. an object that belongs to a group of similar objects. *There are so many pieces to this puzzle.* 3. a work of art, literature, or music. *He practiced the piece of music until he could play it with no mistakes.*

pig *noun* (pig) 1. a mammal with a wide, flat nose, short legs, a thick body, and a short tail. Many people raise pigs for their meat. 2. (informal) a person who is very rude, greedy, or messy. *You're such a pig when you say things like that! | What a pig! He ate all the cookies himself! | My brother is a pig. Look at the mess in his room.*

pigeon *noun* (pi jən) a bird that is very common in cities. It is usually gray with brown, purple, or white marks on its body.

pile *noun* (pīl) a number of things on top of each other, or a mass of material that forms a small hill. *There was a pile of dirty laundry on the floor. | The builders left a pile of dirt behind the new house.*
verb to place things on top of each other. *He piled the wood by the side of the house.*

pilgrim *noun* (pil grəm) 1. a person who takes a trip to a holy place for a religious purpose. 2. (capitalized) one of the English people who came to Massachusetts in 1620 in order to have religious freedom.

pill *noun* (pil) a small piece of medicine that is taken by mouth. *Some pills are hard to swallow.*

pillow *noun* (pi lō) a cloth bag filled with soft material used for resting the head while sleeping. *My favorite pillow is filled with goose feathers.*

pilot *noun* (pī lət) a person who flies an airplane or other aircraft.
verb to operate an airplane or steer a ship. *He piloted the ship through dangerous waters.*

pin *noun* (pin) a thin piece of metal with a sharp point and usually a flat head. Pins are used to fasten or attach cloth, paper, or other materials. *Tom held his pants closed with a pin.*
verb to hold together with pins. *She pinned together the pieces of the dress before she sewed them.*

PIN *abbrev.* (pin) an abbreviation for *personal identification number.* You need a PIN to use an ATM.

pinch *verb* (pinch) to press something hard between two surfaces, especially between the finger and thumb. *My grandmother pinched my cheek. | This machine can pinch your finger if you're not careful.*

pine *noun* (pīn) a tree with soft wood and leaves shaped like needles. The leaves stay green all year.

pink[1] *adj.* (pingk) having the color that results from mixing red and white substances.

pink[2] *verb* (pingk) to cut using a kind of scissors that make a special edge. *The edges of the seam were pinked to prevent fraying.*

pint *noun* (pīnt) a standard unit used to measure liquid. One pint equals 16 ounces. Two pints equal one quart.

pipe *noun* (pīp) 1. a tube of metal, plastic, or other material through which a gas or liquid may flow. *Water comes into my house through a large pipe.* 2. an object with a small bowl at the end of a thin tube that you put in your mouth. You put tobacco in the bowl and smoke it. *My grandfather smokes a pipe.*

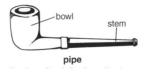
bowl
stem
pipe

pit[1] *noun* (pit) a deep natural or artificial hole in the ground. *They dug a pit to bury the dead animals.*

pit[2] *noun* (pit) the hard seed at the center of certain fruits. *Peaches have a large pit.*

pitch *verb* (pich) 1. to throw hard and with care. *The farmer pitched the hay onto the wagon.* 2. to set up a tent. *The campers pitched their tent on level ground.* 3. in baseball, to throw the ball to the person trying to hit the ball. *She pitched for the entire game.*
noun the high or low quality of a sound or note in music. *The high pitch of the fire siren hurt my ears.*

pitcher *noun* (pi chər) a container with a handle and lip used to hold and pour liquids. *He put a pitcher of iced tea on the table.*

pity *noun* (pi tē) sympathy or sorrow caused by another's pain, bad luck, or suffering. *She has such pity for her sick friend.*

pizza *noun* (pēt sə) a thin, flat piece of bread covered with cheese, oil, tomato sauce, and often meat or vegetables. *A pizza is cooked in an oven.*

place *verb* (plās) 1. to put in a certain spot or position. *Marta carefully placed the baby in the crib.* 2. to ask a store or restaurant for something you want. *We **placed** our **order** for food with the waitress.*
noun 1. a certain area of space used or intended for some purpose. *Let's look for a nice place to eat lunch.* | *Put your keys in a safe place.* 2. a particular point or position within something or among things. *I lost my place in the book.* | *Could you please hold my place in line?* 3. situation or position. *I would hate to be in his place.* 4. a person's home. *Let's meet at your place tomorrow.*
take place to happen. *The meeting will take place at the school.*

plain *adj.* (plān) 1. clear and understood. *It was plain to everyone that she was angry.* 2. without decoration or anything added; simple. *She wore a plain white dress to the party.* | *I like my toast plain.*
noun a large, flat area of land. *People raise cattle on the plains in the western United States.*

plan *noun* (plan) 1. an action one intends to take; aim. *Her plan is to travel in Europe after she graduates.* 2. a way to do something that is decided ahead of time. *You must have a good plan before you build a house.*
verb to develop or think of a way to do something. *He planned to send his children to college.*

Word Builder: plan +
planning: the activity of making plans for a project, business, or government.

plane[1] *noun* (plān) a short form of **airplane**.

plane[2] *noun* (plān) a hand tool with a blade that is used to make the surface of wood smooth or even.

planet *noun* (plæ nit) a large object in outer space that moves around the sun or another star. *There are eight planets in our solar system: Mercury, Venus, Earth, Mars, Jupiter, Saturn, Uranus, and Neptune.*

plant *noun* (plænt) 1. a living thing that has leaves, makes its own food, and has roots that usually grow in the earth. *I have many plants growing in my garden.* 2. a building that has machinery and equipment for making things; factory. *Nina works at the automobile plant.*
verb to put something into the ground to make it grow. *We planted a vegetable garden behind our house.*

plant

Word Builder: plant +
plantings: things that are put into the ground to grow.

plastic *noun* (plæ stik) an artificial substance made from certain kinds of chemicals that can be shaped when soft. *Many toys are made out of plastic.*

Word Builder: plastic +
plastic bag: a bag made of plastic.
plastic wrap: wrap made of plastic, used to cover food.

plate *noun* (plāt) a flat, round dish for food. *I put a slice of cake on each plate.*

platform *noun* (plæt fôrm) a flat, raised surface used as a place to stand or to put things. *The railroad platform was crowded with people waiting for the next train.*

play *noun* (plā) 1. a story written to be acted on a stage. *Our class put on a play for the whole school.* 2. [N] an activity that is meant to relax or amuse. *The parents watched their children* **at play.**

verb 1. to act the part of someone or something for an audience. *She will play an evil queen in the play.* 2. to be in a game or contest. *Let's play soccer.* 3. to make music with. *She plays the piano very well.* 4. to take part in activities that are just for fun. *The children played outside all day.*

Word Builder: play +

player: a person who plays a game.
playful: not serious; wanting to play and have fun.
playground: a space where people play.
playmate: a friend with whom you play.

---

pleasant *adj.* (ple zənt) 1. nice; enjoyable. *It was a pleasant day for a picnic.* 2. having a nice manner. *She is very pleasant to all the customers.*

please *verb* (plēz) to make happy or give pleasure to. *His accurate work pleased his boss.*

interj. used to make a polite request. *Please help yourself to a drink.* | *Would you close the window, please?*

Word Builder: please +

pleased: showing pleasure or feeling pleasure.

---

pleasure *noun* (ple zhər) a feeling of happiness or joy. *Seeing his grandchildren gives him pleasure.*

pleat *noun* (plēt) a flat, even fold that is sewn or pressed in cloth. *She bought a skirt with many pleats.*

pledge *noun* (plej) a serious promise. *She* **made a pledge** *to keep her friend's secret.*

verb to promise. *He pledged his aid to the cause.*

plenty *noun* (plen tē) [N] a full amount or supply. *There was* **plenty of** *food in the kitchen.*

pliers *pl. noun* (plī ərz) a tool that has a pair of jaws connected to handles. Pliers are used for holding, bending, or cutting things.

plot[1] *noun* (plat) 1. the story line or order of events in a book, play, or movie. *The plot of the film was long and complicated.* 2. a secret plan that has an illegal or dangerous purpose. *The robbers formed a plot to steal the painting.*

verb to make secret plans for a bad or illegal purpose. *The men plotted to take over the government.*

plot[2] *noun* (plat) a small piece of land. *There is a garden plot behind the house.*

plow *noun* (plow) 1. a heavy farm machine used to prepare ground for planting. 2. a machine or tool used to move things such as snow.

verb to cut or turn over by using a plow. *The farmer plowed his fields.*

plug *noun* (pləg) 1. an object made of rubber or other material used to block an opening. *Pull the plug to let the water out of the sink.* 2. a device with two or three metal pieces that you put into a power source in the wall to get electric power. *Put the plug into the outlet before you turn on the TV.*

plug

verb 1. to close or stop up with a plug. *They plugged up the hole.* 2. to put a plug into a power source, or to connect a wire to a power source. *Plug the wire to the lamp into the socket on that wall.*

plug in to connect an electric device to a power source. *Will you please plug in the toaster?*

plum *noun* (pləm) a sweet, round, soft fruit with red, purple, green, or yellow skin. Plums grow on trees and have a small, smooth seed.

plumber *noun* (plə mər) a person whose job is to work on pipes that carry water through buildings.

plump *adj.* (pləmp) full and round in shape. *The baby was plump and happy.*

plural *adj.* (plur əl) having to do with the form of a word that expresses the meaning of more than one. The words *books*, *children*, and *knives* are plural nouns.

plus *prep.* (pləs) used when one number or thing is added to another. *Three plus five equals eight.*

p.m. *abbrev.* (pē em) the time between twelve o'clock in the morning and twelve o'clock at night. *We ate lunch at 1:30 p.m.*

pocket *noun* (pa kit) a small piece of material that is sewn onto clothing and left open at the top for holding things. *Ben keeps his house key in his pants pocket.*

pocketbook *noun* (pa kit buk) a small bag used to carry money and personal things. *Sarah took her wallet out of her pocketbook.*

poem *noun* (pō əm) a piece of writing different from ordinary writing in its special form, style, and language. Poems often express emotions and are considered to have beauty.

poet *noun* (pō it) a person who writes poetry.

poetry *noun* (pō ə trē) [N] poems as a group. *We study poetry in English class.*

point *noun* (poynt) 1. the sharp end of something. *The pencil point broke when he pressed on it.* 2. a particular moment in time. *I was at the point of leaving when the phone rang.* 3. the meaning or purpose of a statement or action. *What's the point of that joke?* 4. a special quality. *This horse has many good points.* 5. a unit used for keeping score in certain sports or achieving a grade in school. *She scored sixteen points in the basketball game.* | *She earned ninety points on her test.* 6. a particular place in the world. *We stopped at three points between New York and Florida on our trip.*
verb to aim or direct at something. *I pointed my finger at my nose.*
beside the point not important to the subject that is being discussed. *The fact that you don't like your job is beside the point. You still have to go to work.*
point out to show or tell about something so that someone can see it or know it. *The tour guide pointed out some interesting sights.* | *Please point out the things that you want changed.*

Word Builder: point +
pointed: having a sharp point.
pointer: a tool for pointing at something.

poison *noun* (poy zən) a substance that can kill or seriously harm living beings if it is swallowed, breathed, or taken in. *Parents should keep bug sprays and other poisons where children cannot reach them.*
verb to give poison to; use poison to hurt or kill. *He poisoned the rats that got into his house.*

poisonous *adj.* (poy zə nəs) filled with or containing poison. *Some snakes are poisonous.*

poisonous snake

poke *verb* (pōk) to push with a thin or sharp object. *She poked her brother in the ribs with her finger.*

pole *noun* (pōl) a long, round post or stick made of metal, wood, or some other material. *The flag flew from the top of the pole.* | *Kevin got a new fishing pole.*

police *noun* (pə lēs) 1. [N] a department of a town, city, or state government that protects people and their property and makes people obey laws. *She called the police when she saw someone break into the bank.* 2. [N] members of such a department. *The police taught us about bicycle safety.*

Word Builder: police +
police car: a car in which police officers drive while they are working.
policeman: a man who is a member of the police.
police officer: a person who is a member of the police.
police station: the office of the police in a certain area.
policewoman: a woman who is a member of the police.

policy[1] *noun* (pa lə sē) a set of rules or a plan that is used as a guide for action. *The library policy lets people borrow books for two weeks at a time.*

policy[2] *noun* (pa lə sē) a written contract between an insurance company and the person being insured. *I got a new insurance policy when I bought a house.*

polish *verb* (pa ləsh) to give a shiny surface to. *We polished the furniture before the guests arrived.*
noun a substance used to make something shiny, bright with color, or clean. *This new polish made my boots look new.*

Word Builder: polish +
polished: having been given a shiny surface.

polite *adj.* (pə līt) showing good manners. *Be polite when you greet the guests.*

political *adj.* (pə li ti kəl) having to do with the study or practice of politics, politicians, or government. *He is interested in political issues and always votes.*

politician *noun* (pa li ti shən) a person who holds political office. *Many politicians live in Washington, D.C.*

politics *pl. noun* (pa li tiks) 1. [N] the study of the activities and practice of people in government. *A person who wants to enter government needs to understand politics.* 2. activities or practices of leaders in government. *He was **in politics** for many years before he decided to run for president.*

pollen *noun* (pa lən) [N] the fine, usually yellow, powder made by a flowering plant that helps other similar plants produce seeds.

pollute *verb* (pə <u>loot</u>) to make dirty or harmful by mixing in or adding waste material. *The company polluted the river by dumping oil in the water.*

Word Builder: pollute +
polluted: made dirty by pollution.

pollution *noun* (pə <u>loo</u> shən) [N] poisons, waste, or other materials that cause harm to the environment. *Pollution in the lake is killing the fish.*

pond *noun* (<u>pand</u>) a small body of still water. *Ducks live in the pond near my house.*

pony *noun* (<u>pō</u> nē) a kind of horse that is small in size when full grown.

ponytail *noun* (<u>pō</u> nē tāl) a style in which all the hair is pulled up and tied back so that the ends hang down. *Violet wears a ponytail so her hair doesn't get in her eyes.*

pool *noun* (<u>pool</u>) 1. any small, still area of liquid that has collected on something. *A pool of water formed in the basement after the heavy rain.* 2. a large, deep container that is filled with water and used to swim in. A pool is often in the ground. *My neighbors invited us to swim in their pool.*

poor *adj.* (<u>pur</u>) 1. without money, possessions, or other basic needs. *The community center serves free meals to poor people.* 2. below standard. *She got a poor grade on the test.* 3. having bad luck; experiencing bad things. *This poor woman lost both her husband and her son in the accident.*

Word Builder: poor +
poorly: in a poor way; not well.

pop[1] *verb* (<u>pap</u>) to burst open or cause to burst open with a short, loud sound. *The balloon popped when I stepped on it. | She popped the corn in the microwave.*

pop[2] *adj.* (<u>pap</u>) a short form of **popular**. *Do you listen to pop music?*

popcorn *noun* (<u>pap</u> kōrn) [N] small pieces of corn that open when cooked and can be eaten.

popcorn

popular *adj.* (<u>pap</u> yə lər) 1. liked or enjoyed by many people. *She is popular at school. | That is a popular book.* 2. having to do with or coming from the people. *U.S. senators are elected by popular vote.* 3. designed for or enjoyed by the general public. *This radio station plays only popular music.*

population *noun* (pap yə <u>lā</u> shən) the total number of people living in a country, city, or other area. *New York City has a population of more than eight million.*

porch *noun* (<u>pōrch</u>) a structure or covered space attached to a house. It is used as an entrance to a house and often as a place to relax.

pork *noun* (<u>pōrk</u>) [N] meat from a pig.

port *noun* (<u>pōrt</u>) 1. a place where ships load, or the town or city near this place. *The ship came into the port with a load of fish. | New York City is a port.* 2. a place on a computer for connecting equipment that sends or receives information. *The computer has a port for connecting the printer.*

portable *adj.* (<u>pōr</u> tə bəl) easy to carry or move. *We brought a portable radio to the picnic.*

portion *noun* (<u>pōr</u> shən) 1. a part of a whole. *He read a portion of the book.* 2. an amount of food that is enough for one person. *Do not eat more than one portion of cake or you will feel ill.*

position *noun* (pə <u>zi</u> shən) 1. the exact place where a person or thing is. *Let's **change the position** of the table and put it by the window.* 2. the way something is placed or arranged. *He laid down in a comfortable position and fell asleep. | The heater must be **in** an upright **position**.* 3. a point of view; opinion. *Sarah's parents **took** the same **position on** her going to the party.* 4. an appointed job. *My cousin has a new position as chief of police.*

positive *adj.* (<u>pa</u> zə tiv) 1. sure. *I am positive that she lives on this street.* 2. saying or meaning *yes. I gave a positive answer to his question.* 3. favorable; good. *The coach said positive things about how the team was playing.* 4. having to do with an amount greater than zero. *Jane keeps a positive balance in her bank account.*

possess *verb* (pə <u>zes</u>) to own or have. *He wants to possess more land. | She possesses good writing skills.*

possession *noun* (pə <u>ze</u> shən) something that is owned. *I have many possessions besides my car.*

possessive *adj.* (pə <u>ze</u> siv) of or connected with having or possessing something. In grammar, the words *my, the cat's, the doctor's, our dogs',* and *the children's* are possessive forms.

possibility *noun* (pa sə <u>bi</u> lə tē) something that might happen. *There is a possibility of rain tomorrow.*

possible *adj.* (pȧ sə bəl) 1. able to happen, exist, or be done. *Getting an education is possible for many people today.* 2. being true; likely. *If he didn't answer, it's possible that he didn't hear you.*

Word Builder: possible +
possibly: maybe.

---

post[1] *noun* (pōst) a piece of wood, metal, or other material placed upright in the ground to mark or support something. *The stop sign is attached to a metal post.*
verb to attach to a wall or other surface. *We posted signs for our yard sale on a few telephone poles.*

Word Builder: post +
posting: an announcement that is posted in public.

---

post[2] *noun* (pōst) a position of employment or duty. *She has a post in the shipping department.*

post[3] *noun* (pōst) [N] the system for delivering mail. *A letter sent by post takes only a few days to arrive.*
verb to give someone the latest information. *She posted the news on her Web page.* | *Please **keep me posted** if you hear from the doctor.*

postage *noun* (pō stij) [N] the amount of money charged for sending a letter or package by mail. *Postage for this package is two dollars.*

postcard *noun* (pōst kard) a small card that can be mailed. It has space for a message, address, and stamp on one side. *A postcard requires less postage than a letter.*

post office *noun* (pōst aw fis) an office where mail is received, sorted, and sent out, and where stamps are sold. *Most towns and cities have a post office.*

pot *noun* (pat) a deep, round container made of metal, clay, glass, or other material. Pots are used for cooking and other purposes. *She cooked soup in a large pot.*

potato *noun* (pə tā tō) a root that is eaten as a vegetable. Potatoes usually have brown or red skin and white or yellow flesh.

potatoes

poultry *noun* (pōl trē) [N] birds that are raised for their meat and eggs. Chicken and turkey are kinds of poultry.

pound[1] *verb* (pownd) 1. to hit or strike with force. *The carpenter pounded the nails with a hammer.* 2. to beat hard. *My heart was pounding after the race.*

pound[2] *noun* (pownd) a standard unit used to measure weight. One pound equals 16 ounces.

pour *verb* (pōr) 1. to cause to flow in a steady stream. *Calvin poured milk into his cereal bowl.* 2. to rain hard. *It poured for hours.*

poverty *noun* (pa vər tē) [N] the condition of being poor; a lack of money. *Many people live **in poverty** in the United States.*

powder *noun* (pow dər) [N] a mass of fine, loose grains that are made when a solid material has been ground or crushed. *She put powder on the baby after his bath.*

power *noun* (pow ər) 1. the ability to act, function, or cause things to happen. *People thought the president had too much power.* 2. the ability to control others. *The people feared the cruel leader's power.* 3. a person, group, or nation that has control or influence over others. *The United States is a world power.* 4. energy that can do work. *Electric power changed the way people live.*
verb to supply with energy or force. *Gasoline powers most car engines.* | *That appliance is **powered by** electricity.*

power failure *noun* (pow ər fāl yər) a loss of electric power. *We used candles for light during the power failure.*

powerful *adj.* (pow ər fəl) having or being able to use power or force. *The race car has a powerful engine.* | *The principal is in a powerful position.*

power switch *noun* (pow ər swich) a device used to open or close an electric connection. *Please turn the power switch off to stop the machine.*

power tool *noun* (pow ər tool) a tool that operates by electric power. *Power tools save time when building and repairing things.*

practical *adj.* (prȧk ti kəl) able to be used in everyday activities and experiences. *The new teacher needs practical classroom experience.* | *Is there a practical use for this invention?*

practice *noun* (pr<u>æ</u>k tis) 1. [N] the repeating of some activity many times in order to become good at it. *Claude spends two hours a day at football practice.* | *"Practice makes perfect" is an old saying.* 2. the work of an occupation or profession. *Three of my cousins are in the practice of accounting.*
verb 1. to repeat something in order to do it better. *She practices piano every day.* 2. to work at a particular job. *This doctor practices internal medicine.*

praise *noun* (pr<u>ā</u>z) words that show admiration or respect. *The dog received praise for doing a trick.*
verb to speak well of. *The coach praised the players for their hard work.*

pray *verb* (pr<u>ā</u>) to speak to or make a request of one's god or a holy person. *We prayed that the war would end soon.*

prayer *noun* (pr<u>ā</u>r) words that are said when speaking to one's god or a holy person. *The parents said a prayer for their baby's recovery.*

preach *verb* (pr<u>ē</u>ch) to present or deliver a talk on a religious or moral subject. *The minister preached during the Sunday morning service.*

preamble *noun* (pr<u>ē</u> æm bəl) an introduction to a formal document that serves to explain its purpose. *Many people study the preamble to the U.S. Constitution.*

precaution *noun* (prə k<u>aw</u> shən) something done before an activity to prevent danger or harm. *Check the car's brakes as a precaution before you start your trip.*

precise *adj.* (pri s<u>ī</u>s) 1. stated in a clear way and with details. *Because of the precise directions, we were able to find the park.* 2. exact. *I need a precise count of the people in the room.*

> **Word Builder: precise +**
> **precisely:** in a precise way.

predict *verb* (prə <u>dikt</u>) to say ahead of time that something will happen. *The general predicted an easy victory.* | *They predicted that it would rain today.*

> **Word Builder: predict +**
> **predictable:** able to be predicted.
> **prediction:** a statement saying that something is going to happen.

prefer *verb* (prə f<u>ər</u>) to choose above others as the best liked or most wanted. *He **prefers** carrots **to** all other vegetables.*

prefix *noun* (pr<u>ē</u> fiks) a part of a word with its own meaning that is added to the beginning of another word to change the meaning. For example, *pre* in *prepay* is a prefix that means *before.*

pregnancy *noun* (preg nən s<u>ē</u>) the state or an instance of being **pregnant.** *She ate very carefully during her pregnancy.*

pregnant *adj.* (preg nənt) having one or more babies growing within the body of a female. *Mary is **pregnant with** her first child.*

prejudice *noun* (pre jə dis) 1. an opinion that is formed without knowing or understanding all the facts. *She has a **prejudice against** people who like to hunt.* 2. a hatred or bad treatment of a person or group without cause or reason, usually based on appearance or religion. *There are laws that protect people from acts of prejudice.*

prenatal *adj.* (pr<u>ē</u> n<u>ā</u> təl) before being born or giving birth. *Good prenatal care is important when you are pregnant.*

prepaid *verb* (pr<u>ē</u> p<u>ā</u>d) past tense and past participle of **prepay.**

preparation *noun* (pre pə r<u>ā</u> shən) the act of getting something ready. *Giving a large party requires a lot of preparation.* | *Preparations for the wedding took several months.*

prepare *verb* (pri p<u>ā</u>r) 1. to make ready. *He prepared his house for guests by cleaning.* 2. to make or put something together from different parts. *The cook cut up the meat and vegetables that he needed to prepare the soup.*

> **Word Builder: prepare +**
> **prepared** (1): already made.
> **prepared** (2): ready.

prepay *verb* (pr<u>ē</u> p<u>ā</u>) *prepaid, prepaid* to pay for something before you use it. *You have to prepay when you become a member of the health club.*

preposition *noun* (pre pə <u>zi</u> shən) a word that shows a relation between a noun or pronoun and another word. In the sentence "I went to the bank and asked about a loan," the words *to* and *about* are prepositions.

prerequisite *noun* (pr<u>ē</u> re kwi zit) something required before you can do another thing. *Passing Spanish1 is a prerequisite to taking Spanish 2.*

preschool *noun* (prē skool) a school for children below five years of age. *My children attend a preschool near our home.*

prescribe *verb* (pri skrīb) to order or suggest as a medicine. *The doctor prescribed a cream for his rash.*

prescription *noun* (pri skrip shən) an order written by a doctor for medicine. *Nadia's doctor gave her a prescription for cough medicine.* | *The drugstore **filled my prescription** in ten minutes.*

prescription

presence *noun* (prē zəns) 1. [N] the state or condition of being in a place at a certain time. *Your regular presence at work is important.* 2. [N] the condition of being near in time and space. *The police officers talked with the suspect **in the presence of** his lawyer.*

present[1] *adj.* (prē zənt) 1. existing at this time; current. *The present head of the company has been in charge for two years.* 2. being in a place at the time that you are expected to be there. *All of the students were present in class today.* 3. having to do with the form of a verb that describes an action or state that happens in the current time. In the sentence "I take the bus every day," the verb *take* is in a present form.
noun the period of time between the past and future; present time. *The troubles you have in the present will soon be over.*

present[2] *verb* (pri zent) 1. to give or provide with a gift or prize. *The judges presented a blue ribbon to the winner.* 2. to show. *The theater presented a play by Shakespeare.*
noun (prē zənt) something given as a gift. *She received presents on her birthday.*

preserve *verb* (pri zərv) to keep safe from loss or harm. *The court will preserve the right to freedom of speech.*
noun an area of land or water where plants and animals are protected. *Hunting is not allowed in animal preserves.*

president *noun* (prē zə dənt) 1. the head of government of a nation. A president is elected. 2. a person who leads a company, club, or other organization. A president of an organization can be elected or appointed.

press *verb* (pres) 1. to bear down. *I pressed hard on the suitcase while trying to close it.* 2. to push or force in a particular direction. *Did you press the button for the elevator?*

noun 1. [N] newspapers, magazines, and TV and radio news departments, and the people who work for them. *The press followed the movie star wherever he went.* 2. any of certain machines that act by pushing on something. *Books and magazines are printed on a printing press.*

Word Builder: press +
pressman: a person who operates a press.

pressure *noun* (prē shər) 1. a steady force on a surface. *Put pressure on a cut to make it stop bleeding.* 2. a strong influence or heavy force on the mind or emotions. *He feels a lot of pressure to do well in his job.*
verb to try to influence or force someone into an action. *Her parents are pressuring her to get married.*

pretend *verb* (pri tend) 1. to give an appearance of something being true or real when it is not true or real. *My son pretended to be sick to stay home from school.* 2. to imagine or make-believe. *The children pretended that they were exploring the moon.*

pretty *adj.* (pri tē) pleasing or attractive to the eyes or ears. *What a pretty dress!* | *That's a pretty song.*
adv. used when some quality is of a high degree but not very high; quite; fairly. *She's finding school pretty hard this year.*

prevent *verb* (pri vent) to keep or stop from happening. *Washing your hands can help prevent illness.* | *The police **prevented** the man **from** escaping.*

preventive *adj.* (pri ven tiv) protecting against disease or illness. *Eating healthy foods is part of preventive medicine.*

preview *noun* (prē vū) a short piece of a film or television program shown as an advertisement. *There were many previews before the movie started.*
verb to see or study ahead of time. *The boss previewed her application before her interview.* | *The teacher previewed the film before showing it to the class.*

previous *adj.* (prē vē əs) 1. coming just before another. *His previous car was pink.* 2. earlier. *In previous years, this information was not available on the Internet.*

Word Builder: previous +
previously: before; earlier.

price *noun* (prīs) the amount of money needed to buy something. *The price of gasoline is high.*

pride *noun* (prīd) 1. [N] a feeling of personal value or worth that results from something you have done or can do. *Jack **took pride in** his work.* 2. [N] a sense of one's own value that is too high. *Roger's pride made him hard to like.*

priest *noun* (prēst) a person who has the authority to perform or help at the religious services of some religions.

priest

primary *adj.* (prī mār ē) 1. main; most important. *Deidre's family is her primary concern.* 2. first in time or order. *Jim started primary school when he was five years old.*
noun an early election in the United States, where members of each political party vote for someone from that party to run for office in the general election.

prince *noun* (prins) a male who is a son or other close member of the family of a king or queen.

princess *noun* (prin ses) a female who is a daughter or other close member of the family of a king or queen.

principal *adj.* (prin sə pəl) greatest or first in importance. *The principal job of the police is to keep the peace.*
noun 1. the person who is head of a school. 2. the amount of money in a loan on which you pay interest.

principle *noun* (prin sə pəl) a basic law or belief on which action or behavior is based. *Our country's laws are based on the principles of liberty and justice for all.*

principle or principal?
Principle is a noun that means a basic idea or belief.
Principal is an adjective that means main or most important. It is also a noun that refers to the person in charge of a school.
Compare:
A principle of democracy is "One person, one vote."
His principal responsibility at work is sorting the mail.
The principal made an announcement to the students.

print *verb* (print) 1. to put words and pictures onto a surface using a machine. *They printed thousands of copies of that book.* 2. to write in letters like those of printed type. *The girl printed her name carefully at the bottom of her drawing.* 3. to put a photograph on paper. *The photography lab printed copies of the wedding pictures.*

noun 1. a shape marked or pressed onto a surface. *Her feet left prints in the wet sand.* 2. a photograph copied on paper. *They made prints of the family photo for all the grandparents.*

Word Builder: print +
printed: with writing made by a press or printer.
printer: a machine that prints.

prior *adj.* (prī ər) earlier in time or order; previous. *In prior years, I worked at a different school.*

prison *noun* (pri zən) a locked building for holding and punishing people who have broken the law. *People caught selling drugs will be sent to prison.*

Word Builder: prison +
prisoner: a person who must stay in a prison.

private *adj.* (prī vit) 1. allowing only certain people to take part in or to know about. *They held a private meeting to discuss how the money should be spent.* 2. personal and not to be shared. *I write my private thoughts in a diary.*

prize *noun* (prīz) a reward given to the person who wins something. *He won first prize in the contest and received a car and some money.*

prize

pro *noun* (prō) a reason to support or defend something. *Lana wrote down the **pros and cons** of moving to the city.*

probable *adj.* (pra bə bəl) likely to happen or be true. *Because we arrived at the theater early, it is probable that we will get good seats.*

probably *adv.* (pra bə blē) likely to happen or be true. *If it snows a lot tonight, schools will probably be closed tomorrow.*

problem *noun* (pra bləm) 1. a question or condition that is difficult to understand or to deal with. *Poverty is still a problem that faces our nation.* 2. a question to be discussed or solved. *I spent an hour working on math problems last night.*

procedure *noun* (prə sē jər) steps that must be taken in order to do something. *Follow the proper procedure for leaving the building during a fire alarm.*

process *noun* (pra ses) 1. actions taken to make or do something. *We are learning the process of baking bread.* 2. changes or acts that happen one after another. *The process of growing up takes many years.*
verb to handle, treat, or change something by following certain steps. *That factory processes aluminum into foil.* | *She processes all the invoices for the company.*

> **Word Builder: process +**
> **processed:** having been handled or changed according to a process.
> **processing:** the act of following steps to make or do something.
> **processor:** a person or thing that processes something.

produce *verb* (pra doos) to cause a new thing to come into the world; to make something. *Chickens produce eggs.* | *Our company produces parts for computers.*
noun (prō doos) [N] plants grown for food. *Farmers are getting a good price for their produce this year.* | *That supermarket has the freshest produce.*

> **Word Builder: produce +**
> **producer:** a person or thing that produces something.

product *noun* (pra dəkt) something that is made by humans, animals, or machines that did not exist before. *Our grocery store sells fresh farm products.* | *This store sells all kinds of paper products.*

production *noun* (pra dək shən) 1. [N] the act or process of making or producing. *That factory began production of automobiles eighty years ago.* 2. [N] a thing or amount that is made. *A new kind of seed has increased the farm's production of corn.*

profession *noun* (pra fe shən) a job or type of work that needs special training or study. *He entered the legal profession after finishing law school.*

professional *adj.* (pra fe shə nəl) 1. of or having to do with a certain job or work. *The doctor gave me her professional advice.* 2. doing a job as a way of earning money. *He works as a professional dancer.*

professor *noun* (pra fe sər) a teacher with a high rank at a college or university.

profit *noun* (pra fit) the amount of money made by a business that is more than the amount put in at the start. *The oil company reported a large profit this year.*
verb to gain something good. *He **profited from** his extra hours of piano practice.*

program *noun* (prō græm) 1. a plan of what will be done or take place. *The library has a weekly program for young readers.* 2. a television or radio show. *This TV channel has a lot of good programs.* 3. a set of instructions for a computer to follow so that it can do certain things. *This computer has a new e-mail program.*

progress *noun* (pra gres) 1. [N] a forward movement toward achieving a purpose. *Are you **making** any **progress with** your work?* 2. [N] a forward movement in time or space. *The cars made slow progress through the snow.*
verb (pra gres) to develop in a good way or grow. *She has progressed nicely after a year of cooking lessons.*

prohibit *verb* (pra hi bət or prō hi bət) to not allow, by law or by some other authority. *State law prohibits smoking on buses.* | *The school principal **prohibited** the students **from** playing radios in school.*

prohibit

project *noun* (pra jekt) 1. any activity that takes great effort or planning. *We're working on a new project at work. It will take several months to complete.* 2. a large group of homes, sometimes built with public money. *My grandparents are moving into a housing project for older people.*
verb (pra jekt) to make a good guess about something that is not known. *Can you project the cost of building the house?*

promise *noun* (pra mis) a statement that makes someone feel sure that something will happen or be done. *She made him a promise that she would call.*
verb to state, in a way that makes someone feel sure, that something will happen or will be done. *The children promised to be home before dark.* | *The mechanic promised that the car would be ready by Tuesday.*

promote *verb* (pra mōt) 1. to help something grow, increase, or move forward. *Eating well promotes health.* | *Their company advertises a lot to promote their products.* 2. to move to a higher position. *The boss promoted Mr. Smith from clerk to supervisor.*

promotion *noun* (pra mō shən) 1. a raise to a higher grade or position. *The worker received a promotion to manager.* 2. an effort that attempts to make something grow or increase, especially sales for a business. *The radio promotion of our restaurant brought in many new customers.*

prompt *adj.* (prampt) 1. fast and without pause. *This restaurant is known for its prompt service.* 2. arriving or being ready at the right time. *The fire department was prompt in getting to the burning building.*

pronoun *noun* (prō nown) a word that can take the place of a noun or noun phrase. In the sentence "He gave it to someone," *he, it,* and *someone* are examples of pronouns.

pronounce *verb* (prə nowns) 1. to make the sounds of a word or the sound of a letter. *I'm sorry. I don't know how to pronounce your name.* 2. to state something officially. *"I now pronounce you husband and wife," said the judge.*

pronunciation *noun* (prə nən sē ā shən) an accepted way of saying words. *There are two pronunciations for the word* aunt.

proof *noun* (proof) any material that proves something is true or real. *Scientists are searching for proof of life on other planets.*

proper *adj.* (pra pər) 1. correct or right for a certain purpose. *Shorts and a T-shirt are not the proper clothing for a job interview.* 2. following ideas or rules that have been accepted in society as correct. *They want to get married at a restaurant, but her parents want a proper wedding.*

Word Builder: proper +
properly: in a proper way.

property *noun* (pra pər tē) 1. anything that is owned; all of one's possessions taken as a whole. *The poor man's property included some clothing and little else.* 2. a building or a piece of land. *We plan to build a summer house on our property by the lake.*

propose *verb* (prə pōz) 1. to present or suggest as an idea to be considered. *The council proposed a new bike path around the lake.* 2. to present an offer of marriage. *He bought a ring and proposed to his girlfriend.*

propose

Word Builder: propose +
proposal: something that you propose.

prostitute *noun* (pra sti toot) a person who earns money by performing sexual acts with other people.

protect *verb* (prə tekt) to defend or keep safe from danger or harm. *A fence protects us from our neighbor's dog.* | *The new law protects workers against certain dangers in factories.*

Word Builder: protect +
protective: giving protection.
protector: someone or something that protects.

protection *noun* (prə tek shən) [N] the act of keeping something safe from harm or the condition of being protected. *We lock the doors at night for protection.*

protein *noun* (prō tēn) a chemical compound that is found in all living things and is necessary for life. *Eggs, meat, and beans are good sources of protein.*

protest *noun* (prō test) 1. a statement that says you think something is wrong and needs to be changed. *The management ignored their protests about unsafe conditions.* 2. a formal action of a group of people who want something to be changed. *The employees* **carried out a protest against** *the company's unfair treatment of workers.*
verb (prə test) to state that you disagree or are angry about something. *Many people protested against the plan to raise taxes.*

Word Builder: protest +
protester: a person who protests.

proud *adj.* (prowd) 1. feeling pleased and satisfied because of something one owns or has done. *He is proud of his new car.* | *My daughter is proud of her good grades.* 2. having a very high opinion of one's self. *The proud millionaire refused to ride the bus.*

Word Builder: proud +
proudly: in a proud way; showing pride.

prove *verb* (proov) **proved, proven** to show to be true or correct. *The evidence failed to prove the guilt of the prisoner.*

proven *verb* (proo vən) past participle of **prove.**

proverb *noun* (pra vərb) a short, common saying that expresses something wise or true. *"Actions speak louder than words" is an American proverb.*

provide *verb* (prə vīd) 1. to give what is needed; supply. *The company **provides** the workers **with** uniforms and necessary tools.* | *The rescue team **provided** water and food **to** the victims.* 2. to supply necessary things such as food and shelter. *She **provides for** her children by working hard.*

provoke *verb* (prə vōk) 1. to make angry or annoy on purpose. *Her speech provoked the audience.* 2. to bring out feelings in someone. *The poem provoked feelings of joy.*

prune[1] *noun* (proon) a **plum** that has been dried.

prune[2] *verb* (proon) to cut off or remove branches or other parts of trees or plants. *Jack pruned the branches of the maple tree.*

psychology *noun* (sī ka lə jē) [N] the study of the mind and of the ways that people feel and act. Psychology also includes the study of how to treat problems of the mind and behavior.

Word Builder: psychology +
psychologist: a person who has studied the way people think and act and who treats mental problems.

public *adj.* (pə blik) having to do with all the people in a community. *Our town's most beautiful public building is the new library.*
noun a community of people as a whole. *That beach is not open to the public.*
in public in a place outside your home where other people are present. *They never fight in public.*

Word Builder: public +
publicly: in the presence of many people; in public.

publish *verb* (pə blish) to prepare and print something for the public to read. *I work for a company that publishes magazines.*

Word Builder: publish +
published: having been printed and made available to the public.

pudding *noun* (pu ding) [N] a soft, sweet food that is made by cooking milk, sugar, and a flavor, such as chocolate.

puddle *noun* (pə dəl) a small area of liquid, usually water, on the ground. *The children splashed in the puddles after the rain.*

pull *verb* (pul) 1. to bring closer by using force upon. *She pulled the door shut.* 2. to cause something that is attached to move forward. *The truck pulled the car to the station.* 3. to remove with force from a fixed position. *The carpenter pulled the nail from the board.*
pull over to drive to the side of the road and stop. *The police officer signaled for him to pull over.*

pulley *noun* (pu lē) a simple machine that is used for lifting. A pulley is a wheel or set of wheels that a rope or chain is pulled over.

pulley

pump *noun* (pəmp) a machine that causes a liquid or gas to move from one place to another.
verb to move using a pump or as if using a pump. *We pumped water from the bottom of the boat.*

punch[1] *noun* (pənch) a hard, quick hit with the closed hand. *She gave her pillow a punch.*
verb 1. to hit with the closed hand. *My brother punched someone in the face.* 2. to push or press. *The clerk punched a button on the cash register to open the cash drawer.*
punch in [or] out to record the time of beginning or ending work by using a machine. *At my job, I punch in when I get to work and punch out when I leave.*

punch[2] *noun* (pənch) a sweet drink made by mixing fruit juices and other liquids.

punctual *adj.* (pəngk choo əl) on time. *It is important to be punctual for a job interview.*

punctuation *noun* (pəngk choo ā shən) [N] question marks, periods, and other marks used in writing to help make the meaning clear. *It is important to use correct punctuation when you write.*

puncture *noun* (pəngk chər) a small hole caused by a sharp object. *There is a puncture in the tire.*
verb to cause a hole to be made in something by being sharp or pointed. *The nail punctured my tire when I ran over it.*

punish *verb* (pə nish) to cause someone to experience a thing that is painful or not pleasant because he or she did something wrong. *He punished his son for telling lies.*

punishment *noun* (pə nish mənt) a way of causing someone to suffer or experience something bad for having done something wrong. *Sometimes the punishment for stealing is going to jail.*

pupil[1] *noun* (pū pəl) a young person who is taught by a teacher. *There are 300 pupils in this school.*

pupil[2] *noun* (pū pəl) the small, dark opening in the center of the eye. Light passes through the pupil into the eye.

puppy *noun* (pə pē) a young dog.

purchase *verb* (pər chəs) to get something by paying money for it; buy. *I purchased these shoes at the mall.* *noun* something that is bought. *The clerk helped me carry my purchases to my car.*

pure *adj.* (pūr) 1. not mixed with anything else; made of only one substance. *She's wearing a blouse made of pure silk.* 2. without evil. *The hero had a pure heart.*

Word Builder: pure +
purity: the state or quality of being pure.

purple *adj.* (pər pəl) having the color that results from mixing blue and red substances.

purpose *noun* (pər pəs) the reason that something exists or happens. *The purpose of soap is to clean things.* | *What is the purpose of your visit?*
on purpose done because of someone's desire or intention; not by accident. *He broke his sister's toy on purpose.*

purse *noun* (pərs) a bag used for carrying money and other personal things. A purse is often made of leather, cloth, or a similar material. *Leila keeps her wallet, keys, and a comb in her purse.*

push *verb* (push) to move something or cause something to move by using pressure against it. *I pushed my bed against the wall.* | *He pushed me with his hands.*
noun a strong touch that causes something to move. *She gave the door a push.*

put *verb* (put) *put, put* to move to a particular position or place. *The cashier put the groceries in a bag.* 2. to cause to be in a particular state or situation. *His car accident put him in the hospital.*
put away to return something to the place where it usually stays. *Paul folded his clean clothes and put them away.*
put back to return something to a place. *Please put the book back on the shelf.*
put down to put an object that you are holding onto a surface. *Put that heavy box down on my desk.* | *Put your pencils down.*
put off to delay. *You shouldn't put off paying your bills.*
put on to put something on your body. *Sophie put on her mother's hat.* | *I forgot to put my watch on.*
put out to stop the burning of something. *The firefighters put out the fire in a few hours.* | *They put out their cigarettes.*
put together to build something from parts. *Carol put together a model airplane.*
put up with to accept or live with something bad. *We'll have to put up with this noise until the workers are finished.*

puzzle *noun* (pə zəl) a toy or problem that you solve by thinking or by arranging letters, words, numbers, or objects. *The local newspaper publishes word puzzles every day.* | *It took us a few weeks to finish that jigsaw puzzle.* **verb** to confuse. *The book's ending puzzled me.*

jigsaw puzzle pieces

Word Builder: puzzle +
puzzled: feeling confusion; not knowing the answer.

Q q

qualification *noun* (kwa lə fə kā shən) something that makes a person fit for an activity or job. *Computer skills are a qualification for many office jobs.*

qualify *verb* (kwa lə fī) to make someone fit for a job or activity. *Special training qualifies him to be a teacher.*

Word Builder: qualify +
qualified: having the appropriate qualifications.

quality *noun* (kwa li tē) 1. a feature that makes a person or thing what it is. *Maria has many good qualities.* | *One quality of steel is its strength.* 2. the degree to which something is good or bad. *Shoes of good quality will last a long time.*

quantity *noun* (kwan ti tē) an amount or number. *We bought a large* **quantity of** *napkins for the restaurant.*

quantity, number, or amount?
Quantity is used to tell about either an amount or a number of something.
Number is used to tell about things that you can count.
Amount is used to tell about a mass or group that you cannot count.
Compare:
Ben ate a large amount of ice cream. He ate a large quantity of ice cream.
Beth ate a large number of nuts. She ate a large quantity of nuts.

quarrel *noun* (kwar əl) an angry argument. *My husband and I* **had a quarrel about** *money.*
verb to argue or disagree in an angry way. *After their father died, the two brothers quarrelled over his money.*

quart *noun* (kwawrt) a standard unit used to measure liquid. One quart equals 32 ounces or two pints. *I bought a quart of milk and a quart of juice.*

quarter *noun* (kwawr tər) 1. one of four equal parts of a whole. *I cut the sandwich into quarters.* 2. a coin of the United States and some other countries equal to twenty-five cents. 3. one-fourth of an hour. *quarter past seven (7:15).* | *quarter to seven (6:45).*

quarter

Word Builder: quarter +
quarterly: happening once every three months, or once during every quarter of a year.

queen *noun* (kwēn) 1. a female ruler of a country who is not elected and whose mother or father was usually a ruler before her; a woman who married a king. 2. a playing card that has the picture of a queen. *There are four queens in a deck of cards.*

question *noun* (kwes chən) a sentence that asks for an answer. *There were ten questions on the test.* | *The teacher asked him a question.*
verb to ask a question or questions of someone in a very serious way. *The police questioned him for many hours.* | *His wife questioned him about his decision.*

question mark *noun* (kwes chən mark) a punctuation mark (?). It is used at the end of a sentence that asks a question.

quick *adj.* (kwik) 1. done in a short time; fast. *I made a quick trip to the supermarket.* 2. able to think, act, or learn with speed. *She has a quick mind.*

Word Builder: quick +
quickly: in a quick way.

quiet *adj.* (kwī it) 1. making little or no noise. *That car has a quiet engine.* 2. peaceful and calm. *The house is quiet when everyone is asleep.*

Word Builder: quiet +
quietly: in a quiet way.

quit *verb* (kwit) **quit, quit** to stop doing something. *She quit her job and went back to school.* | *He quit smoking.*

quite *adv.* (kwīt) 1. completely; in full. *She is not quite done with breakfast.* 2. very; rather. *He is doing quite well at his new job.*

quotation *noun* (kwō tā shən) a quoted passage from a book or another source. *"Give me liberty, or give me death" is a famous quotation from American history.*

quotation mark *noun* (kwō tā shən mark) either of a pair of punctuation marks (" "). Quotation marks are used at the beginning and end of a quotation.

quote *verb* (kwōt) to repeat the exact words used by someone else. *He quoted some sentences from a famous speech.*
noun something that is quoted; quotation. *Some amusing quotes came from that movie.*

R r

rabbit *noun* (ræ̱ bit) a small mammal with soft fur, long ears, long back legs, and a short tail.

race[1] *noun* (ra̱s) 1. a sport or test of speed. *That driver has won five races this year.* 2. a political competition. *The candidates are in a close race for president.*
verb to move at high speed. *The car raced around the track. | She raced through breakfast.*

> **Word Builder: race +**
> **racing:** the sport or competition of speed.

race[2] *noun* (ra̱s) a human population sharing certain common physical qualities. *People of many races live in the United States.*

> **Word Builder: race +**
> **racism:** discrimination by people of one race against people of another race.
> **racist:** a person who believes that the people of one race are better than the people of another race.

rack *noun* (ræk) a frame or stand used to hold, hang, or show things. *He arranged the cards on a display rack. | The dresses on this rack are on sale.*

> **Word Builder: kinds of racks**
> **bike rack:** a rack for holding bicycles, usually outside.
> **dish rack:** a rack for holding dishes while they dry.
> **spice rack:** a rack for holding containers of spices.
> **wine rack:** a rack for holding bottles of wine.

radiate *verb* (ra̱ de at) to send out. *The fire radiated warmth.*

radiation *noun* (ra̱ de a̱ shən) [N] waves of energy sent out by sources of heat or light. *Some forms of radiation are dangerous. X-rays are a form of radiation.*

radiator *noun* (ra̱ de a tər) 1. a device in a car that cools the engine. It is made up of metal tubes that hold and cool water and other liquids. 2. a device in a building that uses steam or hot water passing through pipes in order to heat a room.

radio *noun* (ra̱ de o̱) a piece of equipment that receives radio signals and changes them into sound. *I listen to the news on the radio every morning.*

rag *noun* (ræg) a small piece of cloth that is usually used for cleaning. A rag is often torn from a larger piece of cloth that is no longer in good condition.

rage *noun* (ra̱j) [N] extreme anger. *She screamed at her friend **in rage.***

rail *noun* (ra̱l) 1. one of the two long steel bars along which a train moves. *Trains have steel wheels that fit on the rails.* 2. a long bar of wood, metal, or some other material that is attached to posts as part of a fence. *There is a guardrail along the edge of some roads and bridges.*

railing *noun* (ra̱ ling) a long bar that connects posts and is used as a fence or for safety. *Hold onto the railing while you go down the stairs.*

railing

railroad *noun* (ra̱l ro̱d) a road of two connected steel bars along which trains move, or a system of transportation that uses these roads. *The railroad runs through the center of the town. | Before cars were invented, it was more common to travel on the railroads.*

rain *noun* (ra̱n) [N] drops of water that form in the clouds and fall from the sky to the earth. *We had a lot of rain this spring.*
verb to come down as water from the clouds. *It's raining, so bring your umbrella.*

> **Word Builder: rain +**
> **raincoat:** a coat you wear when it rains to protect you from water.
> **rainfall:** the amount of rain that falls in a period of time.
> **rainy:** having a lot of rain.

raise *verb* (ra̱z) 1. to move to a higher position. *I raised my hand.* 2. to cause or help to grow. *My parents raised four children. | The farmers raise beans and corn.* 3. to gather or collect. *The club raised money for a local hospital.* 4. to increase. *They raised the price of gas.*
noun an increase in pay. *She got a raise after six months at her job.*

rake *noun* (ra̱k) a tool that has a long handle and a row of long teeth at one end. A rake is used to gather things lying on the ground or to smooth down soil.

ramp *noun* (rămp) a flat surface that connects two different levels. *There is a ramp from the sidewalk to the building entrance for people who cannot climb stairs.* | *There is a ramp onto the highway from Main Street.*

ran *verb* (răn) past tense of **run.**

ranch *noun* (rănch) a large farm where cattle, horses, or sheep are raised. *There are many ranches in the plains of the United States.*

rang *verb* (răng) past tense of **ring**[2].

range *noun* (rānj) 1. the two points between which something can exist. *In this school, the range of ages is from five to eleven.* 2. a group of different things of the same kind; variety. *This store carries a wide range of shoes.* 3. a large piece of equipment for cooking. A range is an appliance with a stove and an oven. *Their kitchen has a gas range.* 4. a group of mountains. *The highest mountain range is in Asia.*

rank *noun* (răngk) 1. a position as compared to other positions. *New employees start at the lowest rank.* 2. an office or position. *She achieved the rank of general.*
verb to hold a certain position. *The Cubs ranked first at the end of the season.*
rank and file all the ordinary members of a group, not the leaders. *The rank and file voted in favor of the new contract.*

rapid *adj.* (ră pid) very quick or fast. *The police had a rapid response to the emergency.*

Word Builder: rapid +
rapidly: in a rapid way; fast.

rare[1] *adj.* (rār) not often found or seen; not common. *Her necklace contained rare jewels.*

rare[2] *adj.* (rār) cooked for a short time. *He prefers rare steak.*

rash *noun* (răsh) a condition in which red spots appear on the skin. *Allergies can cause a rash.*

rat *noun* (răt) a small mammal with a pointed face and a very long tail. A rat looks similar to a mouse but is larger.

rat

rate *noun* (rāt) a quantity measured in terms of another quantity. *She is paid at the rate of 500 dollars per week.* | *He can run at the rate of seven miles per hour.*

rather *adv.* (ră thər) 1. used to express that you prefer to do something. *I **would rather** drink coffee **than** tea.* 2. in some measure; quite. *He felt rather sad.*

raw *adj.* (raw) not cooked. *She likes to eat raw vegetables.*

rayon *noun* (rā an) [N] a smooth cloth. Rayon is made from a solution of wood tissue that is formed into threads.

razor *noun* (rā zər) a tool with a very sharp blade that is used for cutting hair close to the skin. *Tom shaves his face with an electric razor.*

reach *verb* (rēch) 1. to touch or try to touch something by stretching out part of the body toward it. *Can you reach the glass on the top shelf?* | *He **reached out for** her hand.* 2. to get in touch with. *They can reach us by phone.* 3. to arrive at. *We reached the lake after a three-hour drive.* | *Has he reached a decision?*

react *verb* (rē ăkt) to act in a particular way because of something that happened. *Sue reacted calmly when she heard the bad news.*

reaction *noun* (rē ăk shən) 1. an action caused by something that has happened. *When she saw the snake, her reaction was to scream.* 2. a physical effect caused by a substance. *She had a bad reaction to that medicine.*

read[1] *verb* (rēd) *read, read* 1. to look at and understand the meaning of something written. *My little brother is learning to read.* 2. to show. *The thermometer reads 102 degrees.*

read[2] *verb* (red) past tense and past participle of **read**[1].

reading *noun* (rē ding) 1. [N] the action of a person who reads. *We have to do a lot of reading for this class.* 2. the point shown on an instrument that measures. *The high reading on the thermometer convinced his mother that he was sick.* 3. something that is written; part of a longer written work. *The teacher assigned us readings from our textbook.*

ready *adj.* (re dē) prepared. *I'm not ready to go yet.* | *Can you wait while I **get ready**?*

real *adj.* (rēl) 1. actual or true. *Dinosaurs were real, even though they no longer exist.* 2. natural; not artificial. *Her boots are made of real leather.*

reality *noun* (rē æ li tē) a person, thing, or event that is real. *Her dream of becoming a doctor became a reality.*

realize *verb* (rē ə līz) to understand in a clear way; to suddenly understand. *Do you realize how hard it is to find a job? | I just realized that it is past midnight.*

really *adv.* (rē lē) 1. in fact; actually. *We may not look alike, but we really are brothers.* 2. quite; very. *Your brother is really nice.*

rear *noun* (rēr) the back part of something. *He bumped into the rear of my car.*
adj. being at the back part of something. *Go through the rear entrance.*

reason *noun* (rē zən) 1. a cause or explanation for an action, opinion, or event. *He had a good reason for being late. | What's the reason for the party?* 2. [N] the power to think in a clear way. *The teacher gives assignments that require students to use their reason.*
verb to explain or argue by using reason. *When she didn't meet me for lunch, I reasoned that she had too much work at the office.*

reasonable *adj.* (rē zə nə bəl) 1. using good sense and clear thinking. *The judge made a reasonable decision.* 2. not too expensive. *The price for the jacket was reasonable.*

rebate *noun* (rē bāt) a part of a payment that is returned. *The store offered rebates to customers who bought television sets.*

recall *verb* (ri kawl) 1. to bring a past event into your mind. *Do you recall the day we went to that restaurant?* 2. to have products returned to the factory where they were made. Companies recall a product if it is found to be dangerous or damaged in some way. *The factory recalled the defective bicycles.*
noun (rē kawl) a way for government officials to be removed from office by people who vote. *There was a recall of the governor of California in 2003.*

receipt *noun* (ri sēt) a piece of paper showing that money or things were received. *The cashier at the store gave me my change and a receipt.*

receive *verb* (ri sēv) to get or accept. *He received many cards while he was in the hospital.*

recent *adj.* (rē sənt) happening in the very near past. *Unemployment has risen in recent years.*

Word Builder: recent +
recently: not long ago.

receptionist *noun* (ri sep shə nist) a person whose job is to greet people and answer the telephone in an office.

recharge *verb* (rē charj) to charge again. *You can recharge these batteries.*

recipe *noun* (re sə pē) a list of foods and instructions for cooking something. *This cookie recipe says to mix together one egg, a cup of sugar, and a half cup of butter.*

recipient *noun* (rə si pē ənt) a person who receives something. *Mrs. Harris was the recipient of this year's volunteer achievement award.*

recognize *verb* (re kəg nīz) 1. to know from earlier experience. *She recognized him as her former neighbor. | With his new beard and mustache, I didn't recognize him at first.* 2. to admit, understand, or accept as true. *He recognized his mistake and worked to correct it. | You need to recognize that each person is different.*

recommend *verb* (re kə mend) to speak or write about someone or something in a favorable way. *She recommended him for the job. | I recommend this book if you like mysteries.*

recommendation *noun* (re kə men dā shən) something that recommends, such as a favorable letter. *Good recommendations helped Jennifer get a new job.*

record *verb* (ri kōrd) 1. to put in writing. *The nurse recorded my height and weight in my health chart.* 2. to copy by use of electronic equipment for later hearing or viewing. *This band has recorded hundreds of songs. | I recorded my favorite TV program so I could watch it later.*
noun (re kərd) 1. a written account. *A record of our tax payments is kept at city hall.* 2. the greatest action in a particular field. *She **broke the** world **record** in several swimming events.* 3. written facts about a person's past actions. *Joe does not have a **criminal record.***

recover *verb* (ri kə vər) to return to a normal or healthy condition. *It took a few weeks for Jean to recover from her illness.*

recreation *noun* (re krē ā shən) [N] things that people do to relax or have fun when they are not working. *Taking a yoga class is her favorite form of recreation.*

> **Word Builder: recreation +**
> **recreational:** having to do with or used for recreation.

rectangle *noun* (rek tæng gəl) a flat, closed figure with four straight sides, four equal corners, and opposite sides parallel to each other.

rectangle

recycle *verb* (rē sī kəl) to put used things through a process that allows them to be used again. *The city recycles paper, glass, metal, and plastic.*

> **Word Builder: recycle +**
> **recyclable:** able to be recycled.
> **recycling:** the activity of processing things so that they can be used again.

red *adj.* (red) having the color of blood.

> **Word Builder: red +**
> **redness:** the condition of being red.

reduce *verb* (ri doos) to make less in amount or size. *The teacher reduced the amount of homework this year. | The store owner reduced some of the prices.*

reduction *noun* (ri dək shən) the act of reducing or the state of being less than before. *His reduction in pay was difficult for his family.*

refer *verb* (ri fər) 1. to direct someone to another person for help. *My friend **referred** me **to** a good doctor.* 2. to speak of; to point to something in speech or writing. *Are you **referring to** his wife or his mother? | I don't understand what this sentence is **referring to**.*

reference *noun* (re frəns) 1. a source of information. *This dictionary is a good reference for students.* 2. a report about another person that tells how that person performed in a job. *My last boss gave me a good reference.*

refill *verb* (rē fil) to fill again. *We refilled our water bottles.*
noun (rē fil) an amount that you put into something to fill it again. *This restaurant gives free refills of coffee.*

reflex *noun* (rē fleks) a reaction of the body that a human or animal cannot control or does without thinking. *Breathing is a human reflex.*

reform *verb* (ri fōrm) to make something better that was wrong in the past. *The new president tried to reform the government.*

refreshment *noun* (ri fresh mənt) things to eat or drink that do not make a meal. *Refreshments are often served during a special event or in a public place that is not a restaurant.*

refrigerate *verb* (ri fri jər āt) to make something cold or cool by putting it in a special cold box. *We can refrigerate the leftover food and eat it tomorrow.*

refrigerator *noun* (ri fri jər ā tər) an appliance with a large, cold box where you keep food so that it does not spoil.

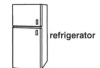

refrigerator

refugee *noun* (ref ū jē) a person who leaves his or her country because of great danger in that country. *Many people became refugees during the war.*

refund *verb* (ri fənd) to return money that someone has paid for something. *The store will refund your money if you have the receipt.*
noun (rē fənd) an amount of money returned. *You should get a refund if you pay too much tax.*

refusal *noun* (ri fū zəl) the act or an instance of refusing. *Her refusal to marry him surprised everyone.*

refuse *verb* (ri fūz) 1. to not accept or agree to something; to say "no." *The bank refused his request for a loan.* 2. to say "no" to doing something; to say that you are not willing. *I refused to tell them my phone number.*

regard *verb* (ri gard) 1. to think of someone or something in a certain way. *They **regard her as** one of their best employees.* 2. to consider; pay attention to. *Children should learn to regard other people's feelings.*
with regard to concerning; about. *With regard to the money, I will send it next week.*

region *noun* (rē jən) an area of the earth's surface that has a certain type of land and climate. *This tree grows only in tropical regions.*

> **Word Builder: region +**
> **regional:** having to do with or belonging to a particular region.

register *noun* (re̲ ji stər) 1. a book used to record names, events, or other information. *The hotel kept a register of its guests.* | *I need a new check register for my checkbook.* 2. a short form of **cash register.**
verb to put your name on an official list. *I registered for four classes this semester.* | *You need to register in order to vote.*

> **Word Builder: register +**
> **registered:** having signed up for something; on an official list.

registration *noun* (re ji stra̲ shən) 1. [N] the act or process of putting your name on an official list. *She is helping with voter registration this year.* 2. an official document that proves that something is on an official list. *The police officer asked to see his car registration.*

regular *adj.* (re̲ gyə lər) 1. normal or usual; not special. *We'll meet at the regular place.* | *My regular schedule is not busy, but this week I have special plans.* 2. following a pattern that repeats. *This bus follows a regular schedule. It comes every half hour.* 3. having or following the most common rule in grammar. *The regular ending for verbs in the past form is* -ed. Worked *and* baked *are regular verb forms, but* went *and* made *are not.*

> **Word Builder: regular +**
> **regularly:** happening at regular times.

regulate *verb* (re̲ gyə la̲t) to control by rules or a special process. *The government regulates the sale of alcohol.* | *Our bodies regulate the temperature inside our bodies.*

regulation *noun* (re gyə la̲ shən) a rule or law that controls or directs people's actions. *When you build a house, you have to follow your city's* **rules and regulations.**

reject *verb* (re̲ je̲kt) to refuse to accept, approve, or believe. *She rejected the job offer.* | *They rejected the beliefs of their parents.*

reject

relate *verb* (ri la̲t) to have a connection with something. *Her question did not* **relate to** *the subject that we were talking about.*

> **Word Builder: relate +**
> **related:** connected by family ties or other relationship.

relation *noun* (ri la̲ shən) a person who belongs to the same family; a relative. *Some of her relations are coming for a visit.*

relations *pl. noun* (ri la̲ shənz) ways that people, groups, or nations communicate or act with each other. *The company tries to promote good employee relations.*

relationship *noun* (ri la̲ shən ship) a connection of some kind. *There is a relationship between exercise and good health.* | *The management has a good relationship with the workers.*

relative *noun* (re̲ lə tiv) a person who belongs to the same family as someone else. *My relatives are coming to visit over the holidays.*
adj. 1. being dependent on something else for understanding or meaning. *How large something looks to you is* **relative to** *how far away it is.* 2. used in grammar to describe a type of connection and relationship between one part of a sentence and another. In the sentence "I know that he is here," the word *that* is a relative pronoun. "That he is here" is a relative clause.

relax *verb* (ri læks) to become calm or less tense. *The workers relaxed during their lunch break.* | *Your muscles will relax after a hot bath.*

> **Word Builder: relax +**
> **relaxed:** less tense; more comfortable.

relaxation *noun* (re̲ læk sa̲ shən) [N] the state or process of becoming calm or less tense. *Margaret does yoga for relaxation.*

release *verb* (ri le̲s) to let something go free; to stop holding something or someone. *They released the prisoners at the end of the war.* | *She released her father's hand.*

reliable *adj.* (ri li̲ ə bəl) able to be trusted or depended on. *A reliable employee always comes to work on time.*

relief *noun* (ri le̲f) [N] the feeling of not having the pain or worry that you had before. *Aspirin gave me relief from my headache.*

relieve *verb* (ri le̲v) 1. to take away pain, worry, or stress. *Hot tea will relieve your sore throat.* | *She relieved my worries about the exam.* 2. to take over the work of someone else. *The night nurse will relieve the day nurse at five o'clock.*

religion *noun* (ri li̱ jən) a set of beliefs that includes a belief about a god or gods. Most religions also have beliefs about death and how the universe was made.

religious *adj.* (ri li̱ jəs) 1. having to do with religion. *The children sang some beautiful religious music.* 2. having strong religious beliefs. *His parents are very religious people, but he is not.*

rely *verb* (ri li̱) to trust or depend on someone or something. *The president **relies on** many advisers.* | *Her boss **relies on** her to lock the office at night.*

remain *verb* (ri ma̱n) 1. to continue in the same way. *He asked her a question, but she remained quiet.* 2. to stay; to not go away or be used. *The thief went into the bank while his partner remained in the car.* | *We bought a hundred paper cups, but now only three remain.*

Word Builder: remain +
remainder: something that remains after other things have been taken away.
remaining: left behind or still present.

remark *verb* (ri ma̱rk) to make a comment or statement. *"You cut your hair," he remarked.*
noun a comment or short statement. *My friend **made a remark** about the clothes I was wearing.*

remedy *noun* (re̱ mi dē) something used to take away pain or cure an illness. *My grandmother had a good remedy for an earache.*

remember *verb* (ri me̱m bər) 1. to bring into your mind from your memory. *I finally remembered his name.* | *Did you remember to buy milk?* 2. to keep in your memory. *They will always remember their wedding day.* | *I remember meeting him at the company party last year.*

remind *verb* (ri mi̱nd) 1. to make someone remember to do something. *She reminded him to take his medicine.* 2. to make someone remember someone or something from the past. *You **remind** me **of** your grandmother.* | *That song **reminds** me **of** when I was young.*

remodel *verb* (rē ma̱ dəl) to make large changes to a room or building. *When they remodeled the kitchen, they put in two new windows and a larger sink.*

remote *adj.* (ri mo̱t) at a far distance in space or time. *They live in a remote area of the state.* | *In the remote past, dinosaurs lived on the earth.*
noun short for *remote control*, a device used to operate a television set or other electronic machine from a distance. *Please hand me the remote.*

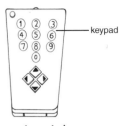
remote control

remove *verb* (ri mo̱ov) to take something off or away. *We removed all the old paint.* | *You need to remove these empty boxes.* | *Please remove your shoes at the door.*

Word Builder: remove +
removal: the act of taking something away from a place.
remover: a liquid that removes something from a surface.

renovate *verb* (re̱ nə va̱t) to put in good condition by making many repairs. *The landlord renovated the building.*

renovation *noun* (re̱ nə va̱ shən) the act or an instance of putting a building in good condition by making repairs. *The renovation of the school building took ten months.*

rent *noun* (re̱nt) the regular payment that you give to the owner of a property for the use of a space. *I have to pay the rent on Monday.*
verb 1. to pay money to use something. *We rent our apartment. We don't own it.* | *We rented a machine to clean our carpets.* 2. to let someone use something that you own in exchange for payment. *The landlord has not rented all of the apartments yet.*
for rent available to live in or use in exchange for payment. *There is a new apartment for rent.*

rental *adj.* (re̱n təl) having to do with the act of renting. *Those students live in a rental property.* | *My parents get rental income from another house that they own.*

repair *verb* (ri pa̱r) to put something in good condition again after being broken; fix. *The car mechanic repaired my tire.*
noun the work of repairing something. *My house needs a lot of repairs.*

repeat *verb* (ri pēt) 1. to say or produce a second time. *The teacher repeated the question.* | *The ship repeated its signal.* 2. to make the same sounds or say the same words that someone else has just said. *The children repeated the words that the teacher read to them.* | *The students repeated the sounds of the letters.* 3. to do or experience again. *You must repeat these safety procedures each time you use the machine.*

repetitive *adj.* (ri pe tə təv) used to describe something that repeats again and again. *Repetitive movements at work can cause an injury called repetitive stress injury.*

replace *verb* (ri plās) 1. to put something or someone in the place of another thing or person. *We need to replace our old refrigerator.* 2. to take the place of something or someone. *Automobiles replaced the horse in the last century.* | *This new manager replaced the old manager a few months ago.*

replacement *noun* (ri plās mənt) a person or thing that takes the place of another. *Her replacement does a better job than she did.* | *If you break that vase, you will have to buy a replacement.*

reply *verb* (ri plī) to give an answer. *Did you reply to your sister's letter?*
noun an answer. *I asked a question but got no reply.*

report *noun* (ri pōrt) a statement or story about something that has happened. *There was a report about the accident in the newspaper.*
verb 1. to present information about something. *He reported the results of the research at the meeting.* | *The soldier reported that he had hit the target.* 2. to give someone's name or description to the police. *I reported the thief to the police.*

Word Builder: report +
reporter: a person who reports the news for a newspaper, a magazine, or a radio or television station.

report card *noun* (ri pōrt kard) a statement from a school or teacher that tells parents about their child's progress in school.

represent *verb* (re pri zent) 1. to be a symbol of something. *People say that red roses represent the feeling of love.* 2. to be one person who speaks and acts for many other people, especially in government. *Every state elects two senators to represent its people.*

representative *noun* (re pri zen tə təv) a person who speaks or acts for a group or community. *She was elected to be our representative to Congress.*

reproduce *verb* (rē prə doos) 1. to make a copy of. *The designer made a model, and the company reproduced it.* 2. to make a new plant, human, or animal. In humans, to reproduce is to produce children. *Plants reproduce in a different way from humans.*

reptile *noun* (rep tīl) a kind of animal whose body temperature depends on the temperature of the air or water around it. A snake is one kind of reptile.

reptile

republic *noun* (ri pə blik) a government in which the people have power through representatives whom they elect.

republican *adj.* (ri pə bli kən) 1. having the nature of a republic. *The United States has a republican government.* 2. (capitalized) of the Republican Party, one of the major political parties in the United States. *Abraham Lincoln was a Republican president.*

Republican Party *noun* (ri pə bli kən par tē) one of the major political parties in the United States. *The mayor is a member of the Republican Party.*

request *noun* (ri kwest) the act of asking for something or a statement that asks for something. *The employees **made a request** for a longer lunch break.*
verb to ask for something. *We requested a bigger table at the restaurant.*

require *verb* (ri kwīr) to make something necessary. When someone requires you to do something, you must do it. *The law requires drivers to have insurance.* | *The school requires physical examinations for all the children.*

Word Builder: require +
required: ordered or demanded; being a requirement.

requirement *noun* (ri kwīr mənt) something that you must do or have. *A high school education is a requirement for entering a university.*

rescue *verb* (re skū) to make someone safe again; bring out of a dangerous situation. *The firefighters rescued three people from the burning building.*

research *noun* (ri sᵊrch or rē sᵊrch) [N] the serious study and collecting of information about something. *Scientists are **doing research** to find a cure for cancer and other diseases.* | *She spoke about her **research in the field of** chemistry.*

Word Builder: research +
researcher: a person who does research.

reservation *noun* (re zᵊr vā shᵊn) 1. a request to save something for a particular person, such as a seat on an airplane, a room in a hotel, or a table in a restaurant. *That restaurant is always busy, so we need to **make a reservation.*** 2. an area of land on which the U.S. government forced Native Americans to live and on which many Native Americans still live.

reserve *verb* (ri zᵊrv) to save for a particular purpose or person. *I'll call the restaurant and ask them to reserve a table.*

Word Builder: reserve +
reserved: saved for a particular purpose or person.

reset *verb* (rē set) *reset, reset* to start something operating again. *When the machine stopped, I checked it and then reset it.*

reside *verb* (ri zīd) to live in a place. *We don't plan to reside here. We're just visiting.*

residence *noun* (re zi dᵊns) a house or any other place where people live. *That building is not a store. It's a residence.*

resident *noun* (re zi dᵊnt) a person who lives in a particular place. *The residents of the building are angry about the noise from the construction.*

residential *adj.* (re zi den shᵊl) having to do with places where people live. *This is a residential neighborhood. You can't open your business here.*

resign *verb* (ri zīn) to leave a job or position. *The president of the company resigned.*

resignation *noun* (re zig nā shᵊn) the act of leaving a job or other position, or a formal letter announcing this. *We were sorry to hear of the manager's resignation.* | *She handed her boss her letter of resignation.*

resist *verb* (ri zist) 1. to fight against or oppose something. *The workers are resisting the new rules.* 2. to keep away or not be affected by. *The jacket is made out of fabric that resists water.* 3. to say "no" to yourself when you want to do something that is not good. *I can't resist chocolate cake.*

Word Builder: resist +
resistance (1): the act of resisting.
resistance (2): a force against the flow of electric current.

resource *noun* (rē sōrs) 1. a source of help or support. *The library is a good resource for information.* 2. a source of wealth. *Oil is an important natural resource for some countries.*

respect *noun* (ri spekt) [N] the honor that someone gives to another person. *My grandparents enjoy the respect and love of our entire family.*
verb to give honor to someone; to put someone in a high position in your feelings. *You should respect your mother.*
with respect to in connection with something; concerning. *I have a few questions with respect to these rules.*

Word Builder: respect +
respected: honored or highly regarded.

respiration *noun* (re spᵊr ā shᵊn) [N] the act of breathing. *Respiration slows down during sleep.*

respirator *noun* (re spᵊr ā tᵊr) a device that you wear over your nose and mouth to protect you from things in the air that are not clean or cause damage to the lungs; a device that helps you breathe.

respiratory *adj.* (re spᵊr ᵊ tōr ē) having to do with the act of breathing. *The lungs are part of the respiratory system.*

respond *verb* (ri spand) 1. to answer or give a reply in some way. *I didn't **respond to** all the questions on the test.* 2. to react. *The boys hit him, but he **responded with** a laugh.*

response *noun* (ri spans) 1. a written or spoken answer; reply. *I wrote to my senator and received a response.* 2. a reaction. *The doctor is happy about the patient's response to the medicine.*

responsibility *noun* (ri span sə <u>bi</u> li tē) 1. [N] the condition or fact of being responsible. *Adults should* **take responsibility** *for their actions.* 2. something that a person is responsible for; duty. *His responsibilities at work include typing and filing.*

responsible *adj.* (ri <u>span</u> si bəl) 1. expected to take care of particular things or to perform certain duties. *Parents need to be* **responsible for** *their children.* | *Don't blame me. I am not* **responsible for** *taking care of the dog.* 2. being the cause of something. *I am responsible for the accident.* 3. having good judgment about what is right or wrong; able to be trusted by other people. *Our baby-sitter is young but very responsible.*

rest[1] *noun* (<u>rest</u>) a time of calm and quiet after work or activity; break. *I needed a rest after lifting all those boxes.*
verb to relax by sleeping or lying down. *I rested on the sofa.*

rest[2] *noun* (<u>rest</u>) 1. [N] a piece or part that remains. *I took a piece of the cookie and gave the rest to my friend.* 2. [N] all the others. *One is black, but the rest are red.*

restaurant *noun* (<u>re</u> strant) a place where you go to eat. In a restaurant, you pay to have a meal that is served to you.

restaurant

restore *verb* (ri <u>stōr</u>) to bring something back to an earlier or normal condition. *It took many months to restore the old house.* | *She was tired, but taking a nap restored her.*

restrict *verb* (ri <u>strikt</u>) to keep within certain limits. *His parents restricted him to his room.* | *Can we restrict our discussion to one topic?*

Word Builder: restrict +
restricted: kept within specific limits; not open to everyone.

restroom *noun* (<u>rest</u> room) a room in a public place with a toilet and a sink.

result *verb* (ri <u>zəlt</u>) to happen because of something. *The accident resulted when the driver fell asleep while driving.*
noun something that happens because of something else or at the end of some activity. *Their success was* the result of hard work. | *The result of the election was surprising.*

Word Builder: result +
resulting: happening as a result.

résumé *noun* (<u>re</u> zu mā) a short written record that tells about a person's education, work experience, and other qualifications for a job. *She enclosed a copy of her résumé with the job application.*

retail *adj.* (<u>rē</u> tāl) having to do with selling things to the people who will use them. *A hardware store and a grocery store are retail stores.*

Word Builder: retail +
retailer: a person or store that sells things to customers.

retire *verb* (ri <u>tīr</u>) to give up a job or career and not work anymore. *When my husband retired, we took a long vacation.*

Word Builder: retire +
retired: having given up a job or life of work.

retirement *noun* (ri <u>tīr</u> mənt) [N] the state of not working anymore after working for many years. *She loved her job, but now she is enjoying her retirement, too.*

return *verb* (ri <u>tərn</u>) 1. to go back or come back. *They finally returned home after midnight.* 2. to put, give, or take back to an earlier place. *I returned the book to the library.* | *Return the form to me after you have filled it out.*
noun 1. the act of coming or going back. *We are always happy to see the return of spring.* 2. a form used to report your income to the government and to figure the amount of tax that you may owe. *You have to send in your* **tax return** *by April 15.*

return address *noun* (ri tərn ə <u>dres</u>) the address of the person who sends a letter. *Write your return address in the top left corner of the envelope.*

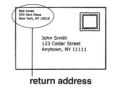
return address

reunion *noun* (rē <u>ūn</u> yən) a meeting of friends, family, or other people who have not been together for a long time. *At my family reunion, I saw many cousins whom I had not seen in years.* | *Do you plan to go to your high school reunion?*

reverse *adj.* (ri v<u>ər</u>s) opposite in direction, position, or movement. *The reverse side of the towel is softer.*
noun 1. the opposite side or opinion. *The reverse of what he said is true.* 2. the gear in a car that causes it to move with the back part first. *Put the car into reverse and back out of the parking spot.*
verb to move or turn in the opposite direction. *She reversed the car into the road.* | *The judge reversed the other court's decision.* | *The candidate reversed his position on the issue of immigration.*

review *noun* (ri v<u>ū</u>) an article in a newspaper or magazine that gives an opinion about a thing such as a new book, movie, or restaurant. *That movie got a good review in the newspaper.*
verb to study or look at something again; to help someone remember what they studied before. *I reviewed my notes before the test.* | *The teacher reviewed the important things that she had taught.*

revive *verb* (ri v<u>ī</u>v) to make conscious again. *A nurse revived him after he hit his head and fell to the ground.*

revolution *noun* (re və <u>loo</u> shən) 1. the act of removing a government by force and putting a new government in its place. *Many people died during the revolution.* 2. a very great change from things in the past. *The invention of the computer chip caused a revolution in technology.*

revolutionary *adj.* (re və <u>loo</u> shə när <u>e</u>) having to do with revolution. *He was arrested for his revolutionary activities.* | *Our company is developing revolutionary new products.*

Word Builder: revolution +
Revolutionary War: another name for the American Revolution.

reward *noun* (ri w<u>ard</u>) something you receive because you did something good. *She got a raise in salary as a reward for all her hard work.*
verb to give something to someone for doing something good. *I rewarded my children for their good report cards by taking them to the movies.*

rewind *verb* (ri w<u>ī</u>nd) *rewound, rewound* to move back to; move back to the original position. *Please rewind the tapes before you return them to the library.*

rewound *verb* (ri w<u>ow</u>nd) past tense and past participle of **rewind.**

rhyme *noun* (r<u>ī</u>m) a word that ends with the same sound as another word. Hop *and* stop *are rhymes for* mop.
verb to end with the same sound as another word. *The word* pan *rhymes with* man *and* fan.

rhythm *noun* (ri thəm) a movement marked by the regular repeating of sounds. *We clapped our hands to the rhythm of the drums.*

rib *noun* (<u>rib</u>) one of the twelve sets of bones that curve around the chest.

ribbon *noun* (<u>ri</u> bən) a narrow strip or band of material used as decoration for hair, gifts, or the like. *I wrapped the gift in pretty paper and tied a yellow ribbon around the outside.*

rice *noun* (r<u>ī</u>s) [N] seeds of certain grasses that grow in wet areas and are eaten as food.

rich *adj.* (rich) 1. having a great amount of money or valuable possessions. *That rich man drives a new car that cost a lot of money.* 2. having large amounts of butter, fat, eggs, or sugar. *We made a rich chocolate cake for dessert.*

rid *verb* (<u>rid</u>) *rid, rid* to cause things that are not wanted to go away. *The new mayor promised to* **rid** *the city* **of** *crime.* | *I'm trying to* **rid** *myself* **of** *my smoking habit.*
get rid of to remove or throw away something that you do not want. *I got rid of all my old clothes.*

ridden *verb* (<u>ri</u> dən) past participle of **ride.**

ride *verb* (r<u>ī</u>d) *rode, ridden* to be carried by a vehicle or animal. *We all rode on the train.* | *She rode on a horse at the farm.*
noun an act of riding in a vehicle or on an animal. *We took a ride in our new car.* | *The ride to my office takes one hour.*

Word Builder: ride +
rider (1): a person who rides.
rider (2): a clause added to an insurance policy to insure specific things.

right *adj.* (rīt) 1. in keeping with what is fair and good. *Helping her was the right thing to do.* 2. true; correct. *She passed the test because most of her answers were right.* 3. proper; appropriate. *His new job was **just right** for him.* 4. being on the side of the human body opposite the heart. The opposite of right is left. *Most people write with their right hand.*

noun 1. [N] the side of the body opposite the heart. *I will walk beside you **on** your **right**.* 2. something that you are allowed to do because of nature or law. *The First Amendment guarantees **the right to** free speech.*

adv. 1. directly; straight. *He walked right toward me.* 2. in this exact place or way; at this exact time. *Your keys are right here! | You should leave right now.* 3. correctly. *This dress does not fit right. | You did not spell the word right.* 4. on or in the direction of the right. *We turned right at the stop sign.*

right away now; without any delay. *We left right away after the hospital called.*

right-handed *adj.* (rīt hæn dəd) having more ability with the right hand than with the left. *My son is right-handed and always writes with his right hand.*

ring[1] *noun* (ring) 1. a small band of metal or other hard material in the shape of a circle. Rings are worn on the finger for their beauty or as a symbol. *My parents wear gold wedding rings.* 2. a band in the shape of a circle used to surround or hold something. *I bought a set of rings to hold my shower curtain up.* 3. an enclosed area for a sports event or circus performance. *In the middle of the circus tent, the elephants walked around in the ring.*

ring

ring[2] *verb* (ring) *rang, rung* 1. to give out a clear, deep sound. *Did the telephone just ring? | I heard the bell on the church tower ring today.* 2. to make a sound by hitting a bell or by similar means. *I will ring the doorbell to see if someone is at home.*

ring up to record or add up on a cash register. *At the checkout counter, the store clerk will ring up your purchases.*

rinse *verb* (rins) to wash off with water. *Be sure to **rinse** the soap **off** the dishes when you wash them.*

rip *verb* (rip) to cut open, off, or apart with force; tear. *The dog ripped open the bag of food with his teeth.*

ripe *adj.* (rīp) finished growing and ready to pick and eat. *The ripe peaches tasted good.*

rise *verb* (rīz) *rose, risen* 1. to move up in direction. *The airplane will rise into the sky after it takes off.* 2. to stand; to get up from a sitting or lying position. *You must rise when the judge enters a courtroom.* 3. to get up from bed. *Every day I rise at seven o'clock in the morning.*

risen (ri zen) past participle of **rise.**

risk *noun* (risk) a chance of getting hurt or losing something. *Smoking increases a person's risk of getting lung disease.*

verb to put someone or something in danger. *She risked her life to climb the mountain.*

Word Builder: risk +
risky: involving a risk or chance of danger.

river *noun* (ri vər) a large natural stream of water that flows toward a lake, ocean, or other larger body of water. *The river was too wide to swim across.*

road *noun* (rōd) a hard, smooth surface for vehicles and people to travel on; street. *The town built a new road from the park to the lake.*

roast *verb* (rōst) to cook or bake with dry heat in an oven or over an open fire. *We roasted a turkey for Thanksgiving dinner.*

noun a piece of meat that you cook with dry heat in an oven. *The butcher sold him three pounds of pork roast.*

roast

rob *verb* (rab) to steal something from a person or place, often with the use of force. *A thief robbed him in the park late at night. | Someone robbed the bank!*

Word Builder: rob +
robber: a person who robs.
robbery: the crime of robbing.

rob or steal?
Both *rob* and *steal* have to do with taking something in a way that is against the law. *Rob* emphasizes the person or place from which something is taken. *Steal* emphasizes the thing that was taken. You *rob* someone of something, but you *steal* something from someone.
Compare:
Someone robbed the store! He stole all the money! Someone robbed John of his wallet. John was robbed. Someone stole a wallet from John. The wallet was stolen.

robe *noun* (rōb) a long, loose piece of clothing worn as a covering.

robin *noun* (ra bin) a small bird with an orange breast, a dark head and back, and a yellow beak.

rock[1] *noun* (rak) 1. [N] a solid mass of minerals that forms much of the earth's outer layer. *Cliffs and mountains are made of rock.* 2. a piece of solid mineral; stone. *He picked up a rock and threw it.*

Word Builder: rock +
rocky: full of rocks or covered with rocks.

rock[2] *verb* (rak) 1. to move forward and back or from side to side. *The ship rocked in the storm.* 2. to cause to move back and forth or from side to side. *I rocked the baby to sleep.*
noun a form of popular music with a strong beat that is usually played loudly on electronic instruments such as guitars.

rocket *noun* (ra kit) a device shaped like a tube that moves at high speed and is powered by gases that are forced out of one end. Rockets are used to send things into the air.

rocking chair *noun* (ra king chār) a chair that rests on two curved pieces of wood that allow it to rock. A rocking chair is used as a place to relax.

rod *noun* (rad) a straight, thin stick or bar. *I bought new curtain rods for the living room windows.*

rode *verb* (rōd) past tense of **ride.**

role *noun* (rōl) the character played by an actor. *I have a large role in the school play.*

roll *verb* (rōl) to move by turning over and over. *The ball rolled down the hill.*
noun 1. a solid tube made by winding material around itself or around a tube or rod many times. *Toilet paper comes in rolls.* 2. a type of bread made into a small, round shape. *I sometimes have a roll with butter for breakfast.*

roller *noun* (rō lər) a tool with a handle and a part shaped like a tube. A roller is used to spread paint on a surface, make a surface smooth, or crush something.

romantic *adj.* (rō mæn tik) causing or showing thoughts and feelings of love. *She wrote a romantic letter.*

roof *noun* (roof) the surface or covering on the top of a building. *The roof of a house protects it from rain and snow.*

room *noun* (room) an area of a building separated from similar areas by walls or doors. *Our house has ten rooms.*

Word Builder: kinds of rooms
bathroom: a room where people wash and use the toilet.
bedroom: a room where people sleep and keep their clothing.
dining room: a room where people sit and eat a meal at a table.
laundry room: a room where people do laundry.
living room: a room where people sit and relax.
storeroom: a room where people store things.

roommate *noun* (room māt) a person who shares another's room, apartment, or home. *My roommate pays half of the bills.*

root *noun* (root) the part of a plant that grows under the ground. Roots take in water and food, and they hold the plant in the soil. *The roots of the old tree were very thick.*

rope *noun* (rōp) pieces of string, wire, or similar material twisted together to make a thicker, stronger line. *We tied a rope to the car to pull it out of the mud.*

rope

rose[1] *noun* (rōz) a flower that has a sweet smell, comes in many colors, and grows on a bush. There are often sharp points on the stem of a rose. *Roses are a traditional gift of love in the United States.*

rose[2] *verb* (rōz) past tense of **rise.**

roster *noun* (ra stər) a list of names of individuals or groups. *I made a roster of the people who play on our team.*

rot *verb* (rat) to decay. *If you leave apples on the tree, they will rot.*

rotate *verb* (rō tāt) to turn on or around a central point. *A wheel rotates on an axle.*

Word Builder: rotate +
rotating: spinning; turning on a fixed point.

rotten *adj.* (ra tən) 1. bad or spoiled; no longer able to be eaten. *We had to throw out several of the apples because they were rotten.* 2. very bad; not at all satisfactory. *No one wants to tell her that she is a rotten singer.*

rough *adj.* (rəf) 1. not smooth. *The rough cloth rubbed against my skin.* 2. something that is hard to do or experience. *A bad storm made travel rough.* 3. not yet perfect or finished. *We have only a rough idea of what kind of house we want.*

Word Builder: rough +
roughly: in a rough way.

round *adj.* (rownd) shaped like a ball or circle. *The earth is round.*
verb to make round in shape. *I rounded the dough into balls for making rolls.*
round off to change a number to a number that is close to it but that ends in zero. *The exact number was 253, but we rounded it off to 250.*
year round during the whole year. *Barbara works year round.*

Word Builder: round +
rounded (1): of a number, estimated or approximate.
rounded (2): of a shape, having curves or like a circle.

round trip *noun* (rownd trip) a trip to a place and then back to the starting point. *We made a round trip from Boston to New York and back to Boston again.*

route *noun* (root or rowt) a road or way of travel from one place to another. *The bus travels the same route every day.*

routine *noun* (roo tēn) a regular course of action. *Brushing her teeth was part of her morning routine.*

row *noun* (rō) 1. a group of things or people arranged in a straight line side by side. *There were eight rows of desks in the classroom.* 2. a line that is made by things or people placed next to each other side by side. *She likes to sit in the front row in class.* | *Her place in the orchestra is in the back row.*
in a row one after another. *She won first prize three years in a row.*

royal *adj.* (roy əl) of or having to do with a king or queen or any members of their family. *The royal wedding was shown on TV.*

rub *verb* (rəb) to push back and forward across something using pressure. *He rubbed his sore arm.* | *I rubbed the spot on the shirt with soap and water.*

rubber *noun* (rə bər) [N] a substance made from the dried liquid from certain tropical plants. Rubber can be stretched and is used to make many things, including tires and balls.

rubber band *noun* (rə bər bænd) a narrow strip of rubber used to hold objects together. *I put a rubber band around the letters.*

ruby *noun* (roo bē) a valuable, dark red stone that is cut and worn as jewelry.

rude *adj.* (rood) acting in a way that hurts or offends other people; not polite. *It was rude to take the gift without saying "thank you."*

rug *noun* (rəg) a piece of thick material used to cover part of a floor. *I spilled wine on their clean white rug.*

rug

ruin *verb* (roo in) to destroy or damage something. *A flood ruined the village.*
in ruins completely destroyed. *The fire left the house in ruins.*

Word Builder: ruin +
ruined: wrecked; destroyed.

rule *noun* (rool) 1. a law or direction that guides behavior or action. *I will play if you teach me the rules of the game.* | *He **broke** many of the school **rules.*** 2. what is usual, typical, or normal. *Most children love sweets, but my daughter is an exception to the rule.*
verb to have authority over; govern. *The king rules the country.*

ruler *noun* (roo lər) 1. a person who governs or leads. *The queen was a strong and wise ruler.* 2. a straight piece of wood, metal, or plastic that is marked off in inches or other units and used for measuring length.

run *verb* (run) *ran, run* 1. to make oneself go forward by moving the legs very fast. *I ran to the bus stop.* 2. to try to be elected to a government office. *She **is running for** mayor in this year's election.* 3. to work or operate; function. *This car runs on electricity, not gasoline.* | *He has been running the business for fourteen years.* 4. to flow or spread. *The river runs fast.* | *Paint is running down the wall.* 5. to move between places at planned times. *The bus to town runs every two hours.* 6. to make something function; operate. *Do you know how to run this machine?* | *He ran a shoe business for twenty years.*
noun the act of running. *He goes for a long run every morning.*

run into to meet someone without planning to. *I ran into my English teacher at the mall.*

run out of to finish using the entire amount of something when you still need it. *He ran out of gas and had to walk to a gas station.*

Word Builder: run +
runner (1): a person who runs.
runner (2): a long, narrow covering for a floor or table.
runner (3): the long, thin metal piece on which a sled slides.

---

rung[1] *verb* (rang) past participle of **ring**[2].

rung[2] *noun* (rang) a bar that forms the step of a ladder; piece between the legs of a chair. *The ladder has twenty rungs.*

runny *adj.* (rə nē) containing too much liquid; flowing. *I don't like runny eggs.* | *My nose was runny because of a cold.*

rural *adj.* (rur əl) having to do with country life. *People in rural areas often live by farming.*

rush *verb* (rush) to act or go fast; hurry. *Don't rush when you are driving a car.*
noun a time of hurry. *I'm in a rush, so I can't stop right now.*

rust *noun* (rust) [N] an orange, red, or brown substance that forms on the surface of some metals that have had contact with water and air.
verb to become rusty. *The fender of my bike is rusting.*

rye *noun* (rī) [N] a grass grown for its grain. Rye seeds are used to make flour for bread and other foods.

S s

sack *noun* (săk) a large bag made of thick paper or other strong material. A sack is used to hold grain, potatoes, supplies, or other heavy things. *The farmer loaded sacks of potatoes onto the truck.* | *The cashier put the groceries in the sack.*

sack

sad *adj.* (săd) not happy. *Steve was sad when his dog died.*

> **Word Builder: sad +**
> **sadly:** in a sad way.
> **sadness:** the condition of being sad.

safe *adj.* (sāf) not in danger; free from harm or risk. *We were safe at home when the storm began.*
noun a strong metal box with a lock that is used for keeping money and valuable things. *Some people keep their jewelry in a safe.*

> **Word Builder: safe +**
> **safely:** in a safe way.

safety *noun* (sāf tē) [N] the condition of being safe from danger. *Sue wears a helmet for safety when she rides her bike.*

> **Word Builder: safety +**
> **safety latch:** a latch that keeps a cabinet or container closed so that you cannot get to dangerous materials.
> **safety shoes:** strong shoes that keep your feet safe from falling or moving objects.

said *verb* (sed) past tense and past participle of **say.**

sail *noun* (sāl) a large piece of cloth that is attached to a boat. Sails move boats forward by catching the wind.
verb to move over the water. *The ship sailed across the ocean.*

sake *noun* (sāk) advantage; good. *For your own sake, you should get to work on time.*

salad *noun* (săl əd) a mixture of raw vegetables usually served with dressing.

salary *noun* (săl ə rē) a fixed amount of money paid at regular times for the work a person does. *My salary is paid every two weeks.*

sale *noun* (sāl) 1. [N] an exchange of goods for money; the act of selling. *There are strict rules for the sale of alcohol.* 2. a selling of goods for a lower price than usual. *The store is **having a** big **sale on** winter coats.*
for sale available to buy. *The house on the corner is for sale.*
on sale available to buy at a lower price. *Bananas are on sale this week.*

sales *pl. noun* (sālz) the business or job of selling. *She has a job in sales.*

> **Word Builder: sales +**
> **sales tax:** a tax on things that are sold, paid by the person who buys them.

salesperson *noun* (sālz pər sən) a person whose job is to sell goods or services.

saliva *noun* (sə lī və) [N] a liquid produced in the mouth that helps people process food. Saliva has no color or taste.

salmon *noun* (săm ən) [N] a silver fish that lives in the ocean but lays its eggs in rivers. Salmon are used for food.

salon *noun* (sə län) a business that deals in fashion and style. *I had my hair trimmed at a beauty salon.*

salt *noun* (sawlt) [N] a white substance that is found in seawater and in the earth. Salt is used for flavoring and preserving foods.
verb to flavor or preserve with salt. *Taste the soup before you salt it.*

> **Word Builder: salt +**
> **salty:** containing a lot of salt.

salute *verb* (sə loot) to show respect with a formal movement such as raising the hand to the forehead. *The soldier saluted the officer.* | *In school, many students salute the flag every morning.*

same *adj.* (sām) 1. not at all different; alike in every way. *I try to treat both of my children in the same way.* 2. not changed; being as before. *He wore the same sweater for three days.*

sample *noun* (săm pəl) a small part of something that shows what the whole is like. *They gave out samples of different cheeses at the store.*
verb to take a small part of something. *Would you like to sample this pie?*

sand *noun* (<u>sæn</u>d) [N] tiny, loose grains of ground rock such as you can see on beaches and in deserts. *The sand on the beach felt soft under my feet.*
verb to polish or make smooth with sandpaper. *Maura sanded the board before painting it.*

Word Builder: sand +
sander: a machine or tool that you use to make things smooth.
sandy: full of or covered with sand.

sandal *noun* (<u>sæn</u> dəl) a light, open shoe that you wear in warm weather. *It is not safe for Dan to wear sandals to work at the factory.*

sandpaper *noun* (<u>sæn</u>d pā pər) [N] paper covered on one side with sand or some other rough material. It is used to smooth wood and other surfaces. *I made the table smooth with fine sandpaper.*

sandwich *noun* (<u>sæn</u>d wich) pieces of bread with food such as meat, cheese, and vegetables between them. *Laura's favorite lunch is a peanut butter and jelly sandwich.*

sandwich

sane *adj.* (<u>sān</u>) having a healthy, normal mind. *She does strange things, but she seems sane when you talk to her.*

sang *verb* (<u>sæn</u>g) past tense of **sing.**

sanitation *noun* (sæ ni <u>tā</u> shən) [N] the study and practice of keeping the public healthy by providing clean living conditions. Sanitation includes removing trash and keeping drinking water clean. *Lack of sanitation is a problem in some small, poor countries.*

sank *verb* (<u>sæn</u>gk) past tense of **sink.**

sat *verb* (<u>sæt</u>) past tense and past participle of **sit.**

satisfaction *noun* (sæ tis <u>fæk</u> shən) 1. [N] a pleasant feeling of having everything that you need or want or of reaching success in something. *She **felt** complete **satisfaction with** the plans for the wedding. | Building the model airplane gave me great satisfaction.*

satisfactory *adj.* (sæ tis <u>fæk</u> tə rē) good enough. *The doctor gave her a satisfactory explanation of the illness.*

satisfy *verb* (<u>sæ</u> tis fī) to give everything that is wanted or needed. *The small snack didn't satisfy her.*

Word Builder: satisfy +
satisfied: happy with what you have; needing nothing else.

Saturday *noun* (<u>sæ</u> tər dā) the seventh day of the week. Saturday comes between Friday and Sunday.

sauce *noun* (<u>saws</u>) a thick liquid served on or with food to add flavor. *She made fish with a cream sauce.*

saucepan *noun* (<u>saws</u> pæn) a deep cooking pan with a long handle. *I heated the soup in a saucepan.*

saucer *noun* (<u>saw</u> sər) a small dish used for holding a cup. *The cat drank milk from the saucer.*

sausage *noun* (<u>saw</u> səj) ground meat or other food that is mixed with spices and put into a tube made from animal parts or some other material that can be cooked and eaten.

save *verb* (<u>sāv</u>) 1. to help someone get away from harm or danger. *He saved the girl who fell out of the boat.* 2. to keep or store for future use. *He saved his dessert to eat later. | They are saving money for their children's education.*

savings *pl. noun* (<u>sā</u> vingz) an amount of money that a person saves. *She has savings of 2,000 dollars in her bank account.*

saw[1] *noun* (<u>saw</u>) a tool with a thin metal blade that has sharp teeth along one edge. A saw is used to cut wood or other things.
verb to cut or shape with this tool. *Harry sawed the wood for the new table.*

Word Builder: saw +
sawdust: dust made in the process of cutting wood with a saw.

Word Builder: kinds of saws
band saw: a power saw that cuts with a metal band that moves around two wheels.
chain saw: a power saw that cuts with teeth linked in a circular chain.
circular saw: a power saw with a circular cutting blade.
hacksaw: a saw with a blade that can cut metal.
miter saw: a kind of table saw that can cut wood at an angle.
table saw: a power saw that is attached to a table and that has a blade shaped like a circle.

saw[2] *verb* (<u>saw</u>) past tense of **see.**

say *verb* (<u>sā</u>) *said, said* to use words to communicate something. *Did you say something just now?*

saying *noun* (sā ing) a familiar statement that often contains advice or wisdom. *"Nobody is perfect" is a common saying.*

scaffold *noun* (skæ fōld) a structure next to a wall or building that holds people and materials. People stand on the scaffold while they do work on the building. *The window washers attached their scaffold to the skyscraper.*

scale *noun* (skāl) a piece of equipment used for weighing. *I weigh myself on a scale every morning.*

scan *verb* (skæn) 1. to read or look at something for a short time. *I scanned the newspaper for the weather report.* 2. to look at or study something with care. *We scanned the clouds for signs of rain.* 3. to use a machine to change an image into data so it can be used by a computer. *I scanned the photographs into a computer and then e-mailed them to my friend.*

> **Word Builder: scan +**
> **scanner:** a machine connected to a computer that turns an image into data.

scar *noun* (skar) the permanent mark that remains after a wound has healed. *The burn left a scar on my arm.*

scare *verb* (skār) to frighten. *The horror movie scared me.*

> **Word Builder: scare +**
> **scared:** feeling fright.
> **scary:** causing fear.

scarf *noun* (skarf) *scarves* a long piece of cloth worn around the neck, head, or shoulders. People wear a scarf for decoration or for warmth.

 scarf

scarves *pl. noun* (skarvz) plural of **scarf.**

scatter *verb* (skæ tər) 1. to throw around in different directions. *The farmer scattered grain for the chickens.* 2. to separate and move in different directions. *The crowd scattered at the sound of thunder.*

scene *noun* (sēn) the place where any event takes place. *They rushed to the scene of the accident.*

scenery *noun* (sē nə rē) [N] the way the land looks in a particular place. *We enjoyed the scenery around the lake.*

scenic *adj.* (sē nik) showing a beautiful view of nature. *We drove on the scenic road.*

schedule *noun* (ske jool) a list of times when certain events will happen. *Do you have a schedule for classes at the community center?*

scholar *noun* (ska lər) 1. a person who has great knowledge, usually from research and study. *My aunt is a scholar of American history* 2. any student. *These young scholars will graduate from high school in two years.*

scholarship *noun* (ska lər ship) money given to students to help pay for their education. *Sally won a scholarship to the state university.*

school *noun* (skool) a place for teaching and learning. *There are classrooms, a cafeteria, and a gym in this school.*

> **Word Builder: school +**
> **schooling:** formal education.

science *noun* (sī əns) a system of studying and learning about things in nature. Chemistry, biology, and physics are all sciences.

scientific *adj.* (sī ən ti fik) having to do with science. *He found a scientific solution to the problem.*

scientist *noun* (sī ən tist) a person who works in or studies a science.

scissors *pl. noun* (si zərz) a tool used for cutting. Scissors have two blades that are joined in the middle. *Use this **pair of scissors** to cut the cloth.*

scold *verb* (skōld) to tell someone, usually in an angry way, that he or she has done something wrong. *The mother scolded her child for spilling her milk.*

scoop *noun* (skoop) a tool with a short handle attached to a deep, curved bowl. You use a scoop to take up food or grain. *The farmer used a scoop to feed corn to the chickens.*
verb to lift things with this tool. *I scooped ice cream into the bowl.*

score *noun* (skōr) total points earned in a game or on a test. *What was the final score of the basketball game?* | *I got a perfect score on the spelling test.*
verb to make a point in a contest. *Mary scored two points in the game.*

scour *verb* (skowr) to clean by rubbing hard. *The cook scoured the dirty pots.*

scrap *noun* (skræp) a small bit, such as a piece left over or thrown away. *I picked up a scrap of paper.* | *They tossed scraps of bread to the ducks.*

scrape *verb* (skrāp) to remove from a surface by rubbing with something sharp or rough. *He scraped the old paint off the house.*
noun an injury or damage from rubbing against something rough. *She fell on the sidewalk and got a scrape on her elbow.*

scratch *verb* (skræch) 1. to cause damage to a surface with something sharp. *The branch scratched the car.* 2. to use the nails on your hand to rub your skin. *I scratched the insect bite on my arm.*

scream *verb* (skrēm) to make a loud, high cry or sound. *The girl screamed in fear.*

screen *noun* (skrēn) 1. a piece of material made of woven wire. A screen covers a window, door, or other opening. *If you don't close the screen, flies will come into the house.* 2. the broad, flat surface on a television or computer on which you see images. *We got a new television with a fifty-inch screen.* 3. anything that hides or protects. *The tall bushes acted as a screen around the yard.* | *They put screens around the patient's hospital bed.*

screw *noun* (skroo) a metal device that fastens. You push a screw into a surface by turning it while pressing down on the head. *We attached the shelf to the wall with screws.*
verb to fasten by turning, often by using this device. *She screwed the lightbulb into the socket.* | *He screwed the screw into the board.*
screwed up (informal) not working well; broken. *This new phone is screwed up. It won't ring.* | *I have to go to the doctor because my knee is screwed up.*

screwdriver *noun* (skroo drī vər) a tool for turning a screw. A screwdriver has a handle for turning and a metal piece that fits the head of the screw. *We need a screwdriver to put the chair together.*

scrub *verb* (skrəb) to clean by rubbing hard. *He scrubbed the pots until they were shiny.* | *The doctor scrubbed his hands before the operation.*

sea *noun* (sē) 1. [N] the salt water covering most of the earth; ocean. *I like to swim in the sea, not in a pool.* 2. a body of salt water with land around it on most sides. *There is a sea in the southern part of the country.*

seafood *noun* (sē food) [N] fish and other sea animals that people eat. Some kinds of seafood are clams and shrimp.

seal *noun* (sēl) a material or object used to close something tight. *Aspirin bottles have seals so that small children can't open them.*
verb to close tight with this material. *Seal the box with tape.*

Word Builder: seal +
sealed: closed tight.

seam *noun* (sēm) the line formed by sewing two pieces of cloth together. *A seam on your dress is coming apart.*

search *verb* (sərch) to try to find something by looking with care. *I searched everywhere in my room for the missing earring.*

season *noun* (sē zən) 1. one of the four parts of the year. The seasons are spring, summer, fall (autumn), and winter. 2. a part of the year in which people do a particular activity. *I can't wait until baseball season.* | *Our family will get together for the holiday season.*

seat *noun* (sēt) a chair or other object for sitting on. *We have six seats around our kitchen table.* | *Please **take your seats** so we can get started.*

Word Builder: seat +
seating: a space where people can sit.

seatbelt *noun* (sēt belt) a belt in a car or airplane that fastens across your lap to hold you in place. A seatbelt is a device for safety. *It's important to fasten your seatbelt whenever you ride in a car.*

second[1] *adj.* (se kənd) next after first.

second[2] *noun* (se kənd) 1. a standard unit used to measure time. There are 60 seconds in one minute. 2. a very short period of time. *I'll be there in a second.*

secondary *adj.* (se kən dār e) 1. coming next after something that comes first. *Our town has three elementary schools and two secondary schools.* 2. not first in importance; less important. *For many people, being rich is **secondary to** being healthy.* | *The secondary roads were not plowed after the blizzard.*

secondhand *adj.* (se̱ kənd ha̱nd) 1. not from the original source. *The story in the newspaper came from secondhand information.* 2. not new; used. *Secondhand books do not cost as much as new ones.*

secrecy *noun* (se̱ krə se̱) [N] the condition of being secret. *He worked on his plans in secrecy.*

secret *adj.* (se̱ krit) not seen or known by others; private. *Mrs. Gross keeps her money in a secret place.*
noun something hidden on purpose, such as knowledge or information. *Don't tell her about the birthday party. It's a secret.* | *Can you keep a secret?*

secretary *noun* (se̱ krə ta̱r e̱) 1. a person whose job is to write letters, keep records, manage mail, and do other things in an office. 2. an official who is the head of a government department. *In the United States, the Secretary of Defense is very powerful.*

section *noun* (se̱k shən) a part that is different or apart from the whole. *I like living in this section of the city.* | *Put the book back in the top section of the bookcase.*

secure *adj.* (si ku̱r) 1. free from fear, worry, or danger. *I feel secure now that I have a good job.* 2. fastened tight. *The box has a secure lid.*

security *noun* (sə ku̱r i te) [N] freedom from fear or danger; safety. *Friends give me a feeling of security.*

Word Builder: security +
security deposit: money paid to a landlord to guarantee payment of rent.
security guard: a guard who gives security by checking people or buildings.
security system: an electric or electronic system that gives security in a building.

see *verb* (se̱) *saw, seen* 1. to use your eyes and receive images. *Can you see the top of the mountain?* 2. to understand; to know. *I don't see what the problem is.* 3. to experience an event using your eyes. *Let's see a movie tonight.* | *I saw the two cars hit each other.* 4. to visit someone for social reasons or for business. *I went to see some friends this weekend.* | *I need to see my lawyer.* 5. to find out; to learn. *I opened the curtain and saw that it was snowing outside.* | *Would you see who is knocking on the door?*

seed *noun* (se̱d) the small part of a plant that grows into a new plant. *We planted seeds in the garden.*

seem *verb* (se̱m) to appear to be or do. *He seems like a nice man.*

seen *verb* (se̱n) past participle of **see.**

seize *verb* (se̱z) to take hold of with force and speed. *The police seized the stolen property.*

seldom *adv.* (se̱l dəm) not often; almost never. *He seldom comes to see us.*

select *verb* (sə le̱kt) to choose; pick. *Please select the song you would like to play.*

selection *noun* (sə le̱k shən) 1. something or someone selected. *Maya is our selection for team captain.* 2. a group from which things or people may be selected. *The market offers a large selection of vegetables.*

selection of vegetables

self- *prefix* (se̱lf) used in front of a word to mean *of, by, to, for,* or *in oneself.* To exercise self-control is to keep control of yourself. To have self-respect is to have respect for yourself. *His self-control kept him from getting angry.*

Word Builder: self- +
self-confidence: a confidence in yourself.
self-defense: the practice of defending yourself against an attack.
self-employed: owning your own business and working for yourself.
self-service: relating to a store where customers must serve themselves.

self *noun* (se̱lf) *selves* one's own being, character, and nature. *He was sick and didn't seem like his old self.*

selfish *adj.* (se̱l fish) concerned only about yourself and not about others. *The selfish boy refused to share his toys with his brother.*

sell *verb* (se̱l) *sold, sold* 1. to give something to someone in exchange for money. *Robert decided to sell his old television for $30.* 2. to offer for sale. *The supermarket sells many kinds of fruit.*
sell out to no longer have something for sale because everything has been sold. *Sorry. We sold out of those shoes this morning.*

Word Builder: sell +
seller: a person who sells something.

semester *noun* (sə me̱ stər) one-half of a school or college year. *My brother will take an art class next semester.*

semicolon *noun* (se mē kō lən) a punctuation mark (;). It is most often used to separate clauses in a single sentence when each clause has its own subject and verb and when there is no word that connects the clauses.

seminar *noun* (se mi nar) a small class at a university that is designed for study and discussion. *The nurse attended a seminar to learn about new medicines.*

senate *noun* (se nət) 1. (capitalized) one of the two houses of the U.S. Congress; similar part of national government in other countries. *The U. S. Senate has two members from each state.* 2. a group of people in government with the power to make laws. *Most U.S. states have a senate as part of their government.*

senator *noun* (se nə tər) a member of a senate. *Each state has two senators.*

send *verb* (send) *sent, sent* 1. to cause to be carried to another place, especially by mail. *I will send you a letter.* | *He sent her flowers.* 2. to cause to go. *I sent him to get food for dinner.*

senior *adj.* (sēn yər) of higher rank. *Mr. Scott is a senior manager at this company.*
noun a student in the last year of high school or college. *The seniors will graduate in June.*

senior citizen *noun* (sēn yər si tə zin) an older person, especially one who is past the age of 65. *Senior citizens get a discount at this restaurant.*

sensation *noun* (sen sā shən) a feeling that you get from one or more of your senses. *She felt a sensation of cold when she stepped in the lake.*

sense *noun* (sens) 1. any of five ways to experience your environment. The senses are touch, smell, taste, sight, and hearing. *Dogs have a very good sense of smell.* 2. [N] the power to reason; judgment. *He has good sense with regard to spending his money.*
verb to feel or experience by means of the senses. *Susan sensed the cold as soon as Rick opened the window.*
make sense to show or be supported by reason and clear thinking. *This paragraph doesn't make sense.*

sensible *adj.* (sen sə bəl) having or showing good judgment; wise. *She's driving slowly in this snow because she is a sensible driver.* | *It was sensible not to walk on the frozen pond.*

sensitive *adj.* (sen sə tiv) 1. feeling emotions in a very strong way. *He is very sensitive and cries easily.* | *My sister is sensitive about being very tall.* 2. showing a strong reaction to chemicals or other things in the environment. *I am **sensitive to** cigarette smoke.* | *Camera film is **sensitive to** light.*

sent *verb* (sent) past tense and past participle of **send.**

sentence *noun* (sen təns) 1. a group of words that expresses a complete idea and has a subject and a verb. 2. a punishment for a particular crime decided in a court of law. *He received a sentence of thirty days in jail for stealing a ring.*

separate *verb* (se pə rāt) to set apart; keep apart. *The teacher separated the two children who were talking during the lesson.*
adj. (se pər ət) not connected; not attached. *I keep my shirts and pants in separate drawers.*

Word Builder: separate +
separated: living apart from each other, as before a divorce.

September *noun* (sep tem bər) the ninth month of the year.

sequence *noun* (sē kwəns) the order in which things follow one another. *Classes at our school follow the same sequence every day.*

serial *noun* (sēr ē əl) a long story that is divided into parts and produced at regular times. *His favorite serial is on TV every day at two o'clock.*
adj. happening one after another. *The people were shocked when they learned of the serial murders.*

serial number *noun* (sēr ē əl nəm bər) an individual number that is given to each one of a set of things that are the same. *Every dollar bill has a serial number.*

series *noun* (sēr ēz) *series* a group of similar things that come one after another. *She read a series of articles in the newspaper.* | *He had a series of back injuries.*

serious *adj.* (sēr ē əs) 1. marked by careful thinking or consideration. *He has a serious decision to make.* 2. important; needing careful thought. *Air pollution is a serious matter.*

servant *noun* (sər vənt) a person whose job is to clean another person's house, cook his or her food, or help the person in other ways in the home.

servant

serve *verb* (sᴧrv) 1. to give help; be of use. *He served as a volunteer at the hospital.* 2. to offer or provide someone food or drink. *The waiter served us dinner and beverages.*

> **Word Builder: serve +**
> **server (1):** a person whose job is to serve customers at a restaurant.
> **server (2):** a computer that serves files to other computers.

service *noun* (sᴧr vis) 1. [N] the work of a person who does things for other people. *The waiter gave us excellent service at dinner last night.* 2. a religious ceremony. *We went to a service at our church.*

serving *noun* (sᴧr ving) an amount of food or drink that is usually taken by one person at one time. *I was hungry, so I had two servings of oatmeal for breakfast.*

session *noun* (se shᴧn) 1. one or more meetings of a court or a government council. *The court is now in* **session.** | *Sessions of Congress begin in January and end in November or December.* 2. the period of time when a school is open for classes. *He took a course during the summer session.*

set *verb* (set) *set, set* 1. to put in a particular place. *Rebecca set the glass on the table.* 2. to decide on. *The library sets a limit on the number of books people can borrow.* | *Paul set goals for his education.* 3. to move down. *We will arrive before the sun sets.*
noun a group of things that go together or are used together. *I bought a new* **set of** *tools.*
set up to put into place; start. *Kim set up a new display in the store.* | *My cousin set me up in business.*

setting *noun* (se ting) 1. the time and place in which something happens. *The setting of that book is Georgia during the Civil War.* 2. all the plates, forks, spoons, knives, and other things for one person to eat with at a table. *The server put out four settings at each table.*

settle *verb* (se tᴧl) 1. to agree on or decide. *We* **settled** *our* **argument** *and shook hands.* | *They* **settled on** *a smaller apartment.* 2. to move to a new place and live there. *They* **settled in** *Florida.*

seven *noun* (se vᴧn) the word for the number 7.

seventeen *noun* (se vᴧn tēn) the word for the number 17.

seventh *adj.* (se vᴧnth) next after sixth.
noun one of seven equal parts of a whole.

seventy *noun* (se vᴧn tē) the word for the number 70.

several *adj.* (se vᴧr ᴧl) not many, but more than two. *There is a gas station several miles from here.*

severe *adj.* (sᴧ vēr) very hard, difficult, or strong. *The prison had severe rules.* | *She is taking medicine for severe pain.* | *We stayed at home during the severe storm.*

sew *verb* (sō) *sewed, sewn* to make or repair with a needle and thread. *Anna sews her own dresses.* | *Aaron* **sewed up** *the hole in his sock.*

sewer *noun* (soo ᴧr) a large pipe under the ground. A sewer carries off the liquid and solid waste of a town or city. *When you flush the toilet, the waste goes into the sewer.*

sewing machine *noun* (sō ing mᴧ shēn) a machine for sewing clothes and other things. *Did you make this jacket with a sewing machine or by hand?*

sewing machine

sewn *verb* (sōn) a past participle of **sew.**

sex *noun* (seks) 1. the fact of being either female or male. *What is the sex of your new baby?* 2. the physical activities of humans and animals that are connected with the purpose of producing babies.

sexual *adj.* (sek shoo ᴧl) having to do with sex. *John and Mary are just friends. They do not have a sexual relationship.*

shade *noun* (shād) 1. [N] the dark area caused when light is blocked. *She sat in the shade of the tree.* 2. a part on a lamp or window that blocks light. *That lamp has a shade made of paper.* | *Pull down the shade so the sun doesn't shine in this room.*

shadow *noun* (shæ dō) the dark image on a surface caused by something that blocks light from the sun. *Your shadow is short in the morning and long in the evening.*

shake *verb* (shāk) *shook, shaken* 1. to move from side to side with very quick, small motions. *She began to shake because she was too cold.* 2. to move something from side to side or up and down with quick motions. *You should never shake a baby.* | *Shake the juice before you pour it.*
shake hands to take the hand of another person and move it up and down. People shake hands to greet each other or to show that they agree on something.

shaken *verb* (shā kən) past participle of **shake.**

shaker *noun* (shā kər) a container that has a lid with holes in it. You fill the container with a substance such as salt or spice. The substance comes out when you shake the container. *The salt shaker and the pepper shaker are next to the stove.*

shall *verb* (shæl) to express future action or to suggest something in question form; used only with *I* or *we*. *I shall leave tomorrow.* | *Shall I call you when I arrive?*

shallow *adj.* (shæ lō) not deep. *We walked across the shallow stream.*

shame *noun* (shām) 1. [N] a painful feeling caused by knowing that you have done something wrong. *She felt shame after lying to her friend.* 2. something that you feel bad about, especially something that is lost or wasted. ***It's a shame*** *that you had to cancel your vacation.* | ***What a shame*** *to waste all that paper!*

shampoo *verb* (shæm poo) to wash your hair or things with hairlike threads. *She shampoos every time she showers.* | *We used a special machine to shampoo the carpet.*
noun a special soap for washing hair. *Wash the baby's hair with a gentle shampoo.*

shape *noun* (shāp) 1. the form of the outer surface or edge of an object. *Each slice of cheese has a square shape.* 2. a physical condition. *People who exercise a lot are in good shape.*
verb to give a certain form or shape to something. *We shaped the clay into a pot.* | *The piece of wood was shaped like a snake.*

share *noun* (shār) 1. a particular person's part of a whole amount. *John paid his share of the rent.* 2. one of the equal parts into which the value of a business is divided. *They own several shares of the company.*
verb to divide and give out. *I shared my potato chips with my friend.*

shark *noun* (shark) a fish that lives in the ocean. Sharks have large jaws and teeth. They eat fish and other animals.

sharp *adj.* (sharp) 1. having a thin edge or a fine point for cutting. *Use a sharp knife to cut the meat.* 2. making a quick and sudden change. *There is a sharp turn in the road ahead.* 3. causing strong, sudden physical or mental pain. *He has sharp pains in his stomach.* | *Her sharp words hurt her friends.*

Word Builder: sharp +
sharpen: to make sharp or sharper.

shave *verb* (shāv) to cut off hair very close to the skin. *Lee shaves with a razor.* | *Carol shaves her legs.*

Word Builder: shave +
shaver: a small machine for shaving; electric razor.

she *pron.* (shē) the female person or animal that is being talked about. *My sister is only three, but she can already count.*

shears *pl. noun* (shērz) a tool that is like a large pair of scissors. *Mr. Greene trimmed the bushes with shears.*

Word Builder: kinds of shears
garden shears: shears for cutting plants in a garden.
guillotine shears: a machine with a heavy blade that cuts through flat material, such as paper, cloth, or metal sheets.
kitchen shears: shears for cutting things in a kitchen.
pinking shears: shears for cutting a special edge on fabric.
poultry shears: shears for cutting poultry into pieces for cooking.
pruning shears: shears for pruning plants.
sewing shears: shears for cutting cloth.

shed[1] *noun* (shed) a small, simple building. You store things in a shed. *We keep the lawn mower and garden tools in a shed in our backyard.*

shed[2] *verb* (shed) *shed, shed* to take off or drop something that covers or grows. *He shed his clothes.* | *The tree sheds its leaves every fall.* | *The dog is shedding.*

sheep *noun sheep* (shēp) a mammal with long hair called wool. People raise sheep for their wool, milk, and meat.

sheep

sheet *noun* (<u>shēt</u>) 1. a large piece of cloth used to cover a bed. *She **changes the sheets** every week.* 2. a thin, broad surface. *The parking lot was covered with **a sheet of ice.*** 3. a single piece of paper. *This package contains five hundred sheets of paper.*

Word Builder: sheet +
sheet metal: a metal formed in a thin, broad piece.
Sheetrock: a brand name of material used to make smooth walls inside buildings.

shelf *noun* (<u>shelf</u>) *shelves* a thin, flat piece of wood, metal, or other material that is attached to a wall or set into a piece of furniture. Shelves are used to hold books, dishes, and other things. *He put the cups and saucers on the shelf.*

shell *noun* (<u>shel</u>) the hard outer covering around a bird's egg, a nut, or the body of some animals. *Crack the shell and put the egg into the pan.* | *Snails, clams, and turtles are animals with shells.*

shelter *noun* (<u>shel</u> tər) a place or structure that gives protection against weather or danger. *During the storm we **took shelter in** the basement.*
verb to protect. *The tree **sheltered us from** the rain.*

shelve *verb* (<u>shelv</u>) to put on a shelf. *The library clerk shelves books that people return.*

shelves *noun* (<u>shelvz</u>) plural of **shelf.**

shield *noun* (<u>shēld</u>) 1. a large, flat piece of strong material carried on the arm for protection. *Long ago, warriors carried shields to protect themselves in battle.* 2. something that gives protection. *The farmer planted a row of trees as a shield against the wind.*
verb to protect. *The man shielded his eyes from the bright light.*

shift *verb* (<u>shift</u>) 1. to move or change position. *The boy shifted in his chair.* 2. to change gears when driving a motor vehicle. *Start the car in neutral, and then shift into first gear.*
noun a regular time period when people work. *He likes working during the night shift.*

shin *noun* (<u>shin</u>) the front part of the leg between the knee and ankle.

shine *verb* (<u>shīn</u>) *shone (shined), shone (shined)* 1. to give off light. *The sun shines.* 2. to aim the light of something. *Please shine the flashlight over here.*

shingle *noun* (<u>shing</u> gəl) a thin, flat piece of wood or other material. Shingles are attached in rows to cover the roof or sides of a building. *The wind blew some shingles off the roof of their house.*

shiny *adj.* (<u>shī</u> nē) having a smooth, bright surface. *He polished his shoes until they were shiny.*

ship *noun* (<u>ship</u>) a large boat that carries people or things through deep water. *The ship crossed the ocean in a week.*
verb to place on and send by ship, truck, or other vehicle. *We shipped a package across the country to our friends.*

ship

Word Builder: ship +
shipping: the department of a company responsible for sending out goods to customers.

shipment *noun* (<u>ship</u> mənt) a quantity of things that are shipped at one time. *The shipment was delayed because the truck had mechanical problems.*

shirt *noun* (<u>shərt</u>) a piece of clothing for the upper part of the body.

shiver *verb* (<u>shi</u> vər) to shake because of cold or fear. *I began to shiver as soon as I stepped outside.*

shock *noun* (<u>shak</u>) 1. a sudden and powerful upset of the mind or feelings. *News of the disaster came as a shock.* 2. the feeling caused by a current of electricity passing through the body. *I got a shock when I touched the wire.*
verb to upset suddenly, in a way that causes strong feelings. *The violence in that movie shocked me.*

Word Builder: shock +
shocked: feeling shock.

shoe *noun* (<u>shoo</u>) a covering for the foot made of leather, cloth, or other material.

shoelace *noun* (<u>shoo</u> lās) a string used for fastening a shoe. *Tie your shoelaces, or you'll trip over them.*

shone *verb* (<u>shōn</u>) a past tense and a past participle of **shine.**

shook *verb* (<u>shuk</u>) past tense of **shake.**

shoot *verb* (<u>shoot</u>) *shot, shot* 1. to hit with a bullet or other thing that flies from a weapon. *The hunter shot a deer.* 2. to fire a weapon. *He shot his gun at the target.*

shop *noun* (shap) 1. a small store. *There is a toy shop downtown.* 2. a place where a person keeps tools and makes or repairs things. *I brought my car to the shop so a mechanic could work on the engine.*
verb to buy or look at the things in stores. *My mother is **shopping for** new clothes.*

Word Builder: shop +
shopper: a person who shops.

shoplift *verb* (shap lift) to steal things from a store. *It is against the law to shoplift.*

Word Builder: shoplift +
shoplifter: a person who shoplifts.
shoplifting: the crime of stealing things from a store.

shopping *noun* (sha ping) [N] the activity of looking for and buying goods in a store. *Some people enjoy shopping at the mall.* | *They go shopping every Saturday.*

Word Builder: shopping +
shopping bag: a bag into which you put things you have bought.
shopping cart: a cart into which you put things you are going to buy.
shopping center: a place with many stores where you can go shopping; mall.
shopping list: a list of things you need to buy.

shore *noun* (shor) the land beside an ocean, sea, lake, or river. *We collected shells along the shore.*

short *adj.* (short) 1. not long in size or time. *Mimi has short hair.* | *I'll be at the office for only a short time this morning.* 2. not tall. *He was too short to reach the top shelf.* 3. having less than you need. *I couldn't buy a movie ticket because I was two dollars short.*

Word Builder: short +
shorten: to make short or shorter.
shortly: in a short time; soon.

shortcut *noun* (short kət) a quicker or more direct way to go somewhere. *I took a shortcut to the store and got there ten minutes faster.*

shortening *noun* (shor tə ning) [N] a solid fat used in cooking.

shorts *pl. noun* (shorts) short pants that stop above the knees.

shot[1] *noun* (shat) 1. an instance of shooting with a weapon. *The police said that two shots were fired.* 2. the act of trying to get points in a game by sending or throwing a ball toward a goal. *Her last shot helped us win the basketball game.* 3. an amount of medicine given by a needle through the skin. *Some people get flu shots every year.*

shot[2] *verb* (shat) past tense and past participle of **shoot.**

should *verb* (shud) 1. used to advise another person or yourself to do something, or to express that some action is a good or important thing for someone to do. *You should stay home. You have a fever.* | *I should go to bed earlier tonight.* | *People should eat healthy foods.* 2. used to express what you believe or expect will happen based on logic. *They left New York two hours ago, so they should be back here soon.* 3. used to express someone's opinion of the correct behavior or state of something, even if it is not what is real. *Children should play outside, not on computers!* | *It's noon. I should be hungry, but I'm not.* 4. used with *if* to introduce a condition that may or may not happen. *If he should call while I'm out, tell him that I will call him back this evening.*

shoulder *noun* (shol dər) 1. the joint that connects the arm to the body. 2. the edge or border of a road where cars can stop. *The driver parked on the shoulder until the rain stopped.*

shout *verb* (showt) to call out in a loud voice. *He shouted to his friend across the street.*

shove *verb* (shəv) to push in a rough way or without care. *The boy shoved his brother out of the way.* | *Rob shoved his shirt into the drawer.*

shovel *noun* (sha vəl) a large tool with a long handle and a wide, flat blade. A shovel is used for digging or lifting heavy material such as earth, snow, or coal.

shovel

show *noun* (sho) 1. a public performance. *Will your son perform in the show at school tonight?* 2. a television or radio program. *My favorite show is on Tuesdays at nine o'clock.*
verb showed, shown (showed) 1. to cause or allow to be seen. *Irene showed her report card to her parents.* 2. to make clear by example; explain. *The teacher showed the class how to do the problems.*

show off to do something in order to attract attention. *Kevin showed off his new car by driving slowly through the neighborhood.*

show up to arrive at a place. *It's important to show up for work on time.*

shower *noun* (<u>show</u> ər) 1. a period of rain that lasts a short time. *The shower lasted only a few minutes.* 2. an act of washing your body with a device that sprays water over your head. *He takes a shower every morning.* 3. a party for someone who is getting married or having a baby soon.

> **Word Builder: shower +**
> **shower curtain:** a curtain that stops water from getting out of the shower.
> **showerhead:** the part of a shower where the water comes out.

shown *verb* (<u>shōn</u>) a past participle of **show.**

shrank *verb* (<u>shræ ngk</u>) a past tense of **shrink.**

shrimp *noun* (<u>shrimp</u>) [N] a small animal with a thin shell and five pairs of legs. Most kinds of shrimp live in the ocean. People catch and eat shrimp.

shrimp

shrink *verb* (<u>shringk</u>) **shrank (shrunk), shrunk (shrunken)** to become smaller or cause to become smaller. *Wool clothing shrinks in hot water.* | *He shrank his sweater by washing it in hot water.*

shrunk *verb* (<u>shrəngk</u>) a past tense and a past participle of **shrink.**

shrunken *verb* (<u>shrəng</u> kən) a past participle of **shrink.**

shut *verb* (<u>shət</u>) **shut, shut** to close by moving something that covers an opening. *Please shut the door.*

shut down to stop the operation of something. *The factory shut down for a month.*

shut off to stop the flow of something, or to stop flowing. *Turn the key to shut off power to the engine.* | *The electricity shut off during the storm.*

shut up to make or become quiet. *He shut up when I walked in.*

shy *adj.* (<u>shī</u>) quiet and not comfortable with other people. *The shy child did not talk to anyone in her class.*

sick *adj.* (<u>sik</u>) 1. having an illness; not well. *Phoebe was* **sick with** *a cold.* 2. having a feeling of needing to throw up. *The amusement park ride made him sick.*

sickness *noun* (<u>sik</u> nəs) a particular disease. *Measles is a sickness.*

side *noun* (<u>sīd</u>) 1. one of the outer surfaces of an object, or one of the lines forming the outside of a shape. *I bumped the right side of your car while I was parking.* | *A triangle has three sides.* 2. the right or left half of a human or animal body. *He rolled over onto his side.* 3. an area away from the center of a space. *She pulled the car over to the side of the road.* 4. one of the ways a thing appears or is understood. *They each told a different side of the story.* 5. one of two opposing groups or opinions. *Are you on my side in this argument?*

side by side next to each other. *They walked side by side.*

> **Word Builder: side +**
> **siding (1):** covering for the outside of a house.
> **siding (2):** railroad tracks off the main line.

side dish *noun* (<u>sīd</u> dish) a small amount of food that is served with the main course. *The restaurant gives a choice of side dishes, including salad and potatoes.*

sidewalk *noun* (<u>sīd</u> wawk) a path for walking along the side of a street or road. Sidewalks are usually made of concrete. *Walk on the sidewalk, not in the road.*

sideways *adv.* (<u>sīd</u> wāz) from, to, or toward the side. *She turned sideways to talk to the person next to her.*

sift *verb* (<u>sift</u>) 1. to pass or force through a screen in order to break up the larger parts. *Cindy sifted the flour and spices for the cake.* 2. to search through something in great detail. *The detective* **sifted through** *the evidence looking for clues.*

sigh *verb* (<u>sī</u>) to breathe out with a long breath because of being sad or tired. *The students sighed when the teacher gave them more work.*

sight *noun* (<u>sīt</u>) 1. [N] the ability to see. *Pilots must have good sight.* 2. something that a person sees. *We saw many beautiful sights on our trip.* 3. [N] a range of what you see at a particular time. *An airplane* **came into sight** *from the west.*

sign *noun* (<u>sīn</u>) 1. something that shows a fact, event, or some other thing. *Her smile was a sign that she agreed.* | *The bruise was a sign of injury.* 2. a mark or symbol that stands for a word or thing. *The sign + stands for addition.* 3. a printed direction, notice, or warning. *I always obey stop signs.* | *Jane hung a For Sale sign on her car.*
verb to write one's name on. *He signed the letter.*
sign in to write your name to show that you have arrived. *Mr. Perez has to sign in at work every day.*
sign up to join or cause to join a particular group, class, or activity. *We signed up for a computer class.* | *I signed my son up for music lessons.*

signal *noun* (<u>sig</u> nəl) a movement or thing that gives directions, warning, or other information. *A red light is the signal to stop.*

signature *noun* (<u>sig</u> nə chər) a person's written name, written by that person, used to sign documents, letters, or checks. *Your signature is required on this document.*

significant *adj.* (sig <u>ni</u> fə kənt) very important; full of meaning. *Graduating from high school is a significant achievement.*

silence *noun* (<u>sī</u> ləns) [N] a lack of sound. *The teacher asked for silence.*

silent *adj.* (<u>sī</u> lənt) making or having no sound. *The cat's steps were silent.* | *The house was silent while everyone slept.*

silk *noun* (<u>silk</u>) [N] a fine, soft thread made by a certain insect, or cloth made from this thread. *She bought a scarf made of silk.*

silly *adj.* (<u>si</u> lē) without good sense or without serious meaning. *Don't waste your time on those silly ideas.* | *The children loved those silly stories.*

silver *noun* (<u>sil</u> vər) [N] a shiny, soft, white metal that is valuable and used to make jewelry and coins.
adj. having the color of the metal silver. *Barbara has silver hair.*

silverware *noun* (<u>sil</u> vər wār) [N] knives, forks, and spoons. Silverware is used for eating and serving food. It can be made of silver or other metals. *Pauline set the table with plates, napkins, and silverware.*

silverware

similar *adj.* (<u>si</u> mi lər) being almost the same as something else. *Lee's handwriting is **similar to** mine.*

similarity *noun* (si mi <u>lær</u> ə tē) a specific point or instance of being similar. *There are several similarities between lions and tigers.*

simmer *verb* (<u>si</u> mər) to cook something for a while but not let it boil. *She simmered the sauce on the stove for ten minutes.*

simple *adj.* (<u>sim</u> pəl) 1. made of few parts. *It was a simple design that used just a few lines.* | *A hammer is a simple tool.* 2. easy to do or understand. *This math problem is simple.*

simply *adv.* (<u>sim</u> plē) 1. in a simple, clear way. *I gave the directions simply so that everyone would understand.* 2. in all ways. *That chocolate cake is simply wonderful.*

since *adv.* (<u>sins</u>) from then until now. *He was in a school play and has been an actor **ever since.***
prep. after a general or particular past time. *There have been many changes in technology since 1990.*
conj. because. *Since we are late, we will have to hurry.*

sincere *adj.* (sin <u>sēr</u>) real and true; not pretended. *The mayor took a sincere interest in the people and their problems.*

sincerely *adv.* (sin <u>sēr</u> lē) with sincere feelings. Often used as a closing in a letter. *I thanked him sincerely for his help.* | *She finished the letter with "Sincerely, Marla Jones."*

sing *verb* (<u>sing</u>) **sang, sung** to make music with the voice. *She sings in the shower.* | *He sang a song from his native country.*

Word Builder: sing +
singer: a person who sings.

single *adj.* (<u>sing</u> gəl) 1. only one. *He had only a single dollar left in his wallet.* 2. of or for one person. *He got a single room at the motel.* 3. not married. *My aunt is single.*

singular *adj.* (<u>sing</u> gyə lər) having to do with the form of a word that indicates only one of a certain kind of thing. *The word box is singular, but boxes is not.*

sink *verb* (<u>singk</u>) **sank (sunk), sunk** to fall slowly to a lower level. *We watched the rock sink in the pond.*
noun a fixed bowl connected to a water supply in a kitchen or bathroom. *Wash your hands in the sink.*

sir *noun* (sər) a polite form of address for a man, usually used in place of his name. *Excuse me, sir, do you know the time?*

sister *noun* (si stər) a female person who has the same mother or father as another person. *I have one brother and one sister.*

sit *verb* (sit) *sat, sat* 1. to be in a position in which you are resting the weight of your body on your buttocks. *She is sitting in a chair.* 2. to be placed or located. *His house sits on top of a hill.* 3. to cause to be seated. *Nancy sat her baby in a chair.*

sit down to move to a position where you are resting on your buttocks. *You don't need to stand. Please sit down.* | *She sat down on the floor.*

sit or set?
Sit describes the state of resting or staying in one place. We also use *sit* when talking about the action of putting a person in a place where he or she will stay.
We use *set* for the action of putting a thing in a place where it will stay.
Compare:
The lamp usually sits on that table.
Mr. Gray sits in that chair all morning.
Laura sat the baby in a little chair.
Luke set the groceries on the table.

site *noun* (sīt) a place for a town, city, building, or event. *This land is the site of the new museum.*

situation *noun* (si choo ā shən) all of the things that exist and that are happening at a particular time and place. *The terrible storm and the slippery road put the drivers in a dangerous situation.*

six *noun* (siks) the word for the number 6.

sixteen *noun* (siks tēn) the word for the number 16.

sixth *adj.* (siksth) next after fifth.
noun one of six equal parts of a whole.

sixty *noun* (siks tē) the word for the number 60.

size *noun* (sīz) 1. how big or small an object is. *This box is the wrong size for your package.* 2. a measure of how large something is according to a scale. *What is your shirt size, medium or large?* | *She wears size 8 shoes.*

skate *noun* (skāt) a shoe with either a blade or a set of small wheels attached to the bottom. Skates are used to move on ice or other hard surfaces.
verb to move along on ice skates or roller skates. *Many people skate on the frozen pond.*

skeleton *noun* (ske lə tən) the set of bones of the body.

ski *noun* (skē) one of a pair of long, narrow, smooth pieces of wood, plastic, or other hard material. People attach skis to their feet to move over snow.
verb to move over snow on these devices. *They skied down the mountain together.*

skill *noun* (skil) an ability to do something well, especially because of training or practice. *After taking this class, her writing skills have improved.* | *He has **a lot of skill** as a carpenter.*

Word Builder: skill +
skilled: having skill.

skillful *adj.* (skil fəl) being able to do something well. *He is a skillful mechanic and can fix any car.*

skin *noun* (skin) 1. [N] the thin outer covering of the body. 2. [N] the outer covering of some fruits and vegetables. *The skin of an apple can be red, green, or yellow.*

skinny *adj.* (ski nē) very thin; having little fat on the body. *He became quite skinny while he was ill.*

skip *verb* (skip) 1. to move forward by jumping on one foot and then on the other. *The children skipped down the sidewalk.* 2. to miss or leave out. *She skipped the fourth grade.*

skirt *noun* (skərt) a piece of clothing that hangs from the waist and is open all around the bottom.

waistband

hem

skirt

SKU *abbrev.* (skū) an abbreviation for **stock keeping unit.**

skull *noun* (skəl) bones of the head and face that protect the brain.

sky *noun* (skī) the air or space above the earth. *There are many clouds in the sky today.*

skyscraper *noun* (skī skrā pər) a very tall building. *New York City has many skyscrapers.*

slacks *pl. noun* (slăks) a piece of clothing that covers the body from the waist down with separate parts for each leg; pants.

slam *verb* (slăm) to shut with force and loud noise. *I slammed the door because I was very angry.*

slang *noun* (slăng) [N] informal spoken language that is made up of new words or new meanings of old words. Slang is not appropriate for serious conversation or writing. *Slang is very popular with high school students.*

slap *noun* (slăp) a sharp hit with an open hand that makes a cracking sound. *She gave him a slap on the face.*
verb to hit with an open hand. *She slapped the fly when it landed on her arm.*

slave *noun* (slāv) a person who is owned by another person and forced to work with no pay or rights.

slavery *noun* (slā vər ē) [N] the owning of people by other people. Slavery is against the law in the United States and most other countries.

sled *noun* (slĕd) a flat piece of wood or other material that is used to travel over snow and ice. *Tommy coasted down the snowy hill on a sled.*

sleep *verb* (slēp) *slept, slept* to be in a state of rest for the body and mind. When people sleep, their eyes are closed and they are not conscious. *I try to sleep eight hours a night.*
noun [N] a state or period of rest for the body and mind. *He needs eight hours of sleep each night.*

Word Builder: sleep +
sleepy: feeling a need for sleep; tired.

sleeping bag *noun* (slē ping băg) a large bag that is very warm. People sleep in sleeping bags on outdoor trips. *My sleeping bag was not warm enough for our camping trip to Alaska.*

sleepwear *noun* (slēp wār) [N] clothes worn for sleeping, such as pajamas.

sleeve *noun* (slēv) the part of a shirt or other piece of clothing that covers the arm. *The sleeves on this jacket are too long.*

Word Builder: sleeve +
sleeveless: without sleeves.

slender *adj.* (slen dər) 1. thin in a way that looks nice. *She looked slender in the black dress.* 2. small in width. *There is only enough room for a slender book on the shelf.*

slept *verb* (slept) past tense and past participle of **sleep.**

slice *noun* (slīs) a flat, usually thin, piece of something, usually food. *She made a sandwich with two slices of bread.*
verb to take from a larger portion by cutting. *She sliced the ham with a sharp knife.*

slice

slid *verb* (slid) past tense and past participle of **slide.**

slide *verb* (slīd) *slid, slid* to move easily along a smooth surface. *The children were sliding on the ice.*
noun 1. a structure that children play on. A slide has a smooth surface down which a person moves. *There are slides and swings in the park.* 2. an image that can be shown on a large screen. The image is on a small piece of film, or it is in a computer file. *We showed the slides from our vacation.*

Word Builder: slide +
slide rail: a rail that slides inside a large rack or case. A drawer or piece of equipment is attached to the rail so that you can pull it out of the rack or case.

slight *adj.* (slīt) small in amount or degree. *There is only a slight difference in the two boys' heights. | I have a slight cold.*

slim *adj.* (slim) 1. thin in an attractive way. *The slim young man looked fit in his uniform.* 2. small in amount or value. *The team had slim hopes for a victory.*

sling *noun* (sling) a wide piece of cloth that you tie around the neck to support an injured arm or hand. *She wore a sling after she fell and broke her wrist.*

slip *verb* (slip) to slide suddenly on a slippery surface. *I slipped on the ice and fell.*
noun a piece of clothing worn under a dress or skirt.

slipper *noun* (sli pər) a usually soft, flat shoe that is easy to put on and take off. Slippers are indoor shoes. *When I come home from work, I take off my boots and put on my slippers.*

slippery *adj.* (sli pər ē) difficult to hold because of a very smooth surface. *The slippery piece of soap was hard to hold in the shower.*

slope *verb* (slōp) to be higher at one end than the other. *The trail slopes down to the pond.*
noun a surface that is higher on one end than the other. *We walked up the slope.*

slot *noun* (slät) a long, narrow opening into which something may be put. *The mail goes in this slot.*

slow *adj.* (slō) 1. not moving fast or not able to move fast. *The slow swimmers were not chosen for the team.* 2. taking a long time. *The patient is making slow progress.* 3. not having much business; not busy. *It was a slow day at the shop.*
verb to make less fast. *The engineer slowed the train.*
slow down to do something less fast or to decrease the speed of something. *Slow down. I can't understand what you're saying.* | *Slow down. You're driving too fast.*

Word Builder: slow +
slowly: in a slow way; not fast.

small *adj.* (smawl) little in size, number, or amount. *They live in a small house.* | *A small crowd gathered in front of the stage.*

smart *adj.* (smart) intelligent; knowing a lot. *The smart boy taught himself how to read.*
verb to feel or cause to feel sharp but not serious pain. *That paper cut smarts.* | *His eyes smarted in the harsh wind.*

smell *verb* (smel) to sense something by means of the nose. *I think there must be a fire, because I smell smoke.*
noun 1. something that can be sensed with the nose. *She likes the smell of coffee.* 2. [N] the sense in the brain that reacts to the working of the nose. *Dogs have an excellent sense of smell.*

smelling salts *pl. noun* (sme ling sawlts) a substance with a strong smell that helps someone wake up if he or she has fainted.

smile *verb* (smīl) to have an expression on the face in which the corners of the mouth turn up. *The baby smiles whenever his mother sings to him.*
noun an expression on the face in which the corners of the mouth turn up. *She gave him a big smile.*

smoke *noun* (smōk) [N] black, white, or gray gases that you see in the air when something burns. *The smoke went up the chimney.*
verb 1. to breathe in and breathe out the gases produced by something such as a burning cigarette. *It's bad for you to smoke cigarettes.* 2. to preserve and give a flavor to something by treating with the smoke of burning wood. *We smoked the turkey with apple wood.*

Word Builder: smoke +
smoke detector: a machine for detecting smoke.
smoker: a person who smokes cigarettes.
smoking: the habit of using cigarettes.
smoky: full of smoke from cigarettes or something else.
smokestack: a large, tall pipe that carries off smoke from a factory.

smooth *adj.* (smooth) not rough; even. *A baby's skin is very smooth.*
verb to make even or smooth. *He smoothed the wood with sandpaper.*

snack *noun* (snæk) a small meal eaten between large meals. *He ate a snack of coffee and cake.*

snail *noun* (snāl) a small animal with a soft body and a round shell on its back. Snails live in water or on land and move very slowly.

snail

snake *noun* (snāk) a long, narrow animal that has smooth skin and no legs. Snakes hunt and eat other animals. Some snakes are poisonous.

snap *verb* (snæp) 1. to break suddenly with a cracking noise. *The branch snapped when I stepped on it.* 2. to close or open with a sharp noise. *The bottle cap snaps on and off.* 3. to cause to make a cracking noise. *The customer snapped her fingers to get the clerk's attention.*
noun a small metal object that is used to open and close something. *My shirt has snaps instead of buttons.*

sneaker *noun* (snē kər) a shoe that has a rubber bottom. Sneakers are worn to play sports. *I need new sneakers to play on the basketball team.*

sneeze *verb* (snēz) to let out a sudden, loud burst of air through the mouth and nose. *My allergy to cats makes me sneeze.*

snow *noun* (sno͞) [N] small, soft, white pieces of frozen water that fall from the sky like rain. *There was so much snow that we couldn't open the front door.*
verb to come down as frozen water from the clouds. *It snowed last night.*
snow in to make people not able to go out because of a large amount of snow. *That blizzard snowed us in last January.*

> **Word Builder: snow +**
> **snowball:** a ball made of snow.
> **snowfall:** the amount of snow that falls.
> **snowman:** large balls of snow made to look like a person.
> **snowstorm:** a storm in which a lot of snow falls.
> **snowy:** full of snow.

snow pea *noun* (sno͞ pe͞) a kind of **pea** with a shell that you eat.

so *adv.* (so͞) 1. to the amount or degree that someone mentions or that is understood by the situation or by the emotion in someone's voice. *She was* **so** *ill* **that** *she could not work.* | *Fifty dollars? I never knew it was so expensive.* | *I'm so happy this project is finished!* 2. also; too. *I ate lunch, and so did she.* 3. used in place of the words or ideas that someone has just expressed. *Is it going to rain? I think so.*
conj. 1. used to introduce a clause showing purpose or reason. *Put on a heavy jacket so you won't get cold.* 2. with the result that. *I was tired, so I went to bed early.*
interj. 1. used to express your understanding of the meaning of what someone just said or did. *So, you think I'm too old to understand.* | *So! You really think you can beat me?* 2. used to bring people's attention back to what you were saying or to some important point or purpose. *So, I was about to tell you what happened last night.* | *So, are we finished with everything now?*
adj. true; based on fact. *She wouldn't say it if it wasn't so.*
or so or about that many. *I'm expecting fifteen or so people at the meeting.*
so that used to introduce a clause showing purpose or reason. *Close the door so that the cold air doesn't come in.*

soak *verb* (so͞k) to place something in a liquid in order to make it wet. *He soaked his white clothes in bleach.*
soak up to take in liquid completely. *The towel soaked up the water.*

soap *noun* (so͞p) [N] a substance used to wash your body or things such as dishes or clothes. *Please wash your hands with soap.*

> **Word Builder: soap +**
> **soapy:** full of or covered with soap.

soar *verb* (so͞r) 1. to fly high and with little effort. *The bird soared over the fields and mountains.* 2. to grow or rise very quickly. *The temperature soared to 100 degrees.* | *Her spirits soared after she heard the good news.*

so-called *adj.* (so͞ kawld) used when you think the name or designation usually given to something or someone is not correct. *That so-called expert couldn't answer any of our questions.*

soccer *noun* (sa͟ kər) [N] a game played by two teams of eleven people each. You get points by moving a ball into a large net without using the hands or arms.

soccer

social *adj.* (so͞ shəl) 1. having to do with human society and the way it is organized. *Education is a very important social issue.* 2. friendly; enjoying the company of other people. *He enjoys parties because he is very social.*

Social Security *noun* (so͞ shəl sə ku͟r ə te͞) [N] a government program in the United States that gives money to people who do not work anymore and people who cannot work. Social Security is paid through FICA.

> **Word Builder: Social Security +**
> **Social Security number:** a number given by the Social Security Administration to identify people who can work in the United States.

social studies *pl. noun* (so͞ shəl stə de͞z) the study of people and their ways of life in the past and present.

society *noun* (sə si͞ ə te͞) all the members of a community or group. *It is important for every society to agree on certain laws.*

sock *noun* (sak) a covering for the foot made of cloth. People wear socks inside their shoes.

socket *noun* (sa͟ kət) a device in a wall where you can connect to a supply of electricity. *Put the electric plug into the socket in the wall.*

soda *noun* (sō də) [N] a drink made with sugar, flavor, and water with bubbles.

sodium *noun* (sō dē əm) [N] a soft, silver-white metal that is a chemical element. Sodium is a part of table salt.

sofa *noun* (sō fə) a comfortable seat with a back and arms made for two or more people; couch.

soft *adj.* (sawft) 1. easy to bend or shape; not firm or hard. *I like to sleep on a soft bed.* | *The metal became soft when we heated it.* 2. smooth; not rough. *She uses lotion to make her hands soft.* 3. quiet or low in sound. *There was soft music playing as we ate dinner.*

Word Builder: soft +
softly: in a soft way.

softball *noun* (sawft bawl) 1. [N] a game that is similar to baseball but played on a smaller field with a larger, softer ball. *Softball is very popular with the adults in our town.* 2. the ball that is used in this game. *She can hit the softball farther with her new bat.*

software *noun* (sawft wār) [N] programs that operate a computer. *He is learning the new accounting software.*

soil *noun* (soyl) [N] the top layer of the earth's surface; dirt. *The farmer prepared the soil for planting.*
verb to make dirty. *The baby soiled her diaper.*

solar *adj.* (sō lər) having to do with or coming from the sun. *This house gets electricity from solar energy.* | *Earth is a planet in the solar system.*

sold *verb* (sōld) past tense and past participle of **sell.**

soldier *noun* (sōl jər) a person who serves in the army and who is not an officer.

sole¹ *adj.* (sōl) single and alone; only. *He was the sole person in the movie theater.*

sole² *noun* (sōl) the bottom of something that touches the ground. Feet and shoes have soles. *Shoes with rubber soles are safer at work.*

sole

solid *adj.* (sa lid) 1. having a firm shape or form that can be measured in length, width, and height. *Cement becomes solid when it dries.* 2. not hollow. *A solid iron bar is very heavy.* 3. made entirely of a single material or thing. *The statue was solid silver.* | *Her dress was solid blue.*

solution *noun* (sə loo shən) 1. an answer to a problem or a way to fix it. *Mary used multiplication to find the solution.* | *The city is looking for solutions to the problem of crime.* 2. a liquid mixed with a solid or gas to make a new substance. *Vinegar is a solution of acid and water.*

solve *verb* (salv) to find an answer to; find a way to fix. *She solved her money problems when she got a better job.*

some *adj.* (səm) 1. being an amount that is not stated, or a number that is more than one but is not stated. *He gave me some money.* | *I have some quarters in my pocket.* 2. not known or named. *Some man stopped to ask about a job.*
pron. certain people, things, or events that are not named or known. *I'm nervous around strange dogs because some are friendly and some are not.*

some or any?
We use *any* in negative sentences about quantity and in questions about quantity. *Some* is not usually used in negative sentences. It can be used in questions if we think that the answer is likely to be yes. We also use *some* when we offer something to someone in order to encourage that person to say yes.
Compare:
Do you have any candy?
I don't have any candy with me now.
I do have some candy at home.
Would you like some coffee?

somebody *pron.* (səm ba dē) a person who is not named or known; someone. *Somebody is knocking at the door.*

someday *adv.* (səm dā) at a time in the future not named or known. *He thinks humans will live on the moon someday.*

somehow *adv.* (səm how) in a way not known or understood. *Our car is out of gas, but we'll manage to get home somehow.* | *Somehow the tiger escaped from its cage.*

someone *pron.* (səm wən) a person who is not named or known; somebody. *Someone forgot to lock the door.*

something *pron.* (səm thing) a thing that is not known or named. *Something smells bad.* | *We have brought something for you to eat.*

sometime *adv.* (səm tīm) at a time not known or certain. *He disappeared sometime last week.* | *Please come to visit sometime.*

sometimes *adv.* (səm tīmz) at times, but not always. *I usually get up early, but sometimes I like to sleep late.*

somewhat *adv.* (səm wət) in some measure or degree; rather. *She is somewhat lazy.*

somewhere *adv.* (səm wār) at, to, or in a place or position that is not named or known. *She bought it somewhere downtown. | My glasses must be around here somewhere.*

son *noun* (sən) a person's male child. *I have a son.*

song *noun* (sawng) a short piece of music for singing. *He listens to songs on the radio.*

soon *adv.* (soon) in a short time. *Dinner will be ready soon.*
　　as soon as at the time that. *I'll call you as soon as I arrive.*
　　sooner or later at some time in the future. *She'll have to admit her mistake sooner or later.*

sore *adj.* (sōr) painful. *He has a sore throat. | Her knee was sore after she fell.*
　　noun a painful place on the body where the skin is broken. *She covered the sore with a bandage.*

sorrow *noun* (sar ō) [N] the feeling of being sad. *We were filled with sorrow when our grandmother died.*

sorry *adj.* (sar ē) feeling sad because you have done something wrong or because something bad happened. *I'm sorry that I lied to you. | I'm sorry your pet died.*
　　interj. used to express that you feel bad that you did something wrong. *Sorry! I didn't mean to step on your foot.*

sort *noun* (sōrt) a kind or type. *What sort of dog is that?*
　　verb to put into groups. *Sort the clothes before you wash them: white clothes in one pile, dark clothes in another.*

soul *noun* (sōl) a part of human beings that some people believe exists and lives on after the death of the body; spirit. *Some religions teach that all people have souls.*

sound *noun* (sownd) 1. [N] anything that people or animals hear with their ears. *The room was filled with sound.* 2. a particular noise. *I woke up when I heard a sound downstairs. | The human voice makes many different sounds.*
　　verb 1. to seem a certain way when heard by the ears. *His voice sounds beautiful to me. | That noise sounds like a bird.* 2. to seem or appear a certain way based on what you have heard or read. *Your vacation plans sound great.*
　　sound out to try to read a word by saying the sound of each of its letters. *You can sound out the word* pot *but not the word* though.

soup *noun* (soop) a food made with small pieces of vegetables, meat, fish, or grains cooked in a liquid. *We ate soup before the main course. | This restaurant serves several soups.*

sour *adj.* (sow ər) having a sharp taste caused by acid. *Lemons, vinegar, and yogurt are some things that are sour. He loves sour candy, but I don't.*

source *noun* (sōrs) 1. the start or cause of something. *Having too little money was the source of his problem.* 2. a person or thing that gives information. *The newspaper article named a government report as its source.*

south *noun* (sowth) [N] the direction to the right of a person facing the rising sun.
　　adv. from, in, or toward the south. *The bus took them south to Florida.*

southern *adj.* (sə thərn) in, to, from, or having to do with the south. *They are immigrants from southern Asia.*

space *noun* (spās) 1. [N] the area that contains the entire universe beyond the earth. *They sent a rocket into space.* 2. [N] an empty area or place. *There's not enough space in the kitchen for a table and chairs.* 3. an area with a particular use. *Your car is in my parking space. | Fill in the spaces on this form.*

Word Builder: space +
spacecraft: a vehicle for traveling in space.

spacious *adj.* (spā shəs) having plenty of space. *Our old neighbors moved into a spacious new apartment.*

spade[1] *noun* (spād) a tool with a long handle and a flat blade that you push into the ground. A spade is used for digging.

spade[2] *noun* (spād) a black figure shaped like a pointed leaf with a short stem. It is used on playing cards. *She needed spades, but she got two hearts.*

spade

spaghetti *noun* (spə ge tē) [N] a form of pasta in the shape of long, thin strings.

span *verb* (spæn) to stretch or reach over or across. *The bridge spans the river.* | *Her life spanned eighty years.*

spare *verb* (spār) to keep from hurting or killing. *The judge spared his life but sent him to prison.*
adj. available for use at a later time. *He has a spare battery in the garage.*
noun an extra tire that you use if one of the tires on a vehicle goes flat. *We keep a spare in the trunk.*

sparrow *noun* (spær ō) a small bird with brown or gray feathers. Sparrows are very common in North America.

spatula *noun* (spæ chə lə) a cooking tool for spreading or mixing. A spatula has a wide, flat blade that can bend. *She used a spatula to put frosting on the cake.*

speak *verb* (spēk) *spoke, spoken* 1. to say words in a usual voice; talk. *Can you speak louder?* 2. to give a speech. *The president will speak at our graduation.* 3. to be able to communicate in a certain way. *He speaks many languages.*
speak out to state your opinion in public. *She spoke out against discrimination.* | *He spoke out in favor of civil rights.*
speak up to talk louder. *Please speak up. I can't hear you.*

Word Builder: speak +
speaker (1): a person who gives a speech.
speaker (2): the part of a radio, TV, or other device where the sound comes out.

Speaker of the House *noun* (spē kər əv thə hows) the leader of the U.S. House of Representatives.

special *adj.* (spe shəl) different, better, or more important than the usual. *A wedding is a special occasion.* | *Gina is my special friend.*
noun a sale of certain things for lower prices. *Apples are on special at the market this week.* | *There was a special on peaches last week.*

special education *noun* (spe shəl e jə kā shən) [N] a program at school for people who find it difficult to learn in a regular class. Special education helps people with disabilities.

specialist *noun* (spe shə list) a doctor who works in a particular area of medicine. *Jane went to a bone specialist when she broke her leg.*

species *noun* (spē shēz) *species* a group of living things that are the same in many important ways. Members of a species can produce young together. *Cats and dogs belong to different species.*

specific *adj.* (spə si fik) certain and exact; particular. *The office is only open at specific times.* | *You need a specific medicine for that disease.*

specimen *noun* (spe si mən) a small amount of matter or liquid from the body used for testing. *Doctors can test a urine specimen to look for drugs.*

spectator *noun* (spek tā tər) a person who attends and watches a public show such as a sports event. *The spectators sat in the bleachers during the football game.*

sped *verb* (sped) past tense and past participle of **speed.**

speech *noun* (spēch) a formal talk given in front of an audience. *The mayor gave a speech at city hall.*

speed *noun* (spēd) the rate of motion. *This car can travel at a very high speed.*
verb sped, sped to drive a vehicle faster than the law allows. *Ted got a ticket because he was speeding.*
speed up to go faster. *Claire drove onto the highway and sped up.*

spell *verb* (spel) to name or write the letters of a word in order. *He can spell Mississippi.*

spell check *noun* (spel chek) a computer program that checks the spelling in a document. *Please use the spell check before you send this letter.*
verb to check the spelling of something by computer. *Please spell check this document.*

spelling *noun* (spe ling) the way letters are used to make words. *It's important to use correct spelling when you fill out a job application.* | *Some words have two spellings.*

spend *verb* (spend) *spent, spent* 1. to use money to buy things. *I will spend my money on a new book.* | *He spent all his money.* 2. to use time doing a particular activity. *He spends a lot of time watching TV.*

spent *verb* (spent) past tense and past participle of **spend.**

spice *noun* (spīs) a vegetable substance with a particular smell or taste. Spices are used to flavor food and drink.

spider *noun* (spī dər) a small animal with eight legs and a body made up of two parts. Spiders catch and eat insects and other very small animals. Some spiders are poisonous.

spider

spill *verb* (spil) to cause to flow or fall from a container. *She spilled the coffee all over her dress.* | *He dropped the sack and spilled the flour.*
noun the material that has flowed or fallen from a container. *Please mop up that spill.*

spin *verb* (spin) *spun, spun* 1. to make thread by twisting. *That machine spins cotton fibers into thread.* 2. to turn fast. *When you turn the fan on, the blades start to spin.*

spine *noun* (spīn) the row of bones in the center of the back of a human or animal.

spirit *noun* (spēr it) 1. a force that some people believe is a part of human beings; soul. *Some people believe that when you die, your spirit lives on.* 2. a being that is not real and not of this world. *He believes that evil spirits live in that cave.* 3. a person's character or energy. *He faced his disease with a brave spirit.*

spirits *pl. noun* (spēr its) a person's general feeling of emotion at a certain time. *I'm usually* **in good spirits** *on sunny days.*

spite *noun* (spīt) [N] the wish to hurt or embarrass a person. *He told my secret out of spite.*
in spite of without being changed or stopped by. *In spite of her best effort, she failed the test.* | *The children played outside in spite of the rain.*

splash *verb* (splæsh) to scatter a liquid. *She splashed water on her face.*

splice *verb* (splīs) to join the ends of two pieces together to make one larger piece. *The electrician spliced the two cables together.*

splint *noun* (splint) a thin, stiff piece of plastic or some other material. A splint keeps a broken bone in place. *Mary wore a splint on her broken finger until it healed.*

splint

splinter *noun* (splin tər) a small, sharp piece of material that is broken off from a larger piece. *My sister pulled a splinter of wood out of my foot.*

split *verb* (split) *split, split* 1. to divide along the length of something. *We split logs for the stove.* 2. to divide or separate. *The road splits here.* | *I hit the rock with a hammer, and it split into small pieces.*
split up to end a relationship. *Nick and Nora split up.*

spoil *verb* (spoyl) 1. to damage something so that you cannot use or enjoy it. *That stain spoiled her dress.* | *The rain spoiled our picnic.* 2. to decay or go bad. *If you don't put the meat in the refrigerator, it will spoil.*

Word Builder: spoil +
spoilage: food or other material that has gone bad.
spoiled: having gone bad; no longer able to be eaten.

spoke *verb* (spōk) past tense of **speak.**

spoken *verb* (spō kən) past participle of **speak.**
adj. expressed using your voice. *Spoken words sometimes get more attention than written words.*

sponge *noun* (spənj) a block of soft material with many small holes that takes in water. *Use a sponge to wipe up the spilled milk.*

spoon *noun* (spoon) a tool with a small bowl at the end of a handle. You use a spoon for eating, stirring, serving, or measuring.

sport *noun* (spōrt) an activity in which people compete against each other. Sports have rules and require certain physical skills. *He likes watching sports on TV.* | *Bowling is her favorite sport.*

spot *noun* (spat) 1. a mark that is different in color from the area around it. *Fido is a white dog with black spots.* 2. a place or position. *Please stay in your spot until your name is called.*
verb to notice or see. *He spotted his sister in the crowd.*

spouse *noun* (spows) a husband or wife.

sprain *verb* (sprān) to hurt the parts of your body that lie between bones by twisting or stretching. *I sprained my ankle when I tripped on the stairs.*
noun the condition caused by twisting or stretching too much at a joint. *He can't operate that machine because of a wrist sprain.*

sprang *verb* (spræng) a past tense of **spring.**

spray *noun* (sprā) water or other liquid flying or falling through the air in fine drops; mist. *I brought insect spray for our hike.*
verb to send out as a mist. *He sprayed water on the plants.*

Word Builder: spray +
sprayer: a tool for spraying a liquid.

spread *verb* (spred) *spread, spread* 1. to open or stretch wide. *He spread the map on the table. | She spread her arms to catch the ball.* 2. to put on in a layer. *Marta always spreads jam on her bread.* 3. to make known to many people. *Spread the news about the meeting.*

Word Builder: spread +
spreader: a machine for spreading something on a surface.

spring *verb* (spring) *sprang (sprung)* to jump up. *The dog sprang to catch the ball.*
noun 1. a curved piece of metal that returns to its original shape after you push it together or stretch it out. *A small spring in some pens makes the point go in and out.* 2. a flow of water from the earth. *We stopped in the woods to drink water from a spring.* 3. the season of the year between winter and summer.

sprinkle *verb* (spring kəl) to drop or scatter in small pieces. *I sprinkled nuts on my ice cream.*

Word Builder: sprinkle +
sprinkler: a machine that sprinkles water.

sprint *verb* (sprint) to run as fast as you can. *He sprinted to the bus stop.*

sprout *verb* (sprowt) to start to grow. *The buds on the trees sprouted in the spring.*
noun a new growth from a seed or root that often is eaten as a vegetable. *She liked to eat bean sprouts.*

sprung *verb* (sprəng) a past tense and past participle of **spring.**

spun *verb* (spun) past tense and past participle of **spin.**

square *noun* (skwār) 1. a flat, closed figure with four straight sides of equal length and four equal corners. 2. a public outdoor space surrounded by buildings. *There are some nice shops around the town square.*

squash[1] *verb* (skwash) to press into a flat mass. *I stepped on the ant and squashed it.*

squash[2] *noun* (skwash) a vegetable with hard skin in many sizes, colors, and shapes. Squash grows close to the ground.

squat *verb* (skwat) to sit on your heels close to the ground. *I saw a coin in the street and **squatted down** to pick it up.*

squeeze *verb* (skwēz) to press firmly together. *He squeezed my hand in his.*

squirrel *noun* (skwir əl) a small, common mammal with a long, thick tail. Squirrels climb well and often live in trees.

squirrel

stable[1] *adj.* (stā bəl) 1. firm or steady; not likely to move. *The table is not stable because one of its legs is too short.* 2. not likely to change or go away. *Lucy is lucky to have a stable job.*

stable[2] *noun* (stā bəl) a building where people keep horses.

stack *noun* (stæk) a neat pile with one thing on top of another. *Carla needs to file that stack of papers on her desk.*
verb to put in a neat pile. *She stacked the wood by the stove.*

stadium *noun* (stā dē əm) a place used for sports events and other outdoor activities. Stadiums have rows of seats that rise up around an open field.

staff *noun* (stæf) a group or team formed to do a particular job. *The office staff has lunch together once a week.*

stage *noun* (stāj) 1. a raised floor in a theater. *The actors walked onto the stage.* 2. one step in a process of growing or making something. *The skyscraper is still in an early stage of construction.*

stain *noun* (stān) 1. a spot or colored mark. *The wine spilled and left a stain on the carpet.* 2. [N] a liquid used to change the color of wood. *We used a dark stain on the table.*
verb 1. to leave a spot or mark on something. *The grass stained her pants.* 2. to give a new color to. *I stained the old chair.*

Word Builder: stain +
stained: having a stain or being colored by stain.

stairs *pl. noun* (st<u>ā</u>rz) a set of steps in a building. *The bathroom is at the top of the stairs.*

Word Builder: stair +
staircase: a set of steps with a railing that goes from one floor to another in a building.
stairwell: a section in a building that contains a staircase with walls around it.

---

stake¹ *noun* (st<u>ā</u>k) a sharp stick that you push into the ground to mark a place or to support something. *We used stakes to hold our tent in place.*

stake² *noun* (st<u>ā</u>k) a share or interest in something. *I have had no stake in the family farm since I left home.*

stale *adj.* (st<u>ā</u>l) not fresh. *We left the bread out overnight, and now it's stale.*

stalk¹ *noun* (stawk) a plant's main stem. *Some flowers grow on tall stalks.*

stalk² *verb* (stawk) to follow in a way that is like hunting. *It is against the law to stalk a person.*

stamp *verb* (stæmp) 1. to push down against a surface with a hard, fast motion. *She stamped her foot on the floor.* 2. to mark something by using a rubber block with ink. *The customs agent stamped my passport.*
noun a small piece of paper that you buy at a post office to pay for mailing. You stick it on something that you want to send. *Bea put the stamp on the envelope before she mailed it.*

stand *verb* (stænd) *stood, stood* 1. to hold your body upright by using your legs and feet; move to this position. *I need to sit down. I'm too tired to stand.* | *People stand when the judge enters the room.* 2. to be in an upright position. *None of the houses were standing after the big storm.* 3. to put something in an upright position. *Stand the ladder next to the window.*
noun a small place or table where someone sells something. It is often outside. *The farmer's stand is open only during August and September.*
can't stand (informal) to hate something. *I can't stand loud noise in the morning.*
stand for to represent. *The letters CD stand for compact disc.*
stand up to move your body into a standing position. *His leg is broken, and he can't stand up.*

standard *noun* (stæn dərd) something that people agree to use as a guide or authority when measuring something. *They want the standards to be the same in every school.*
adj. serving as an accepted model. *This is a standard textbook that is used in all the schools.*

staple *noun* (st<u>ā</u> pəl) a small, thin piece of wire that has a shape like the letter *U*. People use staples to hold pieces of paper together or to attach things to a hard surface.
verb to make two or more things hold together by using a staple. *I stapled the two pages together.*

staple gun *noun* (st<u>ā</u> pəl gən) a tool that shoots a staple into something hard like a wall or wood.

staple gun

stapler *noun* (st<u>ā</u> plər) a tool in a home or office that uses staples to attach papers together.

star *noun* (star) 1. a thing that we usually see as a point of light in the night sky. The sun is a star. 2. a design with five or six points. *The American flag has stars and stripes.* 3. a person who is famous or great in the area of entertainment or sports. *She is a movie star.*
verb to perform the main part in a play or movie. *My favorite actor is starring in the new movie.*
adj. being much better than others; excellent. *He is a star athlete.*

starch *noun* (starch) 1. [N] a white substance that is in many foods. Potatoes and grains are some things that have starch in them. 2. [N] a substance used to make clothing or other material stiff. *She sprayed starch on the shirt before she ironed it.*

stare *verb* (st<u>ā</u>r) to look straight at something with your eyes open wide and not moving. *Children often stare at people who look different or funny.*

start *verb* (start) 1. to begin a movement or activity. *The movie will start at seven o'clock.* 2. to make something begin. *She started the car.* | *The wood was wet, so we couldn't start a fire.* 3. to begin to do something. *He started to read, but the phone rang.* | *He started doing his homework after dinner.*
noun the beginning of something. *We're excited about the start of summer.*
start over to start again. *I made a big mistake, so I had to start over.*

starter *noun* (star tər) a device that starts something. *The starter in my car is broken.*

starve *verb* (starv) to die or suffer from not eating. *People were starving because floods destroyed their crops.*

Word Builder: starve +
starving: very hungry; having no or too little food.

---

state *noun* (stāt) 1. the condition of a person or thing. *The old house was in a bad state after the terrible storm.* 2. a particular condition of your mind or emotions. *Happiness is a pleasant state.* | *She was in a sad state after reading the letter.* 3. an area of land that has a government and is part of a group that makes up a country. *America has fifty states.*
verb to say or write something that you believe, usually in a strong, confident way. *She stated her opinion.* | *He stated that he would never get married again.*

statement *noun* (stāt mənt) 1. an important opinion or piece of information that someone says or writes to other people. *The company made a statement to the newspapers about closing the factory.* 2. a report of your account with a company or bank. It tells you how much money you have or if you need to pay anything. *I receive a statement from my bank every month.*

station *noun* (stā shən) 1. a place or building used as a center of services. *The police brought the man to the police station.* 2. a building where a bus or train stops and where people begin and end traveling. *She drove him to the train station.* 3. a radio or television company; the place on your radio or television where you can find a particular broadcast. *This station plays the best music.*

statue *noun* (stæ choo) a piece of art that is made out of stone, metal, or other material. Statues are often in the shape of humans or animals. *There are some statues in front of the museum.*

Statue of Liberty

status *noun* (stæ təs or stā təs) 1. [N] a person's position or level in comparison with the position of other people. *His status rose when he got the new job.* 2. a person's condition in the view of the law. *What is his marital status? Is he married or single?* | *The company checked her immigration status before hiring her.*

stay *verb* (stā) 1. to spend time in a place. *They stayed at the restaurant until it closed.* 2. to continue spending time in a place or with people; not leave. *Stay with us a few more minutes.*
stay up to remain awake. *She's tired because she stayed up late last night.*

steady *adj.* (ste dē) 1. not moving from a correct position. *The doctor has steady hands.* | *This table is not steady.* 2. having a continuous and regular movement. *We worked at a steady pace until we finished.*

Word Builder: steady +
steadily: in a steady way.

---

steak *noun* (stāk) a large, flat piece of meat or fish usually cooked fast at high temperature.

steal *verb* (stēl) *stole, stolen* to take something from another person without permission and in a way that is against the law. *He didn't lock his bicycle, and someone stole it.*

steam *noun* (stēm) [N] water in the form of a gas that you can see in the air when you boil or heat water. *We cooked the vegetables with steam.*

steel *noun* (stēl) [N] a hard, strong metal made by mixing iron and another metal. It is used to make machines, cars, tools, and many other things.

steep *adj.* (stēp) having a sharp slope. *We got tired walking up the steep hill.*

steer *verb* (stēr) to make something move in a certain direction. *Learning how to steer a car takes practice.*

steering wheel *noun* (stēr ing wēl) a wheel that you turn to control the direction of movement of a vehicle. *The driver should keep two hands on the steering wheel.*

stem *noun* (stem) the main part of a plant that supports the branches, leaves, and other parts. *She likes to eat the broccoli flowers but not the stems.*

step *noun* (step) 1. each single movement of your foot as you walk. *The baby **took** her first **steps** today!* 2. a flat, narrow surface that you put your foot on as you walk up or down to a different level. *He walked up the steps to her house and knocked on the door.* 3. a pattern used in dancing or other types of movement. *We learned a new step in our dance class today.* 4. one act or stage that is part of a process. *The first step is to mix the butter and the eggs.* | ***Follow** all **the steps** carefully.* | *The company **is taking steps** to improve workplace safety.*

step- *prefix* (step) used before another word to show that someone is a relative because of a second marriage of a parent. *When my father married again, his new wife became my stepmother. My stepmother's children are my stepsister and stepbrother.*

Word Builder: step- +
stepbrother: a son of your stepmother or stepfather.
stepfather: a man who is married to your mother but who is not your father.
stepmother: a woman who is married to your father but who is not your mother.
stepparent: a stepmother or stepfather.
stepsister: a daughter of your stepmother or stepfather.

---

stereo *noun* (ster ē ō) a system of equipment for playing sound. *Our stereo has a CD player and two speakers.*

sterile *adj.* (ster əl) 1. completely clean and without anything that can cause illness. *Doctors use sterile tools.* 2. not able to produce babies; not able to reproduce. *The disease caused him to become sterile.*

Word Builder: sterile +
sterilize: to make sterile.

---

stick¹ *noun* (stik) 1. a long, thin piece of wood. *We used sticks to start the fire.* 2. something that has a long, thin shape. *He gave the child a stick of gum.*

sticks

stick² *verb* (stik) *stuck, stuck* 1. to break through the surface of something using an object with a point. *She stuck her finger with the needle.* 2. to attach one thing to another with something sticky. *I stuck the two pieces of paper together with tape.* 3. to be attached or become attached to something. *The cat hairs **are sticking to** my coat.* 4. to enter something and not be able to get out. *The wheels stuck in the mud.*

stick out 1. to be in a position that is not even with a surface. *Be careful. There is a nail sticking out of that piece of wood.* 2. to push something out that is usually inside or even with a surface. *The doctor told him to stick out his tongue.* 3. to be very different so that it is easy for people to notice you. *My daughter is afraid to stick out at school.*

sticker *noun* (sti kər) a small piece of paper with sticky material on the back and writing or pictures on the front. *She put a price sticker on each jar.* | *My children like to decorate their books with stickers.*

sticky *adj.* (sti kē) able to attach to something when touched, or to give the feeling of this ability. *Glue, honey, and paste are sticky.* | *The leaves of that plant are sticky.*

stiff *adj.* (stif) 1. not easy to bend; hard. *This thick cardboard is very stiff.* 2. not able to move freely. *My knees are stiff today.*

still *adj.* (stil) not moving. *The wind stopped, and the trees became still.*
adv. 1. continuing from the past into the present; yet. *He still lives with his parents.* | *Are you still talking on the phone?* 2. used when something is able to happen or remain true, even if something else might seem to prevent it. *He was very sick, but he still went to work.* | *He's not very friendly, but I still like him.*

sting *verb* (sting) *stung, stung* 1. to make a tiny hole in the skin that causes pain. *A bee stung him.* 2. to cause someone to feel a sudden, sharp pain. *If this shampoo gets in your eyes, it will sting.*

Word Builder: sting +
stinger: the part of some insects that causes a sting.

---

stir *verb* (stər) to mix liquids together or move a liquid in a circle using your hand or an object. *She stirred her coffee with a spoon.* | *He stirred cream into his coffee.*

stitch *noun* (stich) 1. one movement of a needle and thread through material when you sew. *When she sews by hand, her stitches are straight and even.* 2. the tiny, single piece of thread that goes through material in one movement in sewing or in repairing a wound in the skin. *He needed four stitches to close the cut on his chin.*
verb to fasten or join with a needle and thread. *He stitched two layers of cloth together.* | *The doctor* **stitched up** *the wound.*

stock *verb* (stak) to supply with goods. *They stocked the shelves with cans of food.*
noun 1. [N] things that you keep that are ready for use or for sale at any time; supply. *My parents keep a stock of extra food in the house.* | *That store has a large stock of shoes in all sizes.* 2. the value of a company, divided into equal shares and sold to people or groups. *They own several shares of stock in a software company.*
in stock in the store and available for sale. *We have several sizes in stock right now.*
out of stock not present for sale in a store. *The shoes I wanted to buy were out of stock.*

stocking *noun* (sta king) a piece of clothing for your foot or leg. A woman's stocking may be transparent and cover her whole leg. *She bought several* **pairs of stockings.**

stock keeping unit *noun* (stak kēp ing ū nit) a number that is given to a specific product in a store; **SKU.** The number is on a small label on the product. People use stock keeping units to keep track of inventory.

stole *verb* (stōl) past tense of **steal.**

stolen *verb* (stō lən) past participle of **steal.**
adj. having been taken in a way that is against the law. *He was charged with possession of* **stolen goods.**

stomach *noun* (stə mək) 1. the organ in the body that processes food. 2. the front part of the body below the chest. *Your pants are tight because your stomach is big!*

stone *noun* (stōn) 1. [N] a hard material like rock. *This old building is made of stone.* 2. a small piece of rock. *She threw a stone into the water.*

stood *verb* (stud) past tense and past participle of **stand.**

stool *noun* (stool) a seat on tall legs and without arms or a back.

stool

stoop¹ *verb* (stoop) to bend the body forward and down. You usually stoop to pick up something from the floor.

stoop² *noun* (stoop) a raised flat area at the entrance to a house. You usually go up some steps to reach the stoop.

stop *verb* (stap) 1. to end the movement of something; make something end. *The police officer stopped the cars.* | *Tim's mother stopped the video when it was time for dinner.* 2. to end an activity. *I stopped smoking last week.* | *We stopped playing the game when we got tired.* 3. to no longer move or continue an action. *The car stopped at the red light.* | *He stopped in the middle of the story.*
noun 1. the act of stopping or state of being stopped. *The car came to a stop in front of our house.* 2. a point where a bus or other public vehicle stops for passengers. *The people waited at the stop for the bus to come.*
stop in to come to a place for a short time; visit. *Could you stop in at my office next week?* | *When you come to Chicago, please stop in to see me.*

Word Builder: stop +
stoplight: a red traffic light.
stop sign: a red sign on the side of the road that tells drivers to stop.

storage *noun* (stōr ij) 1. [N] the act or state of keeping things for future use. *We have to pay for the storage of the furniture.* 2. [N] a place for keeping things. *Your things are safe in storage.*

Word Builder: storage +
storage cabinet: a cabinet in which you store things.
storage closet: a closet in which you store things.
storage room: a room in which you store things.

store *noun* (stōr) a building or other place where you can buy things. *I need to buy bread at the* **grocery store.**
verb to gather and keep for future use. *We store paint and tools in the basement.*

storm *noun* (stōrm) a violent event in weather. In a storm, there may be a lot of rain, snow, or wind. *It's too dangerous to drive in this storm.*

story[1] **noun** (stōr ē) a report of events that really happened or are imaginary. *I read the story about the accident in the newspaper. | I tell my daughter a story before she goes to sleep.*

story[2] **noun** (stōr ē) one level of a building; floor. *That building has ten stories.*

stove noun (stōv) a device that uses electricity, gas, or oil to provide heat for cooking or warmth. *I cooked the vegetables on the stove.*

straight adj. (strāt) 1. without a curve or bend. *He drew a straight line.* 2. without stopping; continuous. *We worked for nine straight hours.*
adv. without turning or changing direction. *Go straight for one mile and then turn left. | He went straight home after school.*

> **Word Builder: straight +**
> **straighten:** to make straight or straighter.

strain verb (strān) 1. to bring something close to its breaking point. *Their frequent arguments strained their marriage.* 2. to hurt or injure something by using it too much. *He strained a muscle while playing softball.* 3. to remove the solid things from a liquid. *She strained the vegetables for her baby.* 4. to pull with energy or force. *The dog strained on its leash.*
noun an injury caused by putting too much force on a muscle. *The strain in his back was caused by lifting heavy boxes.*

> **Word Builder: strain +**
> **strainer:** a tool for straining liquids.

strange adj. (strānj) 1. not usual; odd. *It is strange that she hasn't called me today. | He draws pictures of strange monsters.* 2. not known or familiar. *She is afraid of strange dogs.*

stranger noun (strān jər) a person that you do not know. *She told her child not to talk to strangers.*

strap noun (stræp) a thin, flat strip of material used to attach something or hold objects in a certain way. *She needs a new school bag because the strap broke.*

strategy noun (stræ tə jē) a method or plan of action that you intend to use for some purpose. *What is your strategy for winning the game?*

straw noun (straw) 1. [N] dried stems of certain grain plants. Straw is used to feed animals and to make things such as baskets and hats. 2. a thin, hollow tube of plastic or other material used to suck up a drink. *Sarah drank her soda through a straw.*

strawberry noun (straw be rē) a small, sweet, red fruit with seeds on the outside. Strawberries grow close to the ground.

strawberry

stray verb (strā) to wander away from a group or place. *He strayed from the camp and couldn't find his way back.*
adj. lost, out of place, or without a home. *There are stray hairs all over the bathroom floor. | My family often feeds stray dogs.*

streak noun (strēk) a long, narrow line or mark. *There is a streak of black paint on the wall.*

stream noun (strēm) 1. a flowing body of water like a small river. *We went fishing in the stream.* 2. a continuous flow of something. *I received a stream of phone calls this afternoon.*
verb to flow, as in a current or stream. *Water streamed from the broken pipe.*

street noun (strēt) a public road in a town or city. *Their office is on a busy street with a lot of traffic.*

strength noun (strengkth) [N] the state or condition of being strong. *He had no strength after his illness.*

stress noun (stres) 1. [N] the importance or special attention that you give to something. *Mrs. Berg **puts** a lot of **stress on** good manners.* 2. the louder or longer quality of your voice in one syllable of a word with two or more syllables. In the word *doctor*, the stress is on the first syllable. 3. [N] pressure that causes something to almost break or become injured. It may be physical pressure or mental pressure from problems of life. *The heavy books **put** a lot of **stress on** the shelf. | His job as a police officer gives him a lot of stress. | She is **under a lot of stress** at work.*

> **Word Builder: stress +**
> **stressed:** feeling stress.
> **stressful:** causing stress.

stretch *verb* (strech) 1. to pull something to its full length. *He always stretches his legs after running.* 2. to make something longer or wider. *She stretched the rubber band.* 3. to become longer or wider. *The waist stretches on this pair of pants.*

stretcher *noun* (stre chər) a flat structure with a cloth surface that is used to carry sick or injured people. *They put him on a stretcher and carried him to the ambulance.*

strict *adj.* (strikt) 1. not able to be changed or broken. *That factory must follow strict safety regulations.* | *She was on a strict diet after her operation.* 2. acting according to firm rules. *Mr. Goode is very strict with his children.*

stride *noun* (strīd) a long walking step. *She has a confident stride.*

strike *verb* (strīk) *struck, struck (stricken)* 1. to hit with the hand or a weapon. *He struck me with the back of his hand.* 2. to move toward something and hit it with force. *The car struck a boy on his bicycle.*
noun a stopping of work as a protest for better pay or working conditions. *The workers at the automobile factory* **went on strike** *yesterday.*

stricken *verb* (stri kən) a past participle of **strike.**

string *noun* (string) a thin rope. *He tied a string to his balloon.* | *She fastened the package with string.*

strip[1] *verb* (strip) 1. to take off the outside covering from something. *He stripped the house of paint.* | *She stripped the old paint from the chair.* 2. to take off all of your clothing. *He stripped before he got into the shower.*

strip[2] *noun* (strip) a long, narrow piece of something. *Cut this cloth into strips.* | *We walked along a strip of beach.*

stripe *noun* (strīp) a line of color that is different in color from the area around it. *Tigers have black stripes on their fur.*

stroke *noun* (strōk) a sudden injury to the brain that happens when the flow of blood to the brain is blocked. A stroke can cause damage to various parts of the body. It can also cause death.

strong *adj.* (strawng) 1. having power; difficult to break or damage. *The strong man lifted the heavy stone.* | *Steel is a strong material.* 2. showing great force or energy. *A strong wind blew down the tree.* 3. having a very high degree of something. *That cheese has a strong smell.*

struck *verb* (strək) past tense and past participle of **strike.**

structure *noun* (strək chər) 1. a thing that is made up of different parts that are connected in a particular way. *A human cell is a complicated structure.* | *That new hotel is an interesting structure.* 2. the way in which the parts of something connect with each other. *A carpenter knows about the structure of furniture.*

struggle *verb* (strə gəl) 1. to work on or fight with a difficult problem or situation. *He* **struggled with** *his math homework all night.* 2. to make a strong effort; to try hard. *He struggled not to cry.*
noun a fight. *There was a long struggle between the management of the company and the labor union.*

stub *noun* (stəb) 1. a short piece of something that remains after a larger piece has been used. *It is hard to write with the stub of a pencil.* 2. a piece of paper that remains after an attached part has been used. The stub is often a record or proof that you paid for something. *I deposited my paycheck and kept the stub for my records.* | *Don't throw away your* **ticket stub.**

ticket stub

stubborn *adj.* (stə bərn) not willing to accept change or help. *She is very stubborn and won't do what they tell her.*

stuck *verb* (stək) past tense and past participle of **stick**[2].
adj. not able to move or be moved. *I got* **stuck in traffic** *on the way home.* | *This window is stuck shut.*

student *noun* (stoo dənt) a person who goes to a school or college. *How many students are in your class?*

study *noun* (stə dē) an area of knowledge. *The study of medicine includes learning about diseases.*
verb 1. to try to gain knowledge or skill. *Please don't bother me while I'm studying.* 2. to learn or gain skill in. *He is studying chemistry at the university.*

stuff *noun* (stəf) [N] personal things or any other type of materials or objects. *Will you watch my stuff until I get back?*
verb to fill up a container or opening. *She stuffed the clothes into the washing machine.* | *That pillow is* **stuffed with** *feathers.*

Word Builder: stuff +
stuffed: full.
stuffing (1): a soft food that cooks inside poultry.
stuffing (2): a soft material inside a pillow, cushion, or mattress.

stung *verb* (stəng) past tense and past participle of **sting.**

stupid *adj.* (stoo pid) dull or slow to learn; not smart. *He felt stupid when he locked his keys in the car.*

sturdy *adj.* (stər dē) strong or solid; hard to break. *Your sturdy shelves will hold these heavy books.*

style *noun* (stīl) 1. the manner in which something is said or done. *I like the style of her writing.* 2. a fashion. *Short skirts are back* **in style.**

subject *noun* (səb jekt) 1. the thing that is written or spoken about. *The subject of the book was politics in America.* | *Every time I try to talk to Nina about her boyfriend, she* **changes the subject.** 2. a noun or noun phrase that is one of the main parts of a sentence. The subject performs the action of the verb or is in the state that the verb phrase describes. *The dog* is the subject in the sentence "The dog bit the boy."

subordinate *adj.* (sə bōr də nit) 1. lower in rank or authority. *The workers are* **subordinate to** *the supervisor.* 2. used to refer to a certain type of clause in grammar. A subordinate clause is a clause in a sentence that is not the main clause. In the sentence "If it rains, we won't go," the subordinate clause is *If it rains*. The main clause is *we won't go.*
noun a person who is lower in rank or under the control of another. *The officer gave an order to her subordinates.*

subsidy *noun* (səb si dē) the direct financial help provided by the government to a business, industry, educational institution, or individual. *Many farms get subsidies from the government.*

substance *noun* (səb stəns) a particular kind of matter or material. *She was covered with a sticky substance.*

substitute *noun* (səb sti toot) a person or thing that takes the place of another. *She was the substitute in the class when the teacher got sick.* | *Honey can be a substitute for sugar.*
verb to put or use in place of another person or thing. *She* **substituted** *margarine* **for** *butter in the recipe.*

subtract *verb* (səb trækt) to find the difference in amount between two numbers, or to take away from a whole or larger quantity. *Subtract your current weight from your weight last month to find out how many pounds you lost.* | *To find your net pay, subtract your deductions from your gross pay.*

subtraction *noun* (səb træk shən) [N] the process of finding the difference in amount between two numbers. *Use subtraction to find out how much money is in your account after you make a withdrawal.*

suburb *noun* (sə bərb) an area or community located just outside a city or town. *Many people who live in a suburb go to work in the city.*

subway *noun* (səb wā) a train in a city that carries passengers and travels under the ground. *I take the subway to work every morning.*

succeed *verb* (sək sēd) 1. to have a good result; do well. *You must study hard to succeed in school.* 2. to follow or take the place of. *The president of the company retired, and his son succeeded him.*

success *noun* (sək ses) 1. [N] a person or thing that does well. *The book she wrote was a huge success.* | *He's a great success in the world of computers.* 2. a good result from doing something well. *He has had many successes as an actor.*

successful *adj.* (sək ses fəl) 1. having a good or favorable result. *The business meeting was very successful.* 2. having reached a goal. *The firemen were* **successful in** *putting out the fire.*

Word Builder: successful +
successfully: in a way that brings success; in a successful way.

such *adj.* (sǝch) 1. of a certain character or kind. *I have never eaten at* **such** *an expensive restaurant* **as** *this before.* 2. of the same or a similar kind; like. *You can buy soap, toothpaste, and other such things at the drugstore.*
adv. to the degree that someone mentions, or to the degree that someone can understand from the situation or from the strong emotion in your voice. *It was* **such** *a rainy day* **that** *we decided to cancel the game.* | *Why do you need such an expensive car?* | *They are such nice people!*
such as for example. *This shirt comes in many colors, such as green, red, blue, and yellow.*

suck *verb* (sǝk) to pull into the mouth by using the tongue and lips. *I sucked the soda through a straw.*

sudden *adj.* (sǝ dǝn) happening without notice or warning; not expected. *A sudden noise frightened us.*
all of a sudden suddenly; without warning. *All of a sudden, it started to rain hard.*

suddenly *adv.* (sǝ dǝn lē) without warning, often causing surprise or fear. *He died suddenly of a heart attack.*

suffer *verb* (sǝ fǝr) to feel pain or have a bad experience. *She* **suffers from** *headaches.* | *He* **suffered from** *his mistakes.*

sufficient *adj.* (sǝ fi shǝnt) enough; as much as needed. *The amount of food here will be sufficient for the camping trip.*

suffix *noun* (sǝ fiks) a part of a word with its own meaning that is added to the end of another word to change the meaning. *The suffix -ed in* wanted *gives the meaning of past time. The suffix -less in* hopeless *gives the meaning* without.

sugar *noun* (shu gǝr) [N] a sweet substance made from plants that is used to flavor food.

suggest *verb* (sǝg jest) to tell someone what you think is a good idea to do. *My mother suggested several ways to calm the baby.* | *He suggested that we should go out for dinner.*

suggestion *noun* (sǝg jes chǝn) something that is suggested. *The employees* **made** *some good* **suggestions** *for improving workplace safety.*

suit *noun* (soot) a set of clothes of the same material and color. A suit has a short coat and pants or a skirt.

suitable *adj.* (soo tǝ bǝl) correct for the situation or purpose; appropriate. *I want to buy them a suitable gift for their new house.*

suitcase *noun* (soot kās) a box used for carrying clothing and personal things when traveling. *Kay* **packed** *her* **suitcase** *the night before she left on vacation.*

suitcase

sum *noun* (sǝm) the number or amount that comes from adding two or more numbers. *The sum of ten and ten is twenty.*

summer *noun* (sǝ mǝr) the season of the year between spring and autumn.

summit *noun* (sǝ mit) the highest part. *We climbed to the summit of the mountain.*

summit

sun *noun* (sǝn) the star that is nearest to the earth. The earth receives heat and light from the sun and travels around it.

Word Builder: sun +
sunburn: a burn of the skin caused by the sun.
sunglasses: special eyeglasses that protect your eyes from the sun.
sunlight: the light of the sun.
sunny: having a lot of sun; bright.
sunrise: the time of day when the sun appears to move above the horizon.
sunset: the time of day when the sun appears to move below the horizon.
sunshine: the light of the sun.
suntan: a tan color of the skin caused by the sun.

Sunday *noun* (sǝn dā) the first day of the week. Sunday comes between Saturday and Monday.

sung *verb* (sǝng) past participle of **sing.**

sunk *verb* (sǝngk) a past tense and past participle of **sink.**

super *noun* (soo pǝr) a short form of **superintendent** when it means the person who takes care of a building.
adj. (informal) excellent; very good. *You did a super job preparing for the interview.*

superintendent *noun* (soo pǝr in ten dǝnt) 1. a person who manages or directs an institution or organization. 2. a person who is in charge of the care and operation of a building. *The superintendent fixed the broken window in my apartment.*

superior *adj.* (sə pēr ē ər) much better than others in quality; excellent. *Our department was recognized for superior customer service last month.*

superlative *noun* (soo pər lə tiv) the form of an adjective or adverb that expresses the highest degree of comparison. The words *best*, *fastest*, and *most beautiful* are superlatives.

supermarket *noun* (soo pər mar kit) a large store that carries a wide variety of food and things for the home. *That supermarket has very good fruit.*

supervisor *noun* (soo pər vī zər) a person who is responsible for other people in a workplace. *Her supervisor asked her to work an extra hour.*

supper *noun* (sə pər) an evening meal. *I'm having a light supper because I had a big lunch.*

supply *verb* (sə plī) to provide what is wanted or needed. *The teacher* **supplied** *the students* **with** *pens and paper.*
    noun (plural) materials that you keep available and use whenever you need them. *We keep* **cleaning supplies** *in a separate closet.*

> **Word Builder: supply +**
> **supplier:** a person or company that supplies things.

support *verb* (sə pōrt) 1. to hold the weight of something. *The table top is supported by four legs.* 2. to help during a time of trouble. *She supported me when I was ill.* 3. to provide enough for. *Parents support their families by working.*
    noun [N] the money used to take care of someone's needs. *She gets some support for the children from her parents.*

> **Word Builder: support +**
> **supporting:** giving support to a person or thing.
> **supportive:** giving help to someone who needs it.

suppose *verb* (sə pōz) 1. to imagine or think of something as a possibility. *Let's suppose that we move the couch over to this wall.* | *I suppose I could go to the movies if I could find a baby-sitter.* 2. to believe, but without strong feeling. *I suppose that his plan will work if he has enough time.*
    supposed to 1. used to say what someone should do because of a rule or agreement. *She* **is supposed to** *be at work by nine o'clock.* | *The students* **are** *not* **supposed to** *wear jeans to school, but sometimes they do.* | *I* **was supposed to** *give this to Mr. Sims, but he was not there.* 2. used to say what someone expects or expected because of some rule or agreement. *The check* **was supposed to** *arrive last week, but it's still not here.*

supreme *adj.* (sə prēm) having the highest rank, position, or authority. *He was the supreme general of the army in Europe.*

Supreme Court *noun* (sə prēm kōrt) the highest court in the United States. It has nine judges, who are chosen by the president and approved by the Senate.

sure *adj.* (shur) certain that something is true. *I am sure that this water is safe to drink.*
    make sure to check to be certain. *I made sure that I turned the oven off before I left the house.*

surface *noun* (sər fis) 1. the outside of something. *There are many rocks on the surface of the moon.* | *It's nice to skate on a smooth surface.* 2. a thing or part of a thing that is flat, such as a wall or the top of a table. *That diamond has many shiny surfaces.*

surprise *verb* (sər prīz) to suddenly do something that is not expected. *He surprised her with a kiss.* | *The blizzard surprised the whole town.*
    noun anything that was not expected. *My job promotion was a big surprise.*

> **Word Builder: surprise +**
> **surprised:** showing surprise.
> **surprising:** causing surprise.

surround *verb* (sə rownd) to form a circle around something. *The police surrounded the house.* | *Their house is surrounded by trees.*

surroundings *pl. noun* (sə rownd ingz) all the things around you; environment. *They live in poor surroundings.*

survey *verb* (sər vā) to have a general look at. *He surveyed the landscape.*
    noun (sər vā) 1. a general look at or review of something. *This class is a survey of American history.* 2. the collecting of information on a particular subject from a small part of the public. *They* **took a survey of** *women over forty for their opinions of the new law.*

survival *noun* (sər vī vəl) [N] the fact of continuing to live through dangerous or hard conditions. *Survival is difficult with very little food or clean water.*

survive *verb* (sər v<u>ī</u>v) 1. to continue to live or exist after a terrible event. *Some people survived the airplane crash.* | *Their house survived the storm.* 2. to continue to exist. *This kind of plant can survive in the desert.*

suspect *verb* (sə sp<u>e</u>kt) 1. to believe to be true based on a small amount of evidence. *I* **suspect that** *she likes you very much.* | *The police* **suspected that** *the thief got in through the back window.* 2. to believe someone may be guilty before having proof. *The police* **suspected** *him* **of** *two different crimes.*
noun (s<u>ə</u> spekt) a person who is suspected of doing something wrong. *She is a suspect in the murder.*

suspend *verb* (sə sp<u>e</u>nd) 1. to make something hang from a higher position. *I bought a new light that we can* **suspend from** *the ceiling.* 2. to cause to stop for a period of time. *They suspended the game until the rain stopped.*

SUV *abbrev.* (es <u>ū</u> v<u>ē</u>) an abbreviation for *sport-utility vehicle*. *An SUV is a large car like a truck that can travel off-road.*

swab *noun* (sw<u>a</u>b) a small piece of cotton that is attached to a small stick and is used for cleaning. *The doctor used a swab to clean the child's wound.*

swabs

swallow *verb* (sw<u>a</u> lō) to cause food to go from the mouth to the stomach. *The baby swallowed some cereal.*

swam *verb* (sw<u>æ</u>m) past tense of **swim.**

swamp *noun* (sw<u>a</u>mp) a low area of land that is covered with water. *Snakes and turtles often live in swamps.*

swear *verb* (sw<u>ā</u>r) *swore, sworn* 1. to make a serious promise. *He swore to her that he was telling the truth.* 2. to use angry or bad language. *He* **swore at** *the car when it didn't start.*

sweat *verb* (sw<u>e</u>t) to give off a liquid through the skin. *I was so nervous that my palms were sweating.*
noun [N] the liquid that comes out from the skin. *She was covered with sweat after running.*

sweater *noun* (sw<u>e</u> tər) a warm piece of clothing that is worn on the upper body. *I knitted a sweater for my husband.*

sweatshirt *noun* (sw<u>e</u>t shərt) a thick cotton shirt that is often worn during exercise.

sweep *verb* (sw<u>ē</u>p) *swept, swept* to clear the floor of dirt or dust. *The maid swept the floor with a broom.*

sweet *adj.* (sw<u>ē</u>t) 1. having a taste like that of sugar or honey. *I love this sweet chocolate.* 2. gentle or pleasant. *She is a sweet girl and very polite.*

Word Builder: sweet +
sweeten: to make sweet or sweeter.

sweet potato *noun* (sw<u>ē</u>t pə t<u>ā</u> t<u>ō</u>) an orange root that is eaten as a vegetable.

swell *verb* (sw<u>e</u>l) *swelled, swollen (swelled)* to become larger because of growth or pressure. *The crowd swelled as the night went on.* | *An infection caused his foot to swell.*

Word Builder: swell +
swelling: an area of the body that is swollen.

swept *verb* (sw<u>e</u>pt) past tense and past participle of **sweep.**

swim *verb* (sw<u>i</u>m) *swam, swum* to move through water by moving parts of the body. *My dog swam across the pond to get a stick.*

Word Builder: swim +
swimsuit: the clothing that you wear when you swim.

swimming *noun* (sw<u>i</u> ming) [N] the activity of moving your body through water. *Swimming is my favorite sport.*

swimming

Word Builder: swimming +
swimming pool: a large tub or container of water to swim in.

swing *verb* (sw<u>i</u>ng) *swung, swung* to move or cause to move backward and forward around a point. *He swung the door open.* | *The door swung on its hinges.*
noun a seat hung from ropes or chains on which one sits and moves back and forth for pleasure. *She played on a swing at the park.*

swipe *verb* (sw<u>ī</u>p) 1. (informal) to take something without permission; steal. *Who swiped my pencil?* 2. to move through a special machine that reads information contained in a piece of magnetic tape. *The cashier swiped my credit card and then entered the purchase amount.* 3. to try to hit something by making a sweeping motion. *The cat swiped at the dog's nose.*

switch *noun* (swich) 1. a device that opens and closes an electric circuit. *The light switch is on the wall near the door.* 2. a change. *We made a big switch in our lives when we moved from the city to the country.*
verb to exchange; trade. *The teacher was a little confused when the students switched places.*
switch off to stop the flow of electricity to something. *Please switch off the lights before you go to bed.*
switch on to start the flow of electricity to something. *Read the instructions before you switch on the machine.*

swollen *verb* (swō lən) a past participle of **swell.**
adj. made larger because of infection or injury. *He has a swollen finger.*

swore *verb* (swōr) past tense of **swear.**

sworn *verb* (swōrn) past participle of **swear.**

swum *verb* (swəm) past participle of **swim.**

swung *verb* (swəng) past tense and past participle of **swing.**

syllable *noun* (si lə bəl) a part of a word with one vowel sound. *The word happy has two syllables.*

symbol *noun* (sim bəl) an object or picture that represents something else. *The rose is a symbol of love.*

sympathetic *adj.* (sim pə the tik) feeling or showing understanding. *He is a sympathetic person who listened to me when I was unhappy.*

sympathy *noun* (sim pə the) 1. [N] a feeling of caring for a person who is sad. *I thanked my friends for their expressions of sympathy after my mother died.* 2. [N] an agreement of emotion between people. *I have no sympathy for people who refuse to help themselves.*

symptom *noun* (simp təm) something that happens in the body that shows that there is a disease or something wrong. *High fever, headache, and muscle aches are symptoms of the flu.*

synonym *noun* (sin ə nim) a word that has the same or nearly the same meaning as another word of the same language. *Big and large are synonyms.*

syrup (sirup) *noun* (ser əp) 1. [N] a thick, sweet liquid. *I put maple syrup on my pancakes.* 2. [N] a thick, sweet liquid that contains medicine. *The doctor prescribed cough syrup for my daughter.*

system *noun* (si stəm) 1. a group of things or parts that work together as a whole. *This is a large school system.* 2. a particular way or method of doing something. *We need a better voting system.* | *He's got a system for getting his office work done.*

T t

table *noun* (tā bəl) 1. a piece of furniture with a flat top, supported by one or more legs. *Only four people can sit at our kitchen table.* 2. an organized arrangement of information laid out in rows and columns. *The table in the science book showed the weights of different mammals.*

tablespoon *noun* (tā bəl spoon) 1. a large spoon used for serving or eating soup or other foods. 2. a standard unit used to measure small amounts in cooking.

tablet *noun* (tæ blit) a small, flat, round piece of medicine. *The doctor said to take two tablets before meals.*

taco *noun* (ta kō) a flat, round form of bread made from flour or ground corn and filled with meat, beans, or cheese.

 — taco

tag *noun* (tæg) a piece of thick paper, thin metal, or plastic that gives information and is attached to something. *Everyone was wearing a name tag at the meeting.* | *The price tag shows that this shirt is on sale.*

tail *noun* (tāl) 1. a part of an animal's body that sticks out from the back end. *The dog shakes his tail when he is happy.* 2. the bottom or end part of anything. *You should tuck in the tail of your shirt.* | *The kite's tail waved in the wind.*

tailor *noun* (tā lər) a person who makes or fixes clothes so they fit a person well.

take *verb* (tāk) *took, taken* 1. to cause to be in one's hands. *She took the flowers from me and put them in the vase.* 2. to carry away; remove. *That dog took my hat.* 3. to get something through strength or ability. *The army took the city.* | *He took first prize at the fair.* 4. to use for travel. *She takes the bus to work.* 5. to be part of a class that studies something. *He will take history next semester.* 6. to live through; react to something bad in a calm way. *I can't take this cold weather.* | *He took the bad news pretty well.* 7. to make something necessary; require. *This job takes a lot of time and effort.* | *It takes two hours to drive there.* 8. to carry or lead to a place or in a certain direction. *Please*

take this box upstairs. | *I have to take the baby-sitter home.*

take back to take possession again of something that you gave to another person. *He gave me his bicycle but took it back a week later.*

take off 1. to remove. *Take off your shoes, and leave them by the door.* 2. to go up into the air. *The plane **took off from** the New York airport at noon.*

take over to begin to have control of something. *New management took over the company.*

take-home pay *noun* (tāk hōm pā) [N] the money that you receive for your work after all payments for taxes and insurance have been made. *Sandra's take-home pay is about 400 dollars a week.*

taken *verb* (tā kən) past participle of **take.**

tale *noun* (tāl) a story. *Our grandmother told us tales from the old country.*

talent *noun* (tæ lənt) a natural skill or ability. *He has a talent for music.*

> **Word Builder: talent +**
> **talent show:** a show where several people perform something that they have special skill or ability in.

talk *verb* (tawk) to communicate by speaking. *Can the baby talk yet?*
noun 1. a conversation or discussion. *They had a long talk about school.* 2. a speech given to an audience. *We went to hear a talk at the library last night.*
talk into to convince someone to do something. *I needed to study, but Bill talked me into going to a movie.*
talk out of to convince someone not to do something. *Mary talked me out of wearing the red dress.*
talk over to discuss. *Sean talked over his problems with his parents.* | *Let's talk it over before we make a decision.*

tall *adj.* (tawl) 1. of more than average height. *People who play basketball are often tall.* 2. being a certain height. *Mel is four feet tall.*

tally *noun* (tæ lē) the written record of a total. *Here is the tally of what you owe me.*
verb to find the total of; count or add. *At the end of the game, we tallied our points.*

tame *adj.* (tām) taken from a wild state, but gentle and not afraid of people. *A tame bear travels with the circus.*

tan *adj.* (tăn) having a light brown color.

tangle *verb* (tăng gəl) to be or become mixed up or knotted. *Long hair tangles if you don't comb it.*

tank *noun* (tăngk) 1. a large container used to hold liquid or gas. *The gas tank in a car is behind the rear seat.* 2. a large, strong military vehicle with heavy guns. *Tanks fired at the enemy's position.*

tap¹ *verb* (tăp) to hit with little force. *She tapped her fingers on the desk.*

tap² *noun* (tăp) a device that controls the flow of liquid or gas from a pipe or faucet. *He turned on the tap and began to wash the dishes.*

tape *noun* (tāp) 1. [N] a substance made of plastic, cloth, or paper that usually has glue on one side. It is cut into long, narrow pieces. Tape is used to stick things together. *Paul hung the photograph on the wall with tape.* 2. a long piece of special plastic used to record sounds and pictures. Tape is often inside a cassette. *Kenny watched a tape of his favorite movie.*
verb 1. to fasten, hold together, or fix with tape. *Betty taped her ankle after she twisted it.* 2. to record on tape. *Mr. Garcia taped the school play with his new camcorder.*

tape measure *noun* (tāp me zhər) a tool for measuring length. It is made of a long, narrow piece of cloth or thin metal. *Use a tape measure to find out how long the table is.*

target *noun* (tar git) 1. a thing that you aim at and want to hit. *She shot her arrow and hit the target.* | *The army's target was the weapons factory.* 2. a thing that you want to reach; goal. *His target was to finish the project by December.*

task *noun* (tăsk) a piece of work to be done; duty. *I have several tasks to complete at work today.*

taste *verb* (tāst) 1. to tell the flavor of something by putting it into your mouth. *She tasted the soup to see if it needed more salt.* 2. to have a particular flavor. *This milk tastes sour.*
noun 1. the flavor of something. *Chocolate has a sweet taste.* 2. a small amount of a food. *She had **a taste of** cake.* 3. [N] the ability to know what is beautiful and good. *She has good **taste in** music.*

taught *verb* (tawt) past tense and past participle of **teach.**

tax *noun* (tăks) the money that you pay to a government. The government uses the money to provide services. *Our taxes pay for schools, roads, and many other important things.*
verb to place a tax on. *The government taxes gasoline and cigarettes.*

taxi *noun* (tăk sē) a short form of **taxicab.**

taxicab *noun* (tăk sē kăb) a car that carries people who pay for a ride. *Lisa **took a taxicab** from the bus station to her apartment.*

taxicab

TB *abbrev.* (tē bē) [N] an abbreviation for **tuberculosis.**

tea *noun* (tē) [N] a drink that is made by putting dried leaves of certain plants in hot water. The leaves usually come from a special plant that grows in Asia. *I'd like a **cup of tea** with milk and sugar, please.*

Word Builder: tea +
tea bag: a small bag made of thin paper for holding tea leaves. You pour water over the tea bag to make tea.
teacup: a cup from which you drink tea.
teapot: a pot in which you make tea.

teach *verb* (tēch) *taught, taught* to show someone how to do something or to help someone learn something. *Jenny taught her brother how to tie his shoe.* | *He is teaching me the names of the fifty states.*

teacher *noun* (tē chər) a person whose job is teaching. *He is a teacher in an elementary school.*

team *noun* (tēm) a group formed to play or work together. *A team of scientists worked on the problem.* | *My sister is a member of the volleyball team.*

Word Builder: team +
teammate: a person who is on a team with you.
teamwork: work done together with others.

tear¹ *noun* (tēr) a drop of liquid that comes from the eye. Tears clean the eye and keep it wet. Tears often express sadness or deep emotion. *Donald's eyes filled with tears when he heard the sad news.*

tear² *verb* (tār) *tore, torn* 1. to pull apart or into pieces. *She tore the paper in half.* 2. to damage or make a hole in something by ripping. *The child tore her dress.*
noun the result of tearing. *His shirt has a tear.*

tear down to destroy. *The city tore down the old building.*

tear up to pull apart into small pieces. *She tore up the letter in anger.*

teaspoon *noun* (te̅ spoon) 1. a standard unit used to measure very small amounts in cooking. 2. a small spoon used with tea, coffee, or ice cream.

technical *adj.* (tek ni kəl) 1. needing special skills. *They hired someone to deal with the technical problems.* 2. having a special meaning within a certain field; containing words that have a special meaning. *The word mouse is a technical term when it refers to a computer part.* | *These instructions are too technical. I can't understand them.*

technique *noun* (tek ne̅k) a particular way of doing something. *He learned several techniques for baking bread.*

technology *noun* (tek na lə jī) 1. [N] a field of knowledge having to do with the use of science and industry to help solve common problems of life. *Technology is used to help solve energy problems.* 2. [N] products that are developed using knowledge from science and industry. *Doctors are aided by medical technology.* | *New forms of communication technology include cell phones that can take photographs.*

teenager *noun* (te̅n ā jər) a person of age thirteen through nineteen years. *She has changed a lot since she became a teenager.*

teeth *noun* (te̅th) plural of **tooth.**

telephone *noun* (te lə fo̅n) a piece of electronic equipment that sends and receives sound over long distances. A telephone has a part for speaking into and a part for listening. *Please* **answer the telephone.** | ***Hang up the telephone*** *when you are done with your call.*

verb to call or speak to someone by telephone. *I telephone my mother every week.*

Word Builder: telephone +
telephone book: a book with a list of telephone customers, their numbers, and other information.
telephone number: the number a telephone company gives to a customer.

television *noun* (te lə vi zhən) a piece of electronic equipment that receives sound and moving images that are sent from a long distance. Many people can watch the same programs on television at the same time. *Our new television has a huge screen.* | *I always watch the news* **on television** *at six o'clock.*

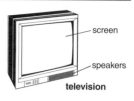
screen
speakers
television

tell *verb* (tel) **told, told** 1. to give information to someone. *He told me that she was sick.* | *She told me about her problems at work.* 2. to express in spoken or written words. *His mother always tells him a story before he goes to sleep.* | *She told a lie.* 3. to command. *Please tell the children to be quiet.* 4. to recognize. *He can't* **tell the difference between** *my twin brother and me.* | *Can you tell if this meat is still fresh?*

tell or say?
Say is used to report the words that someone spoke. The emphasis with *say* is on words.
Tell is used to report an act of communication between people. The emphasis with *tell* is on both the person who receives a message and the message itself.
Compare:
She said that she was sick.
She told me that she was sick.

teller *noun* (te lər) a person who works in a bank. A teller takes in and pays out money.

temper *noun* (tem pər) 1. [N] a state of mind or emotion at a specific time. *He's* **in a bad temper** *today.* 2. a tendency to become angry fast. *Try to control your temper.*

temperature *noun* (tem pər ə chər) 1. the degree of heat or cold in an object or an environment. *The temperature is higher in the afternoon than in the evening.* 2. a condition when the body is warmer than normal because of illness; fever. *John stayed in bed because he had a temperature.*

temporary *adj.* (tem pər ār e̅) lasting a short time; not permanent. *I have a temporary job just for the summer.*

ten *noun* (ten) the word for the number 10.

tenant *noun* (te nənt) a person or group that rents space to live or work in. *Tenants in this building must pay rent on the first day of the month.*

tend *verb* (tend) to be likely to feel or act in a certain way. *He tends to be shy.* | *This dog tends to bark a lot.*

tendency *noun* (<u>ten</u> dən sē) the fact of being likely to feel or act in a certain way. *Babies have a tendency to cry when they're hungry.*

tender *adj.* (<u>ten</u> dər) 1. not tough; soft. *This is a tender piece of meat.* 2. showing love; gentle. *Catherine spoke tender words to her baby.*

tennis *noun* (<u>te</u> nis) [N] a game that is played on a court by two or four people. They hit a small ball to each other over a low net, using a special net attached to a stick.

tense[1] *adj.* (<u>tens</u>) 1. pulled or stretched tight. *My muscles are still tense from lifting those heavy boxes.* 2. feeling nervous and not able to relax. *Elena is tense when she gets home from work.*

tense[2] *noun* (<u>tens</u>) the form of verbs that shows when an action happens. In English, verbs change their form to show past or present time. In the sentence "I stopped the car," the verb *stopped* is in the past tense.

tension *noun* (<u>ten</u> shən) [N] physical or mental pressure. *Michael has tension in his shoulders from working at a computer all day.* | *Not having enough money can cause tension in a marriage.*

tent *noun* (<u>tent</u>) a shelter held up by poles and rope and made of cloth or plastic. *We set up a tent in the forest and stayed there for a week.*

tent

tenth *adj.* (<u>tenth</u>) next after ninth.
noun one of ten equal parts of a whole.

term *noun* (<u>tərm</u>) 1. a word or phrase for something, especially related to a particular job or subject. *Zip drive is a computer term.* 2. a period of time during which something happens. *The president's **term in office** is four years.* | *Larry did not go to school during the spring term.*

terminal *adj.* (<u>tər</u> mi nəl) ending in death. *He has a terminal illness.*
noun 1. a part or point at the end of a wire where you can make an electric connection. *The electrician attached a cable to the terminal.* 2. a place where vehicles stop that is at one end of a road or course of travel. *We met our cousins at the bus terminal.* 3. a screen and small computer connected to a large computer. *Donna's job is to work at a terminal and enter data.*

terminate *verb* (<u>tər</u> mi nāt) to bring to an end. *The company terminated her employment.*

termination *noun* (<u>tər</u> mi <u>nā</u> shən) the act of ending something. *There will be a termination of benefits when you leave this job.*

terrace *noun* (<u>ter</u> əs) 1. a flat surface often covered with brick or concrete outside a building. *We often eat dinner on the terrace in the summer.* 2. a flat, raised section of ground. *The side of the hill was made into terraces for farming.*

terrible *adj.* (<u>te</u> ri bəl) 1. severe or extreme. *She has a terrible case of the flu.* 2. very bad; not acceptable. *Margaret got a terrible evaluation at work.*

territory *noun* (<u>te</u> ri tōr ē) 1. an area of land that belongs to and is governed by a country. *The territory of the United States includes Alaska and Hawaii.* 2. an area of land marked by certain natural features or claimed by an animal as its own. *Animals often fight to protect their territory.*

terror *noun* (<u>te</u> rər) 1. [N] a very great fear. *Spiders fill him with terror.* 2. [N] an act of violence that causes great fear. *The bomb explosion was an act of terror.*

Word Builder: terror +
terrorism: the practice of using terror for political gain.
terrorist: a person who uses terror for political gain.

test *noun* (<u>test</u>) 1. an examination or experiment to find out what something is, what it is made up of, or how good it is. *A blood test is part of a complete physical exam.* | *Tests showed that the water was safe for drinking.* 2. a set of questions or tasks designed to find out how much someone knows about something or about their ability to do something. *She gives us a test at the end of every math lesson.* | *He's taking his driver's test tomorrow.*
verb to check or examine using a test. *The doctor tested my hearing.* | *The teacher tested us on two chapters of the math book.*

Word Builder: test +
testing: the process of giving and taking tests.

text *noun* (tekst) 1. the main part of a printed work, not including such things as the title, headings, and questions. *You can skip the questions at the end of each chapter and read only the text.* 2. [N] words that appear in anything written or printed. *This dictionary has both text and pictures.* 3. a textbook. *Please remember to bring your text to class every day.*

textbook *noun* (tekst buk) a book used for teaching a particular subject. *The students are using a new history textbook this year.*

textile *noun* (teks tīl) cloth. *That factory makes textiles.*

than *conj.* (thæn) 1. compared to or compared with. *She is taller than you.* 2. except; but. *I have no coat **other than** this.*

thank *verb* (thæŋk) to tell someone who has given you something or done something for you that you value the gift or action; to express your appreciation. *I **thanked** him **for** his help.*

thank you used to express thanks. *Thank you for the beautiful flowers.*

Word Builder: thank +
thankful: showing or feeling that you thank someone for something.
thankless: difficult and not likely to be appreciated.

thanks *pl. noun* (thæŋks) a feeling or expression of your feeling that you value something that is given to you. *We want to express our thanks to you for the wonderful gift.*
interj. thank you. *Thanks. You helped me a lot.*

Thanksgiving *noun* (thæŋks gi ving) a U.S. holiday held on the fourth Thursday in November. On Thanksgiving, Americans show thanks for what they have. *Turkey is a traditional food for Thanksgiving.*

Thanksgiving dinner

that *pron.* (thæt) *those* 1. the person, thing, or idea mentioned or understood. *They said she quit, but that isn't true.* 2. the one that is further away or less in mind. *This book is more interesting than that.* 3. a wordused to introduce a clause that describes the thing just mentioned. *The puppy that I chose is now my best friend.*
adj. 1. the person, thing, or matter as mentioned or understood. *That woman from the bank called me again this morning.* 2. used to indicate the one that is further

away or less in mind. *That lamp over there is better for reading.* | *When you said you liked Jim, I didn't know you meant that Jim.*
adv. to such a degree. *I can't run that far without getting tired.*
conj. used to introduce a clause that is the subject or object of the main verb. *That she was angry was clear to everyone.* | *We know that she likes flowers.*

the *art.* (thə or thē) 1. used before nouns or noun phrases to tell the listener that the thing you are talking about is the one that you have already mentioned or the one that is made clear from information that you give in the sentence. *I saw a nice chair and lamp in the store, but I decided to buy only the chair and not the lamp.* | *The window that is in my room is broken.* 2. used before nouns or noun phrases when the thing you are talking about is the only one in the world or is the one that everyone knows. *Look at the moon!* | *The president will give a speech on TV tonight.*
adv. used in comparisons to show that two things happen at the same time. *The older I get, the more I forget things.*

theater *noun* (thē tər) a building where plays, movies, or concerts are presented. *There is a movie theater at the mall.*

theft *noun* (theft) an act of stealing. *Mrs. Jones reported **the theft of** her car to the police.* | *A theft occurred at her office last week.*

their *adj.* (thār) of or belonging to them; a possessive form of **they.** *We went to their wedding.*

theirs *pron.* (thārz) the one that belongs to them; a possessive form of **they.** *Our car is green, and theirs is red.* | *These books are theirs.*

them *pron.* (them) persons or things already mentioned; form of **they** that is used as the object of a verb or that is used after a preposition. *I told them to stay home.* | *When they asked for the money, I gave it to them.*

themselves *pron.* (them selvz) 1. a word used to show that an action is done to or in connection with the same people who perform the action. *Children soon learn to feed themselves.* | *They bought themselves some clothes.* | *They can take care of themselves.* 2. they and no one else. *They built the house themselves.*

then *adv.* (then) 1. at a time in the past. *Life was hard then, but we are all right now.* 2. soon after; next. *The game ended, and then we went home.* 3. as a result of that. *If she stays, then I will leave.*
noun that time. *John broke his leg last month and has not walked since then.*

theory *noun* (thēr ē) a statement that explains why something happens but has not been proven. *The police have a theory about who stole the jewels.* | *The scientists discussed theories about the beginning of life on Earth.*

there *adv.* (thār) 1. in, at, or to that place. *I'll be there in the morning.* | *Go there, and you will see how beautiful it is.* 2. used to call attention to something or someone. *There they are!*
pron. 1. that place. *She sleeps in there.* 2. a word used with the verb *be* to say that something exists or happens. *There are several big trees in front of that house.* | *There was a terrible storm last night.* | *There's a man at the front door.*

therefore *adv.* (thār fōr) for that reason. *The army was not prepared to fight and therefore lost the battle.* | *This product is not what I ordered. Therefore, I am returning it to your company.*

thermometer *noun* (thər ma mə tər) an instrument for measuring temperature. *The thermometer says it is ten degrees outside.*

thermometer

these *adj.* (thēz) plural of **this.** *These clothes aren't mine.*
pron. plural of **this.** *These are the shoes that I want.*

they *pron.* (thā) 1. people, things, or animals already talked about. *If your parents come, they can stay at our house.* 2. people; everyone. *They say it will snow a lot this winter.*

thick *adj.* (thik) 1. large from one side of a surface to the other side; not thin. *These boots have thick soles.* 2. measured from one side to the other. *The wall is six inches thick.* 3. having parts that are very close to each other. *We walked slowly through the thick forest.*

Word Builder: thick +
thicken: to make or become thick or thicker.
thickness: how thick something is.

thief *noun* (thēf) *thieves* a person who steals. *A thief took all our money.*

thieves *pl. noun* (thēvz) plural of **thief.**

thin *adj.* (thin) 1. small when measured from one side to the other or when measured around the outside; not thick. *It's dangerous to walk on thin ice.* | *The children were thin and hungry.* | *Don't use that thin string to tie the package. It will break.* 2. small in quantity and not close together. *The grass is thin under the trees.* | *My hair is getting thin.*

thing *noun* (thing) 1. an object that is not alive. *Please put these things in the drawer.* 2. that which people speak of, think of, or do. *That was a mean thing to say.* | *That is the thing that made me angry.* | *Don't do a thing without telling me.*

think *verb* (thingk) *thought, thought* 1. to judge or reason about something. *I can't answer yet. I'm still **thinking about** your question.* 2. to have an opinion or belief. *I **think of** my parents **as** good people.* | *What do you **think of** the new manager?* 3. to form a new idea. *I need to think of something to get her for her birthday.* 4. to have as an opinion; believe; feel. *I think she's beautiful.* | *She thinks that he's honest.* 5. to expect; believe. *I think he's coming at two o'clock.* 6. to remember or have in mind. *She was thinking how happy she had been.* | *He was thinking of his grandfather.*
think over to give serious thought to. *We are still thinking over our decision.*
think up to invent a new idea. *He thought up an excuse for being late.*

third *adj.* (thərd) next after second.
noun one of three equal parts of a whole.

thirst *noun* (thərst) [N] the feeling that you need or want to drink something. *After playing tennis, I had a terrible thirst.*

Word Builder: thirst +
thirsty: feeling thirst.

thirteen *noun* (thər tēn) the word for the number 13.

thirty *noun* (thər te) the word for the number 30.

this *pron.* (<u>this</u>) *these* 1. the person, thing, or matter that is present or being talked about. *This is my father.* | *Let's talk about this later.* 2. the person or thing that is closer in time or space than any other one of its kind; the one that you see as closer in your mind. *You take that over there, and I'll take this.* 3. the statement or event that is about to come. *I'll play the song now. Listen to this.*
adj. 1. used to indicate a person or thing as the one that is present or being talked about. *What is this game that the kids are playing?* | *Did you already know this man, the one you're talking about?* 2. used to indicate a person or thing as closer than any other of its kind in time or space; appearing to be closer in your mind. *Put the box here in this corner.* 3. used to indicate a statement or event about to come. *Listen to this joke!*
adv. to the degree or extent that is being indicated. *Is it always this cold here?* | *Her homework is not usually this difficult.*

thorough *adj.* (<u>thər</u> ō) complete; considering every detail. *The police made a thorough search of the house.*

those *adj.* (<u>thōz</u>) plural of **that.** *Those boxes have to be moved.*
pron. plural of **that.** *Whose shoes are those?*

though *conj.* (<u>thō</u>) 1. used to connect two parts of a sentence when the meaning of one part seems to disagree with the other. *Though the sun was shining this morning, it was cold.* 2. even if. *He continues to try, though he may never succeed.*
adv. used when a second statement seems to disagree with the first; however. *My brother likes to read. He's not a good student, though.*

thought *noun* (<u>thawt</u>) 1. [N] the act, process, or power of thinking. *Making a good decision requires a lot of thought.* 2. the result of thinking; a single idea. *I have two thoughts about your plan.*
verb past tense and past participle of **think.**

thousand *noun* (<u>thow</u> zənd) the name for the number 1,000.

thread *noun* (<u>thred</u>) a very thin, long string that is used to weave and sew cloth. *She bought thread to match the cloth for the dress she is making.* | *He cut a few loose threads from the edge of the cloth.*

thread and needle

threat *noun* (<u>thret</u>) a statement that someone will harm or punish some person or group. *He used threats to prevent them from calling the police.*

threaten *verb* (<u>thre</u> tən) to say that you will harm or punish some person or group. *The judge threatened to send him to jail.*

three *noun* (<u>thre</u>) the word for the number 3.

threw *verb* (<u>throo</u>) past tense of **throw.**

thrill *verb* (<u>thril</u>) to make someone excited or very happy. *Skiing fast thrills me.* | *Getting a bicycle for her birthday thrilled her.*
noun something that makes you suddenly excited or happy. *It was a thrill to meet the president.*

throat *noun* (<u>thrōt</u>) the part of the body through which food and air pass to the stomach and lungs.

through *prep.* (<u>throo</u>) 1. in one side or end of something and out the other. *Water goes through this pipe.* | *I can't push the needle through this thick material.* 2. by way or means of; because of. *I met them through my father.* | *We learn through experience.* 3. from the beginning to the end of something. *He slept through the afternoon.* 4. up to and including. *The store is open Monday through Saturday. It is only closed on Sunday.*
adj. finished. *When you are **through with** dinner, you should do your homework.* | *If you are through, I'll take your plate.*

throughout *prep.* (throo <u>owt</u>) in, during, or to every part of something. *People celebrated the holiday throughout the country.* | *The party lasted throughout the night.*
adv. in, during, or including every part. *His body is still strong throughout.*

throw *verb* (<u>thrō</u>) *threw, thrown* to send something through the air using your arm. *He threw the baseball over the fence.*
throw away to put something that you do not want in a thing or place that takes it away from you. *You should not throw away things that you can still use.* | *Why are you keeping this old cheese? Throw it away!*
throw up to bring up food and liquid from your stomach through your mouth. *I had a fever, and I threw up.*

thrown *verb* (<u>thrōn</u>) past participle of **throw.**

thumb *noun* (th<u>ə</u>m) the short, thick first finger on the hand.

thunder *noun* (th<u>ə</u>n dər) [N] the loud noise you sometimes hear during a violent rainstorm. *My children are afraid of thunder and lightning.*

Word Builder: thunder +
thunderstorm: a storm with thunder, lightning, and rain.

Thursday *noun* (th<u>ə</u>rz dā) the fifth day of the week. Thursday comes between Wednesday and Friday.

ticket *noun* (ti kit) 1. a small piece of paper that shows that you have paid for something. *You must show your ticket to get into the theater.* | *I went to pick up my shirts at the laundry, but I forgot my ticket.* 2. a notice that a police officer gives that says that you broke the law. *My father got two tickets last year for driving too fast.*

tide *noun* (t<u>ī</u>d) the change in the height of the surface of oceans that happens about every twelve hours. Tides are caused by the pull of the moon and sun.

tie *noun* (t<u>ī</u>) 1. the short form of **necktie**. *He wears a tie to work.* 2. a condition in which each competitor in a game or race has the same number of points. *Our team finally won the game when we broke the tie.*
verb to fasten with something like a string or rope. *He tied the boat to the dock.* | *She tied her hair back with a ribbon.*
tie up 1. to tie someone or something with something like a rope to prevent that person or thing from moving. *He tied up the store owner and stole the money.* 2. to require a lot of time and attention so that you cannot do other things. *My business has been really tying me up recently.*

tiger *noun* (t<u>ī</u> gər) a large, strong mammal in the cat family that has light brown fur with black stripes.

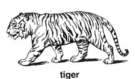
tiger

tight *adj.* (t<u>ī</u>t) having too little space around; too close in fit. *I need new shoes because these are too tight.*
adv. in a close, firm, or safe way. *The glue held the pieces together tight.* | *Her eyes were shut tight.* | *She held her baby tight.*

Word Builder: tight +
tighten: to make tight or tighter.
tightness: the condition of being tight.

till¹ *prep.* (til) up to a certain time; until. *I have to work till six o'clock tonight.*
conj. up to the time when; until. *They watched TV till it was time to go to bed.*

till² *noun* (til) a drawer for holding money in a store. Money from customers goes into the till, and customers receive change from it.

time *noun* (t<u>ī</u>m) 1. [N] the passing of minutes, hours, days, weeks, and years. 2. [N] the amount of minutes, hours, weeks, days, years between the beginning and the end of an event. *How much time do you need to finish the work?* 3. a particular instance or event. *I remember the time you broke your leg.* | *She called me two times.* 4. the period or point when a particular activity or event usually happens. *It's time for dinner.* 5. a moment or moments as shown on a clock or calendar. *What time does the play start?* 6. [N] available moments for an activity. *She never has time to talk.* 7. the period spent at work in a given day or week. *I work **full-time.*** 8. an experience. *Did you **have** a nice **time** at the party?*
verb to record the rate of an action or how long it continues. *I timed his mile run at 5 minutes 40 seconds.*
all the time very often. *I go to that restaurant all the time.*
for the time being just for now; for a short time only. *You can put the box on the table for the time being.*
in time having just enough time to do the thing that you want. *We ran to the train station and arrived just in time to catch the train.*
on time at the correct time for an event that is planned. *I usually get to work on time.*
take one's time to do something without the need to hurry. *You don't have to finish right now. Please take your time.*

Word Builder: time +
time card: a card on which you record the hours you work.
time clock: a clock in a workplace that records the hours people work.
timer: a thing for telling a specific amount of time.

time zone *noun* (t<u>ī</u>m zōn) a region in which all the clocks are set to the same time. The time in each region is different from the time in the next region. *It's four o'clock in the morning in their time zone, so we can't call them now.*

tint *verb* (t<u>i</u>nt) to give a different color to something. *We tinted the curtains pink.* | *She tints her hair.*

tiny *adj.* (t<u>i</u> nē) very small. *This kitten is tiny.* | *She has a tiny house for her dolls.*

tip[1] *noun* (t<u>i</u>p) 1. the end of something that comes to a point; something that is long and narrow. *Touch it with the tip of your finger.* 2. the highest point; top. *There is snow at the tip of the mountain.*

tip[2] *verb* (t<u>i</u>p) to move to a leaning position. *She tipped the bowl to get the last drops of soup.*
tip over to make something fall down that was standing up. *The dog tipped over the lamp.*

tip[3] *noun* (t<u>i</u>p) 1. the money that you give to someone to thank him or her for service. *I gave the taxi driver a good tip.* 2. a small, useful idea. *This magazine has good tips for cooking.*

tire[1] *verb* (t<u>ī</u>r) 1. to take a person's strength or energy away. *Swimming today really tired me.* 2. to make someone lose interest or get bored. *The long speech tired everybody.*

tire[2] *noun* (t<u>ī</u>r) a round, rubber object that fits around a wheel. *My car needs new tires.*

tired *adj.* (t<u>ī</u>rd) 1. needing sleep or rest. *She was tired, so she went to bed early.* | *My legs are tired from climbing those stairs.* 2. bored; having no more interest in doing something. *I'm **tired of** watching TV. Let's go out.*

tiring *adj.* (t<u>ī</u>r ing) causing a loss of strength or energy. *I love my job, but it is tiring.*

tissue *noun* (t<u>i</u> shoo) 1. [N] the material that a plant or animal is made of. There are many different kinds of tissue, such as muscle tissue or fat tissue in humans. *He injured many layers of tissue when he burned himself.* 2. a soft, thin paper that you use to clean an area such as your nose. *Do you have a tissue? I'm going to sneeze.*

title *noun* (t<u>ī</u> təl) 1. a name of something such as a book, movie, or piece of music. *I can't remember the title of the book.* 2. a word used with or instead of a name to show a person's position or occupation. *He uses the title* Doctor, *not* Mister. 3. a legal right to own something such as property or the document that proves it. *She has the title to this house.*

to *prep.* (t<u>oo</u>) 1. in the direction of; toward. *We took the road that goes to town.* | *They're waving to me.* 2. as far as. *We took the elevator to the third level.* 3. indicating something received or owned. *The towel belongs to her.* | *The letter is addressed to you.* 4. in connection with. *She is kind to her brother.* 5. used with; intended for. *This is the key to the house.* 6. used before a verb to show the infinitive or by itself in the place of a verb that is understood. *Do you want to sing? Yes, I want to.*

toad *noun* (t<u>ō</u>d) a small, jumping animal with rough skin, long back legs, and no tail. Toads are born in the water, but they live on land.

toast[1] *noun* (t<u>ō</u>st) [N] thin pieces of bread that have been heated until they become brown. *She always eats toast for breakfast.*
verb to make brown by heating. *We toasted the cheese sandwiches for lunch.*

toast[2] *noun* (t<u>ō</u>st) an invitation to other people to drink in honor of someone or something. *He made a toast to celebrate the wedding.*

toaster *noun* (t<u>ō</u> stər) a small electric appliance used to heat and brown bread or rolls.

tobacco *noun* (tə b<u>æ</u> kō) [N] a plant with large, sticky leaves that people smoke or the leaves themselves.

today *noun* (tə d<u>ā</u>) 1. the day that is right now. *Today is the first day of school.* 2. the present time in general. *The computers of today are smaller and faster.*
adv. on or during the present day. *I'm not going to work today.*

toe *noun* (t<u>ō</u>) one of the parts of the foot similar to fingers on the hand.

together *adv.* (tə g<u>e</u> thər) 1. in or into one group or mass. *She mixed the butter and sugar together.* 2. in or into agreement with one another. *The two sides worked together to solve the problem.*

toilet *noun* (t<u>oy</u> lit) a bowl that is filled with water and that has a seat for a person to sit on. A toilet is used for receiving and taking away human waste.

Word Builder: toilet +
toilet paper: the paper that you wipe yourself with after you use the toilet.

toiletry *noun* (toy lə trē) a thing used in cleaning your body or hair. *Soap and shampoo are toiletries.*

told *verb* (tōld) past tense and past participle of **tell.**

tomato *noun* (tə mā tō or tə ma tō) a soft red or yellow vegetable. Tomatoes grow on plants.

tomato

tomorrow *noun* (tə mar ō) 1. the day after today. *Tomorrow is his birthday.* 2. a future time. *Can you imagine the world of tomorrow?*
adv. on the day after today. *I have to get up early tomorrow.*

ton *noun* (tən) a unit of weight equal to 2,000 pounds.

tone *noun* (tōn) 1. a single sound in music or a sound that is similar to music. *When I heard the tone, I left a message.* 2. the quality or character of a sound. *The tone of the old piano is deep and warm.* | *The teacher spoke to the children in a friendly tone.* 3. a particular type of a color. *He painted his walls a strange tone of green.*

tongue *noun* (təng) the organ in the mouth used for tasting and swallowing and also in speaking.

tonight *noun* (tə nīt) [N] the present night or the night that is coming on this day. *Tonight is a good night to see the moon.*
adv. on or during this present or coming night. *Let's go out for dinner tonight.*

too *adv.* (too) 1. also; in addition. *He's smart, and she is too.* 2. to a greater degree than is wanted or to a degree that makes something not possible. *It is too cold to go swimming today.* | *You're speaking too fast. I can't understand.*

took *verb* (tuk) past tense of **take.**

tool *noun* (tool) an instrument such as a hammer that is usually held with the hands. Tools are used for doing work.

tools

Word Builder: tool +
tool belt: a belt with loops and pockets for holding tools while you work.
toolbox: a box for holding tools.
toolkit: a set of tools in a container.

tooth *noun* (tooth) **teeth** 1. one of the hard white objects in rows in the mouth. 2. something that is similar to a tooth. *This comb has two broken teeth.*

Word Builder: tooth +
toothbrush: a brush you clean your teeth with.
toothpaste: a substance that you put on your toothbrush to make your teeth cleaner.

top[1] *noun* (tap) 1. the highest area, point, or surface. *We climbed to the top of the mountain.* 2. a cover, cap, or lid that goes over something. *Put the top on the jar.*
on top of lying on the surface of a something. *The book is on top of the desk.*

top[2] *noun* (tap) a toy that spins on its point.

topic *noun* (ta pik) a subject of discussion, conversation, or writing. *The teacher gave the students a choice of topics to write about.* | *Can we change the topic?*

tore *verb* (tōr) past tense of **tear**[2].

torn *verb* (tōrn) past participle of **tear**[2].

tortilla *noun* (tōr tē yə) a flat bread made from flour or ground corn.

toss *verb* (taws) to throw gently. *Would you toss me that newspaper?*

total *adj.* (tō təl) complete; full. *I paid the total amount that I owed.*
noun the whole amount. *We spent a total of fifty dollars at the restaurant.*

Word Builder: total +
totally: in every way.

totalitarian *adj.* (tō tæ lə tār ē ən) used to describe a kind of government that has complete control over the people. This kind of government does not allow political parties that do not agree with it. *A totalitarian government came into power after the war.*

touch *verb* (təch) 1. to put one's hand or fingers on

something in order to feel it. *She touched the cat's soft fur.* 2. to be together or come together with another thing, leaving no space between. *The tree branch is touching the window.* | *The paper touched the fire and started to burn.*

noun 1. the act or an instance of touching. *He felt a touch on his arm and turned around.* 2. [N] the sense in the brain that tells you how something feels. *He used his sense of touch to find his way through the dark room.*

in touch together through communicating. *Please **keep in touch** after you move to Chicago.* | *Have you been in touch with your parents recently?*

out of touch not being in communication with someone. *I am out of touch with my high school friends.*

tough *adj.* (tәf) 1. hard to break; strong; lasting a long time. *I have a tough car. I have never had to fix it.* 2. difficult to cut or chew. *I can't chew this tough meat.* 3. hard to control; rough. *My son is afraid of those tough kids in the neighborhood.* 4. difficult to do or understand. *Mathematics is really tough for me.*

tour *verb* (toor) to travel through a place to see interesting or important things. *We toured the mountains of Colorado last summer.*

noun a visit to a place with a person who shows you the important or interesting things. *We **took a tour** of the museum.*

tourist *noun* (tur ist) a person who is traveling for pleasure. *Many tourists come to New York City in the summer.*

tow *verb* (tō) to pull along at the end of a rope or chain. *The truck towed our car to the garage.*

toward *prep.* (twōrd) 1. moving or facing in the direction of something. *We walked toward the center of town.* 2. with respect to. *She was friendly toward the new girl in her class.*

towel *noun* (tow әl) a piece of soft cloth or paper used to dry the face, body, dishes, or other things.

tower *noun* (tow әr) a tall, narrow building or part of a building that rises high above the ground. *The king built a castle with tall towers.*

town *noun* (town) 1. an area with streets, houses, and buildings that is similar to a city, but smaller. 2. the business or shopping area of a city or town. *She went to town to get some groceries.*

townhouse *noun* (town hows) a home in a city that is

part of a row of similar homes. It is connected to other homes by shared walls. *My townhouse was located at the end of the row.*

toxic *adj.* (tak sik) containing poison. *The factory put toxic waste into the lake.*

toy *noun* (toy) any object that can be used in play, especially by children. *The child played with her toy while her mother watched.*

toy

trace *noun* (trās) a very small amount of something. *There was a trace of smoke in the air.* | *The police detective found a trace of lipstick on the glass.*

verb to copy by following the lines of something as seen through a thin sheet of paper. *He traced the complicated drawing.*

track *noun* (træk) 1. a pair of connected metal bars on which trains travel. *The train rode along the tracks through the town.* 2. a path or course laid out for running or racing in sports competitions. *He ran around the track every morning.*

keep track of to record the movements or progress of. *The police kept track of where he was at all times.* | *The store owners keep track of everything that they buy and sell.*

lose track of to lose knowledge of or to no longer be able to find. *We were friends for years, but we moved and lost track of each other.*

tractor *noun* (træk tәr) a powerful motor vehicle with large tires used to pull farm machines. *The farmer pulled the plow with the tractor.*

trade *noun* (trād) 1. [N] the act of buying and selling things, especially things that are produced in one country and sold to customers in another country. *There is a lot of trade between the United States and Mexico.* 2. a means of making money to live; business. *Selling cars was my uncle's trade.* 3. a kind of work that involves special skill with the hands. *He is a plumber who learned his trade from his father.*

verb 1. to buy and sell. *She trades shares in the stock market.* 2. to give in return for something else; exchange. *They traded baseball cards.*

trade in to give an old thing, usually a car, in exchange for a new thing. *Jack will trade in his old truck when he buys a new one.*

trademark *noun* (trād mark) a name, symbol, or other mark used to show who made a product. By law, only the company that makes or sells the product may use its trademark.

tradition *noun* (trə dĭ shən) beliefs and ways of doing things that are passed down from older people to younger people. *Many people celebrate holidays by **carrying out** old family **traditions.***

> **Word Builder: tradition +**
> **traditional:** according to tradition.

traffic *noun* (trăf fĭk) [N] vehicles that are moving along a road or path. *Traffic on the road was busy this morning.*

> **Word Builder: traffic +**
> **traffic cop:** a police officer whose job is to direct traffic.
> **traffic jam:** a large number of vehicles in a road that causes traffic to slow or stop.
> **traffic light:** a box with three lights near a road. The red light means vehicles must stop. The yellow light means vehicles must slow down and move with caution. The green light means vehicles may move forward.

trail *verb* (trāl) to follow behind. *The young child **trailed behind** her parents as they walked.* | *The police trailed the suspect all day.*
noun a path or course through a forest or other rural place. *The group followed the trail through the forest to the top of the mountain.*

trailer *noun* (trā lər) a very large metal container that can be pulled by a car or truck. People can live or work in a trailer. It can also be used to move things.

train *noun* (trān) a group of railroad cars connected together that carry people or things from one place to another. *That train can carry fifty people at one time.*
verb to teach skills or actions. *He trained his dog to catch a ball.*

trainee *noun* (trā nē) one who is being trained. A trainee learns the skills and duties of a new job.

training *noun* (trā ning) [N] instruction that is needed to learn something. *Training is an important part of any new job.*

transact *verb* (trăn zăkt) to perform or be involved in acts of business. *Our company is no longer transacting business with that company.*

transaction *noun* (trăn zăk shən) a single act of doing business. *I **made** two **transactions** at the bank. First, I deposited a check, and then I cashed a check.*

transfer *verb* (trăns fər) 1. to move or carry from one person or place to another. *We transferred our money to our new bank when we moved.* 2. to move from one place or situation to another. *He transferred to New York University from another school last year.* 3. to change from one bus or train to another. *In order to get home, I had to transfer at Central Station.*
noun the act of moving something from one person or place to another. *The transfer of the star player to another team disappointed fans.*

translate *verb* (trănz lāt) to change into the words of another language. *My mother translated the story into English for me.*

> **Word Builder: translate +**
> **translator:** a person whose job is to translate words from one language to another language.

translation *noun* (trănz lā shən) 1. [N] the act of changing writing or speech from one language to another. *She does a lot of translation in her job.* 2. writing or speech that has been changed from one language to another. *Do we have an English translation of this book?*

transmission *noun* (trănz mĭ shən) a system of parts in a vehicle that sends power from the engine to the wheels.

transmit *verb* (trănz mĭt) 1. to send or carry from one person, place, or thing to another. *They transmitted the message to their leader.* | *The television station refused to transmit the program.* 2. to pass on or spread a disease. *Some insects transmit diseases.* | *The doctors are afraid that the child's disease will be transmitted to others.*

transparent *adj.* (trănz păr ənt) letting light pass through so objects can be seen clearly. *Most glass used in windows is transparent.*

transport *verb* (trăns pōrt) to carry from one place to another. *The boat transports cars across the water.*
noun the act of carrying or transporting. *The transport of supplies to the soldiers will require two helicopters.*

transportation *noun* (trăns pər tā shən) [N] the act of moving things or people from one place to another. *In that country, they use buses and trains for transportation more than cars.*

trap *noun* (trăp) a device for catching things, especially animals. *We caught a mouse in the trap.*

trash *noun* (trăsh) [N] anything that is thrown away because it is not wanted. *Did the garbage truck pick up the trash yet?*

> **Word Builder: trash +**
> **trash bag:** a bag for holding trash.
> **trash can:** a large container for holding trash.
> **trash compactor:** a machine that compacts trash, or presses trash into a small space, to make it easier to throw away.

travel *verb* (trăv vəl) to go from place to place. *My father traveled to many countries.*

> **Word Builder: travel +**
> **traveler:** a person who travels.

tray *noun* (trā) a flat, open piece of wood, metal, plastic, or some other material used to carry, hold, or show food, drink, or small things. It often has a low edge. *The waiter carried the food on the tray to the customers.*

tread *verb* (trĕd) *trod (treaded), trodden (trod)* to step or walk on. *They had never trodden that path before.* *noun* [N] the area of a rubber tire that touches the ground. *It is good to have a lot of tread on your car's tires.*

treasure *noun* (trĕ zhər) [N] money or valuable things that have been collected and are considered special. *The queen has treasures worth millions of dollars.*

treasure

treat *verb* (trĕt) 1. to act toward someone or something in a particular way. *The management treats the employees fairly.* | *Her father treats her as if she were a child.* 2. to attempt to cure. *She **treated** her cold **with** hot soup, vitamins, and rest.* 3. to take care of a sick person; give medical attention to. *She **treated** her sick child **with** medicine from the doctor.* | *The doctor treats twenty patients a day.* 4. to pay for food, drink, or entertainment for someone as a kind of gift. *We treated our friends to dinner.*
noun anything considered as a source of pleasure. *Chocolate is his favorite treat.*

treatment *noun* (trĕt mənt) 1. the way a person acts toward another person or thing. *Her treatment of the dog was cruel.* 2. the use of medicine or other means of helping a person get better when sick or hurt. *A good treatment for a cold is to get lots of rest.*

treaty *noun* (trē tē) a formal agreement between two or more countries. *The leaders signed a treaty that ended the long war.*

tree *noun* (trē) a plant that has a long main trunk and many branches. Trees usually grow quite tall. *The tree was covered with leaves.*

trend *noun* (trend) a general course, direction, or tendency. *One bad trend is that many young people do not vote.*

trial *noun* (trī əl) 1. a legal process in which a court decides whether someone is guilty or not. *She proved at her trial that she had not stolen the money.* 2. the act or process of testing. *The new drug is going through more trials to check its safety.*

triangle *noun* (trī ăng gəl) a flat, closed figure that has three straight sides. *The sides of this triangle are all equal.*

tribe *noun* (trīb) a group of people, families, or villages that share the same language, social customs, and ancestors. *She left her tribe to live in the city.*

trick *noun* (trik) 1. a plan to deceive someone. *His lie was a trick to get my money.* 2. an act of skill or magic. *The boy showed his friends his new magic trick.*
verb to deceive someone. *They tricked me into paying twice what this car is worth.*

trigger *noun* (tri gər) the part of a gun that you pull to make it shoot. *He **pulled the trigger** and fired the gun.*

trim *verb* (trim) 1. to make neat or shorter by cutting away some parts. *I trimmed my hair because it was getting too long.* | *He trimmed the bushes.* 2. to decorate. *Our family **trimmed the tree** for Christmas.*
noun material added to decorate the edges of such things as clothing, windows, doors, and cars. *Our car has silver trim on the front.* | *It's a red house with white trim around the windows.*

> **Word Builder: trim +**
> **trimmer:** a tool for trimming something, such as hair or plants.

trip *noun* (trip) the act of traveling from one place to another. *I had to* **make** *two* **trips** *to the store today.* | *My parents* **took a trip** *to Hawaii.*
verb to fall over something. *I* **tripped over** *my son's bicycle in the garage.*

troops *pl. noun* (troops) members of the military; soldiers. *The president sent the troops into battle.*

tropical *adj.* (tra pi kəl) having to do with the tropics; the hot, wet climate in those areas. *The tropical weather made him sweat.*

tropics *pl. noun* (tra piks) the region of the earth that is near the equator and that is known for having a hot climate. *This kind of snake lives only in* **the tropics.**

trouble *verb* (trə bəl) to upset or worry someone. *What is troubling you?*
noun 1. [N] a serious difficulty. *He is* **in trouble with** *the police.* | *I* **have trouble with** *mathematics.* 2. an effort; work. *I'll be happy to feed your cat. It is no trouble at all.*

troubleshoot *verb* (trə bəl shoot) **troubleshot, troubleshot** to search for the cause of a problem. *We'll have to troubleshoot to find out what's wrong with the computer.*

truck *noun* (trək) a large motor vehicle used for carrying heavy loads. *The truck has eight big wheels to support heavy loads.* | *He has a small truck for his plumbing business.*

cab

trailer

truck

Word Builder: truck +
trucker: a person whose job is to drive a truck.

---

true *adj.* (troo) in agreement with fact. *The teacher did not believe that the student's excuse was true.* | *Tell me the true reason that you're leaving.*

Word Builder: true +
truly: in a real or honest way.

---

trunk *noun* (trəngk) 1. the main stem of a tree. *The trunk of the big tree was five feet in diameter.* 2. a large, strong container, often with a lock, used to store or move things. *She brought her trunk into her new room and emptied it.* 3. a large area in the back of a car, used to carry things. *He took the spare tire out of the trunk.*

trust *noun* (trəst) 1. [N] the confidence placed in a person or thing. *They* **put** *all their* **trust in** *the doctors.* | *She* **has** *a lot of* **trust in** *her own ability.* 2. [N] the belief that someone is good, honest, or dependably. *You have* **earned** *my* **trust** *because you have never lied to me.*
verb 1. to have confidence in; to believe that something will produce a good result. *She trusts only her own doctor.* | *I trust your opinion.* | *Don't trust that old ladder! The steps will break.* 2. to believe that someone is good, honest, or dependeable. *It's important to have friends that you trust.* | *Don't leave your money on the table. I don't trust these people.* | *The boss trusts her to count the money.*

truth *noun* (trooth) 1. [N] agreement with the facts; what is real. *There is no truth to that story.* 2. [N] true statements about feelings or things that have happened. *Please* **tell** *me* **the truth** *about the accident.*

try *verb* (trī) 1. to do something in order to achieve some purpose, but without knowing if you will be successful; attempt. *He tried to stand up, but he fell.* | *We tried to finish the project by Friday, but there wasn't enough time.* | *He* **kept trying** *until he found a way to fix his car.* 2. to test something to see if it is good or if it will work well. *Did you try this dessert?* | *Try driving the car before you buy it to find out if it is comfortable to drive.*
try on to put on clothing to see if it is the right size. *She tried on four dresses before making a choice.*
try out to test a thing by using it. *I will try out the bicycle before I buy it.*

T-shirt (tee shirt) *noun* (tē shərt) a soft, informal shirt with short sleeves and no buttons. It can be worn alone or under another shirt.

tub *noun* (təb) 1. a large container with a flat bottom used for washing or storing things. *I washed the dishes in a tub full of soap and water.* 2. a bathtub. *I washed the baby in the tub.*

tube *noun* (toob) 1. a long, hollow piece of glass, metal, or rubber used to hold or carry liquids or gases. *The teacher put water in the tube to begin the experiment.* 2. a small, soft container that is closed at one end and has an opening at the other end. You press on the tube to get things out. *This tube of toothpaste is almost empty.*

tuberculosis *noun* (too bərk yə lō sis) [N] a serious disease that is passed from one person to another through the air. It usually affects the lungs; **TB.**

tuck *verb* (tŭk) to push the end of something into or under something so that it does not hang loose. *When I make the bed, I tuck the sheet under the mattress. | Please **tuck in** your shirt!*

tuck in to make sure a child is covered well before sleeping at night. *Get ready for bed, and I will come up to tuck you in.*

Tuesday *noun* (tooz dā) the third day of the week. Tuesday comes between Monday and Wednesday.

tuition *noun* (too ĭ shən) the charge for instruction at a college or private school. *We pay tuition every year at school.*

tuna *noun* (too nə) [N] a large fish that lives in the ocean and is used for food. Tuna is often sold in small cans.

tune *noun* (toon) notes that make up a piece of music. *He played a tune on the piano.*

verb to make an instrument have the correct sound. *He tuned his guitar.*

tune in to choose a station on your radio or television, or to adjust your radio or television so that you receive a clear signal. *I tuned in the station to hear today's news. | Can you tune in that station any better?*

tunnel *noun* (tŭ nəl) something dug under the ground or under water for cars, trains, and other vehicles to travel through. *We get to the city by going through a tunnel under the river.*

turkey *noun* (tŭr kē) a large bird from North America with brown feathers. People raise turkeys for their meat.

turkey

turn *verb* (tŭrn) 1. to cause to move around a center point. *Turn the key in the lock to open the door.* 2. to change the course or direction of. *Turn the car around.* 3. to change the position of something. *He turned his desk toward the window. | She turned her head to see who was behind her.* 4. to change the nature, character, or color of something. *The witch **turned** him **into** a frog. | The change of season turned the leaves many colors.* 5. to change the direction of one's movement. *Please turn left at the next street.* 6. to change to a new state or condition. *His face turns red when he gets hot. | This milk is turning sour.*

noun 1. the act of turning. *He made a left turn at the corner.* 2. a chance to do an action that is being done by each person of a group in a certain order. *It is your turn to do the dishes.*

take turns used to describe a fair way that two or more people can share in an activity intended for one person only. One person has a turn, then the next has a turn. *The children took turns riding the bicycle.*

turn down 1. to not accept. *That company turned down my job application.* 2. to lower something, such as the heat or noise. *I always turn down the heat before I go to bed.*

turn in to return something to an official person. *Turn in your test to the teacher when you are done.*

turn off to stop the power or flow of something. *Please turn off the radio when you leave the house.*

turn on to start the power or flow of something. *Turn on the light. It's dark in here.*

turn over to turn something to the other side. *Turn over the meat and cook the other side.*

turn up to raise something, such as the heat or noise. *Turn up the radio so we can hear it.*

turtle *noun* (tŭr təl) an animal with a soft body covered by a hard shell. A turtle pulls its head, legs, and tail into its shell for protection. Turtles live in water or on land.

turtle

tutor *noun* (too tər) a person who gives private instruction to a student.

verb to teach individual students, usually outside of a public school. *I **tutor** him **in** English every Tuesday and Thursday.*

TV *abbrev.* (tē vē) an abbreviation for **television.**

tweezers *pl. noun* (twē zərz) a small metal tool that has two arms. Tweezers are used for picking up or pulling out small objects. *I used the tweezers to remove the splinter from my finger.*

twelve *noun* (twĕlv) the word for the number 12.

twenty *noun* (twĕn tē) the word for the number 20.

twice *adv.* (twīs) 1. two times; in two instances. *I called her twice, and she answered the second time.* 2. two times as much or as many. *This is twice the price of what I paid before! | There are twice the number of people here today compared with yesterday.*

twig *noun* (twĭg) a small branch of a tree or other plant. *I broke a twig off the tree.*

twin *noun* (twĭn) one of two children or animals born at the same time to one mother. *I did not know which twin won the race, but they both ran fast.*

twist *verb* (<u>twist</u>) to wind or weave something around something else. *I twisted the rope around the tree to tie up the boat.*

two *noun* (<u>too</u>) the word for the number 2.

type *noun* (<u>tīp</u>) 1. a group of things that are the same in some way. *Educational programs are the only type of TV shows that they watch.* | *That type of dog has long ears.* 2. a style of letters, numbers, and symbols used in printing. *In this book, some letters are in plain type, and some are in bold type.*

verb to write using a machine such as a computer. *I typed my report so that it would be neat and easy to read.*

Word Builder: type +
typewriter: a machine that you use for typing.
typist: someone who prepares documents on a special machine, such as a computer or typewriter.

typical *adj.* (<u>ti</u> pi kəl) having the qualities of a particular group of people or things. *A typical baby walks when he or she is about one year old.*

U u

ugly *adj.* (ə glē) not pleasant to look at. *The accident caused an ugly scar on his face.*

umbrella *noun* (əm bre lə) a device that protects you from the rain. It has cloth stretched over a wire frame that is held up by a long handle. *I carried my umbrella when I walked to work because it was supposed to rain.*

umbrella

unable *adj.* (ən ā bəl) not having the power, skill, or means needed to do something; not able. *She is unable to walk because she hurt her leg.* | *I am unable to visit you today because I have to go to the doctor.*

uncle *noun* (əng kəl) the brother of one's father or mother, or the husband of one's aunt.

uncomfortable *adj.* (ən kəmf rər bəl) 1. not able to feel relaxed in your mind or body; not comfortable. *I'm uncomfortable with people that I don't know well.* | *I'm very uncomfortable in these tight pants.* 2. causing someone to feel uncomfortable. *These shoes are very uncomfortable.*

under *prep.* (ən dər) 1. below; beneath. *There is a lot of dust under the bed.* 2. smaller or less than. *A pack of gum costs under two dollars.* 3. within the group or category of. *You will find the book under the author's name.* 4. subject to the control of. *The country is suffering under its new leader.*

underground *adj.* (ən dər grownd) located, living, or taking place beneath the earth's surface. *We took the underground train from the city to the airport.* **adv.** (ən dər grownd) beneath the earth's surface. *Many animals live underground.*

underline *verb* (ən dər līn) to draw a line under something, usually to show that it is important or that it has a stronger emphasis than other words when spoken. *The teacher underlined the words that he wanted us to study.* | *The important information was underlined.*

underneath *prep.* (ən dər nēth) below or under. *The dog lay underneath the table.*

underpants *pl. noun* (ən dər pænts) pants worn next to the skin under other clothing.

undershirt *noun* (ən dər shərt) a shirt worn next to the skin under clothes on the upper body.

understand *verb* (ən dər stænd) **understood, understood** to know what something means. *Do you understand what you are reading?*

understanding *noun* (ən dər stæn ding) [N] the way you see the meaning of something. *What is your understanding of the rules of the game?*

understood *verb* (ən dər stud) past tense and past participle of **understand.**

underwater *adv.* (ən dər waw tər) below the water's surface. *The children love to swim underwater and look for fish.*

underwear *noun* (ən dər wār) [N] any clothing worn next to the skin under other clothing. *Does this store sell men's underwear?*

undid *verb* (ən did) past tense of **undo.**

undo *verb* (ən doo) **undid, undone** to make free from something that fastens or closes. *She undid the buttons before she washed the shirt.* | *David undid the knot in his shoelace.*

undone *verb* (ən dən) past participle of **undo.**

undress *verb* (ən dres) to remove someone's clothing. *He went into his room, undressed, and went to bed.* | *She undressed her baby and gave him a bath.*

unemployed *adj.* (ən im ployd) having no job; not employed. *Donna has been unemployed for a few months.*

unemployment *noun* (ən im ploy mənt) [N] the state of not having a job, or the number of people who do not have jobs. *Unemployment is high in the city.*

uneven *adj.* (ən ē vən) 1. not smooth or regular; rough. *Be careful when you walk on the uneven floor.* 2. not regular; changing in quality. *The movie was uneven. Some parts were good, but some parts were bad.* 3. not balanced; not fair. *Their side lost because the battle was uneven.*

unexpected *adj.* (ən ik spek tid) not expected; causing surprise. *We greeted an unexpected guest.*

unfair *adj.* (ən fār) against what is just or fair. *Some people think the judge made an unfair decision in that case.* | *It's unfair that we get paid less than they do.*

unfamiliar *adj.* (ən fə mil yər) not known before; unusual; strange. *Unfamiliar faces scare the baby.*

unfinished *adj.* (ən fi nisht) not completed. *I have some unfinished business to take care of.*

unfold *verb* (ən fold) to open or spread out from a folded condition. *Please unfold the sheet and put it on the bed.*

unfriendly *adj.* (ən frend lē) acting in a way that makes people think that you do not like them or care about them. *The new neighbors seem a little unfriendly.*

unfurnished *adj.* (ən fər nisht) without furniture. *Josh rented an unfurnished apartment.*

unhappy *adj.* (ən hæ pē) sad or not satisfied. *He has been unhappy since his divorce.* | *My nephew is **unhappy with** his new car.*

uniform *adj.* (ū ni fōrm) 1. always the same; never changing. *The machine runs at a uniform speed.* 2. without any differences; alike. *The houses on this block are uniform in appearance.*
noun a special suit of clothing worn by all members of a particular group. *People who work in that restaurant have to wear a uniform.*

uninsured *adj.* (ən in shoord) having no insurance, especially health insurance or auto insurance. *Even though she has a good job, she is uninsured.* | *The driver of the car was uninsured.*

union *noun* (ūn yən) 1. a group of states or countries united under a single government. *The U.S. Civil War began when the northern states refused to allow the southern states to leave the Union.* 2. an organization of working people. *The union agreed on a contract that promised fair wages for its members.*

unique *adj.* (ū nēk) being the only one of its type. *Everyone's fingerprints are unique.*

unit *noun* (ū nit) 1. a single thing that is one of a group of similar things. *Our apartment building has twelve units.* 2. a standard amount that is used to measure things. *The foot and the meter are units for measuring distance.*

unite *verb* (ū nīt) to bring together for a common purpose. *The president united the people.*

Word Builder: unite +
united: having been joined together.

United States *pl. noun* (ū nī dəd stāts) a large country in North America that has fifty states. *Washington, D.C., is the capital of the United States.*

the United States

unity *noun* (ū ni tē) [N] agreement among people. *The new mayor brings a spirit of unity to the city.*

universal *adj.* (ū ni vər səl) 1. having to do with the whole world or all people. *Universal peace seems like an impossible dream.* 2. for or affecting everyone. *Some countries have universal health insurance.*

universe *noun* (ū ni vərs) everything that exists, including the earth and stars. *There are many suns and planets in the universe.*

university *noun* (ū ni vər sə tē) a large school that a student may attend after high school. Universities offer several levels of degrees. *Margaret earned a master's degree at the state university.*

unknown *adj.* (ən nōn) not familiar; not known. *That author is **unknown to** me.* | *We walked through unknown streets.*

unlabeled *adj.* (ən lā bəld) having no label. *What is in that unlabeled can?*

unless *conj.* (ən les) except that; on the condition that. *You won't get better unless you take this medicine.*

unlike *adj.* (ən līk) different. *The two sisters were unlike in many ways.*
prep. different from; not similar to. *Unlike my sister, I love to swim.* | *He is completely unlike his father.*

unload *verb* (ən lōd) to remove the load from. *Unload the truck when it arrives.*

unlock *verb* (ən lak) to open the lock of something. *The janitor unlocks the school every morning.*

unlucky *adj.* (ən lə kē) having or giving bad luck. *That unlucky person has lost his wallet again.* | *Some people say it is unlucky to walk under a ladder.*

unnecessary *adj.* (ən ne sə sār ē) not needed or required. *It is unnecessary for you to fill out the entire form.*

unpaid *adj.* (ən pād) not paid; not yet paid. *She took an unpaid leave from her job.* | *I keep my unpaid bills in one place.*

unpleasant *adj.* (ən ple zənt) nasty; not pleasant. *Spoiled food has an unpleasant smell.*

unplug *verb* (ən pləg) to remove from the electric supply. *Turn off the iron and unplug it.*

unsafe *adj.* (ən sāf) dangerous to oneself or other people; not safe. *He is an unsafe driver because he drives too fast.*

unsatisfactory *adj.* (ən sæ tis fǽk tə rē) not good enough. *My boss said my job performance was unsatisfactory.*

unsure *adj.* (ən shoor) not sure. *He is **unsure of** his ability to swim.*

untie *verb* (ən tī) 1. to free from being tied. *Mark untied the dog and let him run in the park.* 2. to undo a knot in. *Jean untied her shoelaces.*

until *conj.* (ən til) up to the time when. *We slept until the sun came up.*
prep. up to the time of. *We worked until evening.*

---

until or by?
By means before a certain time or at that time. *By* is used for an action that happens at one point in time, not for an action that continues over time.
Until is used to express how long an action will continue and when it will end.
Compare:
The children should go to bed by nine o'clock.
The children can watch TV until nine o'clock.
I will be back at the office by noon.
I will be in the office until noon.

---

unusual *adj.* (ən ū zhoo əl) not usual or ordinary. *She had never seen such an unusual bird before.* | *It is unusual for workers in the United States to take an afternoon nap.*

up *adv.* (əp) 1. to, toward, at, or in a higher place or position. *The plane flew up among the clouds.* | *We climbed up to the second floor.* 2. to or in an upright position. *The tent is up.* 3. out of bed; awake. *Are the children up yet?*
prep. 1. at, to, or toward a higher point on something or in something. *The train headed up the hill.* | *The smoke went up the chimney.* 2. at or toward a point that is farther ahead on a certain path. *You can't catch the bus. It's already up the street.* | *She ran up the path as we walked behind.*
adj. having no more time left; being finished. *The time is up, students. Please give me your test papers.* | *The week is up, and he still hasn't paid me.*

up to 1. busy with; doing. *What are you up to this afternoon?* 2. the duty or decision of. *It is up to parents to take care of their children.* | *It's up to you to choose something for dinner.*

update *verb* (əp dāt) to provide with new and current information. *Ruth updated her boss on her progress.* | *They update your payment record when they receive your money.*
noun new information about a particular thing. *The TV is showing frequent updates on the weather.*

upon *prep.* (ə pän) on. *She placed her hand upon his shoulder.*

upper *adj.* (ə pər) higher in place or level. *The child climbed to the upper branches of the tree.* | *People in upper management earn a lot of money.*

upright *adj.* (əp rīt) 1. in a standing position. *The walls of the old house are no longer upright.* 2. right and honest in actions or morals. *An upright person does not lie or cheat.*

upset *verb* (əp set) *upset, upset* 1. to turn something over. *He upset the glass of water.* 2. to make less comfortable; hurt. *Their complaints upset her.* | *Milk upsets his stomach.* 3. to win against an opponent when everyone expects you to lose. *The local team upset the team from the big city.*
adj. causing or feeling pain. *I have an upset stomach.* | *Bill became upset when he heard the bad news.*

upside down *adj., adv.* (əp sīd down)
1. with the part that is usually below on top. *Bobby turned the chair upside down.*
2. so that everything is out of order or confused. *The war turned their lives upside down.*

upside down

upstairs *adv.* (əp stārz) on or toward an upper floor; up the stairs. *He went upstairs.* | *Her room is upstairs.*

up-to-date *adj.* (əp tə dāt) 1. having the most recent information. *We listened to an up-to-date news report.* 2. following or using the newest designs, technology, or ideas. *Those shoes have an up-to-date look.* | *Our company uses the most up-to-date computers and equipment.*

urge *verb* (ərj) to try to persuade someone to do something when you feel strongly about it. *They urged us to stay home because of the snowstorm.*
noun a desire to do something that usually appears suddenly. *She had a sudden urge to eat chocolate.*

urgent *adj.* (ȯr jȯnt) 1. requiring immediate action. *We had an urgent need for water.* 2. expressing a need for immediate action. *We heard their urgent screams for help.* | *They received an urgent phone call from their son.*

urine *noun* (ū rȯn) [N] the yellow liquid that carries waste out of the body. *If you take drugs, a small amount of the drug will be in your urine.*

us *pron.* (ȯs) the person speaking and another or others; the form of **we** that is used as the object of a verb or that is used after a preposition. *They took us home.* | *He gave the money to us.*

usage *noun* (ū sȯj) 1. [N] the way or manner of using or treating something. *The teacher explained the usage of the new words and expressions.* 2. an instance or instances of using something; use. *This is not a correct usage of this word.* | *This old car has had a lot of rough usage.*

U.S. *abbrev.* (ū es) an abbreviation for **United States.**

USCIS *abbrev.* (ū es sē ī es) an abbreviation for *United States Citizenship and Immigration Services.* The USCIS is the government department that deals with people who have moved to the United States and with people who want to become citizens of the United States.

use *verb* (ūz) 1. to bring into service. *I used a computer to type my report.* 2. to spend. *She used her week's pay to buy groceries.*
noun (ūs) 1. way of using. *I like this artist's use of color.* 2. ability to use. *She lost the use of her thumb in an accident.* 3. advantage or good result. *There is no use in fighting.* 4. purpose. *This machine has many uses.* 5. occasion or need to use. *I no longer have any use for this fur coat.*

Word Builder: use +
user: a person who uses something.

used *adj.* (ūzd) 1. having been owned by someone else; not new. *She bought a used car.* 2. familiar with; in the habit of. *I am **used to** strong coffee.* | *I'm not **used to** driving such a big car.*
used to used as an auxiliary verb to describe an action or state that existed in the past but does not happen or exist now. *Brian used to smoke, but he stopped last year.* | *I don't play soccer now, but I used to.*

useful *adj.* (ūs fȯl) having a practical use or purpose. *A dictionary is a useful book.*

useless *adj.* (ūs lis) 1. having no good or practical purpose. *A computer is useless without electricity.* 2. not able to produce the desired result. *All their cries for help were useless.* | *It's useless to try to finish this now.*

usual *adj.* (ū zhoo ȯl) most common; normal. *The bus arrived at its usual time.*
as usual in the usual way; as always. *I went to bed at eleven o'clock as usual.*

Word Builder: usual +
usually: almost always.

utensil *noun* (ū ten sȯl) a tool for preparing or eating food. Knives and spatulas are some utensils.

utensils

utility *noun* (ū ti li tē) a public service or system such as for water, electricity, and gas for heat and cooking. *Rent for this apartment does not include utilities.*
adj. having value because of being useful, not because of a nice appearance. *Nicole wears utility boots at work.*

V v

vacant *adj.* (vā kənt) not in use; empty; available. *There were no vacant seats on the bus.* | *The boss interviewed several people for the vacant position.* | *That apartment has been vacant for six months.*

vacation *noun* (vā kā shən) a period of rest from school, work, or other activities. *We are **going on vacation** this summer.* | *We are **taking a vacation** in the mountains.*

vacuum *noun* (væ kūm) 1. [N] a space or container that has no air or matter in it. Outer space and the inside of a lightbulb are examples of vacuums. 2. a machine that cleans by sucking air; vacuum cleaner.
verb to clean by means of a vacuum cleaner. *He vacuums the rug twice a week.*

valley *noun* (væ lē) a long area of low land between mountains or hills. *A river flows through this valley.*

valuable *adj.* (væl yə bəl) considered to have great worth or importance. *She is a valuable friend.* | *That is valuable information.*

value *noun* (væl ū) the worth or importance of something. *That car has a value of five thousand dollars.* | *She **places** great **value on** education.*

valve *noun* (vælv) a part that controls the flow of a liquid or gas through a pipe. *The plumber closed the valve before repairing the faucet.*

van *noun* (væn) a tall, covered truck or car used to move people or goods. *We loaded our furniture into the van.*

vandal *noun* (væn dəl) a person who destroys or damages property on purpose.

vanilla *noun* (və ni lə) [N] a substance from a plant often used to flavor sweet things such as cake and ice cream.

vapor *noun* (vā pər) [N] tiny pieces of a liquid or solid that float in a gas. *Mist and clouds are made of water vapor.*

variety *noun* (və rī ə tē) a number of different things in a group or class. *They have a large **variety of** vegetables at that store.*

various *adj.* (vær ē əs) of many different kinds. *I have various reasons for wanting a new job.*

vary *verb* (vær ē) to change from time to time. *The weather varies a lot this time of year.*

vase *noun* (vās or vaz) an open container that is taller than it is wide. A vase is used as a decoration or to hold cut flowers.

vase of flowers

VCR *abbrev.* (vē sē ar) an abbreviation for **videocassette recorder.**

vegetable *noun* (vej tə bəl) a plant or part of a plant that is used for food, such as potato, broccoli, or onion.

vehicle *noun* (vē i kəl) a thing used to carry and move people or things. Some vehicles are cars, trucks, and buses. *You can't operate a motor vehicle without a license.*

vein *noun* (vān) a small tube in the body that carries blood to the heart.

velvet *noun* (vel vit) [N] a soft cloth that is covered on one side with many short, cut threads. *She wore a dress made of velvet to the party.*

vend *verb* (vend) (formal) to sell. *Do you have a license to vend merchandise here?*

Word Builder: vend +
vending machine: a machine that sells candy, drinks, snacks, or other small items.
vendor: a person who sells things.

ventilate *verb* (ven tə lāt) to let fresh air enter a space and to let hot air or smoke leave a space. *Open a window to ventilate this room.*

Word Builder: ventilate +
ventilated: having a way for hot air or smoke to leave a space; having a way for fresh air to enter a space.

ventilation *noun* (ven tə lā shən) [N] the movement of air in a space. *Open the window for better ventilation.*

verb *noun* (vərb) a word that expresses an action or state of being. In the sentences "They are sick," "I went shopping," and "He always drives to work," the words *are*, *went*, and *drives* are verbs.

versatile *adj.* (vər sə til) having a number of different uses. *A pocket knife is a versatile tool.*

version *noun* (vər zhən) 1. a particular form of something. *We saw the film version of the story after we read the book.* 2. a description or report from one point of view. *John's version of the accident is different from Laura's.*

vertical *adj.* (vər tə kəl) straight up and down; upright. *His shirt has vertical stripes.*

very *adv.* (ver ē) used to emphasize an adjective or adverb to make the degree of a quality higher. *He is very sad.* | *She runs very fast.*

very, so, or too?
Very is used to express a high degree of some quality.
So is used to express a high degree of some quality that we feel with strong emotion.
We use *too* when there is something that cannot or does not happen because of the degree of some quality.
Compare:
The soup is very hot.
The soup is so hot!
The soup is too hot to eat.

veteran *noun* (ve tər ən) a person who has served in the armed forces during a war. *His grandfather is a veteran of World War II.*

veterinarian *noun* (ve tər i nār ē ən) a doctor for animals.

veterinarian

veto *noun* (vē tō) the power of a government official or group to prevent something from going into effect. *The president's veto sent the bill back to Congress.*

vice president *noun* (vīs pre zə dənt) 1. the title of the elected official in the U.S. government who ranks just below the president. The vice president is also the president of the Senate. 2. an officer of a company or other group who is in charge of his or her own department. *Mrs. Garcia is a vice president at the bank.*

victim *noun* (vik tim) a person who is hurt or killed by someone or something. *The criminal beat his victim.* | *These children are victims of war.*

victory *noun* (vik tə rē) success in a game or war. *The game ended with a victory for our team.* | *The army celebrated its victory in battle.*

video *noun* (vi dē ō) 1. the picture part of television. *We adjusted the video and the sound before watching the show.* 2. a movie or other program that is recorded on a **videocassette.** *We rented two videos to watch tonight.*

videocassette *noun* (vi dē ō kə set) a plastic box that holds tape on which people record and play back pictures and sound.

videocassette recorder *noun* (vi dē ō kə set ri kŌr dər) an electronic machine that records and plays movies or television programs; **VCR.**

view *noun* (vū) 1. the area that can be seen from a particular point. *There is a beautiful view from the top of the mountain.* 2. an opinion or way of thinking about something. *In his view, all children should go to school.*

village *noun* (vi ləj) a small town or community, often in the country. *Ruth moved from her village to the city.*

vinegar *noun* (vi nə gər) [N] a sour liquid used to flavor or preserve food. It is often used in salad dressings.

vinyl *noun* (vī nəl) [N] a tough, shiny plastic. Vinyl is often used to make materials for the inside of a car and for covering floors in a building.

violate *verb* (vī ə lāt) to break or fail to keep. *If you violate the law, you will be punished.*

violation *noun* (vī ə lā shən) an act of breaking a law or agreement. *Sharon got a ticket for a parking violation.*

violence *noun* (vī ə ləns) [N] actions that intend to cause injury, pain, or harm. *Murder and other acts of violence are becoming more common in this city.*

violent *adj.* (vī ə lənt) acting with great force or anger. *The violent criminal was sent to prison.*

virus *noun* (vī rəs) 1. a tiny living thing that lives in other living things and causes diseases. *Influenza is caused by a virus.* 2. a program that can destroy information in a computer. *Viruses are often hidden in e-mail messages.*

visible *adj.* (vi zə bəl) able to be seen. *The skyscraper is visible from across the river.*

vision *noun* (vi zhən) [N] the ability to see; sight. *His vision improved after he started wearing glasses.*

visit *verb* (vi zit) to go or come to see. *We visit our cousins every year.* | *I visited the zoo last week.*
noun an act of going or coming to see a person or place. *I had a good visit with friends.* | *Our visit to the city was fun.*

Word Builder: visit +
visitation: a parent's right to visit a child as ordered by a court in a divorce case.
visitor: a person who visits.

visual *adj.* (v̲i̲ zhoo əl) 1. having to do with sight or seeing. *Painting is a visual art.* 2. using pictures. *The teacher's* **visual aids** *made the lesson easier.*

Word Builder: visual +
visually: with the eyes; by seeing or looking at.

vitamin *noun* (v̲ī̲ tə min) a substance needed for the health and normal working of the body. *People get most of their vitamins from food.*

vocabulary *noun* (vō k̲æ̲b yə lar ē) 1. [N] the words of a language. *We studied English vocabulary in school.* 2. the set of words that a particular person or group knows or uses. *He wants to expand his vocabulary.*

vocation *noun* (vō k̲ā̲ shən) work that you want to do for your whole life. *Being a teacher is not just a job to him. It's his vocation.*

Word Builder: vocation +
vocational: relating to a job or trade.

voice *noun* (v̲oy̲s) the sound that comes from your mouth when you speak or sing. *You have a beautiful voice.*

voice mail *noun* (v̲oy̲s m̲ā̲l) [N] a telephone system that records spoken messages electronically and stores them on a central computer. You listen to the messages by telephoning the main computer. *Many businesses have voice mail.*

volcano *noun* (val k̲ā̲ nō) an opening in the earth's surface through which melted rock, ash, and gases are forced out. *The explosion of the volcano caused a lot of damage.*

volleyball *noun* (v̲a̲ lē bawl) [N] a game in which two teams use their hands to hit a ball over a high net. A team gets a point when the ball hits the ground in the other team's court.

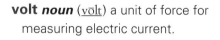

volleyball

volt *noun* (v̲ō̲lt) a unit of force for measuring electric current.

voltage *noun* (v̲ō̲l tij) the force of an electric current.

volume *noun* (v̲a̲l ūm) 1. [N] the amount of space inside an object or the amount of space that an object uses. *This bottle looks bigger than that one, but the volume is the same.* 2. [N] the amount of sound. *Would you please lower the volume on the TV?* 3. one of the books in a series or set of books. *Our encyclopedia has twenty volumes.*

voluntary *adj.* (v̲a̲ lən tār ē) doing something because you want or choose to do it, not because you have to do it. *The president's decision to quit was a voluntary decision.*

volunteer *noun* (va lən t̲ē̲r) a person who offers to work or help without pay. *With the help of many volunteers, we were able to finish the project.*
verb to offer a thing or service freely and often for no pay. *They volunteered their time and efforts to helping other people.* | *I was surprised when my son volunteered to take out the garbage.* | *After high school, he* **volunteered for** *the army.*

vomit *verb* (v̲a̲ mit) to bring up food and liquid from the stomach through the mouth. *He felt very sick after lunch and finally vomited.*

Word Builder: vomit +
vomiting: the act of bringing up food and liquid from the stomach through the mouth.

vote *noun* (v̲ō̲t) the expression of one person's choice in a group decision. *My vote will go to the best candidate.* | *Have they counted all the votes yet?*
verb to express a choice in a group decision. *Who did you* **vote for?** | *My brother is too young to vote.*

Word Builder: vote +
voter: a person who can vote in an election.

vowel *noun* (v̲ow̲l) in English, the sounds represented by the letters *a, e, i, o, u,* and sometimes *y.* The word *pocket* has two vowels.

voyage *noun* (v̲oy̲ ij) a long trip by air or sea, or in outer space. *Many people watched the first voyage to the moon on TV.*

wage *noun* (wāj) (often plural) money paid at regular times to a person for doing work. *Her wages are ten dollars per hour.* | *They get a weekly wage.*

wagon *noun* (wǽ gən) a vehicle with four wheels that is used to carry large or heavy loads. *Often, horses pull large wagons.*

waist *noun* (wāst) 1. the part of the body between the chest and hips. 2. the part of a piece of clothing that covers this part of the body. *The waist of my pants is loose.*

wait *verb* (wāt) to stay in one place until an expected event happens. *We're **waiting for** the mail to arrive.* | *We're **waiting** at home **until** it stops raining.*
noun a period of waiting. *There was a long wait before the movie started.*
wait on to take care of customers in a restaurant or store. *At lunch today, Cora waited on twenty customers.*

Word Builder: wait +
waiter: a person whose job is to wait on customers at a restaurant.
waitress: a woman whose job is to wait on customers at a restaurant.

---

wait for or wait on?
Wait on means to serve a customer, as in a restaurant or store.
Wait for is more common and means to stay in a place or situation until some expected event happens.
Compare:
A nice person waited on us at the restaurant today.
I waited for my son outside his school.

---

wake *verb* (wāk) *woke, woken* to cause someone to stop sleeping. *Please wake me before you leave.*
wake up to stop sleeping or make someone stop sleeping. *I woke up early this morning.* | *The noise in the street woke me up.*

walk *verb* (wawk) 1. to move your body by taking steps. *I walked to the bank.* | *Did you walk or take the bus?* 2. to cause or help to walk, or to walk with an animal or a person to the place that he or she is going. *He walks the dog twice a day.* | *I walked my grandfather to the car.* | *He walked the baby-sitter home.*
noun an act of walking for exercise or enjoyment. *Let's **take a walk** after dinner.*

wall *noun* (wawl) one of the structures that forms a room or divides a space. *He hung the picture on a wall in his room.*

wallet *noun* (wa lit) a small, flat container that is often made of leather and used to hold money, credit cards, and other things. *There is only one dollar in my wallet.*

wallet

wander *verb* (wan dər) to go or walk with no purpose or plan. *We wandered through the halls until classes started.* | *They were lost, so they wandered through the woods.*

want *verb* (want) to desire; wish for. *He wants to go home now.* | *I want some lunch.*

war *noun* (wōr) a time of very great fighting between countries or groups of people. *Her brother died in the war.* | *I hope there will not be **war between** our countries.*

warehouse *noun* (wār hows) a large building or other place where products are stored. *The store has more of those chairs in the warehouse.*

wares *pl. noun* (wārz) things offered for sale. *He displayed his wares in the shop window.*

warm *adj.* (wōrm) 1. having some heat; not cold. *Your hands are warm.* | *Yesterday was cold, but today is nice and warm.* 2. able to hold in heat from your body. *He covered the child with a warm blanket.* 3. full of kind feeling. *She gave him a warm hug.* | *You have a warm heart.*
verb to make warm; to heat. *He warmed the soup for dinner.*
warm up to become warm or to make something warm. *My feet are warming up now.* | *I warmed up your coffee.*

warmth *noun* (wōrmth) [N] the quality of being warm; heat. *The cat loves the warmth of the fire.*

warn *verb* (wōrn) 1. to tell of a possible danger. *They **warned** us **about** the snowstorm.* 2. to advise about some action because something bad could happen. *He warned the children not to play with matches.*

warning *noun* (wōr ning) a signal or notice of a possible danger. *The sign had a warning about drinking the water.* | *Our dad always* **gives** *us* **a warning** *before he gets angry.*

Word Builder: warning +
warning light: a bright light that serves as a warning.

warrant *noun* (wōr ənt) a document that the police must get from a judge in order to do certain things. *The police need a* **search warrant** *to look in your house.* | *The officer said he had a* **warrant for her arrest.**

warranty *noun* (wōr ən tē) a document that you may get when you buy something. It says that the company that made the product will fix certain things for a period of time or will give you a new one if it is damaged.

warrior *noun* (wōr ē ər) a person who fights; a soldier.

was *verb* (wəz) a past tense form of the verb **be** that is used with *I*, *he*, *she*, *it*, and singular nouns. *I was at home yesterday.*

wash *verb* (wash) to make something clean by using water and usually soap. *He washed all the cups.*
noun a liquid that is used as a medicine. *She prepared a wash to treat her red eye.*

Word Builder: wash +
washable: able to be washed in water.

washer *noun* (wa shər) 1. a machine for washing clothes; washing machine. 2. a flat ring of rubber, metal, or other material. You use a washer with a nut and bolt to make a tight fit.

washing machine *noun* (wa shing mə shēn) a machine for washing clothes.

waste *verb* (wāst) to use more or spend more of something than what you really need; not use well. *Don't waste so much paper! It costs money.* | *You waste too much time playing that game.*
noun 1. the act or state of not using something well. *Buying a car like that is* **a waste of money.**

2. [N] something that is not needed or wanted. *That factory puts its waste in the river.*

Word Builder: waste +
wastebasket: a basket or large can that you put garbage in.

watch *noun* (wach) a small clock that people often wear on their wrist.
verb 1. to follow a moving image with your eyes and give it your attention. *I watched the people walking down the street.* | *The TV was on, but I wasn't watching it.* 2. to guard or give close attention to. *My sister is watching the children for me today.*
watch out to pay attention to avoid danger. **Watch out for** *that rock!* | *Watch out that you don't fall.*

watch

watchdog *noun* (wach dawg) a dog that people train to guard property. *The watchdog at the factory barked loudly.*

water *noun* (waw tər) [N] the clear liquid that is in rain. People, plants, and animals drink water and need it in order to live.
verb to put water on something. *He watered the plants around his house.*

watermelon *noun* (waw tər me lən) a large fruit that has a hard green or yellow skin, pink or yellow flesh, and many black seeds.

waterproof *adj.* (waw tər proof) able to keep water out of something. *This watch is waterproof.*

wave *noun* (wāv) the water that rises from the surface of a body of water. *The boat rocked on the ocean waves.*
verb 1. to move gently in the air. *The flag waves at the top of the pole.* 2. to make a signal by moving a hand, arm, or object in the air. People often wave when they see someone they know. *She waved when she saw us at the train station.*

wax *noun* (wæks) 1. [N] a soft, solid substance that is made with fats or oils. It melts when you heat it for a short time. *Candles are made from wax.* 2. [N] a mixture with wax in it that is used to polish a smooth, hard surface. *He washed the floor and put wax on it.*

way *noun* (wā) 1. a road or path that leads from one place to another. *Which is the fastest way home?* 2. an opening that lets you move in or out of something. *The front door is the only way into the house.* 3. a particular direction. *Look that way to see the parade.* 4. a distance. *The store is just a short way from here.* 5. a manner; way of acting. *He spoke in a friendly way.* 6. a means of doing something; how to do something. *Do you know a good way to cook fish?* | *We need a way to solve this problem.*
   by the way used to add something into a conversation that is on a different subject. *By the way, did you know there is no school on Friday?*

we *pron.* (wē) the person speaking or writing and one or more others. *We are friends.*

weak *adj.* (wēk) having little strength or power. *I felt weak after being sick.* | *We could hardly hear his weak voice.*

> **Word Builder: weak +**
> **weakness** (1): the state of being weak.
> **weakness** (2): a special liking for something.

wealth *noun* (welth) [N] a large amount of money or property. *She has money because of the wealth of her grandparents.*

> **Word Builder: wealth +**
> **wealthy:** having a lot of wealth; rich.

weapon *noun* (we pən) an object used to attack or defend. *Guns and bombs are weapons of war.*

wear *verb* (wār) *wore, worn* 1. to have or carry on your body. *He likes to wear rings.* | *She is wearing a skirt.* 2. to become damaged through long use. *The roof is beginning to wear.*
   wear off to become less or disappear over time. *The ink marks will wear off in a few days.*
   wear out to make or become useless through a lot of use. *He wore out his shoes.*

weather *noun* (we thər) [N] conditions outside. Weather includes temperature, rain, snow, sun, and other things. *What is the weather like in Chicago today?* | *I don't like this hot weather!*

weave *verb* (wēv) *wove, woven* to make cloth by passing threads over and under each other. *This machine weaves cotton for jeans.* | *She is weaving a rug.*

web *noun* (web) 1. a thin, open structure made of threads that connect to each other at points. *Many spiders make webs.* 2. [N] a short form of **World Wide Web.**

wedding *noun* (we ding) a ceremony of marriage. *My sister's wedding will take place in a church.*

Wednesday *noun* (wenz dā) the fourth day of the week. Wednesday comes between Tuesday and Thursday.

weed *noun* (wēd) any plant that grows wild in places where people do not want it to grow. *We pulled weeds from our garden.* | *Weeds are a problem for farmers.*
   verb to clear of weeds. *We weed our vegetable garden every week.*

week *noun* (wēk) a standard unit used to measure time. One week equals seven days.

weekday *noun* (wēk dā) any day of the week except Saturday and Sunday. *We go to school on weekdays.*

weekend *noun* (wēk end) the part of the week between Friday evening and Sunday evening. *We went to my grandmother's house over the weekend.*

weekly *adj.* (wēk lē) happening or appearing once a week. *We made our weekly trip to the supermarket.* | *She reads a weekly magazine.*
   adv. once a week; each week. *She takes piano lessons weekly.*

weevil *noun* (wē vəl) a kind of insect that eats plants. The weevil is a problem for farmers who grow cotton.

weigh *verb* (wā) 1. to measure how heavy a person or thing is by using a scale. *The clerk weighed the cheese.* 2. to have a particular amount of weight. *I weigh ten pounds more than I did last year.*

weight *noun* (wāt) 1. [N] the quality that makes something heavy. *There is too much weight in the back of the boat.* 2. how heavy something is. *What is your weight? You look thin.*

weigh

welcome *interj.* (wel kəm) used to express warm greetings to someone who has just arrived. *Welcome! We're glad you could come.*
   noun a warm greeting. *We gave her a warm welcome.*
   verb to express pleasure and kind feelings when someone arrives or joins you. *We welcomed the new people to our office.*
   adj. allowed to do something if you want. *You are welcome to share this food.*

you're welcome used as a reply to someone who thanks you for something. *"Thank you for the gift." "You're welcome."*

weld *verb* (<u>weld</u>) to join metal by using heat. *He welded the parts of the bicycle back together.*

welding torch *noun* (<u>wel</u> ding <u>torch</u>) a tool that uses heat to join two metal things together.

welfare *noun* (<u>wel</u> fār) 1. [N] an official program that gives money and other help to people who need it. *She was on welfare after she lost her job.* 2. [N] the state of being healthy and happy. *My mother thought more about my welfare than her own.*

well[1] *adv.* (<u>wel</u>) in a good, proper, or acceptable way; adverb that expresses the meaning of the adjective **good.** *Her work is going well.* | *He cooks very well.*
adj. healthy; sound. *She didn't feel well today, so she stayed home from school.*
as well also; too. *I ate cake, and I ate a lot of ice cream as well.*
as well as and also. *He is honest as well as kind.*

well[2] *noun* (<u>wel</u>) a deep hole in the ground that people dig to get water, oil, gas, or other things.

well-done *adj.* (<u>wel</u> <u>d</u>ən) thoroughly cooked. *Do you prefer rare or well-done steak?*

well-known *adj.* (<u>wel</u> nōn) known by many people; famous. *He is a well-known actor.*

well-lighted *adj.* (<u>wel</u> lī tid) having plenty of light. *It's pleasant to work in a well-lighted work area.*

went *verb* (<u>went</u>) past tense of **go.**

were *verb* (<u>wər</u>) a past tense form of the verb **be** that is used with the pronouns *you, we,* or *they.* It is also used with plural nouns. *Where are my keys? They were on the table!*

west *noun* (<u>west</u>) 1. [N] the direction in front of you when you face the setting sun. 2. (often capitalized) the western part of a country or area. *He's moving to the West to look for work.*
adj. toward or facing the west. *The west side of the house is bright in the afternoons.*
adv. from, in, or toward the west. *Many new immigrants traveled west in search of a new home.*

western *adj.* (<u>we</u> stərn) having to do with the west. *We watched the sun go down in the western sky.*

wet *adj.* (<u>wet</u>) having water or other liquid within something or on the surface of something. *This towel is wet, but there are dry ones in the closet.* | *Don't sit there! It's wet.*

whale *noun* (<u>wāl</u>) a large mammal that lives in the ocean and swims. Whales look like fish.

what *pron.* (<u>wot</u>) 1. which particular thing or kind of thing out of many possibilities. *What will you wear to the interview?* 2. a word used in a question to get information about a thing. *What did he say?* 3. the thing or things that. *You have to do what the police officer asks.* | *I don't know what happened.*
adj. which one or ones out of many possibilities. *What movie did you see?* | *What kind of music do you like?*

whatever *pron.* (<u>wot</u> e vər) 1. anything or everything that. *Take whatever you like.* 2. no matter what. *Whatever happens, you can depend on me.*

wheat *noun* (<u>wēt</u>) [N] the grain that comes from certain grasses. Wheat is used in making flour for bread and other foods.

wheel *noun* (<u>wēl</u>) a round thing that turns in circles and allows cars, trucks, bicycles, and other things to move. *The back wheel of my bike is broken.*

wheelbarrow *noun* (<u>wēl</u> bær ō) a device used to carry rocks, soil, leaves, and other materials for short distances. A wheelbarrow has one or two wheels, two legs at the back, and handles for a person to push.

wheelchair (wheel chair) *noun* (<u>wēl</u> chār) a chair on wheels that is used by people who cannot walk from place to place.

wheelchair

when *adv.* (<u>wen</u>) at what time. *When will you come?*
conj. 1. at or during the time that. *He will sleep late when he is on vacation.* | *It is not wise to travel when you are sick.* 2. at the moment that. *He smiled when he saw her.*

whenever *conj.* (<u>wen</u> e vər) 1. at any time. *I am ready whenever you are.* | *Whenever he arrives, please tell him to wait for me here.* 2. at whatever time; every time that; when. *Whenever he visited, he brought presents.* | *Whenever the dog barks, the baby cries.*

where *adv.* (wār) 1. at, in, or to what location. *Where do you live? | Where are you going?* 2. from what source or location. *Where did you get that dress?*
conj. 1. in or at what point or place. *Do you know where Peter is?* 2. at which place. *I got a job in a grocery store, where I worked for two years.*
pron. what place. *Where does the new student come from?*

wherever *conj.* (wār e vər) in, at, or toward any place or situation. *She leaves a mess wherever she goes.*

whether *conj.* (we thər) a word used to introduce two different possibilities. *I don't know whether it is snowing or not. | I will be happy whether I go with them or stay here.*

which *pron.* (wich) 1. what one or ones; usually used when there are only a few possibilities. *Which of these three coats is yours?* 2. a word used as a relative pronoun to give information that shows the specific thing or things you are talking about; that. *The hotel which was the least expensive was really the best.* 3. a word used as a relative pronoun to add extra information to a sentence. The information is connected to the word or phrase that comes before the pronoun. *I cleaned my office, which had been a terrible mess. | Their old dog died, which was sad for the children.* 4. a word used after the word *that* to give the meaning of *the thing that* or *what. She never was able to give him that which he really wanted.*
adj. what one or ones out of a certain group. *Which shirt do you like the best of these four?*

whichever *pron.* (wich e vər) whatever or any one that. *Take whichever looks good.*
adj. any, out of all possible choices. *I'll go to whichever movie you want to see.*

while *noun* (wīl) 1. [N] a period of time. *Please stay for a while. | I read my book for a while before I went to sleep.* 2. [N] the effort or time given to something. *It is worth my while to finish school.*
conj. 1. during the time that; as long as. *He watched TV while he was talking on the phone.* 2. although. *While I agree with you about this situation, I cannot agree with you about the other.*

once in a while sometimes but not very often. *I walk home once in a while, but usually I take the bus.*

whine *verb* (wīn) 1. to complain or cry because you do not like something. *My little brother is whining about going to bed early.* 2. to make a long, high cry as a sign of pain or fear. *The dog whined because it wanted to go out.*

whip *verb* (wip) 1. to beat an animal or human with something like a long piece of rope or leather. *He whipped the horse.* 2. to beat eggs or cream. *I whipped the cream for our pies.*
noun a long, thin thing like a rope that is attached to a handle. A whip is used to hit or beat an animal or person.

whisper *verb* (wi spər) to speak softly and quietly. *Please whisper while the baby is sleeping.*

whistle *verb* (wi səl) to make a high sound similar to the sound of a bird. When you whistle, you force air through a small opening in your lips. *My little girl learned how to whistle yesterday.*
noun a small instrument or pipe that makes a high sound by blowing air through it. *The coach used a whistle to stop the game.*

white *adj.* (wīt) having the color of clean snow. *The clouds are white in the clear blue sky.*

White House *noun* (wīt hows) the official home of the president of the United States in Washington, D.C.

who *pron.* (hoo) 1. what person or persons. *Who are you? | Who lives in this house?* 2. a word used as a relative pronoun to give information that shows what person or persons you are talking about; that. *The person who answered the phone was his wife.* 3. a word used as a relative pronoun to add extra information to a sentence. The information is connected to the word or phrase that comes before the pronoun. *Her son James, who writes poetry, is graduating this year.*

whoever *pron.* (hoo e vər) 1. every or any person who; anyone that. *Whoever can pass this test is really smart.* 2. what person in the world. *Whoever lives in that house must be rich.*

whole *adj.* (hol) having the entire amount or length. *He ate the whole cake.* | *She stayed awake the whole night.*

noun an entire or complete thing. *He accepted half, but he wanted the whole.*

as a whole considering everything together without looking at the small details. *You make mistakes sometimes, but as a whole, your papers are very good.*

on the whole in general; looking at everything altogether. *On the whole, I'm very happy.*

wholesale *adj.* (hol sal) having to do with selling things in large quantities to businesses that sell those things to customers. *Sandy runs a wholesale clothing business.*

whom *pron.* (hoom) the form of the relative pronoun **who** that is used as the object of a verb or after a preposition. *Whom does this document concern?* | *He divorced his first wife, whom I've never met.* | *To whom did you address the letter?*

whose *pron.* (hooz) 1. of or belonging to which person or persons. *Whose gloves are those?* 2. the possessive form of **who** or **which**. *The man whose dog bit me took me to the doctor.* | *This was a plan whose purpose was not clear to us.*

why *adv.* (wi) for what reason, purpose, or cause. *Why are you in such a hurry?*

conj. for what reason, purpose, or cause. *I don't know why you didn't call.*

wide *adj.* (wid) 1. reaching across a large area from side to side. *The three of us walked down the wide path together.* | *She likes to wear jeans with wide legs.* 2. having an exact measurement from side to side. *The door is four feet wide.*

adv. to the full distance; completely. *The window was wide open.* | *She opened her eyes wide.*

Word Builder: wide +
widely: over a large distance or among many people.

widow *noun* (wi do) a woman whose husband has died.

Word Builder: widow +
widowed: having become a widow or widower.

widower *noun* (wi do ər) a man whose wife has died.

width *noun* (width) the measurement of something from one side to the other. *That shelf has a width of four feet.*

wife *noun* (wif) *wives* a woman to whom a man is married. *Joe's wife is younger than he is.*

wild *adj.* (wild) 1. living in a natural state. *There are wild animals in the forest.* 2. not following the rules; out of control. *The teacher could not control the wild students.* 3. (informal) approving; enthusiastic. *He's not **wild about** his new haircut.*

will[1] *verb* (wil) 1. used to indicate a future action or condition. *The president will speak on television tonight.* | *His last day at work will be next Friday.* 2. used to express willingness or agreement to do something. *I will help you with that.* | *I asked her about it, but she won't answer me.* 3. used to announce your decision or intention to do something. *She likes both of these watches, but she will take this one.* | *Don't move. I will call the doctor!* 4. used to promise or make someone feel certain about something. *I will finish the work by two o'clock.* | *Don't worry. He will be back soon.*

will[2] *noun* (wil) 1. [N] the power of the mind to choose a course of action or to make a decision. *My father has a strong will.* 2. [N] a strong personal desire or wish. *They took the child **against her will**.* 3. a legal statement that describes what you want to happen to your property after you die. *My father left me his house in his will.*

willing *adj.* (wi ling) ready or wanting to do something. *I am willing to help.*

win *verb* (win) *won, won* 1. to do the best or come first in a game. *Our team won the game.* 2. to get or obtain through great effort. *The people won their freedom after the revolution.*

Word Builder: win +
winner: a person who has won a game or contest.

wind[1] *noun* (wind) air as it moves over the surface of the earth. *A cold wind is blowing.*

Word Builder: wind +
windy: having a strong wind.

wind[2] *verb* (wind) *wound, wound* to cover with or wrap. *He wound the wire around the pole.*

wind up 1. to bring or come to an end. *The party wound up after midnight.* 2. to find yourself in a certain place or situation. *He got on the wrong bus and wound up in Chicago.* | *As usual, I wound up washing the dishes.*

window *noun* (<u>win</u> dō) 1. an opening in a wall or vehicle that lets in air and light. The opening is usually covered by clear glass. *Please close the window so the rain won't get in.* 2. a box that appears on a computer screen. Each program opens in its own window. *There are two windows open on my computer: one for the word processor and one for the Internet.*

windowpane

window

windshield *noun* (<u>wind</u> shēld) a window on the front of a car or other vehicle.

wine *noun* (<u>wīn</u>) [N] a drink that contains alcohol and is usually made from grapes.

wing *noun* (<u>wing</u>) 1. a part of the body of some animals that they use for flying. Insects and birds have wings. *The eagle spread its wings and flew away.* 2. something having the shape or use of a wing. *He likes to sit near the wing on an airplane.* 3. a side section of a building. *My office is in the east wing.*

winter *noun* (<u>win</u> tər) the season of the year between autumn and spring.
adj. appropriate for winter. *Matthew has a new winter jacket.*

wipe *verb* (<u>wīp</u>) to clean or dry by rubbing. *I wiped the wet dishes with a towel.*
wipe out to destroy. *The flood wiped out the town.*
wipe up to remove by rubbing. *Wipe up the crumbs from the table.*

wire *noun* (<u>wīr</u>) 1. a long thread of metal. *The cows were kept in the field by a fence made of wire.* 2. a long metal thread that carries electricity. *The wire runs from the lamp to the outlet.*
verb to put in and attach wires that carry electricity. *The electrician wired the house.*

> **Word Builder: wire +**
> **wire cutter:** a tool that you use to cut wire.
> **wire snips:** a tool that you use to cut wire.
> **wire stripper:** a tool for removing the covering from wire.

wiring *noun* (<u>wīr</u> ing) [N] a system of wires used to carry electricity. *This old house needs new wiring.*

wisdom *noun* (<u>wiz</u> dəm) [N] good judgment and an understanding of that which is true or right. *She had the wisdom to teach her children how to make difficult decisions.*

wise *adj.* (<u>wīz</u>) having understanding and good judgment about what is true or right. *Years of experience have made her wise.*

wish *verb* (<u>wish</u>) to desire; want. *She **wished for** a new car. | You may sit if you wish.*
noun a hope for something; thing that you hope to get. *Close your eyes and **make a wish**. | I hope my wish will come true. | My wish is for good health.*

witch *noun* (<u>wich</u>) a woman who is believed to have magic powers. *Witches are more often thought to do evil things than good things.*

with *prep.* (<u>with</u>) 1. in the company of. *They walked with me.* 2. marked by; having. *Give this to the woman with the red hat.* 3. by using. *You lock a door with a key.* 4. in relation to. *We agreed with each other.* 5. in the same group as; among; into. *He mixed sugar with butter for the cake.* 6. of the same opinion as. *I'm with you on this plan.* 7. due to; because of. *He cried with joy.*

withdraw *verb* (with <u>draw</u>) *withdrew, withdrawn* to take out or remove. *Marta withdrew money from her bank account. | Martin withdrew his hand from the cookie jar.*

withdrawal *noun* (with <u>draw</u> əl) the act of taking money from an account, or the amount of money that is taken out from an account. *Mr. Perez **made a withdrawal of** one hundred dollars from his bank account. | His withdrawal was one hundred dollars.*

withheld *verb* (with <u>held</u>) past tense and past participle of **withhold.**

withhold *verb* (with <u>hōld</u>) *withheld, withheld* to hold something back. *Your boss withholds money from your pay for taxes and insurance.*

> **Word Builder: withhold +**
> **withholding:** an amount that is withheld.

within *prep.* (with <u>in</u>) 1. inside of. *We heard a sound from within the house.* 2. not going beyond the limits of. *I will mail the letter to you within the next two weeks. | It is within a citizen's rights to protest.*

without *prep.* (with <u>owt</u>) 1. having none of or no. *People can't live without food and water. | I don't like shirts without pockets.* 2. not with. *They drove to work without me.*

witness *verb* (wit nəs) to know through direct sight or experience of. *She witnessed the crime.*
noun a person who sees or hears something that happened. *He was a **witness to** the fight.*

wives *pl. noun* (wīvz) plural of **wife.**

woke *verb* (wōk) past tense of **wake.**

woken *verb* (wō kən) past participle of **wake.**

wolf *noun* (wulf) **wolves** a wild mammal that is related to the dog and often travels with its group to hunt other animals.

wolf

wolves *pl. noun* (wulvz) plural of **wolf.** *He got lost in the forest and was attacked by wolves.*

woman *noun* (wu mən) **women** an adult female human. *When a girl becomes a woman, she is expected to decide things for herself.*

women *pl. noun* (wi mən) plural of **woman.** *Six women work here.*

won *verb* (wən) past tense and past participle of **win.**

wonder *verb* (wən dər) to want to know about; sometimes used when making a polite request. *I wonder where she is. | I was wondering if you could tell me his phone number?*
noun a thing or event that causes admiration or surprise. *This huge, beautiful cave is a **natural wonder.** | It was a wonder that she recovered from her illness.*

wonderful *adj.* (wən dər fəl) causing a feeling of pleasure; excellent. *I had a wonderful time on my vacation.*

wood *noun* (wud) 1. [N] the hard material that makes up the trunk and branches of a tree. People use wood to build furniture and houses. 2. (usually plural) a collection of trees growing close together in one area; forest. *I took my dog for a walk in the woods yesterday.*

Word Builder: wood +
wooden: made of wood.

wool *noun* (wul) [N] the thick, soft hair of sheep and some other animals that is often used by people to make cloth. *Jeffrey's winter jacket is made of wool.*

word *noun* (wərd) a sound or group of sounds that has some meaning that other people can understand. Words are a basic unit of language. *I speak only a few words of their language. | Writing new words will help you remember them.*

word processing *noun* (wərd pra se sing) [N] the activity of making written documents with a computer. *The office assistant is an expert at word processing.*

word processor *noun* (wərd pra se sər) a computer or a computer program used to write, change, print, and save text.

work *noun* (wərk) 1. [N] the use of energy and effort to make or do something. *It takes a lot of hard work to build a house.* 2. [C] a project or task that uses energy and effort. *Most of this writer's works were very popular.* 3. [N] a job. *She enjoys her work at the hospital.*
verb 1. to have or do a job. *He works at a bank.* 2. to run or act in the expected way. *That phone doesn't work.* 3. to use or handle. *I learned how to work the new machine.*
work out 1. to solve by making special efforts. *The two groups worked out their problems together.* 2. to do physical exercise. *She works out at the gym.*

Word Builder: work +
workday: the amount of time out of 24 hours you spend working.
worker: a person who works.
worksheet: a sheet of paper on which you do written work.
workstation: the area in a workplace where you do your work.
work-study: a program that helps you find a part-time job to pay for your college education.

workers' compensation *noun* (wər kərz kam pən sā shən) [N] the money that is paid for medical costs if a worker at a company has been injured while doing his or her job.

workmanship *noun* (wərk mən ship) [N] the art or skill of people who work with their hands or with machines. *She takes pride in her workmanship as a carpenter.*

workplace *noun* (wərk plās) a place where people work, such as a factory, office, or store. *You have the right to a safe workplace.*

world *noun* (wərld) 1. the earth, or other planets that might be like earth. *I would like to travel around the world someday.* | *He believes that there is life on other worlds.* 2. the universe and everything that exists. *I think the stars are the most beautiful things in the world.* 3. a particular area or a field of activity along with all the people and things having to do with it. *The United States is part of the Western world.* | *Parents are the most important people in a child's world.* | *The business world is competitive.*

world

World War I *noun* (wərld wōr wən) [N] the war of 1914 to 1918, fought between countries including France, Great Britain, and the United States on one side and Germany and Austria-Hungary on the other. It ended with the defeat of Germany and Austria-Hungary.

World War II *noun* (wərld wōr too) [N] the war of 1939 to 1945, fought between countries including Germany, Italy, and Japan on one side and Great Britain, the United States, the Soviet Union, and other countries on the other. This war ended with the defeat of Germany, Italy, and Japan.

World Wide Web *noun* (wərld wīd web) a part of the Internet. The World Wide Web is made of documents called *Web pages* and *Web sites* that are connected to each other. *We searched the World Wide Web for information on dogs.*

worm *noun* (wərm) an animal with a long, thin, round or flat body with no legs. Worms live in water or on land.

worm

worn *verb* (wōrn) past participle of **wear.**

worry *verb* (wər ē) to feel fear or anxiety. *Don't worry, I'll take care of the problem.* | *I **worry about** my children when they stay out late.*
noun a feeling of fear or anxiety. *He was filled with worry while his wife was in the hospital.* | *She has many worries about how her son is doing in school.*

Word Builder: worry +
worried: feeling worry.

worse *adj.* (wərs) comparative form of **bad.** *That movie was bad, but this one is worse.*
adv. comparative form of **badly.** *I play tennis badly, but he plays worse.*

worship *verb* (wər ship) to give religious honor and love. *Many people come to worship in this church.*

worst *adj.* (wərst) superlative form of **bad.** *It was the worst winter that he could remember.*
noun someone or something that is the most bad or most ill. *Of all the restaurants in town, that one is the worst.*
adv. superlative form of **badly.** *Everyone played badly, but she played worst.*

worth *noun* (wərth) 1. [N] the value of a thing or person. *The worth of that ring is 500 dollars.* | *His worth to the company has increased since he got more training.* 2. [N] an amount of something that can be bought with an amount of money. *He bought five dollars **worth of** flour.*
adj. having a value equal to. *This jacket is worth fifty dollars.*

worthy *adj.* (wər thē) having enough worth or value. *He gives money to community programs and other worthy causes.*

would *verb* (wud) 1. used as a past form of **will** after verbs in the past tense that report speech or thoughts. *They decided that they would go to the movies after dinner.* 2. used to express that an action depends on something else. *If I owned this company, I would make a lot of changes.* | *If I had the money, I would give it to you.* 3. used to form polite questions or requests. *Would you please stop making that noise?* 4. used to describe a typical behavior of someone in the past. *When I was sick as a child, my mother would always make me chicken soup.*
would like used as a polite form of **want** or used when the possibility of doing what you want is not likely. *Excuse me. I would like some more tea.* | *I would like to travel around the world someday.*

would rather used to express that you prefer one thing to another. *I **would rather** live in a small town **than** in a big city.*

would like or want?

Want describes a desire or need for something in an informal manner.

Would like describes a more formal or polite way to express a desire or need for something.

We also use *would like* when we have a desire for something that we think is not likely to happen or is not planned. We use *want* when we are more certain that something will happen.

Compare:
Do you want some coffee? (informal)
Would you like a cup of coffee? (formal, polite)
I would like to go to Spain someday. (It's a wish that I have, but I don't know if it will ever happen.)
Where do you want to go for your vacation? I want to go to Florida. (I will go somewhere, probably to Florida.)

wound[1] *noun* (woond) a cut or other injury to a part of the body. *The soldier has a wound in his leg.*
verb to injure or harm by cutting, piercing, or tearing the skin. *He wounded his knee by falling on a rock.*

Word Builder: wound +
wounded: having a wound.

wound[2] *verb* (wownd) past tense and past participle of **wind**[2].

wove *verb* (wōv) past tense of **weave.**

woven *verb* (wō vən) past participle of **weave.** *She had woven cloth for years.*

wrap *noun* (ræp) [N] a sheet of material, such as paper or plastic, that is used to cover something. *Nancy covered the bowl with plastic wrap.*
verb to cover with paper or some other material. *Please wrap the meat in foil.* | *George wrapped the presents in shiny paper.*
wrap up to finish or complete. *The president wrapped up his speech.*

Word Builder: wrap +
wrapper: a piece of thin material used for wrapping.

wreck *noun* (rek) 1. an action that causes great or total destruction. *His fast driving on the icy road caused a car wreck.* 2. a thing or a person in very bad condition. *That car was a wreck before Chris fixed it up.* | *I feel like **a wreck!***

verb to ruin or destroy. *Fire wrecked that building.*

wrench *noun* (rench) a metal tool with jaws that is used to hold and turn a bolt, pipe, or other object.

wrench

wring *verb* (ring) ***wrung, wrung*** to twist and press tightly. *Please wring the wet cloth over the sink.* | *He couldn't answer and **wrung his hands** in a nervous way.*
wring out to press the water from. *Wring out the wet clothes and then hang them up to dry.*

Word Builder: wring +
wringer: a machine that wrings wet clothes in order to squeeze the water out of them.

wrinkle *noun* (ring kəl) a fold on a surface, such as cloth or skin. *You should iron the wrinkles out of your shirt.* | *Old people have wrinkles on their skin.*

wrist *noun* (rist) the joint between the arm and hand.

write *verb* (rīt) ***wrote, written*** 1. to form letters or words on a surface with a pen, pencil, or some other thing. *Write your name on the paper.* 2. to be the author of something. *She wrote that book.*
write down to write something in order to remember it. *Spell the word out loud; then write it down.* | *I wrote down his phone number in my address book.*
write out to write in full. *Write out the whole sentence.*

Word Builder: write +
rewrite: to write again in order to improve.
writer: a person who writes; author.

writing *noun* (rī ting) 1. letters or words written by someone. *Her writing is hard to read.* 2. a written form. *Can you **put** your ideas **in writing?***

written *verb* (ri tən) past participle of **write.**
adj. done in writing. *The teacher wants a written report, not an oral one.*

wrong *adj.* (rawng) 1. not true or correct. *Your answer is wrong.* 2. not good; bad. *Murder is wrong.* 3. not working in a proper way. *There is **something wrong with** my car.*
adv. in the wrong way. *I did it wrong again!*

wrote *verb* (rōt) past tense of **write.**

wrung *verb* (rəng) past tense and past participle of **wring.**

x-ray *noun* (<u>eks</u> rā) a photograph made
with a special beam that uses radiation
to show what is inside something. *The*
nurse **took an x-ray** *of my leg to see if*
any bones were broken. | *The doctor*
says I need a chest x-ray.

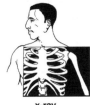

x-ray

verb to take a photograph with this
special beam. *A security guard x-rays all packages that*
people carry onto an airplane. | *A nurse x-rayed my arm.*

Y y

yard[1] *noun* (y̲a̲r̲d̲) a standard unit used to measure length. One yard equals three feet.

yard[2] *noun* (y̲a̲r̲d̲) 1. an open area next to a house or other building. *The children are playing in the yard.* 2. a closed area used for a particular purpose. *Daniel bought wood at the lumber yard.*

yarn *noun* (y̲a̲r̲n̲) [N] thick thread made from wool or another material. *Margaret knitted a sweater with blue yarn.*

yarn

yeah *interj.* (y̲e̲a̲) (informal) yes. *Can I have some pizza? Yeah, take some.*

year *noun* (y̲ē̲r̲) 1. a standard unit used to measure time. One year equals about 365 days. 2. a part of the year that is set apart for a particular activity. *Our school year starts in September and ends in June.*
year-to-date from the beginning of the year to this day. *Year-to-date, or YTD, is often written on the stub of a check for wages to show how much money a person has earned in a year up to the date of the check.*

yearly *adj.* (y̲ē̲r̲ lē) having to do with one year. *Tom got a raise in his yearly salary.*

yell *verb* (y̲e̲l̲) to speak in a very loud voice because you are hurt, afraid, angry, or excited. *The lost boy **yelled for help**. | My mom **yelled at** me because I was late.*

yellow *adj.* (y̲e̲ lō) having the color of the sun, a lemon, or a banana.

yellow pages *pl. noun* (y̲e̲ lō pā jəz) the part of a telephone book that gives information about businesses. *Look under Automobile Repair in the yellow pages to find someone who can fix your car.*

yes *adv.* (y̲e̲s̲) it is as you say or ask; used to say that you agree with or accept something. *Would you like a drink? Yes, I would. | Yes, I agree with your point of view.*

yesterday *adv.* (y̲e̲ stər dā̲) on the day before today. *Carol visited her mother yesterday.*
noun the day before today. *Yesterday was a quiet day for me.*

yet *adv.* (y̲e̲t̲) 1. at this time. *Have they arrived yet? No, not yet.* 2. but. *The weather is sunny yet cold.*
conj. even so. *She has a good job, yet she is not happy.*

yield *verb* (y̲ē̲l̲d̲) to wait and let the traffic from a large road go first. *The yellow sign means you must **yield to** traffic already on the highway.*

yoga *noun* (y̲ō̲ gə) [N] a set of exercises to help you relax and feel well. *Sally teaches yoga at the community center.*

yogurt *noun* (y̲ō̲ gərt) [N] a soft, sour food made from milk that often has fruit added.

you *pron.* (ū̲) 1. the person or persons being spoken or written to. *Can you help me?* 2. the form of **you** that is used as the object of a verb or that is used after a preposition. *Did he hurt you? | What did she say to you?* 3. a person; people in general; one. *You can't drive a car without a license in any state.*

young *adj.* (y̲ə̲n̲g̲) in an early part of life or growth. *My sister is a young child. | Compared to England, the United States is a young country.*
noun [N] animals that have been recently born. *The mother cat is taking care of her young.*

your *adj.* (y̲ō̲r̲) of or belonging to you; a possessive form of **you.** *Put on your hat.*

yours *pron.* (y̲ō̲r̲z̲) the one or ones that belong to you; a possessive form of **you.** *These are my gloves. Yours are on the table. | Is this pen yours?*

yourself *pron.* (y̲ō̲r̲ s̲e̲l̲f̲) 1. a word used to show that an action is done to or in connection with the person that the speaker is addressing, and that it is this same person who performs the action. *Did you hurt yourself when you fell? | You should write yourself a note to help you remember. | Look at yourself in the mirror.* 2. you and no one else. *You yourself must write to them. No one else can do it.*

yourselves *pron.* (y̲ō̲r̲ s̲e̲l̲v̲z̲) plural of **yourself.**

youth *noun* (ū̲t̲h̲) 1. [N] the time of life when you are young. *Hannah had a happy youth.* 2. any young person. *Some youths from the neighborhood offered to help the old couple.*

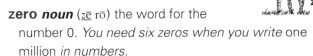

zebra *noun* (zē brə) a large mammal with black and white stripes that looks like a horse. Zebras live in Africa.

zero *noun* (zē rō) the word for the number 0. *You need six zeros when you write* one million *in numbers.*

zip *verb* (zip) to close with a zipper. *Kenny zipped his jacket.* | ***Zip up** your jacket!*

zip code *noun* (zip kōd) (trademark) numbers that are part of the address in mail. Every area in the United States has a different set of numbers. You write the numbers after the state name in an address. The zip code makes it easier to deliver the mail.

zip drive *noun* (zip drīv) (trademark) a computer part that saves information on a special disk, called a *zip disk.*

Ziploc *adj.* (zip lak) (trademark) having a special type of seal used on a plastic bag. You press together strips along the top edges to close the bag. *Sharon packed her sandwich in a Ziploc bag.*

zipper *noun* (zi pər) a thing you use to open and close clothing and bags. A zipper has two rows of teeth and a slide that puts them together or pulls them apart. *Her skirt has a zipper on the side.*

zone *noun* (zōn) 1. an area that is separate or different from other areas because of a particular environment, use, or some other special quality. *These animals live only in tropical zones.* | *In their time zone, it is only six o'clock.* 2. an area in a town or city that has a particular use or that cannot be used for certain activities. *There is a lot of traffic in the business zone.* | *They can't build the factory there because it's a residential zone.*

zoo *noun* (zoo) a place where animals are kept for people to look at. *My children love to visit the zoo to see the lions and tigers.*

Irregular Verbs

Base Form	Past Tense	Past Participle	Base Form	Past Tense	Past Participle
awake	awoke, awaked	awoken, awaked	find	found	found
be	was, were	been	fit	fit, fitted	fit, fitted
bear	bore	borne, born	flee	fled	fled
beat	beat	beaten, beat	fly	flew	flown
become	became	become	forbid	forbade, forbad	forbidden
begin	began	begun	forecast	forecast, forecasted	forecast, forecasted
bend	bent	bent	forget	forgot	forgotten
bet	bet, betted	bet, betted	forgive	forgave	forgiven
bind	bound	bound	freeze	froze	frozen
bite	bit	bitten, bit	get	got	got, gotten
bleed	bled	bled	give	gave	given
blow	blew	blown	go	went	gone
break	broke	broken	grind	ground	ground
bring	brought	brought	grow	grew	grown
broadcast	broadcast, broadcasted	broadcast, broadcasted	hang	hung	hung
build	built	built	have	had	had
burn	burned, burnt	burned, burnt	hear	heard	heard
burst	burst	burst	hide	hid	hidden, hid
buy	bought	bought	hit	hit	hit
catch	caught	caught	hold	held	held
choose	chose	chosen	hurt	hurt	hurt
cling	clung	clung	input	input, inputted	input, inputted
come	came	come	keep	kept	kept
cost	cost	cost	kneel	knelt, kneeled	knelt, kneeled
cut	cut	cut	know	knew	known
deal	dealt	dealt	lay	laid	laid
dig	dug	dug	lead	led	led
dive	dove, dived	dived	leap	leaped, leapt	leaped, leapt
do	did	done	leave	left	left
draw	drew	drawn	lend	lent	lent
dream	dreamed, dreamt	dreamed, dreamt	let	let	let
drink	drank	drunk	lie	lay	lain
drive	drove	driven	light	lit, lighted	lit, lighted
eat	ate	eaten	lose	lost	lost
fall	fell	fallen	make	made	made
feed	fed	fed	mean	meant	meant
feel	felt	felt	meet	met	met
fight	fought	fought	mistake	mistook	mistaken

Irregular Verbs

Base Form	Past Tense	Past Participle	Base Form	Past Tense	Past Participle
mow	mowed	mown, mowed	spin	spun	spun
			split	split	split
overcome	overcame	overcome	spread	spread	spread
oversleep	overslept	overslept	spring	sprang, sprung	sprung
pay	paid	paid			
prove	proved	proven, proved	stand	stood	stood
			steal	stole	stolen
put	put	put	stick	stuck	stuck
quit	quit, quitted	quit, quitted	sting	stung	stung
read	read	read	strike	struck	struck, stricken
reset	reset	reset			
rewind	rewound	rewound	swear	swore	sworn
rid	rid, ridded	rid, ridded	sweat	sweat, sweated	sweat, sweated
ride	rode	ridden			
ring	rang	rung	sweep	swept	swept
rise	rose	risen	swell	swelled	swollen, swelled
run	ran	run			
saw	sawed	sawed, sawn	swim	swam	swum
say	said	said	swing	swung	swung
see	saw	seen	take	took	taken
sell	sold	sold	teach	taught	taught
send	sent	sent	tear	tore	torn
set	set	set	tell	told	told
sew	sewed	sewn, sewed	think	thought	thought
shake	shook	shaken	throw	threw	thrown
shed	shed	shed	tread	trod, treaded	trodden, trod
shine	shone, shined	shone, shined			
			troubleshoot	troubleshot	troubleshot
shoot	shot	shot	understand	understood	understood
show	showed	shown, showed	undo	undid	undone
			upset	upset	upset
shrink	shrank, shrunk	shrunk, shrunken	wake	woke, waked	woken, waked
shut	shut	shut			
sing	sang	sung	wear	wore	worn
sink	sank, sunk	sunk	weave	wove, weaved	woven, weaved
sit	sat	sat			
sleep	slept	slept	win	won	won
slide	slid	slid	wind	wound	wound
speak	spoke	spoken	withdraw	withdrew	withdrawn
speed	sped, speeded	sped, speeded	withhold	withheld	withheld
			wring	wrung	wrung
spend	spent	spent	write	wrote	written

Irregular Nouns and Adjectives

Irregular Nouns

Singular	Plural	Singular	Plural
analysis	analyses	life	lives
basis	bases	loaf	loaves
calf	calves	louse	lice
child	children	man	men
crisis	crises	mouse	mice
criterion	criteria	scarf	scarves
deer	deer	self	selves
emphasis	emphases	sheep	sheep
fish	fish	shelf	shelves
foot	feet	thief	thieves
fungus	fungi	tooth	teeth
goose	geese	wife	wives
half	halves	wolf	wolves
knife	knives	woman	women
leaf	leaves		

Irregular Adjectives

Positive	Comparative	Superlative
bad	worse	worst
far	farther, further	farthest, furthest
good	better	best
little	less	least
much	more	most

Contractions

be

I	I am = I'm
you	you are = you're
he	he is = he's
she	she is = she's
it	it is = it's
we	we are = we're
they	they are = they're
who	who is = who's
where	where is = where's
that	that is = that's
there	there is = there's
here	here is = here's

will

I	I will = I'll
you	you will = you'll
he	he will = he'll
she	she will = she'll
it	it will = it'll
we	we will = we'll
they	they will = they'll
who	who will = who'll
where	where will = where'll
that	that will = that'll
there	there will = there'll

have

I	I have = I've
you	you have = you've
he	he has = he's
she	she has = she's
it	it has = it's
we	we have = we've
they	they have = they've
who	who has = who's
who	who have = who've
there	there has = there's
could	could have = could've
might	might have = might've
must	must have = must've
should	should have = should've
would	would have = would've

had

I	I had = I'd
you	you had = you'd
he	he had = he'd
she	she had = she'd
we	we had = we'd
they	they had = they'd
who	who had = who'd
where	where = where'd
there	there had = there'd

would

I	I would = I'd
you	you would = you'd
he	he would = he'd
she	she would = she'd
we	we would = we'd
they	they would = they'd
who	who would = who'd
where	where would = where'd
there	there would = there'd

not

are not = aren't
is not = isn't
was not = wasn't
were not = weren't
do not = don't
does not = doesn't
did not = didn't
cannot = can't
could not = couldn't
have not = haven't
has not = hasn't
had not = hadn't
must not = mustn't
should not = shouldn't
will not = won't
would not = wouldn't

Some Common Prefixes

A prefix is a part of a word with its own meaning. When you add a prefix to the beginning of another word, you create a new word with a new meaning. The new meaning is related to the meaning of the original word.

Prefix	Meaning	Example	Definition
anti-	against	antifreeze antiaircraft	a substance that stops an engine from freezing against aircraft
co-	together	co-worker co-sign	someone you work with to sign a document with another person
dis-	not	disagree disrespect	to not agree to not respect
ex-	former	ex-president ex-wife	former president former wife
in- il- im- ir-	not	incomplete illegal impossible irregular	not complete not legal not possible not regular, not even
inter-	between; among	interstate international	between states among nations
mis-	wrong; bad	mismanage misfortune	manage in the wrong way bad fortune
multi-	many	multicultural multimedia	having to do with many cultures having or using many media
non-	not	nondairy nonfiction	not dairy not fiction
over-	too; too much	overactive overdue	too active too late, not done on time
post-	after	postwar	after a war
pre-	before; in advance	prearrange prepay	to arrange before to pay in advance
pro-	for; in favor of	pro-America	in favor of America
re-	again	refill rewrite	fill again write again
self-	having to do with one's own self	self-confidence self-control	confidence in yourself control of yourself
semi-	half; not completely	semicircle semiprivate	a half circle not completely private
trans-	across; to another place	transcontinental transplant	across a continent to plant in another place
un-	not	unhappy unreal	not happy not real

Some Common Suffixes

A suffix is a part of a word with its own meaning. When you add a suffix to the end of another word, you create a new word with a new meaning. The new meaning is related to the meaning of the original word.

Suffix	Meaning	Example	Definition
-dom	condition of being	freedom	the condition of being free
		boredom	the condition of being bored
-er, -or	person or thing that does something	collector	a person who collects
		washer	a machine that washes
-ful	amount that fills	spoonful	the amount that fills a spoon
	tending to	harmful	tending to harm
	full of	beautiful	full of beauty
-ist	person who does something	artist	a person who creates art
		machinist	a person who operates a machine
-ity	state or quality	security	the state of being secure
		purity	the quality of being pure
-ness	condition	kindness	the condition of being kind
		darkness	the condition of being dark
-ship	state	friendship	the state of being a friend
		leadership	the state of being a leader
-ward	in the direction of	backward	toward the back
		inward	toward the inside of

These suffixes have a function in grammar. When you add one of these suffixes to a word, you add meaning to the original word or change its part of speech.

Suffix	Function	Examples
-ed	forms the past tense or past participle of many verbs	looked, wanted
-er	forms the comparative of many adjectives	happier, stronger
-est	forms the superlative of many adjectives	softest, ugliest
-ing	forms the present participle of verbs	thinking, going
-ly	makes adverbs from many adjectives	quickly, happily
-s, -es	makes most nouns plural	cats, dresses
		ladies, tomatoes
-s, -es	forms the present tense of many verbs with *he, she, it*	eats, washes

Abbreviations

Abbreviations contain the first letter of a word as well as one or more other letters of that word. When you read an abbreviation, you say the whole word. For example, when you read "Co.," say "company."

apt.	apartment		med.	medium
asst.	assistant		mfg.	manufacturing
attn.	attention		mgr.	manager
Ave.	Avenue		mi.	mile
bldg.	building		min.	minute
Blvd.	Boulevard		misc.	miscellaneous
Bros.	brothers		mo.	month
Co.	company		msg.	message
Corp.	corporation		mt.	mountain, mount
dept.	department		no.	number
Dr.	doctor		oz.	ounce
Dr.	Drive		pd.	paid
dz.	dozen		pg.	page
encl.	enclosed, enclosure		pt.	pint
esp.	especially		qt.	quart
etc.	et cetera, and the like		Rd.	Road
fl. oz.	fluid ounce		Re:	regarding
ft.	foot		sec.	second
gal.	gallon		sm.	small
hr.	hour		Sr.	senior
in.	inch		St.	Street
Inc.	incorporated		tbsp.	tablespoon
Jr.	junior		tsp.	teaspoon
lb.	pound		yd.	yard
lg.	large		yr.	year

Abbreviations

Initializations

Initializations are a short form of two or more words. To read an initialization, say each one of its letters. For example, for "C.O.D.," say "C-O-D" (see-oh-dee), not "cod."

AC	air conditioning, or alternating current	IRA	individual retirement account
aka	also known as	IRS	Internal Revenue Service
a.m.	ante meridiem, a Latin term for "morning"	KO	knockout
ASAP	as soon as possible	LED	light-emitting diode
ATM	automated teller machine	LCD	liquid crystal display
CD	compact disk	MD	doctor of medicine
CD-ROM	compact disk, read-only memory	MIA	missing in action
CEO	chief executive officer	mph	miles per hour
C.O.D.	cash on delivery	MSDS	Material Safety Data Sheet
CPU	central processing unit	N.A.	not available
DC	direct current	OJ	orange juice
DNA	deoxyribonucleic acid	P.E.	physical education
DOA	dead on arrival	p.m.	post meridiem, a Latin term for "afternoon"
DOB	date of birth	PO	post office
DVD	digital versatile disk	PS	postscript
EBT	electronic benefits transfer	PTA/O	parent-teacher association/organization
EKG	electrocardiogram	RIP	rest in peace
ESL	English as a second language	RN	registered nurse
ESOL	English for speakers of other languages	rpm	revolutions per minute
FYI	for your information	SASE	self-addressed stamped envelope
GED	General Educational Development	SKU	stock keeping unit
GFCI	ground fault circuit interrupter	SUV	sport-utility vehicle
HIV	human immunodeficiency virus	TB	tuberculosis
HMO	health maintenance organization	TLC	tender loving care
HQ	headquarters	TV	television
HR	human resources	UFO	unidentified flying object
ID	identification	U.S.	United States
IEP	individualized education plan	USCIS	United States Citizenship and Immigration Services
IOU	I owe you		

Acronyms

Acronyms are a kind of initialization. When you read an acronym, do not say each letter. Instead, read the acronym as if it were any word. For example, when you read "NASA," say "nasa," not "n-a-s-a."

AIDS	acquired immune deficiency syndrome	NATO	North Atlantic Treaty Organization
AWOL	absent without leave	OSHA	Occupational Safety and Health Administration
FICA	Federal Insurance Contributions Act		
NASA	National Aeronautic and Space Administration	SARS	severe acute respiratory syndrome
		ZIP	zone improvement plan

Weights and Measures

Area

American
square inch (sq. in.)
square foot (sq. ft.) = 144 square inches
square yard (sq. yd.) = 9 square feet
acre = 4,840 square yards
square mile (sq. mi.) = 640 acres

Metric
hectare = 10,000 square meters
1 hectare = 2.47 acres

Capacity

American	Abbreviation
fluid ounce	oz.
cup	C = 8 oz.
pint	pt. = 2 C = 16 oz.
quart	qt. = 2 pt. = 4 C
gallon	gal. = 4 qt.

Metric	Abbreviation
milliliter	mL = 1 cubic centimeter (c^3)
liter	L = 1,000 mL = 1,000 cubic centimeters (c^3)

1 oz. = 29.57 mL	1 mL = 0.0338 oz.
1 qt. = 0.946 L	1 L = 1.057 qt.

Time

Unit	Abbreviation
second	sec.
minute	min. = 60 sec.
hour	hr. = 60 min.
day	= 24 hr.
week	wk. = 7 days
year	yr. = 365 days (or 365 1/4 days)

Weights and Measures

Distance (Length)

American	Abbreviation
inch	in.
foot	ft. = 12 inches
yard	yd. = 3 feet = 36 inches
mile	mi. = 5,280 feet = 1,760 yards

Metric	Abbreviation
millimeter	mm = 1/1,000 m
centimeter	cm = 1/100 m = 10 mm
meter	m = 1,000 mm = 100 cm
kilometer	km = 1,000 m

1 cm = 0.39 in.	1 in. = 2.54 cm
1 m = 39 in.	1 ft. = 30.48 cm = 0.3048 m
1 km = 0.62 mi.	1 mi. = 1.6 km

Temperature

Fahrenheit (F)	Celsius (C)	
212°F	100°C	steam point (boiling point)
90°F	32°C	
50°F	10°C	
32°F	0°C	ice point (freezing point)
0°F	-18°C	

Weight

American	Abbreviation
ounce	oz.
pound	lb. = 16 oz.

Metric	Abbreviation
gram	g
kilogram	kg = 1,000 g

1 ounce = 28.35 g	1 gram = 0.0353 oz.
1 pound = 0.45 kg	1 kg = 2.2 lb.

Numbers, Days, Months, Years

Whole Numbers

Numeral	Cardinal Number	Ordinal Number
1	one	first
2	two	second
3	three	third
4	four	fourth
5	five	fifth
6	six	sixth
7	seven	seventh
8	eight	eighth
9	nine	ninth
10	ten	tenth
11	eleven	eleventh
12	twelve	twelfth
13	thirteen	thirteenth
14	fourteen	fourteenth
15	fifteen	fifteenth
16	sixteen	sixteenth
17	seventeen	seventeenth
18	eighteen	eighteenth
19	nineteen	nineteenth
20	twenty	twentieth
30	thirty	thirtieth
40	forty	fortieth
50	fifty	fiftieth
60	sixty	sixtieth
70	seventy	seventieth
80	eighty	eightieth
90	ninety	ninetieth
100	one hundred	hundredth
1,000	one thousand	thousandth
1,000,000	one million	millionth
1,000,000,000	one billion	billionth
1,000,000,000,000	one trillion	trillionth

Fractions

1/2	one-half
1/3	one-third
1/4	one-fourth or one-quarter
1/5	one-fifth
1/6	one-sixth
1/7	one-seventh
1/8	one-eighth
1/9	one-ninth
1/10	one-tenth

Decimals

0.1	one-tenth
0.01	one-hundredth
0.001	one-thousandth
0.0001	one-ten-thousandth

Days of the Week

Sunday, Monday, Tuesday, Wednesday, Thursday, Friday, Saturday

Months of the Year	Number of Days
January	31
February	28*
March	31
April	30
May	31
June	30
July	31
August	31
September	30
October	31
November	30
December	31
Total	365*

*Every four years, February has 29 days and the whole year has 366 days. A year with 366 days is called a "leap year."

States and Capitals

State		Capital	State		Capital
Alabama	AL	Montgomery	Montana	MT	Helena
Alaska	AK	Juneau	Nebraska	NE	Lincoln
Arizona	AZ	Phoenix	Nevada	NV	Carson City
Arkansas	AR	Little Rock	New Hampshire	NH	Concord
California	CA	Sacramento	New Jersey	NJ	Trenton
Colorado	CO	Denver	New Mexico	NM	Santa Fe
Connecticut	CT	Hartford	New York	NY	Albany
Delaware	DE	Dover	North Carolina	NC	Raleigh
District of Columbia*	DC		North Dakota	ND	Bismarck
Florida	FL	Tallahassee	Ohio	OH	Columbus
Georgia	GA	Atlanta	Oklahoma	OK	Oklahoma City
Hawaii	HI	Honolulu	Oregon	OR	Salem
Idaho	ID	Boise	Pennsylvania	PA	Harrisburg
Illinois	IL	Springfield	Rhode Island	RI	Providence
Indiana	IN	Indianapolis	South Carolina	SC	Columbia
Iowa	IA	Des Moines	South Dakota	SD	Pierre
Kansas	KS	Topeka	Tennessee	TN	Nashville
Kentucky	KY	Frankfort	Texas	TX	Austin
Louisiana	LA	Baton Rouge	Utah	UT	Salt Lake City
Maine	ME	Augusta	Vermont	VT	Montpelier
Maryland	MD	Annapolis	Virginia	VA	Richmond
Massachusetts	MA	Boston	Washington	WA	Olympia
Michigan	MI	Lansing	West Virginia	WV	Charleston
Minnesota	MN	St. Paul	Wisconsin	WI	Madison
Mississippi	MS	Jackson	Wyoming	WY	Cheyenne
Missouri	MO	Jefferson City			

* The District of Columbia, or Washington, D.C., is the capital of the United States. It is a city that is not part of any state.

Holidays in the United States

This list presents holidays that many people celebrate in the United States. It does not include all U.S. holidays. There are many other religious, civil, and ethnic holidays that different groups of people celebrate.

Holiday	Day	Observed Purpose
New Year's Day*	January 1	to celebrate the new year
Martin Luther King, Jr., Day*	Third Monday in January	to honor the life of Dr. Martin Luther King, Jr.
Groundhog Day	February 2	to watch for signs of coming spring
Lincoln's Birthday	February 12	to honor the life and works of Abraham Lincoln, the president who freed the slaves
Valentine's Day	February 14	to celebrate love and friendship
Presidents' Day*	Third Monday in February	to honor presidents George Washington and Abraham Lincoln
Washington's Birthday	February 22	to honor the life and works of George Washington, first president of the United States
St. Patrick's Day	March 17	to celebrate with people who came to America from Ireland
April Fool's Day	April 1	to play tricks on people
Earth Day	April 22	to celebrate nature and to remind people to care for Earth and its resources
Arbor Day	Last Friday in April	to learn about and plant trees
Cinco de Mayo	May 5	to celebrate Mexican culture and history and Mexico's victory over the French in 1862
Mother's Day	Second Sunday in May	to remember and honor our mothers
Memorial Day*	Last Monday in May	to honor the memory of servicemen and service-women who died in wars
Flag Day	June 14	to honor the American flag
Father's Day	Third Sunday in June	to remember and honor our fathers
Juneteenth	June 19	to celebrate the freedom of African Americans

Holidays in the United States

Holiday	Day	Observed Purpose
Independence Day*	July 4	to celebrate the anniversary of the signing of the Declaration of Independence in 1776
Labor Day*	First Monday in September	to honor our nation's working men and women
Citizenship Day	September 17	to celebrate the anniversary of the signing of the U.S. Constitution in 1787
Columbus Day*	Second Monday in October	to remember Columbus's voyages from Europe to America
United Nations Day	October 24	to celebrate the anniversary of the founding of the United Nations
Halloween	October 31	for children to dress in costumes, play tricks, and beg for candy
Election Day	First Tuesday after first Monday in November	for citizens to vote in general elections
Veterans' Day*	November 11	to honor the men and women who served in the armed forces
Puerto Rican Discovery Day	November 19	to celebrate the anniversary of Columbus's discovery of Puerto Rico
Thanksgiving*	Fourth Thursday in November	to remember the early settlers from Europe who came to America and to give thanks for what we have
Christmas*	December 25	for Christians to celebrate the birth of Jesus Christ. (Some non-Christians also celebrate Christmas by giving gifts and gathering with family.)
Kwanzaa	December 26–January 1	to celebrate African and African-American culture and values

*These ten holidays are official holidays. Government offices and institutions, such as post offices, schools, and courts, are closed on these days. Many people have a day off from work on these holidays. People who have to work on these holidays often get extra pay.

Countries and Nationalities

Continent: Africa

Country	Nationality
Algeria	Algerian
Angola	Angolan
Benin	Beninese
Botswana	Motswana (sing.), Batswana (pl.)
Burkina Faso	Burkinabe
Burundi	Burundian
Cameroon	Cameroonian
Cape Verde	Cape Verdean
Central African Republic	Central African
Chad	Chadian
Comoros	Comoran
Congo, Republic of the	Congolese
Congo, Democratic Republic of the	Congolese
Cote d'Ivoire	Ivorian
Djibouti	Djiboutian
Egypt	Egyptian
Equatorial Guinea	Equatorial Guinean
Eritrea	Eritrean
Ethiopia	Ethiopian
Gabon	Gabonese
Gambia, the	Gambian
Ghana	Ghanaian
Guinea	Guinean
Guinea-Bissau	Guinean
Kenya	Kenyan
Lesotho	Mosotho (sing.), Basotho (pl.)
Liberia	Liberian
Libya	Libyan
Madagascar	Malagasy
Malawi	Malawian
Mali	Malian
Mauritania	Mauritanian
Morocco	Moroccan
Mozambique	Mozambican
Namibia	Namibian
Niger	Nigerien
Nigeria	Nigerian
Rwanda	Rwandan

Country	Nationality
São Tomé and Principé	São Toméan
Senegal	Senegalese
Seychelles	Seychellois
Sierra Leone	Sierra Leonean
Somalia	Somali
South Africa	South African
Sudan	Sudanese
Swaziland	Swazi
Tanzania	Tanzanian
Togo	Togolese
Tunisia	Tunisian
Uganda	Ugandan
Zambia	Zambian
Zimbabwe	Zimbabwean

Continent: Asia (including the Middle East)

Country	Nationality
Afghanistan	Afghan
Armenia	Armenian
Azerbaijan	Azeri (Azerbaijani)
Bahrain	Bahraini
Bangladesh	Bangladeshi
Bhutan	Bhutanese
Brunei	Bruneian (Brunei)
Cambodia	Cambodian
China	Chinese
East Timor	Timorese
Georgia	Georgian
India	Indian
Indonesia	Indonesian
Iran	Iranian
Iraq	Iraqi
Israel	Israeli
Japan	Japanese
Jordan	Jordanian
Kazakhstan	Kazakh
Korea, Democratic People's Republic of	North Korean
Korea, Republic of	South Korean

Countries and Nationalities

Country	Nationality
Kuwait	Kuwaiti
Kyrgyzstan	Kyrgyz
Laos	Laotian
Lebanon	Lebanese
Malaysia	Malaysian
Maldives	Maldivian
Mongolia	Mongolian
Myanmar	Burmese
Nepal	Nepalese
Oman	Omani
Pakistan	Pakistani
Philippines	Filipino
Qatar	Qatari
Russia	Russian
Saudi Arabia	Saudi Arabian (Saudi)
Singapore	Singaporean
Sri Lanka	Sri Lankan
Syria	Syrian
Taiwan	Taiwanese
Tajikistan	Tajik
Thailand	Thai
Tibet	Tibetan
Turkey	Turk (Turkish)
Turkmenistan	Turkmen
United Arab Emirates	Emirati
Uzbekistan	Uzbek
Vietnam	Vietnamese
Yemen	Yemeni

Continent: Australia and Oceana

Country	Nationality
Australia	Australian
Cook Islands	Cook Islander
Fiji	Fijian
Kiribati	I-Kiribati
Marshall Islands	Marshallese
Micronesia	Micronesian
Nauru	Nauruan
New Caledonia	New Caledonian

Country	Nationality
New Guinea	New Guinean
New Zealand	New Zealander
Niue	Niuean
Palau	Paluan
Samoa	Samoan
Solomon Islands	Solomon Islander
Tahiti	Tahitian
Tonga	Tongan
Tuvalu	Tuvaluan
Vanuatu	Ni-Vanatu

Continent: Europe

Country	Nationality
Albania	Albanian
Andorra	Andorran
Austria	Austrian
Belarus	Belorussian
Belgium	Belgian
Bosnia and Herzegovina	Bosnian, Herzegovinian
Bulgaria	Bulgarian
Croatia	Croat, Croatian
Cyprus	Cypriot
Czech Republic	Czech
Denmark	Dane (Danish)
England	Englishman/woman (English)
Estonia	Estonian
Finland	Finn (Finnish)
France	Frenchman/woman (French)
Germany	German
Gibraltar	Gibraltarian
Greece	Greek
Hungary	Hungarian
Iceland	Icelander (Icelandic)
Ireland, Republic of	Irishman/woman (Irish)
Italy	Italian

Countries and Nationalities

Country	Nationality	Country	Nationality
Latvia	Latvian	Cuba	Cuban
Liechtenstein	Liechtensteiner	Dominica	Dominican
Lithuania	Lithuanian	Dominican Republic	Dominican
Luxembourg	Luxembourger	El Salvador	Salvadoran
Macedonia	Macedonian	Grenada	Grenadian
Malta	Maltese	Guatemala	Guatemalan
Moldova	Moldovan	Haiti	Haitian
Monaco	Monegasque	Honduras	Honduran
Netherlands, the	Dutchman/woman (Dutch)	Jamaica	Jamaican
Norway	Norwegian	Mexico	Mexican
Poland	Polish	Nicaragua	Nicaraguan
Portugal	Portuguese	Panama	Panamanian
Romania	Romanian	Puerto Rico	Puerto Rican
Russia	Russian	St. Kitts and Nevis	Kittitian, Nevisian
Scotland	Scot (Scottish)	St. Lucia	St. Lucian
Serbia and Montenegro	Serbian, Montenegran	St. Vincent and the Grenadines	St. Vincentian
Slovakia	Slovak (Slovakian)	Trinidad and Tobago	Trinidadian, Tobagonian
Slovenia	Slovene (Slovenian)	United States of America	American
Spain	Spaniard (Spanish)		
Sweden	Swede (Swedish)		
Switzerland	Swiss		
Turkey	Turk (Turkish)		
Ukraine	Ukrainian		
United Kingdom	British, English, Scottish, Welsh		
Wales	Welsh		

Continent: South America

Country	Nationality
Argentina	Argentinian (Argentine)
Bolivia	Bolivian
Brazil	Brazilian
Chile	Chilean
Colombia	Colombian
Ecuador	Ecuadoran
French Guiana	French Guianese
Guyana	Guyanese
Paraguay	Paraguayan
Peru	Peruvian
Suriname	Surinamer (Surinamese)
Uruguay	Uruguayan
Venezuela	Venezuelan

Continent: North America

Country	Nationality
Antigua and Barbuda	Antiguian, Barbudan
Aruba	Aruban
Bahamas, the	Bahamian
Barbados	Barbadian
Belize	Belizean
Canada	Canadian
Costa Rica	Costa Rican

Guide to the Word Explorer™

The Word Explorer organizes hundreds of words by their meaning. The purpose of the Word Explorer is to make it easy to find the words you need in many everyday situations.

The Word Explorer has six main parts. They are:
1. Communication
2. Community
3. Everyday Life
4. Human Life
5. Science and Nature
6. World of Work

Each of these parts has several important key words. For example, some of the key words in Everyday Life are *clothes, furniture,* and *vegetable.* The key words in each part are in alphabetical order.

Each key word is followed by word lists that are in groups. The groups show how the lists of words relate to the key word. For example, under *furniture,* there are word lists for these relationships: *parts of furniture, kinds of furniture, places for furniture,* and *actions associated with furniture.* If you could not remember the name of the piece of furniture that you put files in, you might first look under *furniture* and then check the list under *kinds of furniture.* There you would find *file cabinet.* If you had to describe a piece of furniture in writing, you could look under *parts of furniture.* There you would find several words to use in your writing, such as *arm, back,* and *cushion.*

The next page has a table of contents for the Word Explorer. There is also an alphabetical list of all the key words.

Word Explorer Contents

Communication

communication
grammar
language
letter
punctuation
word
writing
written communication

Community

city and town
crime
entertainment
government
recreation
school
sports
transportation

Everyday Life

accessory
appliance
bank
bathroom
beverage
car
clothes
food
fruit
furniture
grain
house
kitchen
meat
money
room
store
vegetable
vehicle

Human Life

arm
body
eye
face
family
foot
hand
head
health
illness
injury
leg
mind
mouth
people

Science and Nature

animal
land
plant
tree
water
weather

World of Work

computer
farm
industry
job
office
restaurant
tool
workplace

Key Word List

accessory
animal
appliance
arm
bank
bathroom
beverage
body
car
city and town
clothes
communication
computer
crime
entertainment
eye
face
family
farm
food
foot
fruit
furniture
government
grain
grammar
hand
head
health
house
illness
industry
injury
job
kitchen
land
language
leg
letter
meat
mind
money
mouth
office
people
plant
punctuation
recreation
restaurant
room
school
sports
store
tool
transportation
tree
vegetable
vehicle
water
weather
word
workplace
writing
written communication

Word Explorer—Communication

communication

examples of communication
announcement, broadcast, conversation, discussion, e-mail, essay, gesture, message, note, notice, sign, speech, symbol, transmission

acts of communication
advertising, announcing, broadcasting, contacting, convincing, explaining, expressing, informing, instructing, inviting, negotiating, persuading, reporting, revealing, sharing, teaching, telling, translating

means of communication
article, billboard, book, brochure, computer, e-mail, film, Internet, language, letter, magazine, memorandum (memo), movie, newspaper, radio, sign, speech, spoken language, telephone, television, text, written language

things important in communication
grammar, idea, pronunciation, subject, tone, topic, vocabulary

grammar

concepts of grammar
adjective, adverb, article, clause, comparative, conjunction, interjection, noun, object, plural, preposition, pronoun, sentence, singular, subject, subordinate, superlative, verb

language

parts of language
emphasis, expressions, grammar, phrases, rhythm, sentences, sounds, stress, syllables, vocabulary, words

actions involving language
advise, announce, answer, ask, communicate, complain, convince, describe, discuss, explain, express, inform, listen, persuade, quote, read, reply, report, respond, reveal, say, speak, talk, tell, think, understand, write

sounds in language
consonant, vowel

letter

parts of a letter
address, body, closing, date, greeting, signature

kinds of letters
business, formal, informal, news, personal

actions involving letters
address, compose, deliver, fold, read, receive, respond, send, sign, write

things associated with letters
address, envelope, paper, postage, post office, return address, stamp, zip code

parts of a letter

date — April 4, 2007

address —
Mr. Lou Grant
1114 N. Main St.
Ithaca, NY 14850

greeting — Dear Mr. Grant,

body —
Thank you for your interest in The Acme Corporation. I have reviewed your résumé, and your qualifications are indeed most impressive. But, unfortunately, we have just filled the position of Human Resources Director.

We will keep your résumé on file, and if a similar position opens soon, we will contact you. Best wishes for your continued success in your current position.

closing — Sincerely,

signature — A.E. Sedgwick

Ann Elizabeth Sedgwick
President,
The Acme Corporation

Word Explorer—Communication

punctuation

examples of punctuation
apostrophe, colon, comma, dash, exclamation mark, hyphen, period, question mark, quotation mark, semicolon

word

parts of words
prefix, root, suffix, syllable

kinds of words
adjective, adverb, article, conjunction, interjection, noun, preposition, pronoun, verb

writing (written communication)

things found in writing
alphabet, letters, paragraphs, printing, punctuation, quotation, sentences, spelling, words

things that use writing
article, book, brochure, e-mail, essay, instructions, letter, list, magazine, memorandum (memo), menu, newspaper, notes, notice, report, text

people associated with writing
author, editor, reporter, writer

things that use writing

magazine

brochure

instructions

list

notice

letter

book

notes

newspaper

menu

Word Explorer—Community

city and town

places in a city or town

airport, apartment building, bakery, bank, bar, barbershop, beauty shop, cemetery, church, clinic, delicatessen (deli), department store, dress shop, drugstore, dry-cleaning store, fire department, firehouse, flea market, gas station, grocery store, hospital, hotel, insurance agency, jail, laundromat, library, mall, market, museum, park, pet shop, pharmacy, playground, police station, post office, prison, repair shop, restaurant, school, supermarket, theater, zoo

areas of a town

block, commercial area, downtown, residential area, zone

people in a city or town

commuter, mayor, pedestrian, resident

crime

kinds of crimes

felony, misdemeanor, violation

examples of crime

abuse, assault, battery, kidnapping, murder, robbery, shoplifting, stealing, theft, vandalism, violation

places associated with crime

court, courthouse, courtroom, jail, police station, prison

actions of crime

abuse, batter, beat, hit, kidnap, kill, lie, murder, rob, shoot, steal

actions associated with crime

accuse, arrest, commit, confess, defend, fine, interrogate, investigate, punish

descriptions of crime

against the law, illegal, violent

results of crime

death, fine, injury, loss, punishment, sentence, trial

people who commit crimes

burglar, criminal, kidnapper, murderer, robber, vandal

people associated with crime

detective, judge, jury, lawyer, police officer, suspect, victim, witness

places in a city or town

gas station   apartment building   bank   restaurant   grocery store

school   park   museum   library   church

Word Explorer—Community

entertainment

forms of entertainment
circus, concert, dance, film, game, movie, play, program, radio, show, sports, television

places for entertainment
bar, club, field, hall, home, library, museum, park, stadium, theater

actions of entertainment
act, amuse, announce, dance, entertain, joke, perform, play, sing, tell

people or groups associated with entertainment
actor, announcer, artist, band, clown, dancer, musician, orchestra, performer, singer, writer

forms of entertainment

radio

game

television

sports

dance

movie

government

parts of government
agency, board, bureau, cabinet, committee, Congress, council, court, department, executive, legislature, senate

parts of the U.S. government
assembly, Cabinet, Congress, executive branch, House of Representatives, judicial branch, legislative branch, Senate, Supreme Court

levels of government
city, country, county, district, federal, national, state, town, village

actions of government
aid, alert, appoint, arrest, defend, elect, govern, guarantee, guard, inspect, investigate, judge, legislate, naturalize, nominate, prohibit, protect, regulate, rule, serve, tax, veto

ways to describe government
communist, democratic, republican, totalitarian

heads of government
governor, king, mayor, president, queen

people associated with government
citizen, governor, judge, mayor, minister, official, police officer, politician, president, representative, senator, vice president, voter

recreation

forms of recreation
bowling, collecting, dancing, drawing, driving, exercising, hiking, listening, painting, playing, reading, relaxing, running, sailing, shopping, skating, skiing, sports, swimming, talking, traveling, walking, yoga

places for recreation
field, gym, home, library, museum, park, stadium, woods

things people use for recreation
album, book, compact disc (CD), computer, digital versatile disc (DVD), e-mail, film, game, Internet, literature, magazine, movie, music, musical instrument, radio, story, tape, video

Word Explorer—Community

school

kinds of schools

college, community college, elementary school, high school, junior high, middle school, nursery school, preschool, secondary school, technical school, university, vocational school

places in schools

cafeteria, classroom, gymnasium (gym), hall, library, locker room, office, playground, restroom

actions associated with schools

draw, experiment, graduate, learn, listen, memorize, participate, pay attention, practice, read, register, remember, study, teach, think, write

things found in schools

blackboard, chair, chalk, computer, desk, locker, table

things taught in schools

arithmetic, art, biology, chemistry, driver education, economics, foreign language, geography, geometry, government, history, literacy, literature, mathematics (math), music, physical education (P.E.), physics, reading, science, social studies, spelling, writing

things received from schools

associate's degree, bachelor's degree, diploma, education, GED, grades, master's degree, report card

people associated with schools

aide, principal, professor, pupil, student, teacher

sports

kinds of sports

baseball, basketball, bowling, boxing, diving, football, gymnastics, hockey, skating, skiing, soccer, softball, swimming, tennis

places for sports

court, field, gymnasium (gym), hill, mountain, pool, stadium

actions in sports

block, bowl, dive, foul, hit, jump, kick, miss, pass, pitch, play, roll, run, score, shoot

things used in sports

ball, bat, glove, goal, helmet, net, protective pads, skates, skis, stick

people and groups involved in sports

coach, league, player, side, team

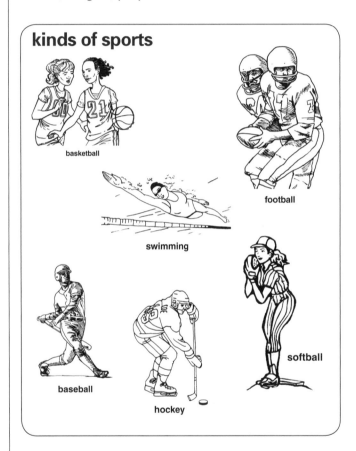

kinds of sports

basketball

football

swimming

baseball

hockey

softball

transportation

kinds of transportation

boat, bus, car, foot, horse, ship, train, truck, vehicle

places used for transportation

air, bus stop, highway, lane, railroad, road, sidewalk, street, terminal, train station, water

actions associated with transportation

commute, drive, fly, ride, run, sail, walk

Word Explorer—Everyday Life

accessory

kinds of accessories
belt, bracelet, ear muffs, earrings, glasses, gloves, handbag, jewelry, necklace, necktie, pin, pocketbook, purse, ring, scarf, sunglasses, tie, wallet, watch

appliance

parts of appliances
blade, button, cord, filter, handle, hose, knob, motor, switch

kinds of appliances
blender, coffee grinder, dishwasher, dryer, fan, freezer, furnace, hair dryer, heater, microwave oven, oven, refrigerator, stove, toaster, trash compactor, vacuum cleaner, washing machine

bank

activities associated with banks
borrow, cash, credit, debit, deposit, exchange, finance, invest, lend, loan, pay, pay back, pay off, save, withdraw

things related to banks
account, balance, cash, check, checkbook, checking account, coin, credit card, debit card, debt, dividend, interest, loan, money, passbook, receipt, savings, savings account, statement

things found in banks
automatic teller machine (ATM), counter, lobby, office, safe, till

people associated with banks
cashier, clerk, customer, guard, loan officer, manager, security guard, teller

bathroom

actions associated with a bathroom
bathe, brush, flush, shave, shower, wash, wipe

things in a bathroom
bathmat, bathtub, cabinet, counter, mirror, shower, shower curtain, sink, toilet, tub

things used in a bathroom
brush, comb, deodorant, hair dryer, razor, shampoo, soap, toilet paper, toothbrush, toothpaste, towel, washcloth

beverage

kinds of beverages
alcohol, beer, cocoa, coffee, cream, juice, lemonade, liquor, milk, soda, tea, water, wine

activities involving beverages
blend, boil, drink, heat, mix, pour, shake, spill, stir

containers for beverages
bottle, carton, coffeepot, cup, glass, jug, mug, pitcher, teapot

kinds of appliances

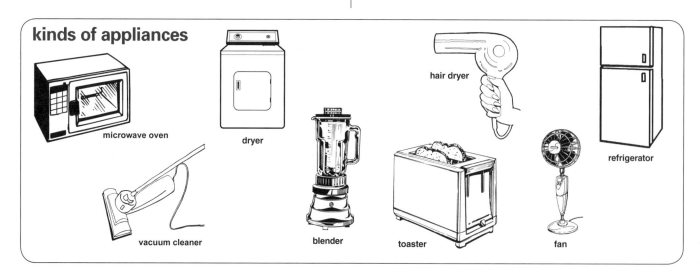

microwave oven

dryer

vacuum cleaner

blender

toaster

hair dryer

fan

refrigerator

car

parts of cars
accelerator, air bag, axle, back seat, battery, body, brake pedal, brakes, bumper, clutch, dashboard, driver's seat, engine, fender, floor, gas pedal, gear, headlights, hood, horn, hubcap, ignition, mirror, motor, parking brake, passenger's seat, pedal, radiator, seat, seatbelt, shift lever, starter, steering wheel, tire, transmission, trunk, wheel, window, windshield

actions of cars
accelerate, brake, drive, go, honk, park, pass, shift, slow, speed, start, steer, stop, turn

people associated with cars
driver, mechanic, passenger

clothes

parts of clothes
button, collar, cuff, pocket, seam, sleeve, zipper

kinds of clothes
blouse, bra, coat, dress, jacket, jeans, jersey, necktie, nightgown, overalls, overcoat, pajamas, pants, pantyhose, raincoat, robe, shirt, shorts, skirt, slacks, socks, sport shirt, stockings, suit, sweater, sweatshirt, swimsuit, tie, T-shirt, underpants, undershirt, underwear, uniform

actions involving clothes
change, design, fasten, iron, put on, remove, rinse, sew, take off, tie, try on, wash, wring, zip

kinds of clothes

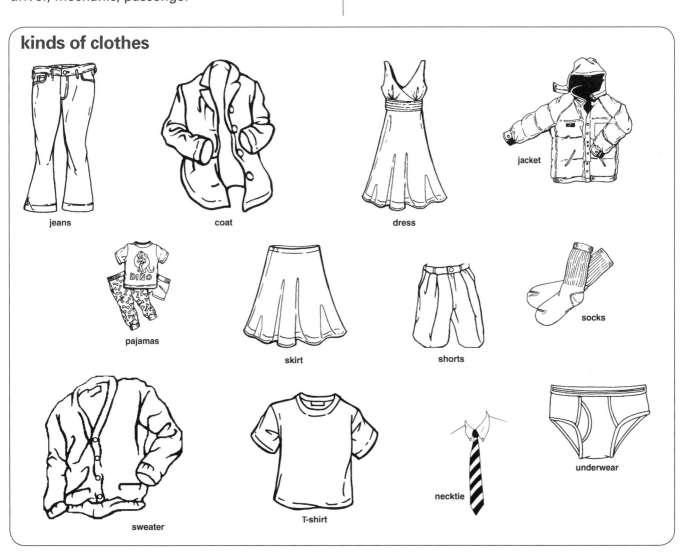

jeans

coat

dress

jacket

pajamas

skirt

shorts

socks

sweater

T-shirt

necktie

underwear

Word Explorer—Everyday Life

food

parts of food
calorie, carbohydrates, fiber, minerals, protein, starch, vitamins

kinds of food
cheese, fish, fruit, grain, meat, milk, noodles, pasta, poultry, seafood, vegetables

places to buy food
grocery, market, store, supermarket

places to eat food
cafeteria, diner, dining room, kitchen, restaurant

places for storing food
bin, cabinet, cupboard, freezer, kitchen, refrigerator, shelf

actions associated with food
bite, boil, cater, chew, cook, digest, feed, freeze, grind, harvest, hunt, nourish, prepare, preserve, refrigerate, salt, serve, spread, swallow, taste, wrap

descriptions of food
bitter, cooked, delicious, fresh, raw, rotten, salty, sour, spoiled, sweet, tough

things for serving food
bowl, china, dish, fork, knife, napkin, pan, plate, pot, saucer, scoop, silverware, spoon, table, tablecloth, tray, utensil

containers for food
bag, can, container, jar, sack, Ziploc bag

people associated with food
baker, butcher, chef, cook, farmer, server, waiter, waitress

events associated with food
barbecue, breakfast, brunch, dessert, dinner, feast, lunch, meal, picnic, snack, supper

ways to get food
farm, fish, garden, gather, hunt, pick, plant

fruit

parts of fruit
core, peel, seed, skin

kinds of fruit
apple, banana, berry, blueberry, cherry, grape, grapefruit, lemon, olive, orange, peach, pear, plum, prune, strawberry, tomato, watermelon

places for fruit
farm, garden, grocery store, market, store, supermarket

activities with fruit
cook, cut, eat, grow, harvest, peel, pick, plant, preserve, raise, store

people associated with fruit
cook, farmer, gardener, migrant worker

things made with fruit
cake, dessert, jam, jelly, juice, pie, preserves, salad, sauce

kinds of fruit

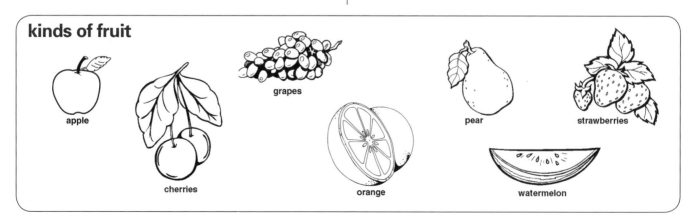

apple
grapes
cherries
orange
pear
strawberries
watermelon

furniture

parts of furniture

arm, back, cushion, door, drawer, leg, pillow, shelf, top

kinds of furniture

armchair, bed, bench, bookcase, bookshelf, bureau, cabinet, chair, chest, coffee table, couch, crib, desk, dresser, file cabinet, rocking chair, sofa, stool, table

places for furniture

apartment, home, hospital, house, office, workplace

actions associated with furniture

close, lean, lie, move, open, place, put, rock, sit

grain

kinds of grain

corn, oat, rice, rye, wheat

activities involving grain

grind, harvest, plant, store

things made from grain

alcohol, animal feed, beer, bread, bun, cake, cereal, cookie, cracker, dough, doughnut, flour, macaroni, meal, noodles, oatmeal, pasta, roll, spaghetti, taco, tortilla

house

parts of a house

attic, basement, ceiling, cellar, closet, deck, door, downstairs, floor, garage, hall, porch, roof, room, stairs, steps, upstairs, wall, window

things found in a house

air conditioning, carpet, curtains, door, fireplace, floor, furnace, furniture, rug

kinds of furniture

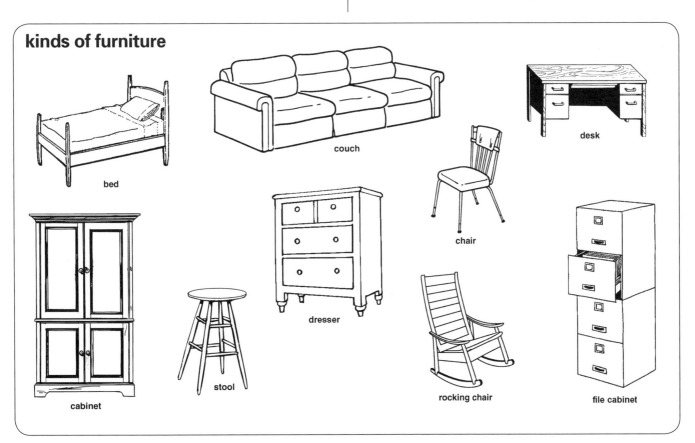

bed

couch

desk

chair

cabinet

stool

dresser

rocking chair

file cabinet

kitchen

actions associated with a kitchen
clean, cook, dry, eat, heat, prepare, wash

things in a kitchen
cabinet, chair, counter, cup, cupboard, dishwasher, drawer, freezer, garbage can, oven, refrigerator, sink, stool, stove, table

things used in a kitchen
appliance, bowl, coffeepot, dish, dishcloth, dish rack, dishrag, dish towel, fork, frying pan, knife, mixing bowl, napkin, pan, plate, pot, salad bowl, saucepan, saucer, serving dish, shaker, silverware, spatula, spice rack, sponge, spoon, strainer, teapot, tray, utensil

meat

kinds of meat
beef, fish, pork, poultry, seafood

animals used for meat
cattle, chicken, cow, deer, duck, fish, goat, goose, halibut, hen, pig, rabbit, salmon, shark, sheep, shrimp, tuna, turkey

ways to prepare meat
barbecue, boil, broil, chop, fry, grill, grind, roast, slice

foods made from meat
bacon, burger, chop, cold cuts, ham, hamburger, hot dog, roast, sausage, steak

things used in a kitchen

mixing bowl

pan

strainer

spatula

knife

saucepan

silverware

shaker

teapot

pot

animals used for meat

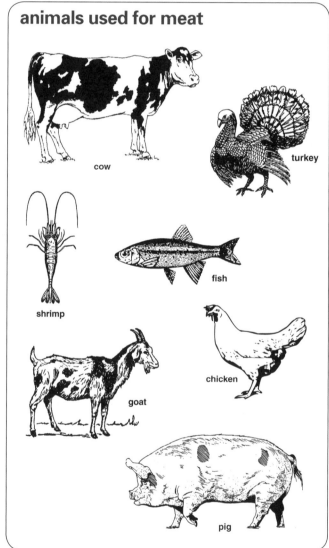

cow

turkey

shrimp

fish

goat

chicken

pig

Word Explorer—Everyday Life

money

places for money
automatic teller machine (ATM), bank, credit union, purse, safe, wallet

actions associated with money
cash, contribute, deduct, deposit, earn, exchange, inherit, invest, lose, make, pay, save, spend, withdraw, withhold

forms of money
bill, cash, check, coin, credit card, dime, nickel, penny, quarter

room

parts of a room
ceiling, closet, door, floor, wall, window

kinds of rooms
bathroom, bedroom, dining room, hall, kitchen, living room

things found in a room
appliance, carpet, curtain, furniture, rug

store

kinds of stores
bakery, clothing store, delicatessen (deli), department store, drugstore, grocery, grocery store, hardware store, liquor store, market, pharmacy, supermarket

places for stores
downtown, mall, shopping center

actions associated with a store
advertise, assist, buy, charge, exchange, guarantee, help, manage, order, pay, purchase, refund, return, sell, shop, try on

people in a store
cashier, clerk, customer, employee, manager, owner, salesperson, shopper, supervisor

things found in a store
aisle, basket, cart, cash register, chair, checkout counter, counter, credit card machine, display case, ladies' room, men's room, rack, restroom, shelf, stock, stock room, storage room

ways of paying in a store
cash, check, credit, credit card, debit card

vehicle

kinds of vehicles
airplane, ambulance, automobile, bicycle, boat, bulldozer, bus, car, cart, helicopter, motorcycle, ship, taxicab, tractor, train, truck

places for vehicles
airport, dock, driveway, garage, gas station, highway, path, road, sidewalk, station, street, terminal, track, trail

actions of vehicles
accelerate, brake, crash, drive, float, fly, go, haul, move, reverse, sail, speed, stop, tow, transport, travel, yield

kinds of vehicles

airplane

bus

bicycle

taxicab

truck

ambulance

vegetable

parts of vegetables
flesh, peel, seed, skin

kinds of vegetables
bean, beet, broccoli, cabbage, carrot, corn, cucumber, lettuce, mushroom, onion, pea, peanut, potato, snow pea, sprout, squash, sweet potato, tomato

places for vegetables
farm, field, garden, grocery, market, store, supermarket

activities involving vegetables
cook, cut, eat, grow, harvest, peel, pick, plant, preserve, raise, store

people associated with vegetables
cook, farmer, gardener, migrant worker

things eaten with vegetables
condiment, dressing, sauce

kinds of vegetables

beet

broccoli

carrots

tomato

corn

lettuce

onion

mushrooms

potatoes

beans

arm

parts of the arm
elbow, shoulder, wrist

body

parts of the body (outside)
arm, back, belly, breast, buttocks, chest, foot, hair, hand, head, leg, neck, skin, stomach, waist

parts of the body (inside)
blood, bone, brain, gland, heart, joint, liver, lung, muscle, nerve, organ, rib, skeleton, skull, spine, stomach, throat, vein

activities of the body
ache, bleed, bruise, catch cold, choke, digest, itch, sneeze, suffer, sweat, throw up, vomit

things used by the body
air, food, minerals, vitamins, water

things that can go wrong with the body
ache, allergy, cavity, cramp, disability, disease, handicap, heart attack, high/low blood pressure, illness, injury, sickness, stress, tension, tooth decay

conditions of the body
alcoholic, alive, allergic, blind, chilly, cold, dead, deaf, disabled, dizzy, handicapped, healthy, hot, hungry, hurt, ill, pregnant, sick, stressed, thirsty, tired, warm, wounded

things worn on the body
accessories, boots, clothes, clothing, coat, gloves, hat, jacket, jewelry, makeup, mask, mittens

parts of the body (inside)

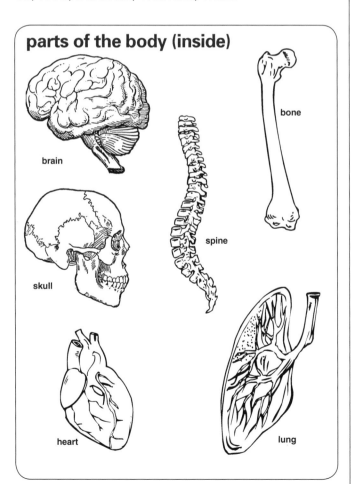

brain

skull

spine

bone

heart

lung

parts of the body (outside)

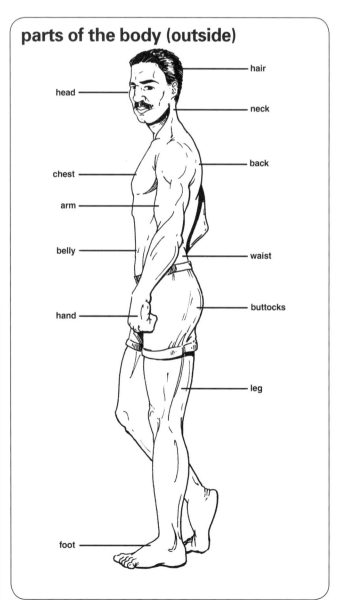

head

hair

neck

chest

back

arm

belly

hand

waist

buttocks

leg

foot

eye

parts of the eye
eyeball, eyebrow, eyelash, eyelid

things worn on the eye
eyeglasses, glasses, goggles, lenses, protective lenses, safety glasses

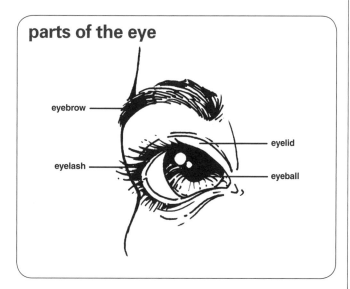

parts of the eye

face

parts of the face
cheek, chin, eyes, forehead, mouth, nose

things put on the face
cream, makeup, mask

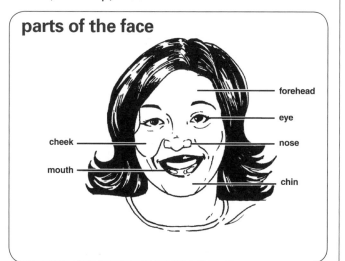

parts of the face

family

people in a family
ancestor, aunt, brother, cousin, dad, daughter, father, grandchild, granddaughter, grandfather, grandmother, grandparent, grandson, husband, in-law, mom, mother, nephew, niece, parent, relative, sister, son, stepbrother, stepfather, stepmother, stepsister, uncle, wife

foot

parts of the foot
ankle, heel, sole, toe, toenail

things worn on the foot
boot, sandal, shoe, sneaker, sock

hand

parts of the hand
finger, fingernail, fingertip, palm, thumb, wrist

things worn on the hand
bracelet, glove, mitten, ring

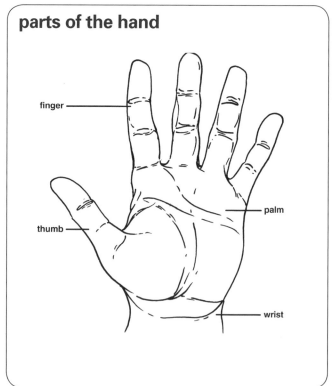

parts of the hand

head

parts of the head
ears, face, hair

things worn on the head
cap, crown, hat, helmet, scarf

---

parts of the head

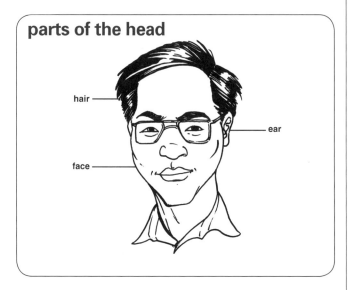

---

health

kinds of health
emotional, mental, physical

places associated with health
clinic, doctor's office, hospital

people associated with health
dentist, doctor, nurse, patient, pediatrician, physician, veterinarian

things that are bad for your health
pollution, poor nutrition, smoking, stress

things that are good for your health
exercise, good nutrition, minerals, rest, sleep, vitamins

illness

kinds of illness
anemia, cancer, diabetes, influenza (flu), measles, mumps, tuberculosis (TB)

symptoms of illness
ache, cough, fever, headache, pain, sneeze, sore throat, stomachache, vomiting

treatments for illness
antibiotic, drug, medicine, operation, pill, rest, syrup, tablet

causes of illness
bacteria, carcinogen, germ, virus

---

injury

kinds of injury
bruise, burn, cut, fracture, scar, scrape, scratch, sore, splinter, sprain, strain, swelling, wound

causes of injury
collision, crash, cut, explosion, exposure, fall, fire, poison, puncture, repetitive stress, shock, slip, strain, stress

treatments for injury
antiseptic, artificial respiration, bandage, first aid, gauze pad, ice, operation, rest, sling, splint, stitches

---

leg

parts of the leg
ankle, calf, foot, hip, knee, shin, thigh

parts of the leg

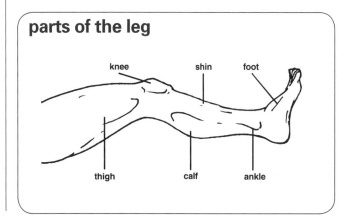

mind

activities of the mind

decide, desire, distinguish, dream, experience, feel, hope, imagine, know, learn, memorize, notice, recall, remember, think, understand, want, wonder, worry

ways to describe a mind

brilliant, clever, crazy, dumb, intelligent, sane, smart, stupid

mouth

parts of the mouth

gums, jaw, lip, tongue, tooth

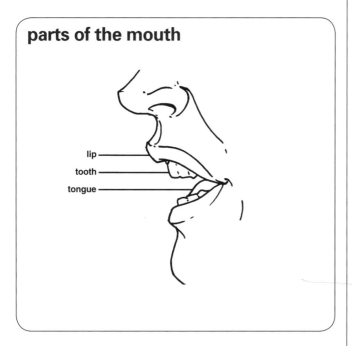

parts of the mouth

lip
tooth
tongue

people

people in different stages of life

adolescent, adult, baby, child, grownup, infant, kid, senior citizen, teenager, youth

marital states of people

divorced, married, separated, single, widowed

events in people's lives

birth, death, divorce, graduation, marriage, retirement

ways people feel

afraid, alert, amazed, angry, annoyed, ashamed, bored, content, depressed, disappointed, embarrassed, excited, frightened, frustrated, glad, happy, hurt, lonely, nervous, pleased, puzzled, relaxed, sad, scared, sorry, surprised, tense, unhappy, upset, worried

physical descriptions of people

attractive, beautiful, cute, fat, handsome, pretty, short, skinny, slender, tall, thin

things that identify people

age, gender, marital status, nationality, race, religion, sex

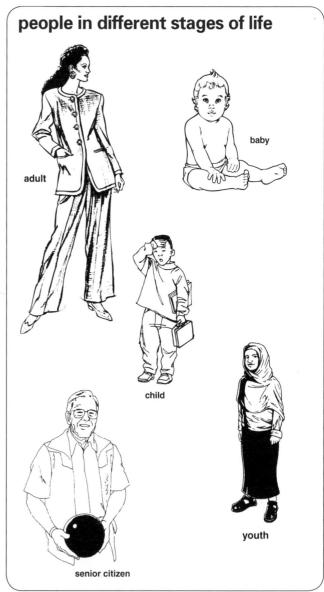

people in different stages of life

adult
baby
child
youth
senior citizen

Word Explorer—Science and Nature

animal

parts of animals
claw, feather, fur, leg, paw, tail, wing

kinds of animals
bird, fish, insect, mammal

examples of animals
ant, bee, butterfly, cat, cattle, chicken, clam, cow, deer, dog, dove, duck, eagle, elephant, fly, fox, frog, goat, goose, halibut, hawk, hen, horse, insect, kitten, lion, louse, monkey, moth, mouse, mule, owl, pig, pigeon, pony, rabbit, rat, robin, salmon, shark, sheep, shrimp, snail, snake, sparrow, spider, squirrel, tiger, tuna, turkey, turtle, weevil, whale, wolf, worm, zebra

places for animals
barn, cage, farm, field, forest, garden, nest, woods, zoo

actions of animals
crawl, eat, fly, hop, jump, leap, run, soar, swim, walk

young animals
calf, chick, cub, kitten, pup, puppy

noises of animals
bark, honk, whistle

examples of animals

ant

bee

moth

frog

dog

horse

hawk

squirrel

wolf

owl

goats

elephant

monkey

lion

land

parts of land
clay, mineral, rock, soil, stone

forms of land
beach, cliff, coast, continent, desert, hill, island, mountain, peak, plain, shore, valley, volcano

uses of land
agriculture, farming, mining, recreation

plant

parts of plants
boll, branch, bulb, cell, flower, fruit, leaf, root, stalk, stem, twig

kinds of plants
bush, flower, grain, grass, tree, weed

places for plants
forest, garden, nursery, woods, yard

activities with plants
eat, feed, garden, landscape, mow, plant, prune, trim, weed

uses of plants
cloth, clothing, fabric, fiber, food, fuel, lumber, material, medicine, shelter, wood

people associated with plants
farmer, gardener, landscaper

parts of plants

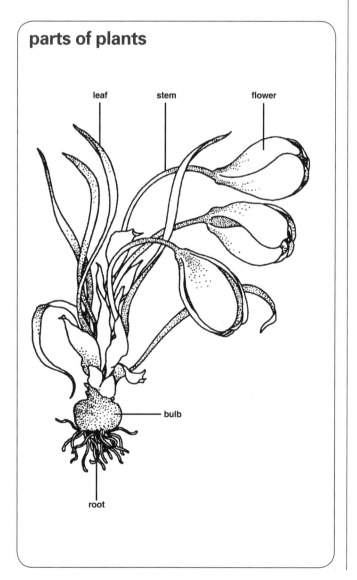

leaf · stem · flower · bulb · root

kinds of plants

bush · grass · tree · flower · grain

Word Explorer—Science and Nature

tree

parts of trees
bark, branch, flower, leaf, needle, root, trunk, twig

kinds of trees
apple, cherry, lemon, maple, oak, olive, palm, peach, pear, pine

places for trees
forest, nursery, park, woods, yard

activities with trees
climb, cut, grow, harvest, plant, prune

water

kinds of water
fresh, salt

bodies of water
brook, creek, lake, ocean, pond, puddle, river, sea, stream

actions involving water
absorb, bathe, boil, float, flood, flush, pour, rinse, shower, sink, soak, splash, spray, swim, wash, wring

actions of moving water
drip, flow, flush, leak

uses of water
bathe, clean, cook, drink, rinse, sail, swim, travel, wash

means of moving on water
boat, canoe, ship

containers for water
basin, bottle, bowl, cup, glass, jug, pail, pool, sewer, sink, tub

containers for water

jug

tub

pail

sink

glass

cup

pool

weather

ways to describe weather
chilly, cloudy, cold, cool, damp, dry, hot, humid, rainy, snowy, sunny, warm, wet, windy

events in weather
blizzard, frost, hail, lightning, mist, rain, shower, snow, snowstorm, thunder, thunderstorm

actions associated with weather
freeze, hail, melt, rain, shine, snow

things useful in different kinds of weather
air conditioning, boots, coat, ear muffs, fan, gloves, hat, heater, hood, jacket, mittens, scarf, snowplow, snowshovel, snow tires, sunglasses, thermometer, umbrella

things measured in weather
humidity, pressure, rainfall, snowfall, temperature

computer

parts of a computer
chip, disk, display, drive, hard disk, hardware, interface, keyboard, memory, monitor, mouse, printer, processor, program, screen, software, zip drive

actions associated with a computer
boot, calculate, compute, copy, crash, delete, input, log off, log on, print, process, save, store, type

things associated with a computer
application, command, compact disc (CD), digital versatile disc (DVD), document, e-mail, file, icon, interface, Internet, network, program, scanner, system, virus, Web, Web page, Web site, World Wide Web

things computers are used for
accounting, bookkeeping, communication, e-mail, games, publishing, recreation, research, word processing

parts of a computer

drive   monitor   screen

disc   keyboard   mouse

farm

parts of a farm
barn, field, yard

kinds of farms
cattle, dairy, ranch

actions associated with work on a farm
fertilize, grow, harvest, milk, pick, plant, raise

people who work on a farm
farmer, hand, migrant worker

tools and machines on a farm
combine, harvester, hoe, plow, shovel, tractor

animals on a farm
bull, cattle, chicken, cow, duck, goat, goose, horse, sheep, turkey

industry

kinds of industry
automobile, computer, construction, electronics, food, garment, manufacturing, mining, oil, petroleum, steel, textile

actions associated with industry
assemble, build, construct, create, form, incinerate, inspect, load, make, manufacture, mine, pack, package, process, produce, sew, weave

places for industry
factory, industrial park, mill, mine, plant

people associated with industry
boss, mechanic, miner, supervisor, worker

things used in industry
assembly line, electricity, engine, equipment, furnace, machine, machinery, motor, oven, pump, robot, supplies, tools

materials used in industry
brass, bronze, copper, fuel, gas, iron, lead, lumber, metal, minerals, oil, petroleum, steel, thread, uranium, yarn

job

people in jobs

actor, actress, adviser, agent, aide, announcer, artist, assistant, astronaut, astronomer, attorney, author, baker, ballplayer, barber, boxer, builder, butcher, buyer, cabinetmaker, chef, clerk, coach, cop, delivery man, dentist, detective, director, doctor, doorman, dressmaker, editor, electrician, engineer, explorer, factory worker, flight attendant, food server, grocer, guard, hairdresser, inspector, installer, janitor, judge, landscaper, lawyer, librarian, mail carrier, mailman, manager, mechanic, migrant worker, miner, minister, missionary, nurse, operator, painter, physician, pilot, player, plumber, poet, policeman, police officer, policewoman, politician, priest, principal, professor, psychologist, receptionist, reporter, representative, salesclerk, salesperson, sanitation worker, scientist, seaman, secretary, security guard, sewer, singer, soldier, superintendent (super), supervisor, tailor, teacher, teller, trainee, tutor, typist, veterinarian, waiter, waitress, worker

requirements for a job

application, degree, education, experience, identification, license, qualifications, skills, training

places to find jobs

agency, bulletin board, classified ad, Internet, job center, newspaper, notice

office

actions associated with an office

accounting, billing, computing, copying, filing, typing, word processing, writing

people who work in an office

assistant, clerk, executive, manager, receptionist, secretary, supervisor

things in an office

bookshelf, bulletin board, cabinet, calculator, calendar, chair, clock, computer, copier, copy machine, desk, fax, file, keyboard, lamp, monitor, paper, pen, pencil, scanner, stapler, staples, tape

things in an office

stapler

pen

copy machine

calendar

bulletin board

lamp

computer

restaurant

places in a restaurant

bar, basement, counter, dining room, emergency exit, employee bathroom, entrance, kitchen, ladies' room, men's room, restroom, storage room, waiting area

actions associated with work in a restaurant

bus, cook, greet, prepare, scour, seat, serve, take orders, wait on, wash, wipe

actions associated with cooking in a restaurant

bake, boil, broil, chop, clean, cut, fry, grill, peel, prepare, slice, wash

people in a restaurant

assistant, chef, cook, customer, dishwasher, host, manager, owner, server, supervisor, waiter, waitress

things found in a restaurant

appliance, apron, bin, cash register, chair, counter, credit card machine, dish, dishwasher, fork, freezer, garbage can, glass, grill, ice machine, knife, menu, mop, napkin, oven, pan, pitcher, plate, pot, rack, refrigerator, silverware, sink, spoon, stool, stove, table, towel, uniform

things served in a restaurant

alcohol, appetizer, beverage, dessert, drink, entrée, food, liquor, salad, sandwich, side dish, soup

things found in a restaurant

cash register

glass

stool

pot

silverware

pan

knife

napkin

chair

refrigerator

garbage can

mop

tool

parts of tools

belt, blade, bolt, clamp, claw, cord, dial, handle, head, lever, lug, nut, pedal, plug, spring, switch

kinds of tools

ax, can opener, chisel, circular saw, clamp, clip, clippers, dispenser, drill, extension ladder, fixed ladder, garden shears, glue gun, hacksaw, hammer, hand drill, hand saw, hedge trimmer, hoe, hook, hook ladder, jack, jackhammer, jigsaw, ladder, laser, level, lever, lug nut, lug wrench, mallet, opener, paintbrush, paint sprayer, pallet jack, pinking shears, pipe wrench, pliers, power drill, power roller, pruning shears, pulley, pump, rake, recharger, rod, roller, roller brush, rolling ladder, ruler, sander, saw, scissors, scoop, screwdriver, shears, shovel, spade, staple gun, stapler, stepladder, straight ladder, table saw, tape dispenser, tape measure, wire cutters, wire stripper, wrench

actions of tools

chop, clip, cut, dig, drill, hammer, hit, insert, pound, remove, screw, slice, splice, split, spray, strip, trim, twist

workplace

kinds of workplaces

agency, assembly line, construction site, factory, farm, office, retail store, shop

actions in a workplace

employ, fire, hire, lay off, pay, punch in, punch out, work

people in a workplace

assistant, boss, co-worker, employee, supervisor, worker

groups in a workplace

committee, staff, team, union

departments in a workplace

accounting, finance, human resources, maintenance, management, payroll, personnel, receiving, shipping

things found in a workplace

equipment, furniture, machines, supplies, tools, uniforms

benefits in a workplace

family leave, holidays, insurance, leave, medical leave, personal days, sick days, vacation

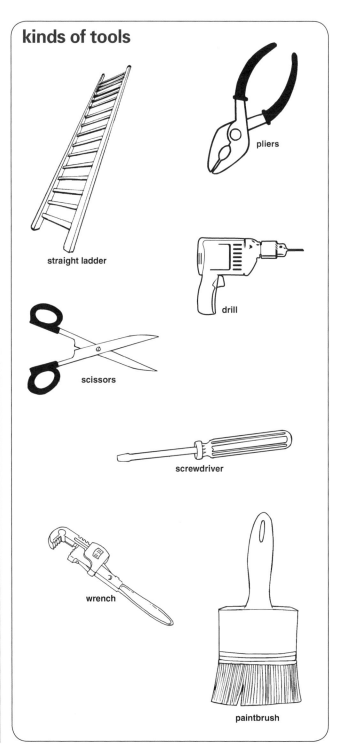

kinds of tools

straight ladder

pliers

drill

scissors

screwdriver

wrench

paintbrush

Defining Vocabulary

The definitions in this dictionary use words from this list of defining vocabulary. Sometimes a definition needs to use a word that is not on this list. This does not happen often. When it happens, you can look up that word in the dictionary to find its meaning.

abbreviation	after	announcement	at	be
ability	afternoon	annoy	ate	beach
able	afterward	another	atom	beak
about	again	answer	attach	beam
above	against	anxiety	attached	bean
abroad	age	anxious	attack	bear
absence	ago	any	attempt	beard
absent	agree	anymore	attend	beat
accept	agreement	anyone	attention	beautiful
acceptable	ahead	anything	attitude	beauty
accident	aim	anywhere	attract	became
according	air	apart	attractive	because
account	aircraft	apartment	audience	become
achieve	airport	appear	author	bed
acid	alcohol	appearance	authority	been
across	alive	apple	available	beer
act	all	apply	avenue	before
action	allow	appropriate	average	begin
active	allowed	approval	avoid	beginning
activity	almost	approve	awake	behave
actor	alone	are	away	behavior
actress	along	area	awkward	behind
actual	alphabet	argue	baby	being
actually	already	argument	back	belief
add	also	arm	background	believe
addition	although	army	backwards	bell
address	altogether	around	bad	belong
adjective	always	arrange	bag	below
admiration	am	arrangement	balance	beneath
admire	American	arrival	ball	berry
admit	among	arrive	band	beside
advanced	amount	arrived	bank	best
advantage	amuse	art	bar	better
adventure	amusement	article	barbecue	between
adverb	amusing	artificial	barely	beyond
advertise	an	artist	base	bicycle
advertisement	ancient	as	baseball	big
advice	and	ash	basic	bill
advise	anger	ashamed	basket	bird
affair	angle	ask	basketball	birth
affect	angry	asked	bath	bit
afford	animal	asleep	bathtub	bite
afraid	announce	association	battle	bitter

312

Defining Vocabulary

black
blade
bleed
blind
block
blood
blow
blue
board
boat
body
boil
bomb
bone
book
border
bored
boring
born
borrow
both
bottle
bottom
bowl
box
boy
brain
branch
break
breakfast
breast
breath
breathe
breed
brick
bridge
bright
bring
broad
broadcast
brother
brown
brush
bucket
build
bullet
bunch
burn

burst
bury
bus
bush
business
busy
but
butter
button
buy
by
cabin
cake
call
calm
camera
camp
can
cancel
candy
cannot
cap
capital
captain
car
card
care
careful
careless
carriage
carry
case
castle
cat
catch
cattle
cause
ceiling
celebrate
cent
center
centimeter
central
century
ceremony
certain
chain
chair

chance
change
chapter
character
charge
chase
check
cheek
cheerful
cheese
chemical
chemistry
chest
chief
child
chin
chocolate
choice
choose
church
cigarette
circle
circular
citizen
city
claim
class
clay
clean
clear
clerk
clever
cliff
climate
climb
clock
close
cloth
clothes
clothing
cloud
club
coal
coast
coat
coffee
coin
cold

collar
collect
college
color
column
comb
combine
come
comfort
comfortable
command
committee
common
communicate
communication
community
company
compare
comparison
compete
competition
competitor
complain
complaint
complete
compound
computer
concern
concerning
concert
condition
confidence
confident
confuse
connect
connection
conscious
consider
consist
construction
contain
container
continue
continuous
contract
control
convenient
conversation

convince
cook
cookie
cool
copy
corn
corner
correct
cost
cotton
cough
could
council
count
country
couple
courage
course
court
cover
cow
crack
crash
crazy
cream
creature
crime
criminal
criticism
criticize
crop
cross
crowd
cruel
crush
cry
cup
cupboard
cure
current
curtain
curve
customer
cut
daily
damage
dance
danger

Defining Vocabulary

dangerous	die	each	entertainment	fact
dark	difference	eager	entire	factory
daughter	different	ear	entrance	fail
day	difficult	early	environment	failure
dead	difficulty	earn	equal	faint
deal	dig	earth	equipment	fair
dear	dinner	east	escape	fairly
death	dip	eastern	especially	faith
debt	direct	easy	establish	faithful
decay	direction	eat	even	fall
deceit	dirt	economic	evening	familiar
deceive	dirty	edge	event	family
decide	disappear	educate	ever	famous
decision	disappoint	education	every	far
decorate	discover	effect	everybody	farm
decoration	discuss	effective	everyone	farmer
decrease	discussion	effort	everything	farther
deep	disease	egg	everywhere	farthest
defeat	dish	eight	evidence	fashion
defend	dismiss	eighth	evil	fashionable
defense	distance	either	exact	fast
definite	distant	elbow	examination	fasten
degree	divide	elect	examine	fat
delay	do	electric	example	father
deliberate	doctor	electricity	excellent	fault
delicate	document	electronic	except	favorable
deliver	dog	else	exchange	favorite
demand	dollar	embarrass	excite	fear
department	door	emotion	excuse	feather
depend	double	emphasize	exercise	feature
dependent	doubt	employ	exist	feed
depth	down	employee	existance	feel
describe	dozen	employer	expect	feeling
description	draw	employment	expensive	female
desert	drawer	empty	experience	fence
deserve	dream	enclose	experiment	fever
design	dress	end	explain	few
desirable	drink	enemy	explanation	field
desire	drive	energy	explode	fierce
desk	drop	engine	explosion	fifth
destroy	drug	engineer	explosive	fifty
destruction	drum	English	express	fight
detail	dry	enjoy	expression	figure
determination	duck	enjoyable	extra	fill
determine	dull	enjoyment	extreme	film
develop	during	enough	eye	final
device	dust	enter	eyelid	finally
dictionary	duty	entertain	face	financial

Defining Vocabulary

find
find out
fine
finger
finish
fire
firm
first
fish
fit
five
fix
flag
flame
flash
flat
flesh
flight
float
flood
floor
flour
flow
flower
fly
fold
follow
food
foot
football
for
forbid
force
foreign
forest
forever
forget
forgive
fork
form
formal
former
fortunate
forward
found
four
fourth
free

freedom
frequent
frequently
fresh
friend
frighten
frightening
from
front
frozen
fruit
full
fun
function
funeral
funny
furniture
further
future
gain
gallon
game
garage
garden
gas
gasoline
gate
gather
general
generally
generous
gentle
get
gift
girl
give
glad
glass
glue
go
goat
god
gold
good
goodbye
goods
govern
government

graceful
grade
grain
gram
grammar
grand
grandfather
grandmother
grandparent
grass
gray
great
green
greet
greeting
groceries
ground
group
grow
grown
growth
guard
guess
guest
guide
guilty
gun
habit
hair
half
hall
hammer
hand
handle
hang
happen
happy
hard
hardly
harm
harmful
hat
hate
hatred
have
he
head
health

healthy
hear
heart
heat
heaven
heavy
heel
height
help
helpful
her
here
herself
hide
high
hill
him
himself
his
history
hit
hold
hole
holiday
hollow
holy
home
honest
honor
hook
hope
hopeful
horse
hospital
hot
hotel
hour
house
how
however
huge
human
humor
humorous
hundred
hundredth
hungry
hunt

hurry
hurt
husband
I
ice
idea
identity
if
ignore
illegal
illness
image
imaginary
imagination
imagine
immediate
immediately
importance
important
impressive
improve
improvement
in
inch
include
income
increase
indeed
independent
indicate
individual
indoor
industrial
industry
infect
infection
infectious
influence
inform
information
injure
injury
ink
inner
insect
inside
instance
instead

Defining Vocabulary

institution	kind	lid	man	mineral
instruction	king	lie	manage	minister
instrument	kiss	life	manager	minute
insult	kitchen	lift	manner	mirror
insurance	knee	light	many	miss
insure	kneel	like	map	mist
intelligence	knife	likely	march	mistake
intelligent	knock	limit	mark	mix
intend	knot	line	market	mixture
intention	know	lion	marriage	model
interest	knowledge	lip	married	modern
interesting	lack	liquid	match	moment
international	lady	list	material	money
interrupt	lake	listen	mathematics	monkey
into	lamb	liter	matter	month
introduce	lamp	literature	may	monthly
introduction	land	little	maybe	moon
invent	language	live	me	moral
invention	large	load	meal	more
invitation	last	loaf	mean	morning
invite	late	local	meaning	most
involve	lately	locate	means	mother
inward	later	lock	measure	motion
iron	laugh	lonely	meat	motor
is	laughter	long	medical	mountain
island	law	look	medicine	mouse
it	lawyer	loose	meet	mouth
its	lay	lose	meeting	move
itself	layer	loss	melt	movement
jaw	lead	loud	member	much
jewel	leader	love	memory	mud
jewelry	leaf	low	mental	multiply
job	lean	lower	mention	murder
join	learn	loyal	mess	muscle
joint	least	loyalty	message	music
joke	leather	luck	messy	musician
judge	leave	lucky	metal	must
judgment	left	lung	meter	my
juice	leg	machine	method	myself
jump	legal	machinery	middle	mysterious
just	lend	magazine	might	mystery
justice	length	magic	mile	nail
keep	less	mail	military	name
key	let	main	milk	narrow
kick	letter	major	million	nasty
kill	level	make	millionth	nation
kilogram	library	male	mind	national
kilometer	license	mammal	mine	natural

Defining Vocabulary

nature
navy
near
nearly
neat
necessary
neck
need
needle
negative
neighbor
neither
nerve
nervous
nest
net
network
never
new
newspaper
next
nice
night
nine
ninth
no
nobody
noise
none
nonsense
nor
normal
north
northern
nose
not
note
nothing
notice
noun
now
nowhere
number
nurse
nut
obey
object
observe

obtain
occasion
occur
ocean
o'clock
odd
of
off
offend
offense
offensive
offer
office
officer
official
often
oh
oil
old
old-fashioned
on
once
one
onion
only
onto
open
operate
operation
opinion
opponent
opportunity
oppose
opposite
opposition
or
orange
order
ordinary
organ
organization
organize
original
other
ought
our
ours
out

outdoor
outer
outside
over
owe
own
owner
oxygen
package
page
pain
painful
paint
painting
pair
pale
pan
pants
paper
parallel
parent
park
part
particular
partly
partner
party
pass
passage
passenger
past
path
patience
patient
pattern
pause
pay
payment
peace
peaceful
pen
pencil
people
pepper
per
perfect
perform
performance

perhaps
period
permanent
permission
person
personal
persuade
pet
photograph
phrase
physical
piano
pick
picture
piece
pig
pile
pilot
pin
pink
pipe
pity
place
plain
plan
plane
planet
plant
plastic
plate
play
pleasant
please
pleased
pleasure
plenty
plural
pocket
poem
poet
poetry
point
pointed
poison
poisonous
pole
police
polish

polite
political
politician
politics
pool
poor
popular
population
port
position
positive
possess
possession
possibility
possible
possibly
post
pot
potato
pound
pour
powder
power
powerful
practical
practice
praise
pray
prayer
prefer
preparation
prepare
present
preserve
president
press
pressure
pretend
pretty
prevent
previous
previously
price
priest
prince
principal
principle
print

Defining Vocabulary

prison	quite	remember	rude	sensitive
prisoner	rabbit	remind	ruin	sentence
private	race	remove	rule	separate
prize	radio	rent	ruler	serious
probably	railroad	repair	run	seriously
problem	rain	repeat	rush	servant
process	raise	reply	sad	serve
produce	range	report	safe	service
product	rank	represent	safety	set
production	rapid	representative	sail	settle
profession	rare	request	salary	seven
profit	rat	require	sale	seventh
program	rate	respect	salt	several
progress	rather	responsible	same	severe
project	raw	rest	sand	sew
promise	reach	restaurant	satisfaction	sex
pronounce	react	restrict	satisfactory	sexual
pronunciation	reaction	result	satisfy	shade
proof	read	return	save	shadow
proper	reading	review	say	shake
property	ready	reward	scale	shame
proposal	realize	rhythm	scatter	shape
protect	really	rice	scene	share
protection	reason	rich	school	sharp
protective	reasonable	rid	science	she
protest	receive	ride	scientific	sheep
proud	recent	right	scientist	sheet
prove	recently	ring	scissors	shelf
provide	recognize	ripe	screen	shell
public	recommend	rise	screw	shelter
publicly	record	risk	sea	shine
pull	red	river	search	shiny
pump	reduce	road	season	ship
punish	reduction	rob	seat	shirt
punishment	refusal	rock	second	shock
pure	refuse	roll	secrecy	shoe
purple	regard	romantic	secret	shoot
purpose	region	roof	secretary	shop
push	regular	room	section	shore
put	related	root	see	short
quality	relation	rope	seed	shot
quantity	relationship	rose	seem	should
quarrel	relative	rough	seize	shoulder
quarter	relax	round	sell	shout
queen	religion	row	send	show
question	religious	royal	sensation	shut
quick	remain	rub	sense	shy
quiet	remark	rubber	sensible	sick

Defining Vocabulary

sickness	so	square	subject	teacher
side	soap	stage	substance	team
sideways	social	stair	subtract	tear
sight	society	stamp	succeed	technical
sign	sock	stand	success	teeth
signal	soft	standard	successful	telephone
silence	soil	star	such	television
silent	soldier	start	suck	tell
silk	solid	state	sudden	temper
silly	solution	statement	suddenly	temperature
silver	solve	station	suffer	temporary
similar	some	stay	sugar	ten
similarity	somehow	steady	suggest	tend
simple	someone	steal	suit	tendency
since	something	steam	suitable	tennis
sincere	sometimes	steel	suitcase	tense
sincerely	somewhere	steep	summer	tent
sing	son	stem	sun	tenth
single	song	step	supper	terrible
singular	soon	stick	supply	terror
sink	sore	sticky	support	test
sister	sorrow	stiff	suppose	than
sit	sorry	still	sure	thank
situation	sort	sting	surface	that
six	soul	stitch	surprise	the
sixth	sound	stomach	surround	theater
size	soup	stone	swallow	their
skill	sour	stop	swear	them
skillful	south	store	sweep	themselves
skin	southern	storm	sweet	then
skirt	space	story	swell	there
sky	spade	straight	swim	therefore
slave	speak	strange	swing	these
sleep	special	stranger	sword	they
slide	specific	stream	symbol	thick
slight	speech	street	sympathetic	thief
slip	speed	strength	sympathy	thin
slippery	spell	stretch	system	thing
slope	spelling	strict	table	think
slow	spend	strike	tail	third
small	spin	string	take	this
smart	spirit	strong	talk	thorough
smell	spoil	structure	tall	those
smile	spoon	struggle	taste	though
smoke	sports	student	tax	thought
smooth	spot	study	taxi	thousand
snake	spread	stupid	tea	thousandth
snow	spring	style	teach	thread

Defining Vocabulary

threat
threaten
three
throat
through
throughout
throw
thumb
thus
ticket
tie
tiger
tight
till
time
tiny
tire
tired
tiring
title
to
tobacco
today
toe
together
toilet
tomorrow
tongue
tonight
too
tool
tooth
top
total
touch
tough
tour
tourist
toward
tower
town
toy
track
trade
tradition
traditional
traffic
train

training
translate
transparent
transportation
trap
travel
treat
treatment
tree
tribe
trick
trip
tropical
trouble
truck
trunk
trust
try
tube
tune
turn
twelve
twenty
twice
twist
two
type
typical
ugly
uncle
under
understand
underwear
undo
uniform
union
unit
unite
United States
universal
universe
university
unless
until
up
upon
upper
upright

upset
upside down
upstairs
urgent
us
use
useful
useless
usual
usually
vacation
valley
valuable
value
variety
various
vegetable
vehicle
verb
very
victory
view
village
violence
violent
visit
voice
vote
vowel
wages
waist
wait
wake
walk
wall
wander
want
war
warm
warmth
warn
warning
wash
waste
watch
water
wave
way

we
weak
wealth
weapon
wear
weather
weave
wedding
week
weekly
weigh
weight
welcome
well
went
were
west
western
wet
what
whatever
wheat
wheel
when
whenever
where
whether
which
whichever
while
whip
whisper
whistle
white
who
whole
whose
why
wide
width
wife
wild
will
willing
win
wind
window
wine

wing
winter
wire
wisdom
wise
wish
with
within
without
witness
woman
wonder
wood
wooden
wool
word
work
world
worm
worry
worse
worst
worth
would
wound
wrap
wrist
write
wrong
yard
year
yearly
yellow
yes
yesterday
yet
you
young
your
yourself
zero